MW00990438

Rising Son

Rising Son

THE LIFE AND MUSIC OF ARLO GUTHRIE

★ ★ ★ ★ ★

By Hank Reineke

With commentary by Arlo Guthrie

UNIVERSITY OF OKLAHOMA PRESS : NORMAN

This book is published with the generous assistance of the Wallace C. Thompson Endowment Fund, University of Oklahoma Foundation.

LIBRARY OF CONGRESS CATALOGING-IN-PUBLICATION DATA

Names: Reineke, Hank, 1961– author. | Guthrie, Arlo, author.
Title: Rising Son : the life and music of Arlo Guthrie / Hank Reineke,
  with commentary by Arlo Guthrie.
Description: [First.] | Norman : University of Oklahoma Press, 2023. |
  Series: American popular music series; volume 10 | Includes index. |
  Summary: "Documents the triumphs and missteps of the singer's fledgling
  record company, Rising Son Records, and traces the chronology of Guthrie's
  mid- to-late career. Also examines Guthrie's role in preserving and shaping his
  father's contributions to American culture and his long-lasting partnership
  with Pete Seeger"—Provided by publisher.
Identifiers: LCCN 2023002404 | ISBN 978-0-8061-9287-1 (hardcover)
Subjects: LCSH: Guthrie, Arlo. | Folk singers—United States—Biography. |
  Guthrie, Woody, 1912–1967. | Seeger, Pete, 1919–2014. | Rising Son Records.
Classification: LCC ML420.G978 R47 2023 | DDC 782.42164092 [B]—dc23/
  eng/20230118
LC record available at https://lccn.loc.gov/2023002404

Rising Son: The Life and Music of Arlo Guthrie is Volume 10 in the American Popular Music Series.

The paper in this book meets the guidelines for permanence and durability of the Committee on Production Guidelines for Book Longevity of the Council on Library Resources, Inc. ∞

CONTENTS

★ ★ ★ ★ ★

INTRODUCTION

In the course of a January 1970 interview published in the *New York Times,* Arlo Guthrie spoke at length about his generation. The folk singer was convinced the rebellious global youth movement would, in due time, bring about a world free of "nationalism, countryism, land-of-the-free-ism." "We're thinking big," Guthrie expounded. "It's world-of-the-free-ism, universe-of-the-free-ism."[1] Not surprisingly, the probing journalist asked Guthrie when he thought this big change might occur.

"You want a date? O.K., 1983," Guthrie responded. "But there'll be a lot going down before that." When pressed why the "arbitrary" year of 1983 was chosen, Guthrie answered, "It isn't arbitrary. That's the year. It has a lot of good numbers. One is creative, nine is completion, eight is infinite, and all good things come in threes."[2] In the end, Guthrie's predicted '83 revolution would not ring in a new age of harmony, peace, and social justice. In America, at least, the only revolution anyone had taken note of was year three of the Reagan presidency.

That's not to say 1983 wouldn't bring about changes. The year proved revolutionary for Guthrie, both personally and professionally. It was the year his fifteen-year-long relationship with Warner Bros. would come to an unceremonious end. Guthrie's usual five-year contract—along with those of such label mates as Bonnie Raitt, Gordon Lightfoot, and Van Morrison—was not renewed. The record company cited decreasing album sales and waning public interest in roots-oriented music as explanation. To be fair, Warner Bros. was not alone in its early-1980s purging of established legacy artists.

Though he might have tested the possibility of new label interest, in 1983 Guthrie instead chose to incorporate a company of his own, Rising Son Records. The trials, obstacles, and successes of his ambitious start-up is—hence the title—an important component of *Rising Son: The Life and Music of Arlo Guthrie.* But perhaps more importantly the present book seeks to document the second act of Guthrie's career, a time when the folk-rock singer was long out of the celebrity spotlight of the late 1960s and early 1970s.

Guthrie's decision to soldier on as an "indie label" musician freed him of corporate meddles, enabling both artistic freedom and ownership of his own music. In a manner of speaking, Guthrie's post-Warner Bros. story is analogous to that of the biblical David and Goliath. Was it possible for a thirty-five-year-old folk singer with no formal business training to make a go of being president of a fledgling record label? And this at a time when the music industry was in flux and access to mainstream radio all but shuttered?

Guthrie's final studio album for Warner Bros., the musically potent but poorly promoted *Power of Love,* entered the Billboard 200 charts in late June of 1981. It would disappear following a four-week run. Though a personal favorite of mine, the slickly produced album had received virtually no publicity nor airplay. It wasn't helpful that Guthrie's fans—at least those of whom were aware a new album had been released—were divided in their opinion of it. For all of its polish and strong performances, *Power of Love* was neither particularly folksy nor particularly rocking. Nor did it demonstrate the sort of energy and music the artist was delivering nightly on stage.

The new album was peculiar to Guthrie's catalog. One critic lamented that the slick disc displayed "more than a little middle-age spread." Looking back, one can understand some of the criticism. In the late '60s and early '70s—the time span of his greatest commercial fame—the singer had routinely bypassed in-person visits with big corporate rock stations, choosing instead to seek out more informal and free-form college and underground outlets. So it was inconceivable to many longtime fans that Guthrie's *Power of Love* seemed designed for commercial airplay on stations offering an exclusive MOR ("Middle-of-the-Road") listening experience.

So who was this Arlo Guthrie anyway? The answer to the question, more often than not, was dependent on the preconceptions of those interested. He was described in the press at various times as "America's next major folk hero," the "Prince of Folk Music," the "Hipster Hero," "the sallow-faced folk singer," the "rebel singer," the "rustic hippie," and the "Successful Anarchist." No one was actually *wrong* in their pinning of such attributions to Guthrie. Such descriptions of him were, in the public's consciousness anyway, a charming hybrid of all of the above. But these were simply tags created to quantify the singer's work and perceived blithe-spirit persona.

In the earliest years of his career, both *Time* and *Newsweek*—displaying a shortfall of editorial imagination—would title their profiles of Guthrie "Woody's Boy." It wasn't surprising: there was no getting around his recognition as the son of balladeer Woody Guthrie. Arlo Guthrie's earliest musical influences were his father's friends and contemporaries: Lead Belly, Pete Seeger, Cisco Houston, Brownie McGhee and Sonny Terry, the Weavers, and Ramblin' Jack Elliott. The rough-hewn sounds these artists had created or preserved would remain essential matter in his musical DNA.

Guthrie was okay with it, for the most part. Being the son of Woody Guthrie had its advantages and disadvantages. "It sets up its own easy things and its own difficult things," he told a journalist in early winter of 1966. "The only thing I resent is when people compare me to my father. I can't compare with a legend."[3] From the beginning—and whether he chose this course or not—Guthrie was destined to serve as a particularly vital link in the chain of American folk music. But his own music wasn't locked in a time capsule. As a teenager growing up in Howard Beach, he was introduced by radio and television broadcasts to such emerging artists as the Everly Brothers, Elvis Presley, Fats Domino, and the Beatles.

There's no denying the Guthrie name allowed the budding artist a measure of inner-circle access. At the insistence of a protective mother, a twenty-two-year-old Bob Dylan agreed to shepherd a sixteen-year-old Guthrie around at the 1963 Newport Folk Festival. Guthrie recalled Dylan rarely spoke directly to him as the two walked about exploring the festival grounds. Dylan mostly introduced his young charge ("Here's Woody's kid") to friends and curious onlookers as if in temporary possession of a trophy.[4] "From my point of view," Guthrie reminisced, Dylan "looked after me well 'cos he basically left me alone, which was fine by me."[5]

In the early '60s, as Guthrie pondered the possibility of a professional career in music, he would hang around the cabarets of Greenwich Village. He carried his guitar along should a desperate club owner have reason to call him on stage in the event "somebody didn't show up, or got sick or drunk or couldn't play or whatever."[6] Even if such calls came only occasionally, his immersion in bohemian street life offered Guthrie an opportunity to hang out with Ramblin' Jack Elliott in the West Village and Ed Sanders and the Fugs in the East.

Though underage, Guthrie would sneak into the Village nightclubs and soak up the vibrant music and arts scene. When night extended into the early morning, he sometimes slept on the couch at Phil Ochs's apartment on Thompson Street. Along with friend John Sebastian, Guthrie copped guitar licks from Mississippi John Hurt, the two young pickers even getting the chance to share a stage with the beloved songster at the Gaslight Café on MacDougal Street.

Guthrie's Greenwich Village days were briefly suspended when he set off for college in September of 1965. His time at school in Montana didn't last long, a four- or six-week spell, depending on the source. He returned to his mother's house in Howard Beach, New York, in late autumn, making the fateful decision to spend the Thanksgiving holiday with friends at the home of Ray and Alice Brock. But as the Brocks' deconsecrated church home was filled with construction materials and other junk, Guthrie and his friend Rick Robbins, "as a friendly gesture," volunteered to take the rubbish to the local dumping ground. The rest, as they say, is history or, at the very least, music history.

In 1966 Harold Leventhal, the cigar-chomping impresario-manager of Pete Seeger, Judy Collins, and many other folk song luminaries, took Guthrie on as a client, arranging bookings for the eighteen-year-old in Boston, New York, Philadelphia, and Chicago. One of Guthrie's original songs gaining attention was a meandering talking blues that, following a number of variations in subject and style, coalesced and bloomed as the "Alice's Restaurant Massacree." He sang the song nightly in coffeehouses and occasionally on New York's WBAI and Philadelphia's WWMR FM radio stations. Guthrie's self-described "anti-stupidity" song proved to be an underground sensation, with people sneaking bootleg copies off the radio and onto their reel-to-reel decks.

Sensing rightfully that money was being left on the table, in June of 1967 Leventhal arranged for Guthrie to record the "Massacree" in a professional setting. Things moved quickly after that. In September of 1967 *Billboard* reported the singer had signed a record deal with Reprise Records, a subsidiary of Warner Bros. Guthrie's debut album was released a short month later, selling more than 200,000 copies by early spring 1968. When he got around to releasing his second album for Reprise in October 1968, his *Alice's Restaurant* LP was still selling well and sitting comfortably on the charts. As Woody's biographer Joe Klein astutely noted, *Alice's Restaurant* "would bring Arlo more fame and commercial success by the age of nineteen than Woody had achieved in his entire life."[7]

To Guthrie's credit, he argued any comparisons made of his own work to that of his father were meaningless. Two years into his career as a recording artist, he mused, "Although I was in [Woody's] shadow until a couple of years ago, I was always of *today*. *His* today has passed, so there was never any feeling of competition."[8] Though Woody, who passed in October of 1967, was no longer physically present, Guthrie recognized the brilliance and timelessness of his father's best work. He chose, from the beginning, to include several of his father's songs in his concerts—and never made apologies for it. The very first time Guthrie played on stage, at age thirteen, he performed a trio of songs composed by his father. "I've always included my dad's songs and I've never felt bad about doing them," he offered. "I love doing them."[9]

He was judicious about selecting songs from his father's expansive catalog. Though Woody's *Dust Bowl Ballads* might have been his most famous cycle of songs, as an established artist in his own right Arlo Guthrie chose to perform those ballads only on select occasions. He allowed that many of Woody's Dust Bowl songs "don't have much meaning for a general audience."[10] The songs of his father's he most often performed over ensuing decades were those he deemed ageless—such ballads as "Deportee (Plane Wreck at Los Gatos)" and "I Ain't Got No Home."

Arlo Guthrie's time in the celebrity spotlight burned most brightly in the years 1968 through 1972. The attention his *Alice's Restaurant* garnered following release would soon be eclipsed by the media storm accompanying the Arthur Penn/United Artists film based on his epic and iconic talking blues. Suddenly Guthrie's personage was everywhere. His photograph appeared on the front covers of such national magazines as *Newsweek* and *Esquire*. Lengthy profiles of him were splashed across the pages of such glossies as *Life* and *Look* and *Playboy*. Revelatory features appeared in the *Saturday Review* and the *New Yorker*. The Guthrie family's musical heritage was analyzed and dissected at length in the Sunday supplements of the *New York Times*, the *Chicago Tribune*, and the *Boston Globe*.

It was a dizzying time. The American Greeting Card company issued a series of moody posters of highways and meadows with overlays featuring the "Soft Touch" poetry of such Arlo Guthrie originals as "Highway in the Wind" and "Meditation (Wave Upon Wave)." To help decorate the funkier walls of college dorm rooms, other companies offered giant black-and-white "Personality Posters" of a floppy-hatted Guthrie playing guitar. It's possible no commercial poster could beat the one in striking Day-Glo orange of Guthrie defiantly gesturing with a middle-finger salute. Guthrie was booked on the talk and variety television shows of such luminaries as Johnny Carson, David Frost, Johnny Cash, and others. He and country singer Marty Robbins would appear as featured guests on an Everly Brothers TV special in July of 1970.

"The Alice's Restaurant Massacree" and Guthrie's subsequent appearance at the Woodstock festival in August of 1969 would forever inform the course of his career. He acknowledged that immediately following Woodstock, the mostly egalitarian music scene would change overnight—rock 'n' roll was now big business. He was caught up in the middle of it for a time, admitting he had become "a new marketable product." He made a small fortune in just a few years' time but spent "it as quickly as I made it."[11] But even before Woodstock, the *New York Times* reported Guthrie's concert appearance fee was not inconsequential, a healthy "$3,000 each, plus a percentage of the gross."[12] There was no longer a need for Guthrie to crash on Phil Ochs's couch. Success enabled a $400 per month apartment rental not far from Greenwich Village's Washington Square Park.

Public acclaim, of course, brought public criticism. Guthrie was the occasional target of journalists put off by his laconic manner and hippie-speak. In 1968, the *Chicago Tribune* coldly dismissed Guthrie's aptitude as a singer, describing his vocals as "thin and ordinary, like anybody's son singing in the shower. Perhaps because he sings with a hayseed accent that is not his own, he has a tendency to mumble many of the words."[13] Again, to be fair, the critic was not alone in this opinion. Following a concert at Tanglewood, Pete Seeger's own mother—a classical violinist—pressed her son to teach "Arlo not to sing so nasally."[14]

Such early criticism—well-meaning or otherwise—was not uncommon at the beginning. Others variously described Guthrie's vocals as reedy, nasal, and tinny. One critic begrudged that Guthrie was, at the very least, capable of making the most of his limited gift. The singer's voice was obviously "not trained," a *Variety* reviewer conceded, "nor does he tax it."[15]

Guthrie's younger sister, Nora, the author, record producer, and president of Woody Guthrie Publications, agreed her brother's speech was a mix of dissonant inflections. Their mother, Marjorie, was determined her children's speech be expunged of their native-to-Brooklyn accents. To this end a drama teacher was hired to give all three of her children (Arlo, Nora, and Joady) elocution lessons.[16] The lessons were only partly successful. It was the belief of some that Guthrie's slow "Okie drawl" was partly picked up from Ramblin' Jack Elliott, who lived on and off with the family in the years 1951–52. The circular irony of all this is that Elliott too was Brooklyn-born, the esteemed folk singer having picked up his *own* drawl from Woody Guthrie's 78-rpm recordings.

The commercial success of "Alice's Restaurant" as both a recording and a Hollywood film allowed Guthrie a measure of financial freedom to ruminate on the things most important to him—which were not always about music. If *Seventeen* was expecting the usual lighthearted celebrity interview with an emerging star, the reporter was in for a surprise. Instead of using the interview as a means to sell records, Guthrie chose instead to ponder a path beyond stardom: "Right now I know I'm in a time of growing and changing, and I don't know where I'm going yet. This is my trip and I'm trying to figure out whether I'm moving in the direction of the spiritual or the material or both. I've got all the material things I need—I'm rich that way in that I don't need very much, really—and the spiritual is something I'm finding in myself."[17]

Guthrie's interest in matters of the spirit was present in his music from the very beginning. This inquisitiveness regarding moral issues organically manifested itself in his lyrics. There were few religions he didn't explore and contrast, searching for their mutual tenets of enlightenment. In 1968 he obliquely described this energy as "The Source," a sort of nondenominational higher power. "I don't go to any particular church," Guthrie would tell Long Island's *Newsday,* "but I walk with whatever it is that's there. Yeah, I'm an established believer. I rap with Him, and that's good enough reason to believe He's there."[18]

It would be incorrect to suggest Guthrie merely "passed through" his religious studies. The most sensible, universal, and charitable aspects of the world's religions and belief systems would inform his life and work in continuum. But he confessed to being particularly interested in religions of the East since he thought those teachings "a little more realistic."[19] Decades later Guthrie, raised in Judaism, admitted, "I've been through it all—Catholicism, Buddhism, Hinduism, and all the other -isms. I love the varieties of devotion. If God wanted every flower to be the same, he would've made them that way."[20]

Such blending of religious thought was already factored in Guthrie's belief system when he was first introduced to his guru, Ma Jaya Sati Bhagavati, founder of the Kashi Ashram in Sebastian, Florida. Through Ma, Guthrie immersed himself in bringing a measure of comfort and friendship to those terminally ill. Such activism was not new to him, as he had done similar bedside visitations as an ordained Brother of the Franciscan Order in the 1970s. Guthrie reflected that the sort of things Ma Jaya taught were "the sort of things that my dad and mom were doing: take care of those that are not as fortunate, take care of those who are in trouble, stand up for the little guys."[21] Guthrie would tell the *Washington Post* in 1968, "It's all right to separate church and state, but we've separated spirit and person. It's not only wrong to treat people like machines, but also to treat a dog just like he's a dog. We are denying the life flow. We are lost in a world of dead things."[22]

It's tempting to suggest Guthrie's interest in issues of illness and mortality is, at least in part, due to his living in the shadow of a possible Huntington's disease diagnosis. There was certainly cause for concern. This hereditary degenerative nerve disease had not only taken the life of his father at age fifty-five, but also that of his grandmother and two of Woody's children from a first marriage.

Though often framed as a "protest singer," Arlo Guthrie has always practiced a brand of politics uniquely his own. There is, of course, no shortage of Woody Guthrie and Pete Seeger Popular Front polemics mixed alongside his personal political sensibilities. Always the iconoclast, Guthrie engaged the hotbed issues of the day to inform but not necessarily define his songwriting. Though often painted as a radical, he wasn't the archetypical angry young man of the '60s. "The scene for young people used to be all anti-everything, marching, protesting," Guthrie mused in 1968. "But I'm not against anything anymore. Now I want to find out what I'm for, not against."[23]

Such independent thinking has caused Guthrie to be considered suspect by those on the political fringes. Some on the left saw his music as less revolutionary in spirit than that of his father. The son would disagree. "I'm more closely aligned with my father than at any time I can remember, he explained. "It seems to me that the struggle we have around the world now is not between right and left as much as between those with too much and those with too little. There are people in this world who actually believe that government works best when it serves those with the most. I'm not one of 'em. I believe government ought to serve everyone about the same even if it's lousy government."[24]

In the final analysis, it's Guthrie's music that will be remembered. Though he would go on limited band sorties in 1969 and 1971, Guthrie was a mostly solo performer in the earliest days of his career, playing guitar, harmonica, and piano on stage. In those early years John Pilla, Guthrie's best friend and producer, would sometimes accompany him on second guitar. This situation changed in the autumn of 1975 when Pilla brought Guthrie to Woody's Roadhouse, a saloon in Washington, Massachusetts. Pilla had become fond of a band named Shenandoah, an incredibly versatile country-rock outfit who played the roadhouse regularly. That night the folk singer surprised everyone when he asked the combo if they'd care to go with him on tour as his backing band. It was an inspired partnership that lasted, with occasional personnel changes, for the next thirteen years or so. Guthrie continued to both tour and record with former members of Shenandoah right up until his final concert in March 2020. Then the world changed with the arrival of the pandemic.

My world changed too in 2020, a couple of months prior to the Covid lockdowns. I was given a medical diagnosis in early January that . . . well, let's just say I was the recipient of a prognosis no patient wishes to hear. By the time March 2020 rolled around I was just starting to emerge from the fog of two months of chemotherapy and radiation treatments. In 2012 my book *Arlo Guthrie: The Warner Reprise Years* appeared, a study written, alas, without the cooperation of the title subject. So it was a complete surprise when, eight years on, I received an email from Guthrie, asking if I had interest in helping him with a book he was contemplating. The new book would examine the second act of his career in music, roughly picking up from the point where my previous book finished off. I wasn't sure how I should respond to the request as I was still feeling weak from my recent health issues. But it was an opportunity I couldn't pass on, so I said "yes."

The following night Guthrie e-mailed me after his gig at Atlanta's Variety Playhouse. It was a short note, reading in part, "I was never into really writing or thinking seriously about an autobiography, but things change.

I'm just kicking the idea around. What I liked about your book was that it wasn't a tell-all kind of biography. It was simply what, where, who, when and some why. But more than that it was readable. . . . There are stories to events that might be interesting to other people, not wildly popular maybe, but for anyone interested it might be fun."[25]

So it was in this spirit that we have assembled *Rising Son: The Life and Music of Arlo Guthrie*, the artist sharing with us—for the very first time—his stories and anecdotes, commentaries and memories. Guthrie's storytelling gift is, I promise, no less entertaining and insightful on the printed page than on stage. My contribution has been providing contextual structure and placing events in their historical timeline. Of course, this being a book about Arlo Guthrie, one can expect the occasional digression. In a review of a Guthrie show in Toronto circa 1969, one truculent critic raged, "There is a limit to how much folk chit-chat (half-completed stories and anecdotes about air trips, what went on backstage before the concert and so on) one can stand without getting a miserable dose of indigestion."[26]

Well, we certainly hope our sidebar discourses will not make you sick. But if you have been a longtime admirer of Guthrie's shaggy-dog storytelling and homespun homilies—or have some interest in the folk singer's musings on the music industry, politics, spiritual matters—I'm confident you are already well prepared to expect the odd narrative detour or two . . . or three. It goes, as they say, with the territory.

While the old adage warns, "The devil is in the details," I contend angels reside there as well. This became readily apparent when I began mapping the timeline of Guthrie's career. Though one might assume there's a predetermined trajectory guiding an artist's life, this is fantasy. It's only after sorting through the minutiae of details, dates, events, successes, near-misses, chance meetings, and back-to-the-wall problem-solves that one can appreciate how a spontaneous moment or impromptu friendship might flash an inspirational spark. Not all great art is the result of divine intervention.

The title track of Guthrie's 1996 album, *Mystic Journey*, seems to support this hypothesis. In its description of a mystical road trip, the song suggests that a moment of magic might ignite at any time by any circumstance: by the stars in the sky, "in the passing of cars/at a table in the bar/in a turn of the cards/in a change of your mind/in the passing of time." I've attempted to chronicle Guthrie's professional career in this light. The singer's ten months of yearly touring afforded him opportunities and observations to see America as his father saw it. An imperfect place, perhaps, but one whose best professed ideals were worth fighting for.

Generally speaking, the music of folksingers now falls well outside the sphere of the pop-music market. That an artist like Guthrie could consistently and dependably sell out theater and nightclub engagements for a half-century mattered little to record company accountants—whose only interest was whether or not such appearances brought with them attendant album sales. Though Pete Seeger managed several pop-folk hit records for Decca in 1950–52 when recording with the Weavers, his subsequent tenure as a solo artist for Columbia was not a commercially successful one—assuming, of course, that one only considers unit sales as the measure. And although Woody Guthrie's legend appears to grow larger with each succeeding decade, the truth remains the balladeer didn't sell too many records in his lifetime.

In contrast, Guthrie's fifteen-year run with Reprise/Warner Bros. was a mostly successful partnership. Though none of the albums issued after *Alice's Restaurant* would chart as high, every album released subsequently would register on both the *Billboard* 200 and the *Cash Box* charts. In 1972, his single of Steve Goodman's "City of New Orleans," culled from his *Hobo's Lullaby* LP, would even sneak into the Top 40—rising as high as number 16 on the *Cash Box* chart. His last few albums on Warner Bros. would similarly chart upon initial release, though their appearances there were not long-lasting. It was disappointing, especially since a lot of great music was not reaching the ears of the general public. But Guthrie wasn't alone in this regard. In the early 1980s the record industry itself was in transition.

In 2016 and 2019 Guthrie suffered strokes, the second of which led to his decision to retire from touring. (Guthrie would announce in November 2022 that he would return to the stage in April 2023—not for a concert tour but for a series of open forum discussions with Robert Santelli of the Grammy Museum). But the folksinger's initial retirement announcement came as a surprise, softened only by the knowledge that Guthrie never intended a career in music. His earliest dream was to live off the grid, to enjoy the serenity and solitary life of a forest ranger. Music would remain an integral part of his life, but only as a private affair, playing songs with friends visiting his woodland sanctuary.

Obviously, Guthrie's dream didn't work out as planned. It was, perhaps, his greatest failure. Guthrie chose instead to live his life on the road, rambling troubadour-style from town to town, city to city, country to country for some six decades. Perhaps his early dream might yet bloom in retirement, singing and playing informally with close friends and family around a campfire. Maybe even sharing a story or two with them. In the meantime, we hope the stories the artist shares with us here in *Rising Son: The Life and Music of Arlo Guthrie* will remind fans of the accomplishments that made up the second act of his career in music. We invite you to ride along with us on Guthrie's ever-searching mystic journey.

Chapter One

THE SUN IS SINKING DOWN, 1981–1982

The recording of Arlo Guthrie's ninth studio album, *Power of Love,* would begin March 1, 1981. The trade magazine *Billboard* was the first to break the news, a brief item noting, "Arlo Guthrie is working on his 10th [*sic*] Warner Bros. LP at the label's Amigo Studios."[1] One month later, *Rolling Stone* also teased that a new Guthrie studio album was forthcoming. "It's going to be called *Power of Love,*" the folk singer told an *RS* correspondent, "which is the name of a T-Bone Burnett song that's on the record."[2] *Power of Love* would be the last of his studio albums issued on Warner Bros., at least for some time. Guthrie recollected his "days spent in the studio making records were winding down, at least as far as Warner's was concerned. But there was still one left to do."[3]

John Pilla, Guthrie's long-standing and musically simpatico compadre, would serve as sole producer on *Power of Love.* Warner Bros. president Lenny Waronker was designated executive producer, the title mirroring his involvement in Guthrie's three most recent albums, *Amigo* (1976), *One Night* (1978), and *Outlasting the Blues* (1979). At age twenty-eight, Waronker, alongside Van Dyke Parks, produced the first Los Angeles sessions of a twenty-two-year old Guthrie in May 1969. Waronker was a relatively new face at Reprise Records back then. In April 1966 Mo Ostin, Warner's general manager, enticed Waronker from his position at Liberty Records, bringing him onboard as an A&R ("Artists and Repertoire") executive at Reprise, a subsidiary label.[4]

The resulting album of that first Guthrie-Waronker collaboration, *Running Down the Road* (1969), served as a template for the studio albums that followed: *Washington County* (1970), *Hobo's Lullaby* (1972), *Last of the Brooklyn Cowboys* (1973), and *Arlo Guthrie* (1974). Guthrie's albums of this period were wonderfully mosaic in composition: a mix of Arlo's original songs with those of Woody Guthrie, Bob Dylan, Hoyt Axton, Mississippi John Hurt, Gus Cannon, and others. Though John Pilla was only obliquely credited as "Spiritual Advisor" on *Running Down the Road,* he and Waronker would coproduce Guthrie's next four albums.

It was with the release of *Pete Seeger & Arlo Guthrie: Together in Concert* (1975), a two-LP set assembled from board tapes of the pair's celebrated 1974 concerts in New York, Chicago, Montreal, and Boston, that Pilla was first credited as the sole producer. When *Amigo* was released in late August 1976, Pilla was again credited solo. Waronker—whose pop music business acumen was in the ascendant—was now listed only as executive producer.

Power of Love was to be recorded in Los Angeles at the Amigo/Warner Bros. Recording Studio, a modest, otherwise nondescript building at 1114 Cumpston Avenue, in North Hollywood:

> **AG**: Amigo Studios was probably our favorite among the vast number of recording studios available to us. It was out of the way, and nearby some decent Mexican food. Don Landee was the usual engineer for the records we made there. Rickie Lee Jones, Leonard Cohen, Randy Newman, and Ry Cooder were at times recording there as well—all of whom I loved.
>
> We had recorded the entire album at Amigo Studios, which by then had changed its official name to Warner Bros. North Hollywood Studios (or something like that), but we had been recording there for many years and referred to it as it was originally known—Amigo Studios.

Power of Love was engineered by the young and brilliant Mark Linett, whose production credits included work on albums by such artists as Randy Newman, Michael McDonald, Los Lobos, and Rickie Lee Jones. Guthrie recalled Linett as a "really good guy with impeccable taste."[5] Guthrie's road band, Shenandoah, was noticeably absent from the new recording. But their contributions to Guthrie's newest effort were reflected in the inclusion of two of the album's best tracks. Steve and Carol Ide contributed one original song to the new project ("Give It All You Got"), and guitarist David Grover a second ("If I Could Only Touch Your Life"). Otherwise no other member of Guthrie's roadhouse rock band contributed to *Power of Love.*

The absence of Shenandoah was by no means a slight. The band had proven to be outstanding musical contributors to Guthrie's most recent and brilliant—if commercially underperforming—LPs *One Night* (1978) and *Outlasting the Blues* (1979). The band's absence on the new album was not conspiratorial. Shenandoah had been working in the New England area long before teaming with Guthrie in the summer of 1975. Simultaneous to Guthrie's *Power of Love* sessions, Shenandoah was cutting tracks for their own project at Spectrum Recorders in Lanesborough, Massachusetts.[6]

When asked why Los Angeles was chosen to record *Power of Love* (Guthrie's previous studio album had been recorded close to home at Long View Farm Studios in Brookfield, Massachusetts), the singer was matter-of-fact in his answer. "I don't like doing the same thing over and over again, and there are some friends of mine in LA that I really wanted to play with and haven't played with in a while."[7] Waronker and Pilla managed to pull together a pretty remarkable team to support Guthrie on the new album, one promising to be his most polished to date. The folk-rock singer was particularly happy to reteam with friends regarded as the crème de la crème of the West Coast session scene: Russ Kunkel on drums and percussion, Jai Winding on keyboards, Bob Glaub on bass, and Leah Kunkel on vocals.

This ensemble, not accidentally, was the nucleus with whom Guthrie had satisfyingly recorded in early summer 1976. "It's a great band," Guthrie offered to *Rolling Stone*. "They're pretty much the same guys I worked with on *Amigo*."[8] Guthrie was pleased to be recording at Amigo studios again. He had only fond memories of working on that album, often citing *Amigo* as his finest effort. It was during those sessions of 1976 that he and his family managed to live the Hollywood celebrity life—if only for a month or so:

> **AG:** On June 19, 1976, we began work on "Amigo," which technically is still probably among the top three records I ever made. We'd rented the old Belgian embassy, which was a big sprawling house on Mulholland Drive, a short distance away from Amigo Studios. It had guest quarters that John Pilla used and a pool. Jackie, myself, and our young kids, Abe and Cathy, loved the place. In fact I could have bought the place, and wanted to, but my manager, Harold Leventhal, was totally opposed to it. He was probably right in that we had little money in those days.

Not all of Guthrie's memories from that working vacation in the summer of '76 were of a musical nature:

AG: A friend of Jackie's gave us a German Shepherd puppy named Max. I loved the dog and took him to work in the rent-a-car. I thoughtlessly left Max in the car one day while we were in the studio, and when John and I returned to the car Max had torn apart the entire vehicle, leaving only wires and gauges dangling where the dashboard had been. Max ate the car.

Neither John nor I wanted to confront the rent-a-car company, so we got Jackie, who was very pregnant with our soon-to-be-born daughter, Annie, to return the car, thinking that the company would look more kindly on a pregnant woman. It was not a problem, as everything was insured, but I never left Max alone in a car again. When the recording came out in 1976, we called it "Amigo" in honor of the studio.

Amigo was, in the estimation of many critics, Guthrie's finest studio album to date. His songwriting talents were certainly affirmed on *Amigo*. The often hard to please Robert Christgau swooned over the new LP, advising Guthrie's latest had him "pulling out my old Arlo albums" for fresh reevaluation.[9] *Amigo* was inarguably the most commercially viable of his studio recordings for Reprise, though Guthrie sighed, "No one paid much attention to it."[10] *Amigo* frustratingly peaked at number 133 on *Billboard's* Top 200 albums chart.[11]

If *Amigo* did not enjoy any substantial commercial success, it likewise didn't receive adequate promotion. Nonetheless, Guthrie suggested *Power of Love* would be, in some respect, an extension of *Amigo*. This was essentially true as both albums featured gorgeous production, brilliant arrangements, and expert musicianship. There was one significant difference: *Amigo* sounded very much like a traditional Arlo Guthrie album, the singer serving as principal or co-songwriter on seven of eleven tracks. *Power of Love*, in contrast, would feature only two Guthrie originals. What both of these new—and very personal—songs shared was a suggestion the singer was tiring of living on the road apart from loved ones.

Aside from the assembled "nucleus," a number of musical guests also contributed to *Power of Love*. Fred Tackett, on break from touring with an evangelized Bob Dylan, contributed a bit of acoustic guitar to one song, electric guitar virtuoso Robben Ford on another. *Power of Love* also featured a number of prominent female singers assisting with primary and backup vocals: Leah Kunkel, Penny Nichols, and Rickie Lee Jones.

AG: Lenny Waronker introduced me to Rickie Lee Jones around that time. She was working on a record in the same place. She accepted my invitation to sing with me on an old song, "Jamaica Farewell." It was one song we both knew, and I was just goofing off with her when, unfortunately, my changing the words a little got recorded and we left it that way on the record.

Leonard Cohen was another old friend recording at Amigo at the same time Guthrie was working on *Power of Love:*

AG: In the middle of the sessions, Leonard Cohen, whom I'd come to know at various events over the years and decades, came into the control booth and said, "Arlo, I'm working on a new record, you want to hear some of it?" I said, "No, your songs are too depressing for me." We laughed. John and I referred to Leonard as 'Laughing Lenny' because his songs were so serious, and our nickname for him was not disrespectful. "You'll really like this one it's much more 'happy,'" he said. So I went over to another studio within the complex and listened to what he was working on. It was the same great stuff as always, but the same depressing material nonetheless. I told Leonard, "Wait a minute! I thought you said it's not going to be depressing!" He and I laughed. "It's less depressing than anything I've done!" he exclaimed. Leonard Cohen actually had a wonderful wry sense of humor.

Power of Love was the slickest and most polished album of Guthrie's entire oeuvre to date. The album was also one of the shortest, the final album's ten tracks clocking in at a mere thirty-five minutes. Such a brief running time was not unusual for, say, a Willie Nelson album revisiting the American songbook. But it seemed a stingy offering from an artist whose signature song *alone* ran 18 minutes and 20 seconds.

The new album kicked off with T-Bone Burnett's "Power of Love." It was a fresh song, the songwriter only recently waxing the track himself on his 1980 solo effort *Truth Decay.* Burnett was a Midwesterner making a name as both a producer and songwriter of the Americana school. He worked with Dylan's Rolling Thunder Revue, subsequently recording a trio of albums for Arista with fellow Revue alumni Steven Soles and David Mansfield. Guthrie is joined on the title track by guest vocalist and old friend

Phil Everly of Everly Brothers fame. The funky rhythmic groove of Bob Glaub's loping bass serves as a great opening volley.

Sadly, *Power of Love* did not satisfy Guthrie's ardent fan base. Many thought the album too slick and not particularly representative of Guthrie's established style. But while the album was undeniably his most lushly produced, it also remains his most underappreciated. The brilliance of the album's opening track was recognized by some, one critic noting Guthrie's "harmonies with Phil Everly on the chorus . . . provide some real electricity."[12]

The album's second track, "Oklahoma Nights," was a fresh song from the pen of celebrated composer Jimmy Webb. Webb's ability to craft a marketable pop song was not in doubt. His successes were legendary. He was the composer of Richard Harris's "MacArthur Park" and the writer of a trio of hit singles for session guitarist and pop country icon Glen Campbell: "By the Time I Get to Phoenix," "Wichita Lineman," and "Galveston." Guthrie's soaring vocal on the last line of "Oklahoma Nights" is pretty remarkable. As a singer best known for his trademark nasal twang, Guthrie rarely dared go that high in vocal register.

"Oklahoma Nights" provides the album with one of its most riveting moments, abetted perfectly by the swelling strains of orchestral strings. After listening to this tour de force performance, one critic wryly offered, "One can only wonder how Glen Campbell let this one get away."[13] Warner Bros. thought Guthrie's rendering was special as well, the company issuing the track as a radio promotional single. Sadly, the promotional 45 did not generate significant airplay.

The album's third track, "If I Could Only Touch Your Life," was a tender love song cowritten by Aaron Schroeder and Shenandoah guitarist David Grover. This wistful song was rare in Guthrie's recorded catalog as it was performed as a duet with Leah Kunkel. Kunkel, the sister of Cass Elliot and wife of *Power of Love* drummer Russ Kunkel, was a much sought-after session vocalist. She was also a songwriter of merit, Guthrie having recorded her tuneful "Walking Song" on *Amigo*. Kunkel's crystal-clear soprano on "If I Could Only Touch Your Life" is as breathtaking as any performance Guthrie and Pilla would capture on magnetic tape.

Warner Bros. believed they still might have a winning radio-friendly track in "If I Could Only Touch Your Life," issuing a second promotional single off of *Power of Love* in August 1981. *Billboard* was impressed. They added the single to their recommended "Pop" music list signaling a "tune predicted to land on the Hot 100 between 31 and 100."[14] Alas, this single too fell through the cracks. In the spring of 1981, Guthrie briefly included the song in his concert dates, vocalist Carol Ide taking on Kunkel's challenging solo—and doing a particularly fine job of it. Sadly, the song would not remain in Guthrie's set list for long, disappearing from his shows by summer's end.

The one song on the album most critics agreed was a highlight was a haunting take on "Waimanalo Blues," with vocalist Penny Nichols singing alongside Guthrie in seamless harmony. The gentle island faux folk song had been composed by Liko Martin and Thor Wold and appeared on the obscure 1975 LP *We Are the Children* (Trim Records) as recorded by the Hawaiian band Country Comfort. One critic gushed, "The way the background vocals on 'Waimanalo Blues' slide from typical *ooh-wah-ooh* into approximation of a Hawaiian guitar is both clever and musically effective."[15]

Not every critic was so moved. Writing in the *Village Voice*, Leslie Berman sourly offered, "The jarring, over-produced Rupert Holmes-goes-to-Antigua "Waimanalo Blues" . . . would fall flat if it were anyone else's album—only Arlo's sincerity saves it from MOR [middle of the road] obscurity."[16] *Stereo Review* took issue, opining "it wasn't until the fourth selection, "Waimanalo Blues," that I found [a track] that I *didn't* think was overproduced."[17] The problem—or, perhaps, strength—of *Power of Love*—was disagreement on the definition of "overproduced." It was all in the ear of the beholder.

Side one of the album closes with the first Guthrie original, the reggae-tinged "Living Like a Legend." The jaunty island rhythms and Guthrie's playful performance partly disguised the desperation of the lyric ("It isn't easy leaving you behind/I'm so tired of living this legend life alone.") Interestingly, Guthrie never considered the track a reggae song, despite its distinctive island flavor. "I think of it as 1950s Black rock 'n' roll out of New Jersey. You have to understand that reggae music is influenced by 1950s rock 'n' roll," Guthrie explained, "by Black singers who were played on the radio in places where reggae comes from. I don't do reggae 'cause I don't come from there. I come from Coney Island in Brooklyn."[18]

The first track on the B-side of *Power of Love* is the album's only up-tempo rocker, the cheery and optimistic "Give It All You Got." The song was cowritten by the husband and wife team of Steve and Carol Ide, occasionally performed by Shenandoah during their warm-up spots on the front end of Guthrie's concerts. While the song jump-starts the album's second side with a bracing dose of roadhouse rock 'n' roll, it contrasts with the otherwise wistful nature of the album's other nine songs. The song seems a stay-the-course response to Guthrie's two offerings of pensive road-weary songs. This track encourages looking forward, to "Say what needs to be said/Get it all out your head/and you'll be back on the road before long."

Yet another highlight is Guthrie's brilliant take on Richard Thompson's "When I Get to the Border." The song first appeared on Richard and Linda Thompson's *I Want to See the Bright Lights Tonight* LP (Island, UK, 1974). The song was one of Thompson's finest to date and Guthrie does it justice. Pilla chose to "Americanize" Guthrie's version, replacing the British songwriter's Celtic-style closing instrumental flourish with a swelling-strings arrangement. Britain's *Melody Maker* mused that Guthrie's cover "never matches the intensity of the composer's original, but is still an astute choice."[19]

The most interesting aspect of the reviews collected of *Power of Love* is there's no consensus on what the album's standout tracks actually are. Just as one critic raves "When I Get to the Border" is the LP's "standout cut,"[20] another dismisses Guthrie's performance on the same as an exercise in "pure escapism . . . man casting off his everyday hassles for fun in sand and sun."[21] The best one can say about the latter critique is the reviewer might be missing the metaphorical component of the term "border."

The third track on the record's flip side was "Jamaica Farewell," the Lord Burgess song Harry Belafonte famously recorded on his 1956 album *Calypso.* Guthrie's version, recorded with Rickie Lee Jones, is a mostly faithful copy of the original, if a bit more playful. It's also the track the harshest critics of *Power of Love* seized upon as the album's nadir.

It's hard to fathom why this was so since Guthrie's version was mostly innocuous. Its inclusion did provide an opportunity for reviewers nonplussed by Rickie Lee Jones's slight pop single "Chuck E's in Love" to sharpen their critical knives. One does wonder if the abundance of reggae and island rhythms present on *Power of Love* was an attempt by Warner Bros. to recast Guthrie as a Jimmy Buffett-style performer (Buffett had scored big with his hit single "Margaritaville" in 1977). The colorful Hawaiian shirt Guthrie dons on the front cover of *Power of Love*—as well as the beach-front photograph on the LP's rear sleeve—suggests this.

The final two songs on *Power of Love* are the only two that would become semi-staples of Guthrie's concert repertoire of the 1980s. The first was Guthrie's own "Slow Boat," a pensive, piano-backed dirge summoning ghosts of lost dreams and the personal cost of choosing a life on the road. The album concludes on a far lighter note with "The Garden Song," written by singer-songwriter David Mallet. Mallet taught the song to Paul Stookey of Peter, Paul and Mary fame, who taught the song to Pete Seeger— who then made it a staple of his concert appearances. Guthrie learned the song from Seeger, adding a verse of his own and embellishing the song in performance with his Will Rogers style spoken asides. Pilla and Guthrie brought in a children's choir to sing on the song's tuneful chorus. This recording marked the professional singing debut of all four of Guthrie's children and two of Lenny Waronker's as well.

The photographs and cover art packaging of *Power of Love* was every bit as colorful and vibrant as the music contained within:

AG: Before the recording sessions, John [Pilla] and I took a short vacation to Hawaii. It came about because Lenny was friends with David Cassidy, who had a home on Crozier Drive, near the town of Haleiwa, Hawaii, on the north shore of Oahu that he rarely used. Through Lenny, David had offered it to us for about two weeks starting February 1, 1981.

We took him up on the generous offer and had a fabulous time. I had acquired a new camera at the time, and we shot the cover of *Power of Love* on the beach outside David Cassidy's house. John was a skilled photographer and I was an avid picture-taker.

Somehow the art department at Warner's couldn't quite make the photos look right, so I suggested they profile the colors within the shots, and blur them so the pictures would pop on the album cover within the same color scheme. That's exactly what they did, and it looked great to me.

In the final tally, the reviews of *Power of Love* were evenly split. While no one suggested Guthrie's latest would be remembered as essential, some accepted the album for what it was. The Saskatchewan *Leader-Post* regarded *Power of Love* a "generally inoffensive product," lamenting only the album's "middle age spread."[22] The *Philadelphia Inquirer* was more positive: "Guthrie has compiled a selection of extremely pleasant songs for this release. He also enlisted some impressive help for studio support, resulting in several strong duets and background vocals."[23]

The most damaging—and widely circulated—review of *Power of Love* was written by *Rolling Stone's* Dave Marsh. In a brief summation syndicated in newspapers across the US, Marsh allowed that while "Guthrie is probably the last great folk-rock singer we have left . . . *Power of Love* doesn't do much to establish the fact." Describing the album as "one of Guthrie's least successful," Marsh blamed the production team for the album's "clunky" rockers and other perceived failures.[24]

Though Marsh wasn't writing headline copy, such large-typeset blurbs as *"Arlo Falls on his Face—Rickie Lee Doesn't Help,"*[25] weren't particularly helpful in moving units from warehouse to record shop. It was sometimes difficult to discern *what* a particular critic's thoughts were regarding *Power of Love*. One of the more memorable read, "Guthrie's new LP is like a midnight drive in a Mustang with the top down and a slight drizzle kissing your face."[26]

AG: *Power of Love* came out in 1981 and it still had some magic between the grooves. Although overall it wasn't my favorite work, it was one of my favorite times. I had no idea it would be the last record I'd make for Warner Bros.

In spring of 1981 Guthrie was due to go back on the road with Shenandoah for a three- week sortie taking them throughout the northeastern US and a bit beyond. But the singer had previously agreed to fly to England to appear on 13 April at a one-off show at The Venue, a London concert hall. The show was to benefit the "Master Musicians of Jajouka," a Moroccan music ensemble of ancient lineage. The North African troupe had gained attention in the West during the 1960s, the exposure opening an avenue to embark on their first-ever European tour in 1980. Things had gone well at first. Many of the earliest dates were played before capacity crowds. But the creaky French touring bus the ensemble purchased to transport them from gig to gig broke down midway through the tour, leaving them in debt for some 7,000 pounds.[27]

One fan of the ensemble was Karl Dallas, a well-respected music journalist and activist. Dallas chose to celebrate his fiftieth birthday in an unselfish manner, staging a benefit for the beleaguered Moroccans. He reached out to Arlo Guthrie and a score of musical friends asking if they

could help. Guthrie was seventeen years old when he first visited London in
July 1965, and Dallas was one of the first people he would meet upon
arrival. Dallas subsequently helped him navigate the then vibrant British
folk-music scene, introducing him to many of its principal players:

AG: In June of 1965, I graduated high school at the Stockbridge School
in Stockbridge, Massachusetts. I had been kicked out a couple of weeks
before graduation, for smoking cigarettes. Well, it was what I had confessed to smoking. However, being so near graduation, the school let
me return to receive my diploma.

I got a job, as an office boy, in Harold Leventhal's office in New York. I
would deliver envelopes to music publishers and other offices in the music
business. Mostly I hung around Harold's office playing music with Pete
Seeger, a client of Harold's. I also hung out with Judy Collins, Theo Bikel,
Harry Belafonte, and others who worked with Harold. I loved being there.

It didn't last long.

On July 2nd, I left New York for a trip to London. I had a guitar and
about three hundred dollars in cash. I was given a contact, a business
associate of Harold's, named David Platz. Platz was a music publisher
who ran Essex Music. I was given his name and number in case of
emergency.

I wandered around London for a couple of days sleeping on park
benches and eating food from street vendors. Finally I decided to get
some real sleep in a movie theater. I walked up to a ticket booth and
asked for a ticket to the movie. The woman asked me if I wished to purchase a ticket for the golden circle, or the silver circle, the purple bal-
cony, etc. There were a half dozen choices with varying ticket prices. I
had no idea what she was talking about: in America there was one
price, and you walked in and could sit anywhere you wanted.

I picked one, walked inside, and sat down—and promptly fell asleep
with my guitar in the seat to my left. I awoke with some guy's hand
crawling on my right leg. "Damn. I picked the wrong circle," I said to
myself. I got up and left the theater.

The event qualified as an emergency, so I went to meet David Platz,
who advanced me some cash, and also introduced me to a friend of his,
a music journalist, Karl Dallas. Karl heard my story and took me home
to his apartment, where he and his wife, Gloria, let me sleep on the

couch in their living room. I was very grateful. Karl and Gloria have remained lifelong friends.

On different nights, folksingers would gather at different folk clubs around London. Karl took me to all of them and introduced me to everyone. Every once in a while, I would sing a few songs. But mostly I loved being in places where people really loved singing, drinking, and performing. I met Alex Campbell and Derroll Adams, both of whom had known Ramblin' Jack Elliott a decade earlier. I also befriended Peter Bellamy, who would form one of my favorite musical groups, The Young Tradition. There were others too numerous to remember, although I was also introduced to Ewan MacColl and Peggy Seeger [Pete Seeger's half sister].

Karl set me up with a little tour of English folk clubs throughout the country. I traveled by bus and train and made my way from place to place, performing some of my father's songs and some of my own. Between gigs I would return to Karl's apartment continuing my stay on his couch.

Though fifteen years had since passed, Guthrie remained grateful for the kindness the Dallas family extended, so the chance to celebrate Dallas's birthday milestone—and help out fellow musicians in distress—could not be ignored. Unfortunately, Dallas's gifts did not extend to stage management. The benefit proved a grueling, marathon-length affair of some seven hours.

Though Guthrie was billed as one of the evening's main attractions—his appearances in Europe being rare of late—he was only one of many to sign on. Others on the program included Roy Harper, Rick Wakeman, Chaka Khan, Davy Graham, Bert Jansch, and a score of others. Dallas booked so much talent the event ran wildly behind schedule, with Guthrie not taking the stage until 2:30 AM. His set was abruptly curtailed at 3 AM, when theater management had enough. Guthrie had barely gotten through "City of New Orleans" and his father's "Pretty Boy Floyd" when all stage power was abruptly cut.[28]

Fans on the continent would have a second opportunity to catch the singer—this time backed by Shenandoah—a few months later. In June 1981 Guthrie was booked on a package tour of open-air concerts to swing through cities across western Europe. Shows were scheduled in and around St. Goarshausen and Nuremberg, Germany; Vienna, Austria; and St. Gallen,

Switzerland. Though the roster changed from city to city, most featured reggae star Peter Tosh and Guthrie as co-headliners. The two men and their bands would play in front of partying, sunlit crowds of thousands.

Some of these festivals were more acoustic-orientated. On 20 June Guthrie performed a solo acoustic set at the *Folkfestival auf der Donauinsel* (Folk Festival of Danube Island), in Vienna. Though he performed two songs from *Power of Love* ("Slow Boat" and "Living Like a Legend"), Guthrie tweaked his set list for this particular show. He thought he might better communicate by singing American folk and blues songs of which the audience might be more familiar. So Lead Belly's "Midnight Special" and Jesse Fuller's "San Francisco Bay Blues" were performed alongside Dylan's "Mr. Tambourine Man" and "Blowin' in the Wind." Near the conclusion of his set, Guthrie brought out British folk-rock stalwart Donovan to great applause. The two '60s icons performed Donovan's "Josie" as well as the traditional country classic "Will the Circle Be Unbroken?"

While touring Europe, Guthrie also appeared on local television— once on a German variety music program and again on a Swiss TV broadcast. The first had Guthrie playing alone on a guitar, performing a short medley of songs of which he was most associated: "City of New Orleans," "Coming into Los Angeles," and a chorus of "Alice's Restaurant." This was followed by a lip-synched performance of "Oklahoma Nights" from the new album. The second performance was an appearance on the Swiss television variety show *Karussell* ("Carousel"). He and Shenandoah bookended the thirty-minute program with performances of "City of New Orleans" and "Living Like a Legend." When asked by the program's host if he wished to convey a message to those watching at home, the visibly exhausted singer flatly replied, "No."[29] On 27 June, Guthrie performed in St. Gallen, the picturesque Swiss festival drawing a Saturday crowd of some twenty thousand.

Just as Guthrie finished up his European adventure, *Power of Love* was released in the US. The album entered *Billboard's* Top 200 album chart as entry number 184 on 27 June—disappointingly stalling in the same position on the second week of release. On 11 July the LP slipped to the number 198 slot and by week four dropped off the Top 200 chart.[30] It wasn't surprising, as rock and pop radio stations were pushing "New Wave" and disco music, two danceable, percussion-driven formats in current vogue. It didn't help that Warner Bros. seemed disinterested in promoting *Power of*

Love. Even Guthrie's most faithful fans in the US were unaware a new album had dropped. Aside from promo singles sent to radio outlets, there were no posters sent to record stores, few print advertisements found in the usual magazines, and no radio or television spots scheduled.

Even prior to the release of *Power of Love,* Guthrie was getting the feeling Warner Bros. was no longer working for their mutual benefit. Performing that spring before a boisterous audience at New Jersey's Ramapo College, Guthrie shared his exasperation. Following the usual shouts to play "Alice's Restaurant," Guthrie responded, "Let me tell you something. Some people make records of songs so that other people will ask to hear them. But I won't do that. I've always made records of songs so I wouldn't ever have to do them again. That gives you time to think of new stuff. It don't have to be better . . . just got to be different. Otherwise you end up doing the same thing all your life. That wouldn't be no fun. That's why we got cheap records."[31]

While on the subject of his records, Guthrie dryly offered, "Warner's doesn't like 'em. It's true." To visually demonstrate how the company was metaphorically dropping the publicity ball, Guthrie held his harmonica in an outstretched hand. "My company puts out records like this," he sighed. Loosening his grip, Guthrie allowed the instrument to drop in an inelegant free fall, watching it crash onto the stage. "It's kind of a fun way of [putting out records]," he remarked. "They like to put 'em out that way." In the words of one band member, Guthrie's pantomime resembled "a bomb falling over Pearl Harbor."[32]

Guthrie's North American summer tour of 1981 consisted of fun events, the shows often played under the stars in cavernous amphitheaters. The first of July began with a joint appearance with Woody Guthrie's old road buddy, Pete Seeger, at New Jersey's Garden State Arts Center. A few days later, Guthrie and Shenandoah crossed the border into Canada for a co-bill with Jesse Winchester at Toronto's Camp Fortune. In a phone interview with a Canadian journalist, Guthrie defended his mosaic style of "folk music," believing the term flexible in definition. He conceded not everyone understood nor appreciated his personal style of working within differing styles and traditions.

This group of people included music industry executives whose record companies preferred working with artists easily labeled and packaged. "The music business doesn't exactly know what to call [my music]," Guthrie explained. "They have trouble with that kind of variety." He believed industry brass preferred artists with a brand. Guthrie was pleased that his own music, even if not in alignment with contemporary pop music trends, held cross-generational appeal. "We get Moms and Dads . . . and then the kids like it too. And we get grandkids . . . it's more of a family thing."[33]

When the journalist asked Guthrie to share his thoughts on Ronald Reagan's recent election as fortieth president of the United States, Guthrie allowed, "It's a real interesting time, for sure." Accepting it was dissatisfaction with Jimmy Carter that allowed Reagan to sweep handily into the office, Guthrie mused, "I think I understand it. . . . I don't always agree with the reasons why it came about, but because I understand it, that scene doesn't scare me."[34] He conceded a lot of Americans were unhappy with Carter's handling of domestic and international affairs.

Carter was chastised at the ballot box for his perceived mishandling of the hostage crisis in Tehran and the Soviet Union's invasion of Afghanistan. Domestically, the president was under fire for rising unemployment numbers and gas pump shortages. While the new administration would inherit some of these issues, Guthrie was certain, in time, Reagan would create problems of his own doing. During his campaign, Reagan made the American people a lot of promises. "It just remains to be seen whether he'll remember those promises and do anything about them,"[35] Guthrie offered.

Guthrie's Ontario Place Forum show with Seeger was one of the largest in which the two would perform. Though one reviewer acknowledged Seeger's performances was greeted with "thunderous applause," Guthrie proved "a more compelling musical presence." The critic conceded Guthrie's "satiric radicalism . . . seems to have been consciously toned down" as the singer "injected only a few pointed political jabs into the show."[36]

Following the Canadian dates, the tour rolled restlessly through New England and the Midwest. On 11 July Guthrie and Shenandoah performed before an audience of six thousand at the Great Northeast Arts & Energy Festival in Ashby, Massachusetts. There was a "Woodstock '69" vibe to the weekend, with concertgoers skinny-dipping and picnicking and dancing and getting along peacefully. Watching events unfold from the stage, Guthrie was transported back a dozen years. "There's a feeling here we haven't seen in quite a while," Guthrie acknowledged. "It would be nice to make this a part of the way we live."[37]

It was a cheerful moment in the middle of a long tour. But Guthrie hadn't been feeling well since returning from Europe. The nagging pains bothering him escalated on the evening of Wednesday, 22 July. He was partway through his show at the University of British Columbia when his health issue came to a head. Midway through the Vancouver show it was clear to bandmates that Guthrie was suffering acute pain and could not soldier on. When the singer exited the stage early with a wobble, his long-serving concert sound engineer, Bruce Clapper, was concerned. Clapper, affectionately nicknamed "BC" by Guthrie, later explained to the local press that the folk singer "looked pretty pale, and he was obviously not comfortable. He wasn't able to talk much."[38]

Guthrie was rushed from the show to the university's Health Science Centre Hospital. The staff first thought the singer was suffering from a kidney stone issue. He was eventually diagnosed with pancreatitis: a painful inflammation causing acute abdominal distress. Clapper stated, "I guess the infection had been building in the pancreas." He conceded several early warning signs had been missed; everyone on the tour assumed the singer was simply dealing with a lingering summertime cold. In retrospect it was clear Guthrie's ill health was partly due to his punishing road schedule. Everyone admitted things had "been pretty hectic in the past month."[39]

It was time for a break . . . if only a short one. Guthrie remained in the hospital for several days, receiving treatment and recuperating. It was obvious that several upcoming dates would need to be cancelled or rescheduled. These included several eagerly anticipated West Coast concerts with Pete Seeger. By Sunday, 26 July, Guthrie was feeling somewhat better, managing to move about with a degree of comfort. He had been released from the hospital and was now resting at a Vancouver motel. Although he was still feeling a bit weak, he was optimistic he could be back on the road "a week from Wednesday."[40]

Guthrie was alone in Vancouver because Shenandoah had already returned to Boston. The band was scheduled to help push the state legislature's passage of a bill designating Guthrie's "Massachusetts" as the state's official folk song. The story behind the honor was, as were so many things in Guthrie's life, grassroots in conception. Guthrie's song was a favorite of Charlene Murphy, a schoolteacher from Chicopee, Massachusetts, who thought it a wonderful tribute to the state. So, in the winter of 1980, Murphy assigned her social studies students to research the present official state song of Massachusetts. The class learned that Massachusetts didn't actually *have* a state song—at least *officially*. The presumed official anthem, "All Hail to Massachusetts" (a march written in 1954 by Wellesley's Arthur J. Marsh), had been adopted in 1966 as a placeholder, but official recognition was never signed into law.[41]

So Murphy sought out Representative Kenneth M. Lemanski to submit a bill calling for Guthrie's song to be officially deigned as such. Once this *Quixote*-like mission caught the attention of the local press, others joined in on the lobbying. The cause was bolstered when children from all over Massachusetts lobbied in support of the bill with a statewide letter-writing campaign. A Boston DJ, interested in doing his part, dusted off the four-year-old *Amigo* track, spinning the song as often as possible. Representative Lemanski submitted the proposal to the House legislature on 3 December 1980. It was now a waiting game, with everyone awaiting government cogs to turn.[42]

On 11 March 1981, Murphy was summoned to the statehouse in Boston to make her case. The teacher brought along thirteen students, several with guitars, to nervously lobby before the legislature. That afternoon the children serenaded the bewildered chamber with Guthrie's song. Three students addressed the lawmakers, one pointing out the Marsh composition was "so little known it is not mentioned in any history book."[43] Though the machinations of government turned slowly, on 9 June the House voted to pass the new bill, pushing approval on to the state Senate.

The idea of Arlo Guthrie's song becoming the official state anthem was an exciting proposition. It was especially endearing as this was no record company ploy conceived to sell discs. Guthrie was barely aware himself what was going on in his behalf. But when informed, the songwriter admitted, "I'm real excited about it. . . . It's certainly a surprise."[44] Things seemed to be going well for the measure, though there were protests by some who thought an open competition for state song honors should first be held. Others expressed concern that Guthrie's song didn't mention the Commonwealth's rich historic, tourist-attracting iconography.

Despite the protests, the Massachusetts Senate passed the bill with enthusiasm. There was one sticking point. In the bill's draft, the state administration committee put in the proviso that Guthrie would need to relinquish the song's copyright . . . which wasn't likely to happen. The House subsequently negotiated an amendment allowing Guthrie to retain ownership. On 7 August 1981, Governor Edward J. King signed the bill into law . . . with a caveat: Guthrie's "Massachusetts" would be designated only as the state's official folk song.[45]

Three days prior to the bill's passage, a healthy Guthrie was back on the road. "Nice to be back working," Guthrie told the crowd at Toad's Place in New Haven.[46] It was the first show after Vancouver, so the ensuing program resembled an open rehearsal. A local newspaper described the evening as "an engaging three-and-a-half-hour marathon," more akin to a Grateful Dead show than a folk-music concert.[47] Guthrie performed "Massachusetts," acknowledging that some folks thought there were far better songs celebrating his adopted home state. Guthrie was O.K. with the protests, sharing a single hesitancy: "Pete Seeger once told me that the only thing worse than *banning* a song is making it *official*."

The following night, Guthrie would take the stage with Pete Seeger for a concert in the round at Long Island's Westbury Music Fair. The critic Leslie Berman was in attendance, sitting alongside her mom ("My mother loved it," she reported).[48] Berman was covering the evening's show for a column she was preparing for the *Village Voice*. It was the critic's opinion that while Guthrie's catalog was sprinkled with gems, his studio albums, no matter how engaging, were unable to "duplicate the genuine enthusiasm of Arlo's shows, where his continuing ability to persuade, activate, and keep the faith is invigorating, provocative, and exemplary."[49]

Surveying Westbury's audience, Berman noted these occasional Seeger-Guthrie pairings brought together two disparate groups. The audiences could be halved between the "I-remember-the-McCarthy-'50s types and kids of the pampered-princess variety."[50] It was for the former that Seeger performed a passionate rendering of "L'Internationale," the Eugene Pottier/Pierre DeGeyter revolutionary worker's song. The radical song had long served as a rallying anthem for adherents of the political left, even having the distinction of once having served as the official national anthem of the Soviet Union.

It was, to some, a disturbing song for Seeger to resurrect. Not everyone thought the anthem appropriate in light of historical events. Following the elder folk singer's annual holiday concert of 1978, the otherwise friendly Seeger fan and critic John Leonard sighed in the *New York Times,* "I won't sing along with *The Internationale,* not even for Pete Seeger in Carnegie Hall. . . . After Stalin and after Cambodia, *The Internationale* is campy if not obscene."[51]

What the Long Island kids thought of the song was irrelevant; few of
the young fans who gathered would have had any notion of the song's ped-
igree. It was simply another Pete Seeger sing-along which everyone was
encouraged to join in on. It *was* difficult not to get swept up by Seeger's
spirit, the singer's gray beard tilted back as he conducted his audience-
chorus with waving-arm gestures. Seeger did concede the Left's making
"*The Internationale*" official was "a big mistake."[52]

Guthrie used "*L'Internationale*" as the springboard to his performance
of "Massachusetts"—still two days away from official recognition. He riffed:

> I was thinking about the other song, you know about making songs
> official and I know what Pete is talking about: because up in the
> state of Massachusetts now, they've been working on trying to make
> one of my songs official—official in the sense that they are going to
> make it an official state song or folk song or something like that.
> Nobody knows what that means, but they're going to do it anyhow.
>
> But it ran into all kinds of problems because all of a sudden
> there were other people who thought their songs would be better
> suited for the job. And I know what they were talking about because
> my song didn't mention Pilgrims, Plymouth Rock; all kinds of
> Massachusetts-New England things. And so I kind of halfway agree
> that my song didn't really have all the things that school kids love
> to sing about.[53]

Guthrie then moved into the story of his "great ancestor" Chief "Guts"
Guthrie. Old Guts, he explained, was a forgotten figure of the clan, a guy
"who lived a long time ago and was a famous Indian writer."[54] The apocry-
phal chief, Guthrie continued, even wrote a poem about the Bay State,
since he "was kind of an historical observer [who] wrote songs that had to
do with Pilgrims and Plymouth Rock and stuff like that. I thought if my
song didn't make it, this song would. So I'm forgetting about my song now
and sending [this one] to the governor of Massachusetts as I think it would
be a better state song."[55] Guthrie then tilted into an acapella rendering of
his playful "Mighty Pilgrim Fathers," its melody lifted from Tom Glazer's
old Union hymn, "Because All Men Are Brothers."

Ten days after the Westbury gig, Guthrie and Shenandoah—sans
Seeger—were back playing straight-ahead folk-rock at Manhattan's Pier 84
at the Dr. Pepper Music Festival. One critic observed Guthrie's audience

was as much comprised of fresh-faced fans than of the thirty- to forty-year-olds one might expect to see: "A surprisingly young crowd turned out Aug. 15 to commune with Arlo Guthrie on the Pier, despite a steady drizzle."[56]

It was true. Guthrie's 1980s appeal was not limited to old hippies or liberal-progressive college students schooling in and around New York City and Boston. Following Guthrie's concert at a déclassé but intimate three-hundred-seat venue in Memphis, another critic observed that many attending "appeared too young to remember 'Alice's Restaurant,' much less Vietnam. But they all seemed to appreciate what they heard."[57]

Directly following the Pier 84 show Guthrie found himself relegated twice to opening-act slots—the first by design, the second by accident. On 16 August, Guthrie was scheduled to appear with singer-songwriter Don McLean of "American Pie" fame at Wolf Trap Farm Park in Vienna, Virginia. Walking out on stage, Guthrie wailed on his blues harp as he and Shenandoah moved into a spirited take of Jesse Fuller's "San Francisco Bay Blues." The energy rarely ebbed throughout his truncated opening set.

The following day, the *Washington Post* conceded McLean, while greatly talented, would have better served as the evening's opener, since "his soft, reflective ballads, simply weren't enough to sustain the momentum Guthrie started."[58] Though Guthrie was scheduled to headline the next night's show at Pennsylvania's Valley Forge Music Fair, the singer was again tasked to serve as opening act. Support artist David Bromberg was running late, the guitarist's flight from Boston delayed due to issues caused by Ronald Reagan's warring with striking air traffic controllers.

Despite the wash of accolades, by mid-August Guthrie decided he had had enough. Though his health had improved since Vancouver, he confessed to homesickness, of missing his wife and kids. He was tiring of the endless string of one-nighters, of engaging the hangers-on, of a life spent traveling America's back roads on a bus. There were also economic concerns. The cost of keeping the band on the road in 1981 was fast approaching $1,500 per day. He admitted he was afraid that carrying the band from gig to gig was fast becoming "a luxury he could no longer afford."[59]

Guthrie's earliest dream was to become a forest ranger, to live Thoreau-like apart from society in tranquil seclusion. It was a dream of making music not as a vocation, but as an activity enjoyed with friends. Instead, he found himself a boss, responsible for routing, meeting payrolls, paying hotel bills, and dealing with bus breakdowns. Then there was the expected wheedling with promoters, nightclub owners, and nosy journalists. "I'm no longer happy to be the person that all this hinges upon," he confessed. "I didn't come into this world to be the head of a pyramid organization."[60]

Guthrie was exhibiting symptoms of a midlife crisis, wishing to transport back to 1965, when he could play, anonymously, on street corners. "Nobody depended on me. I depended on everybody else."[61] He was feeling guilty about not spending more time with his wife and four children. Abe was now eleven, Cathy nine, Annie five, and Sarah Lee three. "I just don't want to be away from my kids anymore," he confessed. "I want to be with them while they're growing up. It's more important to me than making money or singing."[62] A break from touring was soon coming, the folk singer taking off most of September and October, save for honoring his rescheduled West Coast dates with Pete Seeger. Of their show at Berkeley's Greek Theater, a reporter opined, "The teaming of Pete Seeger and Arlo Guthrie is a natural match, bringing together old left and new humanism."[63]

There was another appointment to keep. On the morning of 4 October 1981, Guthrie drove to the village of Croton-on-Hudson, in Westchester, New York. A memorial service was scheduled at the village's Temple Israel. Lee Hays of the Weavers had passed away on 26 August, and Rabbi Michael Robinson was present to greet friends to celebrate the singer's life. That the final send-off of the son of a Methodist preacher from Arkansas would take place in a New York Jewish temple was the least of the bass singer's contradictions. The mourners—perhaps the wrong description, as the memorial was more of a celebration—gathered to commemorate the singer's legacy. Those attending included both local friends and graying comrades.[64]

Harold Leventhal was in attendance, as were the three surviving original Weavers. Composer Earl Robinson, who cofounded People's Songs in 1948 with Seeger, Hays, and Irwin Silber, flew in from California to pay tribute. Robert Sherman, the broadcaster who helmed the popular New York City–area WQXR folk music program "Woody's Children," lightened the atmosphere by reading from the snarky, curmudgeonly letters Hays had written him over the years.[65]

There was never a time in his life that Guthrie had not known Lee Hays. Besides providing the prominent bass vocal to the Weavers' commercial folk-pop sound, Hays was the troupe's most engaging stage personality, mixing into the music humorous shaggy-dog stories and philosophical asides. Anyone who enjoyed sitting through Arlo Guthrie's irreverent between-song soliloquies was listening to the ghost of Lee Hays. Jackie and Arlo named their second daughter, Annie Hays Guthrie, in honor of Lee. At the service, Guthrie sat at the temple's organ and sang a gospel song in Lee's memory.

Guthrie had in fact been pushing the gospel plow of late. On the morning of 8 October, he, Jackie, and the children arrived on the campus of Siena College, a liberal arts school in Loudonville, New York, close to Albany. The college was awarding the folk singer—who wore his trademark blue jeans under a black academic robe—an honorary doctorate in fine arts. The Catholic institution was in the midst of celebrating its "Francis Festival," a weeklong commemoration of the 800th birthday of revered thirteenth-century Saint Francis of Assisi.[66] Though born into a Jewish-Protestant tradition, Guthrie's interests in matters of the spirit led him to study Franciscan Catholicism following a life-changing experience:

> **AG:** On October 27th, 1974, I had a show scheduled at the Santa Barbara Bowl. I had been staying as a guest at the Franciscan Monastery (the Santa Barbara Mission) just up the road. I enjoyed visiting with the Franciscan Brothers, who I found to be dedicated to an honest spiritual life, away from the world of everyday concerns. It was while I was visiting that I had wandered into a chapel off-limits to most people.
>
> I sat down and soon I was observing myself as if from above. I had somehow, inadvertently, left my body, and I could see myself below just sitting quietly. Someone outside the chapel was calling me. I heard them quite clearly, but I couldn't answer from where I was. I believed I had to reenter my body to let them know where I was and that I was just fine. But not knowing how I got out, I had no idea how to return. Somehow I managed to get back inside myself. But I was annoyed that I had been distracted.

The teachings of Jesus Christ had long figured into Guthrie's songs, even before the songs on *Outlasting the Blues* made his interest in Christianity plain. "I have a lot of songs I wrote about Jesus before I figured out who Jesus was," Guthrie told *St. Anthony* magazine. "I'm not Catholic or Franciscan or Christian because I wanted to be. I was compelled by God to follow the direction he was leading me."[67]

Studying under the tutelage of Brothers Michael and Jonathan at a hermitage not far from his Berkshire home, Guthrie was attracted to the charitable and humane tenets of Franciscanism. Saint Francis of Assisi, an Italian preacher, philosopher, and mystic, was canonized in 1228 as the patron saint of animals and the environment. Guthrie's immersion studies eventually led to a conversion to Franciscan Catholicism in 1976. He ascended as a member of the Third Order of St. Francis, the "secular arm of the brotherhood."[68]

Shortly after arriving at the hermitage campus, Guthrie sat in the college friary and chatted with a reporter. "I didn't become involved in Franciscanism because I had a traumatic experience or something like that. I was perfectly happy," he explained. "But it was really a matter of how long did I feel I would be happy not moving, not growing, not doing what I could. I don't think that anybody, on his own, ever really does anything. At some point you have to align yourself with an ideal, with God, with whatever you want to call it."[69]

In his speech that afternoon, Guthrie told students and faculty the same thing: "At some point you have to align yourself with an ideal, with God. . . . At some point you have to realize that—on your own—you can only go so far. I felt that I had gone as far as I could on my own."[70] Following the awarding of the doctorate, Guthrie moved to the on-stage piano, asking everyone to sing along on "Amazing Grace." Guthrie offered the award was merely "another sign, another moment in my life that reaffirms my decisions to be who I am."[71]

Though there would be a handful of trailing concerts into early December, Guthrie's 1981 tour officially concluded at Carnegie Hall in Manhattan. Guthrie and Shenandoah were to team with Pete Seeger at the elder folk singer's annual holiday concert. Though Guthrie had played Carnegie Hall on a number of occasions from 1967 on, the 1980s was the decade in which Harold Leventhal quietly groomed Guthrie as Seeger's successor to the Thanksgiving weekend tradition.

Leventhal had placed an advertisement for the concert in the *New York Times* on 13 November. Two programs were to be staged, afternoon and evening, on Saturday, 28 November. Both shows sold out quickly. The programs were dedicated to the memory of Lee Hays. Leventhal composed an account of Hays's life and times in the 1981 Carnegie *Stagebill,* with Seeger and Guthrie singing several of his songs and offering their own personal reminiscences. It was a night to remember and say goodbye.

1981 ended on a strange note. One of Guthrie's cars was an old Checker Cab, the second of two he owned. It was a quirky automobile, but one with which the singer was enchanted. Guthrie was in the midst of trying to sell off Checker Cab no. 2, placing vehicle for sale ads in the classifieds of a local newspaper. Unfortunately, no one seemed particularly eager to buy the old cab from him, regardless of celebrity provenance. While the vehicle might have held appeal to Checker Cab enthusiasts, the aging auto was no longer sleek and was plagued by mechanical issues.

The situation changed when an unemployed fisherman and Guthrie fan hitch-hiked from Buffalo, New York, to Washington, Massachusetts on Christmas Eve. He traveled to Guthrie's farm hoping to have a personal audience. Though the fan would wait in the December cold until 9:30 PM, Guthrie was nowhere to be found. It was then the fan noticed a key had been left in the ignition of the old cab sitting on property's perimeter. So he climbed inside and whisked the automobile away for a joyride down a country road.

He didn't get very far. The cab broke down a few scant miles down the road, and its driver was arrested. When asked why he thought he could just take off with the vehicle, the fan told police he "didn't think Arlo would mind."[72] In the end, a judge suspended the fan's six-month sentence, recommending two years' probation. This curious incident caused Guthrie to write a brief letter to the *Berkshire Eagle*, asking politely that no one else steal his car.

Following his annual holiday break, Guthrie hit the road in late January 1982, playing several solo warm-up dates close to home. There were three concerts in Connecticut—one at Toad's Place and two at the Shaboo Inn—before Guthrie was to return to Manhattan for a rare nightclub appearance. Playing before two sold-out audiences at Greenwich Village's Bottom Line on West 4th Street—the nightclub sat directly across the street from where Mike Porco's original Gerdes Folk City once stood—Guthrie alternated between a lone acoustic guitar and a piano for an engaging set of songs encompassing his career.

Stephen Holden of the *New York Times* was totally charmed by the evening of stripped-down troubadour music: "Mr. Guthrie has grown into a folk-music institution whose impeccable taste in songs is matched by a zany style of entertainment that is one part absurdist post-hippie wise-cracking and the other part populist storytelling."[73] A critic from *Billboard* offered, "It was like the 1960s all over,"[74] describing the evening's only shortfall as its brevity: both of Guthrie's early and late-night sets ran little more than an hour in duration. These solo engagements were interesting as Guthrie had dusted off an old chestnut seemingly retired from his stage program: "The Alice's Restaurant Massacree."

Just before heading south for a February concert in New Orleans, Guthrie briefly abandoned beer-soaked parlors for a tonier engagement at Manhattan's Waldorf Astoria. He had been asked by the New York regional office of the Democratic National Committee to sing Woody's "Talking Dustbowl" and several other Depression-era songs at the $500 a plate Franklin Delano Roosevelt dinner. The fundraiser was staged to celebrate the centennial of Roosevelt's birth—and to welcome fifty newly elected Democrats to office. That night speakers assailed the policies of the current Republican administration. In his speech Senator Edward Kennedy suggested, "Ronald Reagan must like poor people because he is creating so many of them."[75]

Afterwards Guthrie left on a brief six-city tour of the southeastern US, a short string of solo dates taking him to Louisiana, Florida, and North Carolina. His appearance at Florida's Clearwater Music Hall on 10 February drew a standing room only crowd, but mixed reviews. While the "Alice's Restaurant Massacree" brought the crowd's energy up several notches, one critic carped Guthrie's "original, serious compositions . . . seemed a depressing diversion from an otherwise upbeat, 90-minute early show."[76] This opinion was echoed by a second critic who opined it was only with the "Massacree" that Guthrie won "the warmth of the audience that had been lukewarm up to that point."[77] Between sets Guthrie told reporters he believed "Alice" was, in its own way, as topical in 1982 as it had been in 1967: "The circumstances are essentially the same. As long as the government is of the opinion that without a vote they can just round up young people and stick them in the armed forces, the situation will remain the same."[78]

Guthrie kicked off his first electric show of 1982 with Shenandoah at Philadelphia's Ripley Music Hall. He had caught a winter's cold during the shows down south, causing one writer to note Guthrie's "head cold gave his nasal voice a rough edge . . . inviting comparisons with the early Bob

Dylan."[79] Although the *Philadelphia Inquirer* reported the congested singer "forgot some of the lyrics," he maintained Guthrie's lively arrangement of Seeger's "Sailing Down My Golden River" "worked better than his more recent efforts."[80]

Guthrie had been listening to a *lot* of Pete Seeger of late. *Billboard* confirmed the previous November that Guthrie, John Pilla, and engineers Mark Linett and Jesse Henderson were working at Long View Farms in North Brookfield, Massachusetts. The four were choosing and mixing songs for an as-yet-untitled Warner Bros. double album documenting Seeger and Guthrie's summer 1981 shows. It was remarkable that the set—issued as *Precious Friend* in January 1982—was even considered for release.

The previous Seeger-Guthrie collaborative album, the more folkie-protest oriented *Together in Concert,* hadn't torn up the charts upon release in April of 1975, so a second Seeger-Guthrie double album was something of a commercial gamble. On the album's credits, Guthrie wrote, "Special Thanks to Mo Ostin for signing; Lenny Waronker, for smiling."[81] Such winking dedications suggested hesitancy on the part of Warner Bros. to greenlight the set with enthusiasm.

Precious Friend (the title comes from a song Seeger had written and recorded on his Folkways album *Banks of Marble* in 1974) was released on 27 January 1982 with little fanfare. The album seemingly even caught *Billboard* off guard: the first recognition of the set—awarded "Recommended Pop" album status—was only noted a full month after release.[82] It wasn't helpful that *Precious Friend* was packaged with austerity. Their *Together in Concert* set was handsomely presented. The cover and gatefold—designed by Mike Salisbury—featured the brilliant color photographs of David Gahr, the premier photographic chronicler of the 1960s folk scene.

In contrast, *Precious Friend* was packaged in a relatively plain gatefold of white cardboard. The inspiration for illustrator Dennis Auth's cover art drawing of Guthrie and Seeger was based on a photograph taken by Ruth Bernal. Auth's original black ink illustration was originally commissioned to promote a Seeger-Guthrie concert at Busch Gardens, Williamsburg, Virginia, in May 1981. Guthrie would later use the drawing for souvenir concert tees sold at shows.

The songs and stories comprising *Precious Friend* were sourced from four concerts, all recorded in the summer of 1981: Poplar Creek Music

Theatre 19 July, Pineknob Music Theatre 20 July, Greek Theatre 30–31 August, and the Concord Pavilion 4 September. There are no shortages of great performances waxed for posterity, the set serving as a wonderful souvenir of a memorable series of shows. Though the album offered only one original song of Arlo's (a gentle piano-backed rendering of "Ocean Crossing"), fans were treated to any number of favorites not formally studio-recorded but often performed live: "Please Don't Talk About Me When I'm Gone," Tom Paxton's "I'm Changing My Name to Chrysler," "Will the Circle Be Unbroken?" and "Amazing Grace."

The latter song featured Guthrie's inspirational "John Newton's Slave Ship" soliloquy. His performance of "Amazing Grace" proved a highlight of *Precious Friend,* performed with reverence and intimacy—a pretty nifty challenge to have pulled off before a crowd of seven thousand at San Francisco's cavernous Concord Pavilion. The gospel song had long served as the dependable finale of hundreds of Guthrie's concert performances.

Guthrie also served up several outstanding renderings of his father's classic songs: these include a highly amplified take on "Pretty Boy Floyd" and an absolutely perfect solo on Woody's migrant "Do-Re-Mi" ballad. For good measure listeners were also treated to Guthrie's short stab at his father's sly and winking "Ladies Auxiliary." The song was a seldom-performed "union song" rarity, its existence hardly recalled by anyone other than a small band of Woody's most ardent admirers. The song had been performed—and only on rare occasions—by two of the balladeer's most reverent interpreters: Seeger and Ramblin' Jack Elliott.

Pete Seeger's ministerial presence is ever-present on *Precious Friend.* It must be said for a dyed-in-the-wool, no frills, no nonsense folk singer, Seeger seamlessly meshes with Shenandoah's backing groove throughout. Listening to Seeger's bluesy single-string banjo break on the Jimmy Reed–inspired *Clearwater* anthem, "Sailin' Up, Sailin' Down," is as life-affirming as anything the veteran activist/singer ever pressed on vinyl.

Unfortunately, rock press critics—most of whom displayed little memory of the Weavers or knowledge of Popular Front–era agit-prop folk-music—simply didn't know what to make of the album. Demonstrating little awareness of the Folkways "Hootenanny" LPs of the 1950s, complaints were made of Seeger's omnipresent song-leading. One reviewer suggested, "It is a musically mixed blessing to have the audience participating on so many cuts."[83] There were also the usual barbs directed at Seeger by those dismissive of the folk singer's leftist politics. One review blasted the singer for his "sanctimonious Populism."[84]

Seeger wasn't the only one caught in the critical crossfire. One unkind review took direct aim at Guthrie: "Thematically, the album is a mess. . . . Arlo Guthrie's semi-impromptu raps are certainly not worth recording, certainly not worth reproducing word for word on the album jacket."[85] The *Philadelphia Daily News* argued, "Guthrie isn't old enough yet even to be a nostalgia item, but his voice, style and bloodlines make him sound like he is."[86] One critic confessed that while he wasn't particularly impressed with *Precious Friend*, he conceded judging by the "long ovations" captured, it was clear fans attending the concerts "liked what they heard."[87]

Despite the naysayers, the only real issue with *Precious Friend* is the album's topicality. Though the set shared many similarities with the "Hootenanny" albums Moses Asch issued regularly throughout the 1950s, sonically *Precious Friend* was dissimilar. In the hands of recorder and mixer Mark Linett, no Asch record—regardless of historical import—ever sounded this brilliant. The *Boston Globe* certainly noticed the sonic luster: "Mixed at Longview Farm, the material is as sharp and balanced as if recorded in a studio. Solid performances combined with the excitement of a live audience make it irresistible."[88] *Rolling Stone* too was impressed: "*Precious Friend* is more than a collection of old folk memories. It is memory made alive."[89]

As an item of historical record, *Precious Friend* was an important release. As with *Together in Concert,* the set offers more than great music. Though Seeger and Guthrie would plow through such old chestnuts as "The Wabash Cannonball" and "Old Time Religion," references are made to contemporary events, upending any sense of timelessness. These include comments on the recent passing of both Lee Hays and singer-songwriter Harry Chapin; a long satirical riff on the development of the neutron bomb; acknowledgments of striking PATCO (Professional Air Traffic Controllers Organization) workers; and a mocking take of Tom Paxton's "I'm Changing My Name to Chrysler," a lampoon of the "too big to fail" bailout of Lee Iacocca's ailing automobile company.

The world *was* changing. On 6 February 1982, Pete Seeger found himself a central figure of yet another controversy, having agreed to perform at an argumentative political event at New York City's Town Hall. The program, staged by "Workers and Artists for Solidarity," included many who were well known—and occasionally reviled—for their devotion to radical politics. Members of both the Old Left and New Left were present: Seeger, the writer Susan Sontag, Gore Vidal, Kurt Vonnegut, Studs Terkel, and Paul Robeson Jr. were among those attending.

The radicals gathered at Town Hall were on hand to show support for Poland's *Solidarność* movement and those workers attempting to build an independent trade union in the Soviet bloc nation. Old guard supporters argued the Communist government of Poland was already—*theoretically*—a "worker's state," so there was no need for a strike. The eyes of the West—as well as those in other Eastern Bloc countries—were monitoring the historic protests. There was an assumption Soviet tanks would roll into Gdansk and Warsaw, much as they had in Hungary in 1956 and Czechoslovakia in 1968. This tense situation surfaced a public fracture of the political left.

This wasn't a night for the arts, but the poet Allen Ginsberg offered to read from his works and a bit of music was promised as well. More alarmingly, Pete Seeger, the man whom the *Washington Post* dubbed "America's Best Loved Commie,"[90] was to sing at an event perceived as critical of the Soviet Union. To many aging old-school leftists, Seeger's support of *Solidarność* was upsetting. Many old comrades—who dutifully filled Town Hall to capacity to boo the evening's speakers—saw Seeger's participation as a betrayal. The primary opponent to *Solidarność*, the Catholic church–backed worker's movement, was Poland's Moscow-based puppet masters. In the view of the hardliners, the political agitation in Gdansk was counter-revolutionary, seeded by hostile outside operatives.

The US Communist Party newspaper *Daily World* railed against the forum, one editorial expressing disbelief that "even Pete Seeger" had been persuaded "to participate in meetings on behalf of Polish Solidarity, an openly anti-Soviet effort." "Under the cover of defending human rights," the *Daily World* rued, "the [supporters of *Solidarność*] are in fact providing ideological support for US war policy in the struggle for the survival of monopoly capitalism."[91] The Trotskyite *Worker's Vanguard* newspaper—no friend of the pro-Soviet CPUSA—was equally enraged by the forum. They opined the gaggle of pro-Solidarity artists and writers were not authentic American dissidents because they were now "on the same side of the barricades over Poland as Reagan."[92]

The participation of writer Susan Sontag produced more headlines than Seeger's. She was met with an explosion of angry catcalls when calling out Soviet-style Communism as little more than "Fascism with a human face."[93] It was a troubling night for those who held tight to their dreams of a socialist world. Seeger had a lifelong reticence of *publicly* criticizing the Soviet Union for their foreign interventions and human rights issues. He was obviously unsettled by the anger surrounding him. One journal reported, "Shaking his head and speaking in a sad, tired voice, Pete said that he had hoped that the Polish Communist leadership could have resolved the problems in Poland, but that this did not seem likely now."[94] Seeger expressed cautious optimism that a compromise could still be reached. One headline made note of the folk singer's uneasy straddle: "At a Solidarity rally Seeger sang for Poland, breaking his long critical silence on Communist policies and calling for 'controversy to work its human magic.'"[95]

In the end Seeger decided to support those working to build an independent union—even if this put him at odds with the political organization in which he had invested so many dreams. Seeger's decision was a gift to his critics on the right. Christopher Hitchens registered surprise that such Left luminaries as Pete Seeger and Paul Robeson Jr. had even participated since neither had been previously "seen on a platform critical of the Soviet Union."[96] The *National Review* too was shocked—and perhaps gleeful—when learning of the folk singer's position. They mocked the public change of heart of "Pete Seeger, who by now has provided the guitar accompaniment for one half-century of irresponsible politics."[97]

Biographer David King Dunaway posed in 1981 that Seeger "always had a blind spot to the excesses of socialism-in-the-making."[98] Seeger joined the Young Communist League in 1939 and later signed on as a member of the CPUSA in the early 1940s. He, along with Paul Robeson, were the two most prominent musical heroes of the Old Left of the 1940s and 1950s. Both men simultaneously battled HUAC while holding stubborn to their belief that the Soviet Union's experiment in socialism—while not perfect—might yet serve as the blueprint for economic and social equality and world peace. Though Seeger acknowledged he "drifted out of the Communist Party in the '50s,"[99] he remained—to critics and J. Edgar Hoover's FBI—one of the CP's most famous fellow travelers. If this was so, he was also the most beloved—an ambassador of goodwill and proponent of US-Soviet cooperation.

There were few people on earth Arlo Guthrie respected more than Pete Seeger—as a humanitarian, a social and political activist, an advocate of homemade music, and a stage performer without peer. Seeger was also a longstanding cherished friend of the family and a tireless champion of Woody Guthrie. That said, Arlo Guthrie's politics weren't the same as Seeger's. They weren't necessarily exactly the same as Woody's either. Both Pete and Woody received their political education in the environment of the Depression-era America of the 1930s, and both shared complicated loyalties. Though enemies chastised Seeger as a "songbird" of Stalin and Khrushchev, the folk singer maintained he was an American patriot. A writer from *Rolling Stone* expressed amusement when Seeger sang "all four verses to 'The Star Spangled Banner'" at a benefit for the Communist Party's *People's World* newspaper.[100]

Arlo Guthrie's patriotism was never questioned—except, perhaps, by political antagonists on the fringes who saw commies everywhere. On 4 July 1982, Guthrie was asked to serve as the grand marshal of the Pittsfield, Massachusetts, annual Independence Day parade. He was honored to be asked and especially pleased when parade organizers noted his songs were representative of "Mom, apple pie, and America." Guthrie proudly conceded, "I like that."[101]

Sometimes controversies were nonpolitical. A scant four days after the 4 July parade, Guthrie's name again appeared in local newspapers. A local businessman had recently purchased the old Mapleview Ballroom on Route 8 in Arlo's hometown of Washington, Massachusetts. The new business owner, Woodrow Witter, had plans to convert the former dance hall and rock 'n' roll club into a country and western music venue featuring live music. No one in rural Washington—population 850—was necessarily opposed to that.

But Guthrie was nonplussed when billboards and bumper stickers appeared promoting the new venue as "Woody Guthrie's Roadhouse." Witter made no attempt to contact either Arlo or the executors of the Woody Guthrie estate about the appropriation, and no one in the family was pleased with it. Harold Leventhal advised that he was already "looking into the proper action" to remove Woody Guthrie's name from all advertising.[102] He stood firm in the position the Guthrie estate had "not approved and would never approve" of such licensing.

Woody's son agreed. He told the *Berkshire Eagle* that because he had always been on good terms with Witter, the situation saddened him. "It's rather obvious what he's trying to do. He's using the Guthrie name to attract business, and to do so is a cheap shot. I'm very disappointed. He never discussed it with me. I don't quite know what to do about it. I don't know if it is good to use my father's name since it has nothing to do with him. . . . It gives the impression that I'm involved financially. . . . This is not the case."[103] The Guthrie Children's Trust Fund had been happy to donate funds and the family moniker to the new Woody Guthrie Neurological Center wing at Helen Hayes Hospital in Haverstraw, New York, but not to a private business without charitable component.[104]

Witter's reason for *not* discussing his plans with Woody's son seemed weak tea at best: "If I had asked to use the name and [Arlo had] said 'No,' I would have felt an obligation *not* to use the name." Witter then suggested his nightclub wasn't actually named for Arlo's father at all. The business-man maintained that he was the titular "Woody" and that "Guthrie" was simply the name of a town "famous in the outlaw days."[105] So the pairing of the two was—as he saw it—fair use. This small-town squabble was eventu-ally settled without fuss. Following a message from Guthrie that locals should boycott the enterprise until the matter was amicably settled, Witter relented. His new business venture would simply be called The Roadhouse.

The local newspapers of western Massachusetts continued to brim with Arlo Guthrie miscellany that July. On 10 July, the day of the singer's thirty-fifth birthday, there were reports the folk singer had invested capital in a fledgling Housatonic media company looking to obtain FCC permis-sion to operate a television station. Their aim was to resurrect dormant Channel 51 as a local news and entertainment dial stop. Gary Kaye, the president of the Housatonic Broadcasting Company and a radio producer for NBC, boasted that Guthrie promised to act as the station's "talent scout." He also suggested the possibility of syndicating "some of Arlo's pro-grams for national television."[106]

Guthrie was already something of a television celebrity overseas. A German film crew had recently been following him around, capturing footage of Guthrie performing Woody's songs with Pete Seeger and resting on his coach with Franciscan friend Brother Michael. The film also featured footage of Depression-era hoboes, of Guthrie reminiscing about his father's battle with Huntington's disease, of a father playing with his children in a Berkshire meadow. When the film was broadcast in Australia in Novem-ber 1982, one critic thought the film well done. But he was also saddened that time and age seemed to have diminished Guthrie's '60s hippie activism. The singer appeared "more content to daydream and play his music than campaign too vigorously for any of the causes he once espoused."[107]

On 14 July 1982, the date marking Woody Guthrie's seventieth birthday, Guthrie and Shenandoah were paired with David Bromberg at the Oakdale Music Theater in Wallingford, Connecticut. In a preshow interview Guthrie promised to celebrate his father's natal day by playing "some of his songs later." It wasn't long before Guthrie was asked the "big" question. He was now middle-aged and might "discover one of these days whether he has Huntington's chorea, the fatal disease that killed Woody." It was a personally intrusive question asked unceasingly. The singer's reply was, as usual, a dismissive Doris Day–style response of "whatever will be, will be." "I don't really think about it, strange enough," he answered. "I'm more inclined to be concerned with the same general issues as everybody else is concerned about. Whether it's a nuclear freeze, or what do your kids learn in school, finding a parking place in the summertime in your town . . . things like that."[108]

Though Guthrie resisted being a "poster boy" for the disease, his mother made it her mission to bring attention to and secure funding to battle the neurological disorder. She worked tirelessly for the Committee to Combat Huntington's Disease, the lobbying and information-gathering organization she founded in 1968. Unable to refuse his mother's request for the occasional fundraising favor, Guthrie would dutifully do his part to advance his mother's cause.

During a late summer break in touring, Guthrie joined his mother on the final day of California's Medical Film Festival. The six-day event, held in Walnut Creek, a tony suburb of San Francisco, was scheduled to conclude with an awards ceremony and a gala black-tie fundraising dinner. There, alongside such Hollywood celebrities as the film director Robert Wise and the actresses Helen Hayes, Nina Foch, and Joan Fontaine, Guthrie and his mother shook hands with attendees, asking for contributions for Huntington disease research.[109]

If there was no getting around being the son of Woody Guthrie, there was no getting around being the child of Marjorie Guthrie either. When a college graduate by the name of Aaron Lansky went on a mission to salvage as many aged Yiddish books as he could collect, Marjorie Guthrie wrote the young man offering her own mother's collection. Marjorie's mother, Aliza Greenblatt, was a well-regarded poet, having published several Yiddish-language works in the 1930s and '40s. Lansky was thrilled to accept her generous donation of rare books. He was also shocked when a seed check of $1,000 arrived courtesy of the Woody Guthrie Foundation. The donation was sent to help establish the National Yiddish Book Exchange, then housed at Amherst's East Street School. Both Arlo and his sister Nora attended the inaugural Friends of the National Yiddish Book Exchange kickoff event in New York City, cohosted by their mom and the folk singer/actor Theodore Bikel.[110]

Even after his immersion into Franciscan Catholicism, Guthrie self-identified as a "Catholic-Jew."[111] As youngsters growing up in Howard Beach, Queens, he and Nora had been subjected to underappreciated lessons in Hebrew under the tutelage of a young serious-minded rabbi. Guthrie's mother recalled neither Arlo nor Nora seemed terribly engaged, passing time as disinterested children would by kicking at each other's legs under the kitchen table. The lessons came to an end when a concerned rabbi telephoned Marjorie with the dire warning to "fire the tutor. . . . He's too fanatical."[112] The lessons hadn't been working out all that well in any case, and eventually the tutor, Meir Kahane, simply stopped coming around. "Rabbi Kahane was a really nice, patient teacher," Arlo recalled, "but shortly after he gave me lessons, he started going haywire. Maybe I was responsible."[113] The controversial rabbi, founder of the militant Jewish Defense League, was assassinated in early November of 1990.

Following another benefit—this one to raise funds for an ambulance to serve seven communities in remote areas of the Berkshires—Guthrie headed to a Sunday afternoon gig at the New England Folk and Blues Festival at the Mt. Watatic Ski Area. He was scheduled to share the bill with Bonnie Raitt, Jerry Jeff Walker, Odetta, Josh White Jr., David Bromberg, Taj Mahal, and singer-songwriter Fred Small. The festival was cosponsored by the Massachusetts Nuclear Referendum Campaign, a grassroots organization pushing for a ballot referendum allowing Massachusetts citizens to have a voice on the proposed construction of nuclear power stations in their state.[114]

Though no stranger to antinuke demonstrations, Guthrie told the audience, "I don't think it's good to have only one opinion on nuclear power. As for myself, I don't like nuclear power at all. But it takes all kinds of people, and all kinds of approaches, to get things done. . . . What's great

THE SUN IS SINKING DOWN

is that people are getting excited again. There's just this groundswell of sympathy right now for things that, well . . . are right."[115] This was the sort of grassroots democratic lobbying that had Guthrie's support. Everyone's voice needed to be heard, even if one didn't agree with contrarian views.

Not everything seeming "right" worked out as one might wish. On Labor Day 1982 the Okemah, Oklahoma, chamber of commerce announced their refusal to organize a memorial for native son Woody Guthrie. Chamber president Allison Kelly explained the town simply could not "glorify Guthrie without glorifying his left-leaning background." Citing old *Daily Worker* articles Guthrie had written in the early 1940s, Kelly believed any observance of Woody's contributions to American culture amounted to little more than a "commemoration of a Communist."[116]

To support his position, Kelly regurgitated reports the folk singer had been a "member of the Communist Party's Brighton section in Brooklyn."[117] This *may* have been so, but even Pete Seeger disbelieved it. He maintained that while Woody did once *apply* for party membership, he was turned down—which was probably for the best, Seeger mused, as the itinerant Guthrie "was always traveling, hated meetings and political discussions which used long words."[118]

Arlo Guthrie was soon scheduled to meet up with Seeger at Toronto's O'Keefe Centre. The concert was promoted vigorously and well-attended–perhaps because Seeger's trips into Canada were becoming increasingly rare. The critic from the *Toronto Star* swooned in praise, suggesting Arlo Guthrie as a "keeper of the faith" since "Seeger *is* the faith."[119] Such opinion wasn't universal. One critic thought the mix of Lead Belly, Woody Guthrie, and Bob Dylan songs, traditional music, and antinuclear activism "smacked of complacency." Though impressed by Guthrie's "deadpan humor" and Seeger's "inexhaustible delight in every song," he thought the latter too preachy, exhorting "the crowd to sing along with him—stubborn, proud and dedicated—like a schoolmaster running his pupils through their tables."[120]

Though Guthrie was politically active, he was rarely strident. On 9 October Guthrie and Shenandoah headlined a benefit at Boston's Orpheum Theater. Proceeds from the night's event would benefit the Nuclear Disarmament Project, the American Friends Service Committee, and CPPAX (Citizens for Participation in Political Action). The concert date selection was not accidental. The date near-coincided with what would have been the forty-second birthday of former Beatle John Lennon, assassinated two years earlier.

In a pre-event interview with the *Boston Globe,* Guthrie explained that while he was not a "political singer," he was not averse to getting involved with issues of concern. "I was raised to believe that a person is a human being first and an artist secondary," he explained, "and my commitment to all kinds of ideas is more important to me than my job as a musical artist."[121] Guthrie was moved by Pete Seeger's example of "Thinking Globally, Acting Locally"—the belief that small-town grassroots activism was the most democratic method of bringing people of good will together to influence local and national policies.

"If the 1960s had taught us anything," Guthrie continued, it was "We no longer have one myopic view of what it is to be an American. That's a change that traces back to the civil rights movement, and it's more significant than the Cultural Revolution in China. . . . Disagreeing on fundamental issues—abortion, prayer in schools, nuclear power—does not get you labeled *un-American.* We learned something in the '60s," he mused, "you don't need leaders to have leadership; a groundswell of sentiment can move mountains."[122]

The Old Left shared faith that their building of a socialist world might act as the catalyst for political and social change—even if that meant overlooking the ideologies' trespasses. The New Left didn't see the stodgy, bureaucratic Soviet Union or the People's Republic of China as representative of their sense of idealism. The press tried their best to anoint several figures as leaders of the New Left (Abbie Hoffman, Jerry Rubin, and Arlo Guthrie, et al. were all cited as such). But while many were moved to activism by the civil rights movement and the war in Vietnam, most worked independently of one another. The New Left had no *true* leaders, only a number of personalities. There was no great conspiracy—no matter what the tabloids or the *National Review* conjured up.

Though the son of an Okie balladeer who wrote columns for the otherwise sober communist newspaper *People's World,* Arlo diverged from his father in regard to politics. The younger Guthrie was suspicious of any organization promising *their* way as the only true path. In a fascinating interview with *The Progressive,* he admitted, "When I see what some of the Old Left people did, it scares me."[123] Too many well-intentioned people self-sacrificed and abandoned their capacities of critical thinking to accommodate directives handed down from on high.

There were contemporary parallels. Guthrie noted the problem of obedience to dogma was not exclusively a dilemma of the left: "Interestingly, I see a lot of it in the fundamentalist Right people abandoning themselves in order to form a union with something bigger."[124] Such sublimation to any cause challenged democratic methodologies. Guthrie's own life experience—combined with his immersive studies in spiritual matters—taught him there was no simple, single truth. The CPUSA was notorious for having members follow directives without question. Dorothy Healey, the Los Angeles–based Communist leader later rued, "The only role the Party leaders permitted intellectuals to play was that of providing a rationale for whatever the current Party line might be."[125] Guthrie told *The Progressive*, "What we didn't learn in the Old Left is that we have to be very, very tolerant of somebody else's truth."[126]

Guthrie often referred to the fate of his troubled friend Phil Ochs, a great topical songwriter who would tragically die by his own hand in the spring of 1976. Guthrie filtered Ochs's sad end through the lens of experience—he shared a lifetime's worth of acquaintance with well-intentioned, good-hearted, and totally committed people. Unfortunately, many of the same were often doctrinaire in their beliefs, holding fast to inflexible opinions and worldviews. Guthrie told *The Progressive*, "The thing is, we in the Old Left and the New Left were taught to involve ourselves in the world. Not just to make it better, but to wholly devote ourselves to the world 'til there was nothing left of the person."[127]

Guthrie thought this a fatal mistake, though some friends managed to extricate themselves from old ideas. Guthrie thought Pete Seeger—a man ignorantly branded by enemies as a "useful idiot" of the Communists—was someone who managed to successfully navigate the political storms. Though Seeger never disparaged old comrades who chose to remain in the CPUSA, the antidemocratic and insular tendencies of the organization were among the reasons he chose to leave. No particular event would diminish Seeger's native-son radicalism. He admitted to reading both Communist newspapers and *The Wall Street Journal* to inform and entertain new ideas and tactics.[128]

It had been a process for the senior folk singer. Following visits to Cuba and the People's Republic of China in 1971 and 1972, Seeger became increasingly wary of the socialist world's cult-of-personality fixations. He offered that while the US system too often produced "ambitious and selfish people, whores and wheeler-dealers" it conversely begat "some brilliant non-conformists." Seeger acknowledged the nonconformists in the U.S., at least, "are not killed off. They are not all exiled."[129] By the mid-1970s, Seeger had accepted that changes in political consciousness would likely be evolutionary rather than revolutionary.

Guthrie was quick to point out that while politics were always of concern, he would not allow politics to define him. Though he publicly campaigned for several Democratic candidates over the years (Fred Harris, George McGovern, etc.), "The portion I allow myself to act politically is small. . . . For myself, I think the structure of society is worth a little of my time. Not worth all my time and not worth most of my time—but it's worth some of it."[130] His opinions on politics had not changed during his years in the public eye. In 1969 Guthrie opined while the people in power were not immune to mockery, there were "a lot of good things the Establishment has established." One of those was the US Constitution, a document Guthrie believed remained both relevant and "groovy."[131]

The ensuing years hadn't changed Guthrie's view. "I'm not too thrilled with structures of societies. I'm more concerned with the people that are in them. But this democracy is the best of all the structures. Therefore I'm willing to devote some time to politics, because I'd like to see some of the ideas which make this country so nice and so great restored."[132] Though Guthrie cited Pete Seeger as both teacher and mentor, it's likely the life lessons were reciprocal. In August 1968 when Soviet tanks rolled into Prague to put down a student-led rebellion, Arlo railed, "Everybody puts down hippies. In Czechoslovakia, the hippies stood in front of Russian tanks. I'm sorry, man, but I can't see any Congressman standing in front of a tank."[133] Seeger made no public statement on the Soviet invasion of Prague, but it was during this period Seeger composed his most introspective—and despondent—song, "False from True." The lyrics are telling: "When I found tarnish on some of my brightest dreams/When some folks I trusted turned out not quite what they seemed."

Guthrie credited American activists for helping keep the country's democratic ideals buoyant. He reminded his Boston audience, "It's funny how America keeps changing sometimes. It's strange and it's weird. Remember how years ago we used to have the "Ban the Bomb" marches?" Surveying the mostly young faces in the crowd, Guthrie allowed, "Well, I guess I don't know how old the audience is that's here tonight, but these [marches] used to be really fun. People marching up and down Fifth Avenue, and Europe, and down in Washington and singing songs. Actually, we didn't get much done. Except when the Vietnam War started, there was already a group of people that knew what to do . . . sort of. And I guess they all evolved out of the different things that were going on."[134] Guthrie then asked the young audience to consider their duties as the next generation of activist-patriots.

Such activism was the fruit of the 1960s. One of the pressing issues of the early 1980s was US involvement in the civil war raging in the country of El Salvador. Some saw the conflicts in El Salvador and Nicaragua as the newest proxy wars between the US and the Soviet Union. Prior to performing "Victor Jara," a commemoration of the slain Chilean folk singer, Guthrie observed, "Seems we have other stuff to do in this country than having to send money and guys and guns all over the world. I noticed the president was talking about how much money all the protestors was making from foreign governments the other day . . . and I was wondering how come I never got mine? So I'm telling all you Russians out there, I ain't got my check yet."[135]

The Boston concert ended with the old spiritual "Amazing Grace." Midway through, Guthrie mused, "You know, if we took all the money that we spend on defense for one year, we could solve almost every problem in medicine, almost every problem of poverty, almost every problem of hunger. Not just in America, but all over the world. Just one year. I don't think them Russians would attack us if we just took off *one* year. They'd probably get the same idea . . . they got hungry folks too, you know. Wouldn't that be nice?"[136] Sitting at the piano, Guthrie gently moved from the eighteenth-century hymn to a song of contemporary vintage, John Lennon and Yoko Ono's "Give Peace a Chance."

On 7 November, Guthrie and Shenandoah were still on the road, toplining a bill with Peter Rowan at the newly launched Wax Museum nightclub in Washington, DC. The club had filled 918 of the 1,000 available seats—a pretty impressive number for a Sunday night gig—and *Billboard* reported a take of $8,721 at the box office.[137] The band then moved on to Decatur, Georgia, for a show on Tuesday. The *Atlanta-Constitution* noted Guthrie's audience was nothing if not diverse. There were folks in "braided ponytails and beards" sitting alongside businessmen in three-piece seats, a mix of young and old. The review suggested, "Old protest singers never die; they just protest new administrations and policies."[138] The Decatur gig would be the band's final show on their swing through the Midwest and southeast. There were rumors of a recording session and new album in the works.

It would be some time before fans would hear studio-recorded versions of the new songs Guthrie was now introducing nightly on stage. In early November 1982, industry trades broke the news that longstanding A&R executive Lenny Waronker had been made president of Warner Bros. records. Mo Ostin, now fifty-five, had worked his way from general manager of the Reprise label (acquired by Warner Bros. in September 1963) to his double position as chairman *and* president of the now-combined Warner/Reprise empire. It was Ostin with whom Harold Leventhal negotiated to bring Guthrie on board as a Reprise recording artist in 1967. Lenny Waronker was to assume half of Ostin's professional duties. In 1977, Waronker oversaw Warner Bros.'s successful absorption of Reprise, the company's subsidiary label.[139]

The recording industry was in something of the doldrums as the 1970s drew to a close—and things would not improve markedly in the early 1980s. Of course, a new pop music sensation could still catch public fancy and move a million or so units—but such artists and bands were rare birds and often of the "flash-in-a-pan" school, not "legacy" artists. Many economically distressed record companies found themselves saddled with contracts with artists not generating enough revenue to justify investment. Warehouses were piled high with unsold product by even the most beloved artists, musicians whose albums were not aligned with the ever-shifting trends of the pop music market.

One high-ranking industry executive would crassly tell one probing journalist, "Why are you so interested in having record companies make records with artists that sell 50,000 records? That's something only reviewers and critics want, and we don't make a lot of money off of. But this is the record *business*."[140] It was a cold statement, but one reflecting the temperature of the time. It was in this unsettled atmosphere that Guthrie and John Pilla gathered members of Shenandoah to begin work on the singer's tenth prospective studio album for Warner Bros., tentatively titled *Someday*.

Chapter Two

ARLOCO, 1983–1984

AG: It was a time when our fortunes as touring musicians were going really well, but our record sales were not reflected the same way—and were fairly dismal in comparison to other popular bands. Compared to folk-style musicians, we were big time, but the luster of folk music as a pop-music genre had long worn off, nowhere near as profitable a business as it had once been.

Lenny Waronker had become the president of Warner Brothers, and although he was a dear friend and producer of our records, he was now also obligated to the financial well-being of a major music industry giant. I met with Lenny in his office in the corporate headquarters in Burbank, California, before starting what would have been our fourth contractual five-year term, and we discussed the next project, "Someday." Lenny was frank with me, telling me Warner's was disappointed in the recent decline of sales of our records.

My insistence on making the new record in North Brookfield, Massachusetts, and not on the West Coast was not helping the situation. As I wouldn't be under their direct control, Warner's couldn't help guide the project in a way that would be more helpful—and hopefully more profitable.

One of the reasons I wanted to record at Long View Farms, in North Brookfield, Massachusetts, was I could go home on weekends. It was only an hour and a half drive from my farm to the studio. Long View was a live-in facility, so we could stay there and record after breakfast every day. We'd usually quit before dinner and have the nights off shooting pool or playing cards. The food was great and the staff wonderful people who became like family.

Waronker was not receptive to the idea of Guthrie recording the album in Massachusetts, three thousand miles from Warner's Los Angeles home base. As executive producer and president, Waronker was wary of any artist recording in renegade fashion. It *was* unusual to have an artist work on a new album without corporate oversight. Guthrie was sensitive to Waronker's reticence, suggesting a reasonable compromise:

> **AG:** I agreed that they could oversee the project by having us send a weekly update in the form of a recording to stay apprised of where we were at and how it was going. John Pilla was the official producer of the album so he may have been in contact with Warner's. But I have no memory of him passing along any comments or suggestions to me. So as the weeks progressed we just continued to record as if everything was going well.

Guthrie's ambition to record at Long View Farms made economic sense: it was certainly a cost-saving move. If his albums were not selling in numbers they once had, spending less on a new production seemed a reasonable remedy. The expense of recording in Los Angeles—factoring in the hiring of top session players and technical crews—wasn't the only element inflating budgets. There were other expenditures to consider:

> **AG:** In those days making records took a couple of months or even longer. I'd previously gone to LA with the entire family, and had to rent a home, a car, and all the extras that [go] with not being home . . . with such added expenses as tutors for the kids. These expenses were graciously paid for by Warner's, who would then deduct the costs from any profits going forward from the recordings.
>
> Adding up these expenses, in addition to the costs of recording in their studios at their rates and the salaries of attendant musicians, engineers, and assistants, was un-concerning to me—until the expected royalties from the records were due . . . but not much ever showed up. As a matter as fact it appeared to me that the sheer number of records they were manufacturing, even if they all were sold, would not pay for the costs of making the records. I was confused . . . How could it be possible to lose money on a new record?
>
> It was genius, actually. Warner Bros. simply deducted the monies due them by taking from previous records that had done rather well. I thought to myself, "This is where the real talent is—in the accounting." I wanted to meet with the accountants, as I would want to meet any

really creative people, just to acknowledge the genius at work. And I did. Warner Brothers had released twelve albums of mine (as well as two more with Pete Seeger and myself) in fifteen years and the upcoming *Someday* would have entered us into another five-year contract, and would've been the fifteenth major release.

In the end, Warner Bros. relented and allowed Guthrie to record at Long View. As Guthrie recalled, "We began recording *Someday* in February 1983 at Long View Farm, and it took up a few weeks of March to get it to a point where it was more or less completed."[1] But the satisfaction of having recorded a new album of nearly all original material was dampened when Guthrie's mother, Marjorie Mazia Guthrie, succumbed to cancer at the age of sixty-five, on March 13, 1983, at her home in Manhattan.[2] This remarkable woman devoted the last fifteen years of her life to the fight against Huntington's, the degenerative nerve disease Woody so long suffered. One of the ironies of her passing was she would not witness the first step of the medical breakthrough she worked tirelessly to bring to fruition. In November of 1983 scientists announced they successfully identified the chromosome gene sequence signaling early diagnosis of Huntington's.[3]

Though the recording of *Someday* had been completed, there was postproduction work still ahead. Such studio time allowed Guthrie time to grieve, the folk singer maintaining a low public profile in the months following his mother's passing. *Variety* reported on 27 April that Guthrie was still at work "on his next Warner's LP at Long View Farms in N. Brookfield, Mass."[4] Postproduction work continued, with breaks due to touring commitments, through the late spring of '83. During the first half of May, Guthrie was scheduled to go back on the road for a two-week sortie of small theaters. It was then back to work in the studio to finish off the album. *Billboard* offered a brief notice in its issue of 28 May: "At Long View Farms in North Brookfield, Mass., Arlo Guthrie working on Warner Bros. album, with John Pilla producing and Jesse Henderson engineering."[5]

Though *Someday* would offer less sonic gloss than *Power of Love*, the album was an affirmation of Guthrie's songwriting gift. The album kicks off with "All Over the World," a song praising the worldwide antinuke protests of 12 June 1981. Over a million people crowded into New York's Central Park to protest the escalating arms race, similar protests being held both at home and overseas. Guthrie was unable to attend the Manhattan gathering—he was in the midst of a tour of Europe—but one can date the song's genesis to the same month, Guthrie singing, "I'm on a plane tonight for Germany . . ." It was a beautifully constructed song performed with regularity throughout the early and mid-1980s. Stripped of Shenandoah's graceful backing, "All Over the World" would feature on two live albums on which Guthrie made guest appearances. Both of these pre-*Someday* performances featured only solo piano accompaniments.

"Russian Girls" is one of Guthrie's more unusual originals. When he was visited at home in October of 1983, a reporter found the singer rhythmically nodding his head to playbacks of *Someday* songs slated for release. When "Russian Girls" (described by the journalist as a "song about the women's movement") played, Guthrie admitted the quirky, satirical song might require "a sense of humor to appreciate."[6] It was also the only song on *Someday* to feature a 1980s pop-rock radio-friendly sound.

"Here We Are/Way Out in the Country" is a Beatle-inspired original, two tuneful fragments stitched together *Abbey Road* style. The song has a decidedly Paul McCartney *Wild Life*-era feel with soaring vocal harmonies, a pop-music sensibility, and catchy tempo shifts. In contrast, "Someday," the album's emotive title song, delivers the album's most powerful moment. In a reflective solo piano performance, Guthrie's vocal is never heard more achingly fragile than found here.

Side One of *Someday* closes in a more upbeat fashion with the rocking "Satellite." It's one of the most endearingly optimistic of Guthrie's songwriting efforts, the artist wishing to possess a satellite in which to broadcast goodwill worldwide. It's tempting to see "Satellite" as Guthrie's response to Ronald Reagan's proposed "Star Wars" program, a then much-debated space-missile defense initiative.

The album's flip side kicks off with the perennial concert favorite, "Oh, Mom," Shenandoah drummer Terry Hall's lyrics and Guthrie's music pairing perfectly. The first verse, sung at every live show from this era but peculiarly absent from the studio version, referenced one casualty of the 1960s "free love" movement. Hall's original describes a post-hippie mom hazily trying to identify the biological father of her child: a Virgo, a head shop owner, two freaks from San Francisco, a washed-up surfer, and the lead singer of a rock 'n' roll band were among the suspects. It's likely the verse was excised as the lyrics could potentially offend certain listeners and diminish radio airplay.

The hard rocking "Unemployment Line" is the only non-Guthrie associated song on *Someday*. The song was written by Robb F. ("Rabbit") MacKay, whose "Manzanillo Bay" proved one of the highlights of *Amigo*. Though not a household name, MacKay was a popular West Coast performer and songwriter who recorded a couple of "folk-psych" albums for MCA's Uni record label in the late 1960s. His "Unemployment Line" documented the plight of those who had fallen between the cracks of the era's "Reaganomics" fantasies. That song's political edge is lightened somewhat by "Eli," Guthrie's wistful ode to relaxing on his farm with the family dog at his side.

"Major Blues" is not a traditional blues but a song expressing a veteran's disillusionment at arriving home to a less-than-welcoming reception. The lyrics are opaque: it's difficult to ascertain if the veteran has been betrayed by a former lover or by his country—perhaps both parties chose not to keep promises made. Guthrie's song explores some of the nuances John Prine sketched brilliantly in his metaphorical "The Great Compromise." In several years' time, Guthrie would write a second—and arguably far better—song on the subject of returning veterans: "When a Soldier Makes It Home."

Someday concludes on a gentler note with the curtain-closing "You and Me." Like many of Guthrie's love songs, the composition seems a desperate meditation on clinging to an old love tested by time. There's certainly no sadder lyric on any of Guthrie's album's than the aching couplet "You say you had enough/and that you just don't care." The song was a poignant finale to what seemed the most ambitious singer-songwriter album of Guthrie's career. The next step was simply to take the completed album to Warner Bros.

AG: I took the rough mixes to Lenny Waronker in Los Angeles and played it for him in his Burbank office. It had cost Warner's around $70,000 to get it this far. Usually our records had cost around $250,000 with all the extra costs tossed in. So it was by far way more cost-conscious than anything we'd ever done.

His response was "Well, I don't really love it, but we'll put it out." I didn't really know if that was my old friend or the president of Warner Brothers talking to me. But I simply said, "Considering what happened to the releases you did love, maybe this isn't doing either of us any favors." He asked, "Arlo, what do you want to do?" I told him I just needed another $70,000 to finish it up. He looked at me quizzically and said, "I thought you said it was done."

In fact, it was done, or mostly so. But our contract had an "Artist's Approval" clause which meant that Warner's couldn't release it without my approval or when I considered it finished. I had just made up an amount that seemed reasonable while still being by far less expensive than any of the previous recordings I had done in LA.

Such clauses were only added in the 1960s when record companies had little sense of what was considered popular. New artists and bands were creating things that company executives didn't understand. But they understood it was popular, so they relinquished control in favor of the artists, who were the real creators. It didn't last long. Contracts that didn't contain those kinds of clauses once again became the norm, but for a brief moment they were there and had existed during my most creative time.

"What do you want to do?" Lenny asked me. "You can't expect us to put another $70,000 into a record we don't like." I responded with "Well. You can't expect me to put $70,000 into a record I don't own." The result was that Warner Bros. gave me the record. Lenny and I hugged each other and said goodbye.

I left the music industry as I'd known it. So ended a fifteen-year relationship with Warner/Reprise, amicably and on friendly terms. I was now the proud father of a new record. And they were relieved of one folk singer.

In hindsight, my years at Warner/Reprise were fabulous. Despite my lack of knowing anything about the entertainment business, the creative side, for a time, was geared toward the artists and musicians in a way that made the label a real home. We were thrilled to be a part of that family, especially being part of the company when the headquarters was still a part of the complex of where movies and TV shows were being made. The mid to late 1960s at the Burbank Studios were a hub of creativity unmatched almost anywhere else on earth.

It all changed as things do, but for a time, we were a small part of a big family that included Bugs Bunny. That was amazing and wonderful. Perhaps the most important for me, personally, was the warm relationship I had with Mo Ostin and Lenny Waronker. They made us feel welcomed and treated us extremely well. For that, I will always remain

grateful to have known and worked with them. But times had changed
and it was time to let it all go.

The times *had* changed. The only question now was how to move forward. In an interview with *USA Today,* it was noted that although Guthrie
was no longer associated with Warner Bros. his desire now was to "release
his work on his own label, *Arloco,* or find a smaller company more attuned
to his needs."[7] In a surprising move, on April Fool's Day of 1983—Guthrie's
own Rising Son Records was officially incorporated. Though Guthrie
planned *Someday* as his label's first release of fresh material, there was still
a lot to learn about the machinations, challenges, and pitfalls of running
an indie record company.

It was helpful Guthrie would not sail such uncharted waters alone.
Steve Goodman and John Prine had also recently lost major label deals
with Elektra/Asylum. Undeterred, the ever-optimistic Goodman founded
his own label, Red Pajama Records, releasing two albums, *Artistic Hair* and
Affordable Art, in 1983 and 1984, respectively. John Prine would do the
same. Though courted by other major labels following his drop from Asylum, Prine—along with his longtime manager Al Bunetta and Goodman's
manager Dan Einstein—chose instead to go their own way, founding Oh
Boy Records. Prine decided after the briefest of consideration that a major
label "couldn't do anything for us we couldn't do ourselves."[8] Guthrie
agreed with his friend's assessment. "There used to be a stigma attached to
not being with a major label. And the only thing that broke that was the
economic benefits of not doing it that way."[9]

There was one casualty of the Rising Son incorporation: Guthrie's
relationship with his friend and the producer of *Someday,* John Pilla,
would hit rock bottom. The folk singer recalled 1983 as the nadir of his
career—and life in general. He was trying to build a record company with
little capital to properly invest in it. He and Jackie were talking about
divorcing, his mother was dying from cancer. He wanted to offer Pilla a
position in his startup, but after discussing the legalities of creating a business with a team of lawyers and accountants, Guthrie learned there wasn't
a place on the board for Pilla—at least not yet. To his regret, his old
friend took the news hard and personally. Guthrie was saddened John
"believed that I was trying to oust him from the company."[10] The fact that
Pilla had been self-medicating for years wasn't making the situation any

easier. "I began to have doubts about his ability to think straight," Guthrie sighed.[11]

> **AG:** He went to seek some help. These were the coldest days of our relationship, and thankfully, they did not last a long time. Somehow we were changing, but we weren't doing it together anymore. I wondered if it was due to his worsening physical condition: his heart was beginning to fail, and the drugs weren't helping either. They made him suspicious and paranoid.
>
> There were times when he seemed to be his wonderful old self, and times I wasn't so sure. There were times when we reflected on life and death. We had never been afraid to talk of these things. But there was a restlessness about my friend that I could not reach across. I felt helpless. So did he."[12]

John Pilla was more than a producer, more than a friend. It would be impossible to overestimate his contributions to the music of Arlo Guthrie. Their collaboration could be traced almost to the beginning of Guthrie's career. The dual universe of Guthrie and Pilla had intersected long before each was aware of the other's existence. Guthrie was thirteen years old in February 1961 when his mother took him to catch Cisco Houston at Gerdes Folk City in Greenwich Village. Unbeknownst to Guthrie, John Pilla was there as well. Pilla was only a few years Guthrie's senior, age eighteen. He too was studiously watching Cisco work that night.[13]

John Pilla was a native of Drexel Hill, Upper Darby, Pennsylvania, a Philadelphia suburb. He had been playing the guitar since age twelve, his interest stoked by his enthusiasm for rock 'n' roll. Though self-taught, he immersed himself in guitar studies and became an accomplished instrumentalist within a few years. He couldn't read music—and confessed he wasn't particularly interested in learning the skill. "I found that if I got involved on the technical side too much," Pilla mused, "it tended to get a little duller for me, less interesting."[14] Like many who came of age in the late 1950s and early '60s, Pilla found himself attracted to the folk music craze.

In 1962 Pilla met one of his guitar heroes, North Carolina's Doc Watson, at the Swarthmore Folk Festival. The two became fast friends and, over a period of two years, the nineteen-year-old was given the opportunity to informally study and jam with one of the instrument's masters. In May of 1964, Watson and Pilla performed at Philadelphia's Second Fret, the first of many onstage collaborations from 1964 through 1967. Pilla's reputation as a "musician's musician" was affirmed when Watson brought him into the studio—along with son Merle and bassist Russ Savakus—to accompany him on a new recording project.

Watson waxed *Southbound,* his second studio album for New York City's Vanguard Records, in 1966. The LP included three instrumentals featuring Watson and his protégé in duets, as well as two additional lyric songs with Pilla playing second guitar behind Doc's first. In his liner notes to the LP, Watson offered that aside from being a brilliant guitarist, Pilla was also a gifted songwriter with a "few beautiful compositions of his own."[15]

Pilla's songs, no matter how beautiful, were secondary to his instrumental abilities. He was a sought-after accompanist, especially in the clubs and coffeehouses in and around Philadelphia, the city then "a major spoke in the wheel of folk music," in Guthrie's estimation.[16] Though he rarely worked the coffeehouses of Greenwich Village, Pilla performed regularly on the southernmost end of the northeast corridor, busily gigging in Philly, Washington, DC, and Baltimore. Since his coffee-and-basket-house gigs weren't bringing in enough cash to pay rent, Pilla augmented his income by teaching guitar at the Medley Music Mart and the Main Line YMCA in Ardmore, Pennsylvania.[17] He was a good teacher by all accounts. Guthrie recalled that several of Pilla's guitar "students went on to become professionals."[18]

For all his talent, Pilla didn't have the desire nor ego to stand alone center stage. Though he occasionally supported such headliners as Watson and Mississippi John Hurt, he was more often seen backing less-established musicians at such hip spots as the Main Point in Bryn Mawr, the "In" on Walnut, or the Second Fret on Sansom. He was also a fixture at the Philadelphia Folk Festival, conducting afternoon guitar workshops with the likes of New Lost City Rambler Tom Paley, mountain music specialist Art Rosenbaum, and country blues guitarist "Philadelphia" Jerry Ricks.

Guthrie first met Pilla "during the mid-sixties, as we played guitars and sang at one of the frequent get-togethers back then, called hootenannies." Though he and John did not become instant friends, Guthrie was impressed by Pilla's sparkling guitar and banjo playing. The two continued to bump into each other from time to time because they shared friends central to Philadelphia's folk music scene.[19]

Occasionally, Guthrie and Pilla wrangled for the same audience. In January of 1967, Pilla was supporting Doc Watson at the Main Point during the week Guthrie was to begin a residency at the Second Fret. The *Broadside* of Boston featured regional folk music coffeehouse reports, and the 'zine's Philadelphia columnist enthused, "Arlo Guthrie just finished two weeks at the Second Fret—what a gas! Arlo seemed to be a nineteen-year-old con-glomeration of country hick, city boy, Woody's son, Dylan's brother, and everybody's cousin. He also, by the way, knows how to handle a guitar. He made a special hit here with 'Alice's Restaurant'; nobody can figure out how anybody could learn all those words, especially in a row. And do you know that yesterday three people went around town trying to buy two-inch tall buffaloes. Ask him about that!"[20]

That same column concluded with news about their very own home-town hero, John Pilla. The reporter noted that while Pilla had previously "performed at most all the clubs down here on his own," he recently added a bass player, Chip Bond, to his stage show. The writer offered that while John was presently best known as an accompanist, he predicted the guitar-ist's "name and reputation will continue to grow, we're sure."[21]

Pilla often served as the accompanist to a Cherokee folk singer named Leonda. Though a popular performer on the East Coast folk music circuit—even winning a *Broadside* poll as "Favorite New Performer" in March of 1966—Leonda recorded only a single album by decade's end.[22] While that album, *Woman in the Sun,* released January 1969, didn't make a big splash on the charts, critics were impressed by the singer's "blues-rock-folk groove" and "sensitive, far ranging voice."[23] It was through his friendship and asso-ciation with Leonda that, in autumn of 1966, Pilla managed to get an invi-tation to visit her reservation home in Cherokee, North Carolina.

That fall Pilla and five friends traveled to Cherokee, nestled high in the mist of North Carolina's Smokey Mountains. Having tired of the folk scene, Pilla had been thinking about forming a rock band. Rock 'n' roll was, after all, his first love, and his visit to the mountains gave him the space to reengage. "We wanted to get away from everything except music," Pilla explained, "and down there was the only place I think we could have found freedom and complete peace to do something like that."[24]

The visit brought unintended consequences, Pilla said, recollecting that their arrival in Cherokee, "with our long hair and strange clothes," diverted attention from the indigenous people trying to make a living selling trinkets to tourists. But Pilla managed to find a measure of peace in the solitude of the Smokies. "You could do whatever you wanted to, walk through the mountains or play. . . . It was sort of like our own little Utopia," he recalled wistfully. Regardless, Pilla and his friends returned home to Philadelphia once winter's chill rushed in as "we didn't have the ability really to cope with it."[25]

By 1967 folk music was not trending high on pop-music charts. Dylan had plugged in two years earlier, taking a lot of the folk audience with him, and the Beatles and Rolling Stones were making great records and racking up incredible sales. Pilla was no folk purist—he had even played electric guitar in support of fellow Philadelphian Chubby Checker. He was deeply interested in a myriad of musical styles. Though reared on rock 'n' roll and folk, Pilla described country music as one of his "real loves." He was also experimenting with musical styles from "the Far East, especially India." Interestingly, one of the music forms he didn't care much for was "protest songs." Such rabble-rousing, in Pilla's opinion, brought "a lot of needless commotion."[26]

Ultimately, Pilla's idea of forming a rock band wouldn't work out. By the summer of 1967 he found himself playing electric guitar in Eric Andersen's five piece folk-rock band. But within a year's time the guitarist was conscripted for a project that would forever change his life.

AG: In August of 1968 we began filming "Alice's Restaurant" directed by Arthur Penn. During the previous months I had spent time with Venable Herndon while he and Arthur Penn created the screenplay to be used for the movie.

One problem, as I saw it, was that it only took me twenty minutes to tell my story, but a movie had to be at least ninety minutes long. That meant that they had to invent seventy minutes of fiction to accompany the twenty minutes of real-life adventures they were trying to replicate.

Another problem was that I was not a good actor. I could more or less relive actual events that happened to me, but was far more uncomfortable pretending to relive a fictional account. It was awkward, and I felt that way most of the time. It showed.

The filming of Arthur Penn's *Alice's Restaurant* wrapped in December 1968. Following the editing of the film Guthrie was asked to compose and perform incidental music to burnish the film's soundtrack. "I could think of no one who I had enjoyed picking with as much as John," Guthrie recollected. I searched around until I found him, and he agreed to work on the film with me."[27]

> **AG:** Far more interesting to me was creating the soundtrack for the film, as I had time to create the kinds of sounds I envisioned. Gary Sherman was the musical director for the film and I, along with Gary, enlisted the help of a young man whose musical tastes were very similar to my own. John Pilla and I worked on bringing that sound to the film. We utilized acoustic instruments we were familiar with—dulcimers, autoharps, guitars, banjos—instruments pretty unfamiliar to Hollywood—[these] were the primary sounds we brought to the recordings. This was not rock and roll, this was folk music and I loved it.

With *Alice's Restaurant* in postproduction, Guthrie played a handful of solo shows in the first three months of 1969. In early May of 1969, Guthrie was due back in Los Angeles to begin recording his third LP for Reprise, *Running Down the Road.* Van Dyke Parks and Lenny Waronker were to produce, with *Rolling Stone* promising Guthrie had "written much more material than would fit on a single disc."[28] It was an exciting fresh start for what would be a revolutionary phase in Guthrie's career as a recording artist.

The folks at Warner Bros. and 7 Arts were willing to spend a bit more cash to make *Running Down the Road* a more contemporary record. It was in this spirit that a stellar lineup of musicians was brought aboard to burnish the recording: Clarence White and James Burton on guitars, Ry Cooder on bass and mandolin, Gene Parson and James Gordon on drums, Jerry Scheff and Chris Ethridge on bass, and Milt Holland on percussion. Having worked successfully with Pilla on their recent collaboration, Guthrie invited him to play guitar on the new album as well. In the long run, John's involvement would prove more essential than anyone imagined:

> **AG:** *Running Down the Road* was produced by Lenny Waronker. It was our first attempt at a studio album, as both previous albums had been recorded live. We had a fabulous time in the studio. I enjoyed working with Donn Landee [the engineer], Lenny, and John. Our mutual respect increased even as we began to have serious differences over the project.

It was the beginning of a team effort. And although it was difficult to iron out our differences, all four of us seemed ready to work together again when the project was over. John was ecstatic. He respected Donn Landee and Lenny Waronker and loved working with them. We met other musicians like Ry Cooder and Van Dyke Parks, who became friends as well as coconspirators. John's credit on the album read 'Spiritual Advisor.' It seemed appropriate."[29]

Running Down the Road featured a half-dozen of Guthrie's own compositions, with the songs of Woody Guthrie, Pete Seeger, Gus Cannon, and Mississippi John Hurt filling out the album. There would be no mistaking Arlo's newest as another run-of-the-mill folk music LP. One reviewer described the explosive title track as "an interesting and complex combination of old country and new freaked-out folk. It's kind of like country-on-a-trip."[30] The description wasn't too off the mark. *Running Down the Road* was a modern folk-rock album, Guthrie's most exciting *musical* offering to date.

Following the sessions, Guthrie stayed on in Los Angeles, engaged to play a two-week residency at Doug Weston's Troubadour nightclub on the Sunset Strip. These shows would not offer fans the usual lone-man-on-a-guitar-and-harmonica folk-music show with which they were familiar. Guthrie was now touring with a small band to augment his new sound: John Pilla on guitar, Bob Arkin on bass, and Paul Motian on drums.

This was the band that toured with Guthrie throughout the summer of 1969. There were a lot of big outdoor festivals on the itinerary: appearances at the Mississippi River Festival and the Woodstock Music and Art Fair Aquarian Exposition were scheduled. Guthrie recalled that while he found playing before a crowd of 500,000 at Woodstock mind-blowing and glorious, it was less thrilling to John Pilla. The guitarist wasn't fond of performing before crowds of great size:

AG: John did NOT want to go on the stage. Behind the scenes he was fine, but being in front of a lot of people wasn't his idea of a good time, and there were more than a lot of people there. He went anyway, he could be courageous at times.[31]

The summer and autumn of 1969 also brought a storm of personal and professional changes to Guthrie's life:

AG: On July 25th, 1969, I was playing at the Main Point, a little coffee-shop kind of folk music club in Bryn Mawr, Pennsylvania. It was Jackie's birthday and I had gotten her a little present. Jackie and I were in the basement below the stage, where Jim and Ingrid Croce were opening the show. I said to Jackie, "I have a little present for you." She said, "I have one for you too. I'm going to have your child." I could see she was nervous about informing me, but I was thrilled. I said "Great! We have to move to the country and give him an Indian name."

Then, on August 5th, there was a screening of the forthcoming movie *Alice's Restaurant.* I showed up at the movie theater but the lady at the ticket booth outside wouldn't let me in. I obviously didn't appear to be a movie star. I pointed to the poster behind her and said, "That's me! I'm the star of the film!" She was New York all the way and said, "If you want to go in there, you have to buy a ticket!"

So I bought two tickets to see the movie. I didn't go in right away and stood on the pavement outside the theater when two people came walking by saying, "That's him! That's Arlo Guthrie!" I told them I had two tickets if they wanted to go. I gave the two tickets to the couple and was still left standing on the sidewalk with no way in. Then the producers arrived. Hilly Elkins, Joe Manduke, Harold Leventhal, and Arthur Penn walked me inside the theater, not stopping to explain to the woman in the booth.

I bought some popcorn and decided to watch the movie like a normal person. I couldn't make it through the film. At some point, I left the theater, and returned to my NYC apartment.

He wouldn't stay in the apartment long. One month later, Guthrie made good on his promise to get Jackie that home in the country. The property in Washington, Massachusetts, in the Berkshire Mountains was purchased with money earned from the *Alice's Restaurant* film.

AG: On September 2nd I bought an old farmhouse with a hunting lodge along with 250 acres of land in Washington, Massachusetts. We moved in immediately and began preparing the house for winter. There was no heat other than an old Franklin stove in the living room, and no running water as soon as the temperatures dropped below freezing. The house itself was 250 years old and had no insulation aside from newspapers stuffed into the walls.

Within a short time the house filled up with other friends. My costar in the movie, Geoff Outlaw, and his girlfriend, Tigger, as well as James Taylor and his girlfriend, Maggie, were all living in the house with us. It was kind of crazy, but we all did well. John Pilla rented a house nearby, although he lived with us too for a short while.

On October 9th Jackie and I were married on the lawn between the buildings. It was a perfect fall day. We didn't plan very far ahead and decided about three days beforehand that the 9th would be a good day to get married. There were no announcements other than letting our friends and relatives know.

Despite the lack of preparation, everything went extremely well. Our friend, also living with us, Jim McCormack, and his partner, made our wedding clothes, which were simply gorgeous. Alice Brock created a huge cake. Benno Friedman took photos. Guests arrived by the dozens. My mother and grandmother and Harold Leventhal and his wife, Natalie, arrived by a chartered bus from New York along with other New York friends. Judy Collins sang for us. It was quite a gathering. It was a beautiful fall day. Not a cloud in the crystal blue sky. We were very happy.

The day after the wedding, Guthrie needed to leave his bride behind to set off for Washington, DC. Guthrie's pending show at Georgetown University's McDonough Gym on 10 October was the first of a two-month-long tour. This time the singer was to perform with only Pilla accompanying on second guitar. "It was at this point," Guthrie reminisced, "that I realized John was more than an accompanist, or road manager, or whatever the correct titles were. He was part of my life."[32] "I was spending as much time, maybe more, with him as I was with Jackie. He was family. He went everywhere Jackie and I went: work, home, vacations—everywhere. They were wonderful years. We were young and thrilled to be able to travel, sing songs, and actually make a living at the same time."[33]

When Guthrie performed his final show of 1969, at Carnegie Hall on the day after Christmas, John Pilla was still accompanying and adding the odd harmony or two. The *New York Times* made only a brief acknowledgment of Pilla's contribution in their review, offering only that Guthrie had been "backed by another guitarist."[34] But if the *Times* made short shrift of Pilla's contributions, Guthrie, Lenny Waronker, and Warner Bros. would not.

When Guthrie entered the studio in the summer of 1970 to wax his fourth LP, *Washington County,* Pilla seamlessly transitioned from spiritual advisor to full-fledged coproducer. It was the first of eleven Arlo Guthrie albums Pilla would subsequently produce and arrange—and often play on as well. Their collaborations weren't necessarily Lennon-McCartney in style. They weren't writing songs together. But they were certainly *crafting* songs together, artist and producer tossing around ideas, suggesting musical motifs, bickering over arrangements, and getting on each other's nerves:

> **AG:** By the time we began work on *Washington County,* John had emerged as a skilled producer. He called it being a "glorified gofer." We worked well together, by intuition mostly, or by argument. Like myself, he could be manipulative. He had a natural talent of sensing which emotional buttons to push, at what moment, in order to bring out the best (or the worst) in people. He utilized this ability inside and outside the studio.
>
> Lenny, John, Donn, and I approached working together as equals, although I felt more responsible and therefore more equal. I was not always easy to work with. John challenged my knowledge and my instincts (he drove me nuts), but he believed in the music we were making and took his job seriously. It was always John's self-appointed job to make our sound more "Arlo-fied" and less Hollywood. He achieved that in *Washington County.* It remained his favorite album.[35]

Washington County was merely the first in a sequential trio of meticulously crafted LPs that followed. Pilla was at the control board for *Hobo's Lullaby* (1972), *Last of the Brooklyn Cowboys* (1973), and the eponymous *Arlo Guthrie* (1974). All three albums were not particularly thematic in programming. In the tradition of *Washington County,* Guthrie's next three albums weaved diverse musical styles and traditions together to create an eccentric if perfect tapestry. Such diversity became a hallmark of Guthrie's recordings in the early to mid-1970s. The albums featured an engaging mix of rock 'n' roll, folk, ragtime, gospel, honky-tonk country, fiddle music, banjo breakdowns, original singer-songwriter efforts, and, always, a Woody Guthrie song or two.

The pair scored big with *Hobo's Lullaby,* partly due to the radio-friendly success of that album's single, "City of New Orleans." Their follow-up, *Last of the Brooklyn Cowboys,* released in April of 1973, saw more moderate sales but still enjoyed an eight-week run on *Billboard's* Top 100 albums chart. The eponymous *Arlo Guthrie* first appeared on the *Billboard* charts in early June 1974 but disappeared from the Top 200 chart following a ten-week ride. It was a great album despite disappointing sales.

Some outlets thought the Guthrie-Waronker-Pilla productions a bit ostentatious. The review of *Arlo Guthrie* in *Rolling Stone* was especially damning, charging that the production's "superfluous touches underscore rather than conceal the album's meagerness."[36] Disappointed with the reception, Guthrie agreed it might be time to strip away some of the ornamental musical trimmings. His next album, *Pete Seeger & Arlo Guthrie: Together in Concert*, was a complete reset, the most "folkie" album the artist would issue.

Regardless of the less than stellar reviews the *Arlo Guthrie* album received, the folk singer and Pilla set off for England in July 1974 to play at the Cambridge Folk Festival. It was the only "official" show of a two-week UK vacation—though the friends planned to play a couple of club dates in northern England and Scotland to help defray trip costs. Upon their return to the US, Guthrie and Pilla continued to perform together through the end of October.

Sadly, things were destined to change. On 30 October the two would perform at the Civic Plaza in Phoenix, Arizona. That gig would be their last. On 31 October, John suffered his first heart attack:

> Still in his thirties, John received a quadruple bypass operation. His days of being on the road were numbered, as he could not take the strain of constant travel and performing. He couldn't deal with the normal road abuse of airplanes, rent-a-car agents, and insincere regional record company representatives, the hotels, and the press, let alone the abuses we ingested independently and on purpose.
>
> I had quit smoking weed years before. John had not. There was cocaine, which I could take or leave. Earlier in the decade I took, later in the decade I left it alone. John could not. In and of themselves, these things were little things, but they began to add up.[37]

Though the heart attack effectively ended Pilla's contribution as a touring partner, he remained a brilliant producer: he and Guthrie still had a few more great records to make. Guthrie's sixth studio album, *Amigo*, is often referenced by the folk singer as his personal favorite of the eleven LPs created with Pilla. Guthrie conceded there was, as usual, no shortage of disagreement and friction between the two as *Amigo* was being assembled. But such disharmony was an accelerant lighting a magnificent flame:

> **AG:** My favorite record was *Amigo*, recorded in 1976. And even though we both thought it was our best effort to date, typically we disagreed as to why. It got to the point where we would make three separate mixes of each album: one for the public, one for John, and one for me. That way I could go home with the "good" version, and John could have his version too.
>
> In spite of all the differences of opinion, I still believe that it was the combination of personalities which made *Amigo* great. From a technical point of view, *Amigo* was almost perfection. Every detail down to the smallest degree was fought over with a fury, until a consensus could be reached.[38]

Their collaboration did not end with *Amigo*. Over the next half-dozen years, Pilla produced an additional five Guthrie albums, working out of Los Angeles and North Brookfield. Post-*Amigo* collaborations included a pair of sensational live recordings (*One Night* and *Precious Friend*), both celebrated fan favorites. More essential were the final three studio albums Pilla would produce (*Outlasting the Blues, Power of Love,* and *Someday*). Though *Outlasting the Blues,* in particular, was praised by fans and critics alike, Guthrie's albums simply weren't selling in the numbers they once had. The recording and concert industry was in flux, and Warner Bros. was about to realign their business strategy.

> **AG:** The end of the seventies and the beginning of the eighties found [John] and me close, but not working together as we had in the past. Somehow, we separated not only by distances of the road, but in lifestyle too. We began to drift in different directions. I missed my friend terribly in those days.
>
> Although he could not always travel with me, I needed his help many times, and he would hop on a plane and join me for a day or two until the problems were resolved. He stayed full-time on my payroll for many years, although we worked together less as time went by.
>
> No longer were we playing the nice concert halls, but night clubs and roadhouses became our diet. Warner Bros. began to lose interest in our recordings, due mostly to lack of sales. Sherry (John's longtime

girlfriend) had long since gone, and even Jackie and I had a number of divorce attempts.

Things just seemed to be going downhill for both of us. The albums were getting better and better, however, and we made one every year. We remained close, but reality began to drive a wedge between us. The money stopped coming in.

Still, we were family. We worked on the recordings as we always had. We had it down, and although we still argued about everything, we began to enjoy ourselves more."[39]

On Father's Day weekend of 1983, Clearwater (the organization supporting the sloop *Clearwater* and its agenda of environmental activism) staged the sixth annual Great Hudson River Revival, a two-day fundraising event mixing homespun music, crafts, food vendors, and clog-dancing with environmental and grassroots political activism. Guthrie was a friend of Clearwater from the very beginning, singing at their inaugural Hudson Valley Folk Picnic in June 1968. One of the more anticipated programs of '83 was the joint appearance of Holly Near, Ronnie Gilbert, Pete Seeger, and Guthrie. The pairing was an experiment, just to see how things mixed. The collaboration was successful, opening the possibility of a proper concert tour should schedules align.

Guthrie still wasn't touring aggressively, keeping a low public profile in the months following his mother's passing. But there were commitments to keep. He had earlier signed on to perform with Pete Seeger at several outdoor concerts in July of 1983, with visits to Baltimore, Denver, and Berkeley planned. On 22 July 1983, Guthrie would make his way down to Baltimore's Pier 6 for his first summer concert with Pete Seeger.

In a telephone interview to promote the appearance, Guthrie explained that his concerts with Seeger remained special, and not for reasons one might expect. "Part of the appeal of our shows is the spontaneity," Guthrie mused. "Part of it is the depth perception from the audience. It's not too often you see an old guy up there singing with a young guy." Guthrie thought the three generations faithfully gathering at their concerts were almost the point of the partnership: "That generation gap is nice; it adds a timeless quality to the music. There's an element of a long tradition being continued, of a certain joy in the human spirit being handed down."[40]

In 1982 and 1983 Guthrie was made guest of honor at Pittsfield's 4th of July parade, sweeping down Main Street in a white Cadillac. Guthrie made it plain that being labeled a "protest singer" did not make either him—or Seeger—unpatriotic. "The songs Pete and I sing couldn't be sung in most of the countries in the world," Guthrie conceded.[41] But he acknowledged that even as a youngster living in the land of the free he too often had to "walk through right-wing picket lines" to attend a Seeger concert.[42] He was tired of being pigeonholed as a radical, admitting to being a "real fan" of the US Constitution and the Bill of Rights. "If I didn't care about this country, I wouldn't have been involved in the anti-war or the anti-nuclear movements. . . . I try to write songs and find songs that will enhance the American spirit."[43]

The writer John Steinbeck once said of Woody Guthrie's music, "There is something more important for those who will listen. There is the will of the people to endure and fight against oppression. I think we call this the American spirit."[44] Though there would be some who would never under-stand nor appreciate Woody Guthrie's prominence as a native radical son of America, recognition of his contributions to US culture was slowly shift-ing. Woody wasn't all that famous during his working and most productive years. Ramblin' Jack Elliott mused that while the balladeer was relatively well-known in left-wing circles, "average people didn't know about Woody Guthrie at all."[45]

No matter how tirelessly friends like Pete Seeger, Alan Lomax, and Moses Asch championed Woody's work, the folk singer's name would mostly garner popular-culture recognition through Bob Dylan's invocations. Others were introduced to Guthrie through director Hal Ashby's 1976 film adap-tation of *Bound for Glory*. Arlo Guthrie was not particularly enamored of Hollywood's version of *Bound for Glory*, an earnest if historically inaccurate and highly romanticized account of Woody's 1943 novel.

"There were a lot of good things in it," Guthrie conceded, "but I thought it was kind of frivolous and portrayed . . . Woody Guthrie as sort of a rambunctious kung-fu master, fighting his way through factories."[46] Guthrie was dissatisfied with the casting of actor David Carradine, then of television's popular *Kung Fu* series, as Woody in the fanciful biopic. Guthrie mostly kept his reservations private, as friends were invested, both spiritu-ally and financially, in the film: Guthrie's manager, Harold Leventhal, was serving as coproducer, and blacklisted cinematographer Haskell Wexler was on set too.

Robert Getchell's screenplay could be forgiven for the not-so-small liberties it took in condensing the narrative timeline and historical actualities of Woody's life. But Arlo thought Carradine's humorless portrayal of his father was misguided. The screenplay had so romanticized Woody that the folk singer was reduced to a caricature, a man sitting "on top of freight trains thinking about his destiny and glory, writing songs that he knew would be forever sung in America."[47] Guthrie knew the actual history of his father's American story was more complex and nuanced.

Guthrie had long wanted to make a film that would more properly document his father's life. In the autumn of 1983, cameras began to roll on the PBS documentary *Woody Guthrie: Hard Travelin'*. Guthrie offered there were two reasons helping him decide the time was right to move forward on the project. "The first was that I thought the original Hollywood version, *Bound for Glory,* was such a disaster . . . that something had to be done. The other reason was that there were people whom I had always heard about, but I'd never met—and [I] thought this would be a neat way to meet them."[48]

The raison d'être of the *Hard Travelin'* project was compactly summarized in the film's earliest segment. Arlo is seen rolling westward down a dusty highway on his way to visit several of his father's surviving friends: "I thought it was important to go back and visit with or sing and play music with people who either knew or heard about or who were influenced by my dad," Guthrie's voice-over narration began. "So we started out in Okemah, Oklahoma, in the Oklahoma hills where he was born."[49] Guthrie was, of course, already well acquainted with his father's New York City circle of friends: Pete Seeger, Ronnie Gilbert, Sonny Terry, and Ramblin' Jack Elliott. But working on *Hard Travelin'* gave the singer the opportunity— and the excuse—to visit with several of his father's West Coast friends and family members. These were the folks with whom Guthrie was mostly only familiar through family stories, letters, and biographies. One such person was Matt Jennings, Woody's best friend from boyhood. Jennings was the older brother of Guthrie's first wife, Mary Boyle Guthrie, who was also interviewed in the course of the film. Both spoke openly and honestly of their emotion-testing relationships with Woody. Matt Jennings also demonstrated that he could still capably saw away on his old fiddle, playing along to Arlo's guitar much as he had with Woody back in the 1930s.

Then there was Guthrie's meeting with singer Maxine "Lefty Lou" Crissman who, in 1937, sang on a popular KFVD radio program with Woody in Los Angeles. There was also an opportunity to duet with the irrepressible Rose Maddox, a country and western singer who, with the Maddox Brothers, scored a big regional hit with their cover of Woody's "Philadelphia Lawyer" in 1949. "That single record," Maddox told Guthrie, "sold some eight million copies."[50] If the passing of time had inflated Maddox's timeworn sales memories, Guthrie was too much the gentleman to push her on her cherished recollection.

The point of the whole enterprise was to fill the screen with *real* people, not Hollywood actors. The people introduced in *Hard Travelin'* are the people who lived, worked, drank, fought, and made music with Woody Guthrie. "I was desperately trying to find a way to rectify the image of Woody Guthrie after [*Bound for Glory*]," Arlo explained, initially cautious to move forward with the "Woody Guthrie project."[51] Guthrie confessed that his "hesitancy resulted in my nonparticipation in things like the Hollywood version of *Bound for Glory*."[52] He needed to find the right people to tell a story he believed had not been told well or accurately.

Such hesitancy dissipated following the unanimous critical and public appraisal awarded to *Wasn't That a Time!*, filmmaker Jim Brown's brilliantly constructed and poignant telling of the 1980 Carnegie Hall reunion of the Weavers. Though the film's original theatrical release had played mostly to the art house cinema crowd, it catapulted the Weavers into public consciousness again through a string of successful fundraising broadcasts for PBS. PBS executives were so pleased with the success of the Weavers film, they expressed interest in a second film of similar design.

Though Guthrie had been interviewed and appears in *Wasn't That a Time!*," he could hardly have imagined how this low-budget film would be received and celebrated. "After the success of the Weavers film, it occurred to me that the people responsible for that were people I wanted to talk to about doing a small film on my father."[53] It wasn't too difficult to track down Jim Brown, as Brown had coproduced the Weavers film with Harold Leventhal. It was important to Guthrie that the people involved could be trusted with the undertaking of the task at hand: "These were people I knew directly—or who were peripherally involved with the family. We got together and I found that they had been thinking along the same lines."[54]

Production of *Woody Guthrie: Hard Travelin'* started in October of 1983 in Portland, Oregon, on the banks of the Columbia River, amid the turbines and dams of the Bonneville Power Administration. It was while employed by the Department of the Interior in the spring of 1941 that Woody Guthrie composed his cycle of famed Columbia River songs. "Some of his most beautiful, best-written lyrics were written in these songs," Guthrie told a local reporter present at the filming. "My father defined in a way the best part of the spirit of man in these songs. He was able to capture things in words that usually are best caught only by being there."[55] He also assured that *Hard Travelin'* would be the *real* deal, a proper "document of the people and places where Woody" had been and of the experiences that helped shape his philosophies.[56] Following shooting at the Bonneville Dam, the crew was planning on moving to California, Oklahoma, and Texas.

Woody Guthrie and the Bonneville Power Administration had only recently been in newspapers due to the tireless efforts of Bill Murlin. Murlin, who had been working as an audiovisual specialist for the BPA since 1979, chanced to catch the documentary film *The Columbia*. He noticed Woody Guthrie's name was listed in the film's credit scroll. Having occasionally gigged as a folk singer himself, Murlin was intrigued by the credit and decided to comb through the BPA's "fragmentary files" and trace the history of Woody's involvement.[57]

Woody Guthrie once bragged he had written "twenty-six songs in thirty days" while contracted by the BPA.[58] Though this was essentially true, only a handful of his Columbia River songs had either been recorded or published—or even remembered. In short order Murlin was able to unearth Guthrie's signed original contract of 13 May 1941, with Woody brought on as an "Information Consultant" at an impressive annum of $3,200. This sounded like quite a financial windfall, but since he was contracted only as a "Temporary-Emergency" hire for thirty days work, Guthrie's cash-out was a mere $266.66.[59]

Though Guthrie's work on the Columbia film in 1941 had mostly been forgotten, by August 1983, Murlin had tracked down no fewer than fifteen fragile 78-rpm acetates of songs Guthrie recorded for either *The Columbia* soundtrack or as "amateur recordings made on government disc machines."[60] In September of '83, two more rare recordings ("Jackhammer Blues" and

"Columbia Waters") were found in the possession of a Guthrie fan named Merle Meacham.[61] Murlin was also able to unearth a set of extant lyrics to Guthrie's "Lumber Is King" though, alas, no recording of that particular song would ever surface.[62] This was all amazing stuff, and Arlo Guthrie found this segment of the *Hard Travelin'* documentary among the most rewarding, telling one TV interviewer that through the devotion of Murlin and others he and the crew "discovered a few hundred songs that nobody knew about."[63]

Though a "few hundred" might have been an overreaching estimate, it was true that a score of "new" Woody Guthrie songs *were* being unearthed. One of Bill Murlin's most exciting discoveries was a rousing song titled "Roll Columbia Roll." The song had been in the possession of Ralph Bennett, a former BPA employee now writing editorials for the *San Diego Tribune.* Murlin recollected when Bennett mailed him a tape of the acetate, "It was almost like discovering gold right there on my desk."[64] One of the highlights of *Hard Travelin'* was Guthrie and Murlin's spirited duet on "Roll Columbia Roll." Though Woody's original recording served as the opening song on *The Columbia* soundtrack, that low-fidelity recording would only be issued commercially on *Woody Guthrie: Columbia River Collection* in 1987.

Murlin's work did not escape the notice of either the Guthrie family or of Harold Leventhal back east. Talking of his father's Walt Whitman–like ode to the Pacific Northwest, Arlo told the *Vancouver Columbian,* "My father thought this was beautiful country, but he was also captured by the booming spirit of the place, the feeling that everyone, that ordinary people, could be part of something big and useful and inspiring—like the Grand Coulee Dam. He believed what was happening here was not only good but needed."[65]

Later that October Guthrie needed to take a temporary break from the *Hard Travelin'* filming as he was due in Germany. On 22 October, Guthrie sang before a crowd of some three hundred thousand protesters near Bonn's *Hofgarten* district. The event was one of several dozen anti–missile deployment protests staged across Western Europe: similar peace marches were held concurrently in several other German cities as well as Paris, Vienna, Rome, London, and Stockholm. West Germans were angered by the announcement of a pending NATO-backed deployment of American cruise and Pershing 2 nuclear missiles on their soil. Those protesting insisted their movement was not anti-American in design: NATO's action was a response to the Soviet Union's refusal to remove its own SS20 missiles from its East German client state. Western Europeans were growing increasingly angry of being used as pawns in a maddening Cold War chess game.

Guthrie shared the Bonn platform with such luminaries as former West German Chancellor Willy Brandt and a score of other dignitaries. The Associated Press filed a report that in part read, "Arlo Guthrie, the American folksinger who entertained in Bonn next to a huge papier-mâché globe bristling with mock nuclear missiles, said, 'What started out as a small breeze has now become a big wind, and it is blowing all over the world.'"[66] Guthrie followed up his statement with Dylan's "Blowin' in the Wind" and the civil rights anthem "We Shall Overcome."

Guthrie recollected this continent-stretching day of street protest as "really nice. It was almost like the old days. A lot of people out there and all sort of weird."[67] He admitted his performances of well-worn folk-song chestnuts were by design. "I realized that most of [the protestors] wouldn't be able to put up with me doing a whole bunch of new stuff. It's hard enough understanding each other with the language differences. So I sang a bunch of old songs and it was great. I had a wonderful time."[68]

Guthrie offered praise to those who assembled, marched peacefully and picketed in solidarity. This was a cause worthy of his support, and his visit to Bonn was merely a small contribution "to help end this nuclear threat all over the world. . . . I happen to be here today, and I'll be somewhere else tomorrow."[69] Ridiculing Reagan's handling of a pressing foreign policy issue that might have been better settled diplomatically, Guthrie told American concert audiences upon his return home, "I didn't go over there to say I was *opposed* to missiles. I think everybody ought to have them. I think that's what we're doing. I was over there, 'cause I was afraid that people didn't understand American policy. . . . So I went over to explain it."[70]

A few weeks later, Guthrie would again try his best to explain the vagaries of American foreign policy. On 5 November he was scheduled to play before an audience of rambunctious college students at Rutgers University's New Brunswick, New Jersey, campus. As always, there was something new in the newspapers to reference and riff upon.

Less than two weeks earlier, in the predawn hours of 25 October, the United States had sent a contingent of US Marines and US Army Rangers to invade the tiny island of Grenada, a nation of the British Commonwealth four thousand miles off Florida's shore. One week earlier, the nation's first

Marxist president, Maurice Bishop, had been executed in a *second* Marxist
military coup that Washington believed had been orchestrated to further
Soviet and Cuban interests in the region. The US State Department
defended their decision to invade under the presumption American students might be taken hostage, as well as to "establish law and order in the
country and establish again governmental institutions responsive to the
will of the people in Grenada."[71]

Guthrie was happy to explain the *real* reason behind America's most
recent military incursion:

> Of course I got back and the first thing I realized was that we was
> invading again. It was exciting at first. I thought it was great. . . .
> We need to have the Marines doing something, it's true. But I
> don't think we should stop with little countries like that. I think we
> oughta go really all around and send them everywhere. I don't
> think we oughta stop with certain kinds of governments. I think
> we oughta overthrow them all. We ought [to] go down to El Salva-
> dor next and overthrow that one. . . . I think it would be interest-
> ing. I'm convinced that we're doing this all wrong.
>
> So I just want to say that, just in case there are future, sorta,
> Pentagon-type people here, is that they gotta realize the Russians
> are real good when it comes to educating people. But we gotta
> realize what happens. When they get educated they all want to
> come over here. How many people are sneaking into Russia? How
> many orchestras and ballet dancers are sneaking into Russia? I
> think we oughta let them in from everywhere and educate the
> whole world. That might be interesting . . . and then it might be
> time to take over. Why take over places that need food and educa-
> tion and stuff like that? We already got enough trouble paying
> for stuff.
>
> I think it's okay to invade countries that, first of all, provide
> more beaches for America. We don't have enough beaches left in
> America for people to take vacations and stuff. And for a place like
> Mexico, boy, we get oil too. Not only that, most of the people down
> there want to come up here anyhow. I think we oughta make it a
> state. It's something to do. . . . Of course, I like the way we started
> though. We start small, maybe go down to a country that's tiny and

send in six thousand Marines—ten to one—and come out feeling good. Only America can do that.[72]

With his November tour completed, it was back to work on *Hard Travelin'*. In early December of 1983, *Back Stage* reported shooting had recently been completed at "Cain's Ballroom in Tulsa for a PBS special on the life of Woody Guthrie. It is being produced by the Ginger Group of New York and features Arlo Guthrie, Rose Maddox, and several Tulsa area musicians."[73] The song Guthrie recorded with Maddox and the Oklahoma Swing Band was his father's "Philadelphia Lawyer." It was the song the Maddox Brothers and Rose ("The Most Colorful Hillbilly Band in America") first recorded as a 78-rpm single on the 4 Star Record label in 1949. In December, Guthrie traveled to Pete Seeger's cabin home in Beacon, New York, and ran through several of his father's best-known songs from the 1940s.

With *Hard Travelin'* mostly in the can, it was time to move on. January of 1984 was a break month, time to stay off the road and attend to loose ends. On the evening of 26 February 1984, Guthrie appeared on stage at a half-concert/half-campaign rally for George McGovern. In 1972 the former senator from South Dakota had already vied for—and lost by a staggering margin—the US presidential election to incumbent Richard M. Nixon. Now in 1983 McGovern was again seeking to be the Democratic nominee in the 1984 presidential race. It was a long shot. If McGovern managed to clinch the nomination a second time he would run against another incumbent, Ronald W. Reagan.

The '84 rally was held at the funky Palace Theatre in Manchester, New Hampshire. "A lot of candidates asked for my help," Guthrie told a gaggle of reporters, "but George was the only one I couldn't turn down."[74] That night Guthrie remarked, "George McGovern happens to hold a dear place in my life and it occurred to me that if the election were held with only the candidates voting, I think George McGovern would be president."[75] Despite Guthrie's enthusiasm for his friend's candidacy, McGovern wasn't polling well: a recent Gallup estimate suggested McGovern's prospects had dipped to a mere 5 percent of potential voters in the primary. Undeterred by a series of disappointing showings, McGovern pinned his hopes on a strong show of support in Massachusetts, the only state he carried in his 1972 bid. Guthrie promised to stay onboard the McGovern train . . . at least for the time being.

Hard Travelin' was scheduled to broadcast on most PBS markets on Saturday evening, 3 March 1984. Depending on the market, the documentary was to be followed either by *Wasn't That a Time?* or the Everly Brothers documentary *Rock 'n' Roll Odyssey*. Though New York City would be among the last of the major television markets to broadcast *Hard Travelin'*, WNET managed to get Guthrie to assist in the network's traditional pledge-break segments.

In the early morning hours of 3 March, Guthrie appeared—sleepy-eyed—on NBC's *Today Show*. He was there to promote that night's *Hard Travelin'* broadcast, sharing thoughts on his father's legacy in a tight five-minute conversation with host Bryant Gumbel. When asked what sort of relationship he had shared with his father, Guthrie admitted his childhood was, in some ways, "strange, but that was normal for me. I didn't know it was strange at the time, 'cause when you're a kid growing up, that's just how it is."[76]

He went on to explain that most of the time he spent in his father's company was when Woody was deep in the throes of his increasingly debilitating disease. His memories mostly involved family visits to the Greystone Psychiatric Park, in New Jersey, or Brooklyn State Hospital, a time when Woody "lived in a hospital and we took him home on weekends or went to see him." They spent a lot of time in silent communion, often listening to the LPs arriving almost weekly at their home. So while he, Nora, and Joady didn't enjoy what one might consider a traditional parental relationship with Woody, Guthrie reasoned, "Maybe that's not as a strange as truck drivers who work all the time."[77]

When Gumbel expressed that Woody's life had been mostly one of tragedy, Guthrie countered, "It really wasn't too tragic and that was the great thing." In the course of making *Hard Travelin'*, Arlo had the opportunity to examine his father's life in an "un-tragic" way. "With all the movies and books that have come out that have portrayed [Woody's life] as a great tragedy, it was wonderful for me to get in there," to meet the people who knew him when he was still healthy and creating. "Some parts were tragic," Guthrie allowed," but it wasn't *all* tragic. There were some normal things and some fun things. It was great to go and relive those [times] with people who *didn't* write books or *weren't* in the movies or things like that."[78]

Mostly Guthrie expressed hope that *Hard Travelin'* might "set the record straight for future films. This is not the last piece that's ever going to be made about [Woody], he reasoned. "But at least they'll start from here—with people who were really there." Guthrie also thought the film served as a gift to his own four children. "It's great for my kids: that's why I think I love it. They finally got to know their grandfather in a way that Hollywood can't portray . . . and that was worth it." When asked what Woody would have made of the film, Arlo breathed deeply, replying, "I think he'd be surprised by it. . . . I don't know if he'd like it or not. But *I* like it."[79]

In the PBS studio that night, Guthrie did a little campaigning for the network between broadcast breaks. One of the premiums for PBS viewers was a copy of the soundtrack album of *Hard Travelin'*. It was an impressive collection of Woody's best-known songs featuring Arlo, Pete Seeger, Joan Baez, Judy Collins, Ramblin' Jack Elliott, Holly Near, Ronnie Gilbert, Sonny Terry, Rose Maddox, Hoyt Axton, and Bill Murlin. Guthrie's riffing on the pledge premium was as precious as the film itself:

> If some of the songs seem a little shorter than normal and some of them verses are missing . . . Well, we couldn't fit 'em all in the movie because they said we had to make movies shorter. So on the album there's all the songs . . . There are songs on the album that are not even in the movie at all [but] that we did for the movie. I know there's probably people out there right now who are afraid to pledge money because they think they might get one of these albums in the mail. If that's the case, don't worry. Call up and say, "Look, we'll give you the money, but forget about the album. We don't want the album . . . In which case we'd be very happy . . . Because that means I can take them home and sell them at concerts and stuff like that. So don't worry if you don't want the album. Just say so. But if you want a couple of them, just send them a lot of money. I know there are 500,000 people or more who were at Woodstock who are probably sitting out there, right now, saying "Hey, that's that same guy."[80]

Jokes aside, fans finally had a new Arlo Guthrie "duets" album to enjoy. The soundtrack album to *Woody Guthrie: Hard Travelin'* was released on the one-shot Arloco label. The business address of Arloco was, not coincidentally, the West 57th street address of Guthrie's business manager Harold Leventhal. The album was a perfect companion to the film, allowing fans of the PBS program to hear Woody Guthrie's songs performed by the cast in expanded versions or material unreleased.

The album was produced by John Pilla, mostly taken from Chat Gunter's original recordings for the film. The tapes were later reengineered and mixed at Longview Farm Studios. The only non–Woody Guthrie song included on the album was Goebel Reeves's "Hobo's Lullaby," a favorite song of the balladeer. Arlo Guthrie is featured on eleven of the album's fourteen tracks, his vocal and guitar missing only from Joan Baez's skeletal rendering of "Lonesome Valley," Near and Gilbert's lush piano-backed version of "Pastures of Plenty," and Ramblin' Jack Elliott's seminal take on Guthrie's WWII-era "Talking Sailor."

The album ends with a father and son duet on "This Land Is Your Land." It's a slightly eerie performance not appearing in the film's final edit. Guthrie explained that the idea of synching his vocals with his father's original recording was simply an experiment. "I was just sitting in the studio one night, nothing to do, and I decided to try . . . singing along with my dad. . . . The engineer was off, he wasn't paying attention, and I was sitting there." Guthrie admitted when listening to the first playback he found the result "eerie and strange and very weird. It was almost like he was really there and it was great. . . . It was a *very* strange moment."[81]

AG: I remember sitting in the studio at Long View Farms, when the idea came to me to try and sing a duet with my father. We were working on the *Hard Travelin'* soundtrack at the time.

My father had recorded a version of his "This Land" with three of his original six verses on the recording. And as he had taught me the verses he hadn't recorded, I thought it would be fun to see if I could merge those three extra verses with my voice singing them, and harmonize with him on the chorus.

The first problem I had was that his recording wasn't in any known tuning, but rather off key. It led me to believe that the original recording equipment was running a little too fast, so when it played back it made his voice and guitar sound a little too slow, and lower in pitch. But there was no way to be sure how much it was off. After all, you can tune a guitar a little bit higher or lower. As long as it's in tune to itself, there's no way of knowing if the problem was his doing, or a technical one.

So I went back to the record we were using for his recording and listened carefully for any clue. There were a few tracks where he also accompanied himself on harmonica, and those tracks were also out of tune. That's when it struck me! You can't tune a harmonica. As his harmonica was also out of tune, it had to be an error in the recording process and not one of his doing.

So, we sped up his recording to the next correct tuning. My sister, Nora, was in the studio with me as we listened, for the first time, to an accurate playback. She had tears in her eyes. "That's him! That's the voice I remember!" she cried.

In fact all of my father's records were off to some degree, and no one had paid any attention to it for decades. After this discovery, I could identify which sessions his songs were recorded. The individual songs of his singing had been released as most records are, by choosing the best of the material from a collection of available material without regard to when they were recorded.

But, depending on the pitch I could now tell at which sessions the songs had been initially recorded. All subsequent releases of his songs and records have been adjusted for pitch.

Now, I had the correct key for "This Land" to work with. But, his guitar was not tuned well even to itself. So, in order to play along with him, I had to adjust the tuning on my guitar, so it would sound more like the one he was playing—both would be equally out of tune.

From there we created a framework, a road map to the song, so it sounded as though he was playing while I was singing the missing verses. I had to learn to imitate his style of playing so both instruments complemented each other.

Once that was done, I put the headphones on and began singing. It was an exhilarating experience as my father might as well have been in the next room. The intimacy of his voice in my headphones as our voices merged through the song was completely magical. It was as though we had overcome the years and decades that had separated us. I finally had one chance to sing with my father.

> All this was done long before the digital era, when tempo and pitch could not be adjusted separately. That we were able to do it at that time still amazes me.

Less than a week and a half after the PBS broadcast, Guthrie was off the entertainment pages and back in the hard news section. On the afternoon of 12 March, a crowd of some two thousand supporters congregated near Boston's Copley Square to attend a McGovern rally. Staffers pulled out all stops for the event, hoping to attract the attention of passersby—and television cameras—with a dollop of ballyhoo: a marching band, a hot-air balloon, and Arlo Guthrie were brought in to help create a buzz. Though McGovern's most ardent supporters braved subzero wind chills for the opportunity to hear Guthrie sing a few songs, the writing was already on the wall for the campaign.[82]

Support for McGovern's candidacy was continuing to weaken, even here in Massachusetts, the bluest of states. Guthrie tried his best to encourage supporters to remain faithful. He told the freezing crowd they could be proud because the Bay State was the only one that voted to oust Nixon in '72. "One of the greatest bumper stickers ever is *"Don't Blame Me—I'm from Massachusetts,"* Guthrie reminded them.[83] But McGovern was constantly being referred to in the press as the Democratic Party's "elder statesman." People were looking for someone fresh, for a candidate who might pose a more serious threat to a second Reagan term. A seasoned *Newsday* journalist saw a lot of familiar faces from McGovern's '72 campaign attending. One supporter "gasped" in surprise upon her discovery that Guthrie's famous mop of hair had turned a shade of gray since '72. "We're all getting old," she sighed."[84]

McGovern vowed to bow out of the race should he not receive first or second place in the Massachusetts primary. His third-place finish effectively ended his campaign. McGovern's concession speech was poetically reported by one journalist:

> The end was made official at Boston's Parker House hotel. Though there were enough residual funds in the coffers to allow him to stay in the race through the Illinois primary the following Tuesday, it was clear that George McGovern had just packed in his campaign for the presidency when he turned to folksinger Arlo Guthrie and

asked one last favor. Guthrie picked up his guitar and began to sing. As he did, the hundreds of McGovern supporters who had filled a Parker House Hotel ballroom began to sing with him. "As I was walking that ribbon of highway . . ." That was how it ended, to the strains of "This Land Is Your Land."[85]

Just as one door closed, another opened:

AG: In June I went to visit my old friend Laura Campbell, who lived with Jackie and me at The Farm back in 1969. Laura's brother, Doug, had been a friend and along with Ray Brock and others had helped rebuild the old farm house when I first acquired it.

Laura at the time in 1984 was married to Lenny Baker (of Sha Na Na) and lived in West Tisbury, on Martha's Vineyard, in a gorgeous old house. I would visit on many occasions from time to time.

This particular time, we were talking about things, when I noticed a framed photo on her wall of a woman that intrigued me. It was a picture of Ma Jaya Sati Bhagavati. I asked her about it, and wondered if I could meet her. "I doubt it," Laura said. "It's a closed spiritual community."

Nevertheless, at my insistence, Laura called the ashram in Florida and spoke with Billy Byrom, Ma's first devotee. She asked if I could go visit the ashram. Word came back, "He can come but he comes at his own risk." I said to Laura "Let's go!"

The next day we went to the airport on Martha's Vineyard and boarded a flight to Boston from which we took another flight to Florida, rented a car, and drove to the ashram in Sebastian.

I had previously spent time in religious communities, visiting on retreats at mostly Catholic facilities. So I was not unaccustomed to the isolation of a closed spiritual community. It was a little different, but not uncomfortably so.

What was surprising was Ma (as she called herself). I was ushered into a small hut called The Lion Kuthi, where about a dozen devotees were gathered and seated on the floor before their teacher sitting on a couch before them. I was seated off to the back of the small room, watching with interest as Ma spoke with her devotees on various subjects.

Then Ma turned to me, and asked in a strong Brooklyn accent, "What the fuck are you doing here?"

I was stunned.

I had no answer. I responded that I had come out of curiosity. "Great" she said. "Just sit there."

Although most people would have been somewhat unnerved by the verbal assault through her tone of voice, I had grown up in Brooklyn, as she had. I saw right through her bravado. She spoke the language I grew up with and had learned to overcome. Her mouth was saying one thing, but her eyes were welcoming and wonderful.

I had indeed spent my first years in Coney Island, Brooklyn, New York—and had an accent which reflected it. My pronunciation was so localized that my mother insisted I take elocution lessons, so I could learn to pronounce words properly. Although I couldn't stand them at the time, they came in handy when I began my career as a performer.

I spent my first few years in the same Coney Island apartment on Mermaid Avenue where my older sister Cathy had perished, the result of a faulty electrical system that caused a fire in which she was severely burned. Cathy was rushed to Coney Island Hospital, where she was cared for by her doctors and nurses. But she would not survive the trauma. She was alert, but the fire had burned her so badly that she would not live for long. My parents, who were with her, were devastated.

One evening at the ashram, I was in a large room which was used as a temple. Ma was seated as her sister Shirley walked up to her and pointed at me. "Do you know who that is?" She asked.

"Of course I know who that is! That's Arlo Guthrie, the famous folksinger!" Ma replied.

"No." Shirley said. "That's the brother of the little girl I took care of when I was a nurse at Coney Island Hospital."

I stood there listening while tears formed in my eyes. I had been Woody Guthrie's son, the brother to Joady and Nora, the husband of Jackie, the father of my children. . . . But I had never before in my entire life been acknowledged as my sister Cathy's brother, not by anyone before or since. I was in fact the fourth child born of my father, and the second child born of my mother. My place in the world shifted. I remain the oldest surviving child of my parents.

I stayed at the ashram for a few days, mostly walking around and meeting people. Most everyone was friendly and welcoming, but there was one guy who was not so welcoming. He happened to be a very good-looking guy, tall and lean, but had an obvious dislike for me. I didn't understand it, but there's always one in the crowd that rubs you the wrong way.

I was invited into The Lion Kuthi a few times in those days and, one day, I was seated a little closer to Ma, with about a dozen people. She was going over some breathing techniques and she said to me, "You don't know how to breathe." She called on the one guy, the same guy who we had an obvious dislike for and said to him, "You teach him how to breathe." He said he would. "Now! Take him outside and show him how to breathe now."

We both stood up and began walking out when she added, "You both probably think you don't like each other. But, you've been brothers for so many lifetimes you have nothing more to say. Don't mistake nothing for a negative." It was a teaching that has stayed with me my entire life from then on. The whole thing changed in an instant. And we have remained good friends ever since.

I left the ashram soon after, returning again and again over the following years. It took Jackie about two years to become associated with the ashram, but eventually we would go together and participate in the events going on. It became a safe harbor in our lives—and the lives of our kids.

In late June 1984 Guthrie and Shenandoah flew to the city of Adelaide for their first-ever tour of Australia. The seven-concert tour was to begin 22 June and go through 1 July, but the itinerary was extended to 3 July when a second concert was added at Sydney's Town Hall. One week prior to the band's first show at Adelaide's Festival Theatre, Guthrie took part in a transpacific interview with a journalist from *The Age* newspaper. "What songs might Australian fans expect to hear?" Guthrie was asked. "Haven't worked it out yet," was the reply, but he assured a mix of better-known material with "what we've been doing."[86]

Guthrie seemed more interested in talking about his fourteen-year-old son Abraham "Abe" Guthrie. "He sits around playing synthesizers all day and doesn't do any homework," a sympathetic Guthrie admitted. "He's totally into music."[87] There was little to suggest Abe was destined to be a folk singer. Guthrie allowed his son thought his father's music could be

greatly improved by mixing in a little more rock 'n' roll. It was a period
when heavy metal music ruled the charts. Guthrie's children even suggested he dress up in "leather and spikey-looking things" to enhance his
stage presence.[88]

It was an interesting idea to consider, but Guthrie was content with the
folk-singing path he chose . . . or, perhaps, was chosen for him. "I consider
myself to be within the old troubadour tradition. I go around from place to
place singing about things that go on in other places."[89] He wasn't terribly
enamored with a lot of contemporary music, but he wasn't too concerned.
He was certain new artists would emerge, as they always had, forging new
traditions with new instrumentation. Circling back to Abe's obsession with
his electronic keyboard, Guthrie enthused, "My son, with his synthesizer,
has shown me a few things. To him, the synthesizer isn't supposed to sound
like a flute or like strings. It isn't supposed to sound like a sax—to him, it's
an instrument in itself. What we're waiting for is somebody who knows how
to use this instrument."[90]

A second interview with the *Sydney Morning Herald* was less concerned
with music than with Guthrie's activism. "I think a lot of good things happened as a result of the '60s," Guthrie obliged. "I don't know about Australia, but in the United States at the time there was only one way to be an
American: short-cropped hair, everybody driving the same car, and living
in the same kind of house. If the '60s did anything, it did a lot for individu-
alism." When asked why he finally chose to perform in Australia, Guthrie
replied with a laugh, "Well, I don't really know. It just seems the time's
come."[91]

The Australian shows were positively received. On 26 June, a critic at
the first Sydney concert offered, "Guthrie does not perform a set order of
songs. He tends to play whatever he feels like at the time, which gives all the
more credit to his band, Shenandoah, which played adeptly even when the
songs had not been rehearsed."[92] Another critic reviewing Guthrie's show
at Canberra's School of Music on 29 June was impressed with the singer's
sense of comedic timing and quick wit. When "some overly enthusiastic
members of the audience" boisterously responded in expectation of what
Guthrie might sing next, the singer warned, "You should never clap beforehand. . . . We did and we got Nixon."[93]

The day prior to the Canberra show, Guthrie agreed to a brief interview in a restaurant where he was dining. The discussion centered on the

usual sort of things, but Guthrie made clear that while he was proud to represent the old traditions, his musical vision was not limited by them. "There were a lot of people who were just a few years older than me who were writing about things that were real important to me," Guthrie mused. "Things that I hadn't grown up with. I hadn't heard those views expressed on the radio or in the media until Peter, Paul and Mary and groups like that came along. I thought that when Dylan came along he personalized all of those things. It wasn't just an old folk song anymore. It was new, very innovative and very creative, and I just said 'That's where I've got to be.'"[94] Guthrie thought he made a breakthrough with his writing of the "Alice's Restaurant Massacree": it was a song combining old traditions with the new. He admitted to being a bit "stunned with the reaction that it had. I found myself suddenly becoming a voice for other people and other ideas that were larger than me and larger than anything I had even thought about or knew about."[95]

Guthrie had barely returned from his Australian adventure when he was due to set off on the usual round of July-August shows: a mix of festival appearances, solo concerts, and collaborations with Pete Seeger. On the last weekend of August 1984, Guthrie returned—for the first time in years—to the Philadelphia Folk Festival. The '84 festival was a star-filled event featuring such artists—and old friends—as Ramblin' Jack Elliott, Sonny Terry, Tom Rush, John Sebastian, the Doug Dillard Band, John Hammond, Patrick Sky, and a score of others. "Arlo hasn't been to the festival in five or six years," Gene Shay told the *Philadelphia Daily News*, "and we've certainly missed him."[96]

One of the more anticipated programs of the weekend would be a teaming of Guthrie with Ramblin' Jack Elliott. The acclaimed "James Boswell to Woody's Samuel Johnson," Elliott met up with Guthrie at the latter's home in Washington, the pair driving together to the festival site on Old Poole Farm. The two were slated to perform separately—any plan to collaborate expected but not settled. Elliott was an eccentric performer, not afraid to stretch time signatures or add and subtract musical bars at whim. "Jack and I have spent a lot of time together," Guthrie told the *Philadelphia Inquirer*, "but I think this is a first."[97] He knew fans were expecting some sort of collaboration. When asked directly if he and Elliott would perform together, Guthrie begged off. "It really depends," he replied. 'With me and Jack, you never know. We don't ever rehearse. Jack must know thousands and thousands of songs."[98] They would, to everyone's delight, perform a few Woody Guthrie and Jimmie Rodgers songs together.

One of the welcome results of the Weavers' 1980 reunion at Carnegie Hall was Ronnie Gilbert's return to the concert stage in 1983. Having become involved with the burgeoning "Women's Music" movement—mostly through the influence of the singer-songwriter-activist Holly Near—the Weavers' brassy alto agreed to a series of shows with her new friend. In the spring of 1983, the two played several well-received shows with pianist Jeff Langley. The highlights of those concerts, staged at San Francisco's Great American Music Hall in April and May of 1983, were recorded for the pair's tandem live album *Lifeline*.

In mid-September 1984, Holly Near, Guthrie, Gilbert, and Seeger were to perform together at several formal concerts as HARP, a combining of the first letters of the singers' first names. The tour was a brief one: four shows total, with one in Minneapolis, one in Berkeley, and two in Los Angeles. The last two, both staged at the Universal Amphitheatre on 17 and 18 September, were recorded by Near's Redwood Records label. Plans were made for the recordings to be mixed in the early winter of the following year for an April 1985 release.

The ensemble rehearsed for their tour in New York, the singers mostly plowing through a few old folk chestnuts: songs they could swap verses on without too much effort. Otherwise, aside from a bit of harmonizing or adding a measure or two of accompanying musical flourish, the HARP program consisted of the four mostly doing their own things. Just as Seeger and Guthrie performed together on occasion, Near and Gilbert also managed a successful partnership, attracting a devoted audience of their own.

Near had formed her specialty feminist music label, Redwood Records, in 1973. Since her music and stage manner were unapologetically politically progressive and feminist in content, she was certain she'd never find a niche with Columbia or any similar label. So she decided to strike out on her own from the beginning. "I wanted complete artistic control," she told the *New York Times*, confidently projecting Redwood would gross three-quarters of a million dollars in 1983 alone.[99] The Redwood catalog expanded over the years, recording such other politically conscious or feminist-orientated artists as Sweet Honey in the Rock, Woody Simmons, Ferron, Teresa Trull, Judy Small, and the Chilean folk music ensemble Inti-Illimani.

Ronnie Gilbert had more or less retired from singing on stage when Near, through mutual friend and blacklisted actor Herschel Bernardi, gifted the former Weaver a copy of her 1974 album *A Live One*. In the sleeve notes to that album, Near inscribed "To Ronnie Gilbert: a woman who knew how to sing and what to sing about."[100] The two became friends and, some years later, touring and recording partners. It was following the release of their *Lifeline* album that Gilbert suggested Near and she record a duet of "Pastures of Plenty" for Guthrie's *Hard Travelin'* documentary. Two years younger than Arlo, Near was also introduced to the music of the Weavers at an early age. This wasn't all dissimilar to Arlo's own experience and each, in their own way, found themselves inheritors of a tradition.

If Holly Near had already established a successful record company, Arlo Guthrie was still getting there. On the eve of the HARP tour, he confessed, "The record industry has a hard time with folk artists, because we don't sell a lot of records fast. Ours are the kind of records that can sell for years."[101] Though he suggested he didn't harbor any hard feelings for Warner Bros., he expressed disappointment the company had chosen to delete several of his old albums from the catalog. He wasn't necessarily worried about the financial loss, as "I have always made my living on the road—records are for my fans and to document what we've done."[102] But it was disappointing that Warner Bros. demonstrated little of Moe Asch's visionary, long-range business model.

The HARP shows were marathon affairs. During a Sunday afternoon concert at Berkeley's Greek Theatre, the four managed to cram no fewer than thirty-four songs into their two-hour program. The 8,500 fans who crowded into the Greek to attend the sold-out affair were positively adoring—as were Bay Area critics. The Berkeley concert drew the expected gaggle of nonconformists and radicals. Joel Selvin of the *San Francisco Chronicle* noted the concert brought a convergence of "speeches, pamphleteering, community sing-a-longs and all the traditional hallmarks of such convocations. Many in the all-ages crowd sported T-shirts or buttons bearing messages from the dissident left. . . . Too bad for right-wingers, they don't have this kind of fun."[103]

Things weren't quite as festive at Monday night's program. The atmosphere proved testier when a small but vocal minority booed Near's political avocations. It grew especially contentious when she urged everyone to vote Ronald Reagan out of office on 6 November. The hecklers interrupting with commands to "Shut up and sing!" were not silenced nor directly addressed. In the opinion of the *Los Angeles Herald*, the protestations brought an "intriguing aspect" to the event: "Those who complained [must] have been locked up in a cave for the past thirty years or so. For who else would have come to a concert by [these] four and expected anything other than a couple of hours' worth of left-wing political polemic?"[104]

Despite the heckling, the HARP concerts were public and critical triumphs—even if the four singers differed in their stagecraft. Their multigenerational and diverse program of well-crafted songs, expert instrumentation, and all-around good vibes would, on occasion, flash with disharmony. Near, the only West Coast native, was steadfast in her political convictions and not averse to sharing them. Though the official album trimmed the tense moments, an unedited radio broadcast of the Los Angeles show confirmed some concertgoers were hostile to the political sermonizing.

In contrast, the Seeger-Guthrie mix of politics and music was more bridge-building in tone. Their songs weren't telling people necessarily what to think, only asking people *to think*. "People warned me that Arlo and I wouldn't get along," Near later confessed, "but when we accepted each other's differences, we rapidly became friends."[105] Though Near wasn't pressed on what constituted such "differences," it's likely she and Arlo held contrary views on soapbox politics. In the end, wrinkles were smoothed over quickly. Guthrie couldn't recall any particular moment of friction with HARP. "I think we got along great!" was his remembrance.[106]

Guthrie's solo spots on the HARP program were mostly comprised of songs he had already been performing with regularity in his concerts. Several of his song choices were placed strategically in the program to lighten some of the program's more strident moments: "Oh, Mom," "All Over the World," "City of New Orleans," "President Carter and the Rabbit," "Ladies Auxiliary," and "Mr. Tambourine Man." One newspaper believed "Guthrie provided the most welcome touch of all. Whenever things got too overbearing, he slyly and politely, but firmly, countered."[107] Guthrie accomplished this by sharing an anecdote of folksy humor or singing a specific song he knew could bring everyone together with a laugh or, at the very least, a smile.

One performer with an ingratiating smile would pass away two days after the fourth and final HARP concert. Steve Goodman lost his long battle with leukemia on 20 September 1984. One of the sad ironies of

Goodman's passing is that the singer-songwriter was preparing to go on a nation-crossing tour with Guthrie and David Bromberg. But just before that tour was to commence, Goodman relapsed. It was obvious he would be unable to go on tour. Nevertheless, the irrepressible songwriter chose to remain upbeat and optimistic. This was apparent when Guthrie received a surprise phone call from him. Referencing Willie Nelson's recent cover of "City of New Orleans," Goodman offered Guthrie his "Congratulations, we've got a hit!" "What do you mean, '*We?*'" Guthrie asked, partly taken back that his friend could sound so "awfully happy" considering his grim medical prognosis.[108]

Goodman had reason to celebrate. Willie Nelson's recent recording of "City of New Orleans" did pretty well on the "Country Singles" chart, rising as high as the no. 4 spot in October of 1984, only weeks following Goodman's passing. But Nelson's album of the same name performed even better: it spent a full twelve weeks (mid-August through mid-December 1984) in the no. 1 spot on the *Billboard* "Hot Country" album charts. Goodman explained his "We've got a hit" intimation to Guthrie: Nelson's version was obviously based on Guthrie's 1972 arrangement, not his own. Guthrie suspected the real reason Goodman telephoned was more somber than celebratory. He reminisced that Goodman "called me before he went into the hospital and said that he didn't know what his chances were going to be getting out so he thought he'd say 'So Long,' just in case. . . . We had a real nice, wonderful conversation."[109]

That same September Guthrie would make a splash in the glossy periodical world with the contribution of a thoughtful remembrance in *Esquire* magazine. Guthrie's essay detailed his earliest—and most awkward—stage appearance in February 1961, as a nervous guest of Cisco Houston at Greenwich Village's Folk City. In the early winter of 1961, Cisco, Woody's singing partner, fellow merchant marine sailor, and best friend learned his days were numbered. He had been battling cancer and his two-week residency at Mike Porco's nightclub would be his last engagements. Cisco would pass in April of 1961. "My being born had been his farewell," Guthrie wrote.[110]

In mid-October, Guthrie and Shenandoah headed west, ready to kick off a three-artist package tour. The tour was planned to crisscross the US before ending with a flourish at Boston's Symphony Hall in December. The shows had jokingly been dubbed the *Ménage à Tour,* since the program was originally designed to feature the triad of Guthrie, Bromberg, and

Goodman.[111] That plan was scuttled following Goodman's passing. Guthrie shared that Goodman's absence was not only sad but "quite an irony. . . . I thought after all these years we finally got a chance to put a tour together."[112] Goodman's empty slot on the *Ménage à Tour* was filled by John Sebastian of Lovin' Spoonful fame. Sebastian was a perfect replacement, another old friend whom both Guthrie and Bromberg had worked alongside in their Greenwich Village salad days.

Ticketholders and promoters had been assured the tour would go on as planned. On several shows, when Sebastian was not available to perform due to previous commitments, Doc Watson filled the vacant slot. Guthrie insisted the tour not only serve as a memorial but as a celebration. "This tour is not an obituary for Steve Goodman; we're not sitting around here feeling depressed. The reason Steve wanted to be on this tour with us is that we had a very close philosophy. . . . All of his songs were celebrations of life, not depressing ones, and that's the spirit I think he would have wanted us to convey."[113]

Tapes of the shows demonstrate a relaxed atmosphere where all luminaries found themselves in both central and support roles at one time or another. Off the road for four years to attend fiddle-making school, a reenergized Bromberg brought along a few key members of his reconstituted "Big Band." But to put such an ensemble together in an economically feasible manner, Bromberg needed to employ Shenandoah to fill key roles. It was helpful to him—as it was to Guthrie—that every member of Shenandoah was not only adept on several musical instruments, but were also well versed to perform in any number of disparate styles.

Everyone contributed to each other's sets. On the morning of their gig at the Beverly Theatre on 19 October, Bromberg told the *Los Angeles Times,* "Arlo is like a musical *Mr. Natural.* . . . He lent me his musicians right away—and he's been supportive and helpful all the way."[114] Bromberg insisted these shows were special in many regards: "I've been playing for twenty years," he enthused, "and I've never seen this kind of spirit between two bands: of course, half of my band is [Guthrie's] band, so that could have something to do with it."[115]

The tour's program was representative of authentic musical Americana: there were fiddle tunes, traditional blues, and samplings of old-time string and jug band music, with singer-songwriter musings and nods to such forebears as Mississippi John Hurt and Woody Guthrie. Bromberg remained on stage much of each night, adding his pyrotechnic guitar solos to the evening's program. Sebastian played a few songs from his own catalog of popular songs, colorfully filling in empty patches with bluesy harmonica breaks. And Guthrie traded between his Martin M-38 acoustic guitar and the piano.

This sort of spontaneous musical camaraderie was something that Bromberg, in particular, championed. Though the programs were marked by the appearance of informality, he stressed that the casual on-stage atmosphere should not be mistaken as nonserious music-making. He confessed, "Arlo and I both work in the same way, in that neither of us knows what we're going to play when we go on stage. We've been playing together a lot on the tour, but the good thing is that nobody feels any pressure to make it happen. If I feel like it, I'll go on stage during his set, and if he feels like it, he'll come on during mine."[116] Such adventurous spirit brought a sense of freshness and experimentation to even the most timeworn songs.

A few weeks following the tour's end, Ronald Reagan was reelected president of the United States, having soundly defeated challenger Walter Mondale in a genuine landslide victory. Reagan ultimately won forty-nine of fifty states, Mondale only winning—by the narrowest of margins—his home state of Minnesota and the District of Columbia. Reagan's reelection was the second biggest electoral landslide in US presidential politics. Ironically, the first was Richard Nixon's trouncing of Guthrie's candidate, George McGovern, in the presidential campaign of 1972.

On 17 November, less than two weeks after the election, Guthrie performed with Pete Seeger at Memorial Hall at the University of North Carolina's Asheville campus. Reagan had won nearly 62 percent of the North Carolina popular ballot, capturing all thirteen of its electoral college votes. If the disappointing election results weren't weighing on everyone's mind, they certainly were still weighing on Seeger's. He sighed in rhyme, "I think you and me/Are part of the seventy-three/Who couldn't agree."[117] The "seventy-three" referenced were the percentage of eligible voters who either pulled the lever for Mondale or who, more damnably, chose not to exercise their voting privilege at all. The concert wasn't all grim, though. One of the lighter moments occurred in the midst of Guthrie's performance of "Blowin' in the Wind." Midway through, Guthrie's voice noticeably warbled and rasped. "I sing these songs of Dylan's," he wearied, "and my throat goes weird on me."[118]

Chapter Three

NEWPORT IS HIS JUST FOR A SONG (AGAIN), 1985–1987

In early January 1985, tickets went on sale for "A Tribute to Steve Good-man." The event was scheduled to take place at the Arie Crown Theater in Chicago, the late singer's hometown. Tickets sold out within hours of being put on sale, the tribute to be held later that month. Goodman's man-ager, Al Bunetta, was hesitant to call that evening's concert a "tribute": such attribution sniffed of solemn memorialization. "It's a party in Steve's honor. That's the way he would have wanted it."[1] The organizers had no trouble arranging commitments from the musicians whose lives had been touched by the singer-songwriter. That night everyone performing appeared on stage wearing baseball caps featuring the logo of Goodman's beloved Chi-cago Cubs.

It was a night that would be long recalled by the four thousand Windy City fans lucky enough to score tickets. Before the curtain closed on the nearly five-hour-long program, attendees were treated to performances by Arlo Guthrie, John Prine, Bonnie Raitt, Richie Havens, David Bromberg, the Nitty Gritty Dirt Band, John Hartford, Jethro Burns, Bryan Bowers, David Amram, Bonnie Koloc, and others. Guthrie performed "City of New Orleans"—as everyone expected he would—but also "Will the Circle Be Unbroken?" and his own "All Over the World." Proceeds from ticket sales went to organizations involved in leukemia research.[2] For those unable to attend, the entire program was recorded and released late in 1985 on Goodman's label, Red Pajama Records.

Several musicians performing at the Goodman tribute were booked to play the following night at the 8th Annual Ann Arbor Folk Festival. Since he was already in the Midwest, Guthrie decided to tag along. One newspaper reported, "The biggest surprise of them all—one that drew in the audience's breath—was Arlo Guthrie, fresh from the Steve Goodman tribute on Saturday night in Chicago."[3] Guthrie had flown into Ann Arbor's Hill Auditorium at the University of Michigan with Bonnie Raitt. Raitt too was a survivor of the Warner Bros. roster cleanse of 1983–84, so there was a lot to discuss. Raitt told one writer covering the event, "I wish I could tell you some of the backstage stories Arlo told me on the plane today . . . but I can't."[4]

The early winter of 1985 was a mostly quiet period for Guthrie, staying close to home and tinkering in the recording studio. On 8 March 1985 the singer was recording at Long View Farm when he began to feel unwell, telling John Pilla he was suffering severe stomach pain. Guthrie was attended at the studio by Dr. Louis B. Grace, who suggested he be taken to a local hospital for testing. A receptionist at Long View confirmed Guthrie had indeed been taken ill, adding the doctor suspected the singer might be suffering inflammation of the gall bladder. Guthrie and Jackie drove themselves to the emergency department of Mary Lane Hospital in nearby Ware. The singer was admitted shortly after midnight, and Dr. Grace explained that a series of tests would be ordered so a more concrete diagnosis could be rendered.[5]

On Wednesday, 13 March, the singer was transferred to Massachusetts General Hospital in Boston. John Pilla told the press on 12 March that initial tests ruled out "anything serious." His friend was feeling "much better. . . . He's off medication, and he's on his way back."[6] Pilla's news was comforting, but Guthrie wouldn't be back all *that* soon. The singer would spend more than a week at Massachusetts General undergoing a battery of additional tests.

On 21 March, Guthrie was finally released from care. A hospital official told the press that the singer had suffered a small ballooning, or aneurysm, on a branch of his right kidney artery.[7] Though surgery was not required, it was suggested that the singer rest at home for several more weeks. Guthrie did precisely that, spending a month at home before he was to return to the concert stage on 20 April for a show with Pete Seeger at the Valley Forge Music Fair. Seeger would not be the only graybeard on stage in Valley Forge. Guthrie had grown a moustache and wispy beard while convalescing, making him mostly unrecognizable to fans.

Following the Seeger show and a solo makeup date at the University of Virginia, he was feeling back in form. He immediately flew out of

Charlottesville to Vancouver, Washington, where he had family business. His three-day visit to the Pacific Northwest had been prompted by a request from Washington State Representative Joe Tanner (D-Ridgefield), a distant cousin (Woody Guthrie's mother had been the former Nora Belle Tanner).

It seemed no one in the Evergreen State cared much for the melodramatic "Washington, My Home," the song sanctioned as the official state anthem in 1959. Deciding it was time to freshen things up, the commissioners of Whatcom County introduced a resolution calling for the rock song "Louie, Louie"—a big hit for both the Kingsmen and Paul Revere and the Raiders to replace the stodgy old anthem. There was a curious belief that "Louie, Louie" might somehow act as a catalyst to attract industry and tourists to the area. Old-school supporters of "Washington, My Home" were adamantly opposed to the change, arguing the first two rock groups to chart "Louie, Louie" were not homegrown but natives of neighboring Oregon and Idaho.[8]

Suggestions of more fitting song titles started coming in from all corners. One song, suggested by Joe Tanner, was Woody Guthrie's "Roll On, Columbia." Woody's majestic paean to the Pacific Northwest was, all things considered, a pretty good song to nominate. On 22 April, Arlo Guthrie visited Vancouver, making a bid for "Roll On, Columbia" to be considered. He performed the song for the city council—and for the seventy-five fans who managed to squeeze into the chamber for a listen.[9]

Guthrie's performance caused the Council to unanimously pass Tanner's resolution. There was one caveat. Just as it had been for Arlo's "Massachusetts," Woody's song would only be possibly considered as Washington's official *folk song.* Guthrie was pleased with the compromise, suggesting the resolution was merely another step in the Guthrie family's plan to monopolize the state-song racket.

On Tuesday, 23 April, Guthrie traveled south of Portland, Oregon, to sing several of his father's Columbia River songs to a standing-room-only crowd at the Bonneville Power Administration. When asked what his father would have thought of all the attention "Roll On, Columbia" was suddenly receiving, Guthrie answered, "I think he'd find this awful absurd. It wasn't so much that [Woody] really wanted to come up here," Guthrie continued, only that his peripatetic father simply had "run out of places that he could go safely . . . and I suspect that's why there's a whole lot of people up here."

His father's hire by an official US agency, Guthrie mused, was "the first time the government had shown an interest in him . . . other than chasing him. When reminded his father composed an amazing "twenty-six songs in thirty days" while in the employ of the BPA, Guthrie remarked his father had always been "a prolific writer. He threw away more songs in a week than I've written so far in twenty years of playing."[10]

"He wrote songs to get rich by, and that never panned out," Guthrie explained. "Most of his songs were concerned about the simple integrity of being a human being. He wanted people to feel good about themselves."[11] Guthrie allowed his father would have found it "interesting that forty-five years after he wrote ["Roll On, Columbia"], the song is still remembered by people. The real reason I came out here wasn't so much to promote my Dad's song—I could've gone for "Louie, Louie" myself. One of my songs is Massachusetts' official state folk song, and I just figured that if we could get this through, in another couple of generations, we could have the whole country covered."[12]

Guthrie kicked off the Bonneville event with a measure of historical background. He showcased his father's Oklahoma roots with his playing of "Do-Re-Mi" and "Pretty Boy Floyd," explaining how hard times and the Dust Bowl brought his father—and thousands of other displaced Okies— to seek a new life in California and the Pacific Northwest. Following his set, Guthrie brought out Bill Murlin, the pair reprising their twin-guitar duet on Woody's "Roll, Columbia, Roll." Following the concert, Murlin gifted Guthrie a tape of eleven newly discovered songs his father had recorded for the BPA in 1941.[13]

Guthrie was back in Washington State by Wednesday, playing "Roll On Columbia" in a misty drizzle on the front steps of the state capitol building in Olympia. An hour earlier the House had passed the resolution—brought jointly to the floor by fifty-eight House members—honoring his father's song. Guthrie sat near the rostrum with Rep. Tanner and listened as a tape was played of Judy Collins's melodious performance of the song—taken from the album *A Tribute to Woody Guthrie* (Warner Bros. 1972). Tanner mixed in a bit of politics as well, remarking how Franklin D. Roosevelt's New Deal policies ultimately broke the grip of the eastern power companies, providing citizens of the Pacific Northwest with affordable electric power. Guthrie confessed to the legislators, "Had my father been alive today, he definitely would *not* have been here. It would have scared the Hell out of him." But Guthrie conceded he and the family did "appreciate the effort" made on their father's behalf.[14]

There was a sprinkling of shows in May and June. On 1 June 1985, Guthrie and Shenandoah were on stage at the Temple of Music and Art in Tucson, Arizona, when a thief made off with his bag containing a pair of airline tickets, a crystal pendant, a synthesizer operator's manual, a telephone appointment book, and a favorite shirt.[15] Performing in Tucson was becoming taxing. In a story he would often tell on stage, six years earlier Guthrie was booked to play the University of Arizona. Upon his arrival a smart-alecky journalist advised that Bob Dylan was playing Tucson's Music Hall that very night. "So why would anyone want to come out to hear you?"

Since Dylan was in the period of his career when he was exclusively performing evangelized songs, Guthrie responded with the snarky retort. "Well, if people want to hear those good old Bob Dylan songs, I guess they'll *have* to come and hear me." Having shared a similar interest in exploring Christian tenets, Guthrie was mostly sympathetic to Dylan's restless spiritual search. But he admitted to not being particularly enamored of Dylan's "scorch the infidels" reading of the gospels.

One of the more unusual gigs of 1985 was his concert of 14 June at Boston Harbor. Guthrie was engaged by the folks of Boston's Bestcruise to set up on the deck of the MV *Provincetown II* to entertain a sold-out crowd of "young folks to weathered hippies" standing shoulder-to-shoulder for the two-hour concert cruise. Guthrie played the songs fans expected, such as "The Motorcycle Song" and "City of New Orleans," but he also performed the still unreleased "All Over the World" and "You and Me." While onboard, Guthrie told a newsman that *Someday*—still unissued and now almost two years old—was "probably the finest album I've made. It's a very personal album and I'm waiting for the right time to put it out." The reporter noted that since Guthrie was no longer attached to Warner Bros. the artist was mulling "putting it out on an independent label, though he still hasn't decided yet."[16]

The Bestcruise event was an intimate affair of eleven hundred partygoers. Nothing, however, could have readied Guthrie for the crowd that swelled for a Sunday evening concert planned for 30 June on Hartwood Acres, outside Pittsburgh. This tandem concert with Pete Seeger was to benefit the Greater Pittsburgh Community Foodbank. The local press was

excited about the fundraising event. Four days prior to the benefit, a journalist reached Seeger at his home in Beacon, New York, to discuss.

Seeger promised he'd sing at least a few songs of Pittsburgh origin,
such as "The Homestead Strike Song" of 1892, the Slovak dirge "He Lies
in the American Land," or "Where the Old Allegheny and Monongahela
Flow"—and perhaps even the song he had written with Woody and the
Almanac Singers, "Pittsburgh is a Smokey Old Town." Acknowledging he
had known Arlo Guthrie since he was a child, Seeger mused their collaborations worked as "contrasts in generations, contrasts in styles. Our work
overlaps a lot, but isn't exactly alike." The two never planned a set list prior
to a show, preferring to allow their solo spots to inspire a musical dialogue
of sorts. "I try to surprise him, and he tries to surprise me."[17]

A second Pittsburgh newspaper thought to ring up Guthrie at his
home, hoping to glean the singer's own take. He had been absent from the
Pittsburgh music scene for nearly a decade, with fans eagerly awaiting his
return. The phone call was picked up by Guthrie's mother-in-law, Ellen
Hyde, who explained that Arlo was unavailable as he was "putting up a new
addition on his farmhouse." She, however, was willing to chat, their conversation encompassing grandson Abe's contributions to his father's band,
Joady Guthrie's forthcoming album, and the joy of watching Arlo write
songs at the piano. "When he sits down and composes, I just hang around
and listen," she offered. "He says, 'I hope I'm not bothering you.' Imagine
that!" "I just can't tell you how wonderful a man Arlo Guthrie is," Hyde
continued. "He's my hero, and he's my wife's hero, and he's just crazy about
those kids. You know, a lot of these . . . well, 'rock stars,' I guess you call
them—they've built these beautiful homes and put all their money in
property and things. But Arlo's just given his money away, and you can't
help lovin' him."[18]

Though local newspapers suggested concertgoers arrive at 6 PM for
the 7:30 concert, fans began to trickle in early that morning and continued
to stream into the fairground throughout the afternoon. As the hour of the
concert neared, traffic became completely snarled. In desperation, people
abandoned their cars as far away as two miles from the concert site and
walked along the roadside carrying canned-good donations. In the final
tally, officials estimated the crowd to have swelled between twenty-five to
thirty thousand people, with concert attendees delivering twenty-five

thousand pounds of canned food goods—and $15,000 in cash donations to the food bank.[19]

June of 1985 was a notable month for another member of the Guthrie family. Guthrie's younger brother, Joady, now age thirty-seven, would belatedly join his older brother and his sister Nora (who had released a single on the Mercury label in 1968) as a full-fledged recording artist. Joady had left Howard Beach for a stint at Goddard College in Vermont before moving with his wife, Eileen, to the San Francisco/Berkeley area around 1970. There he worked intermittently as a carpenter and gave guitar lessons. He wrote songs and occasionally performed in small clubs and coffeehouses in and around Berkeley, once landing a steady gig with his band, Duffy and the Nighthawks, at a local Burger King. But ultimately Joady was, by his own admission, too shy to earn his bread on stage as a performing artist.[20]

He was also a bit intimidated to consider music as a possible full-time vocation. Joady was aware that comparisons with Woody and Arlo were inevitable. "I think Eileen and I both felt that if Arlo could make it, so could I," Joady told the *San Francisco Chronicle*. "Those assumptions were behind the whole fantasy of making it big, the money, the recognition."[21] One of Joady's West Coast friends was a mutual friend of his older brother, Country Joe McDonald. The son of left-wing parents, one of McDonald's earliest musical heroes was Woody Guthrie, the singer having even recorded a complete album of Guthrie's songs in 1969. McDonald thought Joady's songs well-crafted, and he coaxed the hesitant progeny of his hero into a Berkeley recording studio in April of 1985 for a two-day session. The result of those sessions was *Spys on Wall Street,* issued on McDonald's Rag Baby Record label in June of 1985.

It was actually a pretty good album, accepting that mostly solo acoustic records were no longer—if ever—in the forefront of popular-music tastes. In the months following its release, a short tour of the East Coast was arranged. On Friday, 7 June 1985, a nervous Joady performed at Greenwich Village's Folk City, opening for singer-songwriter Christine Lavin. To his unwelcome expectation, the advertisement triumphed, *"Joady Guthrie— Woody Guthrie's Son in His N.Y. Debut."* There would be no escaping comparisons. That summer Joady also played a number of gigs in the northeast, including shows at the Iron Horse Coffeehouse in Northampton; the

Prescott Park Arts Festival in Portsmouth, New Hampshire; and Bethlehem, Pennsylvania's, Musikfest—even opening for blues guitarist Lonnie Mack at New York City's famed Lone Star Café.

Following his gig at the Iron Horse, McDonald and Joady visited Arlo at home in the Berkshires. Ellen Hyde recalled Arlo listening to Joady's album and remarking, "Boy, my brother's got more of a voice than I got."[22] Though it was disappointing that Joady's album wasn't receiving the attention it deserved, Country Joe stood by his decision to produce it. "I always liked Joady's point of view, personality, and his choice of chords," McDonald later explained. "He was uniquely different than Woody or Arlo, and perhaps that's what was wrong. But I put my bets into Joady, and I'm still happy I did."[23]

Joady was cut from a different cloth than Arlo and Nora. He could be bristling in assessment of his father, not welcoming of the legend-manufacturing surrounding Woody. In the course of a brief interview for *Broadside* magazine, a writer made note of Joady's cynicism. Listening to a gaggle of young folk singers speak glowingly of his father at that year's Hudson River Revival, Joady sighed, "Woody wasn't the great prophet that he was made out to be. He didn't have all the answers and he didn't know how to take care of himself while he was writing all of those songs."[24]

Though not technically a folk festival, the *Clearwater* sloop's Great Hudson River Revival harkened back to an era when "homemade music" festivals were commonplace. In March of 1985 there were some rumbles that producer George Wein was attempting a resurrection of both the Newport Folk Festival and the Newport Jazz Festival. Although some objected to the restaging of these events—the last Newport Folk Festival dated to 1969—by mid-April Newport's city council agreed to set aside two weekends in August for the return shows. The folk festival, set for the weekend of August 4–5, would no longer be held at the original location, but in Fort Adams State Park, a historic seaside fortress overlooking the harbor.[25]

Things moved quickly following the green-lighting of the events. By early May, Wein received commitments from the crème de la crème of the 1960s folk music revival: Joan Baez, Judy Collins, Doc and Merle Watson, Arlo Guthrie, Taj Mahal, Dave Van Ronk, Tom Paxton, Peter Rowan, Bill Keith, and Jim Rooney had already signed on. That amazing lineup was fine-tuned to perfection in June, with the announcement that Bonnie Raitt,

Mimi Fariña, and Ramblin' Jack Elliott had been added to the schedule. Not wishing the festival to be merely an exercise in nostalgia, Wein and coproducer Robert Jones would bring in some of the less well-known singer-songwriters working the coffeehouse-circuit: Bill Morrissey, Buskin & Batteau, Greg Brown, and David Massengill.[26]

Wein's agreement was that attendance be limited to 6,500 concertgoers per day. Though the producer acknowledged old-school headliners had been brought on to capture the "essence" of the festival, he admitted such celebrity-packing was an expensive gamble, and one that might interfere with the festival's survival interest in turning a profit.[27] Accountants estimated the event would need tickets sales of 95 percent to simply break even on investment. Guthrie was scheduled to play on Sunday afternoon. Saturday's event, featuring Joan Baez, drew a healthy crowd of 5,000, but Sunday's program completely sold out. It certainly didn't hurt that the weather cooperated—skies were blue and cloud-free all weekend—but the box office was what mattered in the end. Wein was able to breathe a bit easier when ticket sales testified to a continuing interest in folk music.

In the weeks preceding the festival, newspapers recounted the iconic past of Newport, usually citing Dylan's going electric and Guthrie's "Alice's Restaurant Massacree" as cultural touchstones. The *Christian Science Monitor* thought Guthrie "the most popular act of the 1985 festival. The sight of him in aviator sunglasses and a green beret, and the sound of the first few chords of his anti-draft anthem, "Alice's Restaurant," brought the entire audience to its feet, cheering wildly."[28] *Broadside,* New York's "National Topical Song Magazine," cynically argued the radicalism of the old guard had clearly dimmed. They contended more political exhortations could be heard at a Bruce Springsteen concert than from those performing on the Newport stage.[29] The resurrection of Newport was also received by mainstream newspapers with muted enthusiasm—and critical brickbats. Arguments were made that Newport was now little more than a weekend retreat for aging boomers. Activists railed there were too few jeremiads against Reagan's meddles in El Salvador and Nicaragua.

The criticisms were noted, if not all accurate or fair. If nothing else, Guthrie's return to Newport was the completion of a circle. Eighteen summers prior, Guthrie's appearance at the 1967 festival changed his life in unimaginable ways. His return to this tony seaside community brought with it a rush of memories:

AG: In June of 1967, Caroly surprised me by showing up at the airport in New York. Because Caroly was best friends with my stepsister Ann, Lou Cooper (Ann's father and my stepdad) knew when she'd be arriving and we went to pick her up. I was thrilled to see her, and she came back to Howard Beach with me. On July 15th Caroly and I went to Newport, Rhode Island, for the Newport Folk Festival. I didn't go as a performer, just another kid with a guitar. We strolled around listening to the performers and enjoyed hanging out in town with all the others who descended upon the peaceful small community.

The festival had set up a free stage where anyone could perform, and I stood on a wooden milk crate and sang "Alice's Restaurant" to about fifty people, at most, who were sitting nearby. Word got around and I was invited to play it again at another stage somewhere in a field. This time there were a few hundred people there.

As word spread, I was invited to perform on the main stage and actually close the event. Pete Seeger and Oscar Brand wondered if I could handle the thousands of people at the closing of the festival, so at the end of "Alice's Restaurant" they added more and more performers who had already performed to join me onstage at the closing of the song. Caroly and I left the next morning, and returned to Howard Beach. That day the headlines (on page 30) in the *New York Times* read "Newport Is His Just for a Song."

The scent of politics lingered in the air a few weeks following Guthrie's return to Newport. On 14 August 1985, HARP was scheduled to play the Ohio State Fair. The gig, the last Guthrie would perform under the anagram, would make national headlines. It would also demonstrate Guthrie's assertion that America had come a long way in dealing with dissenters. Thirty-four years earlier, in August of 1951, the Weavers had been contracted to play eleven sets at the Ohio fair. Upon arrival the Weavers learned the event's director, Howard Foust, had cancelled their controversial appearance, fearing "public disturbances."[30] The Weavers had been branded as Communist sympathizers, and the era of blacklisting and McCarthyism was nigh.

The world had changed. In 1951 Ohio's Democratic governor, Frank Lausche, on behalf of angry complainants, contacted Hoover's FBI regarding the accusations made against the Weavers. In 1985, the state's current governor, Richard Celeste, would make amends by inviting Seeger and Gilbert to return to the state fair. The two former Weavers graciously accepted the governor's entreaty, bringing along Guthrie and Holly Near to celebrate. In a further accommodation, the four singers were even put up for the night at the Governor's mansion.[31]

Though Guthrie was pleased to have been associated with HARP, sharing the stage at the State Fair with a trio holding strong political opinions was challenging. "I figure if you can't laugh at yourself, you can't laugh at anybody else, either—and it's real healthy to laugh at yourself," Guthrie told the New York *Daily News*. "We did a couple of shows with Pete Seeger, Holly Near and Ronnie Gilbert and the shows were so *serious*. Every time I got to the mike, I felt I had to interject some laughter—*anything* to relieve this audience after all the heavy things dumped on 'em."[32]

Guthrie was in New York City to perform at Manhattan's Pier 84, a waterfront venue sandwiched between 12th Avenue and the Hudson River. He was asked to help celebrate the twenty-fifth anniversary of Gerdes Folk City, the tiny Greenwich Village cabaret that launched the careers of so many folk music artists. Bob Dylan's first professional gig had taken place there in September of 1961, and his subsequent fame brought throngs of fledgling folk singers to the club's legendary Monday-night hoots. Even though Guthrie was seven years younger, technically he first performed at Folk City prior to Dylan. That was on that cold February night in 1961 when, at age thirteen, he was called to the stage by Cisco Houston.

Mike Porco, the owner of Gerdes, recalled Cisco as his "favorite," as he was a man with no pretense.[33] He was an unassuming, serious guy—one with whom you could sit and talk and share a drink. Nearly two decades later, in the winter of 1979, Porco began looking to retire. He had been searching for a responsible buyer who might keep his nightclub—and his legacy—afloat. He ultimately offered to sell the club to Robbie Woliver, a literary type with little money. Woliver had been hosting a singer-songwriter program on Sunday afternoons at the club for the past year and a half. He had no cash reserves of his own, but with the financial assistance of two friends, Joe Hillesum and Marilyn Lash, he purchased the club from Porco in May 1980.[34]

It was tough going almost from the beginning: folk music wasn't attracting tourists as it had in the early and mid-1960s. Punk rock and New Wave were the current rage, and Folk City's recent bookings were geared to be more eclectic by design and necessity. You could walk into the club on any given week and still find Odetta, Ramblin' Jack Elliott, or Dave Van Ronk sitting on creaky chairs and coolly doing their thing. But you also might catch two sets of amplified energy-rock from the likes of the Violent Femmes, or Beat Rodeo, or 10,000 Maniacs, or Patti Smith doing *their* thing. Punk rock was the new vanguard of political-protest music.

It was an inescapable reality. The folk singers of the 1960s were aging, many pushing—*gasp*—the age of forty. They hadn't, as some charged, become mossy and soft and apolitical. But with age came wisdom, and some of what they learned was channeled into their present-day songwriting. The *New York Times* tracked down Guthrie for its essay on the forthcoming Folk City celebration, the singer defending his own style of agit-prop song: "I tend to write less and less about the issues themselves and more and more about the kind of people who get involved with them."[35]

"Two years ago," he continued, "a guy came backstage who had been a helicopter pilot in Vietnam. He told me that while everybody else was putting on the Rolling Stones, he used to play 'Alice's Restaurant.' That seemed strange at the time. But I've learned that times change and people change, and I'm pleased with the way things worked out. Twenty years ago, to be opposed to the war in Vietnam was considered unpatriotic. The attitude was *'America—Love It or Leave It.'* Here we are twenty years later and there are serious debates going on about whether we ought to be in Central America, or Grenada or Lebanon, and it is not just a bunch of weird, strange people on one side and well-dressed people on the other. That's a major change and we should congratulate ourselves that it took only 20 years to have a country where you can speak out on something and not be called bad names or be labeled un-patriotic."[36]

Though he had filmed a segment of *Hard Travelin'* at Folk City's second address of 130 West 3rd Street (the club had changed location in 1969), Guthrie had only publicly performed at the nightclub's original location at 11 West 4th Street. "I was frightened beyond terror," he reminisced, but "I always considered that night to be the first night I started as a singer."[37] The event's eight thousand tickets sold out quickly—partly due to newspapers teasing the possibility of Dylan showing up unannounced. Though Dylan would not appear, fans were treated to a marathon-length concert by an amazing array of performers: Eric Andersen, Joan Baez, Buskin & Batteau, Frank Christian, Ferron, Arlo Guthrie, Richie Havens, Melanie, Tom Paxton,

Roger McGuinn, Odetta, the Roches, Tom Rush, Suzanne Vega, the Violent Femmes, Peter Yarrow, Libby Titus, and David Massengill, among them.

Sadly, it wasn't enough. The club was in serious financial straits, the souvenir program hinting at what they were up against, the owners cynically singling out their landlord "for teaching us to multiply by 4."[38] Though the club soldiered on for another seven months, they lost their lease in March 1986, another victim of Manhattan's real estate rent wars. The evening of music on Pier 84 had been video-recorded with highlights cobbled together and issued on VHS and LaserDisc by Rhino Home Video in 1987. Guthrie's contribution was a solo piano-backed version of David Mallet's "Garden Song."

Though Bob Dylan was a no-show at the Folk City celebration—he hadn't toured the US since the autumn of 1981—the rock legend consented to perform at the first Farm Aid benefit scheduled for 22 September at the University of Illinois Memorial Stadium in Champaign. It was Dylan's off-the-cuff remark at Philadelphia's Live Aid famine relief benefit in July 1985 ("It would be nice if some of this money went to the American farmers") that sparked Farm Aid. Dylan's suggestion inspired Willie Nelson to organize a benefit of his own, announcing plans to assist the American family farmer, with a Live Aid–style "Concert for America." The wizened and beloved Texan had already received commitments from Neil Young, Johnny Cash, Waylon Jennings, John Cougar Mellencamp, Merle Haggard, and Bob Dylan.

The list of performers would grow in the coming weeks, with fifty or so additional artists—including Arlo Guthrie—accepting Nelson's offer to help out. Things got off to a good start when several corporations pledged $4 million from the outset. On 28 August 1985, tickets for the benefit concert were put on sale, all seventy-eight thousand general admission tickets selling out within days. For those unable to attend in person, the Nashville Network planned to broadcast the concert almost in its entirety, noon through midnight. There was also a telethon fundraiser established with TNN radio affiliates set to broadcast the event as it unspooled.

Guthrie had planned on traveling to Champaign from a gig in California in style—as a passenger on Merle Haggard's whistle-stop railroad musical caravan. But Haggard's ambitious plan was scrubbed due to logistical and financial tussles with Amtrak. This last-minute cancellation left Guthrie needing to chart an alternate method of getting to Champaign. He was already in California, performing in Berkeley for the thirteenth anniversary of Redwood Records. On the afternoon of 15 September, seven thousand people crowded into the Greek Theatre to catch performances by Guthrie, Holly Near, Ronnie Gilbert, Linda Tillery, and Inti Illimani. The company was also celebrating the sales of the HARP album, released six months prior. By the time of the Redwood concert, more than twenty thousand copies had already sold.[39]

Willie Nelson opened Farm Aid, fittingly, by asking "Good Morning America, how are you?" He called out Guthrie, standing in the wings, to join him on stage. The two traded verses on "City of New Orleans," with a vocal assist from Dottie West. The event was peaceful and, aside from a few technical bugs, the benefit went off without a hitch. Though nearly eighty thousand people were squeezed into Memorial Stadium, local authorities reported fewer than three arrests, twenty-five ejections, and such minor medical issues as twisted ankles, bruises, and scratches. The director of medical services did complain that "Marijuana use was widespread," but this was, after all, a Willie Nelson event.[40]

Guthrie wasn't terribly bothered by the fog of recreational cannabis floating about, simply pleased to be asked to participate in Farm Aid I. When asked how Farm Aid stacked up against Woodstock, Guthrie didn't hesitate in his response: "I think this is nicer overall. Woodstock was meant to be just a normal, commercial concert. And although it didn't end up like that, that's the way it was set up. This from the very start was set up to help a lot of people and I think the feeling here is just tremendous. I think it's better because of that."[41] He also joked that he decided to participate since he was "the only one left who didn't sing with Willie—in the world. So I decided this would be a good time to do something with him."[42]

He was happy to support Farm Aid as there was a history of farming in the Guthrie lineage. Woody's father, Charles, had been both a farmer and a farm realtor in the 1920s and '30s, experiencing tough times long before the dust storms hit. "My grandfather lost a lot of farms during the Depression," Guthrie recalled. "The concert is a wonderful thing because it gets the nation to stand up and say, 'We're behind you.'"[43] Guthrie's experience at Farm Aid inspired him to write one of his best satirical songs—still unreleased—"Down on the American Farm." The song was a favorite of audiences in the mid-1980s, especially in the Midwest. Guthrie's lyrics, sung to the slightly amended tune of "Old MacDonald Had a Farm," offered a primer on the perils of modern farming: "The more you grow, and the more you spend, the less it's worth, to the market in the end." Concertgoers from America's breadbasket knew exactly what Guthrie was singing about.

It was perhaps fitting that Guthrie closed out 1985 as it began, with a series of concerts with Pete Seeger. On Thanksgiving weekend, Seeger and Guthrie teamed at Carnegie Hall, Abe Guthrie adding a measure or two of musical flourish on synthesizer. Arlo Guthrie's previous concert at Carnegie had been at Seeger's Thanksgiving concert of 1981, playing alongside an amplified Shenandoah. This 1985 concert was a more stripped-down affair, similar to the acoustic Seeger-Guthrie pairings of 1974. Moses Asch, the founder of Folkways Records, now age eighty and in failing health, would attend one of the two concerts.

Seeger contributed a set of program notes to the Carnegie *Stagebill* ("A Story You Should Know"). The essay provided a thumbnail history of Asch's career as both a recording engineer and founder of several visionary record companies. Seeger's remembrance noted that in the 1940s, the Asch and Disc labels existed as "a hand-to-mouth operation, often on the brink of bankruptcy."[44] It was Asch who opened his recording studio to Seeger, Woody Guthrie, Cisco, Brownie McGhee and Sonny Terry, and a score of others. By the time of his passing on 19 October 1986, Asch was celebrated as the preeminent documentarian of American folk music, of blues, jazz, spoken-word, science, and anthropological recordings.

On 30 January 1986, WCBY television, the PBS affiliate in western Massachusetts, broadcast *Arlo Guthrie—Live at 57*, a sixty-minute cooperative production of Springfield's WGBY-TV, the WGBH Educational Foundation, and Guthrie's Rising Son International. Though not widely distributed outside of Massachusetts, the program remains one of Guthrie's finest TV appearances, with him and Shenandoah running through a baker's dozen of songs featured in his shows of 1985–86. The program included such nonalbum rarities as Elizabeth Cotten's "Freight Train" and Guthrie's "Down on the American Farm." There were also great performances of Woody's "Do-Re-Mi" and "Pretty Boy Floyd," Dylan's "Gates of Eden," and a blistering version of Guthrie's own "Which Side?" from *Outlasting the Blues*.

The personnel of Shenandoah continued to transform in 1985. Several members, including guitarist and arranger David Grover, drifted out to raise families or work on personal projects. The current incarnation in *Live at 57* featured three veterans: Terry Hall, Dan Velika, and Steve Ide.

They were assisted by the band's newest members, Bob Williams on guitar and pedal steel and Abe on keyboards/synthesizer.

It was in early 1985 when sixteen-year-old Abe began to join his father on gigs, at least during intervals not interfering with school. Guthrie accepted that Abe's musical interests were not necessarily similar to his own. Abe was no folkie. But he was given the opportunity to join the band as his keyboard skills progressed. Guthrie wasn't sure his son would be interested in the offer; he admitted his children really didn't listen all that much to his music—it wasn't their thing. This was the mid-1980s, and his children much preferred listening to the music of Bon Jovi. In the spring of '86 Guthrie explained how he approached Abe to possibly consider getting involved in the family business:

> I don't know that he would play the kind of music that we play as a preference. He loves playing rock 'n' roll with his friends, and I think that's great and that's what he did for a while. He was in one band or another in school, he did a couple of dances here and there. I finally said, "This would work out good, Abe, if you could be good enough to work with us." Which means putting in a lot of time and learning things that maybe aren't as enjoyable. It's worked out real well. I think when he first started out playing with the band he was accepted by the band members not so much because he was my kid as what he was playing. I think over the past year he has begun to add his own musical input that's been appreciated by the other guys.[45]

1986 would prove a watershed year. Guthrie's long-delayed studio album, *Someday*, was, at long last, being readied for release. US fans would have to wait a bit longer to hear the "new" album, but at least the record was being made available *somewhere* in the world:

> **AG:** And so began my next chapter in life as the head of a new family-operated record company—Rising Son Records. We had one record. *Someday* was first released in the UK on actual vinyl, as a record. For the cover we had used a black-and-white charcoal drawing that Jackie had created, but in the UK it was altered and modified to be in color. It would have been great but the dot-matrix looked awful and made Jackie go a little crazy, and so when it was released in the USA the cover went

back to its original black-and-white drawing. There was never a vinyl record made for the US market, as CDs were the newest, most advanced technology, and so *Someday* was released at home in the USA on both cassette tape, and—later—on compact disc.

Guthrie's US fans were mostly unaware *Someday* had been released overseas. The vinyl album was distributed throughout the United Kingdom in 1986 by C.M. Distribution of Harrogate, North Yorkshire, England. C.M. was a roots-music distribution label, still pressing albums on vinyl, as the compact disc medium had not yet caught on in Europe. The company's catalog of artists primarily featured artists based in the UK (The Albion Band, Dick Gaughan, Clannad, Alan Stivell, Dougie Maclean, Dave Swarbrick, etc.), but they also distributed the records of several American indie artists, such as Gene Clark, The Georgia Satellites, Dr. John, Sweet Honey in the Rock, and Rod Piazza. The company also issued a 45-rpm single of Guthrie's "Russian Girls"/ "All Over the World," two songs from the album's A-side.

Since there was no distribution channel available to get *Someday* into record shops, the earliest US copies were available only on cassette and—primarily—sold at concert appearances. "That's the only way it's available, or by mail," Guthrie told the Gannett News Service. "We've started our own record company, Rising Son Records. Why not? I never made any money-making records anyway. I make my money with my shows, always have."[46] But Guthrie was aware he couldn't rely solely on merchandise table walk-up sales. He needed some sort of channel to promote the new album.

On recent tours, Guthrie had been collecting the names and addresses of fans on sign-up sheets. The original idea was to gather addresses to alert fans of future concerts scheduled in their specific area. It was a good idea, but not always practical: many shows were slotted into his schedule belatedly, making time-sensitive postcard notifications inefficient. As he no longer had the Warner Bros. publicity machine to do lead work on his behalf, Guthrie was trying to find a mechanism to communicate directly with his fan base. The patience of the thousands of people who signed over their addresses during the last few years would—finally—be rewarded. In April of 1986, Guthrie's fans discovered a simple two-sided purple 8 × 11 newsletter awaiting them in their mailbox.

Though the mailer wouldn't yet be named as such, the trifolded sheet was the first issue of Guthrie's soon-to-be-celebrated newsletter, the *Rolling*

Blunder Review. It read, "Dear Friend . . . Did you unknowingly request this junk mail by filling in a form at a concert? Maybe you simply (unwittingly) wrote a nice letter. Whatever the reason, you (out of millions of potential victims), are now in possession of a product of our times; that is to say your name is presently on our mailing list."[47]

That first "issue" was sparse in content but still informative. The mailer announced twenty-five provisional dates for his upcoming May/June 1986 tour, which included cobills with John Prine, Pete Seeger, and Judy Collins. In a section titled "Crop Report Spring 1986," Guthrie announced Rising Son Record's first set of releases: "1. Bushels of our new record *Someday.* 2. Heaps of our rereleased *Power of Love.* 3. Chunks of our rereleased *Amigo.* These records are only available on cassette tapes, for now. At some time in the future we may decide to grow them on regular record stuff. But being our own record company (these days), and not having as many options, we decided to grow some high quality, real-time recorded, chrome-type tapes, instead of the regular scratchy kind of records."[48]

The plan to release the new album on cassette made sense in early 1986. Cassettes scored as the most popular format for all prerecorded music sales in 1985. The Recording Industry Association of America (RIAA) reported the popularity of vinyl LPs—once the unchallenged choice of consumers—was showing signs of decline. In 1985 vinyl albums sold in units of 167 million. Which didn't sound all that bad, but it paled in comparison to the 339.1 million units of cassettes sold that same year. The compact disc, first introduced to the US in 1983—a relatively expensive and relative newcomer to the home-music market—was beginning to make headway. But sales of the CD format in 1985 were still rather meager at a mere 22.6 million units sold.[49]

This situation was about to change—and fast. Midway through 1986, the RIAA confirmed the continuing downward slide of the LP as a popular format, reporting sales of only 58.8 million units. Cassettes still reigned as the most popular format—154 million units sold in the first half of 1986 alone, up from 151 million units sold during the first half of 1985. But this format too would soon fall to the compact disc.[50]

The problem with a CD was its retail cost was nearly twice that of a cassette or LP. Though the price of a CD deck was becoming more affordable, relatively few US homes had converted to the new system. Cassette tapes, on the other hand, had improved markedly in sound reproduction with the advent of DuPont's chromium dioxide formulation or "chrome tape," which guaranteed "an undeniable increase in high frequency response." The earliest Rising Son catalogs promised that "All of our tapes are of the highest quality. They are Real-Time recorded on Chrome with Dolby B. All have been recently copied on digital equipment, so as to insure as accurately as possible the sounds of the originals."[51]

One interesting aspect of the first mailer from Rising Son was the company's selling of cassette copies of *Power of Love* and *Amigo*, both Warner Bros. titles. All new cassette releases were being sold with a silver band heralding each as a "25th Anniversary Edition." Guthrie was backdating his entry into the professional music industry to February 1961, the night Cisco called him to the stage. That made 1986 his "Silver Anniversary." He celebrated this milestone by cutting a deal with old friends at Warner Bros.

AG: It was about this time I found out that many of our previous recordings released on the Warner's label were, in fact, out of print. They weren't making them anymore, let alone making them available.

I went out to Los Angeles and met with Lenny and Mo Ostin, and enquired about it. They informed me that sales of my catalog had dwindled significantly and that there was no reason for them to keep the records in print. I realized that there was a world of difference between what Warner's considered reasonable in terms of sales and what a smaller company like ours would consider reasonable. So I pitched them an idea.

I theorized that there was a number under which it would not be realistic for a big outfit like Warner Bros. to keep an album in print, probably somewhere in the 50,000-unit range. On the other hand, for us to manufacture 50,000 would require an expenditure that a small record company couldn't afford. So I suggested that we identify the line below which it wasn't good for them, and above which it wasn't realistic for us. I went further. If a record we made looked like it might go over 50,000 they could release it, and if it looked like under 50,000 Rising Son Records (RSR) would release it.

I went even further. I said that RSR could start manufacturing the records that were out of print, as we had the resources to put out limited supplies ourselves. But, we'd have to come to some agreement as to terms, etc. They thought it sounded like a great idea, and that RSR could acquire (license) the rights to the recordings and start the process immediately. After all, our audience had dwindled, but they hadn't gone completely away.

The deal with Warner Bros. was not only unprecedented but beneficial to both parties. Guthrie boasted in his newsletter that the deal set "a new high for the recording industry and Warner Bros., especially as we know of no other company which has allowed use of their catalogue this way."[52] The odd wrinkle was both Warner Bros. and Rising Son could, should they choose, simultaneously issue the exact same titles. The only catch was Rising Son could only issue a former Warner Bros. catalog title on cassette. Warner's retained exclusive rights to LP sales and reissues on CD. Guthrie offered, "this new agreement was possible because Rising Son is actually manufacturing a different product than Warner Bros."[53]

Warner Bros. wasn't completely generous: they were still holding back several titles, unwilling to license those albums still bringing in a modicum of income: the original *Alice's Restaurant* album, 1972's *Hobo's Lullaby* (featuring "City of New Orleans"), and 1977's *The Best of Arlo Guthrie*. The albums brokered in the earliest deal with Warner Bros. and subsequently re-cataloged as Rising Son Records releases were *Arlo* (1968), *Running Down the Road* (1969), *Washington County* (1970), *Last of the Brooklyn Cowboys* (1973), *Amigo* (1976), *Outlasting the Blues* (1979), and *Power of Love* (1981). Not every title was immediately added to the RSR catalog in 1986. In the early winter of 1987 Guthrie informed newsletter readers that "Final work is being done at this very moment on the re-release of *Outlasting the Blues*. We've had more requests for this record than for almost anything else."[54]

Rereleases of old albums continued to trickle out in 1987 and 1988. But it wasn't until the summer of 1989 that Guthrie managed to add *Hobo's Lullaby* (1972), *Arlo Guthrie* (1974), and *One Night* (1978) to the catalog.

AG: In preparation for our 25th anniversary in the music industry RSR released a special box set of cassette tapes of almost everything we'd recorded, and for that endeavor, Warner's agreed to let us license the few remaining records that they still had in print.

In effect, we had acquired most (but not quite all) the records we'd made. Now that we had our catalog available for the first time in years, I sent the boxed set of cassette tape[s] to Mo and to Lenny under the RSR label, just to make sure that in the future there wouldn't be any

misunderstandings with whoever was running Warner Bros. Records as
to the rights involved.

To celebrate this bringing together of Guthrie's near-complete
back-catalog, RSR issued the aforementioned "Rising Son Cassette Gift
Pack"—a complete set of Arlo's tapes (twelve titles) packed in a black pad-
ded nylon case with "Arlo Guthrie" screened on it. Priced at $99.95
(approximately $8.32 per tape), the handsome package served as the musi-
cal bargain of the century.

Some of this merchandising was still to come, of course. In 1987 the
Rolling Blunder Review issued the first of its "Get Stuff" merchandise offerings. The catalog included several of the company's earliest cassette-tape
releases as well as Guthrie's "Tour 1987" T-shirts (available in silver or tan
or as a special tie-dye). Guthrie soon merged "an older project I had into
the catalog, a record which was essentially the sound track to a film called
Woody Guthrie—Hard Travelin' that had been released years before. Now we
had two records."[55]

The "Get Stuff" merchandising was to become an important part of
the family business. To everyone's welcome surprise there were a lot of
folks receiving the newsletter who faithfully sent in checks and credit card
information to purchase the wares Rising Son offered. In 1987 three issues
of the *Rolling Blunder Review* were sent out to fans. But with Guthrie on the
road—there were over one hundred concert dates in 1987 alone—the staff
at Rising Son found themselves deluged by mail orders. This was causing
issues with vendors and inventory control.

Guthrie hadn't always been on board with the medicine show aspect of
the music business. But he began to understand that the steady stream
of revenue that merchandising provided was an essential component of
Rising Son's operation. "Now that we are no longer recording with a major
record company," Guthrie would write, "we have decided to see if we couldn't
raise enough money in some way to make our own records. Although we
had an attitude problem with T-shirts and stuff for 20 years or so, our philosophy has changed when we were confronted by a simple solution. Income
from T-shirts, tapes, and stuff makes recording possible again. We are making plans at the moment to be recording again soon."[56] There was nothing
dishonorable about merchandising. Blues singers, hillbilly musicians, and
bluegrass bands had been selling recordings and ephemera for decades.

Even Woody Guthrie hawked copies of a songbook (*Woody and Lefty Lou's Favorite Collection Old Time Hill Country Songs*) while broadcasting on KFVD radio in Los Angeles in 1937.

As a new captain of industry, Guthrie hosted the 18 April broadcast of *Yankee Ingenuity* on Boston's WBZ-TV. The program was, according to *Variety,* one of "eight locally produced specials for the first half of 1986."[57] The documentary was a celebration of those New Englanders whose inventions and innovations changed America's method of doing things. In his review of the program, one critic mocked, "The idea that New Englanders may be more inventive than other folks seems at first blush to be another irritating bit of home-town boosterism, especially when host Arlo Guthrie panegyrizes." But he conceded the singer offered a lot of evidence to bolster the argument. "It's the American way," Guthrie suggested, "that special knack for creating inventions that do it faster, better, cheaper."[58]

Business aside, most of 1986 was played out on the concert stage. Two days prior to a show with John Prine at the city's Syria Mosque, Guthrie chatted with a reporter from the *Pittsburgh Press.* He had been on the road with Shenandoah since the first week in February and, with the exception of a few weeks' respite in April, the tour would roll relentlessly on through the summer and beyond. "I've been home about three weeks since Christmas," he explained. "I make a decent living doing this," he acknowledged. "Some years are better than others, but usually because I have a bigger band or crew."[59]

Guthrie also suggested Rising Son's next recording project was already under consideration. "I guess the very next thing will be an album that is mostly stories of mine that have been heard in concert but never have been recorded. I think that's at least half of why people come to see me, to hear some wild and crazy stories."[60] That spoken-word album would not materialize for some time. The reviews of his live album *One Night* had been mixed, with critics citing the A-side's riveting takes of traditional songs and pop standards as brilliant, but the flip side's seventeen-and-a-half-minute monologue, "The Story of Reuben Clamzo & His Strange Daughter in the Key of A," as mildly entertaining on first listen . . . but less so on subsequent visits.

Guthrie's shows with John Prine in the spring of 1986 were fun and ego-free, the performers swapping opening and closing spots on the bill. In Pittsburgh Guthrie treated the crowd of 2,773 to his usual set of songs and stories, but with a resurrected take of Dylan's "Gates of Eden" (waxed for posterity in 1973 on Guthrie's *Last of the Brooklyn Cowboys*). Guthrie had quietly slipped "Gates of Eden" back into the set list in October of 1985. Critics reviewing the concert saw his performance of the *Bringing It All Back Home* classic as the evening's showstopper. "Guthrie hit a high note with a version of Bob Dylan's 'Gates of Eden,'" the *Pittsburgh Press* enthused, a solo acoustic affair tastefully ornamented by Shenandoah and Abe.[61] This opinion was seconded by the music critic for the *Pittsburgh Post-Gazette,* who offered, "Guthrie's voice is probably the whiniest of his peers, but he uses it most beautifully. One surprise was a somber, hauntingly orchestrated reading of Dylan's 'Gates of Eden.'"[62]

In early June of 1986 *Back Stage* reported that Guthrie, a confirmed gearhead, had recently been in Nashville, agreeing to appear before cameras in praise of Dodge trucks. Hummingbird Productions, Inc. of New York and Nashville was engaged by the Detroit-based firm of BBD&O advertising to create the TV spot. The spot was to feature Guthrie "telling tales about a make-believe 'Uncle Jake' who taught him to fish and to appreciate such things in life as a good Dodge truck."[63] The commercial would never see the light of day, though, Guthrie recalling the campaign never really "got past the idea phase."[64]

The campaign might have been short-circuited by Guthrie's very public alliance with striking union workers. On 15 June Guthrie and David Bromberg were to stage a benefit concert for a group of workers striking against the Hormel meatpacking corporation in Austin, Minnesota. The bitter strike was already in its ninth month, Local P-9 of the United Food and Commercial Workers having walked away from their jobs in August 1985, with complaints of wage cuts, working conditions, and benefit freezes. The proposed benefit was to help create a food bank for the workers pushed against the ropes: they were simultaneously fighting Hormel, the banks, the scabs, the justice system, and even the less militant faction of the Food and Commercial Workers Union. The concert, to be staged at Minnesota's Mower County Fairgrounds, would not take place as advertised. Guthrie's appearance was postponed, in the words of one report, due to "a lack of cooperation by Austin authorities."[65] He promised to return.

On July 4 Guthrie was invited to sing again at Farm Aid II at the Manor Downs Racetrack, fifteen miles southwest of Austin, Texas. With seventy-five acts on the program, no artist enjoyed much stage time, but Guthrie's set positively rocked with up-tempo versions of "Pretty Boy Floyd" and "Coming into Los Angeles." There were several additional concert appearances scheduled in July and August, but late summer was an unusually quiet time. This break was necessary as September and October's concert schedule was shaping up to be particularly busy.

On 25 September Guthrie would again pop up on television, this time appearing on a segment of the ABC-TV news-magazine program *Our World*. The topic of the hour-long program was *The Summer of 1969*. The show reminded viewers there was a lot going on in the country at that time: the Manson murders, the "Miracle Mets," the moon landing, Chappaquiddick, and, of course, the Woodstock festival.[66] Guthrie was on stage at the Newport Folk Festival on 19 July 1969, only a few hours prior to the Apollo 11 landing on the moon's surface. He declared that momentous event as "groovy."

Guthrie and Country Joe McDonald were brought on the program to reminisce on Woodstock. Though one critic groused that *Our World* was "nothing special," one highlight noted was the "fabulous recollections by Arlo Guthrie."[67] Guthrie's graying hair had grown out to incredibly long and shaggy proportions in 1986, one review likening his appearance to that of Charlemagne. Otherwise this critic too dismissed *Our World* as nothing more than a "nostalgia news-magazine for boomers."[68]

It was mostly boomers placing their preorders for the home-video release of *Hard Travelin'*. On 30 September 1986, warehouses began to ship the official MGM/UA videocassette to shops and video rentals across the country. Retailers were encouraged to place their preorders for the title by 11 September. The sales sheet touted, "Fans of the Guthries, Baez, Seeger, and even Bob Dylan—one of Woody Guthrie's biggest admirers—won't be able to resist this authoritative and loving account of his quintessentially American music."[69] If Guthrie's fans were unable to find copies at their local retailers, they would not miss out. The videocassette was soon added to the Rising Son "Get Stuff" catalog.

Arlo's name was in the news again that September since the topic of Huntington's disease seemingly could not be discussed without invoking the Guthrie lineage. In September of 1986 scientists began running the first diagnostic tests of individuals believed at risk for the cruel neurological disorder. Blood could now be drawn from those potentially afflicted and sent for genetic analysis. Testing in the New York City area was to be conducted at the Columbia University of Physicians and Surgeons under the direction of Dr. Nancy Wexler. *Newsday* reported Wexler was informed that "Woody Guthrie's son, Arlo, said he won't be tested, even though he has a 50 percent chance of having the Huntington's gene."[70]

The decision to get tested or not was a personal one. Both Guthrie and his sister Nora chose not to take the test. In an essay published in *People* magazine, the singer discussed his decision at length. Though his mother's obsession with finding a cure led her to devote much time and energy to the Committee to Combat Huntington's Disease, Guthrie's decision to *not* test was an easy one. He was already certain that he did *not* have the disease. But he posited should he carry the gene, "I have to ask myself: So what if I have it? Am I going to do something different with my life? If you're going to do something different because you've found out you've got a disease, then you're not living as you should be."[71]

Guthrie recalled the time when Jackie was preparing to deliver one of their children. "A doctor screamed at me, asking me how I could bring somebody into the world who may get sick and live this terrible, tortured life." Though Woody had long suffered—there was no denying that—it was his son's contention that while his "father had Huntington's . . . he lived not just a joyful life, but an important one as well."[72] Though Woody had passed away at age fifty-five, his songs and prose were celebrated not only in America but worldwide. A life needn't be long to be important.

Arlo's brother Joady, too, was ambivalent about taking the test. He admitted the specter of Huntington's had been "a pretty big thing in my life. I have these memories of seeing my father get worse. I tell you, sometimes it's pretty rough now."[73] Though he would not test immediately, Joady eventually choose to undergo the process. He was found free of the insidious Huntington's gene.

Moses Asch, a longtime friend of the Guthrie family, would pass on 19 October 1986. On 23 October there was a memorial service held for Asch on Manhattan's Lower East Side. Asch's friends and colleagues—including such notables as the folklorists Alan Lomax and Ralph Rinzler—spoke respectfully of Asch's work, and Bess Hawes Lomax spoke of the turbulent times Asch documented. Pete Seeger, who recorded as much for Asch as anyone, led everyone through the chorus of the old spiritual "Down by the Riverside."[74]

The question on everyone's mind was the future of the Folkways collection. In years prior to his passing, Asch had entered into negotiations to sell the entirety of his catalog to the Smithsonian Institution. One term of a sale was Asch's insistence the Smithsonian keep every Folkways LP in print. It was important to Asch that the works of the artists, historians, anthropologists, and scientists recorded since 1940 would remain available to scholars, libraries, and the general public. Following his passing, Asch's family continued with negotiations, Ralph Rinzler working diligently to persuade the Smithsonian's board of regents of the collection's cultural importance.

By December the Asch family and the Smithsonian were close to finalizing the terms of acquisition. Michael Asch told the press the archive agreed, in principle, to pay $800,000 for the 2,200-title Folkways catalog.[75] The final deal would be signed in April of 1987. There was already talk of CBS Records being in the early stages of putting together a Folkways tribute album—perhaps even a multidisc set—to assist in bringing the catalog to the Smithsonian. Artists agreeing to participate in the proposed benefit recording were Bob Dylan, Willie Nelson, Bruce Springsteen, Emmy Lou Harris, Sweet Honey in the Rock, Pete Seeger, and Arlo Guthrie. When the list of first-tier celebrities offering to help grew exponentially (U2, Brian Wilson, Little Richard, John Mellencamp), Guthrie joked, "They had to put me on it 'cause I was my dad's kid."[76] It was a modest, self-deprecating statement but, in terms of pop-culture recognition, the son had become at least as famous as the father.

Following the success of *Wasn't That a Time!* and *Hard Travelin'* as PBS fundraising vehicles, the network asked for a new program to feature during their pledge drive campaign of March 1987. So on 3 November 1986, Guthrie found himself in Austin, Texas, helping out the network out again. Tapping the talents of producer Terry Lickona and the production crew of *Austin City Limits*, Guthrie and Shenandoah played host to Pete Seeger, David Bromberg, Jerry Jeff Walker, and Bonnie Raitt for a ninety-minute all-music program. The taping was billed as a coproduction of the Southwest Public Broadcasting Council and Rising Son International.

Guthrie was planning on taking the Austin recordings back to Long View in Massachusetts, where the tapes could be remixed under the supervision of Jesse Henderson and John Pilla. Just as in the old days, Pilla and Guthrie stubbornly argued over the mixes, ridiculing each other's opinions:

We launched into it as always, tempers flaring, ideas pushing against ideas. John always said that I was ten-percent genius and ninety-percent ridiculous. I agreed and when we fought it was always because we disagreed as to whether my new idea was part of the ten or part of the ninety.[77]

The Arlo Guthrie Show would be the final artistic collaboration of Guthrie and Pilla, as John's health—and heart—was faltering. Guthrie recalled their work on the PBS program as special, since "John and I were truly united again. The dark night of our relationship was over. We had come through it all, knowing that it was going to end soon anyway."[78]

During the next year and a half, his life became difficult. He was told that his heart would give out shortly, and he struggled with that information. His physical heart was closing in on its last beats, as his true heart began to open wide. He began giving things away. He judged less. He looked happy at times. He was in pain, but he would get around when he could. We hugged each other saying hello and goodbye.[79]

Three days after the Austin taping, Guthrie traveled to St. Paul, Minnesota, for a benefit concert at Duluth's North Shore Theater. Wearing an "Original Local P-9" cap, Guthrie, surrounded by thirty family members of the strikers, was keeping the promise he made in June. At a press conference, he explained he decided to get involved with the P-9 strike because he saw their struggle as similar to those his father supported decades earlier. "For many, many years my father tried to make life easier for the average working man and working woman in this country," Guthrie reminded the journalists.[80] Though the strike officially ended in September of '86, eight hundred P-9 strikers were still out of work, replaced by scabs who had crossed their picket line.

Though the original June benefit had been scrubbed by local authorities, Guthrie announced that a new date and venue had been arranged. The food bank concert would be staged on 20 November at Minneapolis's Orchestra Hall, with support from Holly Near and folk singer John McCutcheon. The date was chosen to ensure the strikers could manage a Thanksgiving dinner despite their current economic hardship. The benefit attracted some 1,800 concertgoers, bringing between $17,000 and

$20,000 into the coffers, depending on the report. It may have been Guthrie's experience with the P-9 strikers that inspired him to suggest a new recording project with Pete Seeger. Guthrie advised readers of his newsletter of plans for Seeger and himself to "go into the studio and record some of the more unknown works that we have compiled over the years."[81]

In late January 1987, Guthrie and Shenandoah were due to go on a tour that would keep them on the road through July. In addition to the usual round of concert dates in the US and Canada, there was a plan to tour the Far East. Harold Leventhal had been charged to put together a tour of Japan and New Zealand.[82] Guthrie last toured Japan in 1967 as support for Judy Collins. Two decades later he was interested in revisiting that corner of the world. The proposed Far East summer tour would not happen, though. Writing in the *Rolling Blunder Review,* Guthrie sighed that while he and the "remnants of Shenandoah ('Fragmandoah')" had "their kimonos packed," Leventhal and the Japanese promoters had sadly been unable to come to terms.[83]

The Rolling Blunder Review had expanded from a two-sided single paper sheet to a four-page newsletter. By the summer of 1987 the newsletter was being sent to 15,000 subscribers, and it served as Guthrie's primary method of communicating with fans: it supplied upcoming tour information, hinted at recording projects, and offered bits of fragmented musings and other items of miscellany. In one recent issue Guthrie offhandedly revealed that he had *technically* parted ways with Shenandoah.

Only Guthrie's most ardent fans would have likely noted the change: Shenandoah's Terry Hall was still sitting behind the drum kit, and Dan Velika remained on bass. Newcomer Bob Williams had mostly replaced Steve Ide, trading between lead guitar and pedal steel duties. Guthrie's son Abe continued to play keyboards and synthesizer—at least when high school was out of session. Abe was obsessed with music—even if mostly of the heavy metal variety. Guthrie admitted to Long Island's *Newsday* his son's "school work's been kinda going downhill lately."[84]

Though Guthrie did not make it to Japan, a little of Japan made its way to the US. By 1987 the compact disc was embraced by music consumers worldwide. Most of the major labels were beginning to issue new releases of their top-earning artists on CD. And it wasn't only the major labels who recognized the CD was becoming the format of choice. Such independent labels as Rounder Records tested the waters in 1986 with thirty catalog titles offered on CD. Rising Son too was beginning to consider digitizing its own catalog.

To this end Guthrie sent the entirety of his Warner Bros. back-catalog to Dr. Toby Mountain, an engineer at Massachusetts's Northeastern Digital Recording, for remastering. Mountain was trusted as he had a reputation for preserving "the integrity of records as they are converted to CDs."[85] The engineer wasn't interested in reworking the original albums to create a more modern soundscape. "What we do is tweak the recording a little bit," he told the *Boston Globe*, "add reverb a little, or change the equalization so it sounds better. But I object to people trying to redo a record, because there are aesthetic questions involved in that."[86]

There was enough interest to suggest Guthrie's music was deserving of digital preservation. In January, his continuing popularity was affirmed in the *Globe's* annual reader's poll, contributors voting Guthrie, Suzanne Vega, and Peter, Paul and Mary as Boston's most popular folk-music artists.[87] There did seem to be a developing uneasy blending of old-school folkies and introspective singer-songwriters. The fact that both groups plied their art on acoustic guitars conveniently put them under the "folk music" umbrella—but the music they made was mostly dissimilar.

Guthrie hadn't performed at the 1986 Newport festival. Stung by accusations the 1985 event was little more than a "nostalgia orgy," producer George Wein promised the '86 festival would feature a better-balanced mix of established performers and up-and-coming songwriters.[88] "Nostalgia orgy" or not, the festival's 1985 resurrection brought in more than 12,500 concertgoers over two days, netting Wein a profit of some $75,000 and allowing for the staging of the '86 event. But a bleak weather forecast—combined with the absence of such folk royalty as Baez, Guthrie, Collins, and Raitt on the '86 bill—rendered a weak box office. There were only 3,500 paid admissions on Saturday, and five hundred less than that on Sunday, almost half of the previous year's admissions. Some accounts had weekend attendance numbers as low as 4,300 paid admissions. "Folk music is just not where we thought it was," sighed festival codirector Robert L. Jones. "The broad popular base of the music is not there."[89]

Wein argued the festival needed support beyond what "coffeehouse culture" could provide, and he was aggressively courting corporate sponsorship. "There is no pop base in folk music at the moment," he rued, "and that is part of the problem. I don't want to do a reunion every time out."[90]

Wein would get a sponsor in April of 1987 when Nestle Foods offered to foot part of the bill. But it was obvious the festival could not survive without presenting folk music's major players. In early summer of '87 Wein announced Arlo Guthrie would return to Newport—as would Joan Baez, Tom Paxton, John Hammond, Judy Collins, Bonnie Raitt, Johnny "Clyde" Copeland, Billy Bragg, and others.

Guthrie was to perform on Sunday and, to everyone's delight, he again performed the "Alice's Restaurant Massacree." He reminisced about his first appearance at Newport in July of 1967. "I broke four strings" that night, he recalled. "Now, a guitar's only got six . . . so I figured I was in trouble."[91] Performing his signature song two decades on, Guthrie offered, "I wasn't planning on singing this song this afternoon. I wasn't even planning on singing it this decade, until someone reminded me it was the twentieth anniversary. Half the people in this audience weren't even born twenty years ago." Performing a partly rewritten version of "Alice," Guthrie suggested to the youthful crowd when called for draft registration that it was helpful they "know Spanish," a not too obtuse reference to US intervention in Central America.[92]

AG: On July 3rd I left Kashi Ashram, where Jackie and I had been staying, and took off for Nashville, Tennessee. In nearby Hendersonville lived Mae Boren Axton and she was orchestrating a Boren family reunion to which we'd been invited. Her son Hoyt was one of my dearest friends. Mae and I were actually cousins and she was probably the best PR person in Nashville at that time. Mae had also been cowriter with Tommy Durden to the Elvis Presley hit "Heartbreak Hotel." While there I met another cousin, David Axton, who had been the governor of Oklahoma and also a U.S. senator. Jackie and I had a fabulous time in Tennessee visiting friends and family however distant. Hoyt and I had the same model bus, a GMC Scenic Cruiser, and we were making plans to have a cross-country race, although the idea fell through. We returned to the ashram after the event.

With the prospective tour of Japan having fallen through, Guthrie wouldn't work as often as he would have during July—though he still carried a very busy schedule, one most folk singers could only dream of. He had found several other creative projects to pass the time between concert dates. He told Fort Lauderdale's *Sun Sentinel* he was "working on a script based on one of my dad's books called *Seeds of Man*. It's a very difficult book to read because he started it one time, dropped it, then started it again at another place in the story and got sick before he finished it."[93]

Woody Guthrie started writing *Seeds of Man* (first under the working title of *Study Butte* and later as *Foolish Gold*) at his home on Mermaid Avenue in Coney Island, more or less around the time that Arlo Davy Guthrie was born in July 1947. When the 842-page manuscript was delivered to a publishing house in 1949, the editor balked, arguing the massive work was too unwieldly to edit. Woody abandoned the manuscript for a time, taking up the task again of reshaping the novel in 1953. The book was posthumously published in 1976 by E.P. Dutton & Co., Inc. of New York. Arlo Guthrie had long been fascinated by his father's mysterious book. He conceded that since the book—as published—had been heavily edited and reworked, "It doesn't fit in some ways. Nevertheless, it's a great mystical tale about a journey he took to South Texas when he was a young man."[94] Guthrie expressed his desire to complete his screenplay adaptation in 1988.

The past was continually being resurrected. Harold Leventhal arranged "A Tribute to Moses Asch" at New York's Symphony Space on the evening of 10 October 1987. Leventhal was a longtime friend and colleague of Asch, both men taking an uncompromising long-view approach, buffered against the vagaries of the music industry and American culture. "Without Mo, we might never have heard Woody Guthrie, Pete Seeger or their contemporaries: we might never have had a folk revival," Leventhal said bluntly—if accurately.[95] Guthrie was unable to attend the Asch tribute because he was committed to a concert that same night in New Jersey. But during a short break in an otherwise busy tour schedule, Guthrie found time in October to record his father's "East Texas Red" for the upcoming CBS Folkways tribute-benefit album.[96]

That same autumn Leventhal was moderating a series of panel discussions at Greenwich Village's New School for Social Research. Guthrie was among the guests interviewed for Leventhal's course, "American Folk Music: Its Rise and Influence from the '50s through the '70s." Other panel guests included Pete Seeger, Fred Hellerman, and Mary Travers, all clients of the impresario. One of the more intriguing aspects of Arlo Guthrie's re-immersion in the protest-song era of the 1940s and 1950s was a reawakening of his own folk-singing roots. In some ways his path was predestined. In 1968 Leventhal opined, "As far as I'm concerned, my relationship to Woody and the [Guthrie Children's Trust Fund] necessitated my managing Arlo. Arlo is an extension of Woody, and I have an emotional stake in that."[97] Now, nearly two decades on, it was clear Leventhal was quietly grooming Arlo as the heir apparent of a tradition.

There had been no Pete Seeger Thanksgiving concert at Carnegie Hall in 1986. The famed music venue would close its doors in May 1986 to undergo a 50-million-dollar renovation. The concert hall was not scheduled to reopen until December 1986, leaving Seeger's fans looking for something else to do on the Saturday after Thanksgiving. The Weavers had performed at Carnegie Hall in December 1955, and Seeger had performed at the venue—with few exceptions—every year thereafter. Beginning in 1964, Harold Leventhal referred to each new Seeger appearance as the folk singer's Carnegie "Holiday Concert." Beginning in 1976 the tradition moved from December to Thanksgiving weekend. These Thanksgiving holiday concerts would enjoy an incredible forty-three-year run from 1976 through 2019.

Arlo Guthrie was no stranger to the Carnegie stage. In the flush of success following *Alice's Restaurant,* he made his Carnegie debut on 10 November 1967. He would return to Carnegie on subsequent occasions, but only sparingly: at the Woody Guthrie Memorial Concert in 1968; at a solo concert in December of 1968; with John Pilla accompanying him in 1969; with the band Swampwater in March 1971; and at a multi-artist benefit for the Newport Folk Festival Foundation in July 1972. In 1974, Harold Leventhal would pair Guthrie and Seeger for several formal concerts, one taking place at Carnegie Hall on 8 March 1974.

The Thanksgiving weekend holiday concerts soldiered on for years as "Pete Seeger's gig," though the folk singer occasionally brought along friends to help him out. In 1981 Seeger's guests were Arlo Guthrie and Shenandoah, in 1985 it was Guthrie and Abe. The Seeger Carnegie concerts—with or without Arlo—routinely sold out quickly. Critic John Leonard, a big Seeger fan, described the annual pilgrimage as a "cultural brushing of the teeth."[98] Pete Seeger loved playing Carnegie due to the hall's reverberations. He thought the venue's acoustics encouraged people to sing along in the hootenanny tradition. "People like to sing in the bathtub because of the reverberation," Seeger offered, "and that's how they feel at Carnegie Hall."[99] But with Carnegie still shuttered on Thanksgiving weekend 1986, Seeger, now sixty-seven years old and his voice growing wobbly, thought it time to bid adieu to his Carnegie holiday concert tradition.

Though Seeger believed it was time to move on, Harold Leventhal wasn't in accord. Leventhal saw Arlo Guthrie as Pete's natural successor. On the Thanksgiving weekend of 28 November 1987, Guthrie took the stage sans Pete Seeger. To the faithful who gathered at the gilded concert hall each and every year, the change was greeted as a natural passing of the torch. For the next thirty-two years Guthrie would make the trek to Manhattan following Thanksgiving Day. And if Pete Seeger thought he'd not play Carnegie Hall again after his "final" proper concert there in 1985, he would be mistaken.

Harold Leventhal personally penned the "Meet the Artist" program notes in that evening's *Stagebill:*

> Tonight Arlo Guthrie comes to Carnegie Hall, "taking over" the Thanksgiving date that Pete Seeger has performed for more than twenty-five years. Pete is on a "Carnegie leave of absence." It seems appropriate that Arlo, this evening, dedicates a good part of the program to commemorate the twentieth anniversary of his father's death in the fall of 1967 . . .
>
> Arlo, of course, has carried on in the Guthrie tradition, but also very much in his own direction and has developed his own musical concepts, his own style, and his own truncated, baffling, nonsensical, quixotic humor.[100]

As Leventhal indicated, the Carnegie concert was, in part, a tribute to Woody Guthrie. In the weeks preceding the concert, broadsides were pasted on walls throughout Manhattan, advertising "A Special Tribute to Woody Guthrie on the 20th Anniversary of his Death." During his West Coast tour of August 1987, Guthrie had already been experimenting with a set list acknowledging the passing of his father two decades earlier.

On Thanksgiving Day, only two days prior to the Carnegie Hall concert, Guthrie told a UPI correspondent that Saturday night's show would feature his final performance of the "Alice's Restaurant Massacree"—at least for a time. "I won't do it again for about ten years," he pledged, 'cuz it eats up too much time during the concert." It wasn't the first time Guthrie chose to omit the "Massacree" from his stage shows, and the song did have a way of sneaking back onto his set list should the occasion call. "Over the years people would ask to hear it because we hadn't done it for so long," Guthrie mused, "so they just kept asking for it. But other than this tour, I did it when Jimmy Carter reinstituted draft registration and I did it a couple of years ago at the Newport Folk Festival."[101]

It wasn't every day a performing artist chose to mothball his most famous song, so this surprising tidbit of news caused a mild sensation. When a correspondent from Reuters followed up on Guthrie's declaration, the singer allowed himself a bit of wiggle room. "Nothing is written in stone, but unless those loonies in Washington decide to invade somebody, I just can't see doing it anymore. I don't want to be a nostalgia act."[102]

Readers of the *Rolling Blunder Review* had already received notice Guthrie was planning to remove the "Massacree" from his sets. He reminded everyone that 1987—the twentieth anniversary of its recording—would be their last opportunity to sing along "with feelin'."[103] He promised fans not to despair. The talking blues would return in 1997—in time to celebrate its thirtieth anniversary.

A day prior to the Carnegie performance, Guthrie told New York's *Daily News,* "I figure I'll bring it out every ten years, so people who weren't born when I wrote it get a chance to hear it. I changed a few things, but it's basically the same. I think it's fresh." When asked by the tabloid what might fans expect from Saturday night's Woody Guthrie commemoration, Arlo offered, "It's the twentieth anniversary of his death this year. Ordinarily, I can't do many of his songs in my set, 'cause they don't all fit in. But this seems right."[104]

Guthrie had always incorporated several of his father's songs into his set lists (many of the shows in 1986 and early 1987 had in fact kicked off with the dynamic one-two punch of Woody's "Do-Re-Mi" and "Pretty Boy Floyd"), but the shows from autumn 1987 were of a more theatrical nature. Upon taking the stage Guthrie would launch into his father's "Oklahoma Hills," Bob Williams's pedal steel mimicking the song's Bob Wills country-swing stylings. Following that performance, Woody Guthrie's own voice seemingly passed through the son, Arlo channeling the Dust Bowl balladeer as a spiritual medium might. It all seemed a bit weird, but audiences picked up on the Spiritism aspect pretty quickly. This was the time of actress Shirley MacLaine's public and much-ridiculed contention that she had lived a number of "past lives," one even dating as far back as presubmersion Atlantis.

Over the next several songs Arlo as "Woody" recounted a brief overview of his life and times, illustrating periods by skipping through songs
written along the way: "Talkin' Dust Bowl Blues," "Pastures of Plenty," "My
Daddy Rides a Ship in the Sky," and "So Long, It's Been Good to Know
Yuh" among them. The latter song blended with the elder Guthrie telling
of the first song of consequence his son Arlo composed: a ballad about getting out of a grammar school math test. The tribute segment concluded
with "Woody," near the end of his string, hearing his son's recording of
"Alice's Restaurant" for the first time: "My kid, I suddenly realized, could
talk more and say less than anybody I had ever met or imagined. I died
about two weeks later. . . . Some people say it was a coincidence."[105]

★ ★ ★ ★ ★

Chapter Four

ALL OVER THE WORLD,
1988–1990

The crème de la crème of rock music royalty descended upon the Grand Ballroom of Manhattan's Waldorf-Astoria Hotel on 20 January 1988. The champagne occasion was to celebrate the annual induction of new members into the Rock 'n' Roll Hall of Fame. The first two galas celebrated the pioneers of rock 'n' roll: the hillbilly musicians and blues singers who created the sound that inarguably changed the world. The glitzy ceremony attracted much public attention because the first wave of boomers—artists who first made their mark in the 1960s—were slated for induction. The list of honorees was impressive—the Beatles, the Drifters, the Supremes, the Beach Boys, and Bob Dylan.

Not every honoree chose to attend, the rock 'n' roll family being a famously dysfunctional one. George Harrison, Ringo Starr, and Yoko Ono (the widow of John Lennon) were present. Paul McCartney refused to join his former bandmates due to an ongoing legal matter. Mary Wilson accepted for the Supremes, Diana Ross choosing to pass due to "personal family reasons."[1] Scene watchers suggested the real reason was Wilson's disparagement of Ross in a recent autobiography. To top things off, Mike Love of the Beach Boys would give his now-infamous acceptance speech, taking potshots at the "mop-tops," Mick Jagger, Billy Joel, and others. Love later suggested his aggressive speech was the result of not having meditated that morning.

The unfolding personal dramas made for great water cooler talk, but a bit of rock 'n' roll history was made that night. The artists honored were introduced by friends whose own future inductions were almost assured. On hand to distribute awards and testify were Bruce Springsteen, Mick Jagger, Little Richard, Jeff Beck, Billy Joel, Neil Young, John Fogarty, and Elton John. Sitting further back in the ballroom, at the "folk table," were

Arlo Guthrie, Pete Seeger, and Harold Leventhal.[2] They were all nattily dressed, more or less, for the occasion. Seeger wore a rumpled brown suit. Guthrie teased Leventhal for choosing to wear a blue shirt under his suit jacket to emphasize his "workingman's connection."[3] Decades younger than his tablemates, Guthrie was the only one seated at the table dressed with rock 'n' roll flair: he wore a circa 1940s tuxedo with black sneakers and red shoelaces.

The ballroom was crowded with one hundred and fifty tables, nearly every music industry bigshot choosing to attend. Since little actual business was being discussed, Guthrie recalled the folk table as being the most casual. He'd reminisce, "At most of the other tables, entertainers, business-men and women, managers, and so on were seen busy with the world of music industry, while at the folk table everyone began eating as soon as the food arrived. There was little conversation."[4]

The reason the trio were attending was Woody Guthrie and Lead Belly were to be inducted into the Hall of Fame as "Early Influences." Guthrie and Seeger were to accept the awards on their behalf, the former receiving one of the evening's warmest responses with his comment, "You could fig-ure a lot of things in this world, but this isn't one of them. I'm fairly positive if my Dad were alive today, this is the one place he *wouldn't be*. Or else, he'd have shown up drunk. I understand that. You don't have a body long in this life. But you have a spirit. And it's my Dad's spirit that you've helped keep alive tonight. And I think this is why I had to come anyhow, to say 'Thank You.'"[5]

Otherwise, January 1988 was an unusually quiet month. Guthrie was to resume touring with Shenandoah in February, but his first two shows of the year were solo gigs at Florida's Riverside Theater in Vero Beach. He and Roger McGuinn were to play two shows benefiting the Pelican Island Audubon Society. Such environmental fundraisers had become increas-ingly important to him. Guthrie had been working with the Mariners Aid to Sea Turtles since 1982, when organizer Jamie Grosseck enlisted the folk singer to not only stage several benefit events but also to appear on a "Save the Sea Turtles" television spot. On the latter, Guthrie provided a loopy discourse on the migratory patterns of turtles. Despite his tongue-in-cheek approach, the commercial managed to get people talking about a serious matter: two of the three species of sea turtles were now on the govern-ment's endangered list.

Though environmental issues had become increasingly important to Guthrie in the 1980s, he saw the sea turtle plight as part of a much larger and grim picture. "'Environment' is a pretty monstrous word for things," he offered on the eve of the Audubon benefits, but "I guess you can say I'm involved in lots of things that surround us all."[6] The folk singer treated environmental issues much as he would political ones, advocating community involvement. "I have really been into environmental issues, working to change people's minds. Not in a big, flashy way, just working with groups and one-to-one," he explained to the *Miami Herald*. "It's making a difference. Even when you just get people with opposite views to sit down and start talking to each other. That's an accomplishment."[7]

Guthrie was set to embark on an ambitious six-week, thirty-six date winter tour of Western Europe. The sortie would include visits to Ireland, Denmark, Finland, Norway, England, Scotland, Wales, Germany, and Holland. The band would then circle back to the UK for final shows in London and Dublin. A tongue-in-cheek post-tour assessment in the *Rolling Blunder Review* noted the barnstorming of Europe had Guthrie performing nightly "for huge crowds in small venues, and small crowds in large halls."[8]

The tour kicked off on 19 February at Shinrone Community Hall, a small village between Birr, County Offaly, and Roscrea, County Tipperary. One thousand fans pushed into the hall, one observer's olfactory system sensing "the old-fashioned odour of a certain Controlled Substance which was not turf smoke from Clara bog."[9] Since the community hall was essentially a large gymnasium, Guthrie recalled the promoter needed to bring in "the only gear that could handle a show of that size."[10] That gear happened to belong to the Irish band U2, who only recently had recorded Woody's "Jesus Christ" for the forthcoming Folkways benefit album. U2's lead singer, Bono, attended the Shinrone gig, the vocalist's presence causing the usually unflappable Abe to "shake like a leaf in the wind."[11] Guthrie's stage show was typical of the era, though he closed out the evening with a thundering version of the traditional fiddle tune "The Red Haired Boy."

Guthrie and fans both retreated to the Pathe Hotel following the show, the Sackville String Band—his warm-up act from earlier that night—playing a midnight set in the inn's bar. At 1:00 AM, just before a minibus was to whisk him to a Dublin airport for a flight to Copenhagen, Guthrie vowed to return. "It was a real down-home gig," he remarked as he climbed into the van. "I love the place and I would love to play it again."[12]

Guthrie and the band were to perform next at the Metropol in Copenhagen. The city was a favorite of his, one of the first European capitals he played in 1965—if mostly as a street performer:

AG: In 1965 my high school classmate and bandmate, Steve Elliot, had a girlfriend while attending The Stockbridge School: Sekita "Kit" Ornbach, from Denmark. She was quite beautiful and, although I had no personal interest, I thought it would be great to visit her in Copenhagen. I left England by train, which crossed the English Channel, arriving via The Hook of Holland (Hoek van Holland) by boat-train and from there to Copenhagen.

I stayed with Kit and her lovely family for one night before deciding I would be better off on my own. I found myself on what they called The Walking Street (where musicians and artists performed for tourists walking by). I took out my guitar, staked out a spot, and began playing.

I soon befriended an English blues player and songwriter, Rich St. John. After becoming regulars on the street, Rich and I were asked by the local university to hire the entire assembly of street performers as entertainment for an event coming up at the university. The Congress of Industrial Builders was having their annual convention, and the street performers were going to be the entertainment.

At night Rich and I had found an abandoned apartment in a building that was to be torn down. It was across the street from what the locals called "The Bums School." There were a couple of beds with some old dirty blankets in the apartment—but it was shelter. We went there when there was nowhere else to go.

Rich and I wanted to do a real gig and there was one place in town that afforded us the opportunity—The Metropol. Rich arranged through a record company guy he was working with to have us perform at the venue. It took some strings being pulled, but the gig came and went without a hitch.

At least I could say that I'd performed in Denmark at a real venue, not just busking on the Walking Street—and although there's no record of my ever having been at The Metropol, I was.

I also fell madly in love with a young Danish girl, Joy Malcom. With the money—coins of a dozen different currencies from the university event—and a new love, I was profoundly sad to have to leave. But a college career awaited my return home to the states.

At the celebration with fireworks of the eight hundredth birthday of the city of Copenhagen, I bid farewell to Joy, and walked off through the crowded throng on my way to the airport.

I had made enough money from the event at the university to buy a flight from Copenhagen to London, and from there to New York. But it was all in coins and all in currencies from around the world. The Congress of Industrial Builders had come from every country on every continent. I was the recipient of their spare change.

When I arrived at the airport to purchase my ticket there was a long line of people waiting to do the same. When I emptied the bag full of coins on the counter, I heard moans and groans from everyone behind me. But the ticket lady was unbelievable. Faster than a machine, she first sorted the coins by country, then by denomination, and within minutes handed me my ticket. She got a round of applause from the others in line behind me. I left Copenhagen for London and returned to New York.

On tour in 1988 with Abe and members of Shenandoah, I returned to Copenhagen to play again at The Metropol (the same place). I had been in the car to the gig from the airport telling the guys in the band about the beautiful Danish girl I had once loved almost twenty-five years before. They laughed at my story, until the car pulled up to the gig and I said, "And there she is."

Sure enough, Joy was standing at the entrance to the Metropol in Copenhagen, waiting for us to arrive. We walked around the city, catching up before the show. Our lives had run along parallel lines. We'd both married, had kids, had an interest in Eastern spirituality, etc. We wandered through Christiania (a section of Copenhagen taken over by hippies decades earlier), which she had a part in establishing. It was a treasure connecting with her.

1988 would be Guthrie's last tour with Shenandoah . . . at least for some time. Technically speaking, Guthrie's Shenandoah would soon not legally exist. In 1988, an Alabama-based country music group, also calling themselves Shenandoah, rocketed to fame with a couple of best-selling records. That success proved a mixed blessing. The group was sued by no fewer than four other bands touring and recording under the same name. Accruing a half-million dollars in legal expenses in their effort to claim the Shenandoah brand,[13] the chart-toppers were pushed into Chapter 11 bankruptcy.[14] The country music band would eventually, at great expense, buy out all rights to the name in 1992. But due to the ongoing legal wrangle, as early as 1988 European promoters were listing the folk singer's engagements as "Arlo Guthrie and his American Band."

Guthrie and Shenandoah were in the midst of their two-week sortie through Germany, when they received sobering news from back home:

AG: On March 15, 1988, my closest friend, producer, and musical director, John Pilla, passed away from heart problems. I was in Frankfurt, Germany, when the news reached me. John and I began our friendship back in 1968 when I was doing the movie *Alice's Restaurant*. We worked together on the soundtrack for the film and for the soundtrack album that came out afterward.

For the next twenty years, we worked very closely on everything from the stage shows to records, or just sharing time in his darkroom developing film. He was a really fine guitar picker and accompanied me for many years on bass as well as guitar, often with accompanying vocals. When I began working with Shenandoah he'd come out and help arrange the material.

We were closer than brothers. Our last times spent together were at my house for Thanksgiving in 1987, when other friends were visiting. After that he went to Cozumel, Mexico, where he would snorkel and be in the water, where the heart problems were lessened. He passed away a few months later.

John Pilla passed away far too young, at age forty-six. He had returned from Mexico to spend his last days in his hometown of Philadelphia. The 1980s had been a rough time for Pilla, professionally and personally, his substance abuse having tested even lifelong friendships. In Guthrie's published remembrance he recollected:

He went to seek some help. These were the coldest days of our relationship, and thankfully, they did not last a long time. Somehow we were changing, but we weren't doing it together anymore. I wondered if it was due to his worsening physical condition: his heart was beginning to fail and the drugs weren't helping either. They made him suspicious and paranoid.

There were times when he seemed to be his wonderful old self—and times I wasn't so sure. There were times when we reflected on life and death. We had never been afraid to talk of these things. But there was a restlessness about my friend that I could not reach across. I felt helpless. So did he."[15]

The two men *were* brothers in every sense of the word. Though new projects were few and far between, Guthrie and Pilla continued to collaborate—even in nonmusical ways. It was John and Jackie who spent countless hours typing in the names and addresses of fans into a computer database—alerting them via postcard that the folk singer was to soon pass through their area. The database also, and importantly, served as the seed list for the earliest subscribers to the *Rolling Blunder Review*. The *Berkshire Eagle* reported the producer's dying request was a simple one, asking that all "his friends assemble and share their music as a memorial."[16] John Pilla would be missed.

On August 24, 1988, Columbia Records issued *Folkways: A Vision Shared—A Tribute to Woody Guthrie and Leadbelly*. The release of the album was to be supplemented by a film that would air on the Showtime cable-TV network in September. The television program served as an excellent companion to the record and included performances not included on the LP. Guthrie's fans were also happy to learn that the singer had a principal role in filmmaker Jim Brown's newest documentary.

It was interesting that every time Woody Guthrie's public profile seemed to have peaked, another wave of interest would crest. When New York's *Daily News* asked Guthrie to comment on his father's recent induction into the Rock and Roll Hall of Fame and the attendant publicity surrounding the Folkways tribute LP, Guthrie laughed. He suggested his dad would have "gotten a big kick out of it. A real big kick."[17] When Sis Cunningham, cofounder of the radical topical folk song magazine *Broadside* and a former Almanac Singer, was asked a similar question, she answered, Woody would have likely "enjoyed it. That is, as long as he didn't have to participate."[18] The Woody Guthrie she knew was a loner who tended to drift quietly away and disappear into the night. Sis thought it amusing that Woody was getting "more recognition now than he ever got while he was alive."[19]

Guthrie chose to record his father's "East Texas Red" for the Folkways LP. It was a song mostly—perhaps *only*—familiar to the most devoted of Woody fans and scholars. The song's titular character was a sadistic railroad bull causing a world of troubles for Depression-era hobos riding the blinds. There was no extant recording of the song by Woody in anyone's archives, only a lead sheet and set of lyrics included in *The Nearly Complete Collection of Woody Guthrie Folk Songs* (Ludlow Music, Inc. 1963). Arlo Guthrie likely gleaned the song from one or two recordings made in the early 1960s: Cisco Houston included "East Texas Red" on his LP *I Ain't Got No Home* (Vanguard, 1962), and Logan English offered a second rendition on his LP *Logan English Sings the Woody Guthrie Songbag* (20th Century Fox, 1964).

Arlo Guthrie joked he didn't necessarily *want* to record "East Texas Red." The song was "one of those long ballads that nobody really wanted to record for some reason."[20] That may have been the case, but the obscure ballad was one of Woody's finest storytelling efforts, comparative in structure to his masterpiece "Tom Joad." Though the song was rarely performed and not included in Arlo's set lists over the years, he held some fondness for the ballad. He once performed the song on an episode of Chicago's *Soundstage,* but that performance was mostly lost to memory as no one yet had video recorders at home to capture it. That program, titled "Woody Guthrie's America," broadcast in the autumn of 1976, featured Guthrie swapping songs with Pete Seeger, Judy Collins, and Fred Hellerman.

Guthrie accepted he was genetically predestined to sing his father's lesser-known songs. Whenever a Woody Guthrie "event" was in the planning stage, the folk singer sighed, "Nobody ever says 'Arlo, which one would you like to do?'"[21] Other artists would always get first crack at the better-known songs. In a bit of eerie synchronicity, Guthrie recalled recording "East Texas Red" for the Folkways project in October of 1987. Then, just after Christmas of '87, the folk singer traveled to Okemah to buy a 1985 Jeep from a cousin. Driving the Jeep through Texas on the way to his winter home in Sebastian, Florida, Guthrie found himself lost and far from the main highway. He pulled up to a railroad bridge where a weather-beaten road sign read "Kilgore. Longview—9 Miles." It was a revelatory moment. Woody's first verse of "East Texas Red" included the lyric "He worked the town of Kilgore and Longview nine miles down." Now, a half-century later, the son found himself on the very spot of desolate road his father had traveled some fifty or sixty years earlier. "Even though I was still lost," Guthrie recalled, "I knew where I was."[22]

The *Vision Shared* LP would get a second promotional push in autumn of '88 when the accompanying documentary was featured on the Showtime network and offered as an expanded videocassette release in October. The video offered more Arlo Guthrie than the one track allotted on the LP: the VHS tape featured an extended duet of Guthrie and Emmy Lou Harris harmonizing on "Deportee (Plane Wreck at Los Gatos")," a clip of Guthrie and Seeger running through Lead Belly's "Alabama Bound," and a Guthrie solo on "Grand Coulee Dam."

The all-star cast of rock and country music superstars contributing to the project ensured the Folkways LP wouldn't suffer from public disinterest. Some royalties generated would benefit the Guthrie estate, a situation putting the folk singer in an uncomfortable position. "I'm walking that tightrope from being just another person involved in the project and a recipient of it," Guthrie allowed. "I don't want to be pumping something too much that I will eventually benefit from."[23]

Guthrie's participation was benefit enough. The album drew mainstream media attention, newspapers running articles with such headlines as "Arlo Guthrie is back in spotlight after tribute album."[24] The publicity certainly didn't hurt, and Guthrie used the opportunity to ruminate on the record industry, politics, religion, record companies, and, of course, thoughts on the recent Folkways project. The question most asked was a simple one: why has his father's basic one-man-and-a-guitar music endured? It was an interesting question since the folk singer was readying a return to the stage as a solo artist.

In September of 1988, Guthrie would set off alone on a tour taking him from Carrboro, North Carolina, to Carnegie Hall. Woody's songs would be part of the new program, but Guthrie wasn't merely acting as the "good son." Woody's songs remained as relevant as ever, even though four or five decades had passed since their composition. Asked why Woody's music was timeless, Guthrie answered, "I don't know if it's the music itself. I sometimes think that the music is just an excuse to say something else. I'm not exactly sure what that thing is."[25] He added, "It's probably different for different people, but I think somewhere at the root of it all is a kind of spirit that is uniquely American and says something about ourselves with a certain degree of humor but with a certain degree of seriousness. It's a language that we speak. Every time that we seem to look for who we are as a country or where we're going as a nation, we pick up on certain individuals who seem to have expressed it rather well in their own time."[26]

The success of "Alice's Restaurant" enabled Guthrie to claim celebrity apart from that of his father. He wasn't burdened by his lineage, but conceded such stewardship brought expectations and responsibilities. Woody may have died at age fifty-five, but many of his contemporaries were still around—and protective of his legacy. "I have a lot of his peers who still show up at my gigs," Guthrie noted. "Maybe it's because I played with his peers, like Pete Seeger, over the years."[27] For his part, Seeger could estimate Woody's son from a unique opportunity of having worked with both men. "Arlo is his own man," Seeger mused. "He has some of Woody's qualities and a lot of brand-new ones. He's one of the most conscientious musicians that I know. He thinks long and hard about the kind of music he wants to make. Then he gets on stage and, by gosh, he does his level best."[28]

January of 1989 brought talk of a second staging of the Woodstock festival. August of '89 would mark the twentieth anniversary of the legendary "3 Days of Peace and Music." Guthrie was approached by the folks planning a reunion weekend and wasn't opposed to the idea. But he confessed he was a bit wary of signing on too early as the promoters of "Woodstock II" were mostly feeling out "whether they could put together something."[29]

Joel Rosenman and John Roberts were copartners of the JR Capital Corporation, a capital venture business. The two men were investors, admitting to not even being "weekend hippies" when approached to bankroll the original Woodstock event. In early 1969 the two formed Woodstock Ventures, partnering with festival promoters Michael Lang and Artie Kornfield. Since gate-crashers turned the Aquarian Exposition into a free festival within hours, it proved a bad investment. The two estimated a loss of some 1.3 million dollars.[30]

It wasn't until 1980 that Woodstock Ventures went into the green by trading on nostalgia: selling off such trinkets as the fifty thousand unused tickets and posters languishing in storage. Most Woodstock profits came from selling to Warner Bros. the rights to the three-album soundtrack and director Michael Wadleigh's brilliant documentary film. Rosenman and

Roberts had been lying in wait to reinvigorate the brand. The festival's twentieth anniversary seemed the time to strike had, at long last, arrived.

There were going to be hurdles. The two men were already in a wrangle with Warner Bros. over use of the "Woodstock" trademark. Secondly, Max Yasgur's farm was no longer an available rental. The hillside farm had since been sold to a used-car salesman from Brooklyn. In any event, the town of Bethel had long since banned gatherings of more than ten thousand people, a prudent decision considering the wreckage left following the original event.

With the Catskills unwelcoming, Rosenman and Roberts teased out a number of alternate sites. The most ambitious of these was the staging of four *separate* Woodstock concerts: one in the US, one in the Soviet Union, and one in both the Eastern and Western sectors of still-divided Germany. Guthrie was more or less enamored of this idea, even suggesting a fifth show in Africa might be considered. But he thought the promoters had "no real clear-cut focus."[31] He decided not to commit until more concrete plans were made.

It was obvious the recent push for democratic rights in the Soviet Union and Eastern Europe was on Guthrie's mind. He saw the events taking place in the Eastern Bloc as an extension of worldwide calls for more democratic governance. "The struggle today, I think, is the same as it was then," he offered. "It all comes down to treating each other like human beings. It's always 'The other guy can take less because I'm more important' or 'I get more because I'm a guy and that's a woman,' or 'I'm white and that guy's Black.' The solutions are probably gonna be a little different today because the world changes."[32]

Guthrie rarely shared soapbox politics from the stage. He preferred to perform satiric songs, directing Will Rogers–like commentaries at government stupidities. There was, sadly, never a shortage of new outrages to draw from. Pete Seeger once told him, while politics weren't necessarily corrupt in structure, politics tended to "attract the corruptibles." "In my Dad's time, there were different political ideologies that seemed to offer solutions," Guthrie mused, "whether it was capitalist, communist, socialist or one of the ones in between. I don't know if the solution can be found in any one of those ideas. And it took a long time for us to find that out. It took time to find that there are people just as miserable in communist countries as they are in capitalist ones."[33]

In February, Guthrie and Seeger were in Vero Beach to kick off the former's Indian River Festival. The ten-hour concert, staged at Vero's Riverside Park, featured a sampling of national and local talent: Arlo Guthrie and Pete Seeger, Brave New Tribe, the Bone Daddies, Michael Pastorius and the Warning, the Puzzlers, Bill Wharton and Blue House, Ed Gerhard, and David Glover. Any and all proceeds were to go to the Pelican Island Audubon Society.[34]

1989 would mark the second staging of the festival. While the 1989 staging was hampered by cool temperatures, the event still attracted some five thousand fans. Guthrie had been promoting the festival as early as the fall-winter of 1988. "Don't miss this fabulous festival," he urged readers of the *Rolling Blunder Review*. "Bring the kids. Tell your friends. If you don't have any friends, come and make some while you're here."[35] Guthrie partly modeled his festival after Seeger's Great Hudson River Revival. He marveled at Seeger's ability to bring people together for a worthy cause, regardless of personal, political, or social affiliation. He was hoping his Indian River festival could do the same.

"The real problem is when people are divided politically, they don't express their concerns as a community," Guthrie told the *Orlando Sentinel*. "But *everybody* wants a clean environment. Even developers want clean beaches to build their developments near. One of the problems is that people do not generally get together about these things until it is too late. This is a long-term pursuit we're involved with here. But the fabulous thing about the festival on the Indian River is that here is an area where not only can we reclaim the environment but begin to prevent the damage."[36]

On 29 March Guthrie appeared on the PBS science program NOVA. The hour-long episode, titled "Confronting the Killer Gene," centered not only on the recent scientific breakthroughs made in the testing for Huntington's, but also the difficult choice confronting the people most in danger of inheriting it. Guthrie chose to pass on taking the test when first made available. Several years on, he hadn't reconsidered that decision. "I have learned to live every day without looking over my shoulder, without looking back," he offered. "There's a lot of people out there with genetic disorders. After all, the biggest genetic disorder is death."[37]

Geneticist Nancy Wexler, also featured in the documentary, sympathized with Guthrie. She too was in danger of inheriting the gene. Though

Wexler was undecided on whether to take the test or not, she conceded that if Woody Guthrie had taken the test at age eighteen and chosen to "check out" following confirmation of the Huntington's gene, American music would have been cheated out of the nearly one thousand songs he wrote.[38]

By spring of '89 it was becoming apparent that many of the performers of the original Woodstock festival would *not* be going to the Woodstock Ventures reunion. John Sebastian's view was generally shared by several veterans of the original event. "People shouldn't seek to emulate it," the Lovin' Spoonful singer shared. "Woodstock was really the result of a colossal failure. It was not like everyone planned to have this great tribal meeting where everyone would get in free."[39] A few weeks later, Guthrie chimed in: "You can't repeat an event, but you can repeat the spirit of it, if you're not trying to make a lot of money doing it. I thought that all the promoters saying, '*We can do it, we'll charge a lot of money,*' were on the wrong track."[40]

There was already talk that a smaller and less money-obsessed Woodstock celebration might still happen. Intrigued by the suggestion of a Woodstock commemoration in the Soviet Union, Richie Havens announced he was trying to arrange a concert in Moscow in August of '89, one to include Guthrie, Sebastian, and Joe Cocker as cobills. Havens was quickly counseled by a legal team that he could not advertise the program as an official "Woodstock" event: the name was copyright-protected. Should Havens choose to press on, one provisional title suggested was "'69 to '89."[41]

With Havens's plans under consideration, Guthrie's fondness for the beauty and atmosphere of Indian River—just a stone's throw from Ma Jaya Sati Bhagavati's ashram—caused him to begin shopping nearby properties.

AG: On April 1, 1989, Jackie and I purchased The CrabHouse, an old seafood packing factory that had originally been built by the US Coast Guard. We had plans to convert it into a home with a studio for recording.

Guthrie told fans via his June 1989 newsletter it was time for Rising Son Records to look forward. His plan to build a recording studio was now chief among the label's short-term goals:

The idea of having our own recording studio lingered on and at various times seemed remotely possible. In the meantime, we began work on our record company, collecting our catalogue from Warner Bros. and reissuing it. The recording studio took a back seat to other projects.

By the end of this year we will have rereleased all of our record projects contained in the WB catalogue. Our first objective being completed we are looking forward, once again, to recording new records.

This gives rise to the possibility of having our own studios in which to produce our own records. We are considering having other artists join our small label, . . . having signed a mystery artist to be revealed sometime this summer.[42]

The decision to purchase the CrabHouse, described as a "vacant shell on the Indian River," was a gamble. Guthrie admitted he and Jackie "hocked just about everything" to purchase the property—a World War II ammo storage facility of the US Coast Guard.[43] Following the war, the "ghostly pink building" was sold to a private company who transformed the waterfront property into a seafood market.[44] Should Guthrie's recording studio ambition not materialize, the singer joked he could always restore the seafood market to its former glory—the CrabHouse's original clam steamer was "still intact."[45]

Any renovation of the derelict building needed to be put on the back burner, if only temporarily. In the spring of 1989 Guthrie was scheduled to leave for a three-week solo tour, purposefully built around two dates of personal importance. The first was a show in his father's hometown of Okemah, Oklahoma, the second a benefit for his Billings, Montana, alma mater. Both visits would connect Guthrie to ghosts of the past.

On the morning of 13 April, Guthrie unexpectedly was made to confront a third ghost. Morning newspapers were reporting the death, at age fifty-two, of Yippie! activist and author Abbie Hoffman. Guthrie had been friends with Hoffman and Jerry Rubin since his Greenwich Village days. The two had approached Guthrie at the 1968 Newport Folk Festival, asking him if might perform at their "Festival of Life" protest in downtown Chicago in August—the site of the Democratic National Convention. Pete Seeger too was asked, meeting with the young men in Harold Leventhal's

Manhattan office. In the end both Seeger and Guthrie begged off. Seeger counseled they seek a broad representation of "all the different kinds of human beings in the USA" and not just flood Chicago's streets with pot-smoking hippies. Seeger feared such a scenario would play into the hands of the law-and-order types looking for any excuse to brandish nightsticks. "You're not going to have a revolution with a bunch of short-haired older people!" Hoffman and Rubin protested.[46]

So when the disturbing images of clashes between protestors and police outside of the convention flashed across television screens that August, Guthrie was on the West Coast, booked for a week-long residency at the Golden Bear in Huntington Beach, California, Seeger choosing to perform at a Poor People's Benefit at NYC's Lewisohn Stadium. Though neither chose to go to Chicago, both singers were called as witnesses for the defense in the subsequent trial of the Chicago 7.

In his testimony of February 1970 Guthrie explained he chose not to travel to Chicago, concerned that his friends had not secured the proper permits. He told Hoffman and Rubin not only would he not attend but "would, to my best, have other people not attend if the permits were not granted."[47] This absence of permits, Guthrie correctly suspected, would provide an excuse for "police violence." Though all seven defendants would be acquitted on the "conspiracy to riot" charge, five would be found guilty of "crossing state lines with the intent to riot."

Many on the Left dismissed Hoffman as little more than a political clown: the FBI, however, wasn't laughing at his antics. Following a cocaine possession bust in 1974—which Hoffman maintained was an orchestrated frame-up—the activist went underground. During his seven fugitive years, Hoffman underwent plastic surgery and adopted a new persona as "Barry Freed." It was later revealed he had been hiding in plain sight, living on an island in the St. Lawrence River near Canada.

Guthrie hadn't heard from Hoffman since his going underground. In the months following Hoffman's passing, Guthrie's only run-in with his fugitive friend happened in the late 1970s. In a rap excerpted from a show in Hampton Beach, New Hampshire, in the summer of 1989, Guthrie shared the circumstances of that meeting:

> One time I was playing up in this part of the world. I forget exactly
> where I was. I think it was up in, like, Maine or something. It kinda

was weird because a few years ago Abbie Hoffman was still running away from the FBI and I was doing a show and I was talking—like I do most of the time during these shows. And all of a sudden I could hear something like, "Pssst. Pssst, Arlo? Pssst . . ." And I turned around and in the wings they had these drapes and stuff and there was standing Abbie Hoffman. He was supposed to have had some kind of face job so you couldn't recognize him, but I recognized him instantly. Not only that, but he had a kid with him that looked exactly the same. He was a weird guy.[48]

In April of 1989, Abbie's brother, Jack, organized a small memorial in their hometown of Worcester, Massachusetts. Guthrie was unable to attend—he was already two days into his Midwest tour—but Pete Seeger managed to get to Worcester to serenade the mourners. On the very day of Hoffman's service, the coroner ruled the activist's death a probable suicide, post-mortem lab results showing evidence of alcohol and the "residue of about 150 phenobarbital pills."[49] Newspapers played the tragedy as another example of the end of '60s idealism.

Ten days following, Guthrie arrived in his father's hometown of Okemah, Oklahoma—a town long reluctant to celebrate their most famous native. In September of 1965, Woody Guthrie's sister, Mrs. Mary Jo Edgemon, had been invited, to disapproving sniffs, to share memories of her brother at Okemah's free-thinking General Study Club.[50] That meeting signaled a welcome crack in the ice—but only a crack. Following Woody's passing in October of 1967, Marjorie Guthrie tried to donate several of Woody's books and LP recordings to the Okemah Public Library, but her gifts were sadly rebuffed.[51]

Though the situation would change in time, movement seemed glacial. In early May of 1971, Senator Fred Harris (D-OK) introduced a bill commemorating 14 July as "Woody Guthrie Day." But the Okemah Chamber of Commerce voted 7–1 that—even if the bill should pass—no commemoration would be observed in Okemah.[52] Undeterred, on 14 July, 1971, the date of Woody's fifty-ninth birthday, Arlo, Jackie, and Marjorie visited Okemah at the invitation of librarian V. K. Chowning. Chowning chose to not only graciously accept the Guthrie family's donation of books and records, but also helped organize a memorial concert.[53]

That concert was to be staged at Oklahoma City's Mummer's Theater. Sadly, in Okemah, Woody Guthrie was mostly reviled as a probable atheist and—barring any substantive evidence—at the very least a *fellow traveler* of the US Communist Party. Though Okemah and Oklahoma City were physically separated only by a distance of seventy-two miles, philosophically the two communities sat farther apart. The Oklahoma City tribute would feature both Arlo Guthrie and the popular country and western singer Jimmie Driftwood.

On the Wednesday morning of the OKC concert, the Guthrie family wandered about Okemah, visiting the ruins of Woody's old home and meeting with members of the newly founded Woody Guthrie Memorial Committee. Few Okemah residents had been made aware of the family's visit, the committee thinking it best to keep it low-key. There was concern the mere presence of the family might irk locals and cause an unpleasant confrontation. In any event, the Oklahoma City concert was a big success, drawing an audience of some 2,500. But one newspaper suggested the vast majority of fans attending were interlopers arriving from out-of-town *and* out-of-state.

The first sign that Woody Guthrie was no longer thought a pariah by everyone in his old hometown would occur in October 1972. The town council, in a vote of four to one, deigned to have "Home of Woody Guthrie" painted on the bulb of its massive water tower.[54] It was a surprising—and welcome—change of heart. In the years that followed, there would be a gradual—if occasionally grudging—acceptance by Okemah's residents that Guthrie was an important figure, albeit a controversial one. Though Guthrie continued to be the source of some disquiet within the community, many recognized that Woody's cultural contributions were intertwined with the recorded histories of both Oklahoma and the United States.

Such change was partly due to the community-building activities of an outsider. On 1 December 1988 at Okemah's Crystal Theater, a folk singer by the name of Larry Long arranged to bring fifty schoolchildren to the stage to sing Guthrie's songs and read from his prose. Long was not a resident of Okemah; he was a native of Minnesota hired as an artist in residence by Oklahoma's Department of Education and Council of the Arts.[55] The event at the Crystal filled every one of the theater's 450 seats. That night the children read from compositions recounting their own lives as proud residents and Okies. The night's finale had everyone singing along on Woody's "This Land Is Your Land." This remarkable concert was recorded and released as *Larry Long and Children of Oklahoma: It Takes a Lot of People (Tribute to Woody Guthrie)* (Flying Fish, 1989).

One of those clapping loudest was Woody's sister Mary Jo, now sixty-five years old. She *never* allowed anyone talk ill of her brother, so the evening was an emotion-filled event. "I sat there with chill bumps and with tears," she admitted.[56] The program was a triumph for the entire Guthrie family. The Guthries, like so many Okie families, suffered and survived calamity and ostracization. Mary Jo recalled feeling "the warmth of my family all around me. Clara, Roy, Woody, George, Papa and Mama. They too all sat here in this very theatre many years ago. When the children came marching down the aisle and on stage I swelled with pride and the tears came. I knew Woody was watching."[57]

Arlo Guthrie was watching too, if only from afar. Impressed by Long's success, he pledged to help celebrate the release of the Flying Fish LP by planning a concert of his own. The time seemed right. There was some early talk Guthrie might perform at the high school stadium in April, the same week as "Pioneer Days," Okemah's commemoration of the town's founding.[58] But it was later announced the folk singer would instead perform at the Crystal.

The concert was scheduled for Saturday night, 29 April. Though the Crystal's owner was mocked for his belief he could sell more than a few tickets to the program, the concert sold out quickly. So quickly, in fact, the brisk sales had taken many of Okemah's residents by surprise. Many who planned on attending complained that more than two hundred and fifty tickets had been sold to out-of-towners. In a gesture of goodwill, the Arlo Guthrie concert would benefit a scholarship fund for local students. More than $5,000 had already been secured in ticket sales alone.[59]

Not everyone in town was happy that Woody's son was visiting. One agitated citizen—an undertaker and former member of the Okemah town council—was busy putting up signs advertising his displeasure. The signs posted read "Woody Guthrie Was No Hero." Some signs also carried a damning editorial culled from a local conservative newspaper, charging Woody was, amongst other sins, a "militant atheist." Though some in this insular community of 3,500 shared the undertaker's views, the signs angered Guthrie's supporters. So signs were being torn up almost as fast as they were being put up.[60] It was amazing that more than two decades following his passing—and sixty years since his leaving Okemah—Woody Guthrie would remain such a controversial figure in his hometown.

Arlo Guthrie arrived in town the night prior to the concert, sharing a quiet dinner with relatives and trying his best to avoid the press. He did share some thoughts with a reporter who managed to get a few words from him. "I've been walking around the whole town feeling kind of strange," Guthrie admitted. "My grandfather and a lot of his folks grew up here, spent their lives here. I feel like I have encountered my own roots, and I'm real happy about that."[61] When asked his opinion of those who remained hostile to Woody, Arlo sighed, "I don't feel an obligation to push my dad on anyone." Guthrie expressed his belief people were entitled to their opinions, confident his father's "work, his life, can stand on its own. Time and history has spoken for him."[62] Guthrie did graciously refuse the offer to participate in the planned Saturday afternoon Pioneer Days parade and festivities. He thought it would be unfair to local folks more deserving of commendation.

That night at the Crystal Theater, Guthrie walked onstage to a standing ovation. Newspaper reports suggested Guthrie was "clearly nervous," moving directly into a brisk version of his father's outlaw ballad "Pretty Boy Floyd."[63] Following the song, Guthrie allowed, "I work a lot, about one hundred shows a year, but this one's got me scared." He then moved into a somber rendition of "Deportee (Plane Wreck at Los Gatos)." Guthrie chose not to dwell on the controversy his appearance in Okemah had kicked up. The only reference he made was in his winking observation, "I think a lot of good things are happening for my Dad . . . now that he doesn't need it so much."[64]

Two chairs in the theater were, sadly, left unoccupied. "I wish my folks were alive, especially my Mom," Guthrie allowed. "But at any rate, where they are now I know that they are looking down and having a ball, laughing hysterically that this could possibly go on here tonight."[65] Two hours later, Guthrie closed the program with a raucous "This Land Is Your Land" and an impossibly gentle "Amazing Grace." "Thank you for being here," he told the cheering crowd. "And I know that my Dad thanks you also, very much, for this night. God bless you all."[66]

Guthrie's experience in Okemah would linger in his consciousness. Following his appearance at the Crystal, the singer composed a lengthy reflection on the Guthrie lineage. The essay served as an attempt to provide context to his father's "union gospel" politics.[67] By way of explaining his father's life choices, Guthrie wrote at length about his *grandfather's* life and times. He described Charlie Guthrie as a man who wore many hats. Charlie was, at different times in his life, "a court clerk, law officer, prize fighter and a real estate baron,"[68]—someone with strong belief in American ideals:

> [My grandfather] was well educated, writing essays on international affairs. He wrote extensively, defending capitalism from a wave of socialistic ideas that were well rooted in Oklahoma. . . . Charlie Guthrie's ideological defense of capitalism was not the typical mouthing-off of some ignorant local inspired by fear. He had read and understood the theories of Marx and Engels. He was an American individualist and expected each man to stand or fall on his own merit. He had worked hard and it had paid off, convincing him that anyone could do the same thing. He thought these things for most of his life, at least until the combined effects of Wall Street and nature conspired to relieve him of everything he had worked for.[69]

Guthrie went on to explain how his father's family found themselves dispossessed of everything important to them. The Depression, combined with merciless banking practices, was no less sparing of the Guthries than they were of others struggling through the hard times of the 1930s. But Charley Guthrie's family was additionally victimized by other life-changing events: "[The family's] house burned down, his wife became sick and was sent to an insane asylum, and his daughter, Clara, died in a tragic fire. Within an incredibly short time, the Guthries went from having it all, to having it all gone."[70]

It was in this atmosphere Woody Guthrie was, in Arlo's essay, compelled to "awaken from his childhood" and "cross-examine the philosophical foundations upon which my grandfather had built their lives."

> He discovered that it was man's abuse of nature, and not nature itself, that devastated the land. It was man's lust for money and power that led Wall Street to come tumbling down, crushing its priesthood and followers alike. Like Joshua, he sounded its fall.

Knowing he had nothing, my father had nothing to lose. He saw that the fortress built by greed should fall by it justly. Poverty and suffering followed in the wake of economic and natural disaster. Millions of innocent farmers, ranchers, oil field workers, and plain ordinary families were left destitute and alone.[71]

Addressing the charge that his father was a "militant atheist," Guthrie upended the argument, describing his father's lifelong preoccupation with matters of the spirit:

The word "union" came to my father first as a result of his interest in eastern philosophy. He had studied some yoga and read that "yoga" means union. A union between man and God. He practiced meditation and sat absorbed, oblivious to the world around him.

But now the world seemed as if it were screaming in agony, and he could not isolate himself from it. The word "union" became a vehicle to a new life, not just for himself spiritually, but practically speaking, for all those who worked together to build a better world.

He preached his union gospel (in every sense of the word) wherever and with whomever he could. He made friends and enemies because of it. The vision of a world united in a common destiny; where everyday men and women mutually shared in its wealth, pleasure and productivity. . . . In union a better world was possible, and the families of the world were sorely in need of change for the better.[72]

Guthrie's last concert of the spring 1989 tour was a visit to the Alberta Bair Theater in downtown Billings, Montana. Guthrie was no stranger to Billings, having briefly attended Rocky Mountain College in the autumn of 1965. He had actually scheduled the visit to Billings to serve two purposes. The first, and most important, was a benefit concert to help fill the coffers of the Methodist school's scholarship fund. The second was Rocky Mountain College's plan to present him with an honorary doctorate.

Given that Guthrie's high school transcript from Stockbridge School was, at best, spotty, he conceded Rocky Mountain College "was the only school that would take me." It was important in 1965 that he attend college.

This was a period when young men were, in Guthrie's words, "either going to school or visiting Asian nations all-expenses paid." Though the college was to bestow the honor of "Doctor of Music" on him, Guthrie's actual tenure at Rocky Mountain College hadn't lasted long. He was a student for three weeks at minimum, six weeks at the most—it all depended on the recollections of those asked. He jokingly told reporters he chose to depart Rocky Mountain College "just before the phys-ed course changed from bowling to basic training."[73]

In September 1965, Guthrie's college advisor was Jim Taylor. Now, in 1989, Taylor was the college's registrar. In Taylor's opinion, Guthrie seemed a lost soul in 1965. "He was suffering from that 'son of a famous father syndrome,'" he recollected, "trying to find his uniqueness in the world. I think he showed us all that he found it."[74] Guthrie agreed his tenure at Rocky Mountain College came at "a very difficult time in my life. My father was dying; the country was searching for its identity, and so was I."[75]

AG: I left for Rocky Mountain College (RMC) after I'd returned from Europe. RMC was located in Billings, just on the edge of town. I began attending classes immediately . . . and realized I was not a very good student. But I made friends and settled in. My roommate was a great guy, Joe Loos. We began a friendship that has endured since then.

I became involved with a program within the college that sent college students to the nearby Indian reservation to help young kids with tutoring. The program was a great idea, but ultimately didn't do much.

The movie of "Alice's Restaurant" was fictionalized for Hollywood, much to the detriment of RMC. I never had problems in local bars or restaurants, at the college, or in town. Everyone was pretty much friendly to me, and I was happy to be there. Arthur DeRosier was the president of RMC and, with his lovely wife Linda, made my time there welcoming and friendly. I also had a wonderful relationship with the chaplain.

I had a difficult transition with the music theory classes I was taking. After all, I had been a professional musician in the summer of 1965. Okay, not really to any major degree, but I had made a living as a musician even if it was short-lived and [I] wasn't playing Carnegie Hall.

One person from RMC who had a profound effect on Guthrie was college chaplain Reverend Robert M. Holmes. The very liberal-minded Holmes was a free-spirited Methodist: he rode a Harley-Davidson, played jazz piano, and advocated tirelessly for the have-nots and marginalized—unwed mothers, the incarcerated, the gay community, indigenous Americans, and the working poor.[76] Guthrie's reading of different religious traditions would introduce him to a particularly intriguing one. It was an old Viking belief that everyone went to Hell. There was no reward for kindness or for the performing of charitable acts, only the personal satisfaction of doing right unto others. But you were still going to Hell.

After the benefit, Guthrie roamed the campus and visited downtown Billings. The city had certainly changed in the intervening two decades. During a two-hour-long panel discussion held in the school's lecture hall, he reminisced about his days at RMC and took questions. He later offered it was only after watching members of his own crew and the panel fall fast asleep during his ruminations that he "finally fulfilled the promise of an academic career."[77]

There *was* a lot to discuss and ponder. His college experience as contrived for Arthur Penn's film of *Alice's Restaurant* was dramatic, but factually inaccurate. In one of the more memorable scenes in Penn's film, local rednecks toss the long-haired Guthrie through the window of a Billings pizza parlor. Guthrie noted this scenario was completely contrived: Billings didn't even *have* pizza in 1965. Guthrie explained his favorite course at RMC was one concerning the Gospels, and the only books he took with him upon his departure were those pertaining to the origins and comparisons of the Gospels.[78]

Guthrie received his doctorate on Saturday, 6 May. Sitting on the dais, he recalled "so many thoughts flooded his overtaxed mind." He thought back to the autumn of 1965 when his mother "fretted at his leaving for college, using the little money she had to get him there in the first place." He thought back to the early summer of 1984 when he got off the phone with Billy Byrom at the ashram in Florida, suggesting he visit and meet with Ma Jayi Bhagavati, as "It's time to graduate." As he exited from the platform and waded into a sea of well-wishers, Guthrie recollected, his shaking "lots of hands, while he silently wondered whether or not he would ever know what was really going on."[79]

Others, meanwhile, wondered what was going on with the Woodstock twentieth anniversary reunion concerts. There was still chatter that *something* was going to happen. A few days before Guthrie was to perform with Pete Seeger at Clearwater's Great Hudson Revival, the singer volunteered he was still feeling a bit leery. "Nothing's definite at the moment," he conceded. "If it's simply a vehicle for the promoters to make a killing, I won't be there. But if the money raised goes to a worthy cause, I'll do it. If we're going to recreate—or celebrate—Woodstock, it should be in that spirit."[80] It wasn't to be. In July, Roberts and Rosenman gave up on their idea of staging Woodstock II. The idea fell victim to legal wrangles and corporate infighting between Woodstock Ventures and Warner Bros.

Richie Havens's idea of a series of "'69 to '89" revival shows, however, would go forward. "We aren't planning on having any corporate sponsors," Havens told reporters when discussing his alternate Woodstock. "We want to generate some kind of consciousness again. This will be the real Woodstock reunion."[81] But due to scheduling conflicts, Havens's tour would not include Guthrie because the folk singer's summer schedule was already booked solid. Though Guthrie's presence would be missed, Havens's program suffered no shortage of Woodstock veterans: Melanie, John Sebastian, Country Joe McDonald, Rick Danko and Garth Hudson of The Band, Buddy Miles, and the Hendrix-less "New" Band of Gypsies would all take part.

That summer Guthrie would again share the stage with Seeger at a 4th of July celebration at the Koussevitzky Music Shed at Tanglewood in Lenox, Massachusetts. There had been a lot of recent discussion in the media about patriotism and the American flag. Two weeks prior to the 4th of July event, the Supreme Court upheld the First Amendment right to burn the flag in protest. The court's decision was an unpopular one, and letters and editorials in newspapers bristled with outrage.

At Tanglewood, Pete Seeger—no stranger to free-speech tangles—briefly addressed the subject. Just prior to the recitation of his poem, "The Torn Flag," the singer mused that since he had "been reading the newspapers and all this nonsense about the American flag, I thought I'd recite a poem I wrote about twenty years ago. I'd been singing at a college in the South—Tennessee, as I remember it. In the afternoon I took a nap in the Student U. dormitory and at the foot of the student's bed was a big American flag. At the other end of the student's bed was a big picture of Leon Trotsky. I didn't know which was *camp*."[82] "The Torn Flag," a poem often misinterpreted by detractors, expressed Seeger's desire that America live up to the best of her ideals. The Lenox concert concluded on a far more upbeat note, with Guthrie and Seeger harmonizing on the question, "Good morning, America, how are you?"

As August neared, newspapers were filling with Woodstock reminiscences and "Where Are They Now?" retrospectives. Guthrie's most public nods to the anniversary were twofold. He contributed an essay to a special Woodstock edition of *Rolling Stone,* now a glossy mag far removed from its pulpy counter-cultural beginnings. The second commemoration took place on Monday, 14 August, one day prior to the anniversary of his original appearance at the festival. With the assistance of Abe on keyboards, Guthrie performed a rocking version of his Woodstock anthem "Coming into Los Angeles," on NBC-TV's *Today Show.* On the day following, a new adventure was set to commence:

> **AG:** On August 15, 1989, we left for what we were calling "The Blunderman's Fabulous Adventure." It was a two-week tour arranged by our friend, Gil Markle, who was the owner of Long View Farms. We had recruited a busload of friends and fans who wanted to visit places in Europe together with me. Gil had a business which essentially arranged for young people through their schools to do the same thing. I wanted to know if his expertise in that area would translate to taking individual adults on similar adventures. We visited Heidelberg, Lucerne, Zermatt, St. Moritz, Innsbruck, Vienna, and Munich, with usually a couple of days in each place to wander around or partake of guided tours. Gil had hired two women to act as guides and, together with them and a busload of friends and fans, we had a great adventure.

Guthrie first teased the idea of taking his fans on a European adventure in the early winter of 1989. He wrote, "If enough people could be convinced to make the journey overseas for two weeks or so, . . . the costs to those going would be extremely favorable even with the devalued dollar." The trip was not necessarily an extension of a proper concert tour of Europe, though Guthrie hoped to "tie in some concert and festival" dates when planning the adventure, provisionally set for August. Bringing a busload of fans was an interesting idea. Guthrie joked, "Imagine selling out a show in Europe to a group of Americans who've filled the joint so that no Europeans could get in." In his promotion of the adventure, Guthrie opined, "You'll see yourself in places you've only dreamed of. And when you return home after your journey, you'll have a lifetime of memories to share with others, even if they're not interested."[83]

Many readers of Guthrie's newsletter thought the whimsical idea was likely a joke. But there were enough trusting souls who chose to contact the Rising Son Records office at "Wailers Wharf." By June 1989, it became apparent the offer to travel throughout Western Europe with Arlo Guthrie was a serious one. It was suggested that those interested in the "Journey to Blunderland" needed to get their applications in quick. 16 June 1989 was the cutoff date so airfare arrangements and hotel bookings could commence.[84]

Sometime earlier Guthrie was asked to narrate and compose incidental music for a book and cassette collection of favorite children's stories. Kay Chorao was already a highly regarded illustrator of children books. One of her most popular titles, *The Baby's Story Book,* had been published by E. P. Dutton in the autumn of 1985. The target demographic for her handsomely produced hardcover was preschoolers, ages one to four. Chorao's more-or-less-faithful retellings of the most classic children's fables, fairy tales, and nursery rhymes were purposely kept brief as not to strain "the brief, wriggly attention spans of lap sitters."[85] The recording session was scheduled for December 1988.[86]

In July of 1989 *Back Stage* reported Manhattan's Michael Sporn Animation had been engaged to produce a "limited animation version" of Chorao's book, with Arlo Guthrie name-checked to provide the soundtrack.[87] Chorao's book was only one of several to be ported over to home video. Such celebrities as James Earl Jones, Judy Collins, and Mia Farrow would also lend their voices to several of these children's cassette and book releases.

Joshua Greene, a producer of children's films, was inspired to bring the Chorao and Guthrie collaboration to home video when noticing his own son chose to "bypass books for more stimulating forms of entertainment." "For better or worse, we are raising a generation of viewers and listeners," Greene conceded. "Kids are tuned into their cassette players and televisions from an early age. . . . It's a matter of letting video and audio cassettes reinforce and enhance the reading experience. . . . Not all parents feel comfortable reading. Besides, it's not so much reading as communicating, and the most effective people for that are storytellers."[88]

There was no denying Guthrie's gift as a storyteller. In February of 1989 Guthrie informed fans that a book and cassette combo—as well as a forthcoming VHS tape—of *The Baby's Story Book* would soon be available. If Guthrie's decidedly non–rock 'n' roll contribution to children's literature seemed odd, it actually was not. The same folks who had grown up listening to his music were now parents themselves. In that light, the children's project made perfect sense. Those with a sense of folk music history also understood that Guthrie's contribution was simply another part of his family's lineage.

In the 1940s Woody Guthrie recorded a number of 78-rpm folios of children's songs for Moses Asch's Disc Records, including *Songs to Grow On: Nursery Days* (Disc 605, 1946) and *Songs to Grow On: Work Songs for Nursery Days* (Disc 602, 1947). Woody also recorded a number of 78-rpm singles on the Asch-associated children's label, Cub Records. Pete Seeger too had been recording children's songs since the 1940s. One of his earliest sets for Disc, *Songs to Grow On: Lullabies and Rounds* (Disc, D-1, 1946), was a two-record 78-rpm set of the imprint's Young Folksay Series. The most notable difference between Arlo's Chorao soundtrack and those earlier works was the absence of guitar and 5-string banjo. The soundtrack to *The Baby's Story Time* was scored entirely on synthesizer, giving the project a sonically modern sheen.

Despite the nontraditional musical settings, Guthrie saw his contribution as a component of folklore. "Folk music is made up of as much storytelling as songs," he explained when discussing his involvement. With a tinge of regret, he added, "For a big part of our lives, we've lost the ability to tell stories or relate them."[89] He approached the narration as a personal challenge. He would be, in some ways, an actor again. "When you're not seeing the person who's speaking, you really need to animate your speech," he explained. "Especially for kids, it's important when they first hear it that it has enough depth to keep their interest, but not so much that they can't follow it. And humor is a big part of that."[90] Guthrie's personal favorite on *Baby's Story Time* was his reading of "The Gingerbread Boy."

These were the *really* "old school" bedtime stories—many dark in nature, certainly not in tune with the "self-esteem building" yarns currently in vogue. One critic from *Billboard* charged Guthrie's narration was more raffish than Raffi: "Although toddlers will probably find the animation amusing, those old enough to distinguish may find the endings of some of the tales—which are generally true to the originals—quite disturbing."[91] Several of Guthrie's own children found the tales grisly, and one critic warned parents *Baby's Story Time* was "definitely not for babies."[92] But the same reviewer conceded the video "does an admirable job of retelling some old favorites, thanks largely to narrator Arlo Guthrie. Guthrie has a wonderful range of voices, from a fox's sly growl to a hen's cackle. . . . There's a sweetness and sense of comfort in the familiar tales, and Guthrie's wry, conversational voice does much to make both parents and children appreciate the stories all over again."[93]

Though no longer a constant presence on television in the 1980s, Guthrie continued to pop up every now and again. More often than not, the singer was seen in PBS re-telecasts of *The Arlo Guthrie Show* or *Pete Seeger & Arlo Guthrie: Together in Concert.* Younger viewers knew Guthrie through multiple repeats of his appearance on Jim Henson's *The Muppet Show,* singing songs with a cast of puppets . . . and being caught in a compromising embrace with Miss Piggy. But in September of '89, in the wake of the *Woodstock* anniversary mania, it had become increasingly easy to catch Guthrie on the tube.

On 5 September the singer was a guest on TNN's *Nashville Now* cable program. Then, only a few nights later, Guthrie was one of several Woodstock veterans featured on the CBS program *Woodstock: Return to the Planet of the '60s.* The latter wasn't well constructed, unnecessarily marred by interlaced pseudo-hippie comedy bits. The program's saving grace was its inclusion of several "lost songs" from the '69 festival. A *Daily News* critic echoed the sentiments of many interested only in the music: "What's annoying about the musical presentation is that two of the most interesting songs, Arlo Guthrie's 'Walkin' Down the Line' and Jimi Hendrix's 'Star-Spangled Banner' are truncated so severely they're suggestions more than songs."[94]

Guthrie's 1989 tour would come to its more or less official conclusion with two Thanksgiving concerts at Carnegie Hall. One tabloid suggested, "There are three things in life that you can count on—death, taxes, and Arlo Guthrie's annual appearance at Carnegie Hall around Thanksgiving time each year."[95] The Carnegie solo shows of 1989 were constructed similarly to 1988's program. One review mused, "On Friday (the first of two nights), Guthrie was so dependable he duplicated his show of last year, song for song. But since music is only part of an evening with Arlo Guthrie, the song selection is not what matters."[96]

This was essentially true, as many enjoyed the shaggy-dog stories nearly as much as the music. But it was also true that the running times of Guthrie's between-song monologues were beginning to exceed the musical segments. This was acknowledged by one *New York Times* critic: "At Friday night's concert, Mr. Guthrie spent more time talking than he did singing and playing. . . . To his credit, Mr. Guthrie is a polished raconteur, a kind of post-hippie, East-coast folk-answer to Garrison Keillor. But he is also a superb folksinger from whom one could have wanted a bit more music and a bit less rambling, no matter how amusing."[97]

Circulating bootleg tapes confirmed a preponderance of what the *Daily News* called Guthrie's "stream-of-consciousness" ramblings.[98] This trait was something of a family inheritance—though not every critic realized it at the time. In 2002 a live recording of a Woody Guthrie performance from New Jersey's Fuld Hall in 1949 was issued on CD as *The Live Wire*. Nearly half of that recording consisted of Woody's spoken asides, his wife Marjorie gamely attempting to coax her husband to move on to the next song. The occasional complaint from the audience "to sing something" was not uncommon at an Arlo Guthrie concert. It was a "suggestion" the folksinger would hear—and address—from the very beginning of his career. During his residency at Gerdes Folk City in 1965, a drunk catcalled, "Don't talk. Play music." Guthrie answered, "Everything's music."[99]

Most folks accepted Guthrie's on-stage loquaciousness as a genetic inheritance. Shortly after the Carnegie show, he conceded he was, for lack of a better word, "compelled" to tell stories. Guthrie suggested his style of stagecraft was likely inspired by his admiration for the Weavers and, especially, the dry, shaggy-dog tales spun by Lee Hays. The Weavers, Guthrie reminisced, "used to talk or tell jokes between songs, and I found that really nice, almost as like they were speaking to you personally in the audience, not just going on stage with a bunch of rehearsed songs."[100]

Guthrie's performance style was, from the very start, low-key and unassuming. He was rarely announced to the stage with show-biz flourish: he mostly ambled out unannounced, asking how everybody was doing. It was deceptively easygoing, but his performances were thoughtfully considered. Guthrie's style was conversational, one bridging the invisible divide between artist and audience. Even in such a grand setting as cavernous Carnegie Hall, Guthrie could conjure an intimate, living-room feel.

Guthrie had written his own program notes for the 1989 Carnegie Hall booklet. He suggested even the closest of friends should not be thought of as monolithic in their personal worldviews:

> My personal life is somewhat of a mystery to me. Although it's fun to be mysterious at times, it isn't always convenient. People want to know what you are, as if it made some kind of difference. Lots of people want to have something special in common with folksingers. They'd like to share their views on religion, pollution, nuclear power, human rights, truth, justice, and the American way with someone who sees things the same way.
>
> I have come to the conclusion that we are one person with a few billion faces, so we can see things in a lot of different ways.[101]

Guthrie was now in year three of having taken over the Thanksgiving weekend Carnegie gig from Seeger. In doing so, he not only inherited a tradition but a good section of the elder folk singer's older—and more political-minded—audience.

A few weeks prior to the Carnegie concerts, history was in the making. The German Democratic Republic had been engaged in an internal political crisis spiraling out of control. On 9 November 1989, and scrambling to hang on to power, the Communist government took the unprecedented step of opening passage through the long-sealed Berlin Wall. The directive not only allowed its citizens to travel freely between the east and west sectors of Berlin—for the first time since 1961—but to emigrate west should they so choose.

It was the beginning of the end of the post–WWII Cold War era. Though supporters of the East German Communist Party were steadfast in their belief the discontent had been orchestrated entirely by American and West German interventions, the protests in the streets of Leipzig and elsewhere were homegrown. At the forefront of the street demonstrations were ordinary East Germans pressing for democratic rights. Their demands included the simple privilege of traveling outside of the GDR to vacation or visit with relatives and friends.

Guthrie watched the historic events unfold live on television, as did Washington bureaucrats. One night President Bush pronounced that the GDR's decision was not only a "dramatic happening for East Germany" but for the cause of freedom worldwide.[102] This was true, but there was also a lesson for US hardliners to learn. America need not support murderous right-wing generals, fund mercenaries in Latin America, or deploy the CIA to undermine "unfriendly" governments worldwide. Sometimes it was best to not act the role of the world's policeman.

At Carnegie Hall Guthrie was doing his best to explain his thoughts on the best course forward for US foreign policy: "I guess the point that I thought [Bush] missed was that everybody from the sort of 'leftist' countries. . . . Guthrie paused. "Well, it wasn't like people were streaming into the Communist nations of the world. You know what I'm getting at?"

Silence.

"No?" Guthrie tested, noting the pensive quiet. "Well, it looks like most people were trying to leave, or, at least 'lots.' What I don't get was why we are so afraid of leftist governments anywhere. Especially seeing as how they're doing these days. And all at their own expense. . . . We're not even funding that. You know what I'm saying?"[103]

In December of 1989, Guthrie confirmed that his crew had been recording all of his solo shows that year. These recordings were not meant to languish in his personal library. There were plans to go through the tapes and cobble together an album featuring the tour's best moments. While it would have been easier to record a single concert or two, Guthrie wasn't enamored with this reasonable, economic model. "With me it's not like you just record a bunch of shows and quit recording. Something good could happen anytime."[104]

There was certainly no shortage of great performances to choose from. Many of the songs featured in 1988–89 were raw, stripped-down versions of songs previously recorded. Since going solo in the spring of 1988, Guthrie had reintroduced a few neglected songs from his back-catalog, treating them to fresh, dramatic solo rearrangements: "My Front Pages," "Gypsy Davy," "Highway in the Wind," "I Ain't Got No Home," "Pretty Boy Floyd," "Victor Jara," "Coming into Los Angeles," "Key to the Highway," and "Darkest Hour," to name only a few. On the piano side, fans of Guthrie's "Shades of '89" tour were treated to nightly outings of "The Garden Song," "City of New Orleans," "Last to Leave," and "Amazing Grace." There were also occasional revisits of such old favorites as "Last Train," "Gaubi, Gaubi," "Slow Boat," and "Me and My Goose."

The only new song introduced in 1989 was Guthrie's "When a Soldier Makes It Home." It was the artist's best "protest" type song in years, one that immediately captured audiences' attention. In August of 1989 Guthrie offered the sheet music to the song in the pages of the *Rolling Blunder Review*. Not yet completely at ease with computers, the songwriter rued, "This is the first time I have tried to create sheet music to one of my songs. The process of getting it onto this format through the computer was beyond torture."[105] Guthrie dedicated the song to the veterans who had returned home without fanfare or acknowledgement—and, by extension, to the families of those serving.

January of 1990 was relatively quiet. Guthrie was considering bringing other artists to the Rising Son label, but there were no definite plans. There was some chatter that Ramblin' Jack Elliott might record for the label. Elliott allowed that Guthrie's wife, Jackie, had been at work producing a new album of his. Elliott had recently spent two weeks in the studio recording Woody Guthrie songs, accompanied by the Moody Family, bluegrass pickers from Charlotte, North Carolina. The details are a bit hazy. Elliott suggested the session was not for RSR but for the Moody's label, Lamon Records. But he also mentioned that Jackie was sending the tapes to Arlo for review. He added Guthrie wasn't particularly happy with the quality of tapes being sent him.[106]

Elliott didn't seem to be offended. He admitted he hadn't heard any of the tapes from the session and completely trusted his friend's judgement, since "Arlo is definitely the best renditioner of Woody Guthrie's songs."[107] In Guthrie's own hazy recollection, the Elliott album was likely never intended to be a RSR release. "I don't think Jackie was 'producing' Jack's record, but may have been assisting in the production," he recalled. "Normally a producer is responsible for the financial aspects of any given project. I do remember the project, but it's hazy and vague. RSR at one time did study the feasibility of having other artists on the label, but after looking into the financial liability of such an endeavor, we decided against it, choosing to only do projects with members of the family. So, there may have been some talk, but it never materialized."[108]

There was apparently interest in bringing folks outside the family onto RSR. In January of 1989, Guthrie was coy in his announcement of a Los Angeles "meeting with a mysterious character to sign a contract to produce a secret New Age album; one of those crystal-powered type meditative albums."[109] He had assigned this "new secret RSR project" the designation "LA/VDK." Eagle-eyed readers of the *Rolling Blunder Review* believed the mysterious "VDK" was an acronym for "Leslie van der Klam," a fanciful character appearing intermittently in his newsletter. But no one knew for certain. Guthrie's newsletter was, from its inception, less a promotional tool than an eccentric mélange of tour dates, recording news, recipes, memories, editorials, narrative fiction, reader's letters, and nonsense. In its pages, everything published in the *Rolling Blunder Review* was made real, even when things seemed *unreal* . . . or something like that.

The real events generated the most attention. Guthrie would pull out all the stops for the third staging of his Indian River Festival. The event, scheduled for 10 February 1990, featured an amazing lineup. Guthrie would perform, as always, but the bill was also to feature Kris Kristofferson, The Marshall Tucker Band, The Outlaws, Queen Ida, Nicollete Larsen, Rick Danko, The Brave New Tribe, The Puzzlers, Xavier, the River Rats, David Grover, and Ed Gerhard. With an asking price of $12.50 per ticket, the festival was a music lover's bargain of the century. This year the festival was cosponsored by the Pelican Island Audubon Society and the Kashi Church Foundation.[110]

Guthrie would spend most of early winter of 1990 on the road. Following Indian River, the folk singer packed his guitars and headed off on a tour taking him throughout the southeastern US. In March, he was to swing into Texas, New Mexico, and Colorado for a number of shows, many with singer-songwriter Eliza Gilkyson slotted as the opening act. The tour would then move on to the Midwest for several more concerts before moving eastward—and back home. Guthrie's 1990 shows were, as they had been the previous year, all solo gigs. Audiences settling into their seats prior to the concerts were welcomed to the sight of a bare stage, dressed only with a couple of guitars and harmonicas, an electric piano, and a barstool.

The folk singer was actually wearying of playing the role of solitary troubadour. In his teasing article "Guthrie Goes On Through Life Alone," the singer conceded he tried to coax a few musicians to help him out on this first leg of the 1990 tour but was too late in asking. "I've talked to a couple of the guys and they've made other plans. I guess I didn't get around to asking them in time for this trip."[111] Although many of the songs featured on the 1989 solo tour remained, Guthrie kept things interesting by re-introducing a few old favorites back into the shows—Mississippi John Hurt's "Creole Belle," Dylan's "Mr. Tambourine Man," "Ukulele Lady,"

"St. Louis Tickle," "Buffalo Skinners," "Oklahoma Nights," and "Can't Help Falling in Love" among them.

Guthrie also introduced a new song to his program, "Keep the Dream Alive." He had been moved to write the pensive song following the nostalgic Woodstock media storm of 1989. In nearly every interview that year, the folk singer was asked, "Arlo, what happened to the dream?" Guthrie was never certain if they understood his answer, but explained there was no single dream. Everyone who traveled to Yasgur's farm brought their own dreams with them. In one of the more intriguing lines of the song, Guthrie compared his own life course with Woody's: it was a "shared journey of a father and a son/and though at times they're different/they're still one."

The twentieth of April 1990 would mark the twentieth anniversary of the founding of Earth Day. The city of Boston was planning a special commemoration, with Guthrie asked to perform. Sitting at his computer a few days prior, the singer knocked off an intriguing essay on the subject. Past experience told him what was to expect. There would be a single-day media storm blanketing newspapers, radio, and television—all featuring interviews and commentaries by TV pundits, scientists, New Agers, astronauts, and activists. There would be town hall meetings and streams of bleak newsreels documenting "industrial waste, Los Angeles smog, New York garbage, South American rain forests (if they still exist), and heavily populated cities in Asia."[112]

Nonetheless, Earth Day served as an important ringing of the alarm. The Boston celebration was to be held at Hatch Shell on the Commons. Police and newspaper accounts estimated that nearly 200,000 people would flow through the area, listening to an afternoon of music and impassioned speechifying. Guthrie was only one of dozens of musicians on hand to offer support. Others scheduled included Livingston Taylor, Phoebe Snow, the band Treat Her Right, the Del Fuegos, and Tom Rush.[113] As the schedule was tightly scripted, Guthrie's set would last only twenty minutes and total three songs.

Guthrie could hardly have turned down the invitation to play. But he shared that while the celebration was important—attracting much needed attention to the cause of environmental issues—he recognized there were ecology-centered groups working tirelessly year-round without attention. Environmental activism had been partly taken up by musical friends, a welcoming trend. Guthrie had already staged a trio of Indian River festivals,

Don Henley was a vocal proponent of the Walden Woods preservation project, and Pete Seeger had been the central figure of Clearwater's eco-fests
since 1968. "I didn't want to get involved in so many things that were specifically Earth Day-orientated," Guthrie explained. "Because that's the
kind of thing we do all the time."[114]

All the same, Guthrie told the crowd in Boston, there was plenty of
work to do, even if only in their own backyard:

> Hey, it's fun to be here, 'cause it's so much fun for me to wel-
> come so many people—especially the people who were up here
> before from all over the world and from all over the country—to
> the state I love the most. 'Cause the truth is, you know, it's nice to
> think about the whole world, but you got to do stuff in your own
> hometown. And if we did that all over the world, we'd find it a
> nicer place to be, I'm sure."[115]

A month later Guthrie returned to Boston Commons. On 12 May, an
unseasonably cold and windy Saturday afternoon, Guthrie was to perform at a benefit supporting "freedom and human rights in China and
Tibet." The event was organized by Harvard's Kennedy School of Government, with fellow students from Boston University, Boston College, Mt.
Holyoke, and other area colleges attending in solidarity. One organizer
promised, "The concert would celebrate non-violence in bringing about
reform, and . . . encourage the re-initiation of dialogue in China."[116]

The date of 12 May was not chosen at random. One year earlier, 13
May 1989, university students from China's capitol city had begun a
mass hunger strike to protest government corruption, the lack of free
speech, joblessness, and human rights abuses. This very public protest
in Tiananmen Square caused great embarrassment to the government.
The protests were planned to coincide with the 15 May visit to Peking of
Soviet premier Mikhail Gorbachev. With sympathetic supporters pouring
into Tiananmen Square, the meeting with the Soviet delegation was hastily moved to the airport and martial law was declared on 20 May. The Red
Army brought in some 250,000 troops to put down disturbances. By early
June more than one million protestors had gathered in the square, tanks
and troops moving in soon after to disperse crowds. The military's cleans-
ing would lead to the killing of hundreds and the arrests of ten thousand
citizens.

Taking the stage at the Boston Teach-In, Guthrie wasn't sure what songs to sing, what words to say, or how he could help:

> I was thinking on my way here. There's a Professor [Robert] Thurman who lives out—or used to live out—sort of nearer to where I live. I was listening to a tape of his, to a talk he was giving the other day, talking about a world that spends most of its money when it's talking about defense and stuff like that. Or people whose job it is to go around and knock off other people . . . or tell 'em what to do or control them in some way. And how in places like Tibet there are whole armies that are supported by the people. Whose main job it is to create an atmosphere of peace and love and stuff like that. Armies of monks, walking around or living somewhere, or just gentle people.
>
> And I guess when I was thinking about what it is that I could say, that I could do myself, what it is that I could suggest that we begin to do here is to think we need herds of people whose main job it is to be peaceful. And that means we have to support them. And I don't care if they're monks or they're not or just average people walking around. And somehow or other, wouldn't it be nice to have herds—flocks—of us walking around, allowing ourselves and everybody else to live in the world and create a place.
>
> Not over in China, because we don't live there—at least most of us. And not over in Tibet or over in Eastern Europe but right here in town. Where there's a lot of people in trouble all the time. They don't know what to do. They don't know how to be peaceful. They don't know how to just relax and enjoy each other's company and stuff, I guess. That's something we could do for each other, right now.
>
> And it would be a good idea to start to think that when you do that you add that dimension to the world. That's something each individual can do. You can't do it as a herd, you can't do it as a group. Nobody can tell you as a flock which way to fly. That's something only each person can do for themselves. And when you do that, you add that to the world.[117]

In a day filled with angry speeches, Guthrie thought it best to remain optimistic. But in the days following the rally on the Commons, Guthrie seriously discussed the political implications of the China/Tibet situation in a commentary published in the *Rolling Blunder Review*. In an unusually bristling essay, Guthrie charged "the situation in both countries has been worsened by the lack of a uniform policy from leaders in western nations."[118] He cited how the West's sanctions imposed on apartheid South Africa "produced some movement (although not nearly enough)," wondering aloud why a similar strategy had not been implemented to address China's human rights violations:

> The arguments suggest that Black South Africans are better able to endure the hardships that would certainly result from such economic sanctions, than are their Asian neighbors. This policy seems, at the very least, racist, and at the most, inconsistent with the wishes of those who have to endure them.
>
> Media coverage of events in Tibet has been relatively nonexistent. China, for example, has recently proposed "self-determination" for the people of Tibet. That's great, until you realize that China has poured more of her own people into Tibet than were there to begin with. There are more Chinese in Tibet than there are Tibetans. One can only speculate as to who will be the determiners.[119]

If the Chinese government wasn't happy dealing with outside agitators, local groups of Massachusetts-based land developers and politicians weren't pleased about dealing with troublemakers *they* deemed outsiders. Chief among the troublemakers was the musician Don Henley, a founder of California's soft-rock band The Eagles. Henley was against developers' plans to construct an office park and condominium complex on the edge of Walden Woods.

Henley, a noted activist in antinuclear and environmental causes, had chanced to learn about the Walden Woods development plan while watching a CNN television segment. One of the singer's heroes was the man deemed "the father of the modern environmental movement," Henry David Thoreau.[120] Thoreau, a revered naturalist-poet-transcendentalist, was, inarguably, the Woods' most notable past resident. Thoreau had famously written about the quiet splendors of the area in his 1854 work *Walden*. The ambitious construction plans of developers were mutually unwelcomed by historians, environmentalists, and admirers of Thoreau's works.

The backlash against the plan kicked up a very public bit of dust. Henley was dismissed as a meddler in affairs of no local import to him. Walden Woods was in candidacy for protective inclusion on the National Register of Historic Places. With such designation not yet having been conferred, Henley was pressing for acknowledgement of such, preferably sooner than later. It wasn't only the developers and local government officials who were angry with Henley's protestations. Even those with established liberal *bona fides* reprimanded protestors for not considering how construction of affordable housing units might assist the area's working poor.

Others argued that Walden Woods was not the idyllic, secluded retreat it had been in 1845–47. Walden Pond had long since been subdivided by both a multilane highway and a trailer park. The location of the small cabin in which Thoreau lived now sat adjacent to a garbage dump. The *Wall Street Journal* was cynical of the protest, suggesting, "More than a few locals think it's a bit ironic that jet-setting stars are claiming kinship with the frugal Mr. Thoreau."[121] The article suggested the protest was a smoke screen for the residents of neighboring Concord to keep out the "undesirables" an affordable housing complex might attract.

Undeterred by such criticism, Henley pressed forward, scheduling two benefit concerts at Worcester's Centrum. The second program of 25 April featured a reunion of former Eagles Henley, Glen Frey, and Timothy B. Schmidt, along with Bob Seger, Jimmy Buffett, Bonnie Raitt, and Arlo Guthrie. Guthrie opened the three-hour-long concert with a "pair of folk tunes"—as per a newspaper account—before exiting after his performance of "Massachusetts." Guthrie teased he was leverage against the "outsider" criticisms leveled against Henley and others. "The organizers were looking for a little localness . . . I guess that's me," he opined.[122] Guthrie would also contribute an essay to *Heaven Is Under Our Feet: A Book for Walden Pond* (Stamford, CT: Longmeadow Press, 1991).

Guthrie's summer tour would prove to be a half-vacation of sorts, responsible only for delivering half an evening's program. Though there was a smattering of solo concerts June through August, more often than not Guthrie would share the stage with Pete Seeger on summer's front end, with John Prine on summer's back end. There was never a need to rehearse a program with Seeger. Their tandem concerts had long been free-form affairs:

AG: On February 24th, 1974, I went to visit Pete in Beacon, New York, at Harold's insistence we rehearse for upcoming shows. Harold just didn't really understand how Pete and I worked. Pete would often say, "Arlo! You never want to over-rehearse." I whole-heartedly agreed. I loved the spontaneity Pete and I brought to the stage. But, nevertheless I went to spend a few days with Pete and we goofed off playing and singing together, while Toshi [Pete's wife] provided sustenance. We never got around to what would even remotely be considered a rehearsal.

When Guthrie first formally toured with Seeger in 1974, the revered folk singer was just shy of fifty-five years of age. Pete Seeger was now seventy years old. Though he had semiretired from touring, this only meant he had cut down on his inexhaustible globe-trotting. Seeger was content to stay close to his home on the banks of the Hudson, crewing with the sloop *Clearwater* and singing in support of environmental and political causes in his own backyard. "Think Globally, Act Locally," had been Seeger's mantra since returning from a controversial visit to North Vietnam in 1972.

Time had not diminished Seeger's interest in radical politics, though he posited he was now an advocate of gradualism rather than revolution. He traveled to Nicaragua in both 1983 and 1988 to show solidarity with the leftist Sandinista government that deposed US-backed dictator Anastasio Somoza in 1979. In concerts back home, the folk singer made sure to teach audiences several songs—in gringo Spanish—that he picked up on his visits to Latin America. But Seeger was aware there were also things to do at home. Even though he fretted that his voice wobbled and his hands were no longer dexterous, Seeger continued to crisscross the country and perform at benefits for righteous causes. Seeger explained his summer shows with Arlo Guthrie were his only "proper" concert tour dates and, for the most part, the only paying ones. Seeger was aware his concerts with Guthrie enabled him to engage the hearts and minds of a big audience. "I'm used to singing for only a few hundred people," the folk singer mulled. "But now when I go on tour with Arlo Guthrie, we play at huge fairs with 20,000 to 30,000 people watching."[123]

Music critics reared on pop music were not always conversant with Seeger's place in history. Those in non-accord or openly hostile to Seeger's leftist politics often unfairly sharpened their poison pens when Seeger and

Guthrie visited town. The previous summer, one critic rued, "Pete Seeger turned 70 this year and, alas, his age shows. . . . The edge and melody to his voice has sagged."[124] Others suggested those who turned out had only purchased tickets to catch Guthrie's set, as Seeger was now an aged relic of a time out of mind. Others, with a better sense of history and performance art, noted Seeger possessed a rare gift. He could easily engage young listeners with his music, even put them at ease: "With his nonchalant, avuncular manner, Seeger made singing along seem the most natural thing in the world."[125]

In the summer of 1990 Guthrie would also share the stage with new friends. The band Xavier, featuring Abe Guthrie on keyboards, Randy Cormier on bass, and Tim Sears on guitar, was formed in 1984. Like any startup rock band—and they definitely were a *rock* band—Xavier initially played local gigs, performing at high-school events and all-age shows. In 1984, Abe and his friends were around fifteen or sixteen years of age. In early 1990, this earliest configuration of Xavier passed into history when Cormier moved on. Abe's abilities on the keyboard had blossomed during this period. The absence of Cormier's bass forced Abe to refine a steady left hand on his keyboard since *someone* had to cover the bass lines. It was a skill that would serve him well in coming years, even if its importance was missed at the time. In any event, Cormier's departure might have signaled the end of the band had a new opportunity not presented itself.

In July and August of 1990, Guthrie was to set off, for a second time, on a US cobill tour with singer-songwriter John Prine. In announcing the tour with Prine, the folk singer offered in his newsletter, "Mr. Guthrie has been threatening to bring Xavier, the rock and rollster band of which his son, Abe, is a partner in crime. They have been working up some tunes together for a different occasion and may be interested in pursuing life on the road during the month of July. Mr. Guthrie thought that it might be a nice way of introducing the youngsters to his audience, some of whom may be in the same age group."[126]

The band with whom Guthrie would work wasn't Xavier as originally constituted but, as recollected by the folk singer, a hybrid of Xavier and "a couple of local bands. Abe and Tim were still there, but they had added Darren Todd, Jason Webster, and Jason McConnell. Sean Hurley and Darren switched back and forth as bass players. I had fun with these guys immediately. It was great seeing them on the first tour when they realized that people were sitting there listening to them. No one ever did that before. It was usually high school kids jumping around with nothing in mind other than high school kids jumping around."[127]

Besides being a great opportunity for Xavier, the change also afforded Guthrie the chance to front a rock 'n' roll band again. It had been almost two years since he decided to go the solo folk singer route. So his gigs with Xavier offered a fresh, vibrant energy to his upcoming stage shows. Guthrie also had the opportunity to reintroduce songs from his back-catalog that brightened with a brisk folk-rock backing.

Guthrie and Xavier were scheduled to play Nashville's Jackson Hall in August. Prior to the show, the singer was asked to weigh in on the Recording Industry Association of America's tangle with aggrieved moralists. The music industry was pressed to agree that any pop music lyric featuring "explicit" content (sex, violence, drugs, etc.) must carry a parental warning sticker. Rap and heavy metal were the primary targets of such industry self-censorship. One problem with the RIAA's capitulation was the question of what an "explicit" lyric actually *was*. If every song referencing sex, violence, drugs, or alcohol—regardless of genre—needed to carry a warning label, a *lot* of stickers would need to be affixed.

Such censorship was hardly new—and Guthrie was an early victim of it. In spring 1971, a Philadelphia disc jockey was fired for playing Guthrie's "Coming into Los Angeles," the song accused of "celebrating" the smuggling of drugs into the country. Station's owners fretted over losing their broadcast licenses due to an FCC ruling that radio stations were obligated to "pre-screen records with lyrics tending to promote or glorify illegal drug use."[128] Brewer and Shipley's "One Toke Over the Line" was also pulled from rotation, as were others directly or indirectly referencing drug use. The Tipper Gore–led movement to brand certain music as unwholesome seemed censorship pure and simple. Guthrie mocked the RIAA's capitulation: "The fact that people can spend their time thinking about all that stuff when there are disasters going on all around us is kind of silly, I think. The fear of music is more harmful than bad music."[129]

Following the conclusion of his tour with John Prine, Guthrie was summoned to attend a champagne luncheon organized by the Walden Woods Project. On the afternoon of 13 August, the group gathered to celebrate the National Trust for Historic Preservation decision to recognize Walden

Woods as an endangered site. A press conference was called to announce a tentative deal involving the purchase of a twenty-five-acre parcel of Walden Woods.

The deal included the provision that the construction of the affordable housing units—a very big sticking point—would go forward, possibly to an area three-quarters of a mile from the original site. The land purchase was expensive, but everyone agreed the deal satisfactorily addressed most of everyone's concerns. Guthrie shared a toast with a host of friends who lent talents to the cause: Don Henley, Bonnie Raitt, John Hall of the band Orleans, Aimee Mann, and Tom Scholz, the lead singer of the band Boston. They were joined at their "Victory Picnic" by a gaggle of environmental activists and sympathetic politicians. Guthrie told *USA Today* the Walden victory was an important one: "There are very few people who understand what it means to be human. Thoreau had the courage to delve into those mysteries."[130]

That same August, there was, again, no shortage of media coverage of the Woodstock anniversary, but the festival's twenty-first anniversary wasn't as exhaustively trumpeted as it had been a year earlier. On 15 August 1990—twenty-one years to the day of his 1969 appearance at the festival—Guthrie returned to Bethel to perform a "clandestine concert" organized by singer-songwriter Will Hoppey.[131] Three thousand pilgrims in tents and campers gathered on the fringes of Max Yasgur's farm to soak up music and vibes and resurrect spirits of the past. That afternoon Xavier played a couple of songs on the makeshift stage, with Guthrie joining in soon afterward and playing an hour-long set of his own. There was no media attention, no promoters looking to make a fast buck, no media hoopla surrounding the intimate commemoration. Walking off-stage, Guthrie reacted, "It's been some day. The whole of '69 happened again today."[132]

If the small Woodstock gathering brought a warm glow to Guthrie's heart, few gigs in 1990 proved as satisfying as his visit to Denmark's Tønder Folk Festival a week later. The singer's trip to the festival would be his only European show of 1990. This year's event held the promise of being more special than ones previous. For the very first time, fans from Eastern Bloc countries were free to travel to Tønder.

If that wasn't reason enough to celebrate, Pete and Toshi Seeger and their grandson Tao Rodriguez also agreed to perform at the festival.

Seeger was a much-admired figure on both sides of the Iron Curtain. In January of 1967, he was granted permission to perform concerts in both East Berlin and West Berlin, even appearing on an East German TV special. Following his visit, the state record label, Amiga, issued a variant of Seeger's *We Shall Overcome* LP in the DDR. It was a decision that would backfire on them.

The album partly caused East German teenagers to be belatedly swept up in the western folk-pop music craze—a craze on the wane elsewhere. German teenagers adopted Seeger's version of the civil-rights anthem as musical arsenal in their own struggle. Less than two months following Seeger's visit, the official Communist Party newspaper *Neues Deutschland* railed against the adoption of "We Shall Overcome" "as a sort of hymn."[133] The name of the freewheeling East German Hootenanny Klub was formally changed to the *October Klub*. The newly sanctioned name was less Western in its provenance and better reflected the glories of Russia's 1917 revolution.[134]

If anyone doubted Pete Seeger was one of folk music's most beloved performers, it was soon made evident when he and Guthrie took the stage at Tønder. In the years following the concert, Guthrie recalled their appearance at Tønder as one of the most memorable of his career. Seeger, Rodriguez, and Guthrie wove a musical spell that still conjures chills when viewed today (blessedly, a good portion of their set was filmed and broadcast on Denmark television).

The finale of the evening's concert was to conclude with the entire cast of performers on stage, Guthrie taking the lead on the old Carter Family classic "Will the Circle Be Unbroken?" That song should have brought things to a fitting close, but after the stage was cleared the audience simply refused to leave their seats. Without prompting, the audience spontaneously began to sing "We Shall Overcome," the crowd swaying back and forth as they sang the old civil rights–era song to an empty stage. Suddenly Pete Seeger, the man who brought the song to Europe during his 1960s travels, poked his head out from the wings. He made his way to Guthrie's electric piano, silently sat down on the bench and began to chord along. In short order, the entire cast slowly reassembled onto the stage and joined in with the audience's singing on the chorus. It was goose pimple time. It was 1963 again.

When Guthrie returned home to the U.S., he discovered fewer folks were in residence at home. Daughter Cathy had headed off to attend college in San Diego, Annie to school in Florida. Abe too was soon to depart, preparing to go on a club tour of the South with Xavier. Guthrie was scheduled to fly to Barstow, California, where a crew was filming the theatrical feature *Roadside Prophets*. The film was to be written and directed by Abbe Wool, a cowriter of the edgy biographical drama *Sid and Nancy*. That 1986 film documented the stormy, doomed relationship between Sex Pistol's bassist Sid Vicious and his girlfriend Nancy Spungen. *Roadside Prophets* would mark Wool's first official directorial effort.

The assembled cast was an odd mix of Hollywood actors and working musicians. John Doe of the band X and Adam Horovitz of the Beastie Boys would play the film's two primary characters, two motorcyclists searching out intangibles in the deserts of Nevada. During their desert trek, the pair would meet an assortment of eccentrics: Arlo Guthrie, John Cusack, David Carradine, and Dr. Timothy Leary.

Writing in the third person, Guthrie suggested he accepted the role of gas station attendant "Harvey" since the part "was so small that he could actually memorize all of his lines on the way to the set from the motel where he will be staying. . . . I didn't actually read the script, I just read the part they asked me to do, so I can't tell what the movie is about," with the exception of "It has motorcycles and I'm like this old biker who says something."[135]

Guthrie wasn't the only one unable to explain what the film was about. Following the film's regional rollout in autumn of 1991, the *New York Times* dismissed *Roadside Prophets* as "a boys-on-bikes American odyssey drenched in an attitude of would-be hipness."[136] A critic from *Billboard* conceded while "audiences might get some chuckles from cameo appearances by such countercultural relics as Arlo Guthrie and Timothy Leary . . . in the end *Roadside Prophets* delivers tame comedy, feeble drama, and no payoff."[137]

Most reviews were middle-of-the-road in appraisal, though many mocked the film for its "self-conscious existentialism" and "hip-absurdism."[138] The film was mostly written off as a time-waster of middling interest, dismissed as a poor man's successor to *Easy Rider*. Some critics were less sparing. The most damning review came courtesy of the *Los Angeles Times:* "For those who doubted it, the reality of *Roadside Prophets* is that the '60s are officially dead."[139]

January 9, 1999: Guthrie enjoys a two-week New Year's break at Mokuleia, HI, before flying to Scotland for the *Celtic Connections* concert at Glasgow's Royal Concert Hall. Photo by Jackie Guthrie, author's collection.

Wandering the streets of Gallup, NM, prior to a concert at the El Morro Theatre. February 4, 1999. Photo by Arlo Guthrie, author's collection.

With Willie Nelson at the "Arlo Guthrie & Friends: Ridin' on the City of New Orleans" Hurricane Katrina relief benefit at Tipitina's, New Orleans, LA, December 17, 2005. Photo by John Claeys.

On the road to Durango.
The Guthrie Family Legacy
tour. Durango, CO, May 5,
2007. Photo by Arlo Guthrie,
author's collection.

"Kid, I want you to go over and sit down on that bench that says Group W."
The Guthrie Family Legacy Tour, Ft. Lewis College Community Center,
Durango, CO, May 6, 2007. Photo by John Claeys.

Performing at the Woody Guthrie Folk Festival's "Pastures of Plenty" stage, Okemah, OK, July 14, 2007—Woody's 95th birthday. Photo by John Claeys.

Backstage at Okemah, Oklahoma's Woody Guthrie Folk Festival, July 14, 2007. Photo by Henry Diltz.

Enjoying a cup of coffee prior to sound check at the Wortham Center for the Performing Arts, Asheville, NC. February 15, 2008. Photo by Amelia Burns.

On the piano. Sherman Theater, Stroudsburg, PA, November 9, 2008. Photo by John Claeys.

Sherman Theater, Stroudsburg, PA, November 9, 2008. Photo by John Claeys.

A performance with Keith Lockhart and the Boston Symphony Orchestra. Bethel Woods Center for the Arts, Bethel, NY, August 22, 2009. Photo by John Claeys.

At home in Washington, MA, May 17, 2010. A brush-up before his performance with the Boston Pops at Symphony Hall the following night. Photo by Arlo Guthrie, author's collection.

Guthrie in formal attire feeling "like a penguin." Preparing for an upscale meal during a transatlantic sail on the Queen Mary 2. New York to Southampton, England, July 23, 2010. Photo by Arlo Guthrie, author's collection.

With Judy Collins. Sharing a laugh during the first show of their post-Thanksgiving co-bill tour of 2011. Union County Performing Arts Center, Rahway, NJ, November 27, 2011. Photo by John Claeys.

Pondering a pint at "The Nines," Queen's Arms Pub, South Kensington, London, January 3, 2012. Photo by Jamie Burton.

"My Old Friend." Visiting Izzy Young at the Folklore Centrum, Stockholm, Sweden. January 12, 2012. Photo by Marti Guthrie.

Guthrie arrives in Bergen, Norway, January 23, 2012. The midpoint of his solo "Scandinavian Winter Adventure Tour." Photo by Marti Guthrie.

With Pete Seeger on stage at Clearwater's Great Hudson River Revival, June 16, 2012. Photo by John Claeys.

In need of roadside assistance. A flat tire strands Guthrie and singer-songwriter Jess Klein on their autumn tour of Ireland, September 2012. Photo by Marti Guthrie.

On the road from Mullaghmore Harbour to Sligo, Ireland. At the Pier Head Hotel. January 20, 2013. Photo by Marti Guthrie.

Trying to keep warm prior to the final show of the "Here Comes the Kid" tour leg at the Hawk's Well Theatre, Sligo, Ireland. January 22, 2013. Photo by Marti Guthrie.

With Pete Seeger and Abe Guthrie. The final Guthrie & Seeger Thanksgiving concert at Carnegie Hall, November 30, 2013. Photo by John Claeys.

"Kids, this piece of paper's got forty-seven words, thirty-seven sentences . . ." The Alice's Restaurant 50th Anniversary Tour, Berklee Performing Arts Center, Boston, MA, October 9, 2015. Photo by John Claeys.

Afternoon sound check break on the Alice's Restaurant 50th Anniversary Tour. O'Shaughnessy Auditorium, St. Paul, MN, October 25, 2015. Photo by Marti Guthrie.

A man and his motorcycle: Earl's Hideaway Lounge, on the banks of the Indian River, Sebastian, FL, March 10, 2017. Photo by Marti Guthrie.

Not so "Hard Travelin'." A folk singer and his touring buses. Key West, FL, January 26, 2018. Photo by Marti Guthrie.

Taking a brief respite in Mokuleia, HI, the middle of the first leg of the winter/spring "Re: Generation" tour. April 25, 2018. Photo by Marti Guthrie.

Picking on the ornate Gibson J-200 Vine at Nashville's CMA Theater during the early winter leg of the "Alice's Restaurant—Back By Popular Demand" tour. February 13, 2019. Photo by Eric Brown.

Resting in Mokuleia, HI, April 4, 2019, prior to bringing the "Alice's Restaurant— Back By Popular Demand" tour to Australia. Photo by Marti Guthrie.

August 15, 2019: "The spot you're standing, it's Holy Ground" (Woody Guthrie). Arlo visits the original site of the Woodstock festival, Bethel, NY, fifty years to the day of his 1969 performance there. Photo by Marti Guthrie.

★ ★ ★ ★ ★

Chapter Five

SON OF THE WIND, 1991–1993

F ollowing the success of Guthrie's 1989 summer odyssey, plans were in the making for a second adventure. In the summer of 1990 *Rolling Blunder Review* subscribers were advised to keep their calendars clear because a "Blunderman's Fabulous Adventure II" was in the works. This planned January 1991 tour would take Guthrie and a busload of "Blunderites" on a "Holy Land Pilgrimage." Visits to Tel Aviv, Haifa, Mt. Carmel, the biblical city of Acco, the Dead Sea, Jericho, Bethlehem, and Jerusalem were scheduled, with an optional extension to press on to neighboring Egypt. This second adventure was to be something of a family affair. The trip was organized by Jack Hyde, Guthrie's father-in-law, with family members onboard. Fans interested in making the pilgrimage would depart Miami for Israel on 6 January 1991.[1]

But plans were scuttled when Iraq annexed neighboring Kuwait in August of 1990, the invasion meeting with swift international condemnation. *Operation Desert Shield,* a multinational coalition of military troops, assembled in the Persian Gulf. As late as November of 1990, Guthrie counseled readers the pilgrimage was still on despite the fact that "events in the Middle East have changed fairly dramatically in recent months."[2] He was too optimistic. On 29 November 1990, the UN Security Council demanded that Iraq remove its troops from Kuwait. Should they disregard the warning, coalition forces would employ "all necessary means" to expel them. With tensions ratcheting up, Guthrie cancelled his participation. On 16 January 1991, *Operation Desert Storm* was inaugurated, and the US-led coalition began carrying out intensive bombing sorties on Iraqi cities and military targets.

Guthrie was at the CrabHouse, watching television as the bombs rained on Tehran. Though uncomfortable seeing US troops used to protect "someone else's interests"—many believing the US was putting the

interests of oil companies and dynastic, antidemocratic Saudi Arabia above
all else—Guthrie chose to focus on the soldiers called to fight. "We had
to learn a big lesson in Vietnam," Guthrie reasoned, "that we need to support those people who are in the Middle East even if we disagree with the
policy."[3]

With cable channels broadcasting war news 24/7, Guthrie "wondered
with sorrow how newspapers and TV networks could get swept up into
the whirlwind of military scenarios so exclusively." It wasn't that the war in
the Middle East was not an important story, but it was hardly the *only* story
worthy of coverage. "Around the entire globe millions of men and women
are still living with AIDS, millions of children are still starving," Guthrie
offered. He sighed that the war coverage was so suffocating that other cases
of human suffering were receiving "almost no media attention at all."[4]

Guthrie was in Florida organizing the fourth annual Indian River Festival. A day prior to the benefit, he received word Silvio Ottavio Conte, a
sixteen-term Republican member of the US House of Representatives, had
passed at age sixty-nine. Some of Guthrie's friends on the Left were con-
fused by the singer's admiration for the former Republican senator from
Pittsfield, Massachusetts. But Conte had served as one of the more liberal-
minded Republicans in the House. He broke with the GOP in his opposition
to the war in Vietnam and had only recently voted against US involvement in
the Gulf War. Conte was also an important champion of Marjorie Guthrie's
fundraising efforts on behalf of Huntington's research.[5]

In 1968 Guthrie had been approached by Conte's office, asking if he
might assist in his candidacy. Guthrie agreed to help out Conte's reelection
bid since the senator "had been wonderfully helpful with my Mom." Guthrie reminisced that Conte was "the only Republican I ever did anything
for, much to the chagrin of a lot of people [for whom politics had] become
a way of life and who could not understand how a young folk singer could
be supporting a Republican candidate—especially in the late '60s and
early '70s."[6]

Guthrie provided a few radio spots to promote Conte's campaign, but
the two men remained friends for the next two decades. "Whatever he said
he was going to do, he did. And if he couldn't do it, he would say so," Guthrie recalled. The singer admitted to not being a fan of "blind ideology."
"The counterculture had their own agenda," Guthrie conceded, "and
supporting Republican candidates was not part of that agenda, no matter

what their record was."[7] Conte was a GOP maverick, reviled by many on the Right due to his willingness to allocate funds for social programs benefitting "healthcare, housing, scholarship funding, and home heating assistance."[8] He was one of the good guys.

The Indian River Festival was scheduled for the weekend of 9–10 February at the County Fairgrounds outside Vero Beach. In a significant change, Guthrie resigned from the festival's board of directors. He asked Paul Smith, his booking agent, to take over the responsibilities of organizing the event. The endless grind of touring, of building Rising Son Records, of acquiring his back-catalog, of writing and editing the *Rolling Blunder Review,* of converting the CrabHouse into a second home and recording studio—all were taxing, time-consuming, and *expensive.* Looking over his portfolio, Guthrie sighed, "I need another *Alice's Restaurant—real* soon."[9]

"I loved working with everyone [on the festival], but there's only so many creative moments in each day," Guthrie explained, "and I've spent them on getting things started. Now, there are very capable friends who can take it from here, so I can get back to thinking weird thoughts and playing music."[10] The plan to make the Indian River Festival a two-day weekend affair (à la Seeger's Great Hudson River Revival) was scrubbed. The festival would be staged only on a single day. This year's edition would be particularly attractive in that it would feature two heavy-hitters: Don Henley of the Eagles and Michael McDonald of the Doobie Brothers.

Henley's involvement was a favor returned for Guthrie's assistance in the battle to save Walden Woods. McDonald was a longtime friend, Guthrie having even contributed a bit of autoharp to the Doobie Brother's 1974 Warner Bros. album *What Were Once Vices Are Now Habits.* McDonald was hesitant to sign on to play benefits. It wasn't always clear to him where the money was *really* going. But he expressed confidence this wouldn't be the case here. "I know that Arlo is a forthright guy and his heart is in the right place," McDonald explained. "If he is involved with the project, there won't be any surprises. You have to be very careful."[11]

Guthrie was to close out the festival with Xavier backing. Expectations were high. The previous year's benefit brought in 8,000 music fans, raising nearly $25,000 dollars for the Pelican Island Audubon Society and the Kashi Foundation. Kashi was founded in 1976 as a 501(c)(3) nonprofit by Ma Jaya Sati Bhagavati. Guthrie believed it was important to contribute to Kashi because "We've got a plague going on and people need to be educated about the fact that there are people who are dying, people who need to know someone cares without making a judgement."[12] In the days leading up to the festival, the board was confident this year's event would attract some 15,000 fans.

The weather, however, wouldn't cooperate. Morning temperatures were in the high 40s and rose in painfully slow increments. Though the festival did attract 15,000 fans, the box-office wasn't reflective of the turn-out. Guthrie chose to focus on the positives, describing the festival as "wonderfully successful." "We didn't make much money, but we didn't lose any either. We did make a lot of people happy, and folks are more aware of the environmental state of things than they were before the festival took place."[13] Guthrie was scheduled to go on directly following Henley, but there was an hour-long gap between sets. "In an effort to leave quickly," Guthrie reminisced, Henley's roadies "unplugged everything that looked like it might be attached to something important."[14] The entire stage had to be rewired for Guthrie and Xavier, the long delay and plummeting temperatures causing many to fold their lawn chairs early.

That February Guthrie played a handful of solo shows in the southeastern US, before reteaming with Xavier for an extensive month-and-a-half-long tour of the West. Tickets to those shows, mostly held in theaters and large clubs, were moving quickly, selling out completely, or falling just short of doing so. One exception was Guthrie's shows at the famed Troubadour nightclub on Los Angeles's Sunset Strip. The Troubadour rarely hosted established or up-and-coming singer-songwriter types anymore, as it had in the past. The club now catered to younger audiences interested in heavy metal, and most of these bands were booked as "pay-to-play" acts, required to sell a predetermined number of tickets if they expected remuneration for their performance.

As the Troubadour's glory days were clearly in the rearview mirror, the club had mostly ceased taking out advertisements in the newspapers. As such, there was practically no press given to Guthrie's return to Los Angeles in the city's weeklies or dailies. Though Guthrie's box-office value went well beyond a "pay-to-play" scenario, he'd joke that this practice might actually have helped sell tickets this go-round, all three shows being, in his words, "painfully under-attended."[15] The brightest moment came when distant cousin Hoyt Axton climbed onto the stage and sang his "Joy to the World," a huge hit for Three Dog Night in 1971.

If this recent visit to the Troubadour was disappointing, the nightclub itself would forever remain special in memory:

AG: In March of 1969, I flew out to the West Coast and met with Van Dyke Parks as he was going to help produce the first album of mine to be recorded without the oversight of Fred or Harold. It was a break from the New York scene and allowed me to experiment in the recording studio.

My girlfriend Caroly flew out to meet me on the 19th, and on the 21st we began recording *Running Down the Road*. It was a sonic departure from anything I'd previously done, and I had some of the finest LA musicians to work with. When Caroly and I returned to New York, we broke up and she moved out of my apartment April 1st. We remained great friends afterward, but we just weren't meant to be a couple.

John Pilla, Gary Sherman, and I began the recording sessions for the soundtrack to the "Alice's Restaurant" film in late April. At the same time I began fixing the vocal recordings for the film—looping. Both the soundtrack and looping continued throughout May at various studios in New York.

By June 3rd we began mixing the soundtrack for the record in Los Angeles. Then, on the 5th, I began a week stint at the Troubadour. I was accompanied on the trip by my brother by marriage, Richard Cooper. Richard's father, Lou Cooper, had married my mother. Richard and I had become quite close and, as a matter of fact, the very first voice in the "Alice's Restaurant" movie you hear is Richard's.

Richard was in the dressing room at the Troubadour, when Jackie Hyde walked in. I was onstage doing my thing. Jackie heard that I was Woody's kid, which, to her, meant Woody Allen. And that I had written a "Motorcycle Song." So she assumed I was a biker . . . who was Woody Allen's son. Nonetheless, Jackie looked at Richard and said "I'm going to marry your brother."

My stay at the Troubadour was extended beyond a week as Neil Young had to cancel his expected appearance. I played there for another week. When I left Los Angeles, I took Jackie with me. We had fallen in love and wanted to be together. She left her job at the Troubadour although she would remain friends with owner Doug Weston until he passed away decades later.

I had to get back to New York for Pete Seeger's first fundraiser for the Clearwater project, a wooden sloop that he envisioned would sail up and down the Hudson River and act as a focal point for his efforts at cleaning up the river. The event was called The Hudson Valley Folk Picnic.

Guthrie's visit to Los Angeles in March 1991 was less memorable than his 1969 experience. Following the Troubadour shows, the folk singer developed what he thought was nothing more than a seasonal cold. But the cold stayed with him for the next several weeks, and when the tour hit Seattle, the bug had not diminished. So he decided to visit a Seattle walk-in clinic and have his swollen glands checked out. Though it was confirmed he was suffering from an aggressive cold, he also learned the stabs of lower-body pain he had been experiencing for "some seven or eight years" were the result of a ruptured hernia. Recalling his hospitalization in Vancouver in1981, Guthrie once again blamed this recent medical issue on the "Curse of the Northwest."[16]

Guthrie had not been feeling well when he visited Oakland's Scottish Rite Temple a few weeks earlier. He had been a participant in "Reaching Out," one of ten sessions administered by Ram Dass. Ram Dass (the term means "Servant of God)" was the former Richard Alpert, a Harvard-expelled psychedelic drug coresearcher and friend of Timothy Leary. Ram Dass studied under the tutelage of guru Neem Karoli Baba, a devotee of the Hindu deity Hanuman. Ram Dass was a well-known public figure, achieving success authoring books on spiritual matters: his 1971 book "Be Here Now" would ultimately sell some two million copies. Dass had studied in the mid-1970s with Guthrie's own guru Ma Jaya Sati Bhagavati, though teacher and student would later have a falling out.

Guthrie thought it "unbelievable" that he and Ram Dass had not met previously considering they shared spiritual interests and mutual friends.[17] Guthrie was one of several musicians asked to play a few songs at the seminars. Peter Gabriel, Bob Weir, Rob Wasserman, and Bobby ("Don't Worry, Be Happy") McFerrin also dropped by to provide a measure of meditative music. Many of the sessions were featured in the documentary film *Ram Dass: A Change of Heart*. That film received a limited arthouse theatrical release in February of 1994 and was issued on videocassette in 1998.

Following his hernia diagnosis, Guthrie chose to push through the remaining half-dozen shows left on the schedule. One of the remaining shows booked was his now semiannual visit to Rocky Mountain College. Following a benefit show at the Alberta Bair Theater, a reception was held at Billings's Radisson Northern Hotel, their chef promising to serve "Authentic Recipes from the Original Alice's Restaurant!" Guthrie wasn't able to visit long, telling dignitaries he hoped "next time I'll be feeling a little better and will be able to sit back and catch up on things."[18] The tour's final show was at the University of Utah's Kingsbury Hall in Salt Lake City. Immediately following, Guthrie and Xavier parted ways. The band boarded the bus for their return to Massachusetts. Guthrie would go west and undergo hernia surgery at the University of California's San Francisco Medical Center.

Just before checking himself into UCSF, Guthrie visited Los Angeles. Ma Jaya was already there, having earlier asked Guthrie to accompany her on a three-day visit to hospitals and hospices. Ma wasn't a medical doctor: Guthrie took pains to point out to cynics Ma didn't "fix" anyone." Instead, he explained, Ma "brings a little unconditional love to those who are having a hard time remembering what it was like to be treated like a human being. The world can be a lonely place sometime. It's bad enough out there for people who are well, let alone for those who have cancer or AIDS or some other terrible disease. You can become an outcast overnight, like the lepers of Christ's time. A little tender loving care is rare these days, but it's needed more than ever."[19] Such sickbed visitations were not new to him. As a Franciscan Brother of the Third Order, Guthrie and friends from the Hermitage had done much of the same.[20]

When finally checking in to UCSF, the singer expressed trepidation about going under the knife. His fears lessened when a bearded anesthesiologist arrived at his bedside—with a copy of the *Alice's Restaurant* LP, and the request it be autographed. The anesthesiologist promised he would personally administer the sedatives prior to the operation. Writing of the experience, Guthrie recalled, "This was a very auspicious sign as far as the folk singer was concerned. He not only decided to undergo the surgery, but he actually looked forward to it. Unfortunately, the anesthesiologist was so good that the folk singer missed the whole operation, and the drugs were so good that the folk singer had no memory of experiencing them. 'What a waste,' he thought."[21]

Guthrie's visit to the hospital and his subsequent convalescence caused him to postpone several East Coast dates booked that spring. He was still feeling the postoperative effects when he performed in late May at an open-air concert to benefit the Behringer-Crawford Museum in Covington, Kentucky. "I only thought Arnold Schwarzenegger types got hernias," he confessed. I haven't been pumping iron or anything."[22]

The summer of 1991 was relatively quiet. In early June, Guthrie again shared the stage with Pete Seeger and Tao Rodriguez at concerts in Minneapolis and Chicago. These were followed by a few low-key solo appearances at small outdoor festivals closer to home. July's schedule was almost entirely empty save for a big "classic rock" revival held at the Poplar Creek amphitheater near Hoffman Estates, Illinois. Radio station WCKG's "Psychedelic Celebration" concert, held 28 July, featured Guthrie, Three Dog Night, John Kay and Steppenwolf, Dave Mason, and Robbie Krieger of the Doors.

Guthrie's time off the road wasn't unproductive. But there were challenges:

AG: Jackie and I began playing with computers. We had entered the names and addresses we'd collected over the years at our gigs. There was probably about six thousand people on our mailing list, but we'd never sent anyone any mail. After we entered the name and addresses on this newfangled device, we decided to try and print them on peel-off stickers, just to see if we could do it.

The names were printed, and the computer asked Jackie if she wanted to "initialize." She had never before seen the term used before, and she thought, "Why not?" So we mistakenly erased the entire computer.

Luckily, we still had the hard-copy names and addresses printed out, so we stuck them on postcards which essentially said, "We know you've added your names and addresses to our database over the years, but we've never actually contacted you. If you wish to remain in our database, please let us know." We received several thousand responses which began a mailing list we would use for decades, building it up over time to be over sixty thousand.

One of Guthrie's missions in spring and summer of 1991 was to get Rising Son Records' product out into the world. The label had been enjoying reasonable success through their selling of CDs and cassettes through mail order and at the concert merchandise table. By spring of 1991, Guthrie reported, "Distribution of Rising Son's record catalogue is picking up very well in the retail world. Most of the continental U.S. is now being supplied with RSR tapes and CDs. There are still some gaps, but hopefully they will be filled in soon. Overseas, things have been slow for the company, but recently we've been asked for some of the titles in Germany. This is a good sign."[23]

Along with seeking out distribution channels, Guthrie was also readying a new CD for release in autumn. The new album was to be titled *All Over the World* (RSR 0002), its name lifted from one of the songs featured. This new collection promised, in Guthrie's words, to contain "many of the folk singer's favorite songs which he did not write but wishes he had. The songs were recorded from the early seventies through the early eighties and, surprisingly enough, they fit together really nicely."[24] The new CD was not originally conceived to be marketed; rather, Guthrie compiled this collection of personal favorites to bring to radio stations as a promotional tool.

In his notes to the austerely packaged original edition, Guthrie offered, "I visited a radio station (once) and they gave me a CD version of an older collection of mine, asking me to pick some songs for them to play while I was there. There was only one song that seemed appropriate. I left feeling that it would be a good idea to release a new collection quickly, in case I ever got stuck in that situation again."[25] The thirteen-song collection presented songs from his back-catalog that shared a general geographical component. Selections would revisit both specific locations ("Massachusetts," "Oklahoma Nights," "Miss the Mississippi and You," "City of New Orleans"), with nods to Hawaii ("Ukulele Lady" and "Waimanalo Blues"), the Soviet Union ("Russian Girls"), and Mexico ("Manzanillo Bay," "Evangelina," and "When I Get to the Border").

The only song that didn't seem to fit was Guthrie's live recording of Ed McCurdy's "(Last Night I Had the) Strangest Dream." The antiwar song was a People's Songs favorite, but the odd man out in an otherwise thematic album. The song was chosen because the Iraqi war was then raging in the Middle East. The album also had a nondescript plain white insert that highlighted the collection's geographic aspect, a subtitle offering it as a "recollection of songs from *All Over the World.*"

Guthrie was very pleased with this middle of the road, decidedly *musical*, collection. He described *All Over the World* as a group of superbly arranged songs "which the folk singer thought may play well on radio, although none of the songs are Top-40 types. All these songs are about places, thus the title. Listening to songs that were recorded over the years, it's interesting to note how well they work together. RSR decided to make it available to everybody."[26] Guthrie teased the album served as "A good collection for people who don't have anything, and want some idea of what the folk singer is like when he's around people with violins."[27]

The release of *All Over the World* sparked a particularly productive period in Guthrie's recording career. During August through December of 1991, Guthrie would spend a great deal of time at Derek Studio in Dalton, Massachusetts, working diligently on two new recording projects:

AG: In 1991 a new project began. It was called "Woody's 20 Grow Big Songs," a collection of my father's songs and artwork that my sister Nora had first brought to Harper Collins, the book publisher. They were happy to become involved, but I was somewhat suspicious of working within the publishing industry. HarperCollins put out a large book with attached cassette (on the RSR label), and had raised expectations of sales within a given time period, and I made sure contractually that if those expectations were not met, the work would become the property of RSR. Warner Bros. was also involved and had released the project as a CD on the Warner label. It did well for them and was nominated for a Grammy Award in 1993.

We utilized the entire family singing along together to create the songs. My brother Joady, my sister Nora, and all of our kids gathered together to bring the songs to life, something I knew our parents would have loved. It still holds up well, and remains the one project we were all took part in producing.

The first rumor a children's recording project might be in the offing came via a brief mention in the spring 1991 issue of the *Rolling Blunder Review,* with Guthrie describing a recent meeting with old boss Lenny Waronker. Waronker expressed interest in having Guthrie record a children's album for Warner Bros. Guthrie admitted that while he would have preferred "to do a regular record," he conceded he "would love to do a children's project also."[28] The only things holding him back from getting to work on such an album were touring commitments and a proper contract offer from Warner Bros.

The album that resulted, *Woody's 20 Grow Big Songs*, had been, in some sense, in the making since 1948. In widely circulated interviews with the Associated Press, *Publishers Weekly*, and the *Los Angeles Times*, Guthrie and coproducer/sister Nora shared accounts of how this forty-year-old project finally came to fruition. The project was originally conceived as a partnership of Woody and Marjorie Guthrie, one celebrating the life of their first child, Cathy. The child tragically perished, age four, in 1947, in a house fire at Guthrie's Coney Island home.

Woody's original dedication to Cathy Ann's memory would have been written circa September 1948 as there's a reference to Arlo Davy's "climbing up into [his] fourteenth month." Woody's foreword was equally uplifting and heartbreaking, a tribute to Cathy, "whose smile and whose laugh we try to catch parts of to make our hearts laugh, to make our books dance, today and tomorrow."[29] Woody also dedicated the songbook-in-the-works to three children from his previous marriage as well as to Arlo Davy Guthrie, his second-born with Marjorie. Woody would write of Arlo in his preface, "You have played the mouth harp and danced now since you were twelve and a half months old, and have always been able to sing rings around me and stomp dance a circle around Marjorie. You'll give us all kinds of songs, games, jokes, joshings, dances, newer things to think and hope and to do in new ways."[30]

Though Woody decorated the pages of the manuscript with his own artwork, Nora explained, "The music was written out by my mother, who was musically literate."[31] The book featured twenty songs Guthrie had written for his children, particularly for Cathy, in the years 1943–47. There were extant recordings—commercially issued or available as reference acetates—of Woody singing eighteen of the twenty songs included in the book. The problem was several of the songs not issued by Disc Records in 1946 and 1947 were not readily available for reference. Asch was a notoriously bad record-keeper, and many of Woody's unreleased recordings had not been properly catalogued. Arlo Guthrie explained of the twenty songs featured on the *Grow Big* album, "Ten or twelve Woody recorded. Some have been available as children's records for forty years. Another eight or ten have probably not been recorded."[32]

There were two songs, Woody's "Mailman" and "Little Bird," that survived only as a set of lyrics with a simple lead sheet. Technically, one song didn't even possess the latter. "Little Bird," Guthrie recollected, "didn't have music."[33] If Guthrie was to tackle the assignment of bringing these songs to life, it would require a proper musical collaboration with his father. Guthrie remarked that some of the simple lead sheets his mother had sketched seemed unfamiliar to him. "Some of songs I remembered had different melodies than the written versions. I did them the way I remembered them in most cases."[34] Nora agreed several of the melodies notated seemed odd, adding, "The way Woody sang some songs was different than the way it was in the book. We had to change the book because we couldn't change Woody."[35]

A year or so prior, no one in the family was even aware this unpublished manuscript existed. So it was to everyone's surprise when, in 1990, a parcel containing the original manuscript arrived on Harold Leventhal's desk. As Guthrie recollected, "No one even knew this book even existed. It was lost when I was fourteen months old."[36] The manuscript might have been lost for all time had it not been for the foresight of a school librarian in Bronxville, New York. "It was found one and a half years ago at Sarah Lawrence College on a dusty shelf in an old manila envelope," Guthrie continued. "My mother was teaching dance there in those years."[37] Nora recalled her shock when she looked through the manuscript. "When Harold showed it to me we flipped out. We had never known about it."[38]

The idea that the manuscript's existence had not been noted—or even rumored—by Woody's biographers and scholars was mind-boggling. It was more surprising that Arlo and Nora's own mother never made mention of it. This was a woman well aware of her husband's contributions to American literature and music, she being a self-appointed curator of his work long before there was any serious interest in it. "Our mother catalogued everything. For her not to even mention this book means she totally forgot about it," Guthrie conceded.[39]

There was one person still around from those days, however, who *did* recall Woody and Marjorie having worked on the project. After learning about the proposed children's songbook, Arlo Guthrie recalled, "The first person I mentioned it to was Pete Seeger . . . and he knew what it was right away, though he'd never mentioned it in the twenty years we'd been working together."[40] Guthrie offered that the resurfaced manuscript would prove an important contribution to his father's canon as it best "represents Woody's philosophy. Learn to play with your kids and take their world as seriously as you take your own. Be real and share with each other."[41]

Woody Guthrie was mostly celebrated as "the Dust Bowl Balladeer," the author of *Bound for Glory*, and the father of the modern protest-song movement. But Woody saw the writing of his children's songs as no less important. Arlo Guthrie explained the reason Woody's children's songs were so unique was that they were written from a child's perspective. "Your world expands as you get older. Sometimes adults try to make that big world fit onto a little kid. . . . That was Woody's genius. The world that little kid is in, tying his shoes, is as important to that kid as making a big deal in real estate is to some guy. Woody would take that kid seriously."[42]

Though biographers focused on the instances when Woody Guthrie did not act as an ideal husband or father, Arlo's reminiscences were different. "Woody had time for us and for all the kids in the neighborhood," Guthrie recalled. "He didn't 'make time.' He was interested. He was really there. He was able to get into our world and play with us and not make it less important than his own world or the real world."[43]

Once the shock of discovery had passed, it was decided that the songbook should, at long last, be put into production. That was the easiest of decisions to make. Its publication would not only serve as a tribute to their sister Cathy, but the songbook project was the single surviving collaborative work of Nora, Joady and Arlo's parents. There was some early talk of issuing a companion CD to the songbook. This would make sense since, according to Guthrie, "Kids don't read music. Having a songbook for children almost required that they know what the songs sound like."[44] The question was how to move forward with such a recording.

It isn't entirely clear whether the idea to record the songs as a project involving the entire Guthrie family was Arlo's alone. There are some who credit Harold Leventhal with making the suggestion. The idea of bringing the entire family onboard was only one of several under consideration. "Originally, it was going to be Woody's singing only," Nora explained. That plan was scuttled when, according to Nora, "Arlo had a brainstorm one day. He called me up one morning and said, "Hey, let's do us singing, with Woody's vocals."[45] As Arlo remembered the progression, "We were going to have Woody's songs. Then it was going to be Arlo and Woody. Then the idea came, why don't we make it a family project? This is a book for families."[46]

Of course, Guthrie had already recorded a "duet" with his father on the soundtrack album for the *Hard Travelin'* film in 1983. Technology had progressed considerably since that night when, on a lark, he synced his vocals with his father's original recording. But an attempt to record an entire album in a similar matter would prove to be a far more challenging task. In the summer of 1991 singer Natalie Cole had recorded a best-selling duet of "Unforgettable" with her late father, the bandleader Nat King Cole. It was a lovely record, seamlessly blending daughter and father together on tape. But few would disagree that singing along with a slick professional like Cole was not the same as trying to sing along with Woody Guthrie and his out-of-tune guitar.

"When Natalie Cole sings with Nat 'King' Cole, Nat 'King' Cole had made his records for a record company," Arlo recalled. "There was a band, they all played in time, everybody was in tune. Woody Guthrie probably just went in there and sang the songs as fast as he could. They were done for documentation purposes."[47] The original Asch masters the Guthrie family could work from were neither slickly recorded nor lovingly archived. "We knew [Woody had] recorded probably at least half of the songs," Arlo continued. "The problem was he did not record them all to be released commercially. He had recorded them for publishing purposes. In a lot of instances, those recordings were not in good shape."[48]

The decision was made that having the entire family singing along with Woody was the most proper way of moving forward with the recording project. The album would be coproduced by Arlo and Nora with their childhood friend Frankie Fuchs. Their idea was to set aside a few days in August, when the offspring of Arlo, Joady, and Nora were still on summer vacation from school. The process would be fun and easy. As Guthrie remembered, the idea was to simply sing "along with Woody where it seemed appropriate and [start] from scratch on the rest."[49] But any notion the album could be effortlessly dashed off in a few days' time was put to rest immediately.

The "couple of days" recording scenario as envisioned would morph into a five-month-long recording commitment revolving around school schedules and Guthrie's touring commitments. The sessions producing *Woody's 20 Grow Big Songs* album were recorded intermittently throughout the months of August and December at Derek Studios. The musicianship on the recording was impeccable. Guthrie drafted several old friends from Shenandoah (David Grover, Dan Velika, and Terry Hall) to serve as the principal backing musicians. That core of musicians would be complemented with artful, tasteful assists from the fiddle and mandolin breaks of Rick Tiven and the jaunty accordion playing of John Culpo.

The person causing the biggest problem on the recording, predictably, was Woody Guthrie. "It was hard enough to sing along with Woody Guthrie when he was alive, let alone on a fixed recording," Guthrie allowed. "The guy had very little sense of time and meter."[50] In her liner notes, Nora described the problems the family had trying to sing along with Woody: "Half were out of tune, the rest were just . . . 'Out.' We heard Woody put extra beats where no man had gone before. We heard keys hovering strangely between those we had learned from our music teacher. We heard words combining dialects from Oklahoma, Texas, and Coney Island."[51]

The family was forced to reconvene and reassess. Though he had passed away nearly a quarter century earlier, it was obvious Woody Guthrie remained the bandleader. "Woody's music was basically untouchable," Guthrie reasoned. "The only thing we could do was try to digitally remove some scratches from the old acetate recordings. Technically and musically, we did fairly astounding things."[52] What was becoming more obvious was that everyone involved had to start taking the recording sessions more seriously. This project was going to take some earnest work if it was to come off successfully.

Guthrie thought the collaboration of Woody and the grandchildren he had never known was important for personal reasons. He recalled that while his own kids had some notion of who their grandfather was, he was mostly a figure from the distant past, Pete Seeger's old road buddy. "We didn't impose the family tradition on our own," Guthrie mused. But he held out hope the project might ultimately bring children and grandfather together. "When my girls first got into the studio, they came wearing makeup and tight skirts," Guthrie reminisced. "And all of a sudden, here's this old man singing with scratchy sounds. So it was interesting to me when they came out with 'Hey, Grandpa's cool, where'd he get these words, man?'"[53]

Which didn't mean everything fell easily into place following such revelation. The recording brought tension as well, Guthrie describing several sessions as a "pressure-cooker environment that boils off all diplomacy."[54] Interestingly, the children of Arlo, Nora, and Joady were circumnavigating the sessions better than their parents. They were less invested in the family drama. "We were all flashing back to when we were little kids," Arlo sighed.

"It makes you remember why families go in different directions, especially when we had to be on such good behavior because all of our children were there."[55] Nora would write, "The immense amount of work it would take to turn these solo performances into a cohesive and artistic piece of work brought strange new colors to our previously glowing faces. . . . Along the way we had a lot of good laughs, as well as a few good fights, and even a couple of sad cries."[56]

There were also moments of magic, and those moments were perfectly captured. Though Arlo Guthrie's memories of his father dated back to the family home on Mermaid Avenue, these were mostly hazy recollections of Woody sitting at a desk "typing and writing."[57] Working on *Woody's 20 Grow Big Songs* would reunite Arlo, Nora, and Joady in some strange way. "When you've got a set of headphones on and you're singing along with the voice coming through them, all that time and distance are gone," Guthrie recalled. "That person you're singing with could be in the next room. It was wonderful to be there and feel very raw feelings with people who are our family."[58]

Woody's 20 Grow Big Songs was only the first of two recording projects that Guthrie was in the midst of orchestrating:

AG: The real beginning of RSR, however, was a record I had envisioned totally apart from anything we'd begun for Warner's, and was something I'd been longing to do for years. It was a collection of old cowboy songs, or songs associated with that genre. It was called *Son of the Wind*. It was the first project entirely ours. We recorded it just up the road in Dalton, Massachusetts, in Greg Steele's Derek Studios, a small facility up a steep flight of stairs, the same studio we used for the *Grow Big* sessions earlier. Greg owned and operated the small but lovely facility, and engineered all the projects we did there.

David Grover, of Shenandoah, produced the record, as we were using mostly musicians from the road band, with extras brought in to fill out the songs as warranted. To this day it remains one of my favorite recordings as we tried to faithfully execute the old songs. I remember telling the band not to play anything heard after 1950. I wanted it to be authentic as possible.

If work on the *Woody's 20 Grow Big Songs* album consumed Guthrie's days, this second recording project consumed his nights. In September of

1991 he proudly announced he had recently completed work on *Son of the Wind*. Though *Son of the Wind* would be the third album released on the Rising Son label, it was the first one recorded totally independent of Warner Bros. Though the album wouldn't feature any new material, the songs Guthrie chose to include had long been part of his musical DNA. "I have waited a long time to make a record of these kind of songs. That time has finally come," Guthrie wrote. "I've made lots of records for everybody else. I made this one for me."[59]

Son of the Wind featured a dozen songs collected from old cowboy ballads and traditional folk songs. These were the songs Guthrie gleaned from his father's old 78s as well as from the records of Woody's cousin Jack Guthrie, Cisco Houston, and Ramblin' Jack Elliott. The songs that made up *Son of the Wind* were not dry academic recording exercises with Guthrie singing reverently into an aged ribbon microphone. This was an especially bright and completely musical album. Guthrie and coproducer David Grover drafted a crack band of old friends to breathe new life into these creaky old cowboy songs. Only one song, Jimmie Rodgers's "When the Cactus Is in Bloom," had been previously recorded by Guthrie.

Son of the Wind also featured a couple of classic Woody Guthrie songs. These included the western outlaw ballad "Dead or Alive," originally recorded by Woody on 19 April 1944, and the mandolin instrumental "Woody's Rag." The latter tune was relatively familiar through Pete Seeger's recording with the Weavers. On *Son of the Wind,* the instrumental is brilliantly paired with Woody's talking blues "Hard Work." Several traditional songs, such as "Buffalo Gals" and "I Ride an Old Paint," had been recorded by Woody and Cisco Houston in the 1940s, the tracks seeing belated issue on LPs on the Folkways and Verve/Folkways labels. That said, Guthrie attributed his reworks of "I Ride an Old Paint," "South Coast," and Gene Autry's "Ridin' Down the Canyon" to Ramblin' Jack Elliott, a preeminent interpreter of Woody's songs.

The ballad "Utah Carroll" had been recorded as early as the 1920s by the Cartwright Brothers and, more famously, by Marty Robbins on his seminal LP *Gunfighter Ballads and Trail Songs*. But Guthrie's version shares little resemblance to those two, his version possibly gleaned from the folk singer and former Weaver Frank Hamilton's Folkways recording of 1962. He admitted this was by design. "My father taught me to distrust everything anybody else taught me," Guthrie would write. "I rearranged his songs and stories to fit the way I remembered them."[60] He also took Cisco Houston's early advice on keeping arrangements simple. That's not so say *Son of the Wind* was not brightened by fresh arrangements and expert musicianship. The real magic was how tastefully it was executed. The album was also the most traditional folk music record that Guthrie would commit to magnetic tape. Of Woody, Jack, and Cisco, Guthrie offered. "I grew up listening to these guys sing these songs and the older I get, the more I realize how important it is for us to hand down these stories and songs to future generations. Some people think a folk singer is someone who just sings their own songs. That's a shame. It's like being of the tradition, rather than in it. I've taught myself to make any song I like, my own. This is the secret of all great spiritual teachings: claim nothing as yours and everything belongs to you."[61]

The autumn of 1991 brought forth other flashbacks. One year earlier, Guthrie had been visited by a television crew interested in filming, in Guthrie's words, a "Whatever Happened to Him?" segment.[62] The crew wanted footage of the folk singer standing on the front lawn of the "Alice" church in Great Barrington. Alice and Ray Brock had sold off the property in 1970 with ownership of the building passing to a number of different renters and proprietors over the years. The present owners were two artists, Roland and Ellen Ginzel. The Ginzels permitted Guthrie and the crew access and, following the filming, they mentioned they would soon be putting the church on the market.

It was an interesting morsel to digest. Briefly inspecting the church interior through a window, Guthrie despaired of the renovations made to the sanctuary in the intervening twenty-five years. Regardless, he saw beyond the interior changes. He enthused, "Much of the old feelings can still be felt: there is STILL something there."[63] The Ginzels's asking price was $350,000, an enormous amount of money, especially as the property was only valued at $200,000. If Guthrie was considering an offer, there was a pressing problem. He and Jackie had only recently purchased the Crab-House. The idea of juggling two expensive mortgages bordered on economic lunacy.

But the idea remained intriguing. It dawned on him that the people he might turn to for help were the seventy thousand fans either subscribing to the *Rolling Blunder Review* or active on his mailing list. He wasn't asking his readers to send cash, or at least not yet. He was simply gauging interest, asking for fundraising ideas so a purchase might be possible. The Rising Son office received no shortage of responses—but many dismissed the idea as impractical. There was one interesting suggestion. The church could be set up as a nonprofit should it serve the community in one capacity or another.[64]

Guthrie was intrigued by the concept of returning the church to its original purpose—as a house of worship, but one with no agenda other than being responsive to community needs. The church could then again serve as a place where people might heal, pray, and meditate. Many of the activist types Guthrie met out on the road were wonderful and generous people: but many subjugated their own well-being in the pursuit of altruistic goals. This was apparent in the years following the end of the Vietnam War. Many activists found themselves rudderless. Without an all-consuming cause, some turned their energies to religion, some to drug experimentation, some to off-the-grid lifestyles.

These thoughts had been on Guthrie's mind for some time. The folk singer mused in 1991, "I don't see happiness as a cause-and-effect thing as I once did. I found that if I really wanted to be happy, then it couldn't be dependent on other people or what shape the world is in. Some people think like, 'Somebody's wearing a fur coat—I can't be happy. Somebody's starving—I can't be happy. Somebody's in a war—I can't be happy.' I had to unlearn that and recognize that my happiness was inborn and natural."[65]

If Guthrie was mulling over a reconsecration of the church, he was still lacking the money to do so . . . and the time to do it. The Ginzels wanted a sale to go through as quickly as possible, the couple having already vacated the premises. Guthrie came up with the idea of moving the offices of Rising Son Records into the church and renting space with an option to buy once funds were secured. This seemed like a good idea, but one requiring more than the seller's blessing. It would also involve the tricky navigation of having a residential property rezoned for professional use.

To that end, on 5 September 1991, Guthrie's lawyer, Harris Aaronson, appeared before the selectmen of Great Barrington. He assured all present that Guthrie was active in securing loans for the first down payment. The attorney allowed he recognized any such move would require a special permit: one allowing two full-time staffers and three part-time employees to administer the duties of Guthrie's record company and planned foundation. It was understood the approval of such a permit required all five members of the Zoning Board of Appeals to vote in accord.[66]

Guthrie needed a lot of cash. To help facilitate the purchase, he turned to the readers of his newsletter. He optimistically predicted that—with their financial assistance—Rising Son could move into the church as early as 1 November. Though that date came and went without anything happening, the rent-to-buy scenario allowed Guthrie breathing space to continue with the fundraising. He expressed "hopes that a final sale can take place within a few months," writing:

> The folk singer, because he is a folk singer, is not now, and may never be likely to purchase the property personally. Therefore, he has created an entity which has filed for tax-exempt status with the IRS and the Commonwealth of Massachusetts. The entity is called The Guthrie Center.
>
> We sincerely hope that The Guthrie Center will be able to provide many more services to the local and global community than we were able to provide under the present circumstances. If we've learned anything from the likes of Woody Guthrie and Pete and Toshi Seeger, it's that groups of ordinary folks can do things impossible for individual folks to do.[67]

The folk singer then made a sensible pitch: If all seventy thousand folks on the mailing list could send $5 toward the purchase of the church, the Guthrie Center would have the necessary $350,000. Recalling his visit to the Vietnam Veterans Memorial Wall in Washington, DC, Guthrie described "how powerful a wall of names can be. The sense of agony and pain, as well as pride and courage of those men and women who gave their lives two decades ago couldn't be remembered better, except if they were still with us." It was Guthrie's intention that everyone who donated five bucks would have their name enshrined on "a wall of peace."[68]

On 19 November, the selectmen of Great Barrington unanimously voted to approve the zoning change. It was a welcome decision, if a nervous one. Advised of the—highly fictionalized—scenes played out in the *Alice's Restaurant* movie, one board member asked Guthrie to promise there would be "No motorcycles in and out the front door." "We gotta remember that the movie was a movie," Guthrie reminded those a bit wary of his intentions. "I never had a bike there."[69]

Others asked for Guthrie's assurance that no freewheeling hippie cele-brations would take place on site. That was not his plan, of course, though his petition made plain his intent to establish the Guthrie Center as a 501(c)(3) nonprofit. The Guthries to be honored by the appellation were his father and mother. The *Berkshire Eagle* reported the Guthrie Center would be devoted "to the study and promotion of the relationship among music, culture, and values."[70] This was Guthrie's dream, but he admitted to still being in the process of trying to raise funds so he could actually pur-chase the church. He was also aware the board's welcome decision was only one of two approvals necessary for Rising Son to be allowed to conduct business.

The end of the touring year concluded, more or less, with the tradi-tional Thanksgiving weekend concerts at Carnegie. There was a lot to be thankful for in 1991, but with so much activity he hadn't the chance to compose many new songs. Guthrie warned fans in his program notes, "You won't hear a lot of new songs tonight. I've started a whole lot of them, maybe I'll sing just the beginnings."[71] The *New York Times* cautioned Guth-rie's "yarn-spinning has become at least as important as the songs in his shows."[72] This was not entirely true as Friday night's concert totaled some twenty-one songs, and Saturday's nineteen—a pretty generous selection considering the "Alice's Restaurant Massacree" was in the mix both nights. Guthrie even managed to introduce one new song of spiritual dimension that weekend, "Wake Up Dead."

In his notes, Guthrie summarized the most important milestones of the past year: the recording of the still-in-progress *Woody's 20 Grow Big Songs* and the recent release of *All Over the World*. He also offered having "just finished an album of songs I've been waiting years to record. It's called *Son of the Wind*. This is the record that a lot of old friends have been waiting for. As I write these notes, it's down at the local manufacturing plant, so it may not be available tonight. Check the lobby anyway." He also shared his plans regarding the establishment of a foundation at the old church "to help serve those of us who are in trouble." "We need your help immediately," he'd write. "There's all kinds of stuff going on."[73]

Hoping fans might contribute a few dollars to the cause, Guthrie had been setting up donation canisters at concerts. Since his concerts at Carne-gie Hall attracted an audience of well-heeled Manhattanites, Guthrie hoped the donation jars might fill generously. Though there were contributions made both nights, the Carnegie donations totaled less than at his smaller gig at New Britain, Connecticut's grungy rock-club The Sting less than a week later. In some ways, Guthrie was not surprised. "My Dad told me when I was a kid, if you're hungry, don't go to the rich people's door. Go to the poor folks. They'll feed you."[74]

Though the Ginzels had lowered the church's asking price to $300,000, it was becoming obvious Guthrie's appeal for donations would require going outside his fan base—the Ginzels were giving the singer a March 1992 deadline to come up with the funds. With the clock ticking, Guthrie gave an interview to the *New York Times,* suggesting his mission to reclaim the church as a spiritual center was an important one. "For a large group of us the church symbolizes the same spirit that drove the controversies of the '60s—civil rights, the peace movement, the women's movement." Guthrie insisted his mission was not based on personal nostalgia. The pro-democracy movements in Eastern Europe and in the People's Republic of China were proof enough, "The same spirit is still moving people around the world."[75]

A week later, Guthrie played host to a film crew from TV's *Entertainment Tonight.* He was also the subject of an article in the widely read glossy celebrity weekly magazine *People,* speaking of his desire to return the church to the "family of the '60s." Guthrie reminisced, "Most of the songs on my first few albums were written on the organ by the altar. It was a very creative place for me."[76] This comment echoed an earlier one made to the *Times.* Guthrie suggested he had composed more than twenty of his earliest songs in the church. He added, "I think there are a couple more in there."[77]

AG: In January 1992 I bought the Old Trinity Church from Roland and Ellen Ginzel. With the help of hundreds of friends, we were able to put a down payment on the building that had previously been the home of Ray and Alice Brock, and was the main location setting for the film *Alice's Restaurant* that was released in November 1969. The following year, in January, Ma came up from Florida, and reconsecrated the church.

The folk singer was happy to share the good news that the "Guthrie Center at Alice's Church stopped paying rent. It was now ours. Now it became a matter of keeping it."[78] The decision to purchase the building was economically tenuous. The Guthries remortgaged their farm in Washington, Massachusetts, putting it up as collateral while convincing the Great Barrington Savings Bank to guarantee a loan. To celebrate the turning over of the keys, newspapers reported, incorrectly, that Guthrie had sent out 4,500 invitations to the rededication ceremony. This was *partially* true, at best. Postcard notifications had been sent to subscribers of *the Rolling Blunder Review*. But since the majority of readers weren't from the Berkshires, it was mostly a polite gesture—there was no consideration that most would attend. Guthrie conceded the large number of folks who *did* show up was unanticipated.

On Thursday evening, 30 January 1992, hundreds of supporters and well-wishers—including Alice Brock, former police chief William J. ("Officer Obie") Obanhein, Tigger Bruenn (who sang Joni Mitchell's "Songs for Aging Children" during the wintry burial scene in the *Alice's Restaurant* film), and Ma Jaya Sati Bhagavati—descended upon the former Episcopal church at 4 Van Deusenville Road. Though the well-wishers gathered in good faith, the celebration sparked no small controversy in this otherwise placid western Massachusetts hamlet.

The selectman of Great Barrington had approved Guthrie's use of the building as his professional address, the administrative office of Rising Son Records. But it was with the provision that the building's capacity be limited to no more than fifteen people as the capacities of the aged structure's septic system was meager at best. So it was to no one's surprise when the police arrived midway through the ceremony, informing the hundreds of congregants that they were illegally parked and tickets would be issued. Guthrie advised, "Well, the cops just came. The first time I got arrested, it worked out good. But it may not work out that way again."[79]

The parking situation would be the least of the evening's troubles. In an incense-scented ceremony, Guthrie looked to have a portion of the sanctuary reconsecrated as "Ma's Hanuman Gar,"[80] Hanuman, being the Hindu God of Service. To demonstrate, Ma, who dedicated much of her life in service to the terminally ill, brought along a friend suffering the devastating effects of the AIDS virus.

Ma's characteristic Brooklyn-bred brashness—a personality type the Coney Island–born Guthrie was accustomed to—wasn't completely embraced by all gathered at or reporting on the ceremony. There were some mutterings, even amongst friends, that Ma, once described by

Guthrie as "a Jewish-Christian-Hindu from Coney Island," was an outsider essentially upstaging local luminaries in attendance.[81] Visiting from her Florida ashram, Ma seemed omnipresent. Photographs of the fifty-one-year-old were prominently displayed in the sanctuary, and several of her abstract paintings adorned the walls.

There were also a lot of folks expressing displeasure when Ma made the metaphorical vow to "bring death to the community and teach the community about death."[82] Others were shocked when Ma kissed the cheek of the ailing AIDS patient—and then had her ten-year-old son do the same. This at a time when so little was understood about the devastating disease. Ma insisted her words and actions were misinterpreted. The concept of "bringing death" was merely a response to the community's ignorance and anxiety, "the whole fear of AIDS and homeless children. What I want them to do is accept death as a part of life."[83]

Misunderstood or not, it was the belief of several members of the community that Guthrie had been disingenuous regarding his intentions. In early February, angry neighbors brought their concerns to a special meeting of the board of appeals. "We welcomed him into the neighborhood with open arms, and he stabbed us in the back," raged one petitioner.[84] "He bamboozled the neighborhood, and he bamboozled the town," cried another.[85] There was no hiding the fact that many were primarily upset with Ma's pronouncements. There were inferences that Ma had a Svengali-like influence over Guthrie. Others were fearful Great Barrington would soon be overrun by swarms of AIDS patients, abused children, and the homeless.

One suggestion made to the board was to consider "a guru bylaw," one effectively revoking the Guthrie Center's business zone status.[86] Though no decision was rendered that night, one sympathetic selectman sighed that it did appear Guthrie had not been "totally honest" with his intentions when filling out his original application.[87] Guthrie was stung and angered by many of the things he had been reading and hearing in the local press. He was particularly unhappy with the latter charge. "I've been called a lot of things in my life," he said, wearily. "Dishonest is not one of them."[88]

In a letter presented to the selectman, Guthrie reminded the board that he *had* outlined his plans for the center's "outreach efforts" to assist "AIDS victims, people in hospices, and abused children during public hearings on his special permit application last fall."[89] There was nothing disingenuous in his application. Addressing the concerns regarding his relationship with Ma, Guthrie answered, unapologetically, "Ma is my guru and my teacher who inspired me to do the kind of work we do here." He conceded in his letter of 3 February the "enthusiasm and fervor (and therefore their statements)" of friends "went far beyond the limitations to which the property is subject," but he left it at that.[90] There were attempts to downplay Ma's excitations of 30 January. "Ma did get overrun by her enthusiasm," Rising Son's Sharon Palma allowed. "She did come on strong, and I can understand that she frightened a lot of people."[91]

Guthrie was due on the road for a month-and-a-half-long tour of the western US in February and March. He then planned to take time off in April to check on the ongoing rehab of the CrabHouse. Guthrie played additional gigs in Georgia and Florida while making his way to Sebastian. Two days prior to his solo concert at Sarasota's Players Theater, Guthrie told a reporter, "I've just finished a new album, *Son of the Wind*, that's all cowboy songs. I figure these songs have gotta get handed down to the next generation. We do two of my Dad's songs, and a Gene Autry song, "Ridin' Down the Canyon," and others most people haven't heard like "Utah Carroll." They're such great stories, you kind of get locked into them. It's getting a great response." Guthrie was hoping his new album might receive thoughtful critical attention and sales. Should the new album find "an appreciative audience," he hinted, "other recordings of this nature will be made in the future." The journalist noted Guthrie was already in the "process of collecting the songs for the next in what promises to be a fabulous collection. A series perhaps."[92]

The *Son of the Wind* project was personally satisfying. "It's something I've been wanting to do for twenty years but I couldn't because it wasn't commercial enough," he told another reporter. "Warner Bros. certainly wasn't interested in it."[93] Unfortunately, in the months after its release, *Son of the Wind* went nearly unnoticed. There were some brief reviews in folk-music journals with limited circulation. But while distribution channels were slowly opening, there were still too few record shops carrying Rising Son product. Without a big marketing push, many fans were simply unaware that a new record had been released.

AG: *Son of the Wind* was released in 1992, with no budget or events scheduled for promotion. It just was there. But we released it anyway.

Then later in 1993 we were playing a place called "The Mangy Moose" in Teton Village, Wyoming, for a couple of nights. It's out in the middle of not much.

As we were setting up the stage that day, an old craggy looking rancher came in and asked where Arlo Guthrie was. I had no idea who this guy was, or what he could possibly want. Maybe he had a daughter he was concerned about. . . . I introduced myself, and asked what I could do for him. He just looked at me and said, "I just came by to thank you for making that CD *Son of the Wind*. Nobody makes songs like that anymore, so I just thought I'd come over here and thank you for doing it." Relieved, I thanked him and asked if he wanted a couple of comps for the performance later that evening. "No," he said. "I don't go to shows, I just came here to thank you." And he walked away.

I thought about that for a long time, wondering how a record with no promotion and no advertising got into his hands to begin with. I began to realize that the music and songs get to where they need to be. RSR didn't need advertising to get it to that guy. The music industry isn't all it's cracked up to be. Our job was to create the kinds of records that get into the right hands, people who appreciate it for what it is, and not worry too much about how that happens. Rightly or wrongly that is how we've been operating ever since.

The recent storm of activity continued unabated. Following the recording of *Woody's 20 Grow Big Songs* and *Son of the Wind*, Guthrie found himself in the studio again, working on two brand-new projects. The first was for the soundtrack of a film with the provisional title of "Woody Animation Project." The sessions were recorded on the West Coast at Los Angeles's Music Grinder Studio on Hollywood Boulevard and at Track Record Studio in North Hollywood. The sessions were produced by Frank ("Frankie") Fuchs, coproducer of the *Grow Big* album.[94]

Guthrie's soundtrack was to accompany a VHS cassette release issued in 1997 as *This Land Is Your Land: The Animated Kids' Songs of Woody Guthrie* on the FHE (Family Home Entertainment) label. The companion CD featured the shared vocals of Woody and Arlo. While some dismissed the releases as sort of lesser companions to the original *Grow Big* album, the soundtrack featured several standalone tracks. It *was* true five of the songs reworked on *This Land Is Your Land* had been included on the earlier album: "Howdi Do," "Riding in My Car," "Jig Along Home," "Bling Blang," and "All Work Together." But songs singular to this release included Woody's "Mail Myself to You," "Grassey, Grass, Grass," "So Long, It's Been Good to Know Yuh," and, of course, "This Land Is Your Land." Concurrent with the VHS release, Rounder Records of Cambridge, Massachusetts, issued the soundtrack on CD as *This Land Is Your Land: An All-American Children's Folk Classic* (Rounder Kids CD 8050).

A second project conceived in early 1992 was a two-song cassette single released as a *Special Limited Edition—2 Songs* (RSR 0006): "Norman Always Knew"/"Massachusetts." "Norman" was Norman Rockwell, the beloved illustrator of all things Americana. The town of Stockbridge had long celebrated their most famous native son, whose folksy illustrations featured on covers of the *Saturday Evening Post* brought him deserved acclaim. Stockbridge established a Norman Rockwell Museum in 1969, and Guthrie's cassette, released in July 1992, was sold only through RSR mail order, at concerts, and at the museum's gift shop.

The cassette's fold-out J-card (the paper card in the cassette case) was certainly memorable. The cover featured Rockwell's famous "Triple Self Portrait," the inner sleeve featuring a recreation of that same image, with Guthrie similarly posed, sitting on a stool with paintbrush in hand. "Norman Always Knew" was not a Guthrie original, having been written in 1990 by Connecticut's Steve Vozzolo and Joe Manning. Manning was pleased with Guthrie's recording and happy sales of the cassette would benefit both the refurbishing of the Rockwell Museum and the Guthrie Center.[95] The song would also get a very public airing later that summer during Guthrie's July 4th concert at nearby Tanglewood.

One of the more unusual Guthrie recordings to come to market in 1992 was a book-on-tape release from Berkeley's Audio Literature Company. In the spring of 1992 the company issued a two-cassette abridged version of Woody Guthrie's *Bound for Glory*, first published by E. P. Dutton back in 1943. The release was one of several autobiographies of American musical and literary icons issued. The *Bound for Glory* package was part of Berkeley's "Musical Heritage on Cassette" series and featured a near three-hour reading of novel sections by Arlo Guthrie. The session had been recorded at Derek Studios in Dalton, Massachusetts, with Greg Steele engineering.

Though there were generally fewer reviews of books-on-tape than of books published in the traditional manner, nearly every review cited *Bound for Glory* as one of the best. The *St. Louis Dispatch* was impressed, suggesting Arlo successfully managed to carry off "an accent that could very well be that of the Oklahoma folksinger." Though the tape featured a straight reading of Woody's original text, the review noted a welcome musical flourish was offered when Arlo chose to sing the "stanzas of the song that provided the book's title."[96]

One critic thought Guthrie's genetics allowed him to perfectly capture his father's "laid-back, friendly, conversational style." The reviewer mused, "There's more to it than that, though. What is it about a son reading his father's book? Is it that he really is simpatico with the story, that he actually does enhance the words and the ideas? Or does it just seem like that? . . . . There's just an overall haze of richness, of 'rightness' about the recording."[97] The *Bound for Glory* audiobook was belatedly nominated for "Best Spoken Word or Non-Musical Album" for the 36th annual Grammy Award ceremonies, losing to Maya Angelou's poem *On the Pulse of Morning.* Angelou's poem was fresh in memory, having been famously read by the poet at the 20 January 1993 inauguration of President William J. Clinton.

The summer of 1992 brought a third "Blunderman's Fabulous Adventure." Guthrie's new plan was to fill the cabins of the Mark Twain–era paddlewheel steamship, the *Delta Queen,* with friends and fans. The planned seven-day tour (June 13–20) was to push off from St. Louis and sail down the Mississippi River to the port of New Orleans. The ship's accommodations promised luxury: five meals a day in addition to an afternoon tea and a midnight buffet. Guthrie promised that several musical friends would be coming along to provide entertainment augmenting that of the *Delta Queen's* own swinging dance band.[98] Guthrie was booked to perform three onshore concerts at three ports of call: St. Louis, Memphis, and New Orleans. The first concert, at St. Louis's Westport Playhouse, was scheduled to take place on Friday, 12 June, the eve of the Saturday launch.

The tour itself got off to an inauspicious start. Everyone had to be bussed from St. Louis to Hannibal when a damaged lock stranded the *Delta Queen* downriver. So the adventurers were stuck in Hannibal until late Sunday, when the lock issue was finally resolved. Everyone was pretty happy to leave Hannibal since all onboard were being attacked by hordes of giant insects attracted by the ship's bright lights.[99] The delay in sailing also caused Guthrie's second concert at the Peabody Alley of Memphis's Peabody Hotel, to be rescheduled for the week following. Guthrie's final concert was to take place at the Audubon Institute of New Orleans. For that occasion, Guthrie cheerfully banged out a few verses of Tom Paxton's "Goin' to the Zoo."

Guthrie was due back in the Berkshires soon afterward. He had been booked to play a 4th of July holiday concert with Judy Collins at Tanglewood. The concert date with Collins rekindled great memories. Guthrie had accompanied the crystal-clear soprano on a tour of Japan at the very beginning of his career:

AG: In May of 1967 I accompanied Judy Collins to Japan. Mimi Fariña opened the shows. Then I would come out and after an intermission Judy would close the gigs. Bruce Langhorne was Judy's accompanist and Irene Zacks (from Harold Leventhal's office) was the tour manager.

I remember getting off the plane in Tokyo with lots of flashing camera newsmen on the tarmac. They had never seen a real live hippy before, and I tried not to disappoint them by wearing tall yellow boots, lots of fringe, and a big floppy hat, never mind the long hair.

The first thing I noticed was how polite everyone appeared to be. All of our business however, had to be dealt with by either Bruce Langhorne or me, as no Japanese businessman would even consider doing business with women. That kind of put Irene in a difficult position.

She was a towering redhead, far and away taller than most people in Japan at the time. As tour manager she was in fact responsible for the business part, but cultural differences negated her role, and she had no choice but to go between Bruce and the promoters in every city.

I had first met Mimi when we together attended Indian Hill Music and Art Camp in Stockbridge, Massachusetts. She was a couple of years older than me, and that difference became less important as we grew older. She had studied dance with my mother, and she had a dancer's grace in everything she did, which I found very attractive. On our trip together in Japan the differences vanished completely and we had a wonderful, albeit short, romance. We remained friends until her untimely passing in 2001.

The Judy Collins tour was relentless—thirty-two shows in thirty days. On our last day there I succumbed to food poisoning and hallucinated alone in my hotel room. I was happy to leave, although I had many wonderful moments and memories.

Guthrie learned a lot about stagecraft on that tour with Collins. Just prior to the Tanglewood show, Guthrie reminisced to the *Berkshire Eagle* how that visit to Japan ultimately shaped him as a performer:

> The trip to Japan with Judy Collins was very, very important to me. I was singing before thousands of people, none of whom understood a single word I was saying—this was back before the Japanese were English-literate—and my normal performance was to talk a lot and tell funny stories. Aside from that, they didn't understand me. Not just my language and my words, but they didn't understand the philosophy, they didn't understand the person. They'd never seen a person with yellow boots up to his knees, with long hair and weird shades. They didn't get it. I was a curiosity, an oddity, like a new fruit or vegetable. Judy Collins, they understood—she was a nice, beautiful girl with a gorgeous voice who played guitar and piano.
>
> So I realized that I was going to be on tour for one month . . . and that at not one of these shows was there going to be any one person who would get it, who would get me. So I just loosened up and said the hell with it, I'm just going to get up there and say whatever I want. And I did. I just made up stuff. I started making up songs and tunes and stories, and you know what? They liked it. They really liked it. I had a great time in Japan.
>
> From that point on I started having fun on stage. I had sort of exposed myself to an unknown force and I didn't die. I didn't burn up in flame. I was no longer a frightened little kid. I was somebody who couldn't sing in tune but certainly had an engaging style.[100]

Guthrie's set at Tanglewood was interesting on several levels, not the least of which was his being backed by two bands. Though Xavier served as his primary backing group, Guthrie also performed a mini-set with several of his old bandmates from Shenandoah. The press coverage differed wildly. One local newspaper described the concert glowingly as "an intimate and nostalgic musical reunion with . . . two icons of '60s folk music."[101] This view contrasted sharply with that of a *Boston Globe* correspondent dismissive of the event's "Doonesbury generation" demographic: Collin's set was described as "sad," Guthrie's as "stupefying." Even the closing performance of "This Land Is Your Land" was assailed, the ideologue critic suggesting sourly the song was performed "without a trace of the irony that Arlo's father, Woody (a true rebel with a clear Leftist agenda), always brought to it."[102]

If anyone thought Guthrie would be bullied from performing "This Land Is Your Land" in a manner perceived nonsacrosanct . . . well, they'd be mistaken. On 12 July 1992, Guthrie was to perform at New York City's Rumsey Playfield in Central Park for a *Summerstage* commemoration of Woody Guthrie's 80th birthday. Guthrie was joined on the program by friends old and new: Pete Seeger, Nanci Griffith, Suzanne Vega, Billy Bragg, and the Disposable Heroes of Hiphoprisy. In a preshow notice, Guthrie offered that his father was at the vanguard of "a global musical culture that respects liberty, freedom, justice. What we have seen in Tiananmen Square, in Eastern Europe, in Central and South America, is equally, if not more, the result of ideas expressed through music than any political ideology." He was most impressed that his father's topical song had remained relevant. "It is fabulous that there is a whole new generation of people discovering not just the fact of his being, but what he stood for."[103]

It was important the eightieth birthday celebration was not an exercise in nostalgia. Nanci Griffith had recently recorded Townes Van Zandt's "Tecumseh Valley" with Guthrie on her album *Other Voices, Other Rooms* (Elektra). She described Guthrie as having the "purest voice in folk music."[104] Griffith was pleased to be invited to perform and she certainly knew Woody's songs: she acknowledged her father as a "huge Woody Guthrie fan." She was impressed by Nora Guthrie's request that performers "not just to sing Woody Guthrie songs, but songs where, as writers, we were influenced by him."[105] The former Texas Agriculture Commissioner, Jim Hightower, was to serve as master of ceremonies. Hightower, a syndicated political columnist with a populist Democratic bent, offered, "What Woody Guthrie believed and put into his songs and writings is that it's the people who count, not the politicians; the people, not the parties and the media; the people, not Wall Street."[106]

Aside from performing a handful of shows in Europe in late August, Guthrie stayed relatively close to home in the late summer of 1992. During the first week of August he and Ma organized a two-day symposium at the Guthrie Center, "Shakti Initiation—An Intensive Retreat." Shakti is a Hindu spiritual practice in which one confers their energies to another. The retreat promised that those signing on would be taught "techniques

for relieving stress through meditation, spiritual songs, and yoga and discussion groups."[107] Sadly, this event too would bring condemnation from
Guthrie's neighbors and selectmen. One cynical, if ironic, headline crowed,
"Guthrie's anti-stress retreat creates tension in Barrington."[108] The public
cries included the usual complaints of outhouses and parking. But the whis-
pered ones concerned Guthrie's teacher-student relationship with Ma and
their bringing of AIDS victims and abused children into the community.

The folk singer wasn't going to back down. The retreat would proceed
as scheduled. Guthrie would write that the participants "came with the
desire to grow and learn, with a curiosity of what is, with stuff to deal with
and stuff to let go of. Some came to learn how to live, some to learn how to
die, and some to learn both, as many reasons as there were participants."
Two Hebrew scholars, Schachter and Eve Ilsen, were engaged to speak on
the second evening of the retreat. During a candle-lit ceremony, Guthrie
marveled at Eve's "incomparable singing of the Song of Solomon." It was
the song "Jesus had probably listened to his mother sing," Guthrie mused,
"but this might be the first time the old church had ever sung it there. It felt
right."[109]

There was no separation between music and good work. On a September Sunday, Guthrie was to perform at the Great Meadows Amphitheater,
outside Uniontown, Pennsylvania. The concert was to benefit a community
food bank and several local activist groups. It was merely one of any number of similar benefits he agreed to. In a preshow interview, Guthrie confirmed that while he wasn't going to perform any songs from the best-selling
Grow Big Songs album, he was "planning to do a first outing of this in
November." He said the possibility of a series of *Grow Big* concerts was not
yet settled since the family was "going to have to rehearse a lot to take this
on the road."[110]

The irony wasn't lost on Guthrie that the Warner Bros.–issued *Grow
Big Songs* CD was his only album, at present, that a record store browser
could find easily. Guthrie was proud the *Grow Big* album was "breaking
kids' record sales and is also gaining *lots* of media attention."[111] The fact
that it was a great album was only part of its success. The new CD was enjoying the sort of promotional push that only a major label could muster.

The patchy distribution of Guthrie's Rising Son Records releases was
now the front-and-center issue. Guthrie knew he could produce a great
independent record. The problem now was getting people to hear them. In

December of 1992, Guthrie appealed to newsletter readers to "go into as many record stores, large chains, and smaller independently owned stores" and ask store managers about their distribution channels, scour their catalogs, and collect such record store information as addresses and phone numbers so Rising Son could contact owners directly. "THIS IS NO JOKE!' Guthrie assured, "We think this will be a wonderful way to exploit our readers." Readers were also asked to report on radio stations who still had Guthrie's music in rotation or would spin "Alice's Restaurant" on Thanksgiving. "Are there stations that might play AG's music if they were made more aware of our present new releases and activities?" he wondered.[112]

In early November of 1992 Guthrie was the recipient of a *Points of Light* honor. The award was created in 1990 by America's forty-first president, George H. W. Bush, and was designed to honor Americans engaged in charitable work. The letter had been sent to Guthrie from the office of C. Gregg Petersmeyer, assistant to the president and director of the Office of National Service. The award was conferred for "the fine example of generosity you have set for your fellow Americans."[113] No one missed the irony that this honor was signed off on by a former director of the Central Intelligence Agency. Still, it was a validation of the charitable work they were doing at the Guthrie Center. It was also an acknowledgement, of sorts, that there were Americans hurting and in need. "I was actually quite pleased," Guthrie admitted, seeing the award as recognition, "not so much for us, but for the people we try to help."[114]

Though Guthrie was now being *officially* recognized as a national hero, not everyone in the Berkshires held him in similar regard. Shortly following the news of the award, Guthrie announced plans to host a $1,000 a plate Thanksgiving dinner at the church. The invitation, sent out to four hundred well-heeled dinner guests, attracted both attention and controversy. Guthrie's philanthropic dinner invitation gently tweaked the noses of those locals holding ungenerous opinions of him: "Come and enjoy the frenzy your presence will create as our neighbors go nuts, the media goes berserk, and I go to the dump once again. . . . We are not a religion. We are a diverse collection of strange people from many different religious backgrounds who share in common the belief that the best way to solve our own problems is to help somebody who has more problems than you do."

While the planned "Thanksgiving Dinner That Couldn't Be Beat" attracted a lot of media attention, it was not to be. A week prior to the event, Guthrie cancelled the benefit because RSVPs had been under-whelming. Thanksgiving dinner would still be served, with meals doled out free of charge. Everyone who volunteered to mend and repair the church, anyone who regularly visited or ran errands for the elderly, anyone in need of a hot meal or simply lonely for company was invited to Thanks-giving dinner.

As for the benefit, Guthrie sighed that he was "sorry it didn't work out."[115] The Guthrie Center desperately needed money so they could con-tinue their charitable work. The press was, as expected, cynical in their reportage of the cancellation. The snarky headlines were at least cleverly crafted: "A Second Massacree for Arlo," "Guess Who's *Not* Coming to Din-ner?" and "You *Can't* Get Everything You Want at Alice's Restaurant."

The day following Thanksgiving, Guthrie made his annual trek to Car-negie Hall. This weekend's concerts would be particularly special. The folksinger had gathered Nora, Joady, and family onto the stage to celebrate the *Woody's 20 Grow Big Songs*. In his program notes, Guthrie also offered his fans a "Happy Anniversary," thanking them for their loyalty: "I've been on the road for almost 30 years. It's been interesting." To celebrate the milestone, Guthrie advised he was forfeiting a large-scale celebration and would instead go back to the starting point . . . if only for a couple of months: "I'm adding another twist, starting next week! I've decided to buy a pickup truck, take off by myself, and enjoy my 'Solo, Alone, By Myself' tour for the next several months. It'll be me and my truck, and I may be showing up in places you never expected to see me, so keep an eye out!"[116]

Guthrie had recently purchased a new black diesel four-wheel-drive Dodge pickup truck and found a novel method of paying it off: by going out on the road in December for a brief solo tour. December, traditionally, was a month few shows were booked. The most interesting aspect of this new string of dates—set to start on 4 December in Carlisle, Pennsylvania, and finish off on 19 December in Woodstock, New York—were the ven-ues. Most shows booked were in small, intimate club settings. Some of the nightspots were so small fewer than seventy-five fans could be seated. Only one venue booked—the University of Vermont's Ira Allen Chapel in Burlington—had the capacity to seat as many as three hundred fans.

One journalist called the Rising Son Records office to ferret out the *real* reason the singer—who had just played two sold-out performances at prestigious Carnegie Hall—was choosing to play on a cramped coffeehouse stage or in a saloon. Sharon Palma explained the reasoning was simple. "He wanted to get back in touch with the people who are like him—back to his roots where he started. He said, 'Find places that I wouldn't let Paul [Smith, Guthrie's booking agent] book me into otherwise, and see what we can come up with.'" Palma assured Guthrie was "a people person and hasn't really had the chance to be that lately."[117]

It was a return to the early coffeehouse days of 1965 and 1966—with one exception. This was no "basket house" situation: the more intimate the setting, the steeper the cost of admission. The higher ticket prices did not deter the faithful. The cabarets were packed to capacity, with last-minute allowances made for SRO patrons to gather at the bar. There was no longer any need for Guthrie to pass the hat as he had in '65. As long as he had a guitar, he wouldn't starve. On the downside, he was reminded of the perils of booking shows in December: two gigs were postponed due to a winter storm blanketing the northeast under several feet of snow. But he pushed on.

> **AG:** In January 1993, I decided that it would be a good idea to get back to performing the way I'd begun—alone. I bought a new Dodge diesel pickup truck and headed out. I had a high shell covering for the bed of the pickup that kept the instruments and luggage out of the weather. It was, after all, January. I took along a neighbor, Maya Payton, to help with merchandise, and we took off.
>
> Maya was a gorgeous young girl from down the road in Becket, Massachusetts. I should point out that her being on the road was not an intimate relationship, but an opportunity for her to get out of the existence of living with not much nearby, in the hills, and a chance to see the country with a trusted friend. The year began as we headed to Michigan for a couple nights at The Ark, which I always loved playing.

Just as he was preparing to push off to Michigan, Guthrie received welcome news. On 7 January 1993, the American Academy of Recording Arts and Sciences announced the nominees to be recognized at the 35th annual Grammy Awards show. One of the five recordings chosen for the "Best Album for Children" category was *Woody's 20 Grow Big Songs*. It was a satisfying acknowledgment of the creative vision and sweat that produced the brilliant album. The press rang the Rising Son Records office in hopes of scoring a comment. Since Guthrie wasn't around, Sharon Palma handled the calls. She told one reporter, with a hint of understatement, "We're very, very excited about this."[118]

The album would face some stiff competition. It was one thing to compete against *Alvin and the Chipmunks in Low Places,* but the *Grow Big* album was also set against, of all people, Pete Seeger. The aged folk singer too had been nominated for his album *Pete Seeger's Family Concert.* In the end, Guthrie, Seeger, and the Chipmunks would all lose to Disney's *Beauty and the Beast.* Seeger, however, would not go home empty-handed. The Academy would recognize his contributions with a well-deserved Lifetime Achievement Award. To everyone's surprise, Seeger chose not to attend. As the awards were passed out in Los Angeles, Seeger was in Beacon, New York, working diligently on a book about songwriting. "I couldn't spare the time to go out," Seeger obliged, "but it is quite an honor."[119]

Guthrie too wasn't in attendance. He was already midway through his tour of the western US:

> **AG:** My idea was to get to the warmer West Coast only stopping along the way for a few shows. After The Ark, we drove to Woodstock, Illinois, for a night at The Opera House, a small venue that I also loved playing. We then deadheaded to The Coach House, another favorite and familiar music venue in San Juan Capistrano, California. It was a lot warmer in California too, and I was happier being on the West Coast.
>
> Maya returned home about halfway up through California, leaving me to finish the tour on my own. Not everyone can endure the road for long. I played around thirty-six shows during the tour up the West Coast before returning home on the northern route at first, then diving southward through Montana, Idaho, Wyoming, Colorado, New Mexico, and Texas. From there I was back in decent weather. I returned to The Farm during the last few days of March.

The weather hadn't been accommodating. Guthrie described his tour of the Pacific Northwest and western states as one "hell of a journey. I've been through five separate snowstorms, three major squalls, and two good ice rains, not to mention the regular winter weather that flows from one end of the country to the other."[120] Following two frostbitten gigs at the appropriately named Glacier Grande in Whitefish, Montana, the gauge on Guthrie's truck registered the outside temperature as twenty-five degrees below zero.

On 19 February Guthrie was scheduled to begin a three-night residency at the Gallatin Gateway Inn, on the edge of Bozeman. During his residency, Guthrie visited the Gibson Guitar Factory. The famed guitarmaker had opened new factories in Bozeman and Memphis in 1989, and many guitar enthusiasts thought the company's new models rivaled those of its glory days. Guthrie instantly fell in love with a newly minted J-180 guitar, one of two just off the production line. It was the type of guitar that the Everly Brothers played. Guthrie recalled the Everlys as "heroes, and the first record I ever actually purchased was theirs." "There are songs in this guitar," Guthrie mused, justifying the expensive purchase.[121]

The solo concerts were lonely, introspective ones. Guthrie's tour diary, published in the March 1993 issue of *The Rolling Blunder Review,* documented the realities of the on-the-road life of a touring musician: less-than-luxurious hotel accommodations, an endless search for something decent to eat—sometimes *anything* to eat—of lousy coffee, and one-nighters on cramped stages no larger than "a double-bed."[122]

Things picked up a bit in mid-March as he headed south for shows in Texas, Louisiana, Tennessee, and Kentucky. On 22 March, two days prior to a gig in New Orleans, Guthrie received news scientists had managed to isolate the renegade gene that brings on Huntington's disease. A reporter tracked down Guthrie, who was resting in a hotel just off the French Quarter. The singer acknowledged he wouldn't change his own mind about being tested for the gene, but was nonetheless happy to learn of the breakthrough. It wasn't only a victory for the medical community, but a vindication of his mother's work in getting scientists to seriously research the disease. "I'm sure wherever she is, she is smiling right now," Guthrie offered. "There was very little known about the disease when my father became ill in 1952. My mother educated herself to the point where she knew more about the disease than most of the doctors who were trying to deal with it."[123]

In Nashville, Guthrie made a rare television talk-show appearance on the Nashville Network's program *Miller and Company* with host Dan Miller. The two shared a lengthy and interesting conversation, touching on a variety of subjects: the creation of the *Woody's Grow Big Songs* album, Bob Dylan, Woody's eclectic archive of 78-rpm records, the accusations of his father's membership in the Communist Party, and of Guthrie's own heavily redacted FBI file.

Since the Huntington's news was fresh, Miller brought up the uneasy subject. Guthrie responded philosophically: "Sometimes you got to trust in God. You got to live your life as though you're not going to be here tomorrow, anyway. If you can do that, it doesn't matter if you're gonna get sick five or ten years from now." He explained with so many sick people already in need of attention, it was selfish to perseverate on whether or not he'd *remain* healthy. "I got a fabulous teacher in Florida," Guthrie continued. "Her name is Ma. She's a wonderful lady. She took me by the hand one day years ago and brought me into a bunch of places where she goes and visits people who are sick from AIDS, from cancer, Alzheimer's . . . all kinds of stuff. And I suddenly realized me, with my little gene problem—if it's there—is nothing. There are people who need help *right now*. There are people who are dying *right now*. There are people who are alone *right now*."[124]

AG: Mid-April 1993. I returned to Montana in the Red Hanuman Bus (a 1975 Eagle), with Dennis LaChapelle driving me and Abe's band, Xavier. We were back to a full sound on stage, as we'd done in the previous years. The bus deadheaded to Missoula for our first show and continued working our way back home. There were a few breaks during the next few months, but essentially Xavier and I covered a lot of territory doing our gigs. There were a few solo shows included, when the venues weren't large enough to have a full band on stage.

In April of 1993 the former Indian River Festival would move from Vero Beach to the campus of Brevard Community College in Melbourne, Florida. The benefit would no longer be held in February, as had been tradition, but was scheduled for mid-spring. Since the new location no longer had a geographic tie to Indian River, the festival was rechristened "Arlo Guthrie's Great Music Festival." All proceeds would go to the Indian River lagoon project, the Pelican Audubon Society, and several AIDS-related education and care groups.[125]

Woodstock MC Wavy Gravy hosted the day-long event. This year's festival featured less star power than previous years, Guthrie and the Outlaws being the day's biggest box-office draws. There was an effort to attract younger listeners to the college campus, with no shortage of alternative rock and heavy-metal bands booked: Xavier, of course, but also the Giant Hairy Nevus, Lost City, Scoobee Doos, What!, Relative New Point, Tribulations, and Arrow. The youngest concertgoers would be served as well. David Grover entertained at the children's stage, as would Guthrie in a special set designed for kids.[126]

It was Guthrie's intention to make certain that his festivals brought out families and communities to celebrate together. "We've tried to become a real community event," Guthrie told the Cocoa-based *Florida Today* newspaper. "Everybody wants beautiful beaches and clean water and those things. The question is, how do we go about getting it? The movement for change doesn't start with the Congressman or Governor. It starts with the community. We need to make friends with each other in our community because we can see change."[127]

In June, Guthrie was back in Los Angeles at UCLA's Drake Stadium for the "Troubadours of Folk" festival. Cosponsored by Ben & Jerry's Ice Cream and Rhino Records, the weekend folk festival boasted an amazing lineup: Ramblin' Jack Elliott, Judy Collins, Beausoleil, Janis Ian, John Hammond, Richie Havens, John Prine, Odetta, Roger McGuinn, Bob Gibson and Hamilton Camp, Tish Hinojosa, Peter Case, Jimmie Dale Gilmore, the Kingston Trio, Taj Mahal, Joni Mitchell, Richard Thompson, Leon Redbone, and Peter, Paul and Mary. There was even a special one-off "unplugged" set featuring Jefferson Starship.

At the press conference, Ted Myers, an A & R coordinator at Rhino Records, suggested environmental concerns had supplanted Vietnam-era protest anthems as the primary subject of topical songwriting. Though Guthrie didn't necessarily disagree with the assessment, he saw the movement as a continuum: "A lot of today's concerns are the same ones we had back then. I was in the environmental movement in the late '50s, as part of the 'Ban the Bomb' protests. Pete Seeger's Hudson River Revival was over two decades ago, and the Sea Turtles benefit concerts I did were years ago. . . . The environment was always an issue. We're still cleaning up this mess."

The two-day festival was filmed, select excerpts appearing on Rhino's *Troubadours of Folk: The Greatest Gathering of Folk Musicians in 25 Years.* Three of Guthrie's performances from UCLA were included in the set: "Garden Song," "Darkest Hour," and "I Can't Help Falling in Love." The latter song—made famous by Elvis Presley—had become something of a Guthrie standard since he first started singing it on his tours with Shenandoah. It was the folk singer's belief that if the tune wasn't yet considered a traditional folk song, it would be someday. He joked that even Pete Seeger—not generally considered a rock 'n' roll disciple—knew the song and could plunk out its melody on his 5-string banjo.

AG: On August 8, 1993 Pete, Xavier, and I were playing in Vienna, Virginia, at Wolf Trap, and the show was filmed and recorded. It was a magical night, and RSR released it as a two-CD set called *More Together Again* the following year (1994). Jesse Henderson (the head engineer) and I mixed the show for audio at Long View Farm probably around September–October 1993.

Pete and I had performed over a dozen times at Wolf Trap beginning in the late 1970s. But this one particular night had a magic to it, and we were thrilled that it had been recorded. In fact, to this day as of this writing, our most viewed video on YouTube is of me singing "Can't Help Falling in Love with You" from that night.

I remember getting to the venue at about 3 PM, when we would typically arrive to set up for the evening's performance. The catering and dressing rooms were located directly beneath the stage. Pete and I eagerly looked forward to the catering as it was usually a great setup. Pete spied a really big chocolate cake on one of the tables, and immediately cut what looked like a small piece of cake. He left that piece and took the rest of the cake into his dressing room. He emerged about twenty minutes later asking aloud, "Anybody want the last piece of cake?" I laughed. That was Pete behind the scenes.

The following month Xavier and I kept touring, mostly in the Midwest.

Guthrie was to perform at Ohio's Cuyahoga Heritage Festival on 27 August. The date fit nicely into his schedule as he was due in Chicago the following day. Several days prior, Guthrie agreed to an interview with the *Akron-Beacon Journal*. Matters of religion and spirituality were very much on Guthrie's mind, and the interview was limited to questions regarding faith and spirituality. Though both of his parents had been raised in the religious traditions of their Protestant and Jewish upbringings, Guthrie conceded that as his parents grew older, "they sort of merged their philosophies into something uniquely their own."[128] Seventeen years earlier, Guthrie had discussed this spiritual blending with *Rolling Stone:* "From my mother, I got the whole Jewish mind thing, you know, asking questions. From my father, I got the idea that the answers to the questions don't make a god-damn bit of difference."[129]

There was no one true path. Since founding the interfaith Guthrie Center, the singer had been telling of a chance encounter with a local preacher. The churchman was asking—with a hint of wariness—what sort of religious institution Guthrie was presiding over. "Well, it's a Bring Your Own God Church" was his response. It was a "smart-alecky" retort made in the moment, but not untruthful. Guthrie would later share a more expansive explanation of his personal brand of spirituality: "It's difficult to say I'm this or I'm that, especially when I enjoy a wide variety of opportunities to celebrate . . . or to just look at those things which I find extraordinarily beautiful. And that can be hearing some of the old Jewish hymns or those gospel songs. Or, standing out chanting with some Native Americans under a clear sky. To me, it's all the same. It's all different faces of the same Creator."[130]

AG: Toward the end of August, I went to Chicago for a meeting of "The Council for a Parliament of the World's Religions." It was a big long name for an event, but it was accurate. One of the founders of the event was an old and dear friend of mine, Brother Wayne Teasdale, a Franciscan monk. We'd met decades earlier and had remained friends.

I was well established by now as a member of Kashi Ashram in Sebastian, Florida. Ma Jaya Sati Bhagavati was my friend, mentor, and guru, and had established the ashram decades earlier. Kashi was a thriving interfaith community with focus on service to anyone, and in those days the AIDS pandemic was sweeping the world. We served the community of people dealing with AIDS, much to the displeasure of some neighbors. Ma's mission in Chicago became clear, she would make AIDS and the care of families and friends living and dying be among the concerns at the interfaith community. I was totally behind this effort to bring awareness and compassion to many in communities of faith who had been ostracized from religious groups around the world.

Upon arriving in Chicago, Guthrie was asked about his interest in Ma's teachings. "She took me by the hand and took me to the hospitals and hospices, and took me to see people that nobody goes to see and nobody seemed to care about," he told the *Chicago Tribune*. "I know I sound crazy when I talk about this, and it's really difficult to put into words because no words can describe it. There was this bright light and everything was known to me, and it was just total love. I was just free to be what I was. Afterwards, I realized I was speaking when all this happened, because I think I was afraid of disappearing into that light. Now I realize it was my ego trying to hang on, and we need to get past our egos."[131]

The conference was the second meeting of the Parliament of the World's Religions. The first also convened in Chicago—in 1893—so this revisit was long overdue. The exiled Buddhist spiritual leader, the High Holiness Dalai Lama, was also in attendance, calling for unity. "All religions carry the same message: compassion, forgiveness, love," he pleaded, "and each philosophy, each tradition, has a powerful mechanism to do good."[132]

Newspapers tended to report only on the controversies of the summit. Despite occasional flare-ups, more than two hundred and fifty religious leaders and eight thousand pilgrims attended the week-long conference at the Palmer House Hilton. One of the Parliament's goals was to compose a declarative "Global Ethic" on which all signatories could agree. For all its good intentions, this document too would cause controversy. Some delegates thought the proposal "too Western" in its tenets and sought revisions.[133]

Guthrie would participate on several panels, including a workshop titled "Towards a Civilization with a Heart." The small room at the Palmer House was unable to accommodate the number of people wishing to attend, so a decision was made to move the discussion into the hotel's corridor. The discussion was interrupted when hotel security arrived, advising the blocking of the corridor was a safety issue. The panel reconvened on another floor of the hotel but was, again, asked to disband due to safety concerns. This time everybody refused to move.[134]

AG: There were over two hundred delegates selected from almost every religious institution of any merit at the Parliament. There were probably upwards of two thousand representatives at the hotel, and the two hundred delegates were the voting members of the interfaith community. And after meeting for days, the delegates met to vote on the ten most important things they could do as a group. AIDS was not mentioned. It infuriated Ma, and she went ballistic on the delegates gathered there. She wasn't someone to be taken lightly.

Following the event, I did a concert in Chicago as part of the Parliament proceedings. It was also a fundraiser for them. During the concert, I'd found out that one more thing was added to the list of things they could do. AIDS and the problems people were facing became important. Much thanks to HH the Dalai Lama for recognizing Ma's important contribution to the assembly, and insisting that she be allowed to be heard. He could be convincing.

The concert, at Grant Park's Petrillo Bandshell, was less impressive than it should have been. Not only was the event poorly advertised but hundreds of chairs allotted to Parliament dignitaries were left unoccupied: the concert was absentmindedly scheduled to take place during the Parliament's closing ceremonies. Guthrie was only one of several musicians performing. Others scheduled were a New Age pianist, a reggae band, and the singer-songwriter Kenny Loggins. The program was to conclude with a group of Drepung Loseling Monks chanting and reciting Buddhist scripture.[135]

It wasn't the usual Sunday-in-the-Park concert experience. The *Chicago Tribune* asserted Guthrie's set provided one of the "shinier moments" of the generally lackluster, poorly attended event: "Arlo Guthrie . . . livened things up a bit when he came out and began an East-meets-West hootenanny with a sitar player." If nothing else, Guthrie's set served as a metaphorical musical sample of the conference's best intent. "It makes for better music when everyone does their own thing," Guthrie offered the sparse crowd. "Just like at the Parliament."[136]

Guthrie was to set off on a tour of mostly East Coast shows in the last three months of 1993. There were only a handful of shows in mid-October since Guthrie was busy working on the tapes that would produce the *More Together Again* album. Earlier in October, he had been visiting hospices in the Los Angeles area with Ma. While in the City of Angels, the two were invited to chat with Guthrie's old friend William J. "Bill" Rosendahl on his cable-television civic affairs program. On 7 October 1993, folks tuning into Century Community Cable were treated to *A Public Affairs Special: A Conversation with Arlo Guthrie and Ma.*

Things took an odd turn as the program was about to close. "At the end of the cable show," Guthrie recalled, Rosendahl said, 'I hear you're doing a television show, congratulations.' Before I could say, 'What are you talking about?' he signs off and the show ends." The only explanation, Guthrie figured, was Rosendahl's contention that "his cable show goes to Hollywood, where a lot of producers are."[137]

Which was apropos of nothing. Then, only a week after the broadcast, Guthrie received a phone call from a producer at Hollywood's Steven Bochco Productions:

AG: In late 1993 I met Stephen Bochco in Los Angeles, to audition for a part in a newly conceived television series called *Byrds of Paradise*. The show was created by Charles H. Eglee and Channing Gibson, produced by Stephen Bochco's production company. The thought of working as an actor in Hawaii agreed with me. Initially, I was only supposed to be acting in the first episode, but I had a recurring role as the show took off. It was one of the best times of my life.

★ ★ ★ ★ ★

Chapter Six

MYSTIC JOURNEY, 1994–1996

T wo weeks after his appearance on Bill Rosendahl's cable TV show, Guthrie found himself back in Los Angeles. He had been summoned to audition for a role in a new television show. Charles H. Eglee, a screenwriter who had worked with producer Steven Bochco on TV's *NYPD Blue,* was now the executive producer of the Hawaiian Island–based drama *Byrds of Paradise.* He reminisced there was little doubt Guthrie would get the role. Eglee recalled, "Arlo came out and on the last line of the scene he was reading, he finishes making his pitch to get the housekeeper job and says, 'So, listen man, I just hope I get the gig.'" At that moment series creator Bochco "looked over and said, 'You just did.'"[1]

In an interview with the *Boston Globe,* Eglee shared additional insight into why Guthrie was cast as Alan Moon. "Well, we needed to find a 47-year-old hippie to play that part, so we went through all kinds of lists. . . . When this idea of Arlo came up, everybody just went, 'Yeah, yeah.' The casting office was already familiar with Guthrie's work through Arthur Penn's *Alice's Restaurant.* "And because he's a performer and is something of a storyteller," Eglee continued, "there was something very compelling about him."[2]

The television drama *Byrds of Paradise* told the story of Sam Byrd (Timothy Busfield), an educator who uproots his family upon acceptance of a position as headmaster at Oahu's tony Palmer School. Byrd and his three children, Harry (Seth Green), Franny (Jennifer Love Hewitt), and Zeke (Ryan O' Donohue) are welcomed warily by island natives. As transplanted "outlanders," the Byrds are not conversant with Hawaiian customs or lifestyle. Sam chose to accept the position in hopes of buffering his children from a recent family tragedy. Sam's wife, Holly, had been murdered in a bungled robbery near their Connecticut home. How the grieving Byrd family deals with the impact of this loss, with teen angst, budding romances, and navigating their new lives as strangers in a strange land would provide the series' storylines.

The characters as written are realistic. Guthrie's Alan Moon is, frankly, the only character that is comic-book in construction. In the very first episode, Moon, a graying '60s remnant, is one of several candidates who show up at the Byrd family's door, looking to secure a housekeeping gig. Not surprisingly, the shaggy-haired hippie with the stoned countenance doesn't get the job.

In an early episode we're given a bit of Moon's backstory by Rex Palmer (Warren Frost), the school's moneyed founder. We learn Palmer's son and Moon were business partners for a time in the late 1960s—that business centering on the cultivation and distribution of cannabis. The pair were eventually arrested for trafficking their product, Moon taking the fall so his friend could plea-bargain down his own involvement. In doing so, father Rex's reputation as an upstanding community member was saved. Having served out a prison sentence of several years, Moon would return to Oahu, scratching out a living in a world he no longer recognizes.

Though Guthrie looked the part of an aging hippie, he took pains to point out he *wasn't* Alan Moon. Having lived through the experience of the *Alice's Restaurant* film, Guthrie was acutely aware some folks had trouble separating reality from fiction. He couldn't change that. Guthrie sighed, "I know when they see this show they'll say, 'I knew that Arlo was growing dope all along."[3] To be fair, fans of the folk singer were primed to accept such a scenario as truth. Guthrie's stage show—especially in the late 1960s and early 1970s—was awash with stories involving illegal substances. Well into the 1990s, Guthrie's own "Get Stuff" mail-order catalogs also sold (nonhallucinogenic) seed packets with teasing names as "Grow Some Weed(s)" and "Hippie Starter Kit."

Guthrie cautioned that while Alan Moon might look "like me and we come from the same era . . . he doesn't have a real sense of humor. He's in his own zone, doesn't have a global concept of things. No, that's definitely not me, though I know people may not believe that."[4] He conceded, "This character's real different from me. I don't know if the guys who hired me know that. They never really asked me if I grew dope, they never asked all those kinds of personal things." Since the producers of *Byrds of Paradise* had "discovered" Guthrie on the Rosendahl cable show, Guthrie assumed, "What they saw on the TV interview was someone who looked like and spoke like the character they had written."[5]

As a relic of the '60s, Alan Moon is a personable, good-natured sort. On the other hand, he's a pretty self-involved character. When trying to enroll—at age forty-seven—at the Palmer school of tweens and teens, he accuses Sam Byrd and dean of students Healani Douglas (Elizabeth Lindsey) of "ageism" when they balk. But whether dancing alone to a DJ or reminiscing about his days as a fan following Frank Zappa's tours, Alan Moon serves as the program's much needed light-relief character. There aren't a lot of belly laughs in the series. The teleplays of *Byrds of Paradise* tackle an assortment of serious emotional and cultural issues.

Guthrie admitted that when asked to audition for the role, he initially expressed disinterest, as his musical career was going well. It was only when told the series was to be filmed entirely on location in Oahu that his interest deepened. He simply loved the Hawaiian Islands:

AG: I had spent time in Hawaii off and on again since my first visit in 1967 on the way to Japan, with Judy Collins and Mimi Fariña. Together we were doing a tour of Japan, and we stopped in Hawaii to break up the trip. I was back July 18, 1970, for a show at The Waikiki Shell (Honolulu's big outdoor venue) with Linda Ronstadt. The day after the concert I took part in a peace rally at Kapiolani Park Bandstand almost across the street. I have very fond memories of that event.

He was also happy to learn that the role of Alan Moon was relatively small. A more substantial role would require the memorization of extended dialogue. When he first arrived on set in December of 1993, he was nervous, but anxious to do his best. Though one television critic offered sourly, *"Memo to Arlo—you're not TV's worst actor, but don't sell the gee-tar,"* Guthrie wasn't about to phone in his performance.[6] When the filmmakers suggested, "Arlo, just be yourself," he understood instinctively that being himself really wasn't an option. "But being Arlo's self," Guthrie reflected, means "he wouldn't be doing the things he's doing in the show. So I have to pretend that I'm being somebody else. I'm not a trained actor, I've never pretended to be, and I'm having a real good time making up for that deficiency."[7]

AG: When the chance came to work from Hawaii for an extended period of time, I rented a small place in Mokuleia, nearby Haleiwa Town, back again on the North Shore. Luckily it was just across the road from where *Byrds* was being filmed, at least for many of the exterior shots. The movie studios were just outside of Waikiki Beach, so many times I had to drive the forty-five minutes to work very early in the morning. I loved staying in Mokuleia, and driving through the sugar cane fields of this remote part of Oahu.

I invited Jackie to come out numerous times, but she was busy with her own projects and had no interest in taking time off from that to be in Hawaii. So I lived by myself in a little cottage. Jackie would return there with me over the coming years, however, and we both really enjoyed the time we spent there.

On days when I wasn't needed, I would walk out the door of my cottage and go to the beach. There were miles of totally empty beaches on that part of the island. As I was laying on the sand one morning, a totally naked older man and woman walked up to me and asked why I was wearing a bathing suit. I didn't think I'd quite heard or understood what they were asking. It turned out I was laying on the sand of a nude beach. I don't know if it was really designated that way, but for them it appeared to be so. I had the feeling that traditional Hawaiian culture wasn't quite ready for a bunch of naked white people to be parading up and down their beaches, so I let the old timers go by without further conversation and resumed my quiet time alone and clothed.

While Guthrie was sunning himself on the beach, Jackie was across the country freezing in Manhattan. The 36th annual Grammy Awards were held on 1 March at Radio City Music Hall. Jackie was attending should her husband receive an award for his reading of the Woody Guthrie *Bound for Glory* audiobook. Though he didn't win, Guthrie was satisfied his work on the project was recognized by the Academy. Two of his recordings had now been nominated by Grammy voters in consecutive years. His only regret was not entering *Son of the Wind* into competition. It surely would have been a contender in the "Best Folk Recording" category. But working and sunning in Hawaii seemed pretty decent consolation.

AG: The cast members were people I actually liked, and got along with. Tim Busfield, Seth Green, Jennifer Love Hewitt, Ryan O' Donohue, and Elizabeth Lindsey were the primary actors, and I was very fond of every one of them. My particular role—that of a goofy forty-five-year-old hippy returning to high school—was something I had fun portraying.

So the news was devastating to the cast when, on a blue Monday, 9 May 1994—and only two months following its premiere—ABC announced cancellation of the series. Network brass cited the show's poor ratings, although there were whispers the production costs of shooting on Oahu were prohibitively expensive. In any event, the show was over. Guthrie was disappointed, but he laughed when well-meaning folks offered words of consolation. When he responded that it was okay, that he would "just have to go back on the road," they looked puzzled. "Oh, you sing too?" they'd ask.[8]

While *Byrds of Paradise* didn't catch on with the public at large, the series was celebrated by islanders themselves. The Hawaii *Tribune-Herald* noted the islands had not only lost a vehicle in which to tell their stories, but "dozens of local actors, technicians, and other crew members" were now unemployed.[9] The director of the island's Department of Business, Economic Development and Tourism calculated that the show had, in its short six-month lifespan, put ten million dollars into the local economy.[10]

Within a day or two of the cancellation there was a groundswell asking ABC brass to reconsider. A number of the island's radio stations and two of Honolulu's biggest newspapers asked fans to write and phone the network to register their support. Advocation for the program's reinstatement came from all corners: the NAACP, the Tribal Leaders of Traditional American Indian Councils, from schoolchildren from the islands and points well beyond.[11] Sadly, the petitioning was not enough. The *Byrds of Paradise* would remain flightless.

AG: The show aired on ABC TV from March 3 to June 23, 1994, during the 1993–94 season, and we had done thirteen episodes (twelve of which were aired), before it was cancelled.

Guthrie was saddened by the cancellation. He offered his thanks to those readers of the *Rolling Blunder Review* who had written or called ABC to make their voices heard. "Too bad we got cancelled," he would write, "but that's how it goes. I'm going to miss working with the friends I made both in the cast and in the crew. I never experienced anything like that before. I had a chance to be an equal in a company of truly wonderful people."[12] Though everyone blamed ABC for the cancellation, Guthrie was aware that some in the network were supportive of the series. It was the stockholders fretting over the show's lagging Nielsen rating who brought it down. As with the record business, everyone wanted a quick turnaround on investment.

It was ironic that Steven Bochco, who brought violent, sexual, and grim envelope-pushing stories to television, had delivered the thoughtful, culturally sensitive *Byrds of Paradise* to the small screen. Guthrie thought it interesting, "While there are groups of people walking the Halls of Congress deploring violence on TV, we have not received much support from them, so far. Here's a show where no one is getting shot, stabbed, investigated, mutilated, sexually harassed, made fun of, and demeaned as a human being. You would have thought that there would have been an outpouring of support from what is generally referred to as the religious right."[13]

While his fellow cast members had to scramble for new work, Guthrie seamlessly slid back into touring. Even as *Byrds of Paradise* was filming, the singer managed to slip away on occasion for a few West Coast gigs. On 13 February, Guthrie performed at a benefit for the Seva Foundation at San Francisco's Masonic Auditorium. He was only one of many performers on the program, others including Bob Weir, Graham Nash, David Crosby, Paul Kantner, Jorma Kaukonen, Jack Casady, Richie Havens, Wavy Gravy, and Country Joe McDonald. One of the songs performed by Guthrie that night, "Can't Help Falling in Love," was recorded and issued on the compilation CD *Sing Out for SEVA*.

Then, in mid-March, during another break from filming, Guthrie arranged shows in Redondo Beach, San Juan Capistrano, and Ventura. This brief tour culminated at a "Generations" show at San Diego's Copley Symphony Hall, on 26 March. That program, a benefit for AIDS research, featured Willie Nelson, A. J. Croce, and Guthrie. So there was never a time that his old Martin M-38 guitar was allowed to gather dust.

On the morning of the San Diego concert, Guthrie discussed *Byrds of Paradise,* musing the program had faced stiff time-slot competition: it certainly wasn't helpful to be scheduled against the wildly popular animated series *The Simpsons*. Guthrie acknowledged his acceptance of the Alan Moon role was partly motivated by an interest in making the general public aware he was still working, not "just a name in a crossword puzzle. A lot of people haven't seen me in a long time," he ruminated. "I make folk songs and there's not a whole lot of publicity in that."[14]

Guthrie's name would soon return to the spotlight. As 1994 would mark the twenty-fifth anniversary of Woodstock, a tsunami of retrospectives expectedly surfaced on TV, in print, and on film. There was no shortage of attendant controversy. Plans were announced to produce a blockbuster Woodstock of the '90s. A lot of corporate money was poured into the staging of Woodstock '94, with marketing and ticket prices bordering on the obscene.

The record companies were getting ready for the big push. Warner's planned on rereleasing the original *Alice's Restaurant* album on CD. Guthrie was sent a complimentary copy while on location in Hawaii, and he was on the phone with a journalist when the disc arrived in the mail. Removing the shrink-wrap from the case, Guthrie couldn't help but feel a nostalgic twinge. He was transported to autumn 1967 when he was sent the acetate of his very first album. Since acetates degraded quickly after each play— perhaps after five or six spins on the turntable—one had to be selective with whom they'd share first listens. Guthrie recalled,

> My mom was there, and I told her, "You gotta listen to it." I wanted her to come and sit down and hear this great new album I had made.
>
> She told me, "No, I'll listen to it from here."
>
> I said, "No, come over here and listen."
>
> She said, "No, I'll just do the dishes and listen from here."
>
> She didn't want to listen to it the way I wanted to, and it was the first time I realized that people have different ways of listening to music. Me and my friends would balance the speakers, and sit in just the right position . . . and it was so important to hear every little thing.
>
> But not to my mom. That's when I gave up thinking too much about how people were going to hear me.[15]

As for a proposed Woodstock commemoration, Guthrie was noncommittal. He hadn't been asked to perform at the big corporate event, but another company was looking to put on a more low-key festival the same weekend. The details were sketchy. Guthrie was on tour in Texas when the subject of Woodstock came up during the course of a preshow interview. "I think if they would have put on a free festival, I would have definitely gone," he mused. "The upcoming one is a lot of money, and I just don't think that's the way to celebrate the spirit of the event that actually took place."[16] But as August was still some time away, everything was still on the table.

There were other things to occupy Guthrie's time and attention. In the final week of March 1994 Rising Son Records issued *Arlo Guthrie & Pete Seeger: More Together Again,* the set capturing the recording of their 8 August 1993 concert at Wolf Trap Farm Park. Though he and Pete served as the prominent vocalists and instrumentalists, they were supported by Seeger's grandson, Tao Rodriguez, and all three of Guthrie's daughters— Cathy, Annie, and Sarah. Instrumentals and backing harmonies came courtesy of Xavier, with Abe on keyboards. The album would be the last of a trio of double album sets documenting three separate decades of Seeger and Guthrie collaborations.

In his notes to the album, Guthrie wrote,

> I know there will never be another night like this one—where generations of Guthries and Seegers got together with generations of friends and neighbors and sang their hearts out.
>
> We have captured one of those rare moments in the personal histories of everyone involved in the project. The thousands of voices singing these songs, new and old, are not unique to one generation or another. They are more than a concert hall or a city. They are the voices of a nation and a world that on any given night can be heard singing together—we just happened to have recorded one of those nights. What makes it extraordinary is that it is not unusual.[17]

Guthrie dedicated *More Together Again* to the memory of Paul Smith. Smith was not only his booking agent, but a friend. He was the principal figure behind Route 183 Productions, a North Hollywood company incorporated in the spring of 1973. Smith had previously worked for an agency charged with the handling of Guthrie's bookings—a firm with which the singer had become increasingly dissatisfied. Relieving that particular agency of their duties, Guthrie asked Smith to take over the booking of his tours. "Things started getting better right away," he recalled. In a poignant recollection written directly after learning his friend had passed, Guthrie offered an emotional, personal obituary. With Smith's acumen and assistance, Guthrie recollected, "We went from playing those bars and road houses back to the theaters and auditoriums where we were able to do our shows right."[18]

Guthrie escaped serving in Vietnam despite 1-A status. Smith was not so lucky, and the scars of his service forever haunted him. "I know that fucking war in Vietnam never ended for you," Guthrie wrote. "If you got a couple of hours of uninterrupted sleep at night, you were lucky. If I could have changed that, you know I would have—we talked about it. We laughed about it too. If people knew all the battles you've been fighting for all these years, they'd be surprised that you lasted as long as you did. You were stronger and braver than most people knew. But I knew."[19]

AG: Even as *Byrds of Paradise* continued to air publicly through June, we had wrapped up the season of shooting in mid-May. On May 12th I flew back to Massachusetts when Abe and I began a series of concerts that took us through the year—including a trip back to Tønder, Denmark, with Pete. In fact, Abe and I toured together for a couple of years taking us all over the country, and occasionally overseas.

From Tønder, Abe and I travelled to Italy and Sardinia for a few shows, returning later in the year for a full tour of Italy that December.

As Abe and I crisscrossed the country, Jackie was busy overseeing the building of our home in Roseland, Florida. She would meet up with us at various places, to take a break from construction and see some friends we'd come to know—especially on the West Coast, where she was from. We had rented a house in Sebastian, Florida, on Harris Drive, which was where Jackie and the girls lived and where I would return between tours when I wasn't at The Farm.

We stopped renting the house in 1996 when Jackie moved in with our dear friend Bill Rosendahl in Santa Monica. She was working on a project of hers we called "The Troubadour Project" and needed to be in LA. She had grown very fond of Doug Weston, who started the Troubadour in West Hollywood, which was where I met her in 1969. And as he lay dying, she would visit him often. His club changed hands at that time—and all of Doug's archives were being unceremoniously tossed into a dumpster behind the club. Jackie rescued as much as she could.

As August and the Woodstock anniversary loomed, there was no escape from the steady drumbeat of the campaign. There was certainly a need for the hype as a lot of money was on the line. The ever-expanding list of "A list" artists invited to perform at the "official" event ensured the wallets of sponsors and fans would be duly lightened. But to many others Woodstock '94 was antithetical to the spirit of the original event.

There was an alternative. Fifty miles away from the main event near Saugerties, the town of Bethel was planning to celebrate in an appropriate manner. This competing celebration was either cheered or ridiculed—one's feelings based primarily on their tolerance for nostalgia. Three days prior to Guthrie's appearance at the "alternative" Bethel '94 weekend, many of that event's performers held a dry run at Brooklyn's "Return to Woodstock" concert. That program, part of Coney Island's Seaside Summer Concert Series, was held on the boardwalk just off Ocean Parkway and Sea Breeze Avenue. The concert featured *genuine* Woodstock veterans: Guthrie, Canned Heat, Country Joe McDonald, and Melanie. The event was also free to the public . . . although high-rollers could enjoy premier seating for a mere sawbuck.[20]

A misty rain was beating down on Coney Island that afternoon. Guthrie mused that it was a sign—a true Woodstock reunion required such precipitation. But he was also saddened his old Brooklyn neighborhood was looking pretty rough, suffering more from dampened spirits than damp weather. In his introduction to his father's "Pretty Boy Floyd" that night, the singer shared that Woody,

> realized even before he was writing songs fifty or sixty years ago, something a lot of people still don't understand. And that is the more laws you make, the more criminals you produce. Seems like every time someone wants to get elected for something, they got a new law to pass. I'd love to see someone run sometime just to figure out what laws we could get rid of 'cause they're piling up. It's hard to tell outlaws from regular people lots of times, anyways. And I noticed that sometimes history don't move in the right

direction. There's more people living under the boardwalk tonight than when I was a kid. And that's not right. More people without houses, more people without food and stuff like that.[21]

The Bethel celebration almost didn't happen. On 1 August, the Shea Entertainment Company announced the cancellation of the program due to lackluster presales. Only 1,675 tickets had been sold, causing nervous financial backers to tap out. John Scher, the rock promoter coproducing the big-ticket Saugerties show, practically sneered. Calling Shea's Woodstock weekend little more than an "oldies show," Scher dismissed the Bethel event as a sad relic of the Aquarian Age, one appealing only to aging boomers. "I'm not surprised that the concept of doing a nostalgia festival geared to 40-to-50-year-olds didn't work," he opined tartly. "But it's sad."[22]

But if Scher thought the old guard was out of the game, he was in for a surprise. The desire to celebrate the spirit of the original festival was strong, and the rescue of the event would come courtesy of Richie Havens. Teaming with promoter Bernard Fox, Havens asked his friends to come out and play just to see what might happen.[23] The idea seemed crazy: not only was there no time to properly organize a show, there wasn't even a stage. When the pilgrims began to congregate in Bethel for the weekend, there was no live music to be heard through Saturday afternoon. The field was filled with people hanging about in campers and tents, partying and listening to vintage bands through boom boxes. No one was sure if there would be any live music at all.

That changed around one o'clock that afternoon. The gathered faithful watched as Guthrie's tour bus pulled onto the grounds. "I heard about what was happening on the radio and decided to come," Guthrie told reporters. "This just sounded like the right spirit of Woodstock." When asked about his noninclusion in the "official" Woodstock '94 event, the folk singer laughed, "Hey, I didn't even want to come to *this* when it was organized."[24]

Guthrie acknowledged he had no idea when he might perform—but likely at some point after stage construction was completed. A crew of volunteers had worked all of Friday night to construct something resembling a stage. The first incarnation was a single flatbed truck with speakers mounted at the sides. Several other flatbeds were brought in, with plywood flooring nailed tight to conjoin trailers and smooth out gaps.

Then, midafternoon on Saturday a torrential downpour lasting a hundred minutes soaked everyone and everything. This caused construction of the makeshift stage to be temporarily halted.[25]

Sitting on the steps of his bus and surveying the chaos—people ducking for cover and the field turning into a soggy bog—Guthrie mused the vibe was "feeling pretty familiar right now."[26] This was going to be a true Woodstock celebration. Guthrie didn't seem to mind the anarchy—and there was a lot of it. He even helped direct traffic as cars continued to pour onto the site. "I didn't want to go to this when it was organized," he admitted. "It's a feeling that's kind of familiar, with . . . all the volunteers out there building the stage, people coming together."[27] He admitted, "I wasn't going to do this as an organized thing. But once it became free, I decided to come."[28]

The live music didn't get off the ground until nearly 10:00 PM, when Melanie walked out on stage. Guthrie and Abe followed, finishing well past midnight. Afterwards, the stage was ceded to a number of local bands who jammed into the wee hours. On Sunday, the determined fans who braved Saturday's raging rainstorms were rewarded with sets courtesy of Havens, Peter Yarrow, and Mountain.[29]

In the closing days of August, Guthrie escaped the Woodstock madness, traveling to Denmark for two sets at the Tønder Music Festival. Directly afterward, he moved on to Italy and Sardinia. The biggest of these gigs was a solo set at the *Ai Confini Tra Sardegna E Jazz* festival on 3 September. Guthrie confided his visit to Italy was mostly a working vacation. He offered that while "the pay sucks," the sumptuous meals made the brief tour worthwhile.[30] The European shows proved to be his last vacation for some time. Upon returning to Massachusetts, Guthrie was to begin work on a long-delayed recording of a new studio album:

> **AG:** During the last three weeks of September of 1994, we began work on *Mystic Journey*, a new album of mostly original material that had been waiting in the wings for a chance to be recorded. The project was recorded once again just up the road, in Dalton, Massachusetts, at Derek Studios. I used Abe's band, Xavier, as the predominant sound, and brought in other musicians when it seemed like a good idea.

The new album originally carried the more playful *Disguise the Limit* as its working title. While Guthrie had hardly been inactive in the decade following *Someday*, a new studio album of mostly original material was long past due. *Mystic Journey* marked Guthrie's welcome return to songwriting, having penned nine of the album's eleven tracks. Only two of the original songs would be familiar to fans. "When a Soldier Makes It Home" had first been introduced to his stage show in 1989. Guthrie's "Stairs" was a more obscure original, the song appearing infrequently during his concerts of 1987. Once Guthrie went solo in 1988, the folk rock–propelled "Stairs" had been quietly dropped from his sets.

Though Guthrie's albums for Warner Bros. had a mostly mosaic quality about them, *Mystic Journey* was differently constructed. "Previously, I'd put out albums reflecting the various strains of music I was interested in," he offered. "You'd hear something rock-y, alongside a bluegrass tune, then a folk ballad, because that's how I perceived music to be. That's how I listened to it, omnivorously. But I think it was too much for the new fans. So for this one I wanted a cohesive album which was all of one piece, reflecting a particular style."[31]

If the album's sonic fidelity was consistent, its content was not. "The album sort of developed organically; it wasn't a preconceived unit," Guthrie mused. He offered that the new album "wasn't meant to be cohesive. It's just a group of individual songs that I thought fit together fairly well."[32] He told another journalist, "*Mystic Journey* just took time to grow. Most of these songs are fairly new, not more than three or four years old. There are a few songs that have been around for a while. I've had a chance to let some of the ideas mature. I think they've aged somewhat gracefully on this record."[33]

Several of the songs appearing on *Mystic Journey* reflected Guthrie's interest in matters of spirituality and mortality. The singer would write in the album's notes, "This record is dedicated to Ma Jaya Sati Bhagavati and to those for whom these songs were written and sung. Your faces are forever in my heart—who cared enough to cry. To the mourners of this passing age—courageous enough to laugh. And to those whom we shall never forget."[34]

Three of the songs on *Mystic Journey* were clearly influenced by Ma's teachings and by both Ma's and Guthrie's bedside visits to those suffering illness and loneliness. During certain periods Guthrie explained that he and Ma had visited as many as one hundred ailing people in a single day.[35] There was a consensus—amongst journalists, at least—that Guthrie's interest in issues of mortality was the result of living his life under the cloud of a possible Huntington's diagnosis.

Perhaps. "Some of us are going sooner and some of us are going later, but we're all going," Guthrie reasoned. "I think if you expect people to be compassionate, you've got to show some compassion to those who are going now."[36] One of Guthrie's stage raps was with the world in such sorry shape, "there was never a time that you could do so little and have it mean so much to people." This lesson was confirmed by his brief but meaningful bedside visits. "I had always thought you had to sit with somebody for hours and hours. I didn't know that you could spend just a little time with someone and that you could make the difference."[37]

It's impossible to calculate the influence the hospice visits had on Guthrie's mindfulness. "We visit a lot of people who are right now dealing with HIV and AIDS, and their caregivers," he reminded. "We also work with people who are near death, especially with children, and most of those are AIDS-related."[38] If critics thought these bedside visits interfered with his artistic output, the singer found the opposite to be true. "You know what? It fills your life," he explained. "You could be doing a lot of other things in this world, but nothing fills your life like sharing it with somebody in the most important moments of their life. Aside from being born, the only other important thing is leaving."[39]

The bedside visits and Ma's tutelage had a profound effect on Guthrie, providing inspiration for several songs on *Mystic Journey:* "Some of the songs are songs that I think create a sense of reality for people who are dealing with very important issues at certain times of their lives. . . . So a lot of the songs on here are dealing with life and death issues and spirituality."[40] Ma directly inspired Guthrie's "Doors of Heaven," one of the album's loveliest songs. During one of their visitations he and Ma found themselves in their vehicle between stops. "We were driving down the road and she just had that thought, 'If all the doors were closed in Heaven, where would all the angels go?' "That's a song," he thought to himself. Almost simultaneously, Ma turned to him, suggesting, "You know, there's a song in there."[41]

Though the song remains one of Guthrie's most beautiful compositions, others thought it treacly and impossibly utopian in vision. Critic Colin Harper described "Doors of Heaven" as a "well-meaning but horribly 'Imagine'-esque piece of whimsy that will probably be a minor hit for somebody."[42] Of course, having your song compared to John Lennon's best known post-Beatles classic was, at best, dubious criticism.

If Guthrie was even aware of Harper's remark, it's likely he would have ignored it. Lee Hays once defended Pete Seeger's alleged naiveté and sense of optimism by saying, "It's the bright side of the mirror that does the work."[43] This, seemingly, was Guthrie's view as well. He was proud of his work on *Mystic Journey,* assuring fans the new album contained something "out there for everyone. In our lives, in this world, we're dealing with death and destruction on all sides. So what we have to do is get through it, find a way to enhance the experience of living."[44]

Guthrie's new songs were, in essence, similar to those composed by his father and Seeger. "Anyone who knows my work won't be surprised by the songs here, or the themes," he told journalist David Hinckley. "I've never had much patience with people who say that we're wasting time here. Like my Dad, I've tried not to dwell on the negative stuff—certainly not where you say things are so bad there's no point in trying to do anything about them."[45] In a subsequent interview, Guthrie took pains to point out that while he was not trying to compare his work to that of his father, he acknowledged, "We're doing a lot of similar things and I love that. I think it means something to people." Guthrie also offered, "We're not just playing guitars . . . we're continuing the ideas and values that accompany these songs. There's a wonderful feeling in tradition."[46]

Though critics doted on the album's spiritual theme, only three or four songs on *Mystic Journey* fit such a narrow definition. Guthrie's view of "spirituality" was pretty expansive: "To me, all songs are spiritual songs," he explained. "I don't care if it's disco or rap or country or whatever. Spiritual to me is how you choose to live your life and where your heart is. That's where your spirit is."[47]

The title track of *Mystic Journey* was not a Guthrie original. The song had been composed by a busking musician named James Rider, and it had come to Guthrie's attention a decade earlier when he was visited at The Farm by Ramblin' Jack Elliott. Elliott was accompanied by a girlfriend, Barbara Dodge, and a young man named James Rider. Dodge had made Rider's acquaintance on a New York Metro North train bound for Clearwater's annual festival. Elliott described Rider as a "big, tall, skinny, gangling Canadian kid with a big black cowboy hat and a guitar and harmonica" who played "just like Bob Dylan." In Elliott's recollection, Rider and Dodge smoked "a joint together on the train" and became fast friends.[48]

In Elliott's estimation, Rider became an "adopted son for a couple of weeks. . . . A real nice kid. He was singing on the streets all 'round New York. His name was Rider James Riley. Or 'James Rider,' as he later changed his name. And he was very good, but he never got past the basket house stage."[49] Following that afternoon at Clearwater, the three would visit Guthrie at The Farm in Washington, Massachusetts. Rider slipped Guthrie his self-produced cassette of original songs. In Guthrie's opinion most of the songwriter's efforts were "sappy love songs," even telephoning Rider afterward to say so. But one song stood out, the Kerouac-style *On the Road* travelogue "Mystic Journey." Guthrie told Rider that he was going to record the song at some point. It was a real firecracker.

The second non-Guthrie composition on the album was the beautiful—and mostly forgotten—treasure "You Are the Song." The song's evocative melody had been composed late in life by silent film legend Charlie Chaplin for an unrealized film project. The tune was reportedly sketched as a loving tribute to the actor's wife, Oona. The lyrics were later added by songwriter Glen Anthony. Guthrie was not the first to record the song. In 1977 a Pittsburgh-based pop music vocalist and nightclub performer, Charlie "Doc" Stewart, issued the song as the A-side of an obscure single on the Diane Records label. Guthrie recalled Chaplin, the "Little Tramp," as "one of the heroes of my parents . . . and me."[50]

While the three weeks of working in the studio on *Disguise the Limit* were productive, the album was still unfinished when October rolled in. Guthrie was hoping he might find time in November to get back into the studio, but opportunities were limited: he was scheduled to head out for a two-month-long tour with few breaks. October's shows were solo acoustic gigs—well, Arlo and Abe, sans Xavier—venues ranging from intimate coffeehouses to theaters. One of the tour's earliest stops was a two-night residency at Dayton, Ohio's Canal Street Tavern. While there the singer noticed a poster advertising an upcoming gig by "The Hawaiian Slack Key Guitar Masters: Cyril Pahinui, Leward Kaapana, and Keola Beamer."

While on a tour of Hawaii in the 1970s, Guthrie had played on a program with both Cyril Pahinui and his father, Gabby Pahinui. Gabby was a legendary slack-key guitarist, having contributed to Ry Cooder's 1976 Warner Bros. album *Chicken Skin Music*. That collaboration led to Pahinui recording his own album for the label with Atta Isaacs and Cooder: *The Gabby Pahinui Hawaiian Band, Vol. 1.* Gabby passed away in 1980, but son Cyril was preserving his legacy by offering his own mastery of the slack-key guitar. The style was, as Pete Seeger might say, the result of disparate traditions getting "All Mixed Up." Though slack-key was mostly identified with native Hawaiian music, the guitar was brought to the islands by Spanish and Mexican *vaqueros.* The Hawaiian contribution was adding a slide and distinctive open-tunings.

Guthrie was reacquainted with Cyril on the set of *Byrds of Paradise.* On the show's closing episode, Guthrie and Cyril can be seen sitting beachside on Oahu's north shore playing the former's "Moon Song." Guthrie had already recorded "Moon Song" for *Disguise the Limit* back in September but, upon learning his friend would be on the mainland and as close by as Ohio, he desperately wanted Cyril to add his own filigrees to the existing recording. Arrangements were made for Cyril to fly into Albany, New York, where he would be met by Abe.

"How do I know what he looks like? Abe asked his father.

"Just look for the guy who's freezing," Guthrie replied.[51]

The finished recording served as the album's opening track, the guitars of Guthrie, Pahinui, and Ed Gerhard weaving a dreamy, wistful luster.

In 1985, Harold Leventhal had conspired to have Guthrie assume ownership of Pete Seeger's Thanksgiving weekend concerts at Carnegie Hall. Due to a Carnegie renovation project, there was no program in 1986. But from 1987 through 1992, the weekend was Guthrie's alone. These were a mix of solo shows, concerts backed by members of Shenandoah, and programs with Xavier—even an evening with the entire Guthrie clan gathered together on stage. The one person missing was Pete Seeger. Guthrie really wanted to bring his old friend back to Carnegie, and he convinced Seeger to return at the 1993 staging. The two had shared a concert date earlier that same year, the evening the *More Together Again* concert was recorded. In his program notes for the Carnegie '93 show, Guthrie wrote, "Pete said that the audience at Wolf Trap had been one of the best crowds he had ever heard. It was the voices at that show which inspired Pete to join us for these concerts."[52]

The 1993 show went so well that Seeger agreed to perform again on Thanksgiving weekend 1994. Guthrie allowed that the two programs would mark "the first time since that last Carnegie show that Peter and I will be on stage together. We have a lot of catching up to do." Guthrie thanked Harold Leventhal for making the event possible: "These concerts at Carnegie Hall with Pete Seeger are part of a long tradition of families and friends coming together. And they're coming in from everywhere in the world."[53]

Guthrie would meet with Seeger on one more occasion as 1994 came to a close. On 3 December, Guthrie was in Washington, DC, to attend, of all things, a dinner hosted by the US State Department. Guthrie had visited the White House once before—back in 1980 directly following the inauguration of Jimmy Carter as president. But Guthrie's current presence in the White House's East Room was less surprising than that of Pete Seeger. Seeger, looking uncomfortable in an ill-fitting tuxedo borrowed from his father's closet, was one of five artists to be presented—by President William J. Clinton—with a prestigious Kennedy Center Honor. The Kennedy Center Awards were given to Americans recognized for a lifetime of achievement in the performing arts.

Clinton introduced Seeger as "an inconvenient artist who dared to sing things as he saw them. He was attacked for his beliefs, and he was banned from television."[54] The president also noted that despite all the attempts to silence him, Seeger continued to sing for the causes of civil rights and peace. Guthrie wasn't the only one to note the irony of Pete Seeger getting an award from the US government. Guthrie told the circle of journalists covering the event, it had been "a long way from the McCarthy hearings to the State Department" for Seeger. This was a reference to the folk singer's 1955 appearance before the House Un-American Activities Committee and its contempt of Congress admonishment. But Guthrie teased that the "best reason I had for coming was to see Pete in a tux tonight!"[55]

The *New York Times* noted the irony as well, describing the septuagenarian as someone having "spent more time singing outside Washington's halls of power than within them."[56] It had been a year of belated national recognition for Seeger. In October, he had been presented with the equally prestigious National Medal of Arts, Clinton describing the banjo picker as having "had a personal impact on my life, and I daresay, the lives of every American citizen."[57] But even at age seventy-five, Seeger remained a lightning rod for controversy. These late-age acknowledgements were celebrated by some, decried by others.

Things would get particularly nasty as the Kennedy Center Awards program neared. Several days before Seeger received the honor, a *Washington Post* reporter visited him at his home in Beacon, New York. The resulting feature, "America's Best Loved Commie," was neither condemning nor fawning. It simply painted a portrait of a free-thinking man of conviction *and* contradiction. It was clear time had not dimmed Seeger's political radicalism. But he now allowed for the possibility of the coexistence of socialism and free-market capitalism. "I tell socialists, every society has a post office and none of them is efficient. No post office anywhere invented Federal Express."[58] Seeger told the *New York Times,* "I'm sure that they've looked at both sides of the question, and they decided to give the award to me for my music and try to ignore my politics."[59]

Not everyone was willing to ignore Seeger's politics. Eric Breindel, the editorial page editor of the Rupert Murdoch–owned *New York Post,* contributed a vicious essay, railing against Seeger ("a man who stood by Stalin") and disparaged any official commemoration of this "career soldier in the American Communist army."[60] On the morning of the Kennedy Center's television broadcast, *Post* critic John Podhoretz also attacked Seeger. In Seeger's induction, host Garrison Keillor had introduced him as a man "singing about freedom and justice and about people who work hard and about our country." Such testimonials sent Podhoretz into fits of rage. By celebrating Seeger, Podhoretz argued, the country was honoring "this song-stylist of Stalinism, this troubadour of tyranny, this Horace of Ho Chi Minh homiletics."[61]

Seeger shrugged off the attacks. He had been through all of this before. "When anybody says I'm a Communist," Seeger mused, "I say, 'Yup, just like the American Indian. There was no thievery, and no wealth either, among the Indians."[62] As uncomfortable as it was for right-wingers to see Seeger receive the award, it wasn't easy for Seeger to allow himself to be fawned over in such an extravagant manner.

On the afternoon of the star-studded celebration, an "elegant brunch" was served at Washington DC's swanky Ritz-Carlton. Pete and Toshi Seeger were in attendance, the folk singer dispensing with the formal tuxedo for a "brown striped sweater and pants, a blue flowered shirt and well-worn Nike sneakers." The well-heeled crowd of Washington insiders was catered with silver trays of crab cakes, salmon, lamb, pastries, and endless bottles of

champagne. Seeger's discomfort was obvious. "I'm eating too much," he
sighed. "And when I think of all the starving people in the world, my conscience gets to me a bit. Other than that," Seeger conceded, "it's a very
interesting experience."[63]

That night at the gala—some paying as much as $5,000 to attend—
short films were played, each capsulizing the career of an inductee. The
recapping of Seeger's controversial life was, not surprisingly, the most
political. Keillor briefly explained how the folk singer's songs were woven
tightly into the American fabric. A musical tribute would follow with the
Choral Arts Society of Washington singing Lead Belly's "Good Night,
Irene," a song the Weavers topped the charts with in 1950.

Guthrie performed next and, along with Pete's grandson Tao, he sang
Seeger's "If I Had a Hammer." He commented, "Pete, years ago when some
well-intentioned folks were trying to replace the national anthem with
'This Land Is Your Land,' you suggested it wasn't a good idea. You said the
worst thing you could do to a song was to make it *official*. . . . I'm wondering
what we're going to do now that *you've* become official."[64]

The segment closed, as one might have expected, with everyone singing Woody's "This Land Is Your Land," Guthrie handling lead vocals.
When Guthrie got to Woody's "Private Property" verse, he slyly slipped in a
line of topical protest. Instead of incanting the original ("As I Went
Walking/I Saw a Sign There/and on the Sign It Said, "Private Property"/
But on the Other Side/It Didn't Say Nothing/That Side Was Made for You
and Me," Guthrie replaced "Private Property" with "Proposition 187." The
cameras quickly cut to Seeger in the loge, clapping in approval at Guthrie's
pointed political gesture. Proposition 187 was a contemporary and controversial hot topic. Californian voters approved a ballot initiative that would
deny undocumented people access to emergency health care, public school
tutorship, and other state-administered services. Critics of the initiative
found the measure inhumane and xenophobic.

Directly following the performance, Guthrie was cornered by reporters. He admitted to not advising producers he was going to include the
"Proposition 187" verse. But the moment felt right and, after all, this was
Pete Seeger they were celebrating. "You have to be your father's son, just at
times," he calmly responded to the brouhaha. "I didn't know if I was going
to do it or not," he mused, thinking the response from the political types
attending was "kind of positive."[65] When asked if Guthrie's small protest

verse might be edited out of the broadcast, the show's producer replied, "We put on the show that happened. . . . It's not a big deal."[66] The verse was included on the CBS broadcast of 28 December.

The night's Kennedy Center celebration should have been the climax of a very busy year . . . except it wasn't. The day afterward, Guthrie, Abe, and Xavier boarded a plane and embarked on a two-week, ten-show tour of Italy. "Xavier and I stuffed our faces with a zillion kinds of pasta," Guthrie recounted.[67] The tour marked the end of Abe's tenure with the band. As he had been backing his father on keyboards for some duration, he no longer had the time to devote his energies to the band he helped form. There were no hard feelings. The remaining members of Xavier would rebrand as "Lord Hill."

Guthrie returned to the US just before Christmas, forsaking the snow of Massachusetts for the sun of Florida. Actually, there was no family to return to in Washington. Jackie, Annie, and Sarah were living in a rental because the CrabHouse was still being rehabbed. The rental home was situated close to the Kashi Ashram, such proximity allowing Guthrie to visit with Ma and check in on friends. Ma was still working tirelessly with those afflicted with AIDS. Guthrie would sadly write during his absence, "Almost all of the children with AIDS I had played with on my earlier visits had died. As had most of the adults." There were a few folks who soldiered on courageously, and he made sure to pay them all a visit. Guthrie recalled, "The smiles of recognition from them will always remain fixed in my heart."[68]

While in Florida, Guthrie discovered his booking agency hadn't scheduled any of his now-traditional early-winter gigs out West. So he called a friend in Taos, New Mexico, asking him to book as many shows as he could in a week's time. He then had Amy Feld at Rising Son help fill in gaps in the schedule and extend dates beyond New Mexico. The tour was pulled together quickly. It began on 22 January 1995 at Albuquerque's Kimo Theater and finished a month and a half later at the Civic Center in Farmington, New Mexico.

Guthrie wasn't long into the tour when he suffered another of his "three-week cold-flu-whatever things." But Guthrie believed his appearance on Boulder, Colorado's "E-Town" radio show might have been "the worst sounding evening recorded as far as my voice is concerned." Rough vocals aside, Guthrie was pleased he had the opportunity to perform several songs from his forthcoming *Mystic Journey* album. "Abe and I unleashed some new material on the radio," he reminisced, "and, aside from how it sounds, we had a great time."[69] Otherwise the tour was a success— although poor Dennis LaChapelle had to navigate Guthrie's bus through no fewer than "three snowstorms, four rain squalls, and one blizzard."[70]

Midway through the tour Guthrie received word his daughter Annie had given birth to a son, Shiva Das Marquis Guthrie. It was Guthrie's second grandchild, Abe and Lisa's son, Krishna, having been first. Guthrie joked his choice of a name was "Curly." But he sighed, "Being a grandfather doesn't give you the same clout as you had being a father. Well, if he can put up with that name, I guess I can too."[71]

Though Guthrie toured throughout the spring and early summer of 1995, he cut back on the number of shows booked, playing mostly in the northeast. He returned to Boston's Hatch Shell on 22 April for the city's annual Earth Day celebration. Some eighty thousand people streamed through the Esplanade for the eight-hour-long afternoon of speeches and music, Guthrie sharing the bill with Al Kooper, Eddie Money, Mike and the Mechanics, Paula Cole, Jesse Colin Young, and many others. The speeches and sets that day were more somber and less strident than usual. Four days earlier the Alfred P. Murrah Federal Building in Oklahoma City had been bombed, killing 168 people, including nineteen children.

There were happier occasions worthy of celebration. On 22 June Guthrie appeared on stage at the Grand Hall of Cooper Union in Manhattan for a show commemorating the career of folk singer Oscar Brand. Brand was celebrating the fiftieth anniversary of his folk-music radio program on WNYC. The Canadian had been broadcasting his "Folksong Festival" since 1945, encouraging folk singers living near or passing through to visit. The show was a labor of love. Since WNYC was publicly funded, Brand was not paid a penny for his time and talent. It was a tradeoff. With no sponsors, his show suffered few censorship issues. "The station has never told me what to play," Brand proudly told the *Daily News*. "It's been a great run."[72]

Joining Guthrie at Cooper Union were old friends Peter Yarrow, Dave Van Ronk, Odetta, Richie Havens, Tom Paxton, Josh White Jr., and Eric Weissberg. Brand was instrumental in helping Guthrie get started as a professional musician some thirty years earlier. Brand admitted with guilt the only reason he invited a nineteen-year-old Arlo Guthrie to play at his American Music Festival in February 1967 was his being "Woody's kid." It was a professional courtesy. At that Carnegie Hall event Brand asked performers to limit themselves to a set of twenty-five minutes. So he was shocked when Guthrie sighed that, in his case, twenty-five minutes might be "one song."[73]

The reasons Guthrie was staying close to home in the late spring/summer of 1995 were twofold. The first was a desire to polish the tracks on the forthcoming *Mystic Journey* album. With postproduction of the album completed, the next step was getting the album engineered and readied for distribution. The other reason was Guthrie's decision to embark on a second long-delayed recording project:

AG: In July of 1995 we began work on a remake of "Alice's Restaurant." The original 1967 record was recorded in one or two days, before a live audience in a recording studio in New York. In effect, it was a live recording. The people gathered for the event had been friends or acquaintances of my manager, Harold Leventhal, or my producer, Fred Hellerman of the Weavers. As all those in attendance had already heard "Alice's Restaurant" (probably more than once), they were happy to be there, but not especially present in their response to the material. After all, how many times can you laugh at the same joke? Laughter had to be imported at various pivotal moments of the song. The B-side was equally difficult for me, as there was almost no rehearsal, and before a live audience there was no "take two" or even "Why don't we learn the song?" Musically it was awful. But it did rather well despite all that.

I remember bringing the test pressings of "Alice's Restaurant" to my friend's apartment that November, standing outside the door knocking and saying, "I got the album! I got the album!" Inside I heard them say, "We got the album, come on in!" I couldn't imagine how they'd got ahold of my album so soon. I had just received it myself.

I realized it was not my album everyone was excited about, but rather the Beatles album, *Sgt. Pepper's Lonely Hearts Club Band*, that had just been acquired by them that same day. I listened to *Sgt. Pepper* realizing that everything made before it had suddenly become obsolete, even the stuff that had been made that day.

On November 22nd *Alice's Restaurant* was released as an album by Reprise Records. I wasn't particularly happy with the album as it sounded awful to me. It had been hurriedly produced. Together, Harold and Fred owned publishing companies. With the article in the *New York Times*

and the sudden interest in me, Harold had struck a deal for me with Mo
Ostin of Reprise (Warner Bros.) Records to release a record as soon as
possible. He picked Fred to produce the recording. I had sold the publishing rights to "Alice" and the other songs on the record to Appleseed
Music (one of Harold and Fred's publishing companies), for a buck some
months before. That's how it was in those days.

Nevertheless, I wanted a chance to do it again, and it seemed that
the thirtieth anniversary of the original was a good excuse to do it. So, in
1996 we rerecorded the B-side in our own studio at The Farm, with Abe
doing the engineering. The A-side was from a concert we recorded at the
Church (The Guthrie Center) down the road. *Alice's Restaurant—The
Massacree Revisited* was released later that same year.

Guthrie's idea for rerecording the *Alice's Restaurant* album had long sim-
mered. As early as November 1988, the singer was telling the press he was
simply waiting for the right moment. "It's just the matter of getting the right
recording of the right timing of the right audience on the right night," he
suggested.[74] When pressed when Guthrie might get around to this new
recording project, Rising Son office manager Sharon Palma thought it
could happen sooner rather than later, but "with him you never can tell."[75]

Guthrie's desire to rerecord the album was somewhat odd. In the summer of 1988, Warner Bros. allowed him to issue the original *Alice's Restaurant*
album on cassette. But it was only a gesture of half-goodwill: the company
retained the rights to issue the original album on CD should it choose to do
so. Guthrie told *Guitar World Acoustic* one of the reasons he chose to rerecord
the entire record was "because it was the one album I couldn't get back from
Warner Bros. I said, "We have ways of dealing with that."[76]

The 1995 sessions wouldn't mark Guthrie's first attempt at rerecording
his famous talking blues. He had been working on a rerecording of "Alice's
Restaurant" as early as 1976. "It wasn't something that we would try all the
time," Guthrie admitted. "Doing 'Alice's Restaurant' every night would
drive anybody nuts. But we would still use all of the new portable recording
equipment on occasion to see if we couldn't get an updated version of it.
And we never could." More often than not, his attempts sank due to reasons
beyond his control. "In the thirty minutes or so that it would take to do the
song, there would always be somebody coughing, a glass breaking, a plane
going by, a train hitting something. Something would always go wrong."[77]

In June of 1995 Guthrie announced plans to record his updated version of the *Alice's Restaurant Massacre* at the Old Trinity Church. This time out, he wasn't going to rely on a one-take performance, hoping to recapture magic in a single session. The song would be played in its entirety on four consecutive nights, the best moments of each performance seamlessly blended together in postproduction. As was the case with the original session of 13 June 1967, the song would be performed before a live audience—there would be no canned laughter to augment. The sessions were set for the evenings of July 5, 6, 7, and 8 with only fifty tickets sold for each performance at $20 per guest. All proceeds from ticket sales would benefit the operation of the Guthrie Center.

On Wednesday night, 5 July, Guthrie picked up his guitar and—sitting on a stool before three microphones—ran through a single warm-up number, "Ukulele Lady." Sitting behind the soundboard was Abe, serving as the album's coproducer, with Greg Steele of Derek Studios engineering. This new version of the "Massacre" would exceed the length of the original by approximately two minutes. Over two decades, Guthrie had added "historical footnotes" to the original. The most famous of these noted the 18 minute and 20 seconds running time of the original was suspiciously the same timing of the infamous erasure on Nixon's damning Watergate tape. Though Guthrie's interest was to create a more-or-less faithful rendition of the original album, he assured fans he was "not pulling a Meatloaf," a reference to the 1993 album that reunited the rocker with songwriter Jim Steinman on *Bat Out of Hell II: Back into Hell*. The new *Alice's Restaurant* CD "isn't a sequel," Guthrie promised. "It's really the same song. It's updated a little bit."[78]

Guthrie appeared visibly nervous on this first night of recording. "This is kind of a very weird night for us," he allowed. "So if we look dazed, that's why. Some people may not have seen me for a while—or ever—and when they saw this being advertised, I'm sure some of them said, 'Hey, is that guy still alive?' Well, yeah, I am."[79] But the singer's anxiety had less to do with his performance than with any number of factors beyond his control.

The decision to rerecord the song in the church was one invested with obvious cyclical symbolism. Whether or not it was a wise choice was another thing altogether. The church was not a proper recording studio, a room sealed off from noise leakage. "I couldn't resist the temptation to try and pull this song off here," he conceded. "The thing is, trying to do a record anywhere is hard. Trying to do one here, especially when the song is a half-hour long, is going to be interesting. There's a train that goes by here about four times a day. I'm waiting for that train to come by."[80]

That first night the song went by without a hitch: no train whistles, no breaking glasses, no coughing spells, no rustling of chairs. The crowd sang along dutifully on the song's final chorus. "That was pretty good," Guthrie smiled following an exhale of relief. "Now all I have to do is sing it exactly the same way the next three nights so we can merge the best parts of the song into one." The song that brought Guthrie his greatest success was also an albatross. "You know the next important song I write will be one of those short little two-minute numbers."[81]

Though Alice Brock wasn't in attendance that first night, she was at Thursday night's session. There was, sadly, one celebrated figure who couldn't attend. "I miss Officer Obie," Guthrie sighed on Wednesday. "I wish he were here. He would have enjoyed this."[82] Indeed, former Stockbridge Police Chief William J. Obanhein had passed on, age sixty-nine, on 11 September 1994. Obanhein had retired from the force in 1985, having been caught up in an imbroglio caused by his old-school police tactics. When asked to comment on the chief's passing, Guthrie recalled Obie as "the quintessential small-town cop." "Bill and I became friends during the making of the movie," Guthrie recollected, "and we remained friends. He was a wonderful actor. We talked about doing a sequel together for twenty-five years. I'm going to miss him."[83] Alice Brock, who described Obanhein as a "fascist" in the late '60s, also got to see the chief's other side over the years. He was a troubled man who suffered a divorce and the loss of two children in tragic circumstances. "He was a very sweet man, and he was a very good cop," Brock conceded. "I certainly will miss having him on earth."[84]

The rerecording of the *Alice's Restaurant* album would be the last major recording project Guthrie would undertake in 1995, as the imminent release of *Mystic Journey* was to take priority. But that didn't signal any dearth of creativity as the year wound down. In fact, the singer was planning to dip his toe into the choppy waters of the publishing industry.

Guthrie was no stranger to the world of book publishing. In April 1968, New York City's Grove Press published Marvin Glass's ninety-two-page illustrated version of Guthrie's *Alice's Restaurant* opus. Then, in 1969, New York City's Amsco Music published *This Is the Arlo Guthrie Book,* a collection of Guthrie's writings and lyrics with an assortment of rare photographs and ephemera tossed in for good measure.

So it was with surprise twenty-five years later that Guthrie returned to the world of publishing with a children's book. The slim hardcover, titled *Mooses Come Walking*, was published by San Francisco's Chronicle Books in the autumn of 1995. The colorful tome received a lot of attention upon release, partly since it was a collaborative effort. The book's illustrations came courtesy of Alice Brock. Alice too was no stranger to the world of publishing, having written three books herself: *The Alice's Restaurant Cookbook, How to Massage Your Cat*, and the semibiographical *My Life as a Restaurant*.

In his introduction, Guthrie allowed that his poem "Mooses Come Walking" was written as he gazed out the window of an airplane and looked out over the clouds. He wasn't sure why he was thinking about mooses as he had "never thought or wrote about moose before."[85] But he scrawled out the short poem on the back of an envelope and slipped it into his pocket. Guthrie's memory of the creation was soon challenged by one member of his entourage who said the singer had in fact composed the poem on his tour bus. Guthrie wouldn't contest the moment or place of inspiration. "I was either on a plane or a bus going out west," he obliged. "There are two versions of this. One from somebody who was there who said I was on the bus, and one in my own mind that said I was on a plane. I'm not exactly sure. I might have read it on the plane after I got off the bus. In any case, I was on my way to Hawaii and all of a sudden a moose poem showed up."[86]

Guthrie faxed a copy of the poem to office staffers and things got out of hand almost immediately. Suddenly he was being barraged with photos of moose, candles carved as moose, and "all kinds of moose stuff."[87] More alarming was when he and Abe chose to communicate with one another exclusively through moose poetry. It had, in Guthrie's words, "become a nightmare."[88] He began to recite "Mooses Come Walking" at concerts beginning in November of 1994—and audiences loved it, many suggesting he turn it into a book. When he finally came around to the idea that his poem might actually be worthy of publication, he thought Alice Brock should illustrate it as "ever since I've known her she's been drawing things."[89]

Surprisingly, Brock accepted the assignment, though she later complained, "I ended up doing all the work."[90] She researched and carefully studied moose photographs for inspiration, but after months of indecisiveness and preliminary sketches, she decided to toss out any traditional moose renderings. She settled on creating the cartoon-ish, goofy, and extremely loopy animals seen in the final product.

The book might not have circulated far beyond Guthrie's concert merchandise table had it not been for a positive review ("Arlo with Antlers") in
the erudite *New York Times*.[91] It's of no little matter that the newspaper
offered a dense and detailed six-paragraph review of a 102-word poem.
The glowing *Times* review was the first of many to follow. In December
Guthrie and Brock set off for book-tour stops in Lenox, New York City, and
Philadelphia. Hundreds of fans and readers lined up in the cold to have
copies signed. Wringing his weary sore hand, Guthrie suggested he might
end up looking like a moose himself if the long line of folks awaiting signatures didn't dissipate.

No one anticipated the first printing of *Mooses Come Walking* would sell
out within three weeks of publication—just before the busy holiday sales season was set to kick off, no less. "There isn't one available in the whole world,"
Guthrie sighed. "The idiots, they didn't print enough, and now we've missed
the Christmas season. The second printing won't be out 'til February."[92]
Bookshops and Rising Son would belatedly receive back-ordered cases of the
second printing in early spring of 1996. Though the book did lose sales
momentum due to the delay, its success hardly went unrecognized.

Guthrie's interest in moose lore sparked his reputation as an authority
on all things moose-related. "I'm the moosemaster of Massachusetts," he'd
tell the *Berkshire Eagle* in a boast. He wasn't, of course, at least not officially,
but the offices of Rising Son had become a repository for a deluge of
incoming "moose materials." Fans were sending him any and all sorts of
moose ephemera they'd stumbled across. Sitting amongst these treasures,
Guthrie reasoned his adopted state might as well rename itself "Moose-a-
chusetts."[93]

The fictional moose appearing in the pages of Guthrie's storybook
were now almost as famous as an actual one. As a longtime resident of the
Berkshires, the singer was acquainted with the legend of "Old Bill." "Old
Bill" was still around—if only in a "sort of" way. His stuffed head and massive antlers were on display at the Berkshire Museum in neighboring Pittsfield. "Old Bill" was a beloved moose who roamed the hills of Washington's
October Mountain Forest at the turn of the century. His story was first told
in Walter Prichard Eaton's 1920 tome *On the Edge of the Wilderness*. The
moose was doted upon and left to his ways by residents until a hunter—
unaware of the unofficial protection status granted him by locals—brought
"Old Bill" down with a rifle shot.[94] In December of 1995, the seventy-fifth

anniversary of "Old Bill's" tragic end, a local author asked Guthrie to write an introduction to his forthcoming book *Walter Prichard Eaton: The Odyssey of Old Bill, the Berkshire Moose.*

Guthrie obliged. As the Berkshire's self-proclaimed "mooseologist," he could hardly refuse. He contributed a ten-stanza poem celebrating the life of "Old Bill." Guthrie's penchant for dark humor was evident in the poem's subtitle, "He's Just Ahead in Pittsfield." When asked by a reporter if he might someday consider putting his own moose poem to music, Guthrie demurred. "I don't plan on it at this point. This is not a song. This is litera-ture."[95] If nothing else, the appearance of a second Moose poem caused fans to ponder Guthrie's promise that "Mooses Come Walking" was merely the first of his series of "Collected Moose Poems."

There were few states in the US that Guthrie had not yet visited in his thirty-odd years of crisscrossing the country. On Saturday 16 September Guthrie scratched one such state off the list when he performed at South Dakota's Deadwood Jam. The event was founded by John McEuen of the Nitty Gritty Dirt Band. Jonathan McEuen, John's son, was to kick off the festivities. His band was followed by blues singer Keri Leigh, country singer Sylvia, McEuen, Poco, Guthrie, and the Fabulous Thunderbirds. These were the sort of festivals Guthrie enjoyed playing, the ones where you could meet with old friends under a tent "without the surrounding madness of a big city gig." He also noticed that he and his contemporaries shared some-thing in common. "You can always tell the '60s bands from the ones that came along later because the guys set up their own stuff."[96]

Of course there were the old guys and then there were the *really* old guys. As Guthrie and Abe skipped across the US on a string of one-nighters, Pete Seeger was in South America, touring under the auspices of the United States Information Agency. The folk singer, accompanied by his grandson, Tao, was to perform in Paraguay, Brazil, Argentina, and Chile. Though Seeger brought along any number of Spanish-language songs, he admitted being nonconversant in the tongue. He sang them, by his own description, in "gringo-Spanish." So Tao's presence was particularly helpful as he spoke the language fluently, thus allowing his grandfather to more easily navi-gate about.

Upon their return, Seeger and Tao accompanied Guthrie and Abe at the Carnegie Hall Thanksgiving concerts. This year's shows were stripped-down affairs: old-school hootenannies featuring old songs and old stories.

Guthrie had only performed with Seeger at a single concert earlier in the year—at Connecticut's Oakdale Theater in August—but these annual gatherings at Carnegie remained special. In his program notes Guthrie offered the "evenings at Carnegie Hall with Pete Seeger and myself have become, for me, the highlights of a year of living on the road."[97]

Though Guthrie wouldn't perform the "Alice's Restaurant Massacree" at Carnegie '95, a few weeks prior Rising Son had placed an ad in the trade industry publication R&R (Radio & Records). The ad alerted station managers the "new" *Alice's Restaurant: The Massacree Revisited* could be "On Your Desk by Nov 22nd." The notice continued, "Arlo Guthrie was arrested on November 27, 1965. . . . 30 years later, Arlo returned to the scene of the crime."[98] With the new CD ready for release, the question now was would anybody else?

On Monday evening, 17 January 1996, Guthrie was back in formal attire. The singer was surrounded by pop music glitterati attending the eleventh annual Rock 'n' Roll Hall of Fame induction ceremonies. The event was again held in the Grand Ballroom of the Waldorf-Astoria Hotel. The Class of '96 inductees included David Bowie, Jefferson Airplane, the Shirelles, Pink Floyd, Gladys Knight and the Pips, and the Velvet Underground.

Guthrie was attending as he and singer-activist Harry Belafonte had been asked to induct Pete Seeger into the Hall of Fame as an "Early Influence"—the category created to celebrate performers "whose music predated rock and roll but had an impact on the evolution of rock and roll and inspired rock's leading artists." This was the second time Guthrie was asked to help induct a pioneer, having already accepted the award on behalf of his father eight years earlier.

Belafonte's praiseful introduction was the longest of the night, clocking in at nearly seven and a half minutes—and causing Seeger to shuffle uncomfortably in the wings. If Belafonte's speech went on a bit too long, his testimony was genuine and heartfelt: the calypso singer too had endured the ignominy of the blacklist. "If I were to pick the fifth face on Mount Rushmore," Belafonte mused, "I would nominate Pete Seeger. For those of us who have looked upon art as a curious gift, a troublesome gift, an awesome gift, looking for ways to turn this gift to some constructive use . . . many of us were fortunate that, in our lifetime, Pete Seeger lived."[99]

When Belafonte ceded the stage to his copresenter, Guthrie got an immediate laugh with his comment, "I think Harry just said it all, frankly . . ." But he pressed on:

> You know, I'll just mention this one thing. It's almost fifty years ago now that "Goodnight, Irene"—that Pete was shown-singing with the Weavers—it was almost fifty years ago that it was on the charts and went to number one. I can't think of a single event in Pete's life that is probably less important to him . . . and I think he's still embarrassed by it. And I think that says more about his willingness to be here tonight. There are a lot of branches to this rock 'n' roll thing and somewhere in these branches there are these voices singing so many different things. And the one thing that I don't think we should ever forget—and that Pete has reminded me all of my life—is that when we sing together nobody can take us down. As a country, as a people, as friends and families.[100]

Upon induction, Seeger ambled onto the stage, his 5-string banjo draped over his shoulder. After receiving his trophy, the seventy-six-year-old briefly held the award aloft—before walking directly off the stage without a word. The New York *Daily News* noted the folk singer "accepted his induction with a smile and absolute silence. Now that's a new one."[101] Some saw Seeger's refusal to speak as dismissive of award shows and rock music. Seeger explained that wasn't the case. He had simply forgotten to bring along his hearing aids. He didn't understand a single word of what was being said of him, good or bad.[102] It was probably for the best. The $1,500 a plate dinner was already awash with performers gushing about hit records and glory days. It was clear award shows weren't part of Seeger's scene.

Following the conferring of awards, the traditional late-night on-stage jam commenced. At the 1988 event, Guthrie performed alongside the likes of Bob Dylan, George Harrison, and Stevie Wonder. While it was fun to share the stage with so many legends, Guthrie found several of them "a little distant." The 1996 ceremony was more relaxed since Guthrie could jam alongside members of Jefferson Airplane and Pink Floyd, genuine friends with careers contemporary to his own. Guthrie reminisced, "These were my buds! I had a great time playing with some of those guys onstage, just goofing off and catching up—'where you been for 25 years?' that type of thing."[103]

Rising Son began shipping copies of *Mystic Journey* as January passed into February. There was little fanfare, though the New York *Daily News* helpfully made mention of its imminent release. The short blurb included Guthrie's comment: "It took me ten years to regroup. There was a night back in about 1983 when Warner Bros. let Bonnie Raitt, Gordon Lightfoot, Van Morrison, and me all go at once. Obviously, especially with Bonnie, they've had reason to realize they were being hasty. I think I'm the last one to get out there again."[104]

Though largely ignored by the rock press—the most popular music magazines had morphed into glossy promotional tools for the heavy metal and rap music industries—Guthrie's touring allowed for regional promotion of the new CD. In the final week of January, he set off for his traditional West Coast tour. On the morning of his appearance at the Coach House in San Juan Capistrano, Guthrie conceded his last few albums hadn't been necessarily commercial—but he was perfectly alright with that. "One of the great things about having your own record company is that not everything needs to be commercial. You can make these special project records for people who love them."[105]

The new tour was smoothly rolling along . . . until, predictably, Guthrie arrived in the Pacific Northwest. There *did* seem to be some sort of curse plaguing appearances there. After a show at Portland's Aladdin Theater, his next three concerts in Washington State were cancelled. Guthrie's bus and equipment truck were marooned due to road closures caused by the Columbia overflowing its banks. The "misty crystal glitter" waves of the Columbia—as eloquently memorialized in his father's song of 1941—stranded the son fifty-five years on, "holed up in a Portland Hotel room" awaiting waters to recede.[106]

In late February, Guthrie had a half-dozen shows scheduled in the far drier climes of New Mexico. Chatting on the phone with the *Albuquerque Journal*, Guthrie shared why it had taken him so long to get back into the record-making game. "It took me a while to get through our 'what are we gonna do stage,' and then actually figure out what to do. We started our own record company and we got some of the old records we had made on Warner's back . . . and it took me some years to generate enough sales of those to pay for the making of new records. The days when somebody was going to give me a couple of hundred thousand dollars and say 'Here, Arlo, go make another one,' those ended."[107]

Having your own record company brought pitfalls and benefits. *Mystic Journey* took time to be realized as Guthrie had spent the better part of a decade studying the machinations of the record business. "I was not someone who knew anything about manufacturing or distribution," he acknowledged. On the plus side, recording *Mystic Journey* allowed him— save for economic restraints—complete artistic freedom to make the record he wanted: "It was nice to make an album without anybody looking over my shoulder. It came together without any preconceived notion of what the thing should sound like."[108]

AG: The reviews of *Mystic Journey* were disappointing, as many were focused on the lack of humor and overall sadness in a few songs. Personally, I thought it had plenty of humor, but it was understated. Maybe the reviewers were just having a bad day. Either way, it's still one of my favorite albums.

The album was released in 1996 and it did rather well for us despite the lack of good reviews. However, the reviews were right in one way. I began to realize that, although making records was creatively exciting, it wasn't having the same positive impact evident in our live performances.

It was true that a number of critics, weaned on the stage shows and Guthrie's lengthy Will Rogers–Mark Twain like soliloquies, found *Mystic Journey* devoid of the singer's trademark humor. This wasn't completely the case, but the humor was more subtle. A case in point was Guthrie's own "All This Stuff Takes Time." On first listen, the track sounds like an homage to such mid-60s folk-rock classics as Dylan's *Bringing It All Back Home* or *Highway 61 Revisited*. And while it was true that *Mystic Journey* offered a number of spiritual ruminations, it was by no means a somber album. Many reviews were, in fact, positive in assessment:

"On *Mystic Journey*, Arlo continues his life mission of confounding fans and foes alike. This time around, it's done by recording a rootsy, folk rocking set of tunes, a long haul from the gently paced acoustic album most fans expected." (*Toronto Star*)[109]

"In recent years, Arlo Guthrie has re-released many of his old Warner Bros. records on his own label, done a terrific album of cowboy songs, a live album with Pete Seeger and re-recorded *Alice's Restaurant*. Now comes the fine *Mystic Journey*, his first "regular Arlo album" in a decade. There's full production on most of the songs and, although I wish some of them were a little more spare, I have no hesitancy in recommending *Mystic Journey*." (*Sing Out!*)[110]

"Arlo's voice is as infectiously reedy as ever, with more of a Dylanesque harmonica wheeze; Abe's work on the Hammond B-3 organ is fulsome, and the band is extremely homey. Chalk up a nice comeback for a good soul." (*Morning Call*)[111]

"Arlo Guthrie is an icon for many folk musicians and a revered performer. His wry wit in his live on-stage stories have become things of legend. So whenever Arlo adds something to his repertoire, it is a sought-after commodity. *Mystic Journey*, with its full-band sound, has been a long time coming for Guthrie. His previous studio album, *Someday*, was released in 1986. On *Mystic Journey*, Guthrie is joined by his son, Abe, members of his former band, Shenandoah, and of his most recent collaboration, Xavier. Abe Guthrie co-produced the album with his father, and his addition of synthesizer to the mix is every bit as musical, though a bit mystical, as the piano his father formerly played on his albums." (*Dirty Linen*)[112]

These were the "first wave" reviews of the new album. The album would actually get a second, fresh look in the summer of 1997, when *Mystic Journey* slowly found its way into record shops. But Guthrie admitted his frustration that it would take Rising Son through the autumn of 1996—at the earliest—to get *Mystic Journey* into wide distribution. One couldn't miss the sarcasm of one brief item found in the April 1996 edition of the *Rolling Blunder Review:* "It's true! Reports coming in to the offices of the RBR have confirmed that a copy of folksinger Arlo Guthrie's newest recording, *Mystic Journey*, was actually seen in a store. Sources close to the folksinger could not identify the location of the store where the sighting had taken place. They also maintained that the story, however improbable, was true."[113]

The early-winter tour of 1996 had been intensive. The tour's first date was scheduled on 25 January in San Diego and concluded on 7 April in Oshkosh, Wisconsin. Though no one would have refused Guthrie a well-deserved vacation break, everyone was caught off guard when he asked his driver to pull over and let him off at a Wisconsin airport. On impulse, he made the decision to fly to Hawaii for rest and relaxation. His decision came as a surprise to the staff at Rising Son. Back in Massachusetts, everyone stood around pondering his absence as stage equipment and three months of laundry were unloaded from the bus.[114]

Guthrie would spend the next several weeks in Hawaii doing not much of anything. He was visited by a reporter while in Oahu, who found the refreshed singer living in a cottage on Mokuleia Beach. "I love Hawaii, man," he explained. "Been coming here for twenty-eight years and have a lot of dear friends here. In the old days . . . I did a free show at the bandstand and the next day we played the Shell with Linda Ronstadt. It was great."[115] Guthrie's memory was spot on. He had played a band-backed set at Honolulu's Waikiki Shell in July of 1970. The concert attracted some seven thousand listeners and impressed a local critic then with a set of "irresistible irrelevance." That review, published in the *Honolulu Star-Bulletin,* was glowing—despite describing Guthrie's singing as "not very good. The tone is nasal, the texture so-so, the range limited."[116]

Guthrie explained he was visiting Hawaii to work out the staging of a free concert on the island. It would be an expression of gratitude "for all the 'aloha' that's been given to me in twenty-eight years of visiting."[117] Guthrie was hoping to stage the concert sometime in December, a possible springboard for an ambitious world tour that would take him to Europe, Japan, Australia, New Zealand, and Israel. Though that tour didn't transpire, Guthrie did make it back to Hawaii in February of the following year.

He was due back in Massachusetts in early May for a series of shows scheduled mostly around the northeastern US. The tours were important. Not only was he able to perform his new material in front of an appreciative audience, but the concerts gave him the opportunity to promote the new album in the press. Guthrie was happy to talk to reporters about the song cycle of *Mystic Journey.* Several critics rightfully cited "When a Soldier Makes It Home" as one the album's standout tracks. But many were misinformed that the song was written in the wake of the Persian Gulf War. Guthrie corrected the error, advising that he had been performing the song since 1989. He was happy to discuss his reasons for writing it. Being against war in general wasn't equivalent to being anti-soldier. Speaking of the Vietnam War, he said, "There were terrific people who fought, who stayed, who left. I grew up with all of those guys and we made different decisions. Tough decisions. But today we're still friends. That's what I wanted to say."[118]

One reason "Soldier" was likely seized upon as one of the album's highlights was simply that its theme was familiar, a protest-style song meeting expectations. But the song wasn't an early-1960s Phil Ochs–style anthem. Like so many of his father's best songs, "When a Soldier Makes It Home" was timeless. "We were trying to make a record that talked to the way the world was today and talked in terms that were at the same time poetic but not fuzzy," Guthrie shared. I hope it'll speak to a lot of people, especially young people. We're living in a time when it's not fun to be a young person."[119]

Although Guthrie's music was no longer enjoying any appreciable amount of mainstream radio play—Thanksgiving being a one-day exception—young people continued to comprise a good portion of his audience. They were seeking something intangible. Rap artists and heavy metal bands were the engines driving album sales. But most pushed theatrical fantasies, at best, or promulgated violent imagery or the subjugation of women, at worse. Guthrie wasn't an aging codger. But he did believe his generation shared a common dream: one far more progressive than the "plastic dreams" in current vogue. "We had a lot of idealism. We didn't have a lot of the problems that we have today. We weren't being divided on so many issues. We seemed to have a vision of the future where we could enjoy diversity. So much of that stuff has now gotten into the hands of the loudmouths around the world that are trying to divide us on everything."[120]

In September of 1995, Guthrie advised readers of the *Rolling Blunder Review* that his decade-old newsletter would no longer accept subscriptions.[121] The newsletter had served as a great vehicle to keep fans abreast on tour dates and new recording projects. Subscriptions had peaked at 60,000 readers, but by the summer of 1993, subscriptions began to trail off. Guthrie admitted that while he had fun publishing the newsletter, it was becoming a chore to get an issue out on schedule. There were other projects more deserving of his time and energy.

Starting with its spring 1993 issue, the *Rolling Blunder Review* discontinued printing tour dates. Though the absence seemed odd—there was certainly no shortage of shows scheduled—the office was continuing to send out notification postcards to fans. The postcards were still important because not every fan was a newsletter subscriber. The decline in subscriptions was a little disheartening. In the summer of 1993 Guthrie offered, "There are fewer of you now than there has ever been before. At one time, years ago, we sent this stuff to over 60,000 people across the country and the world. We began the RBR with more people than we send it to today. If the trend continues, it will make more sense to get together and talk, rather than to go through this elaborate written ritual. I would like that very much."[122]

In 1993, three issues of the newsletter were published, but in 1994 and 1995 only two. In 1996, the newsletter bounced back to three issues, but the publishing schedule was erratic. There were times when Guthrie turned the contents of the newsletter over to members of his office staff. The "Letters to the Editor" section remained an essential component. It was a fun and lively forum for fans to share *their* thoughts and stories, joys and complaints. Some letters generated a sly or humorous response from Guthrie. The singer appeared to enjoy engaging with fans, hearing what was on their minds while sharing what was on his.

Then something pretty remarkable occurred. In the summer of 1996 a computer whiz and admirer of Guthrie's music, Dave Downin, created an Arlo Guthrie fan site on the World Wide Web. It's difficult not to over-state the importance of the site, deemed *arlo.net,* as it was among the first and most easily navigable fan sites established for any artist. Downin would build arlo.net section by section until it became *the* clearing house for all things Guthrie: discographies, tour dates, photo galleries, interviews, articles, merchandise offerings, tape-trading lists, guitar tablatures, lyr-ics, album reviews, games, and even a chat board. The most visited sec-tions of arlo.net were the interactive forums where fans—and the folk singer himself—could discuss politics and music and books and lifestyles and nonsense.

Though arlo.net didn't *completely* supplant the *Rolling Blunder Review* as Guthrie's primary communication tool with fans, it certainly made the newsletter less essential. Curious fans could now easily follow the singer's itineraries online with a click of a mouse. Guthrie was supportive of the venture. Downin's creation had become an important meeting place. "It's a community of people that hang around," Guthrie offered. "It's replaced the old town square."[123] The site also served as a useful platform from which to announce all news coming from Rising Son Records. Tour dates could now be updated in real time within minutes of confirmation.

Though arlo.net didn't necessarily hasten the demise of the *Rolling Blunder Review,* the website was—inarguably—more expansive in its reach. Guthrie's printed newsletter soldiered on for a number of years after the inception of arlo.net, but the majority of his fans now received news and updates via their computers. The website also facilitated bringing Arlo's disparate fan base together. Many online acquaintances made on arlo.net would develop into meaningful real-life friendships.

Just as arlo.net was being launched, Guthrie and Abe were to set off for the UK in July of 1996. Guthrie was to play two shows at London's Border-line nightclub, then set off on a seven- show tour of Ireland. The gigs would include two appearances at the Róisín Dubh as part of the Galway Arts Festival and a pair of shows at Whelan's in Dublin. Guthrie's Whelan's show of 24 July was recorded and broadcast a week later on Ireland's RTÉ radio network.

Guthrie's personal life was similar to anyone's at middle age. Just as the youngest family members were splintering off to pursue their own dreams, the eldest members were saying their goodbyes. Earlier in the year, Guthrie and Jackie would attend a memorial service for Jackie's mother, Ellen Hyde, who had passed away, at age seventy-five, on 8 March. Ellen Hyde had been a light of the family from the very beginning. When Jackie first brought her future husband around, her mother admitted she was "shocked" by the news of their impending marriage. "At first, I mistook his ways as arrogance," she admitted, "but he was really shy."[124] Hyde called her future son-in-law "Ar," collecting mementos of his career and baking "oodles" of her homemade burritos whenever he passed through Salt Lake City. "Arlo loves my burritos, as hot as I can get them," she proudly declared. She needed to bake his burritos separate from others she'd prepare. "No one can take them as hot as Arlo," she confided.[125]

Guthrie learned his mother-in-law was ailing during a stopover at Seattle's Back Door nightclub. Three days later Guthrie was in Salt Lake City performing "Amazing Grace" and "Will the Circle Be Unbroken" at his mother-in-law's service at the Waterloo Chapel Ward House. Following his musical interlude, Guthrie took a seat in the front pew. A bishop teased from the pulpit, "Arlo and I are a lot alike. But there is one big difference— he has talent." Without missing a beat, Guthrie answered, "I thought you were going to say I had more hair."[126]

Guthrie remembered how those too-infrequent visits with his mother-in-law made Salt Lake City a favorite stop. Jackie had already traveled out to her mother's bedside when it became evident her days were numbered. Guthrie recalled, with the family gathered, "We had a wonderful time together, goofing around and reminiscing and nothing was left undone or unsaid. Grandma's huge family all showed up and we sent her off as best we could. . . . We are all still getting used to the idea that we can't call her up and get together every once in a while. But I guess we'll be together again soon enough. In our family, losing our Grandma will be the most important event of 1996."[127]

1996 brought joyful moments as well. In early August, Abe married Lisa White at a ceremony at the Church.[128] The newlyweds didn't have time for an extended honeymoon as the groom and his father were due back on the road by mid-August. That tour would take them through October with few breaks. With Guthrie's four children all fully grown or coming of age, he admitted being less burdened by guilt when out on the road for months on end.

Guthrie's newfound freedom would abruptly end that summer when everybody returned home. Cathy was the first to return, having finished college in San Diego. Jackie, Annie, and Sarah also returned to Washington County from their secondary home in Florida. Cathy and Annie, the two eldest, also brought their boyfriends along with them. This caused Guthrie to remark that his home in the Berkshires was beginning to resemble that of TV's "Walton's Mountain."

In September the singer did allow himself a short break from touring. On 3 September, Guthrie found himself in Los Angeles for a small acting role on the short-lived television series *Relativity*. The romance-drama had made its debut in September of 1996, part of the ABC network's fall schedule—surviving only seventeen episodes before the network pulled the plug. Guthrie appeared in the series' sixth episode, "Fathers," broadcast 26 October. The singer played "Mick Hillis," an eccentric "music editor/critic of an alternative weekly," but the role was little more than a cameo.[129]

Though Woody Guthrie had been inducted into the Rock and Roll Hall of Fame, the institution had never arranged a proper retrospective of the folk singer's life and work. This changed in September of 1995 when the Rock Hall mounted a special display of folk music artifacts to their exhibit. As the primary custodians of the singer's works, Harold Leventhal, Nora Guthrie, and the members of the newly established Woody Guthrie Archives were asked to lend items for display. The resulting exhibit also acknowledged two of Woody's musical contemporaries, Lead Belly and Pete Seeger.

Following the success of that exhibit, Robert Santelli, director of the museum's education and programming, thought a more in-depth look at

Guthrie's life and work should be considered. Santelli met with Leventhal and Nora in the spring of 1996 to plan what would be the first of the museum's American Music Masters series. The multiday event, *Hard Travelin': The Life and Legacy of Woody Guthrie*, would include a museum-worthy curation of rare Guthrie family photographs and ephemera, a film festival, and several staged hootenannies at Cleveland-area rock clubs. An academic conference of Guthrie scholars was also assembled to put the commemoration in context. Plans were made to close the celebration with a concert to benefit the work of the Woody Guthrie Archives.

Guthrie was asked to give a keynote speech at the conference on 28 September—though he was only tasked with the chore when writer and broadcaster Studs Terkel was unable to attend. The impromptu speech Guthrie made that afternoon was somewhat familiar to his fans: fragmented memories of growing up in Coney Island, the folk music boom, and a retelling of Woody's "Mama and the Papa Rabbit in a Hollow Log." He recounted,

> [My father] exists today in a lot of people who are here, not just me. And he exists in ways that mean different things to different times. I think one of the wonderful things about my dad that I learned from him—not from him personally, but from his work—was his propensity toward wanting to be himself. I didn't just learn it; I also appreciated it. I began to realize some of the sacrifices that a person has to make when you're dealing with things like being free: free in every moment to pursue and to be who you are. There's a price that has to be paid for those things. It's not easy. You're not born with that. Things have to happen to you. You may have to lose things. . . . This freedom that you have just doesn't spring up from nowhere; it comes from life's experiences, which are not always easy to deal with.[130]

The all-star concert set to take place the following night was held at Severance Hall at Case Western Reserve University. Tickets had been scooped up quickly when news leaked that Bruce Springsteen was to perform. The list of artists signing on included both surviving friends of Woody's (Ramblin' Jack Elliott, Fred Hellerman, Harold Leventhal, and Pete Seeger), and Guthrie's own family (Arlo, Abe, Cathy, Sarah Lee, Nora, and Cole and Anna Rotante, Nora's son and daughter). But the concert

also featured a number of musicians influenced by Woody's music and
spirit.

Though Springsteen was the biggest name on the bill—the rocker hav-
ing been belatedly introduced to Woody through Joe Klein's 1980 biogra-
phy of the singer—the "Boss" was not alone in declaring his alliance to
Guthrie. Joining to celebrate were a staggering array of acolytes: Dan Bern,
Billy Bragg, Ani Difranco, Joe Ely, Alejandro Escovedo, Jimmie Dale
Gilmore, Peter Glazer, John Wesley Harding, the Indigo Girls, Jorma
Kaukonen, Jimmy LaFave, David Lutkin, Country Joe McDonald, David
Pirner of Soul Asylum, the actor Tim Robbins, and Syd Straw. Bruce Spring-
steen was to perform next to last, singing several songs before bringing on
Arlo for a duet on "Oklahoma Hills." That song served as a segue to Arlo's
own set: a mix of Woody's songs with a few of his own: "Dust Storm Disaster,"
"My Daddy Flies a Ship in the Sky," "When a Soldier Makes It Home," and
"Doors of Heaven."

Guthrie closed the three-hour-long evening by asking everyone to join
him on his father's "Hard Travelin'" and "I've Got to Know." He then
brought Pete Seeger out to rapturous applause. They sang "This Land Is
Your Land" and "Hobo's Lullaby" as a finale, one newspaper noting that
Seeger's appearance perfectly "completed the circle. His voice was worn,
his banjo out of tune, but his spirit was in perfect pitch."[131]

The Rock Hall's symposium of all things Woody Guthrie would beget
both a concert recording, *'Til We Outnumber 'Em: The Songs of Woody Guthrie*,
and a book, *Hard Travelin': The Life and Legacy of Woody Guthrie*. The CD was
worth the small investment, but notable for what was omitted from the
final track listing. Happily, the album did include the only "official" recording of Arlo Guthrie singing his father's "Dust Storm Disaster." An expanded
version of the lengthy concert—admittedly a bit of a financial gamble for
Righteous Babe Records, Ani Difranco's indie label that issued the title—
might have better captured the spirit of the event. The book, edited by
Santelli and Emily Davidson, would arguably better serve those curious to
learn more about Woody Guthrie's life and legacy.

On 11 through 13 October, Guthrie was among the tens of thousands
visiting Washington, DC, for the unfurling of the AIDS quilt. The purpose
of the quilt was to bring attention to the disease ravaging communities
throughout the US and the world. The quilt consisted of some 36,000 to

40,000 panels, each measuring six feet in length and three feet across—
the size of a casket, with many panels representing a person lost to the disease. It was a Herculean effort bringing the quilt to Washington. The panels
weighed somewhere in the neighborhood of forty to forty-five tons and
were brought to the Capitol via railroad. More than 1,600 volunteers were
on hand to help stich the panels together.[132]

The assembled quilt would stretch from the base of the Washington
monument to the steps of the Capitol, the length of twenty football fields
or fifteen city blocks. Though the panels had been displayed in sections
since the quilt's inception in 1985, the DC event was the first to bring the
collection together. Greg Lugliani, the communications director for the
Names Project Foundation, shared that AIDS was now the leading cause of
death in men between the ages of twenty-five and forty-four, with women of
similar age not far behind in the grim ranking.[133]

Guthrie met up with members of the Kashi Ashram and Ma in DC,
being one of hundreds agreeing to read names of the dead during a solemn ceremony. Guthrie was also among the hundreds of thousands taking
part in a memorial candlelight vigil. It was a moving tribute, but Guthrie
noted there were few songs being sung. The absence of music was sadden-
ing. Guthrie would write a lovely essay on the vigil, collecting his memories
in a thoughtful, beautifully written remembrance:

> A little more than a month ago I was in Washington DC for the last
> unfolding of the entire AIDS quilt. It stretched out for over a mile
> with forty thousand panels representing seventy thousand names.
> I walked back and forth looking for the friends I'd known. I saw a
> friend I knew on every block of that mile. And I marched with a
> few hundred thousand others holding candles against the oncom-
> ing night sky where we held a vigil before the Lincoln Memorial.
>
> I remembered the times, when I was a kid and as I grew up,
> that I marched along with Pete Seeger and others—Ban the
> Bomb—Civil Rights—End the War in Vietnam—No Nukes—
> Clean Air and Water and so on. We sang and shouted, chanted
> and laughed, and took note of who we were and where we thought
> we were headed. We were determined that if the world was going
> to hell, it wasn't going quietly. We hoped that future generations
> would continue to believe that if we all could stick together long

enough, we stood a chance of celebrating a victory against the greed and stupidity that was plainly in evidence everywhere.

I was remembering and thinking about these things as I walked quietly along the somber streets of Washington, DC. I wondered why nobody was singing. There were occasional attempts at getting through an entire song, but the songs died down when no one knew any more verses. And how many times could you sing about being a gentle angry people without being weary too? We were singing for our lives, passing by our friends who had already lost theirs.

I missed the ring of Pete's loud banjo that you could hear for a few blocks in any direction. I missed hearing the songs that gave us a strength to keep walking, talking, thinking, and singing. The prerecorded music and songs being pumped through the loudspeaker system at the Lincoln Memorial did not move the weary marchers or give them strength. We stood around waiting for it to end so we could eventually hear the speakers.

I wondered if the organizers were old enough to have remembered a time when we didn't let the radio and the TV, the CD or tape player, do our singing for us. When singing was part of our lives. And I counted myself blessed beyond measure for the songs I knew and the memories they held.[134]

That same October Guthrie was back on the West Coast—San Diego, this time—for another shot at TV stardom. He had been hired by producers of the USA Network's long-running *Renegade* action series starring Lorenzo Lamas. In this one-off episode, Guthrie was perfectly cast as Jamie Jackson, a former member of the radical Weatherman group. His character was living underground and on the run from the FBI, accused of planting a bomb at a chemical lab manufacturing napalm. That 1972 bombing reportedly killed Jackson's friend, Warren Adrian (Adrian Sparks), a simpatico radicalized college professor.

As a result of his off-hours bombing of what he thought was an empty building, Jackson landed on the FBI's Ten Most Wanted list. He had been squeaking by as a solo guitar player and singer at such déclassé saloons as Dusty's and the Rattlesnake Café. Our first glimpse of Jackson is at the former, performing under the alias of "Deke Martin," his gray-white locks dyed completely black. (He later explains to his captors that he's forced to dye his graying hair black "every time a Republican gets elected"). The song "Deke" is singing when we first meet him is Guthrie's own "When a Soldier Makes It Home."

Jackson narrowly escapes being nabbed by pursuing FBI agents at Dusty's, though a pair of bounty hunters catch up with him several weeks later during his set at the Rattlesnake Café. Jackson, now using the modified alias of "Martin Deacon," is snared in the middle of a rendering of "City of New Orleans." But as the bounty hunters negotiate Jackson's turn-over to the Feds, the two begin to question the guilt of their prisoner, a self-described "criminal of conscience."

Guthrie's role in this *Renegade* episode ("Top Ten with a Bullet") is expansive. Not only does the singer give a great performance as Jamie Jackson, but admirers are also treated to several musical snippets. In case anyone was curious whether Guthrie ever put a melody to "Mooses Come Walking," the answer can be found here. Guthrie chords along on a lilting version of "Mooses" to an audience of refugees from war-torn El Salvador. Working with the refugee children was a court-ordered restitution for Jackson's decades-old bombing. The episode was first broadcast on 3 January 1997, and a bit later in other markets.

Guthrie really enjoyed working on TV. "The nice thing about acting," he recalled, "is that it gives me a chance to explore myself in a way that I can't really do when I'm singing on stage. I get to be somebody else."[135] The singer admitted he wasn't terribly happy with the *Alice's Restaurant* film because he was tasked to play himself. The opportunities afforded him on *Byrds of Paradise, Relativity,* and *Renegade* were more satisfying. "These things I'm doing now are pleasurable," he confided. "I get to have the fun of acting."[136]

Despite having fun working on television, Guthrie confessed he didn't watch TV often. There were exceptions. As he was a lifelong "Trekkie"—a fan of TV's *Star Trek* series—it was with excitement that he received a call from the producers of *Star Trek: Next Generation.* They were looking to cast Guthrie in a future episode. But the timing was, sadly, off. Guthrie already had concert dates scheduled on the days of the production shoot. "It was the one show I really wanted to do," Guthrie sighed. "I can only hope we get a call in the future."[137] Sadly, a second call did not come.

Radio fame was still an option. On 26 November, Guthrie was at the Old Trinity Church to record a program slated for broadcast on Thanksgiving, two days hence. The program, produced by Rob Frankel for the ABC Radio Network and Radio Today Entertainment, was titled the "Alice's Restaurant Thanksgiving Massacree Concert." Guthrie was calling it the "first annual" staging, hoping the radio program might kick-start a new holiday tradition. It was no secret the playing of "Alice's Restaurant" on Thanksgiving Day had become a tradition on FM dials, so this radio show was simply an extension of that heritage. Guthrie explained, "We're trying to start a tradition of being on the radio at least one day a year. . . . It seems we have Thanksgiving sewn up. Next year, we'll work on another holiday—like Groundhog Day."[138]

Though the radio crew brought in their own production team, Guthrie drafted Bruce Clapper to engineer. He also assembled two members of Shenandoah (David Grover and Terry Hall) to sit in on guitar and drums, with two alumni from Xavier (Abe on keyboards, Sean Hurley on bass) to augment. The ensemble was also graced by the accordion of John Culpo, who had earlier sat in on recording sessions for *Son of the Wind*, *Mystic Journey*, and *Woody's 20 Grow Big Songs*. Though the concert itself was two hours long, the plan was to select an hour's worth of material for broadcast. Among those attending were Alice Brock and Rick Robbins, the latter of whom fatefully dumped the trash with Guthrie in 1965.

Since the "Alice's Restaurant Massacree" was the program's obvious selling point, only four non-"Alice" performances were broadcast: "City of New Orleans," "Mooses Come Walking," "Gabriel's Mother's Highway Ballad #16 Blues," and "This Land Is Your Land." It was a compact program, a bit of a "Greatest Hits" package for casual fans. Songs excised from the final program included "Ukulele Lady," "Ring-Around-a-Rosy Rag," and "Amazing Grace." More disappointingly, two great songs from *Mystic Journey* were also cut: "Moon Song" and "Doors of Heaven."

One of the more spontaneous moments occurred when Guthrie invited Alice Brock to the stage. The two chatted a bit about their *Mooses Come Walking* collaboration. The increased sightings of Canadian moose in Massachusetts caused Guthrie to suggest this anomaly was an obvious result of the recent signing of the North America Free Trade Agreement (NAFTA). Brock, now a resident of Provincetown, suggested moose were even making their way south to the shoreline of Cape Cod. These creatures were, Alice explained, "Salt Water Mooses."

"They're not as big as these mountain mooses," she continued.

"How big are they?" Guthrie asked.

"Well, I've never seen one totally out of the water, so I couldn't really say," Brock deadpanned.[139]

The radio show was sent out to stations across the country. Any monies raised through sales or from the donations of listeners were to fund the physical restoration of the Old Trinity Church, consecrated in 1830. The creaky building was beginning to show its age: peeling paint exposed wood to damaging wet weather, the roof leaked, and the original stone foundation was crumbling.

Guthrie confided to readers of the *Rolling Blunder Review* that each month's mortgage payment left little money to put toward the church's rehabilitation. He was hoping the radio show might generate enough cash so necessary repair work could commence. As November passed into December, Guthrie was uncertain if the radio show had been "worth doing," but he remained optimistic. "If it is successful as a fund raiser," Guthrie wrote, "it could mean a new era for the old church."[140]

★ ★ ★ ★ ★

Chapter Seven

ARLO VS. THE ORCHESTRA, 1997–1999

AG: Rising Son Records continuously manufactured and sold the entire collection of our own projects along with those recently acquired from Warner Bros. through our office via mail. We realized that we needed to partner up with some kind of distribution company to get the catalog in retail stores if we wanted to move beyond our mail-order business.

We entered into a distribution deal with Koch Records to put our catalog out on their label and distribute it throughout the North American market. We were finally getting somewhere, as our products entered into the retail market and were widely available.

Michael Koch was the founder of Koch International USA, Port Washington, New York. Koch had moved to the US from Germany in 1987, having made a small splash as "a specialist record company in the German-speaking market."[1] His company was, in its first years, involved mostly as a CD-pressing broker, but moved into the area of distribution in 1990. Koch's primary interest was distributing European and American classical music recordings on compact disc. Deluxe pressings of classical music recordings on vinyl had long held appeal for audiophiles, but their loyalty to the LP was being tested. Koch caught whiff of the preference change from analog to digital, and the company maneuvered into recognition as "one of the two leading independent classical distributors in the country."[2]

The company was also looking to other genres to nurture growth outside of classical and foreign-language titles. They worked closely with Shanachie Records of New Jersey, a roots-based label specializing in fiddle and Irish music. Koch soon went from merely pressing that label's new releases to distributing them nationally. That success paved the way for

Koch to handle distribution of other such roots-based indies as Sugar Hill and Smithsonian Folkways.

The company continued to burnish their catalog by catering to consumers whose musical tastes—jazz, cabaret, soundtracks, theater—fell outside mass consumer interest. But the money-making pop market wasn't one that could be ignored. In 1994 Koch distributed the music of several indie-rock labels and, in 1996, even made inroads into the urban/rap music market. That same year Koch Records USA was incorporated, the label issuing back-catalog titles of such country artists as Charlie Rich, Ray Price, and Merle Haggard.

On 15 February 1997, *Billboard* announced that Arlo Guthrie had signed an "exclusive North American distribution pact" with Koch. The article revealed the company had plans to distribute the entirety of Guthrie's back-catalog on compact disc. It was also rumored that the Koch editions might even be "rereleased in expanded editions under the agreement."[3] This was exciting news for Guthrie's fans, as bonus tracks were coveted items. The addition of bonus material had proved a successful strategy to get fans to repurchase albums already in their collections.

Though eleven of Guthrie's albums would eventually be published by Koch from 1997 through 2000, it was to some disappointment that none would see issue in expanded editions. This call wasn't Koch's. It was Guthrie who chose to forego adding bonus material. He'd later state that he looked upon the albums in his catalog as "works of art, they're like paintings, they're done."[4] This decision was sound, if a disappointment to fans hoping to finally hear the rumored Guthrie's outtakes of Mississippi John Hurt's "Louis Collins" or his own "Café Harris Rag," "Hold On to Me," and "Band Song." But at least the albums as originally conceived would be stocked in record shops and made available again.

Guthrie's decision to partner Rising Son with Koch made financial sense. The partnership allowed Guthrie to divorce himself from the time and expense of marketing his records. Koch already had the distribution channels open and flowing. One of the Koch releases was a rebranding of *Mystic Journey*, still very much a "new" album in every sense. Guthrie wasn't harboring fantasies of *Mystic Journey* going double platinum, but if the record did take off and Rising Son was asked to deliver 200,000 copies to meet demand, his modest label wasn't capable of absorbing the risk.

Guthrie was aware that if he went to a CD manufacturer with such a large order, he'd be in debt for a half-million dollars—at a minimum. Should distributors return them in three months' time, saying, "We tried, but it didn't sell," that would, effectively, signal the end of Rising Son.[5] The deal struck with Koch was favorable in other regards too. The most important of these was that Rising Son retained ownership of the recordings. It was agreed Guthrie could continue to issue the albums on cassette since Koch's interest was exclusive to CDs. Guthrie was also pleased the majority of his albums on Warner Bros. would be made readily available in shops.

The first of the Koch/Guthrie titles set for release in May and June of 1997 were 1969's *Running Down the Road* (KOC-CD-7949), 1970's *Washington County* (KOC-CD-7950), and 1974's *Arlo Guthrie* (KOC-CD-7953). Though Guthrie's albums were not reissued by Koch in order of their original release, it did appear the CDs were issued with holds on sequential numbers. Koch had no rights to issue the original *Alice's Restaurant*—Warner Bros. was going to hold on tight to that album. But Guthrie's second album from 1968, *Arlo*, was issued as (KOC-CD-7948), with 1996's *Mystic Journey* as (KOC-CD-7960). Since there were no Koch releases for 7955, 7957, and 7958, this suggests these numbers were reserved for possible future progressive reissues of *Together in Concert* (1975), *One Night* (1978), and *Precious Friend* (1982). Though the first two albums would eventually be issued on CD by Rising Son, none of the trio received a Koch release. Though no reason was given, there were reports Koch was unable to secure rights to *Pete Seeger & Arlo Guthrie: Together in Concert*.

On the eve of the first Koch reissues, Guthrie was excited about the prospect of his albums getting back into record stores nationwide. He shared that another old recording had recently been exhumed for possible release. "We will also be putting out the soundtrack for a documentary film that was called *Hard Travelin'*," Guthrie promised. It's a record with a lot of well-known people singing my Dad's songs. We just located the master tapes about a week or so ago. I haven't even told Koch about it."[6] The *Hard Travelin'* soundtrack would eventually be issued on CD but, again, not by Koch. Regardless, it was an exciting time and while the CDs were top-notch, Guthrie's partnership with Koch would not extend beyond their contractual five-year obligation:

AG: Unfortunately, we also discovered that our records on the Koch label were also being sold overseas in direct violation of our contract. No royalties were ever recovered from those sales. Not that they were huge, but there was no way to know, and so we ended our relationship with Koch on November 1, 2001, and decided to go it alone.

But in 1997 that dissolution was still in the future. It was time for Guthrie to get back on the road:

AG: I began working in January 1997, deadheading out to Tulsa, Oklahoma, from The Farm for a gig at Cain's Ballroom, which I simply loved. It was pretty much as it had been for decades and decades, with colorized portraits of well-known cowboy or country-western artists hanging on the walls. It really was an authentic ballroom, not in name only but the real deal—a dance hall Oklahoma style. Back from the days when country and western music were two different but equally important genres. We played the venue quite often and always loved returning.

Midway through his January-March tour, Guthrie kept his promise of playing a few shows in Hawaii. Though he originally planned to use Hawaii as a springboard to a proposed tour of Japan and Australia, those Pacific dates hadn't come together as wished. With his working vacation on the Hawaiian Islands over, Guthrie returned to the US mainland mid-February for a concert at the Temple Beth-El in San Mateo, California. Already missing Hawaii's "warm tropical breezes and the big blue Pacific," Guthrie sighed, "This isn't a gig. This is a sacrifice."[7]

Professionally, however, Guthrie's "Alone—Solo (By Himself Again)" tour allowed the singer to shake up his set list. He described the exercise as a "slow process of adding and deleting songs and stories from the road shows."[8] It was a tricky proposition. Hardcore Guthrie fans longed to hear deep cuts from old albums, even wishing "Alice's Restaurant" might get a well-deserved rest. But Guthrie wasn't playing the usual circuit. His tours were taking him to small towns across the US often playing new venues before fresh audiences coming out for the first time. These fans came to the shows with the expectation of hearing "City of New Orleans," "The Motorcycle Song," "Coming into Los Angeles," and "Alice's Restaurant." Guthrie often answered requests for certain songs with resignation. As he was already thirty-odd years into his career, he replied he had only the same two hours of stage time that he had at the very beginning of his career. It was impossible to satisfy everyone's requests.

AG: We worked our way through the southwest and ended up in San Diego for a show at 4th & B, and from there northward along the coast until we came through Montana and ended that leg in Salt Lake City. From there we drove back to The Farm.

I didn't stay long, as I left for Austria a couple of weeks later for a tour of Austria and Germany, with one show in London before a short tour of Denmark and Sweden.

I decided not to fly back the usual route but take the cheap flights through Iceland. I left Copenhagen April 21st and flew to Reykjavik for an overnight stay before returning from there to Boston. I arrived in Iceland knowing no one. I hailed the one cab at the airport and asked to be taken to a nearby hotel—any hotel. It was evening and I was hungry. I checked into a hotel and asked if they had a restaurant. The young girl behind the check-in counter said they did, and led me into an empty restaurant, and asked if I wanted to see a menu. . . . I guess the same girl who had checked me in was also the waitress. I just hoped she wasn't also the cook. But, after a few polite words of conversation, she gathered that I was a musician heading for Boston. With that discovery, she abruptly left the hotel saying, "Wait right here!"

As I had nowhere to go, I waited until she returned a few minutes later—with a guy I had met once in my hometown of Stockbridge, Massachusetts. Rúnar Júlíusson was the head of a famous Icelandic band in the 1960s called Hljómar. They had made records at Shaggy Dog Studios in Stockbridge decades earlier when I became acquainted with them. It was crazy that he'd be so nearby, but there he was, and we had some fun catching up over a few beers. I flew back to Boston the following day smiling at the good fortune of finding an old friend along the way.

I had a couple of shows to do when I got back from Europe. Both were in North Carolina: one was Merlefest and one at the Grey Eagle Tavern. I'd known Doc Watson from previous tours where we shared the same bill. He'd been a mentor to me, even if he hadn't known it. As high school kid—we'd listen to his recordings down to the finest detail to figure out what he was doing. No one previously had played so well and so clean. He was someone whose playing was truly inspirational to me personally.

My friend John Pilla had accompanied Doc for a short while back in the 1960s. And John's style of playing clearly reflected Doc's influence—which is one of the reasons John and I had gravitated toward one another. When Merle died prematurely as the result of an accident, Doc held a festival in his honor and called it Merlefest, and I performed there on April 26, 1997. From there we drove to Black Mountain, North Carolina, for a gig at the Grey Eagle Tavern. I drove home to The Farm after those shows.

I finally had enough time at The Farm to get some things done. Jackie and I had bought the place on September 2, 1969. It was two hundred and fifty acres of forest abutting watershed areas and state forest, on a dirt road with two houses. Although we'd made extensive renovations to the buildings, we hadn't done much to the property itself, and I was determined to reseed the lawns and pastures. I had purchased a roto-tiller attachment for my farm tractor and prepared the ground for seeding.

Following his return, Guthrie advised the selectman of Great Barrington of his interest in staging a series of fundraising concerts at the church during the summer. The concerts were designed to bring public attention to the activities of the Guthrie Center, as well as to bring in revenue to support those charitable activities. Guthrie promised to limit attendance to one hundred and twenty-five fans. He advised that tentative weekends in June, July, and August had already been penciled in. The matter was taken up on 30 April during the selectmen's meeting, and there was, as expected, dissent.

The Guthrie Center's zoning permit of 1992 allowed for only fifteen office staff members to be onsite, the selectmen suggesting then that there were "other areas where concerts can be given without doing it in a residential area."[9] But there was seemingly less hostility to Guthrie's special permit request, the board promising to work with his attorney to discuss possible options.

Nearly lost in the whirlwind of activity in early winter of 1997 was the VHS release of *This Land Is Your Land: The Animated Kids' Songs of Woody Guthrie*. The tape was released on 25 March as a companion video to the CD issued earlier by Rounder Records. The reviews were entirely positive for both releases, the *Hartford Courant* assuring suspicious readers that while Woody Guthrie "was famous for his leftist activism . . . this video contains no political content."[10] The *Chicago Tribune* described the CD as "Americana at its jubilant best."[11]

> **AG:** On May 13th, in the middle of turning up the soil, my old friends Ramblin' Jack Elliott and Rick Robbins showed up for a visit. It was hot and dusty, and I needed an excuse to take a break. Their visit was perfectly timed. I'd known Jack for as long as I could remember. He had been a friend and companion of my father since back in the early 1950s. I'd always admired Jack as he was uniquely himself and never would allow anyone to characterize him in a way that compromised his idea of who he was, and what he was doing. It was from Jack's shows I attended as a young teenager that I saw the potential of doing an entire evening—a show. Others before him had been singers of songs, but no one had yet tied the songs together with tales and stories that were equally—if not more entertaining—than the songs themselves. It proved to become a valuable lesson for me.

Elliott, a longtime friend of the family, had traveled to Great Britain in 1955, recording a number of seminal discs of rough-hewn American folk music for several English labels, including Topic Records of London, 77 Records, and even the British arm of Columbia Records. He was the first US-based performer to introduce the songs of Woody Guthrie—in authentically dusty and gritty musical settings—to British and European audiences. By the time Pete Seeger received permission to travel to Great Britain in the autumn of 1959 following his brush with the House Un-American Activities Committee, Guthrie's songs were already well-known throughout London's folk and skiffle music scene due to Elliott's advance work.[12]

Though Elliott returned to the United States for a brief time in late 1958, this "folk singer's folk singer" returned to stay in 1961. His residency at Gerdes Folk City in July 1961 drew a rave review from the *New York Times*, and the singer famously mentored Bob Dylan, then a recent arrival to the Greenwich Village folk music scene. Elliott also recorded a series of seminal albums for the Prestige-International label that were studied by every aspiring folk-guitarist. Although Elliott wouldn't—or couldn't—comfortably transform himself into a folk-rocker after Dylan's ascension, he remained a celebrated and much sought-after performer on the US folk and coffeehouse circuit.

Rick Robbins was another old friend whose personal history, like Elliott's, was forever intertwined with Guthrie's:

AG: Rick Robbins was a classmate of mine in high school. He had been expelled one year earlier than my own expulsion a few weeks before I was supposed to graduate in June 1965. I was allowed to show up and get a diploma, however.

During the mid to late 1960s Rick and I were both friends of Ray and Alice Brock, and we found ourselves in their converted church spending time playing music together and goofing off. It was Thanksgiving 1965 that Rick and I that took a VW microbus full of garbage to the wrong place.

During the years that followed, Rick and Jack had become friends, and Rick became Jack's road companion, driving him from gig to gig, taking care of the aging folk singer.

Though Robbins chose not to pursue music as a vocation, as a high school student he purchased his first guitar after being captivated by an album of Ramblin' Jack's. Robbins belatedly recorded his own debut album, *Walkin' Down the Line,* at age fifty, a score of musical friends accompanying him, including Elliott and Guthrie. Guthrie's contribution was a fun duet with Robbins on Floyd Jenkins's hillbilly classic "Low and Lonely." It was a song gleaned from Elliott's 1962 *Country Style* LP.[13]

AG: I left Massachusetts to attend Ma's birthday celebration at the ashram. I returned home to The Farm to prepare for the upcoming Further Festival. I was hired to be the master of ceremonies and sing a few songs during set changes. The Further Festival would highlight various former members of the Grateful Dead who had created their own bands, and they would obviously also do some material together. It was a huge undertaking and large venues require a lot of work to go smoothly.

The summer of 1997 was the second staging of the Further Festival. The "Further" in the title was the psychedelic bus of Ken Kesey's "Merry Band of Pranksters." The jam-band festival was inaugurated so that surviving members of the Grateful Dead and kindred artists could continue their musical explorations after the passing of guitarist Jerry Garcia. Guthrie was performing a concert with Pete Seeger at Connecticut's Oakdale

Theater when he learned of Garcia's passing. That night Guthrie offered that the Grateful Dead was "one of the last great spontaneous bands— people who were not afraid to experiment as they were doing it. This was not pre-recorded music."[14]

Bob Weir formally announced the second staging of the Further Festival in April of 1997. Though the slate of performers had not yet been finalized, the lineup would be Dead-centric. There had been some speculation that tour producer John Scher was courting Bob Dylan to join the roster, but the bard was already committed to a tour of Europe.[15] That tour was abruptly cancelled when Dylan was hospitalized in May, suffering severe chest pain due to histoplasmosis, a rare fungal infection causing painful swelling of the heart sac. The singer's illness made front-page news around the world.

The thought of losing Dylan was something fans and critics were not ready to accept. Guthrie recalled the "week where we were wondering whether Bob Dylan was going to survive. I felt sad and empty at the thought of a world without him." Guthrie recollected the time Dylan "exploded and became for us like a warrior-poet who put images and words that we didn't even know we were thinking about for everybody to hear and see. I've learned so much from him, I don't even want to start thinking about it."[16]

The performers of Further '97 were announced in May. The original tour was to encompass twenty-one shows, but brisk sales allowed the itinerary to expand to twenty-nine. Bands and artists performing included Rat Dog (Weir and bassist Rob Wasserman), the Black Crowes, Mickey Hart and Planet Drum, Bruce Hornsby, moe, Jorma Kaukonen and Michael Falzarano, and Dead lyricist Robert Hunter. Weir announced "old pal" Arlo Guthrie would serve as master of ceremonies.[17] The folk singer was also slated to sing and play a few songs during band changes, as well as sit in on jams when mood and circumstance permitted.

Some thought Guthrie's invitation to join the Further tour was a curious one. Though not necessarily a jam-band sort of artist, Guthrie's connection to the music of the Woodstock/1960s era was solid. There was always a solid block of Grateful Dead fans in attendance at his concerts— particularly at shows in the late 1970s and early 1980s, when Guthrie routinely traded blistering guitar breaks with Shenandoah's Steve Ide and David Grover. Guthrie admitted his own family was perplexed by the offer to host Further. "When I told my kids about it," Guthrie offered, "they asked me 'Why you?' I told them they were looking for someone who could talk and say something at the same time." He also had already conjured his own subtitle for the upcoming tour: "The Night of the Living Dead."[18]

There were several good reasons to consider the assignment. Guthrie explained he accepted "for two reasons. The most important one is I thought it would make me nervous. I've been on the road now for thirty years. I'm very comfortable doing it, it sustains me, [but] on the other hand, it doesn't always challenge me. When someone asked me if I'd like to be the MC and play some songs, my mouth was going to say 'No,' and, all of a sudden it said, 'Wait a minute, that's *different*. So I'm a little nervous and a little apprehensive—and because of that, I know I *have* to do it.'"[19] But he also saw a natural "kinship between that audience and my audience." While he had enjoyed a passing friendship with the Dead's Bob Weir and Mickey Hart, he admitted that was "years and years ago. They aren't close friends of mine; we have not hung out in decades." Then, recalling Wavy Gravy's notion, "If you can remember the '60s, you weren't there," Guthrie laughed. He and the ex-members of the Dead "might be more friends than we actually remember."[20]

Guthrie's appearance before tens of thousands of music fans adorned in tie-dye—many too young to be of the Woodstock generation—undoubtedly helped freshen his own fan base. He admitted to being a champion of music festivals. There was a tangible strength-in-numbers vibe present. "I think what happens is that it becomes so big it can't be regulated, can't be policed to each fine little detail. You can get away with things you can't get away with on the street."[21] Which sounded like an open invitation for attendees to bring their own stash along—as if they weren't going to anyway.

AG: Starting in West Palm Beach, Florida, at the Coral Sky Amphitheater on June 20th, we ended the tour in Irvine, California, at Irvine Meadows some six weeks later on August 3rd. Personally, I had a great time hanging out with old friends and filling up stadiums from coast to coast. It was also challenging for me, because the crowd had come to see and hear members of the Grateful Dead and not a folk singer. Nevertheless, I made the transitions as smooth (and as quickly) as possible— and regaled the audience with tales and songs that were short and digestible.

The tour mostly went off without incident. The festival was elastic by design, lasting anywhere from six to ten hours. The only wrinkle occurred when tour buses rolled into Buffalo's Darien Center Amphitheater on 8 July. Guthrie would soon find himself thrust into a controversy not of his making. The Performing Arts Center at Darien had been employing non-union stagehands, locking out twenty members of the International Alliance of Theatrical Stage Employees Local no. 10. The union's president tried to get the news to Guthrie, but the singer was in mid-travel, unaware of the protest.[22]

"Given the short time I've had to look into this," Guthrie told a local newspaper upon arrival, "I'm pretty sure that I don't know what is actually going on."[23] Guthrie would perform at Darien Lakes. Though reports never specifically described the singer as a strikebreaker, the idea of Woody Guthrie's son crossing a picket line was worthy of a newspaper blurb. But it was unwelcome bad press and terribly unfair: no other performer had been called out. The incident was mostly forgotten by 10 July, the occasion of Guthrie's fiftieth birthday. The folk singer celebrated hitting the half-century on his bus, the tour moving from Toronto to Hershey, Pennsylvania, for a performance on 11 July. Fans at the Hershey show interrupted his sets with shouted birthday greetings. Acknowledging the wishes Guthrie sighed, "A lot of time's gone by, but not a lot has changed."[24]

The Further tour rolled on for fourteen more shows, wrapping on 3 August in Irvine. Though it seemed a vacation was in order, the singer instead pressed on with a solo tour.

AG: I left the Further tour thankful for the opportunity—and with a new merchandise girl. Jessica Kelly joined our crew immediately following the conclusion of the Further Festival. She was young, funny, vivacious, and completely comfortable traveling from place to place every day. She could count too. You wouldn't believe how many people we'd gone through over the years, some who really couldn't do basic arithmetic. Being a merch person is a lot of hard work. We had an entire catalog of stuff, to which we added the usual T-shirts and accessories and it all had to be organized and accounted for every day.

From California we traveled east going through Grand Junction, Colorado Springs, and Fort Collins in Colorado before deadheading back to the East Coast. After a few more shows in the Midwest, I returned to Chicago for another meeting of the Council for a Parliament of the World's Religions. This was a much shorter event occurring November

8, 9, and 10. Just three days. I also played a Tribute to Steve Goodman at the Medinah Temple on the 13th. Steve's family was in the audience, and I got so nervous with them being there, I screwed up the words to his song "The City of New Orleans"—which I had been singing for twenty-five years. Nevertheless I had a good time revisiting with friends of Steve's in his home town of Chicago.

Guthrie's request that he be permitted to host a series of summer benefits in Great Barrington was made less pressing once he was conscripted for Further. But the Old Trinity Church was still in desperate need of cash so their community outreach work could continue. An editorial in the *Berkshire Eagle* was cautiously supportive: "It seems apparent that Arlo Guthrie's plans for a series of eight small concerts conflict with the conditions of the special permit for the Guthrie Center. . . . It seems just as apparent, however, that the concerts will benefit the not-for-profit organization and won't be so large as to be unmanageable."[25]

The special permit was eventually granted, with four sequential October dates set aside for the benefits. The shows proved special for several reasons. The first was the concerts' reunification of Guthrie with members of Shenandoah. Guthrie's surprise appearance with the band at the Berkshire Music Festival back on 4 May had sparked talk of a reunion. "We had so much fun together last spring," Guthrie explained. "I didn't even know I was going to be able to be there. But we had a great time."[26]

The church concerts were also special because they would also serve as recording sessions. The previous year's Thanksgiving show for ABC radio had been enough of a success to give it another go—this time with a special twist. The single 1996 program was transmitted via satellite to thirty-five radio outlets. This time Guthrie planned to record all four shows and select the best performances from the resulting six hours of recordings. Once edited into a tidy sixty-minute package, the program would be pressed to CD. The discs would then be shipped by Radio Today to two hundred radio stations for broadcast.[27]

Guthrie's West Coast cable-TV friend, Bill Rosendahl, also brought a production crew to film one of the concerts for broadcast in the Los Angeles area. It was a big deal for the Guthrie Center. The expansive radio and television coverage provided a wonderful opportunity to promote the church's mission. "We want to become a prominent part of life in Berkshire

County," Guthrie offered to the *Berkshire Eagle*. "The radio show will give us the opportunity to reach hundreds of thousands of people, so this is a big event for us." When asked how his life might have unspooled had he not been arrested on Thanksgiving Day 1965, Guthrie pondered the question. "I think about that myself sometimes," he replied. "This whole thing hangs by a very thin thread."[28]

The Rosendahl program allowed fans from far afield to enjoy the October benefit. Guthrie assembled a band of "old friends," including David Grover on electric guitar, Terry Ala Berry on drums, Carol Ide on vocals, John Miller on bass, and Abe on keyboards. He performed "Alice's Restaurant," of course, but the TV segment also included takes on "Ukulele Lady," "Gabriel's Mother's Highway Ballad #16 Blues," "St. Louis Tickle," "City of New Orleans," and "This Land Is Your Land." In a bit of musical irreverence, Guthrie pondered how the course of popular music might have veered had Bob Dylan played ukulele. The band then kicked into a torrid ukulele-driven rendition of "All Along the Watchtower."

Rosendahl managed to corral Guthrie for an interview. As he was an old friend, Guthrie was comfortable commenting with sincerity on what Alice's old church meant to him: "We recognize that everybody has their way and not one way is more right than another way. In a world like this, we can't afford to live where only some people are right and everybody else is wrong. We have to make room and learn to live with people who have different opinions about what's real. And this place has become that. I couldn't have asked for a better thing to happen. Even in my wildest crazy imagination—and I have a good one—I would have never thought this place would be that."[29]

When Rosendahl suggested the church's ecumenicalism mirrored Guthrie's own multistrand religious beliefs, the singer conceded his lifelong spiritual interests had "totally screwed up" his life:

> I mean, there's no question about it. I was born in Brooklyn, New York. I had a Jewish mom. My dad was one of those Protestants from Oklahoma. And somehow because they both live in me, I knew that those kind of people could exist together. There didn't have to be all the problems and confusion. It was already inside me. And later on in my own life as I went on and on, I also moved myself into other traditions. Other ways of thinking about things.

Whether it was just standing outside on a hill looking at stars at night. . . . There is a whole lot of people for whom that is religion. Or the Buddhist tradition. Or the Hindu tradition. Or this or that or whatever it is. . . . I envisioned a place that was sort of like me. A physical place. Because I knew if it could exist in me, I knew there was hope for [the world] outside of me.[30]

With the tapings completed, Guthrie was due to set out on the final tour of 1997. Just before setting off for shows at The Ark in Ann Arbor, Michigan, the singer was to be honored as a recipient of the Huntington's Disease Society of America's newly inaugurated "Woody Guthrie Award." The three children of Woody and Marjorie had always made themselves available to assist the society in small ways, but none had committed to its work as tirelessly as their mother. Nora confessed, "I felt I lost a big part of my mother to the group, and when I grew up it was a huge relief *not* to participate."[31] Though Arlo periodically helped his mother canvas for research funding, he too was not interested in becoming "a poster boy for Huntington's."[32] Guthrie watched as his mother became "somewhat obsessed" working for a cure, her selfless dedication unmatched.

The family's immersion back into their mother's work with the Huntington's Disease Society of America (HDSA) was mostly the result of Nora's taking on a leadership role in the organization. "Coming back after fifteen years since my mother died gave me some breathing room," Nora explained. Everyone interested in the Guthrie family was aware of Woody's musical legacy. But Marjorie's activism was every bit as important—if less recognized—than her husband's cultural contributions. It was in this light that Nora conceded, "Someone from the family should be part of it." With Nora's involvement, the society went from having raised some $250,000 toward Huntington's disease research to bringing in nearly four times that amount. There had been hope among HDSA advocates that the Guthrie family's connection to the music industry might help them raise additional funds through benefit concerts and recording projects. "There is a lot of support from the artists I already work with," Nora told *Billboard,* "and I'll do what I can to bring them to HD."[33]

So on 16 October, members of the HDSA gathered to celebrate their achievements at a $350 a plate dinner at the Marriott Marquis Hotel in midtown Manhattan. There would be three separate awards for the honorees:

the Marjorie Guthrie Leadership Award, the Guthrie Family Humanitarian Award, and the Woody Guthrie Award. Arlo Guthrie was presented
with the latter, a press release noting the folk singer "epitomizes his father's
work in the world of music."[34] Guthrie was reluctant to accept, obliging,
"Receiving this is really for my mom. This organization was her life. It's an
exciting time with all the new discoveries about the disease, and I'm a little
saddened she couldn't be here to see it, because we're really getting somewhere." He also noted the link between people suffering from Huntington's
and people suffering from AIDS. Suffering was suffering, and he recognized those afflicted with the latter were often "dealing with the same
issues as Huntington's disease."[35]

One person attending the banquet was choreographer Sophie Maslow,
now a spry eighty-six years of age. It was Maslow who first brought Marjorie
to Almanac House in January of 1942. The pair were hoping to convince
Woody to assist on Sophie's production of *Folksay*. Fifty-four years on, Arlo
was surprised to see Sophie again. "I hadn't seen Sophie for two or three
decades, and she had been like an aunt to me," Guthrie recalled. "She was
really one of my mother's best friends."[36] That night Maslow asked Guthrie
if he might reconsider an offer made several years earlier: to take on his
father's role in a new production of *Folksay*. "I would love to," Guthrie
answered. This was a heartening response. As Maslow recalled with a frown,
"When I asked you about twenty years ago, you refused."[37] Guthrie replied
he didn't recall the offer, but he would certainly consider it now. Their
Folksay partnership would, sadly, not happen, as Sophie Maslow passed on
in 2006.

In the autumn of 1997, the Koch CD reissues of Guthrie's *Running
Down the Road, Washington County,* and *Arlo Guthrie* albums finally hit record store bins. It had been some years since these albums were made
widely available, so their reappearance in shops was something worthy of
celebrating. *Folk Roots* magazine was among the first to welcome them:
"Brother Arlo Guthrie has been witnessing for most of his recorded
career. While affiliations with hillbilly, synagogue, church, and ashram
have shifted, his compositional fix on Biblical [*sic*] themes has remained
bedrock; a Gospel sun around which orbits such humanistic concerns as
migrant labor, quantum physics, family, penniless dignity, and account-
able government. Woody Guthrie's mischievous mysticism twinkles
through Arlo's spirited covers from downtrodden America's folk hymnal,

and his own wildly irreverent country-ish rags, ballads, blues, and shit-kicker rockers."[38]

Guthrie's year closed, as traditional, with a series of small club dates and the Thanksgiving weekend concert at Carnegie Hall. The singer's hope that his appearances at summer's Further Festival might help bring fresh faces to his shows seemed to have come to fruition. Guthrie told the *Boston Globe* his playing on the tour—combined with his recent television appearances on *Byrds of Paradise, Relativity,* and *Renegade*—caused "a lot of new people [to say], 'Hey, let's go see that guy.'"[39]

Although Guthrie's gigs in November and December included a handful of theater and college dates, most shows were booked as multinight visits to the best-known folk clubs in the northeast: the Canal Street Tavern in Dayton; the Rams Head Tavern in Annapolis; the Iron Horse in Northampton; the House of Blues in Cambridge, Massachusetts; and Jonathan's in Ogunquit, Maine. Such intimate residencies were refreshing, connecting him to his more modest beginnings in the business. On the eve of the Cambridge gigs, Guthrie told the *Globe* his past one-nighters at Boston's Symphony Hall, Harvard's Sanders Theatre, and Berklee Performance Center "didn't give us much chance to hang out and talk to people, which we used to do. I've really missed hanging out and attracting off-the-street people to the shows."[40]

In January of 1998, Berkshire newspapers were reporting Guthrie's interest in buying the eighty-year-old Kresge Building in downtown Pittsfield. The *Berkshire Eagle* reported Guthrie had even signed a purchase agreement, though a final sale was contingent on a number of as-yet-unspecified conditions. A few days earlier a reporter tracked Guthrie down in Austin, Texas, where the singer was to soon perform at the city's La Zona Rosa nightclub. The folk singer confirmed negotiations to purchase the property, partly to house the offices of Rising Son. He also hinted at other ambitious plans for the space. "All I can tell you is at this point about four weeks from now, we'll know what the story is."[41] There were still a number of contingencies needing to be worked out.

In 1992 the offices of Rising Son moved from Guthrie's home to the Old Trinity Church in Great Barrington. But six years into ownership of the latter, Guthrie was still struggling to meet monthly mortgage payments and perform necessary repairs. He continued to look to fans for a bit of financial support, asking for their assistance through donations and paid memberships to the Guthrie Center. As it was a very innocent bit of fund-raising, Guthrie was taken back when several potential donors pointedly asked why they were being asked to fund the office space of a privately owned record company.

The truth of the matter was the donations of fans and sponsors *weren't* funding Rising Son Records at all. Trying to calm the fears of potential donors, Guthrie explained RSR "was in the building to pay rent to the church in order to help the church buy the building. So no one was donating *anything* to a record company." But the singer sympathized as to why some might see an element of impropriety. He admitted the arrangement was confusing since both his record company and the foundation shared space "in the same building with the same people answering the phones."[42]

Guthrie tried his best to allay any misunderstandings to readers of the *Berkshire Eagle*. But it was evident it might be best to physically separate the offices of his record company from the church. "We have been looking for a place to move the business," he offered, conceding "the not-for-profit organization located within the church needs to have a separate identity and not be seen as part of our for-profit stuff. When we ask for funds or endowments, we don't want them to confuse what we're doing as a charity with what we're doing as a normal company."[43]

It was a difficult decision. While separating the Rising Son office from the church removed any appearance of impropriety, moving would incur a burdensome financial responsibility. The singer acknowledged he had been interested in doing business in downtown Pittsfield. Though the town was always announcing intentions to rejuvenate its lackluster Main Street, nothing ever seemed to come of it. Several years earlier Guthrie had mulled over purchasing Pittsfield's old Palace Theater, but bureaucratic red tape and zoning issues frustrated plans time and again.[44]

Guthrie's purchase of the Kresge building was—temporarily, at least—mothballed in late February 1998. The singer was one of two potential buyers who pulled out of a deal. The attorney for the present owners would only say that both interested parties "withdrew their agreements when conditions of those agreements were not satisfied."[45]

AG: I began 1998 continuing the solo shows I had been used to doing. Jessica, Dennis, and I drove to Austin for a series of shows that took place in Texas, and some out of way places were on our schedule, including a stop in Alpine, Texas, at Rail Road Blues, a small venue. But the folks were more than friendly, and we had a great time playing a gig for them.

Guthrie described his six-week winter tour as "not very unusual; a normal January trekking southward through the Carolinas and Georgia, then over into Tennessee and Oklahoma, down through Texas into New Mexico to follow the warm weather. This year brought us farther south into Texas than we had ever been."[46] The singer was pleased to get a chance to visit the "Big Bend" part of Texas. This was the territory his great grandfather, J. P. Guthrie, had worked in as a ranch hand in the 1890s. Following five shows in Texas, the tour rolled through New Mexico and Arizona, finishing with a half-dozen shows in Colorado. Guthrie recalled, thanks to the effects of the *El Niño* jet stream, Colorado's highways "were free of snow and ice and our travels through the Rockies were easier than they had ever been."[47] It had been a successful six weeks. Jessica was joined by her twin sister, Jennifer, for a week or two as the tour passed through the West. Guthrie recalled that the sisters managed to collect "more donations to the Church and sold more stuff than anyone had ever done. What a team!"[48]

AG: We returned home in late February. I had a couple of weeks off . . .

Guthrie made it home in time to catch a bit of the 40th annual Grammy Awards telecast from Radio City Music Hall on 25 February. Although the songs for the *This Land Is Your Land* soundtrack had been recorded back in 1992, the album wasn't issued until 1997. In January of 1998 the slate of Grammy honorees was announced and Guthrie again found an album of his in the running for "Best Musical Album for Children."

Just prior to the nomination, a newspaper managed an interview with the album's producer, Frankie Fuchs, a Guthrie family friend. "These were obscure publishing demos done on one microphone captured on tiny reels," Fuchs recalled, musing on the original tapes Woody recorded back in the years 1944–52. Fuchs conceded that while the album was "not sonically pristine, I didn't try to make it like that, either." Similar to the *Grow Big* album, *This Land Is Your Land* featured several studio-enabled "duets" between Woody and Arlo. "I wouldn't call ours electronically enhanced," Fuchs told the *Los Angeles Times*. "Woody's performance was on acetate, which we transferred to digital and then back to analog so we could record along with it. It's not perfect by any means."[49]

It seemed the majority of people making the best children's records of value were the folk singers of an earlier age. Guthrie's Grammy competition included Taj Mahal, John McCutcheon, Eric Bibb, Art Garfunkel, and John Denver. There was a sense of *fait accompli* that the award would go to Denver, the singer-songwriter having died in a tragic plane crash a few months prior to the show. "I forgot about the Grammys all day," Guthrie admitted, "until I got home late and found out that John Denver had won."[50]

AG: Abe and I had been planning a tour that would take us around the world. It was coming up soon but was not very practical financially. However, a travel agent friend of mine told me there were unlisted special fares available on British Airways that would substantially reduce the cost if you could follow their rules. The major rule was you could only go in one direction, without backtracking more than a few times. You could stay in one place as long as you wanted (within reason). This allowed us to go from the East Coast to Ireland to India, through Australia to Los Angeles and back to where we started—all first-class and cheaper than simply going overseas and back. We jumped on it.

During the Irish part of the tour we were playing in Galway for a few nights at The Roisin Dubh and my old friend Donovan jumped onstage and played some songs with us. The crowd went crazy, and we had a lot of fun swapping songs. In Ireland there's a special gift the locals have. They can sing along with you on songs they've never heard before. It was self-evident that particular night.

From Ireland we flew to London, where we had a flight to India after a day off, so we stayed with my old sweetheart, Caroly. I had met Caroly in 1966 on a tour I was doing in the UK. And we were instantly attracted to each other. I was nineteen and she was a close friend of Ann Cooper, whose father, Lou Cooper, was married at that time to my mother, Marjorie.

In Guthrie's reminiscence, "Caroly and I were mostly inseparable until we parted in late 1968." He could still recall, in vivid detail, the occasion of their first meeting:

AG: On December 1st, 1966, I traveled back to England, where my friend Karl Dallas had set up a small tour of twelve shows. I did a gig in Brighton at the Stanford Arms Folk Club at Preston Circus on December 4, and my stepfather's daughter, Ann, came to the show. She was living in London at the time. She brought along her friend, Caroly Davis. Caroly and I hit it off extremely well and became boyfriend–girlfriend almost immediately. Caroly accompanied me on the remaining shows in England. I visited her often where she was living in her parents' flat nearby the Hempstead section of London.

I also did a TV show hosted by Jane Asher for the BBC TV. It was a variety show of current events, book writers, performers, popular people, etc. On the show was one man who intrigued me, a holy man from India, Baba Hari Dass. He'd taken a vow of silence but would answer questions using a small blackboard he carried with him.

On air he was asked the usual meaning-of-life questions, but as the show ended and he was still in the studio, Caroly and I walked up and asked him, "Do you know any good Indian restaurants around here?" Hari Dass broadly smiled and wrote, "Finally! Someone with a real question!" He wrote the name and address of what turned out to be a fabulous Indian restaurant in London, called Gaylord's. Caroly and I visited there many times.

At the end of my 1966 tour, Caroly and I went to Davos, Switzerland, for the holidays. Neither of us were skiers, but we enjoyed ourselves immensely, visiting the sights, and eating at restaurants. The train to Davos from Zurich ended with a horse-drawn sleigh ride from the train station to the hotel. It was magical. We parted after a few days and I returned to New York, while Caroly went back to London.

Caroly and I remained close friends throughout the years, and I stayed with her in the same flat she'd lived in when we met. Every time I'd go overseas, which was quite often, I'd stay with my old friend. Although we were no longer lovers, we were dear friends and I always looked forward to visiting her for a few days, catching up on our lives, and going out together to restaurants we both loved. On April 17th and 18th, 1998, Abe and I camped out on her floors for a couple of nights, and left the next day, April 19th, for our grueling flight to New Delhi, India.

Luckily, we had friends in New Delhi. Richard Celeste (the former governor of Ohio) had become the American ambassador to India during the Clinton administration and he was a friend. We were met by his staff at the airport and whisked away to stay at The Roosevelt House—the American embassy in New Delhi. Abe and I stayed for a week in New Delhi, venturing out as much as we could to check out the country.

As it happened, we were there just as the Kumbha Mela was taking place—a festival that takes place every twelve years bringing countless seekers and people of all kinds to important spiritually recognized places. One of those places was in Hardwar, on the banks of the Ganges River.

Ma had given me special instructions concerning her recently departed sister, Shirley. I was to go to the Ganges and ritually bathe in the flowing waters before following her instructions. So we rented a car and driver and took off for Hardwar just as the festival was getting underway.

Millions of people were heading there at the same time, and the roads were packed with every form of transportation available during the last thousand years. There seemed to be one rule for those on the roads—the right of way belonged to the biggest vehicle. It was beyond my imagination that so many people could be in such chaotic circumstances, but there were no accidents and no one appeared to be overly concerned. I followed Ma's instructions and we returned to the embassy later that same day.

We also attended a charitable gala with Richard Gere, who was headlining the event, a fundraiser for people and families suffering from AIDS. Abe and I didn't have any formal clothes, let alone bring them with us. So we had to go shopping for the event. What impressed me was that the men's clothing store had about a dozen employees in a small shop. One opened the door, one led you to the right counter, where another reached up on the shelves and handed the clothes to yet another, who saw that they were the proper size. Another led you to the counter, where a clerk packaged the clothing and another took care of the financial arrangements. I thought to myself, if we did that in America, everyone would have a job.

Now that Abe and I had formal Indian clothing at our disposal, we were better able to attend the usual functions at the embassy. One evening they held an event for the movers and shakers, mostly Americans who held corporate positions in India—the head of Pepsi, the head of McDonalds and the like, as well as various military types in positions of authority. These were not typically people in my circle of friends. I had lived most of my life believing these were the very kinds of people we were opposed to. Boy, was I mistaken.

I had a chance to chat with the guy in charge of the McDonalds Corporation for all India. He was a very nice guy, who was telling me how hard it was to operate in a country where they don't generally consume beef. Not only that, but American Big Macs are made with lettuce, virtually unknown in India. In order to sell Big Macs in India, they first had to switch to some other source of protein. Then they had to teach farmers how to grow lettuce. It was too far to import it from anywhere else. To grow lettuce, you need irrigated fields—also unusual there. As the Indian government had no money for these changes to be made from traditional farming, the expenses of doing so had to come from the corporations themselves.

Local farmhands were not educated enough to read the warnings or instructions for the fertilizers or pesticides they had to use. So schools had to be built to educate people, and hospitals had to be built to take care of those who'd become unwittingly contaminated. All for a world-wide corporation to sell Big Macs. It went on and on.

All the corporate guys had similar stories. There were military guys there too who'd served in Vietnam, or at that time, and risen through the ranks. After the evening began to wind down, Richard Celeste asked if me and Abe could do a little impromptu performance. We did and watched as our songs brought tears to the eyes of our soldiers there—who thanked us afterward and said, "It's good to be reminded of who we are."

We left India after a few more days and headed to our next destination, Australia. Abe and I were pretty sick by the time we'd arrived—having spent just enough time in India to deal with the foreign creatures lurking in the food and water. Luckily we had a few days off to recuperate.

This was my second trip to Australia, the first being in 1984. For this tour Richard James became our new friend and promotor, and he put together a series of eight shows in many parts of the country. In those days, we had to have a local Australian on the bill with us, so we hired a local singer-songwriter, Jodi Martin, to open the shows for us. She was just fabulous to work with and we become dear friends.

The Australian tour was to kick off on 12 April at the Byron Bay Blues Festival in Brisbane and finish up two weeks later on 26 April at Lismore's Star Court Theatre. There was talk the US embassy in Canberra might provide the Guthries a formal welcome. To Guthrie's relief, that official greeting would not happen. "I don't know about this 'official welcome' thing," he told Sydney's *Morning Herald*. "It's not good for the hippie image." The *Herald* acknowledged that Guthrie managed "to hold true to his music and values at an age when most have succumbed to the creeping conservatism of the older generations." But he did wonder if time had frayed his radicalism, since fewer protest songs flowed from his pen. "As I get older," Guthrie answered, "it's not a matter of becoming conservative. But I say to all those people who come up with [protest] things for us to do now, 'You go do it, I'm busy doing something else.'"[51]

In Guthrie's case, that "something else," was working alongside Ma. Guthrie tried to explain Ma's role in his life: "She dragged me into all these places and people I didn't really have a connection with. And there I was at the parades and rallies and it introduced me to a new group of people who had something to fight for. Somebody needed to stand up with these people." Guthrie was quick to correct the inference that his brand of folk music was out of step with the times. Wasn't getting people together to sing along Seeger-style on old songs passé? Guthrie would have none of that, suggesting such camaraderie was a counter-reaction to an increasingly commodified society "where people have no sense of *real*. You can say that sort of music is old-fashioned, but I don't care because I know it's true."[52]

Guthrie also would run into an old friend while visiting Sydney, the singer-guitarist Roger McGuinn. Guthrie and Abe were soon to appear at the city's Seymour Centre, and McGuinn was resting, having just finished a residency at Sydney's Basement nightclub. The friends were invited to a luncheon at McGuinn's hotel, the meeting arranged by a journalist interested in getting two musical icons of the '60s together. The reporter opined that both artists enjoyed "the good fortune of being in the right place at the right time,"[53] their legacies giving them the credentials that allowed both to enjoy sustained careers. But the interview became animated when the writer suggested the new generation was getting tired of listening to the music of their parents.

A gauntlet had been thrown. "When we were in our prime—not just us but all our friends—there was something unique going on," Guthrie fired back. "We were the first generation in the entire history of the world that actually grew up in the shadow of instant destruction. We knew that if we kept going the way we were, the possibility of destroying ourselves was reasonable. Everybody started doing things differently just to get out of the tradition. Those traditional values had to change. The one tool for this change was music. It was the universal language around the world at the time. It's not anymore. We had moved into talking about real important stuff . . . and having fun was a necessary ingredient of all of this. We believed that we could do this. We believed if we were true to ourselves and honest enough and didn't give up, didn't sell out, we would survive."[54]

When the journalist defensively parried that "folk-rock" music was simply "not the music of today," Guthrie argued, "You're wrong. All the kids today are going to Roger and our shows and they're listening to all the music that we made much more than I was listening to Frank Sinatra when I was growing up. Our music is about real things. It is not created just for entertainment."[55]

The visit to Australia was, in fact, not all about entertainment. Guthrie had a break between his concerts in Adelaide and Perth, and one of his desires was to pay a visit to the Marjorie Guthrie Center. Guthrie's mother first traveled to Melbourne in November of 1979, scheduled to speak at the country's first Huntington's disease conference in neighboring Balwyn. She had no medical degree, of course. But she had lived through the experience of watching her husband lose himself to the disease. "Here was a young professional performer; a man in the prime of his life," Marjorie told *The Age* on the eve of the conference, "who very unexpectedly became moody and lost his balance. He voluntarily walked into a hospital and said, 'Something is wrong.'"[56] She was determined to find out what that something was.

Marjorie's mission to educate people about Huntington's disease inspired scientists and geneticists to deeply research it. Australia honored her commitment with the branding of the Marjorie Guthrie Center, a care facility designed to allow victims to carry on their lives with dignity. Arlo hadn't been able to visit the center on his 1984 tour of Australia, so his visit was long past due. He was inspired by the work being done for the benefit of Huntington's patients. Caregivers were appointed with simple but helpful tasks, ones benefiting both the patients and their families. The singer would write, "My visit to the Marjorie Guthrie Center was really wonderful. People have been studying the effects of Huntington's disease for about three decades now. And they made a very interesting discovery in Perth. Seems like in most places around the world, including the US, people with Huntington's disease were stashed away in hospital wards. The drain on family life, having to personally care for someone with the disease, was just too much for most average people to handle. So folks were put in facilities where they could receive some full-time care."[57]

Guthrie explained how in Australia a team of good Samaritans visited families caring for HD patients. They took patients on small adventures, to intermingle with others or simply be attended to. Having had the experience of living with someone suffering Huntington's, Guthrie realized how important it was for family members to be given a rest from time to time, no matter how small. Australian researchers discovered that bringing patients into social situations would slow "the effects of disease . . . considerably." Guthrie mused that such treatment was more humane and less costly than warehousing patients in hospital wards or asylums. The program also allowed families to "stay together as long as possible" before institutionalization became a necessary option. He continued, "I wondered years ago what my own life might have been like if we'd had those kinds of services available when I was a kid growing up in a Huntington's disease family. Even today most of our care seems archaic viewed against the care people receive in Perth."[58]

> **AG:** From Australia we flew to Honolulu for a day off there, then continued on back to New England via Los Angeles for an overnight stop. The days of fifteen-hour flights were getting to be a little too much for me, and I preferred to break up the flights, even staying overnight if need be. I still love going from Australia to Hawaii, because I can't wrap my head around the international date line. In effect you get to Honolulu the day before you left Australia. It always seems like a free day—one that doesn't count.

Guthrie had barely shrugged off his jet lag when he appeared before the cameras of WRBG-TV at Pittsfield's Park Square. Newspapers were reporting the folk singer's purchase of the old Kresge building. The singer had managed to line up investors to help with the $100,000 purchase. It was Guthrie's intention that the Rising Son office would occupy the second and third floors of the building, with the street-level entrance hosting a restaurant and nightclub.[59]

On the following Friday, Guthrie was at The Farm, rehearsing for an unusual Saturday-night gig in Maine. He stole away just long enough to share his desire of transforming the Kresge building into a performance space. He suggested the proposed nightclub was to be modeled after the House of Blues in Cambridge. Though his original vision for the Kresge building hadn't included any plans for a nightclub, Guthrie had long mulled bringing a performance space to downtown Pittsfield. The town's two old theaters, the Capitol and the Palace, were first choices, but those plans were scuttled for a number of reasons. Though not the funky old theater he originally envisioned, Guthrie thought the Kresge's first floor could serve as "a very unique and special space." "I've been hoping for something like this since I moved up in '69," he explained. "It took a little time. But with everyone else doing what they're doing, this could be a really fun time for Pittsfield."[60]

The press conference was brief since he had to return to rehearsals at The Farm. The newspaper made a brief mention of the folk singer's unusual "current project"—to marry his folksy brand of music-making with "symphony orchestras."[61]

AG: I first met John Nardolillo May 9, 1996, when he barged into my dressing room at Lincoln Center in New York, saying, "I know I'm not supposed to be here, but before you have me thrown out I want to share an idea with you." He didn't appear to be crazy, so I listened while he spoke of trying to incorporate my songs into a symphonic setting. The idea intrigued me. He wanted to give it a proper name, but as far as I was concerned it was Arlo Versus the Orchestra, as I found it difficult to imagine. It took a couple of years to organize the idea into reality.

The idea seemed crazy. Nardolillo didn't even hold a ticket to Guthrie's show at Lincoln Center's Alice Tully Hall. He was a concert violinist trained at the Cleveland Institute of Music and the Peabody Conservatory in Baltimore. He was presently playing violin for the Annapolis Symphony, while concurrently conducting a youth orchestra in Washington, DC. Nardolillo, at age twenty-four, was also mostly broke. He admitted to slipping inside the Tully when, at the interval, he managed to mingle with the smokers outside. He then pushed his way into the hall when the crowd reentered the theater at the curtain bell.[62]

Nardolillo had been introduced to Guthrie's music through his parent's record collection. Listening from the wings, Nardolillo had a revelation: "Wouldn't it be completely wild and nutty to hear Arlo with an orchestra?"[63] After bluffing his way backstage, he proposed the folk singer might consider working with symphonic backing. Guthrie wasn't opposed to the idea. "I had been thinking about doing some different things than the normal Arlo shows," Guthrie explained. "You reach a point where everything is easy creatively. I'd get up there night to night and do good shows. I wanted to do other things."[64]

But when first introduced to the proposition, Guthrie wasn't quite sure what to make of it. He thought the kid standing in front of him seemed "too young to even know about a symphony orchestra or even who I was."[65] But it was moments like this when Guthrie took inspiration from Marilyn Monroe's observation, "Ever notice how 'What the hell?' is always the right answer?"

> **AG:** We hired a guy named Ari Myers to write the orchestra charts, someone neither of us knew very well, but he seemed like a reasonable person. My agent, Mark Smith, was essentially more familiar with symphony orchestras than he was with folk singers. So this was a natural for him and he began talks with various venues around the country, contracting dates for what we then called "An American Scrapbook." I still called it "Arlo Versus the Orchestra," but that was more of a private reference and not a selling point when Mark began booking the shows. It was essentially an entirely new thing for me to be working with symphony orchestras on stage. As Mark began filling in the calendar with the orchestra shows, Ari Myers began working on the charts— although he wouldn't respond to requests to see them or to let us know how it was going.

The first "American Scrapbook" concert was scheduled at the Maine Center of the Arts in Orono on Saturday night, 9 May 1998. The plan was for Nardolillo to conduct the Bangor Symphony Orchestra on that first performance. Nardolillo would kick off the program with selections from Leonard Bernstein's Overture to "Candide," Hershy Kay's "Cakewalk Suite," and Aaron Copland's ballet "Rodeo." Guthrie would then take the stage, moving directly into a symphonic "City of New Orleans." That, at least, was the plan.

> **AG:** Two weeks before the first show was scheduled we still had no charts, and a lawyer for Ari Myers had called my office demanding more money before anything would be sent to us. A week before our first try at a show in Orono, Maine, we heard from the guy saying the charts were done. We were desperate to have them in our hands. I'd spent around $20,000 for Ari Myers to complete the work and get it to us. It had to be paid in full before he would send anything. After sending the guy the money, the charts arrived—and they were awful. What was created was mostly unusable. We were devastated.
>
> With a few days before the premier of "An American Scrapbook" in Orono with the Bangor Symphony Orchestra, John brought the principal players of his own Metropolitan Symphony to my house, and they sat around recreating and rewriting the charts for the orchestra to play. John's assistant, Kathy Swekel, tried her best to keep things organized, but even her natural orderliness was put to the test. Nevertheless she kept it all organized as the parts flew across the dining room table.
>
> Then the most wonderful thing happened. The Boston Pops had booked the second symphony show at Symphony Hall in Boston, but they wanted to include a gospel choir in one of the songs. They needed an arrangement. The pianist John had brought to my living room, Jamie Burton, turned out to be a truly gifted choral arranger. Jamie and John at first tried to use the Ari Myers charts and simply add the choral section, but it proved to be impossible. So they rewrote the entire piece for orchestra with choir which, as it turned out, was magical.
>
> Meanwhile, John's principal players were still creating the orchestral parts in the tour bus on the way to Maine. Despite the road sickness that overtook some of the musicians, and the frenzy of trying to organize all the sections, we got it done and performed a wonderful two nights for the folks in Orono on May 9th and 10th.

Incredibly, those two off-the-radar concerts came off without a hitch. A music critic from the *Bangor Daily News* described the evening as "among the most raucously enjoyed concerts in recent Maine Center history . . . and will undoubtedly make its mark as one of those truly American moments in music history."[66] Guthrie's back-catalog was given new life in majestic, string-swelling settings, with "City of New Orleans," "Darkest Hour," "Streets of Laredo," "Last Train," "You Are the Song," "This Land Is Your Land," and "Goodnight, Irene" among those recast. During the course of the program, Guthrie would tell the story of how his father had recently become "official" on a US postage stamp. The honor was, in Guthrie's view, "a stunning, final defeat." Later on, Guthrie—decked out in formal black concert attire and cowboy boots—acknowledged, "I never thought I'd see me looking like I do at this moment. I feel like my Dad. This is a stunning defeat for me."[67]

Self-deprecating humor aside, it was obvious the magic created on stage wouldn't have happened without the Herculean team effort to salvage the worthless charts first sent. It was also obvious to Guthrie that Jamie Burton was the best man to hone the charts to perfection:

AG: At some point, after the frenzy of the first series of orchestra shows had worn down, I hired Jamie to completely rewrite all the charts from scratch. His arrangements were simply gorgeous and complimented my own material, never intruding on the original source material. We even created breaks in the music so I could continue to tell my wild stories within the songs—and then have the orchestra reunite with me as I picked up from where I diverted.

A second "American Scrapbook" concert was staged at the Kennedy Center in Washington, DC, on 25 May, though, in some ways, that show was a simply a warm-up for the big night to follow:

AG: On May 26, 1998, I performed at Symphony Hall with The Boston Pops with special guest Gil Shaham, and I was thrilled to be working with such an incredible violinist. We performed together doing one of my own ragtime compositions that had been orchestrated especially for the event by Pat Hollenbeck (longtime arranger for the Pops). Pat would later create an orchestral version of my "Coming into Los Angeles" that was simply stunning and wonderfully fun.

I had originally titled the ragtime piano piece "Week on the Rag" and had released it as such on an earlier Warner Bros. record. For this event, however, the name was changed to "Arlo's Rag" as my sense of humor was a little too over the top for the attendees that evening. This was, after all, the classical world.

The good notices soon piled up, with offers to perform "An American Scrapbook" in other concert halls beginning to roll in. Guthrie acknowledged he wasn't really breaking new musical ground. There had always been a link between folk song and classical music. "I grew up in a classically trained world as well as the 'back porch' folk music world," he'd explain—no doubt remembering those difficult childhood sessions sitting on a piano bench aside a formal instructor. "I really love both of them, and this is the first time I've had a chance to combine them in my own life. What we're trying to do is to create an American style of symphonic music that is able to tell the stories that are normally reserved for folk singers."[68]

It's interesting to note that in the midst of his symphony hall dalliances of 1998, Guthrie chose to dedicate a week in June to the recording of a bluegrass album of Woody Guthrie songs:

> **AG:** On June 8th, Jackie and I went to Branson, Missouri, with Dennis and Jessica to record an album of my father's songs with The Dillards. It was originally called "32¢" in honor of my dad becoming a postage stamp of that value. The Dillards—Rodney and Doug Dillard, Mitch Jane, and Dean Webb—had pioneered a style of playing and harmony that greatly influenced the Byrds, The Eagles, and American bands in general. They were pivotal to the music scene in Los Angeles and were friends of mine from back in the day. They were authentic and no group of musicians was more suited to help record the songs my father had written. We had a great time in the studio in Branson going through the material and making great progress.

The town of Branson had become a vacation destination for fans of country music. Though Branson's fame wouldn't supplant that of Nashville, the little Missouri town was giving Music City a run for its money. In 1983 Roy Clark of TV's *Hee Haw* fame built his Celebrity Theater in Branson, bringing in a score of friends and fellow performers. By the early 1990s a number of other performers—including many aging stars unable to tour as aggressively as they once had—organized their own cozy theaters. Branson had become, essentially, a Las Vegas–style home base where fans could flock to hear favorite artists old and new. There was never an afternoon or evening where live music fell silent.

Unlike Nashville, Branson was not considered a recording center. Guthrie nonetheless booked a week at Branson's Caravell Studios. His decision to record there was simply due to his friends, the Dillards, being based there. It was also helpful that Rodney Dillard was vice-president of operations at Caravell. Dillard had a vested interest in seeing Branson considered an alternative country music recording mecca. Describing Branson as "a petri dish," Dillard recognized the opportunity for growth. "If you attract the artists and the writers and musicians," he explained, "it creates a synergy that feeds itself. At the same time that our live entertainment industry is growing, we could see a wellspring of new artists and new ideas, which becomes something in its own right."[69]

Dillard's optimism was echoed by music industry insider Joe Sullivan, a booking agent helpful in bringing a score of rock and country music acts to Nashville, Branson, and beyond. Guthrie wrapped the recording of *Thirty-Two Cents* on Tuesday, 17 June, pleased with the sessions. Sullivan was also pleased that Guthrie's time in Branson had been productive. He offered, "Anytime you have an artist the stature of Arlo who chooses a particular studio and location in which to record and goes away with good things to say, that can only have a positive effect on that aspect of our industry."[70]

Though Guthrie had recorded a number of his father's songs in the past, he had never waxed an all-Woody Guthrie album. The idea to record the album in the bluegrass style would differentiate *Thirty-Two Cents* from the folksier ones that had appeared with regularity in the 1960s. Guthrie's decision to record the album appeared spontaneous. Dillard had only been contacted in May to make the arrangements.

Guthrie had worked with the Dillards before. Doug Dillard's sparkling banjo breaks were prominent on any number of records the folk singer had waxed for Reprise, including *Washington County, Hobo's Lullaby, Last of the Brooklyn Cowboys*, and *Arlo Guthrie*. In 1976 Guthrie appeared with Rodney and Doug on the album *Woody Guthrie's We Ain't Down Yet* (Cream Records CR-1002). That album, coproduced by Don Gallese and Rodney Dillard, was one of eight LPs on the heels of Hal Ashby's *Bound for Glory* biopic. As for *Thirty-Two Cents*, one report suggested a total of seventeen Woody Guthrie songs had been recorded at Caravell between 8 June and 16 June. Though the original plan was for the album to be released concurrent with the US Postal Service's issuing of its Woody Guthrie stamp, the resulting CD album of thirteen songs would not see release for a decade.

AG: Unfortunately, the technology we were using to record was fairly new, and multiple machines were out of sync, so it took another decade for the technology to advance enough for us to fix the original recordings. By the time the record came out ten years later, the cost of a first-class postage stamp had increased, so we added "Postage Due" to the title of the recording.

Guthrie was still unaware of the serious issues plaguing *Thirty-Two Cents* when called to perform on the National Mall in Washington, DC, on 26 June. His appearance was part of the Smithsonian Folklife Festival's celebration of the US Postal Service's honoring of four singers in the Legends of American Music Series: Woody Guthrie, Lead Belly, Sonny Terry, and Josh White. Guthrie was joined in the celebration by White's son, Josh White Jr., as well as Bernice Reagon and the Willie Foster Blues Band. When the moment came for the unveiling of the stamps, Guthrie informed the postmaster general he "wasn't surprised to know there was a picture of my Dad in the Post Office. I was, however, surprised to discover it was worth thirty-two cents."[71]

1998 was something of a watershed year for Woody Guthrie, a pretty impressive feat for someone who had passed some three decades earlier. In June 1998, just as Guthrie was finishing up recording the tracks to comprise *Thirty-Two Cents,* Elektra was about to issue the Billy Bragg and Wilco *Mermaid Avenue* CD. Nora Guthrie served as both the impetus and the executive producer of the *Mermaid Avenue* project. Nora and Bragg first met at the Woody Guthrie 80th Birthday Concert in Manhattan's Central Park in July of 1992. Nora was impressed with Bragg. "He has a way of getting a message across without being pompous, the same way Woody did," she recalled.[72]

In 1995 Nora offered Bragg unfettered access to "over a thousand" of Woody's typescripts. These were songs and poems without music notation nor an extant recording. If Arlo's recent Woody Guthrie project revisited mostly familiar songs, Nora's vision was different. As Bragg recalled, Nora asked him, in effect, to work "*with* her father to give his words a new sound and a new context."[73] Bragg soon brought in the Americana band Wilco to collaborate. It wasn't that Bragg was incapable of writing or adapting melodies to accompany Guthrie's lyrics, but he thought, as a Brit, he was ill-suited to carry out the task without musicians demonstrating an *American* sensibility. Nora wasn't concerned that Bragg was British. "There's been a little controversy about getting an English guy," she conceded, "but the songs don't have borders or language or religions. That's what Woody taught. When you look at the words—they're meant for all over, for all time."[74]

Visiting the Woody Guthrie Archive in Manhattan, Bragg sorted through twelve boxes containing nearly one thousand unpublished songs: songs that tackled subjects well beyond the tropes Guthrie was best remembered for. Bragg decided from the outset he wasn't going to craft "a folk record." He was looking to create an album where Woody's lyrics were reconstituted "in the spirit of super-sonic boogie."[75] He brushed off criticisms he was ill-suited to bring these obscure Guthrie songs to life. "Of course there were lots of more obvious people who could have done it," Bragg acknowledged, suggesting Pete Seeger, Ry Cooder, Bruce Springsteen, and Arlo as four natural choices. "There's a logic to all of those names—but, with respect," Bragg mused, "over the years they have all given us their take on Woody."[76]

Mermaid Avenue was a critical smash and modest commercial success, earning a Grammy nomination in January 1999 in the Contemporary Folk Album category. Ironically one of its competitors was Ramblin Jack Elliott's *Friends of Mine,* a disc featuring Elliott's duet with Arlo Guthrie on Gene Autry's "Riding Down the Canyon."

Some wondered why Arlo Guthrie wasn't included on *Mermaid Avenue.* One critic suggested Guthrie, if nothing else, had "genetic entitlement" to the songs.[77] Bragg assured he had chatted a bit with Arlo and the conversation was friendly. He never directly asked why Guthrie didn't choose to make a similar record of his father's "lost" works, but he assured readers that Nora's brother was "completely behind this project."[78] Having sorted through the thousand sets of lyrics in the Woody Guthrie Archive, Bragg was satisfied that Guthrie could still mount a similar project should he choose to do so.

"If we had recorded the last few fragments, the last twelve songs," Bragg allowed, "I would feel it was [Arlo's] inheritance. But there are so many more songs to choose from."[79] There were still boxes of original material to mine through. Bragg suggested that should the *Mermaid Avenue* project kick-start a series, then "if Arlo wants to have a go, or Dylan wants to have a go, there's plenty of stuff there. Everybody can have a go, and maybe find a different angle on Woody than the one I've particularly locked onto."[80]

Guthrie was aware of the thousands of unpublished works buried in his father's notebooks—songs scrawled on the back of envelopes, on cocktail napkins, and in composition books. As early as 1976 Guthrie mentioned his consideration of "doing an album of songs by Woody that no one had ever heard." While Woody's songs from the 1930s and 1940s were his most celebrated, Guthrie believed his father's works from the 1950s were among "his most amazing."[81]

Guthrie was impressed with *Mermaid Avenue*. Though the CD contained fifteen songs, Bragg acknowledged that a total of forty songs had been recorded. An additional fifteen tracks from the sessions were issued in 2000 as *Mermaid Avenue Vol. II*. Though the second CD introduced a number of worthwhile songs to the canon, the consensus was this more rock-orientated edition didn't measure up to the original. Guthrie admitted that while he "loved the first of the series," he was less enamored with the second.[82] Regardless, Guthrie thought Bragg and Wilco managed to create an entirely new set of "Woody Guthrie standards, and that's an amazing feat, I think."[83]

Billy Bragg coasted into Okemah that July, bringing along a selection of songs from *Mermaid Avenue*—as well as several from his own politically charged repertoire. Bragg was set to kick off Okemah's celebration of all things Guthrie with a program at the Crystal Theater on 14 July, Woody's 86th birthday. As was his style, Bragg wasn't deflective of Guthrie's radicalism, occasionally shocking even those holding liberal views. Bragg peppered his between-song patter with discussions on how the communists helped beat back the fascists in World War II. Speaking of what he described as "socialism of the heart," Bragg conceded he was preaching to the choir. "I have a dreadful feeling," Bragg reconciled, "that if somebody were to put a bomb in this building, it would set back the left-wing in Oklahoma by a generation."[84]

Bragg's digressions likely made a few members of Okemah's chamber of commerce shuffle uncomfortably. The town had recently voted, four to one, to rename a section of State Highway 27—historically known as "Division Street"—to "Woody Guthrie Street." Then, on Saturday, 18 July, a life-sized bronze statue of Woody was unveiled downtown.[85] It was demonstrative,

all things considered, of a pretty remarkable shift in the town's reconcilia-
tion with their native son.

Since Bragg hadn't shared the Guthrie family's earlier experiences of
being vilified in Okemah, he likely underappreciated the miraculous
embrace of Woody by the town's residents and governing councils. Arlo
Guthrie was acutely aware of the amazing changes. In 1971, he and his
mother had to meet in secret with the few residents wishing to honor
Woody. Now, in 1998, the town was staging a festival in his honor. Guthrie
reflected that such commemoration "would have left my family speechless"
only a few decades earlier. "One can assume that neighbors and friends of
the Guthries are somewhat dazed and amused by these changes," Arlo
would write. "There are a few who are actually angered by the changes
imposed on them. But times change and we all adapt—like it or not."[86]

In 1998 it was also becoming apparent that the Guthrie musical lineage would extend beyond the children of Woody and Marjorie:

AG: August 27th I was playing in Holyoke, Massachusetts, at their
annual "Celebrate Holyoke" event, and my daughter, Sarah Lee, joined
me and Abe for the first time together onstage. We all kept playing
together for the rest of the year.

Sarah Lee had been living in Los Angeles for most of the past year,
singing and playing the guitar—often in the company of Johnny Irion, a
new beau. Like Sarah Lee, Irion was a musical transplant, not native to Los
Angeles. Though he forged a love of music in his native North Carolina, it
was only after attending a military school in Virginia that he decided to try
his hand at learning a musical instrument. As his skills developed, he
joined several Carolina-based indie bands, such as Queen Sarah Saturday
and Dillon Fence. He would first meet Sarah Lee in June of 1997 when she
and her father, on tour with the Further Festival, passed through Raleigh.[87]

Sarah Lee was working the tour as road manager, and Johnny was
attending as a friend of singer Chris Robinson of the Black Crowes, an act
on the bill. It was through Robinson's prodding that Irion moved to Los
Angeles, where the rock music scene was vibrant and less insular than that
of North Carolina. Sarah Lee joined him in Los Angeles shortly thereafter,
introducing him to a slice of Americana of which he knew little. Irion
acknowledged he really didn't know all that much about folk music, especially the tradition personified by Woody Guthrie and Pete Seeger. He

conceded that hooking up with the Guthrie family—as well as their circle of friends and collaborators—expanded both his musical skills and his mindset. He described this immersion as going to musical college.

Like most musicians their age, Sarah Lee and Johnny scrambled: gigging around the Los Angeles area for small change and trying to arrange bookings. They were looking to develop original songs and carve a niche for themselves. There were bumps in the road. In August of 1998 Arlo Guthrie announced Sarah Lee had chosen to join the family band "when there was nothing left to eat in her apartment."[88] As both a singer and guitarist, Sarah Lee was slowly building her skills and stage persona. Much as her father had done in 1965, she gradually developed as a performer while on stage. The difference was her father managed to hone his skills off the radar. He often played in front of small coffeehouse audiences for a few dozen people, sometimes less. Sarah Lee, in contrast, was expected to hold her own in front of large audiences at her dad's concerts. Trying to live up to a father's legend was commonplace for each new generation of Guthries.

Guthrie's fans were welcoming of Sarah Lee, the proud father noting his audience was "very enthusiastic over the additional Guthrie on stage. Sarah will be on stage more and more as time goes on as they work up tunes on the road."[89] It was the beginning of a fulfillment of one of Woody Guthrie's dreams. Guthrie had written in June of 1947—the eve of Arlo's arrival on 10 July—that he dreamed of forming a family band. It was to be a playing and singing troupe he referred to as "The New Improved Modern Cannonball Guthrie Family."[90] That Guthrie Family band would, at long last, slowly assemble, and Woody's songs would remain part of it. After the Guthrie Center benefit shows in mid-October, Arlo, Abe, and Sarah boarded the bus for a US tour taking them through the end of the year.

While out west, Guthrie was asked to tape a segment of Bill Maher's irreverent topical news talk show *Politically Incorrect*. One topic discussed was the call to impeach President Clinton over an alleged indiscretion with a White House intern in the Oval Office. Guthrie seemed a bit out of place on a vociferous panel that included Republican National Committee spokesperson Genevieve Wood, the conservative political satirist P. J. O' Rourke, and the Emmy-winning actress Camryn Manheim. The program was mostly people yelling at each other, reflective of the nation's divisive political climate. When Guthrie finally got a chance to offer a few words, he suggested the sexual act alleged to have been committed would, if nothing else, would inspire "young people to political office."[91]

AG: I ended the year after roaming around the East Coast doing a series of solo shows, with the exception that Pete Seeger and I reprised our Thanksgiving show at Carnegie Hall together.

Guthrie had been trying to convince Seeger to join him again at Carnegie, but the aging singer, soon to turn eighty, begged off. He sighed that his singing voice simply wasn't what it used to be. But Guthrie was persistent and, with the assistance of Harold Leventhal's prodding, the two convinced Seeger to return. Seeger was to be advertised only as a "Special Guest" as he had no intention of performing more than a few songs. But during the sound check, Seeger appeared to be in pretty good form and spirit. So he agreed to come out at the very beginning of the show . . . just to see how things might progress.

Things went extremely well. To many longtime attendees, the two sold-out Thanksgiving concerts of 1998 were among the finest of the Guthrie-Seeger pairings, perhaps *the* finest. At the program's conclusion Seeger stood beneath the arch of Carnegie's stage door puzzled at the cacophonous standing ovation. The fervent applause swelled in intensity as Seeger cast glances from the parquet, to the dress circle, to the upper and lower balconies. The pair's final song on the second program was, somehow fittingly, "Hobo's Lullaby."

The two concerts would have not transpired without Harold Leventhal's intervention. On the eve of the Carnegie programs, the *New York Times* ran an article detailing Leventhal's career as concert impresario. It was a long overdue acknowledgment of the man whose tireless work on behalf of scores of activist-minded performers had brought many of folk music's most notable practitioners to public attention. Always reliable for a good quote, Pete Seeger offered, "Harold's a remarkable person, totally honest with a great sense of humor. He did something extraordinary for the Weavers. He stuck his neck out and had faith in us when others wouldn't. You might say he had faith in America, too."[92]

AG: Jackie and I began 1999 back in Mokuleia for a little over two weeks. On January 1st we rented the same place I had spent months at while shooting *Byrds* five years earlier. It was a wonderful time to spend together. We strolled the beaches and visited friends. But mostly we just spent time together. We'd been married thirty years and were still in love. It was truly a magical time as the kids had grown and began having kids of their own.

After our vacation I got back to work heading to Glasgow, Scotland, for a gig there—Celtic Connections—this time accompanied by Abe and my daughter Sarah Lee.

I introduced Sarah Lee to the stage gradually. At first she'd join us for a few songs at the end of the show, but as her experience grew, so did her time on stage. Her new husband, Johnny Irion, was a great songwriter/guitarist in his own right, and Johnny and Sarah Lee became part of my stage show. For the next twenty years we toured together often. Eventually, Sarah Lee began to open the evenings on her own.

The sixth annual Celtic Connections festival at Glasgow's Royal Concert Hall was a late booking, an opportunity offered when scheduled headliner Lyle Lovett was unable to make the event. The cancellation left organizer Colin Hynd scrambling for a replacement artist of similar box-office stature. "We were very lucky to get Arlo," Hynd told *Scotland on Sunday*, noting that Guthrie's booking "was the result of having a very good relationship with the people who act as his agents in this country who persuaded him that Celtic Connections was the perfect festival to act as a showcase for him."[93] Guthrie's set was well-received, with Scotland's *The Herald* trumpeting,

> Contributions to America's vast catalogue of songs don't come much bigger than Woody Guthrie's, and while books have been written and films made about his life, hearing his philosophy and how some of these songs came about from his offspring's mouth turned into one of the real pleasures of this festival.
>
> Although granted Son of Messiah status on America's folk scene, Arlo Guthrie went on to have his own career, championing great songwriters such as Steve Goodman and going through chuckleworthy experiences in the process. . . . and while the raconteur outpaces the troubadour in Arlo, the outcome is an entertaining flip through a family album.[94]

A critic from Edinburgh's *The Scotsman* celebrated Guthrie as an artist with "a direct link to the classic American roots music."

> This link comes in the amiable form of Arlo Guthrie, son of folk legend Woody and contemporary of Bob Dylan, whom he sounds remarkably like although he is as affable and chatty as Dylan is curmudgeonly. He is more than willing to regale the audience with serpentine tales of the Sixties counter-culture, so much so that he practically makes a stand-up comedy routine out of his recollections, with some songs thrown in by way of musical illustration. Guthrie is a fully paid-up member of the Woodstock generation. With his mane of wavy grey hair, he looks like God or at the very least the Grateful Dead's Jerry Garcia, which in hippie circles is pretty much the same thing. His songs may be indelibly infused with his father's tradition but he relishes his place in the Greenwich Village scene.[95]

The Guthries barely had the chance to unpack upon arriving home. The traditional early-winter US West Coast tour was to commence on 3 February in Albuquerque, New Mexico, and finish in Portland, Oregon, on 28 February. The tour included a string of one-night stands in Montana, Colorado, and Washington State. After their gig at Portland's Aladdin Theater, Guthrie and Abe would board a plane for a quick visit to a music trade industry show in Frankfurt. As Guthrie recalled, he and Abe "showed up at the world's largest music trade show convention of the year and played a few songs—the longest flight for the fewest songs I'd ever done."[96] At the show, he and Abe got to talk shop with luthier John Pearse, of guitar-string fame, and with the technicians at Kurzweil, the manufacturers of keyboards and synthesizers.

Guthrie's visit to Frankfurt was, in part, to promote a new addition to the Martin Guitar Company's line of Limited Edition series of artist-inspired acoustic instruments. In July of 1997 the famed guitar manufacturer announced their collaboration "with songwriter Arlo Guthrie to create two limited edition guitars, a six-string 0000–28H AG and a 12-string 000012–28H AG." Only thirty of each were crafted, each numbered sequentially and personally signed by both Guthrie and C. F. Martin IV. The guitars were limited to thirty in recognition of the thirtieth anniversary of the release of the *Alice's Restaurant* album. Guthrie's own Martin M-38 guitar was used as the template. The guitars, made from gorgeous Sitka spruce and rosewood, featured custom mother-of-pearl inlays, including one depicting the Old Trinity Church on the instrument's headstock. A label pasted inside promised, "A portion of the proceeds from the sale of this Limited Edition Arlo Guthrie Signature Model support the Interfaith Church Foundation at The Guthrie Center which is housed within the original and notorious church building, formerly Alice's home, in Great Barrington, Massachusetts."

The visit to Frankfurt was little more than a whistle-stop, the musicians due back on the West Coast to recommence their US tour. On their way to a concert in Richland, Washington, the Guthries paid a visit to old friend Bill Murlin, the folk singer and song archivist. Murlin was still working for the Bonneville Power Administration (BPA) and provided the Guthries the rare opportunity to visit the subterranean tunnels running beneath the Bonneville Lock. This visit necessitated that each member of the touring party be loaded singly into a claustrophobic steel cage and dropped deep into the catacombs. It was part of the dam even Woody hadn't the chance to visit in April of 1941. Guthrie was impressed that "the names of some of the guys who built the dam decades earlier were still legibly scratched in the concrete walls."[97]

Guthrie found himself back in a recording studio in early summer of 1999. The pop singer Jennifer Warnes had called, advising of her plans to record Guthrie's "Patriot's Dream" for her forthcoming CD *The Well*. Guthrie's initial response was "Why?"[98] Warnes, who scored a monster Top 40 hit with Joe Cocker for "Up Where We Belong," explained, "My friend Leonard Cohen told me that our job as artists is to keep our antennas up really high and listen for impulses that are out there in the community. I want my music to serve the community, and I had a sense that it was time for something to gather us."[99] Warnes asked Guthrie if he might consider sharing vocals on the track. He agreed, flying into Pasadena, where, he recalled, Warnes managed to bring his "old song to life. She sings and looks as beautiful as ever. It was such a joy. Not since Nanci Griffith asked me to sing with her on Townes Van Zandt's song "Tecumseh Valley" had I had as much fun."[100]

Guthrie was to return to Okemah for the second annual Woody Guthrie Free Folk Festival on 14–18 July. The singer was scheduled to kick off the festival at the Crystal Theater for an evening billed as "Arlo Guthrie and Friends." Guthrie's friends that evening would include the Kingston Trio and Country Joe McDonald. The singer-songwriter Ellis Paul served as the evening's MC. Festival organizer Don Gustafson told the *Daily Oklahoman* that Arlo pledged to support the yearly celebration of his father under two conditions: "First, it always [has] to be a free event. Second, you never pay anyone to play."[101] The second condition, Gustafson recalled, was to ensure any performer invited to perform demonstrated a true allegiance to Woody's work and spirit.

August of 1999 marked the thirtieth anniversary of Woodstock, with newspapers and TV carrying the usual nostalgic musings and "Where are they now?" stories. Guthrie commemorated the anniversary with an appearance at the unofficial "Another Day in the Garden" festival in Bethel. It was a one-day event featuring genuine Woodstock alumni such as Richie Havens, David Crosby, Johnny Winter, Melanie, Leslie West, Country Joe McDonald, Rick Danko, and Garth Hudson. While cynics dismissed the "Garden" show as yet another nostalgia trip for aging boomers, the musicians hoped to make the event a *true* day of peace and music. The corporate-backed hucksters who staged the "official" Woodstock 1999 event a month earlier were still cleaning up the mess left behind. The Woodstock '99 event was plagued by fires, looting, property damage, sexual assaults and small-scale riots.

"The word 'Woodstock' is out," sighed one fan who witnessed the carnage of the "official" Woodstock '99 event. "It's been blasphemed."[102] The alternative Day in the Garden promised to be a low-key, friendlier celebration, with twelve thousand fans gathered peacefully on the rolling hills of Max Yasgur's old farm. Guthrie wasn't apologetic Another Day in the Garden was peopled—on stage and those attending—by members of the old guard. "I think it will be a little nostalgic," Guthrie conceded in a pre-show interview. "There's a lot of aspects to this to me personally that mean more than just going to another gig."[103]

Actually, there were almost as many young people enjoying the Day in the Garden as there were old-timers. Some of the youngsters were even on stage. Guthrie wasn't the only artist bringing along musical offspring and family members. David Crosby brought along his new group CPR, performing alongside his wife and son. Crosby enthused the event as a "great evening" of music—no matter what the Gen X critics sniffed. "In a row, there was Richie Havens, Arlo Guthrie and his family, and me and CPR," Crosby beamed. "And the three of us together put the people on just a trip . . . and they just didn't know what to do. They were absolutely jazzed beyond belief. It couldn't have been better."[104]

Musically, Guthrie didn't rely on nostalgia, playing only one song ("Coming into Los Angeles") from the seven he had performed at the original festival in 1969. Midway through the sixty-minute set he ceded the stage to Sarah for interpretations of Gillian Welch's "Orphan Girl" and Pete Seeger's "Sailing Down My Golden River." Guthrie chose to stick close to his 1999 set list playbook, mixing Woody's songs with traditional material, a few of his own classics, and two songs from *Mystic Journey*. Recalling what he could of the original Woodstock, Guthrie joked, "I don't remember much about the first time I was here. I had to wait for the movie to come out."[105]

Though there was a handful of shows booked in September, it was mostly a quiet time. Midway through the month Guthrie traveled out to Jorma Kaukonen's Fur Peace Ranch in Pomeroy, Ohio, for a three-day guitar workshop. There he taught his personal style of guitar playing—a mix of licks and filigrees gleaned from the playing of Brownie McGhee, Mississippi John Hurt, Doc Watson, and Ramblin' Jack Elliott. Near month's end, Guthrie returned to New Mexico for the third annual gathering of the Tewa Women United's Mother Earth Celebration,[106] and a Nuclear Free Future ceremony held outside of Los Alamos. Los Alamos was chosen as the site to award peace prizes since the town's name had been sullied, in the description of an organizer, as "the birthplace of the bomb."[107]

October saw the staging of the annual concerts to benefit the Guthrie Center. The benefits were originally to consist of three shows, but when all three hundred $50 tickets sold out, a decision was made to add a Thursday night program. Rising Son called this year's event "Arlo Guthrie's Annual Thanksgiving Revival Fall Fundraiser," asking fans to join in on the "last big church event of the millennium."[108] There were no television cameras or radio broadcasts planned in 1999, so the shows were more relaxed and casual, with friends stopping by to sit in and help out.

There was more to celebrate in the days ahead. On 16 October, friends and family gathered at Guthrie's home in Washington to attend the wedding of Sarah Lee and Johnny. The day was filled with music. John Nardolillo conscripted several friends to play a program of elegant string arrangements. Irion's friends from Los Angeles played a bit of rock 'n' roll, as would Abe and Xavier. Pete Seeger plunked on his 5-string banjo and had everyone singing along on a few old songs. The couple set off for a honeymoon in Hawaii shortly afterward. The news of Sarah Lee's marriage was reported in the *Rolling Blunder Review:* "The father of the bride was at a loss for words until recently due to the emotional strain of losing a daughter. When interviewed for this article he could only say, 'There's more where she came from.'"[109]

Guthrie closed out October with three symphonic shows. The first was with the Metropolitan Symphony Orchestra at the Lisner Auditorium in Washington, DC. This was followed by two shows with the Delaware Symphony Orchestra at the Grand Opera House in Wilmington, Delaware. Guthrie told a Wilmington newspaper that the symphony shows offered him the welcome opportunity "to combine two very early influences of my life. My mother would dance to Copland's music in performances with the Martha Graham Company. As a kid I would go see her, just as I went to see my dad's friends play in folk clubs. So this is not alien or new to me. To put both parts together in one night, in one moment, I think is an incredible thing." Guthrie also didn't see one musical form as more "elevated" than the other. "Professionalism exists whether you're playing classical music or folk music, or anything else," he contended. "When you have developed musical skills over decades, they become very unique, and when you marry them to those other professionals, very interesting things happen."[110]

Shortly following his final symphony show of the year, Guthrie returned to the CrabHouse, but his time there was not peaceful. Jackie Guthrie was, in Arlo's remembrance, "in a hospital bed recovering from her second breast cancer surgery in as many weeks. This will be the first Thanksgiving when our family will not be able to be together." Guthrie shared that everyone was choosing to remain optimistic that things would go well. He acknowledged that Jackie would be facing "an ordeal during the coming year," suggesting the "prayers and wishes of our friends and family will help."[111]

Guthrie composed his thoughts while on flight from Florida to Windsor Lock's Bradley Field airport, the station servicing the Hartford, Connecticut, and Springfield, Massachusetts, areas. He had commitments to perform a half-dozen shows before closing out his year with what broadsides described as "The Umteenth Annual Thanksgiving Holiday Concert" at Carnegie Hall. There would be no Pete Seeger to share the stage this year. The Carnegie Hall concerts had become, in the words of critic John Leonard, a "cultural brushing of the teeth, obligatory," ceremonies of an ongoing tradition.[112] Guthrie's program notes read,

> If it were not for these concerts at Carnegie Hall, the world would seem a very different place. It's gone beyond annual. These evenings together, at least for some, have become ritual. They have become moments through which we move into the years and the decades yet to come, while still remembering those that have gone on before.
>
> It was around 1955 that Harold Leventhal produced the Weavers at Carnegie Hall. They made it an annual pilgrimage until the early 1960s, when Pete Seeger took over. I joined Pete sometime during the early 1970s. And then for the next thirty years, more or less, Pete continued the tradition with or without me until just a few short years ago. I'll be doing pretty well if I can keep up with Pete for the next thirty years.[113]

Considering the emotional duress everyone was under due to Jackie's health issue, it was an amazing night. It was a more subdued evening of music, not as raucous as the previous year's reunion concerts with Seeger. Though Seeger was absent from the 1999 show, his grandson, Tao Rodriguez, performed during the evening's second set, singing songs associated with his grandfather. Sarah sang a few solos, and would duet with her father on Woody's "The Sinking of the Reuben James." One thing was evident: Just as Seeger often used the Carnegie stage to introduce kindred musical spirits to his audience, his successor was now doing the same.

AG: The day after my annual Thanksgiving show at Carnegie Hall on November 27th, I left for South Africa. It was the next installment of The Parliament of the World's Religions, and this time I accompanied Ma as part of her entourage.

The purpose for attending was essentially the same as it had previously been: a chance to prod the major religious leaders of the world into doing more when it came to AIDS. People were still dying, and across the world those who had become infected were stigmatized by outdated ideas on culture, status, and sexual orientation.

We went to present and to add panels to the Names Project Quilt and participate in other activities relating to the pandemic. It was extremely important to put faces and names on the numbers, so that everyone understood it was their neighbors, families, and friends who were enduring the unendurable.

The 1999 gathering of the parliament was to be in Cape Town. The conference attracted nearly 8,000 pilgrims, spiritual leaders, activists, and scholars. Three separate sites simultaneously hosted workshops and discussion panels, occasionally offering some entertainment to keep spirits high. Speakers at the conference included his HH the Dalai Lama, Nelson Mandela, and the German theologian Hans Kung. The world's problems weren't settled by the conclusion of the two-week-long conference, everyone agreeing there was still a lot of work ahead.

Guthrie was attending as a delegate. He had originally become involved with the parliament's missions through the founding work of his Franciscan friend Wayne Teasdale. On the third day of his visit, Guthrie and Ma traveled outside of Cape Town to visit a tiny shantytown called New Rest. Guthrie offered that despite evidence of poverty, the "place was immaculate. We handed out some simple things, pencils, paper—things people had little access to for school, etc. I played a few songs in an old truck that had been flipped on its side to become a stage."

One of Ma's missions was to continue to press awareness of those afflicted with AIDS and other life-threatening diseases. South Africa was certainly a place to bring this issue to the forefront. The country, per capita, had one of the highest rates of AIDS infections anywhere in the world. On 1 December Guthrie was at the University of Cape Town for the unfolding of the AIDS Quilt. It was an attention-grabbing demonstration designed, in Guthrie's words, to remind the world's religious institutions that "their lack of understanding and their silence concerning those around the world suffering with the disease is not the best they can do." Though it was discouraging that the rallying cry was not being taken as seriously as he wished, there were still encouraging and enlightening moments:

AG: One evening at a gathering in a very large venue, I was seated far from the stage as different people made presentations. I was talking to the person next to me when I heard the sound of a drum coming from the stage. I said, "You know that sounds like Olatunji." The person next to me said, "That is Olatunji."

I thought to myself, that couldn't possibly be true. I had gone to see a show in New York that Olatunji had given in or before 1959, but that was some forty years earlier. I bought his recording *Drums of Passion* and wore the grooves off of the album. I quickly opened the program notes and was shocked that, indeed, it was the same guy—Olatunji.

More than the shock of being informed as to his identity, I wondered how I could recognize the playing of a drum. Something in the way he played was identifiable as him. There was no melody, there were no chords, nothing I'd learned as a musician to identify a person or piece of music. It was simply a drum. Forty years after first hearing him— within only a few seconds—I knew who it was without knowing how I knew it. That is the nature of a master.

It was just the first of many shocks I had that evening. Imagine if you were in a room with a few thousand people and George Washington walked in. Not a guy in a George Washington outfit, or an actor, but the real George Washington. Imagine what you'd feel.

That was the feeling in that venue when Nelson Mandela, the undisputed father of the country, walked in. The crowd spontaneously began singing the South African national anthem, and tears were streaming down thousands of faces of every color and persuasion. It was almost too much to handle emotionally.

After a few more days in Cape Town after the conclusion of the parliament, Ma and most of her entourage, including myself, took a trip to Botswana for a safari adventure. It was amazing, as I'd never seen so many wild animals outside of a zoo before.

Our few days out in the wild were not really roughing it: we were staying in a very nice camp, protected at all times by locals with rifles, and evening dinners were like from a restaurant. Nevertheless, it was truly magical and the sounds of big creatures sounded close in the night, even if they were in reality far off.

We were in Africa for a little over two weeks, and I was home in Massachusetts with the family for Christmas.

★ ★ ★ ★ ★

Chapter Eight

IN TIMES LIKE THESE, 2000–2010

AG: On January 14, 2000, I bought a bus—a 1989 Prevost XL. It didn't have the same capacity to hold an entire band, but it did have some more privacy for me, with a bedroom and shower built in. Unlike previous buses (this was our fourth), it didn't get a name. It was just "The Prevost."

In comparison to the usual pattern, Guthrie's early-winter schedule was relatively light. Beginning 5 February, the Museum of the City of New York hosted *This Land Is Your Land: The Life and Legacy of Woody Guthrie*. The exhibit was heralded as the "first full-scale museum exhibition" of his father's life and work.[1] This wasn't *technically* accurate. An earlier exhibition tracing Woody Guthrie's legacy had already been staged in 1999 at the Gene Autry Museum of Western Heritage in Los Angeles.

Nora Guthrie served as principal organizer of both exhibitions. Woody's work as a singer, writer, and radical had been well documented, but often at the expense of his other talents. His work as an artist who dabbled in painting and sculpture was less well-known. A generous sampling of Guthrie's art was published in the lavish volume *Woody Guthrie: Art Works* (Rizzoli, 2005). The sizable tome included a reproduction of Woody's hand-painted postcard announcing the 1947 birth of Arlo Davy Guthrie.[2]

Few folks outside the inner circle were aware how wide-ranging Woody's artwork was. The Guthrie Archive held some six hundred sketches, doodles, political cartoons, watercolors, and paintings. Nora suspected what was already catalogued was a mere tip of the iceberg since Woody often gave away—or trashed—a good portion of his creations. On the eve of the exhibit's opening, Arlo offered that it was important to examine this avenue of Woody's creativity. He noted when his father "left Oklahoma to seek his fortune, he didn't leave with a guitar. He left with paint brushes.

He really had studied art. He took correspondence courses. He was serious about it."[3]

There were other events to consider in the first few months of 2000—some sad, others cautiously optimistic. Traveling west for shows in California and Arizona, Guthrie paid a visit to Jack Hyde, his ailing father-in-law.[4] Hyde would pass on shortly after that visit. And soon there was another serious issue of great concern: In March of 2000, Jackie was diagnosed with breast cancer and underwent chemo and radiation therapy. Treatment was successful and she was cancer-free after about a month.

Though he was only fifty-three, such recent events caused Guthrie to reflect on his midlife situation. Following his father-in-law's passing, Guthrie wrote, "My own parents have been gone for decades. And now with Jackie's mom and dad gone, we've had to step up to the realization that we are next to depart in the natural order of the coming and going of the generations. It is a very peculiar feeling I could not have imagined when I was younger. I have begun to realize that I have more loved ones on the other side of the mountain than I do on this one."[5]

In the spring of 2000, Guthrie joined Pete Seeger, Tao Rodriguez, the San Francisco Mime Troupe, several political figures, and a gaggle of historians at a reunion of the Veterans of the Abraham Lincoln Brigade (VALB). The sold-out event at the Borough of Manhattan Community College would celebrate the sixty-third anniversary of the 2,800 Americans who fought "the Good Fight" in Spain 1937. The Abraham Lincoln Brigade had joined an international team of *brigadistas* to combat the Axis-supported fascist takeover of the Spanish Republic.[6]

That afternoon, Guthrie and Seeger sang a few songs together, but the music played only a small part of the program. Seeger was held in high esteem as a long-standing friend of the VALB. In the autumn of 1943, Seeger had used his weekend pass from the US Army base in Fort Meade to travel to New York City. The singer had convinced Moses Asch to record a folio of songs commemorating the *Songs of the Lincoln Brigade* (Asch 330).

One of the six songs recorded at that session by Seeger and friends was "Jarama Valley," Jarama being the site where the first American shots were fired—and the earliest American casualties recorded. Woody Guthrie, not present at the Asch session of '43, had also recorded "Jarama Valley" (its melody lifted from the old folk song "Red River Valley"). Guthrie's version was less well-known and went unreleased until 1962, when it was belatedly included on the Folkways album *Songs of the Spanish Civil War, Vol. II.*

Arlo Guthrie too would record "Jarama Valley" for the CD *Spain in My Heart: Songs of the Spanish Civil War* (Appleseed Records). Seeger is also present on that recording, sprinkling in a bit of 5-string banjo and providing context with a voice-over narration. "Jarama Valley" wasn't Guthrie's first track to appear on Jim Musselman's Appleseed label. In 1999, Guthrie joined Seeger in Manhattan to record the Woody Guthrie–Pete Seeger rarity "66 Highway Blues." The song had been written—but never recorded—by the two friends while journeying to Pampa, Texas, in June of 1940.

"66 Highway Blues," as performed by Seeger and Arlo, was issued on the multi-artist release *The Songs of Pete Seeger: If I Had a Song Vol. II.* The song might have been lost to time had it not been included in the songbook *Hard Hitting Songs for Hard Hit People.* In his introduction to "66 Highway Blues," Woody wrote, "I had part of this tune in my head, but couldn't get no front end for it. Pete fixed that up. He furnished the engine, and me the cars, and then we loaded in the words and we whistled out of the yards from New York City to Oklahoma City."[7]

With the engine and boxcar in place, Arlo Guthrie brought the locomotive into the station. The recording was one more example of the Guthrie children's helping to bring the half-finished or forgotten works of their parents to fruition. It was a complex, occasionally bittersweet inheritance. Harold Leventhal once sighed that Woody "wasn't the greatest husband or father in the first place," and became "even more physically removed" from the lives of his wife and children due to a decade of institutionalization at life's end.[8] Nora conceded that while her parents—both artists—didn't handle their parenting roles in any traditional manner, both left behind legacies that allowed their children "to collaborate with them in a mature way."[9]

Sometimes family plans wouldn't work out. But it was not for lack of trying:

AG: About this time Jackie and I had purchased the old Kresge Building (55 North Street) in Pittsfield, Massachusetts. We had planned to build a performance space with attendant bars and restaurants. It was a major commitment, and the city of Pittsfield had agreed to make changes to accommodate our financial investment in the restoration of the downtown area. However, none of the promises by the city were kept. What changes they did make made the area look like a 1950s school yard, completely destroying the old-style brick in favor of glass and concrete. It was a disaster from our point of view. We kept at it for three years, and finally sold the building.

Guthrie's spring 2000 touring schedule was light. There was a performance at "Rails to Trails" under St. Louis's Gateway Arch in early June, followed by four dates at Disney's EPCOT in Orlando, Florida. It was then off to Europe:

AG: On June 12, I left Florida for a tour overseas. I initially stayed for about a week with Caroly in London. We had dinner together with the British poet Adrian Mitchell and his wife, Celia. Adrian had written the poem I changed into a song about the Chilean folksinger, Victor Jara.

On May 9th, 1974, I had been invited by Phil Ochs to join with other performers at the Felt Forum in New York. It was called "The Friends of Chile" and a fundraiser to help deal with the calamitous American intervention on behalf of the bad guys in Chile. Phil was joined by Bob Dylan, Dave Van Ronk, Pete Seeger, and others.

Before I was to perform my songs, a woman named Joan Jara handed me a poem written about the murder of her husband, the Chilean folksinger, Victor Jara. He'd been rounded up and tortured in a football stadium with thousands of other Allende supporters. Sociopathic guards—supported by American foreign policy—told him to play his guitar while they broke his hands. Then he was killed by gunfire.

The poem had been written by Adrian Mitchell. I took the words onstage with me and, placing them on a piano, improvised the rudimentary outline of a song which I would later record and release on my record *Amigo* (1976). The song was simply called "Victor Jara."

Now, twenty-six years later, Adrian and I had a lovely time arguing politics and things in general. Sadly he passed away a couple of years after our get-together.

I then flew from London to Vienna, where the Austrian tour would begin. Hans Theessink and I did the few shows together. It was a short tour with only four gigs, the most important being the Donauinsel Festival in Vienna. It was organized by Hans and Milica Theessink, Milica being the driving force behind it.

On June 29 I left Europe on just about one of the most horrendous journeys I'd ever undertaken: Linz to Vienna, Vienna to London, London to Los Angeles, and finally Los Angeles to Portland.

From there I had to drive to Jacksonville, Oregon, for a gig at the Britt Pavilion on the 30th. Going east to west, I could make it because of the time zones involved.

From Jacksonville, I traveled around and did my shows in the northwest, the most notable one being in Saratoga, California, at Mount Montalvo with my dear friend Judy Collins.

I continued going east through Okemah, my father's hometown, where I participated in the Woody Guthrie Folk Festival. Then onward to the eastern states. I never actually made it all the way home. From Batavia, Illinois, I flew out of Chicago and went to Los Angeles where I had to do a voice-over soundtrack to accompany the movie *Alice's Restaurant*—now made possible by it being released in a digital format.

About that time I was also attempting to create my own TV series called "The Last Resort," which I had written as a screenplay. My son-in-law, Johnny Irion, and I had become quite close working together with Sarah Lee on stage. Johnny's aunt, Gail Knight Steinbeck, had set up numerous visits to TV production companies throughout Los Angeles, and she and I made the rounds trying to pitch my screenplay for a pilot to an eventual series. In early August of 2000 I met with the network producers in what proved to be a vain attempt to get someone excited about the idea.

In essence, it would have been a series about my resurrecting the CrabHouse as a fictional recording studio with live-in accommodations: every week a new popular band would come to record their latest projects. They would interact with the staff in ways that would allow the viewer to get to know them more personally but also include the recording of new material. There were a lot of very humorous interchanges between the recurring staff members, and I was excited by the idea of using the CrabHouse as a location, mostly because it was great visually and because the use would pay for the construction being televised.

For the pilot episode I had written in Spinal Tap as the band, because I thought they were timely, and because Christopher Guest ("Nigel Tufnel") and the band had proven themselves to be accomplished actors and wonderful musicians. Chris was an old friend from high school days (he played mandolin in my band, and we were in the same class). I thought I would have a great time working with them. I spent about two weeks pitching the idea to no avail and eventually gave up and went home.

Guthrie's autumn tour was a bit more of a rock 'n' roll affair. He was again backed by Xavier, with whom he had not performed for a number of years. Things went so well the folk singer closed out 2000 by inviting Xavier along for his annual Thanksgiving concert. Guthrie summed up the year's events in his program notes:

> I've learned more real history through songs than by studying facts and remembering important dates. The heart of the matter is exposed in the words and melodies about love and hate, war and peace, joy and sorrow, one thing and another.
>
> Our personal histories get caught up with each other from time to time as we move from one generation to another. I am now about the same age that Pete Seeger was when I first began singing with him in this very hall 30 years ago. Earlier this year I joined up with Pete and sang a few songs for a reunion of the Lincoln Brigade vets here in the city. People of all ages sang the songs of the Spanish Civil War—the songs that told their stories. Their songs keep the hopes and dreams alive for us.
>
> The songs of my own generation echo into the next, just as the truths of my father's generation have found a home in me through the songs. Take a look around tonight and you'll see that there are people of all ages seated around the hall. There is no one single moment when the truths of one generation pass on into the next, but when it does, it does so in song."[10]

Though 2001 would bring chaos to America and the world, the year began with no portend of what was on the horizon. There was a sprinkling of winter shows, both solo and with the symphony. The singer was also asked to lecture on "Contemporary Folk Art: Treasures from the Smithsonian American Art Museum," in Coral Gables, Florida.[11] In early spring, Guthrie was asked to assist on a new project in the works:

AG: On May 5th, Jackie and I went to do a video with Ramblin' Jack Elliott organized by Happy Traum. Happy arranged for us to stay at a nearby inn called The Wild Rose. Happy had a series of videos created to be informative about various techniques of playing guitar, and had wanted to do one with Ramblin' Jack. He thought I'd be of some help wrangling Jack so he wouldn't get off-topic during the video sessions. The inn-keeper was a lovely woman who made us feel welcomed. Her name was Marti Ladd, and we became friends almost immediately. After a few days Jackie and I returned home to The Farm.

On June 31st we returned again to EPCOT for a three-day stint at The American Theater. I had Abe's band, Xavier, along with Sarah Lee and Johnny with me onstage. We loved performing during their annual Flower Power events, as part of their botanical exposition. The stage was decorated in bright psychedelic colors. On one side it said "Peace" and on the other side it said "Love." I remember coming back in the following years, and the word "Peace" had been removed. They said "Peace" was too controversial. I thought that was funny. The following year, they removed "Love." I guess that was likewise too controversial for EPCOT. A week after the final show at EPCOT, my name was added to the Celebrity Walk at the Brooklyn Botanical Gardens, in New York.

September of 2001 was to provide a welcome respite from touring, with only two shows scheduled in the first half-month: a solo show in Con-necticut followed by a concert at the Murat Theatre in Indianapolis to celebrate the twenty-fifth anniversary of Habitat for Humanity.[12] But the latter show was cancelled due to the September 11 attacks in New York and Washington, DC. Stages across the country went dark as America came to grips with the tragedies of that day. The week should have been more joyous, as Guthrie's granddaughter, Jacklyn, was born to Annie only five days prior to the events of 9/11.[13]

Guthrie was shaken by the shocking carnage of 9/11, the morning's hor-rors rebroadcast in endless loops. The interfaith Guthrie Center was instru-mental in getting their small corner of America through the sadness. With pundits on every channel talking about the role religion played in the attacks, Guthrie mused that the events of 9/11 actually taught the world a lesson. "These days, the battle lines, if you want to call them that, are between the fundamentalist and everybody else. Every religion has got its crazies."[14]

On 16 September, former Shenandoah guitarist David Grover arranged "A Music Memorial for Kids" at Pittsfield's Park Square. Grover had long been working as a children's music entertainer, and the intention of the gathering was to help children cope with the psychological fallout of the tragedy. Literature was distributed advising parents on how to discuss the events of 9/11 with their kids—and where mental health services could be found. Near the end of Grover's ninety-minute program, Guthrie sang "This Land Is Your Land." For families unable to attend, the event was broadcast on Springfield's public television station, WGBH, as "A Musical Memorial for Families."[15]

There was a backlash against people of Middle Eastern origin and Islamic faith in the wake of the 9/11 attacks. It was in this light the folk singer asked a local Muslim to discuss the tenets of Islam as a guest at the Guthrie Center's Summer Speaker Series on 26 September. Tensions were running high. There were reports of communities in the Middle East— and the US—celebrating the attacks. The media images were played up and angrily denounced on television and radio. The guest speaker acknowledged that while a section of fundamentalists, "subverted by many Middle Eastern political entities," existed within the Muslim world, their actions were non-Islamic.[16] But not many people were yet willing to hear that message. "The War on Terror" would officially be launched two weeks later, the US and allies invading Afghanistan to oust the Taliban government.

One of the few concert events not cancelled in the wake of 9/11 was Farm Aid. Willie Nelson thought it important to hold the annual benefit as scheduled. "Never has a Farm Aid concert come at such an important national moment," Nelson told the press. "We are all called to do what we can to strengthen our country. Farm Aid has a long history of responding to natural disasters, from droughts to floods to hurricanes and tornados. Never did we imagine that we would be responding to a disaster caused by terrorists."[17] The 2001 Farm Aid event was held near Noblesville, Indiana, and Guthrie was again asked to perform. It would be his seventh Farm Aid appearance.

There was no question of Guthrie not accepting the invitation. In a telephone interview, he mused it was "important to stand up when people are doing the right things." Willie Nelson was, in his opinion, "a real patriot, someone who seems to care more about his friends and neighbors in the long run." In Guthrie's view, Nelson was an honest broker. "This is an era when people are distrustful of a lot of organizations," he offered. "And there are frauds and scammers out there."[18] Willie was not one of those people. The wizened Texan shared an activist streak that Guthrie appreciated. "There are so many things that are negative and positive in the world," he commented. "I'm like an old Boy Scout: If you can't add something positive, at least leave it alone."[19]

Though most concert halls and Broadway theaters were shuttered in the weeks and months following the attacks, Guthrie managed to stage three concerts to benefit the ongoing work at the church. He returned to the road in late October for concerts in Connecticut and New Jersey. Prior to one of his Jersey concerts, Guthrie chatted with a reporter, refusing to let the 9/11 event upend his personal belief system. He was proud that the patriotic musical tributes on the radio included his father's "This Land Is Your Land." Guthrie expressed faith that his father "would be very happy. The song is about people's lives counting regardless of race, economic status or whatever. It's still great today . . . much like many of my dad's songs."[20]

Guthrie was certain America would get through this dark episode. "I think we're going to go on living and we're going to do it well." He believed all great civilizations were tested, the better ones learning how to best manage crisis and adversity. "We've only been an empire for hundreds of years. Humans are very creative. We'll find a way out of this. Most of us around the world want to live in peace. There are a few lunatics out there, including in this country. Hopefully we'll survive this and protect our country."[21] Guthrie shared his hope that the tragedies of 9/11 might even allow the Muslim world to enjoy a "spring awakening" of its own.

On Thanksgiving weekend at Carnegie Hall, Guthrie performed "An American Scrapbook" with the University of Kentucky Symphony. On the afternoon following, Guthrie sang at a concert to benefit gravelly voiced singer and guitarist Dave Van Ronk. Van Ronk, a staple of the Greenwich Village folk scene since the 1950s, was ill with colon cancer and facing six months of chemotherapy. The benefit concert, held at the Bottom Line cabaret in Greenwich Village, was billed as "A Concert for a Friend" and featured several of the folk-blues singer's most prominent musical buddies: Peter, Paul and Mary; Tom Paxton; and Guthrie. Tickets sold out quickly, and $25,000 dollars was raised to help the ailing singer.

Guthrie's short set included such finger-picking guitar favorites as his own "Ring-Around-a-Rosy Rag" and the traditional "St. James Infirmary." The latter blues was a Van Ronk favorite, the guitarist partial to Josh White's version. One wag noted, due to his previous night's program at Carnegie Hall, Guthrie's singing on "City of New Orleans" "sounded a little raspier than usual." Guthrie acknowledged his pipes were not at a premium. "I lost my voice a little last night—not that many people noticed." When fans in the cabaret requested "Alice's Restaurant," he begged off. "We were at home a little while ago, and I tried to do it," he explained. "I got halfway through. Couldn't remember the rest. I looked over at Abe. He said, 'It's something about the draft.'" The audience laughed. Sarah Lee couldn't help either. "I remember all *my* dad's songs," he reprimanded.[22] Though the benefit was successful, Dave Van Ronk would pass on 10 February 2002.

In January of 2002, Rising Son Records issued the second non–Arlo Guthrie release on the label. On 11 January, Great Barrington's Club Helsinki hosted an album release party for their newest addition to the catalog: Sarah Lee Guthrie's eponymously titled debut album. (Xavier's *Full Circle* CD from 2000 was the first non-Arlo RSR release).[23] Sarah Lee's album featured eleven original songs and one cover. She was backed on the project by her brother, several former members of Shenandoah, Xavier, Tao Rodriguez-Seeger, Johnny Irion, and Bobby Sweet. Her father assisted on only one song, a cover of Hoyt Axton's "In a Young Girl's Mind." The song had become a standard of Sarah Lee's set since joining her father on the road.

With Sarah Lee and Johnny working on their own music and booking their own dates, Guthrie would go back on the road alone for a string of shows in late January through late February. Most were solo acoustic, though he performed "An American Scrapbook" on three successive nights with the Omaha Symphony Orchestra. Then, in early March, the singer added a teaching credit to his resume:

AG: On March 3 through 8, 2002 I went, at Ma's direction, to teach yoga through an arrangement with the Omega Institute in Rhinebeck, New York. I had about a dozen students and we were housed at Hacienda Sueño Azul, Horquetas de Sarapiqui, Sarapiqui, Costa Rica. It was quite beautiful, and I had a pretty good time teaching meditation and kundalini yoga. For about a week we did a few hours of guided meditation each day and generally enjoyed ourselves in the pristine beauty surrounding the area.

The singer repeated this course in a workshop titled "Available Space." "Available Space" was the title of an impromptu instrumental composed by old friend Ry Cooder when an LP-in-the-works clocked in short. Guthrie's interest in meditation was genuine. He extolled awareness of "Chitikash, the heart space above the head. Placing one's self, one's awareness, in this place, we act without attachment. This is my best me—to swim without drowning, to walk without exhaustion, to think without unnecessary desire—these kind of things are more complimentary [*sic*] to my nature as I continue my journey."[24] The sessions would be repeated in early May at a second workshop. There was, of late, a lot to meditate upon:

AG: I returned March 9th to the CrabHouse, where Jackie and I virtually camped out in the one room that was usable. We had a series of extension cords that ran out the window to the electric service on a pole connected to the defunct dock. It was kind of crazy, but we had a great time imagining that someday the place would be inhabitable.

We'd bought the CrabHouse in 1989, and immediately set about making it a home. We had borrowed enough money for the construction. But in 1992 Hurricane Francis roared through Florida and the price of construction materials soared. We'd had most of the work done, about 80 percent finished at the time, but the bank would not deviate from the allotted construction loan. It would be impossible to finish. So it had sat for years with no windows, and different storms deteriorated what had been already built.

As it was under construction, there was no insurance available, and it became a total loss; add to that we still had to pay back the loans. Jackie and I still went there every day, having coffee in the morning, and we spent years camping out in what was left of the building. She went through her chemo and radiation treatments there while I began working at a fevered pitch back on the road.

There was another development that spring. It was a more joyous event, but one requiring some sensitive handling:

AG: On May 28, 2002, my son, Isadore Prudencio Guthrie, or Simon, was born in Pittsfield, Massachusetts. His mother, Susie, had been working for us as our merch girl for a short time, and we'd had a brief affair on the road. She became pregnant as a result. Naturally, it put a strain on my marriage to Jackie, but Jackie was absolutely remarkable and helped me considerably, showing compassion and understanding.

Guthrie was in the middle of his spring-summer tour of 2002 when he received news of Simon's birth. His summer itinerary included a number of high-profile shows with Judy Collins, beginning in June and ending Labor Day weekend. There was a short break in the middle when Guthrie was to perform at Denmark's Tønder Folk Festival. The 2002 festival was to serve as a record release party for a project that was years in the making:

> **AG:** Derroll Adams was someone I'd met many times over the years beginning in the mid-1960s when, in Europe, folk clubs were where traditional folk music could be celebrated. Derroll passed away in February 2000, leaving a legacy of friends who had been greatly influenced by his wit, his warmth, and his style of playing—notably among them was Donovan, whom I'd also known for years. Another was Hans Theessink, the Dutch-born blues singer/player who had mastered the nuances of that genre to great acclaim in Europe. Hans and his wife, Milica, had become dear friends of mine over the years.
>
> At some point after Derroll had passed away, Donovan, Hans, and I began working with other friends of Derroll to produce a record in tribute. The project was finally completed in 2002, and it was released and distributed in Europe on Hans's Blue Groove label. In the US it came out on our label (RSR). It was called *Banjoman*, and it remains one of my favorite recordings. Hans Theessink was the go-to guy to put all of the recordings of individual songs into a collection for the record. He did an amazing job.
>
> The album featured quite a cast of performers too: me, Hans Theessink, Ramblin' Jack Elliott, Donovan, Allan Taylor, Barney McKenna, Dolly Parton, John Sheahan, Ralph McTell, Billy Connolly, Happy Traum, Wizz Jones, Tucker Zimmerman, and even Derroll Adams himself, posthumously. All proceeds from the recordings went to Derroll's family. It is an exquisite work with a fabulous and informative accompanying booklet.

Banjoman: A Tribute to Derroll Adams had a summer 2002 release in Europe, with the US issue following near year's end. But the project's genesis had been long in the making, Guthrie's friend and coproducer, Hans Theessink, having first written about it to Derroll's wife, Danny, in April of 1998. Derroll Adams was still alive when Hans told Danny of plans to coordinate a tribute album.[25] Born in Portland, Oregon, in 1925, Adams was revered in European folk music circles. The banjo player and artist had been working at a logging camp in Blue River, Oregon, in 1956 when he received a letter from London written by his old singing partner Ramblin'

Jack Elliott. Jack asked Derroll to consider joining him in England for an adventure and a little music. Elliott and his wife, June, had arrived in London in September of 1955. It was a fortuitous time for the newlyweds to visit as their arrival coincided with England's skiffle music craze.[26]

Elliott brought to England the songs of Woody Guthrie and the American West, both of which he interpreted in authentically dusty replications. Like Adams, Elliott too was a virtual unknown in the US, but landed on England's shore with a measure of professional distinction. He had not only traveled with Woody Guthrie, but had even lived with the Guthrie family in 1951–52. Elliott was, along with Sonny Terry, one of the last musicians to record with Woody during a session for Moses Asch in January of 1954. Elliott's first "professional" solo recording would be issued by Jac Holzman's newly founded Elektra label on the 10" disc *Bad Men and Heroes* in 1955.[27]

Elliott quickly became a cult artist in England. He made a reputation for himself singing nightly in folk clubs, at pubs, and busking on street corners. While in London, Elliott recorded several records for a number of British labels. Once established, Elliott summoned old pal Derroll Adams to join him. Derroll arrived at London's Victoria Station on 15 February 1957, and together they performed their rough-hewn songs in the cabarets and streets of England, Paris, Italy, Belgium, Spain, and other Western European locales.[28]

Elliott eventually returned to the US in November of 1960, establishing himself as a fixture on the Greenwich Village folk music scene. But Derroll stayed on in Europe, eventually settling in Brussels. His friendly, welcoming, and philosophical nature—combined with his expert 5-string banjo-playing and sepulchral singing style—would influence a generation of skiffle musicians. Many of Derroll's disciples—most notably Donovan— achieved prominence in the rock and folk music scenes of the early 1960s. Guthrie reflected that Derroll Adams was many things in his lifetime—"a wild man, Zen Buddhist singer and songwriter, and a drunk." Guthrie also acknowledged Derroll as a master of his art, "It's hard to say what a master is until you meet one," he noted, "and then you can only say, yeah, he's one."[29]

Though Theessink hoped the ailing singer would live long enough to hear the album tribute in full, Adams only heard bits and pieces of an incomplete project. He passed away at his home in Antwerp on 6 February 2000. Though Derroll lived long enough to hear roughly 80 percent of the tracks recorded, he sighed that all the contributors were male. There should be at least one female voice included. To everyone's surprise, Adams suggested that pop-country singer Dolly Parton contribute.

Guthrie responded, "Derroll, she never heard of you or nothing . . ."

"I don't care," he answered. "Get Dolly."

As this was a dying man's request, it was one that couldn't be ignored. So Guthrie was tasked to try to get Dolly Parton involved with the project. As he explained, "I wrote her a letter. 'Dear Dolly—You don't know me, but let me tell you about another guy you never heard of.' I didn't expect an answer. Two weeks later I got a letter saying, 'Arlo, love your stuff. Will be happy to do it.'"[30] When schedules aligned, Parton and Guthrie recorded A. P. Carter's "Dixie Darling" at Jack Clement's legendary Cowboy Arms Hotel and Recording Spa in Nashville.

Their recording was one of the standout songs of *Banjoman*—an album already brimming with classic performances. The CD was beautifully constructed, chock full of spirited takes, all done coolly, as Theessink mused, in "Derroll's Way."[31] There was some concern the album might be a tougher sell in America. Guthrie promised US listeners—most of whom knew Adams, if at all, only through a few tracks included on long-out-of-print Ramblin' Jack Elliott LPs—they would soon "feel the Banjoman's wonderful spirit come through this recording."[32]

There was a spirited second—if decidedly more outside-the-canon—CD issued in autumn of 2002. The polka king, Jimmy Sturr, released *Top of the World*, an uplifting album of Americana songs. Guthrie was conscripted to add vocals on accordion-driven versions of "City of New Orleans" and "This Land Is Your Land." When questioned why Guthrie was asked to contribute, Sturr explained, "When 9/11 happened I thought, 'I want to do something patriotic,' and the first thing I thought of was 'This Land Is Your Land.' At first, we were going to sing it with just us guys in the band, but then I thought, 'Who would be better than Arlo for that song?' Arlo has such a great style." Sturr said he regarded Arlo Guthrie "as the East Coast Willie Nelson."[33]

As 2002 neared its close, Abe called his father to say the completed mixes of the Woody Guthrie songs recorded with the Dillards back in June of 1998 were being readied for mastering by Toby Mountain at Northeastern Digital Recording, Inc.[34] The previously compromised recordings had been salvaged through a combination of painstaking determination and technological advancements.

To celebrate, Guthrie invited the Dillards to join him at Carnegie Hall, where he, Pete Seeger, the Mammals, Sarah Lee, Johnny Irion, and Abe were to celebrate "Woody Guthrie's 90th Year." The evening, as it turned out, was more a celebration of Woody's spirit than his songs. The evening was mostly a night of old friends mixing songs in the style of a 1950s hootenanny. Against expectations, Guthrie chose not to perform any of the *Thirty-Two Cents* songs with the Dillards.

On the night prior to Carnegie Hall, Guthrie performed at Newark's New Jersey Performing Arts Center. He recalled that "Newark was more like a rehearsal for the next evening at Carnegie Hall. It was moody and paced a little too slowly with everyone trying to find a way to compliment [*sic*] the occasion without stepping on anyone else's toes. . . . The next evening everyone made some adjustments in their sets and we blew the roof off of Carnegie Hall." Guthrie was happy to see that both shows had sold out. He conceded the concerts were less a tribute to his father than to eighty-three-year-old Pete Seeger, "although no one ever said as much." It was the first time Seeger would sing at Carnegie Hall with Guthrie since their concerts of 1998.[35]

Guthrie, Abe, Sarah Lee, Johnny, and pedal steel guitarist Gordon Titcomb would spend most of January 2003 out west. Sarah Lee and Johnny had become an integral part of the revue, often opening shows with a set of their own. "When you work with your own kids as musicians, the relationship becomes more than a parent and a kid," Guthrie explained. "Musically, they get into a zone. They've got this look in their eye and it doesn't matter how old they are or where they come from or even if they speak the same language—the music defines the relationship."[36]

Such ties were in evidence on 5 February 2003 when Guthrie performed at Nashville's Ryman Auditorium. The night at the Ryman was heralded as "The Woody Guthrie 90th Year Celebration." The list of performers was dizzying, top-heavy with leading members of the folk and Americana scenes. Among those joining the Guthrie family were Alison Brown, Guy Clark, Slaid Cleaves, Ramblin' Jack Elliott, Cathy Fink and Marcy Marxer, Nanci Griffith, Corey Harris, Janis Ian, Jimmy LaFave, Eliza Gilkyson, the Old Crow Medicine Show, Ellis Paul, Peter Rowan and Tim O'Brien, Marty

Stuart, James Talley, Rob Wasserman and DJ Logic, Wenzel, Gillian Welch, David Rawlings, and the "Native American Punk Band," Blackfire.

The concert was to serve as the final act of Nashville's monthlong celebration of Woody Guthrie. On 8 January the Belcourt Theatre hosted a Woody Guthrie film festival, and on 12 January the Bongo Java/Fido Coffee Shop hosted an exhibition of materials from the Woody Guthrie Archives. There had also been a seminar on Woody Guthrie's life held at the Country Music Hall of Fame. That night at the Ryman, Marty Stuart, serving as MC, pressed for Woody's induction into the Country Music Hall of Fame.[37] By all rights he should have already been there, but his radical politics had made some voters cautious and others hostile to the idea.

Nora Guthrie admitted that some of the evening's performers—whose interpretations were not necessarily informed by country music—left many of the Ryman staff less than enthused. Nora defended those artists, telling one reporter, "I respect their way of thinking and doing the material. I never say, 'Woody wouldn't do it that way.' Woody would have hated me for doing that."[38] In truth, there were still plenty of old-school performers on the bill to tether the songs to Woody's homespun originals. There were Guy Clark ("Pretty Boy Floyd"); Nanci Griffith ("Do Re Mi"); and Ramblin' Jack Elliott ("Pastures of Plenty" and "Talking Sailor"). Guthrie, performing his father's "Dead or Alive," would close out the evening. Following the concert, a critic from the *Tennessean* optimistically suggested that Woody Guthrie's induction into the Country Hall of Fame now "had an air of inevitability about it."[39] As of this writing, Woody Guthrie remains unrecognized by the Country Music Hall of Fame.

> **AG:** In March 2003, I began imagining our barn being remodeled from an actual barn, where we'd kept horses, cows, goats, sheep, and smaller animals, to become a studio and office space. I did preliminary drawings and sketches, although actual construction would be three years later.

Remodeling plans had to be put aside as Guthrie was scheduled to perform on 13 March at Jacksonville's Florida Theater. The concert was a benefit to see that Beluthahatchee—the home of a desolate grove of low-hanging cypress trees, a man-made lake, and an assortment of blue herons, possums, squirrels, alligators, and ospreys—might be preserved as a wildlife refuge. To some, Beluthahatchee was more than just a nature sanctuary. In the description of the *Palm Beach Post,* the swamp served "as a workshop for students of literature, the environment, human rights, and American folk culture."[40]

A promising step had already been made in that direction. The Friends of Libraries designated Beluthahatchee as a "national literary landmark," one of only sixty-four sites in the US to be so honored.[41] Three great American writers had written novels or historical tracts in or about the region. The African-American novelist and anthropologist Zora Neale Hurston wrote affectionately about Beluthahatchee in her book *Go Gator and Muddy the Water*. It was one of several essays Hurston wrote on southern culture and folklore when employed by the Federal Writer's Project wing of the WPA in the late 1930s.

One of Hurston's correspondents was Stetson Kennedy. William "Stetson" Kennedy was an amateur folklorist who collected songs in Florida and neighboring southern states. He would later write extensively about racial injustice and integration issues of the South. Following his infiltration into a local chapter of the Ku Klux Klan, Kennedy made a number of enemies. His experiences with the clandestine organization were collected and published in such works as *Southern Exposure* (1946) and *I Rode with the Ku Klux Klan* (1954).

These were not Kennedy's first works of note. An earlier book, *Palmetto Country*, published in 1942 as part of Erskine Caldwell's "American Folkway Series," caught the attention of a voracious reader up north: Woody Guthrie. The two men struck up a correspondence and Guthrie eventually visited Kennedy—living in an abandoned bus on the edge of Beluthahatchee—in November of 1951. Guthrie's experience caused him to compose at least two song-poems: "Beluthahatchee Bill" and "Beluthahatchee—Place of Freedom."

One of the realities of visiting Kennedy was guests needed to be able to handle a firearm. His exposés had made him a target. So Woody was assigned daily rifle practice on a World War I firearm in the event of an incursion. There was, happily, no such incident during Guthrie's visit, but Kennedy reportedly did wake the singer from a deep slumber in an alcohol-inspired mock practice-attack.[42] Guthrie returned to Beluthahatchee in 1953—this time in the company of third wife, Anneke, and Jack Elliott—and worked diligently on his *Seeds of Man* manuscript (later to be published posthumously in 1976). Kennedy, no longer in residence, had chosen to wait out the McCarthy years in London.

Arlo Guthrie knew all about Stetson Kennedy, but the Beluthahatchee benefit was the first time the two would meet. Near the concert's end, Kennedy gifted Guthrie the very rifle—a long-stem rose sticking from its barrel—his father had handled back in 1951. Guthrie accepted the gift, promising to display it up north. In turn, Guthrie gifted the eighty-six-year-old Kennedy with the plaque designating his old stomping grounds as a literary landmark. Stetson Kennedy passed away on August of 2011, age ninety-four, mourned but not forgotten. In May of 2012 Guthrie headlined a program honoring Kennedy at the 60th annual Florida Folk Festival.

If there was no escaping being the son of Woody Guthrie, there would soon be no escaping acknowledgement as the grandson of Aliza Greenblatt:

AG: On December 20, 2003, I joined The Klezmatics at the 92nd Street Y in New York, for a performance of "Holy Ground." It was a collection of my father's lyrics set to music by various members of The Klezmatics, a wildly popular klezmer band, all really talented performers. They had put together a limited edition of the project on CD called *Happy Joyous Hanukkah*. It was a CD package that actually folded into a dreidel. They released a more substantial version of the work in 2006 called *Wonder Wheel*.

The collaboration of Woody Guthrie's lyrics and the Klezmatics' music could be dated to 31 July 1997. That's the evening the classical violinist Itzhak Perlman brought his Jewish-music program, "In the Fiddler's House," to Tanglewood. The night was a celebration of Klezmer, a mostly instrumental music associated with the Jews of Eastern Europe, particularly of Poland. One audience member that night was Nora Guthrie. Nora recalled that while listening to the program, she thought, "My grandmother would love this. It reminds me of songs she sang to us."[43]

One of the songs the Klezmatics played was "Fisherlid" ("Fisherman's Song"). The title meant little to Nora until, after the show, Perlman asked if she enjoyed the song, as it had been written by her maternal grandmother. Aliza Greenblatt was—among other things—a published Yiddish poet of distinction. Over several decades she published her work in a number of tomes: *Lebn mayns* (My Life, 1935), *Tsen lider mit gezang* (Ten Poems with Music, 1939), *Ikh zing* (I Sing, 1947), *Ikh un du* (Me and You, 1951), and *In si-geyt baym yam* (In Sea Gate by the Ocean, 1957).

A light suddenly went on. Much as she had with Billy Bragg, Nora suggested the Klezmatics look through the score of her father's unpublished lyrics. The archives housed a trove of songs Woody had written from biblical texts as well as others addressing the Jewish historical experience. Nora explained that through interactions with his mother-in-law in the 1940s, Woody "was discovering Jewish culture and writing about it as he went along. These songs aren't religiously Jewish—they're culturally Jewish. They reflect Woody's world and his perception of what the Jewish story is."[44]

Arlo Guthrie recalled his father and grandmother sharing a "kinship of spirit." He had shared one as well. "In every family you hope there is one person that gets you. It's usually not a parent. It's a connection with a person that you can't put into words. *Bubbe* got me." Guthrie offered Bubbe (grandmother) as "the poet of the family, and her spirit was very close to mine."[45] Nora recalled Bubbe and Woody were—despite their dissimilar backgrounds and upbringings—soulmates. They were poets interested in progressive unionism and anti-fascism. The bond the Guthrie children had with their grandmother was also practical. Nora remembered that she and her brothers looked forward to visiting their grandparents. Bubbe "was the only one that fed us. My mother didn't cook. My father would take us to Nathan's. That was his idea of breakfast, lunch, and dinner."[46] Arlo was in agreement, recalling his father describing Marjorie as the "fastest can-opener east of the Mississippi."[47]

Though not directly involved with the production of *Happy Joyous Hanukkah,* Guthrie was amazed by the sympathetic treatments given by the Klezmatics of old song scraps left behind, most written between 1944 and 1954. "The way the Klezmatics have treated each one is unique and special, and I was absolutely thrilled with what they did," he said. The band managed to make each song their own, which, in Guthrie's opinion, was "how it should be done."[48] The concert at Kaufman Hall of the 92nd Street Y in Manhattan was the premiere of the program *Holy Ground: The Jewish Songs of Woody Guthrie.* Arlo Guthrie and singer Nancy McKeown joined the Klezmatics that night as special guests.[49]

In December of 2003 the very last issue of Guthrie's *Rolling Blunder Review* rolled off the press. Over a period of seventeen years, forty-four issues were published, with occasional fluctuations in page counts and mailing schedules. In recent years, two or three issues had been published annually. In 2001, no issue was published, and only a single newsletter hit mailboxes in 2002. The final two issues were published in 2003. There was no indication in the December 2003 issue that no. 44 would be the last.

Politics would occasionally mix with Guthrie's spiritual musings in the RBR, but the final issue took no prisoners. Guthrie's "If I Were the President" essay touched on nearly every tripwire of American and global politics. Few issues escaped comment: trade, terrorism, the war on drugs, universal access to health care, family farms versus corporate multinationals, the Israel-Palestine conflict, and China's meddling in the affairs of Tibet—all were fair game. There was even a rebuke against the US government for training "recruits from foreign countries in order to prop up lousy governments unpopular with their own people."[50]

Guthrie wanted America to live up to the values it espoused. That meant supporting people around the world who "want to breathe free. It means we oppose those who want for themselves what they would deny others. It means an end to supporting policies of nations that are anathema to the ideals in our Bill of Rights and the never-ending evolution of our Constitution."[51]

Guthrie's libertarian streak was becoming evident, as was his belief the present system needed "some more good Republicans. There doesn't seem to be enough of those." In a prescient opinion, Guthrie suggested that while it was important the GOP remain a loyal opposition player, it needed to shift "a little to the left so that the wacko factor becomes less influential."[52]

The *Rolling Blunder Review* had already been supplanted in the spring of 2001 by the appearance of the *Guthrie Center Newsletter*. While not necessarily designed to replace the RBR, the center's first issue noted it was conceived because "a lot of new stuff [was] happening at the church and it wouldn't all fit in the RBR what with all those folksinger ramblings."[53] Abe's wife, Lisa, would take a leading role in getting the newsletter out to the dues-paying members of the Guthrie Center. The new publication served much as any traditional church newsletter would. There were items on fundraisers and rummage sales, lectures and special programs, local events and the church's ongoing music series.

It was a time of change. Guthrie, now fifty-six, would immerse himself ever more deeply in the workings of the Guthrie Center. "The older I get the more time I would actually like to spend at the Center, trying to do some of the programs myself," he admitted. "Road life is great and I love it, but I need to quit doing it so much. You figure you've only got so much time left and you want to squeeze in all the things that are important."[54]

It was fortunate Guthrie still enjoyed road life since plenty of shows were booked for the new year. His first of 2004 was with Judy Collins at Sarasota's Van Wezel Performing Arts Hall. Guthrie then returned to a few low-key gigs at coffeehouses and high school auditoriums in the northeast. Afterward, he—along with Gordon Titcomb, Sarah Lee, and Abe—set off for the warmer climes of the West Coast. "This is sort of a chance to relive our old tour up this side of the country," he'd tell the Santa Rosa *Press-Democrat*. "We used to call it the San tour. We'd start in San Diego, and go up to San Juan Capistrano, San Luis Obispo, San Francisco, and, a couple of times, Santa Rosa."[55] Guthrie would spend five days in San Diego at the Folk Alliance conference, appearing on a couple of panels while mixing in a little music.

That spring Guthrie would spend Mother's Day weekend in a nontraditional manner, conducting a Kali Natha Yoga workshop at the Old Trinity Church with Swami Krishnapriya. He remained in the Berkshires since he was scheduled to perform the first of his annual benefit concerts at the church that following weekend. It was then back on the bus for a tour of the southeastern US. The month of June was no less busy—though he needed to trade his bus for an airplane to get to the next series of gigs:

AG: In June 2004, Abe, Gordon, and I did a ten-show tour of Australia, organized by Richard James. The show in Sydney was recorded and released by RSR as *Arlo Guthrie—Live in Sydney*, which was a two-disk live recording. I had come to realize that my strength as a performer was better captured during live performances than typical sterile studio recordings. Even the few who reviewed it seemed to appreciate the difference.

Prior to arriving in Australia, Guthrie was contacted by the Academy Award–winning cinematographer Haskell Wexler—the man who so beautifully photographed the Woody Guthrie biopic *Bound for Glory*. The filmmaker asked for Guthrie's participation on a new project in the works. Wexler, a man of the political left, was working on the film version of *From Wharf Rats to Lord of the Docks: The Life and Times of Harry Bridges*.

Harry Bridges, an Australian by birth, immigrated to America in 1920 and gained notoriety as a radical labor leader of California's waterfront.

Bridges was both celebrated and reviled for his success in organizing a series of port strikes in the 1930s. In 1933 he signed on with the International Longshore and Warehouse Union of San Francisco, a particularly militant and red-baited branch of the Congress of Industrial Organizations. The port strikes crippled the docks and brought Bridges to the attention of US authorities. In 1941 the government, looking for an excuse to deport the Aussie, charged him with engaging in subversive activities and having ties to the Communist Party USA. Even though Bridges had been granted citizenship in 1945, his battle to remain in the US lasted through 1953, when the Supreme Court overturned his earlier conviction for perjury.

In the summer of 1941, several of the Almanac Singers—including Woody Guthrie, Pete Seeger, Lee Hays, and Millard Lampell—were singing in support of the union movement. In June of 1941, the four gathered in a New York City recording studio to record "Song for Bridges." The session was coordinated by Eric Bernay of Keynote Records, the same company that previously issued the Almanac's *Talking Union* folio. Bernay was an early champion of the Almanacs, selling the group's earliest 78-rpm records—as well as a number of other politically left records—at his Music Room shop on West 44th Street in Manhattan.

Bernay issued "Song for Bridges" on what is now an impossibly rare 78-rpm disc that same year. That song, its melody adapted from the old folk song "Little Old Sod Shanty," had been hastily cowritten by Seeger, Hays, and Lampell on the eve of the group's departure for a labor-organizing tour that would take them to the West Coast. Unbeknownst to all, Woody had already written a song about the labor leader, "The Ballad of Harry Bridges." It was a song he had never recorded but had performed in 1939 on his KFVD radio program.[56]

Sixty-five years after the radio broadcast, Arlo Guthrie agreed to assist Wexler with the project. With Gordon Titcomb accompanying on mandolin, Guthrie recorded "Song for Bridges" on the afternoon of his Sydney concert on 12 June. Since the crew was already at the Seymour Centre, Wexler also filmed the entirety of that night's concert. The tapes were later mastered by Toby Mountain at Northeastern Digital. The resulting album, *Arlo Guthrie: Live in Sydney*, was issued in 2005, a mostly unedited documentation of a night's concert experience circa 2004.

The Harry Bridges project became something of a family affair. Sarah Lee recorded, for the very first time, her grandfather's "Ballad of Harry

Bridges." The song appeared on the 2008 soundtrack album *Step By Step: Music from the Film From Wharf Rats to Lords of the Docks*. This multi-artist CD also featured contributions from Pete Seeger, Jackson Browne, Ciro Hurtado, Tim Reynolds, and David Mora. It also featured Guthrie and Titcomb's gentle fingerstyle guitar and mandolin instrumental take on the 1895 Australian "bush ballad," "Waltzing Matilda."

> **AG:** On July 5, 2004, Jackie sent me photos of the clay tile roof that I'd finally saved up enough money to install on the CrabHouse. I was at The Farm in early July after returning from Australia while she was overseeing the project in Sebastian. I was thrilled with the photos, as we finally had some protection from the elements, and they looked great. The construction had been on hold for nearly twelve years. Two days later, on July 7, 2004, Abe's family, including Lisa, his son, Krishna, and daughter Serena joined the tour for a loop from the East Coast to the West and back. We left The Farm on July 7 and headed to Hampton, Virginia, to a small venue we'd come to love—The American Theater. From there we deadheaded to Okemah for the Woody Guthrie Folk Festival.

On his way to Okemah, Guthrie was to attend a somewhat surprising ceremony in Oklahoma City. On 14 July, the occasion of Woody's 92nd birthday, Guthrie was to help celebrate the unveiling of a portrait of his father that was to hang, in permanence, in the rotunda of the state capitol. The portrait, a creation of artist Charles Banks Wilson, was greeted with fanfare and speeches. Guthrie confessed he wondered how many of the faces of the people already hanging in the gallery would be remembered one or two hundred years hence. It will be "interesting to see if my dad will be one of them," he remarked.[57]

Guthrie performed a brief three-song set of his father's works at the event. Following "The Sinking of the Reuben James," Guthrie apologized for being a bit out of breath: the air conditioning unit in his bus had died four days earlier and Oklahoma in July was a testing month of scorching heat. He conceded his playing the capitol was still preferable to "standing out in that field they got out in Okemah." Afternoon temperatures at the Woody Guthrie festival often exceeded 100 degrees. "Noting that my dad has always been controversial in some way or another," Guthrie added, "I have proposed to the town of Okemah that they celebrate his life on the day he died. Which would be October and a Hell of a lot colder . . . and then *everybody* would be able to celebrate whether they liked him or not."[58]

Things had gotten a lot better in Okemah as people began to understand who Woody Guthrie was: who he chose to stand up for and those he chose to stand against. Guthrie told the *Daily Oklahoman* that too much emphasis was made on his father's politics. "Frankly," Guthrie mused, "if my dad's politics were as people imagined them to be, I don't think he would have been part of our family, either."[59]

"A lot of people talk about his politics," Guthrie continued, and they "have tried to summarize my dad in that context. When he was first well-known, for example, they called him the 'Dust Bowl balladeer,' because that's what the first record was about. Then, he became the voice of the millions of people who had to just up and leave and go to California—the John Steinbeck tradition. Then, for a while, he was the voice of the left-wing struggle in terms of union songs—the better working conditions guy. He was involved in a lot of things, but they're no longer the central focus—they're just a small part of him. He not only wrote love songs, he wrote songs for kids—songs that are still being played today, still being sold today, and still being made today."[60]

AG: After a show in Salt Lake City, the bus broke down, and we rented a couple of big cars to haul the family and crew along with the gear to Teton Village, Wyoming. Dennis stayed with the bus while Abe and his family took one car and Gordon and I took the other. After a day of driving we arrived in Teton Village. We'd been to the place before, doing gigs at The Mangy Moose, but this was a bigger event—The Grand Teton Music Festival—at Walk Festival Hall. We had a chance to visit the Moose again while we were there.

The following day (July 26) my old and dear friend Raine Hall (who just happened to be living nearby) arranged for us all to go with her to visit a large wilderness area which was owned by a rancher friend of hers. It was a magical event. We had a kind of cookout along the banks of a pristine river, where Gordon, Abe, and myself played some music just for the fun of it. Not a performance, but an old-style gather-round-the-campfire type event. It took hours to get to this spot and hours to get back, all on horseback and a chuck wagon or two. After a gig in

Reno a few days later we deadheaded back to The Farm, arriving there around the 3rd or 4th of August.

There was no real break in the summer schedule. After Guthrie's proctoring of three days of workshops at the Omega Institute, the band set off for another full four months on the road:

AG: On November 27, 2004, I invited The Klezmatics to perform at Carnegie Hall doing the songs from the "Holy Ground" show we'd done just under a year earlier.

It had been nearly a year since Guthrie had first performed with the Klezmatics at Kaufman Hall. That night proved so successful that Guthrie and the group embarked on a five-date tour taking them to Albany, Manhattan, Los Angeles, Berkeley, and West Palm Beach. The Albany date was to serve as a dress rehearsal for Carnegie, one reviewer describing the performance "as a fascinating mix of the unusual and the familiar."[61] The second concert at Carnegie Hall was performed before Guthrie's legacy audience—concertgoers aware of the motherlode of unrecorded and unpublished material Woody "scribbled from a hospital room or typed on an old typewriter in Coney Island."[62]

In his program notes Guthrie acknowledged his sister Nora as "one incredible person," getting Woody's unpublished work into the hands of so many talented artists. Through her work at the archive, Nora managed to breathe "new life into the body of work created more than 50 years ago." On a personal level, Guthrie opined the marriage of Woody's Judaica-centric lyrics with the Klezmatics' vibrant music invoked memories of days long gone. "The Klezmatics took these lyrics and created new songs, some of which will surely become classics," Guthrie wrote. "I must admit that for me personally it was interesting to hear what they did with songs that were about personal family history—'Dancing around a Hanukkah Tree'— What family in their right mind even has a Hanukkah Tree? A burning bush . . . maybe! It brought back my childhood world that was unique and extraordinary."[63]

AG: After our annual Thanksgiving show at Carnegie Hall, I took off for a vacation in Hawaii. I only stayed about ten days before resuming the "Holy Ground" tour on the West Coast for a couple more performances.

We concluded the tour at the Kravis Center, in West Palm Beach, Florida, on December 30th.

The reviews of the *Holy Ground* tour were glowing, the *Los Angeles Times* describing the Disney Hall concert as a "richly rewarding program." The editor might have, arguably, chosen a better headline for the otherwise appreciative review: "Dust Bowl Meets Matzo Ball."[64]

AG: On February 20th I began a vacation retreat by myself back in Hawaii at the same place I'd been going to for years—Mokuleia. It was only for a week, but I needed the break. We resumed touring in Columbia, Missouri, in early March. At that time I had Abe, BC, Sarah Lee, and Johnny on the road for the shows I was doing at the time. I hired Carey Bramer, who I renamed "Killer," as my tour bus driver. She was a terrific gal we'd met in an Italian restaurant in Pittsfield, Massachusetts. She was working as a waitress, but had a great attitude and wanted to get out of Dodge. It worked for both of us.

For the remainder of the month and during April, Jackie and I were investigating the possibility of buying Bucksteep Manor, a rundown manor house with some barns and about five hundred acres of land, a couple of miles away from home in Massachusetts. We thought it might be possible to create a town center for our town of Washington, which had none. It would have camping, a bakery, bar, restaurant, skating rink, post office—all the things you would expect a town to have. Finally in August with a deal mostly in place, we hired a guy to do an extensive survey of the property. The result was not good. Problems with well water, asbestos, and other hidden treasures came to our attention.

In June of 2005 Guthrie embarked on the first leg of his "Alice's Restaurant 40th Anniversary Massacree Tour." Sarah Lee and Johnny were an integral part of those shows. The two had been busy working on their own music during the last two years, releasing both the EP *Entirely Live* and *Explorations*, an ambitious studio effort of mostly original music. By late summer of 2005, Guthrie issued his newest release as well:

AG: In late August 2005, *Live in Sydney* was released by RSR. After almost a decade since the release of *Mystic Journey*, it felt great to finally get some new product out there, even if there were no new songs. The idea was that a live album was more a document of what we were doing at the time. So, that even if someone tired of hearing the stories over and over again, the record becomes representative of my performances and not the experience of being in a studio developing new material.

There actually were a few "new" songs sprinkled throughout the set. *Live in Sydney* included two Guthrie originals. The first was the haunting guitar instrumental "Haleiwa Farewell (Haleiwa Blues)," a concert favorite written during his *Byrds of Paradise* tenure. The second was "My Old Friend," a wistful reminiscence of friends now gone. The CD also featured a number of concert cover song favorites not yet captured on an official recording: Len Chandler's "Green Green Rocky Road," Derroll Adams's "Portland Town," Kris Kristofferson's "Me and Bobby McGee," and the traditional blues "St. James Infirmary." Rising Son announced the release of *Live in Sydney* with a press release of 25 August. They promised that Guthrie's new album intertwined "the music and stories that have endeared him to audiences for more than forty years."[65]

Technically speaking, *Live in Sydney* was the *second* live Guthrie concert recording of 2005. This other would prove one of the singer's rarest releases, made available only as a fundraising tool to a select group of professionals. On Thursday evening, 18 August 2005, Guthrie performed at a private event in Washington DC, the opening session of the 113th annual meeting of the American Psychological Association. Guthrie's forty-five-minute program was recorded and made available as an exclusive release to members of the APA.

In his notes, the APA president offered, "Today, as we face major national and international conflicts among groups related to cultural and religious differences, Arlo's music, message, and current educational and cultural efforts parallel those of psychology. . . . Arlo works to give voice to those victimized by social injustice. He also strives to stimulate a deeper understanding of, and tolerance among, the peoples of the world."[66] That night Guthrie allowed to his bemused audience of psychologists, "The whole world is so nuts right now, I guess you guys are pretty busy."[67]

On 3 October 2005, Guthrie's manager, Harold Leventhal, passed away, age eighty-six, at Manhattan's New York University Medical Center. Nora Guthrie confirmed the news of the impresario's passing to the *New York Times*. Guthrie was finishing up the last few dates of his southern swing of the "Alice's" tour when he learned the news. "With all of the history that he'd had with the Weavers," Guthrie reflected during a long-distance telephone interview, "he really was a connection between my dad's era and the world of the late '60s."[68]

It was one of the few public comments Guthrie made in the days following Leventhal's passing. But there was no mistaking Guthrie's affection for the cigar-chewing manager with the thick Bronx accent. In his program notes to 2003's "Tribute to Harold Leventhal Concert," Guthrie would write eloquently of the friendship the two shared. Leventhal was a guiding light of the American folk music revival, his list of clients not only legendary but historical. Guthrie recalled his brief employment, age seventeen, as a useless office boy—watching as the leading lights of folk music and entertainment passed through Harold's West 57th street suite: Fred Hellerman, Pete Seeger, Ronnie Gilbert, Theo Bikel, Bob Dylan, Judy Collins, Phil Ochs, Peter, Paul and Mary, and countless others visited the office to plan concert tours and recording sessions. Guthrie offered,

> These were the same people who, up until then, I had only seen from a distance on stage, and from the stage these were the people who were at the cutting edge of the struggle to change the world through songs.
>
> Sometime around the mid-1960s, I traded my office space for the open road. For almost forty years Harold and I have laughed, argued, fought, triumphed, cried, and celebrated together.
>
> I have very mixed feelings about Harold but as I write this I realize that they are the kind of mixed feelings that one would have for a father or a son. The triumphs and disappointments we share with each other are deep. And at the center of that depth beyond the business of ordinary events is an extraordinary love. I truly love this man. There is no good way to thank him for being Harold. There is no good way to murder him either. Such is life—such is love.[69]

AG: On August 29th, Hurricane Katrina made landfall and swamped New Orleans. We watched, with millions of other people, the catastrophe unfold live on TV and were determined to help in some way.

In late August of 2005, Hurricane Katrina hit the southeastern US, causing billions of dollars in damage and bringing death to some eighteen hundred citizens. One of the cities most affected was New Orleans. The city's levees and flood walls had given away, unable to withstand the hurricane winds and the rising water table. Nearly 80 percent of New Orleans was completely underwater, with power and emergency services all but lost. Tens of thousands of residents, unable to get out of town before Katrina hit, were left stranded.

Like millions of others watching the tragedy unfold on television, Guthrie sent donations through such relief agencies as the Red Cross.[70] But he was hoping to do a bit more.

Guthrie reasoned the major relief outfits would provide basic necessities: food, water, and clothing. But as a singer and guitarist, Guthrie was acutely aware of New Orleans's role in the development of American music. It was impossible to overestimate the import Bourbon Street had on US music and culture. Guthrie reckoned New Orleans was, either directly or indirectly, responsible for the "rock 'n' roll that we're hearing, all of the country music, all the bluegrass and blues, I mean, all of that tradition starts in New Orleans. It doesn't start in Hollywood, or New York, or Nashville or something like that, great cities, but it all started here in New Orleans about one hundred years ago."[71]

The moment that Guthrie realized he might be able to help friends and colleagues in New Orleans came in a moment of inspiration. In early October, a news teletype scrolled across the bottom of his TV screen, advising that Amtrak was going to resume service to the beleaguered city for the first time in more than a month after the flooding. One of the trains to service the Crescent City was the "City of New Orleans." It was a sign:

AG: Our schedule as usual ended every year at Carnegie Hall on the Saturday after Thanksgiving. From there we would celebrate the holidays, with everyone able to return to their homes, friends, and families. So, as usual, our calendar was open after the show at Carnegie Hall. We hastily arranged to do a fundraising tour aboard the City of New Orleans—the actual train. The idea was to do a few shows along the route from Chicago to New Orleans that would raise money and instruments for musicians in New Orleans who had just lost everything during the storm.

Within an hour of announcing our intentions, I got a phone call from Richard Pryor (who I knew wasn't doing well), who voiced his enthusiasm for our idea. I'd never spoken with Richard Pryor beforehand, and was overwhelmed by his support, generosity, and spirit. Others, including old friends, signed on and within a few days we had a show worth going to. Amtrak offered us two train cars which were part of the old City of New Orleans train that Steve Goodman had written about. Willie Nelson, Ramblin' Jack Elliott, and a host of others volunteered to be part of the event, which would culminate at Tipitina's over three nights. The proceeds of monies and instruments donated would go through a foundation well equipped to handle it, making sure it went into the right hands.

Our friends at The Ark, in Ann Arbor, Michigan, gratefully, booked us so we'd have some way to pay for the rest of the two-week journey. I took Jackie and the family in the old tour bus, and headed for The Ark about the 1st of December, which we played on the 3rd. My daughters Cathy and Annie managed to put together the entire event in a little under two weeks, which is pretty remarkable. And they worked as stage managers for all the events. Herding cats is generally preferable to organizing musicians, but they did it.

The first official show was on December 5th, at the Old Vic in Chicago, with Cyril Neville, Kevin Kinney with Drivin' N' Cryin,' Sarah Lee Guthrie and Johnny Irion, Abe Guthrie with Xavier, Ramsay Midwood, John Flynn, the Burns Sisters, Jack Neilson, and Gordon Titcomb. The shows continued with some performers having to come and go, having previously booked themselves for normal gigs. But from night to night we had full houses with people doing everything they could to support the cause.

Guthrie's caravan arrived in the Crescent City in mid-December. A CNN reporter tracked the singer down to discuss the tour on the network's *American Morning* program. Guthrie remarked it was sort of fitting that the tour's first show was at Chicago's Old Vic since that theater was "right around the corner from where I first heard the song 'City of New Orleans' thirty-five, forty years ago." The Chicago kickoff was successful despite being pulled together at the last minute. But Guthrie acknowledged once they hit the road and headed south "the crowds got bigger and bigger, better and better because we had the lead time."[72]

Originally only one show was planned at Tipitina's. But once word got out that Willie Nelson had signed on, tickets moved so quickly that a second night was added. Guthrie expressed his desire that all receipts from ticket sales assist the not-so-famous musicians playing in and around the city. He breathlessly offered, "The best idea would be to support the kind of people. . . . playing for tips, bars, the nameless guys who may not have their name in lights or something like that, but the guys who are working on the street and whatever, and to get some instruments back into their hands. So we're working with a number of different foundations, the Tipitina's Foundation, the Music Cares Foundation, the Gibson Guitar Company. Amtrak came through for us, and so we've got a number of people that will help us get these instruments in to people who they've been working with for a long time."[73]

AG: We played Chicago, Kankakee, Champaign, Effingham, Carbondale, Memphis, and finally New Orleans. Overall it was a huge success, and we raised a lot of money and earned a great deal of goodwill. The train tour ended mid-December and we deadheaded home to The Farm to celebrate the holidays, and the coming New Year.

By January 2006, once everyone was home, Jackie and I returned to Mokuleia and stayed for a little over two weeks, long enough to recoup from the train tour, and to prepare for the upcoming "Alice's Restaurant 40th Anniversary Tour." The Alice Tour began at the end of January and continued into mid-May.

The Thanksgiving holiday of 2005 marked the fortieth anniversary of the events providing the genesis of the "Alice's Restaurant Massacree." The *Alice's Restaurant* album and subsequent Arthur Penn film brought a commercial success Guthrie hadn't dared dream of. His earnings enabled him to build both a successful career *and* a beautiful home in the Berkshires. It was appropriately ironic that dropping out of Rocky Mountain College in 1965 was the best move of his life. The six months after his departure would irrevocably change the course of Guthrie's life:

AG: In November of 1965, I left RMC for the Thanksgiving holiday and knew at the time I would not be returning. A few months of being in Montana, isolated from the rapidly changing world elsewhere, motivated me to make the move. I headed home to Howard Beach on November 21st.

Within a few days I found myself up in Great Barrington, visiting my friends Ray and Alice, at their deconsecrated church. I had decided to spend the holiday with them rather than with the family in New York. On November 24th, I drove up to the church for the Thanksgiving holiday. The next day, Thanksgiving, my friend Rick Robbins and I carted away some rubbish (mostly construction materials) that had collected in the church. Ray had asked us to take the stuff to the dump in his VW Microbus, and we obliged, trying to be helpful.

Rick and I found the dump closed for the holiday, so we went to another place that I knew had been used for disposing that kind of material. We unloaded the VW there, and returned to the church, where we had a Thanksgiving dinner that couldn't be beat. Alice had cooked up a storm of good food.

The next morning, Rick and I were seated around the kitchen table when the phone rang. Alice answered the phone and within a short time she looked at Rick and me and said to the caller, "I didn't! But I think I know who did." She hung up. The police chief of Stockbridge, Bill Obanhein, had called and said that he'd found an envelope with Ray's name on it, among other illegally disposed items, at a site in town.

Rick and I were told to go pick it up and dispose of it properly—and that before doing so had to stop off at the police station and have a chat with the chief. Rick and I went to the police station, where we were arrested and handcuffed. We sat in back of the chief's cruiser and were taken to where we'd left the trash. When we returned to the police station, Alice came and bailed us out of jail. A court proceeding would take place the following day at the Lee Courthouse before Judge Hannon.

That evening, Ray, Alice, Rick, and I sat around the dinner table. The talk was that Alice was considering opening a restaurant in Stockbridge. It made sense. She was cooking for a lot of people anyway, why not turn that into something that people would actually pay for and enjoy?

I strummed my guitar and created the chorus to "Alice's Restaurant." We all laughed and made up verses to go along with the tune. We included the events of the day, extraneous thoughts, whatever seemed relevant and humorous. Eventually the song died down and we resumed regular conversation.

The following day, Chief Obanhein, Rick, and I arrived at the court-house. The chief had multiple photographs of the trash, but they were not entered into evidence as Judge Hannon was blind. We pleaded guilty anyway. We were ordered to remove the garbage, dispose of it properly, and fined $25 each for the offense.

Rick and I returned to the scene, removed the garbage, and returned to the church after taking the garbage to the real facility, which had been reopened after the holiday. I returned to Howard Beach after a day or two, and thought no more of the incident. I spent the holidays of Hanukkah and Christmas with my mother, brother, and sister in How-ard Beach.

On January 11, 1966, I somehow got up to Pete Seeger's house. I went there to purchase a red 1957 MGA. It was a fabulous car and Pete was selling it to me for around $800 (I think it actually belonged to his son, Danny). My mother was horrified. She said, "Arlo! Folksingers don't drive sports cars." I answered, "Mom! Pete Seeger is selling me the car!" You couldn't get more authentic a folksinger than Pete. So she had nothing left to say. End of conversation.

When I got to Pete's mountaintop home in Beacon, New York, the car was sitting in the driveway. I couldn't wait to take it for a spin. But Pete wanted to first show me the quirks and intricacies of the MGA. I sat in the passenger seat as Pete took the car down the steep gravel driveway to the two-lane highway beneath his home. Pete was talking about the gauges and other oddities, but what got my attention was that he was driving on the left side on the two-lane road. I thought maybe I ought to say something—but it was Pete Seeger and I was a kid. So I kept my mouth shut and he continued driving along the banks of the Hudson River.

The road itself was kind of hilly and winding. As Pete was looking at the gauges and explaining the details to me, I looked up ahead and saw the twin stacks of an 18-wheeler coming our way a few hills away. By the time I was going to mention it to Pete, the truck had disappeared into the valley ahead.

Pete was explaining how the back seat, which was a simple bench, folded up and down. He had his face turned toward the back of the car, while I was still looking ahead and saw those twin stacks coming into view again. This time the truck was heading up one side of the hill and we were going up the other. I yelled, "Pete! We're on the wrong side of the road!" He grasped the situation and immediately changed lanes. "My God! I thought I was in England," he said. That was the last time I completely trusted anyone who I believed was smarter than me.

I had three real gigs coming up. The first was at the Main Point in Bryn Mawr, Pennsylvania, opening for Josh White. The second was at Lena Spencer's Caffé Lena in Saratoga Springs, New York. The third was in Chicago, at a place called Poor Richard's. My intention was to take the car I'd just purchased and drive to the gigs. My mother was very concerned that a nineteen-year-old would be out alone, so she hired a friend to accompany me. Chuck Bowbeer was a nice enough guy, but the thought of having a hired hand along irked me. I had dreams of doing this sort of thing alone.

Nevertheless, Chuck and I set out on January 21st to my first real gig on the road, driving a few hours away to Lena's. It was January and the heat in the MGA was barely warm. We were cold when we arrived. But Lena was gracious and filled us with hot drinks. Not having a set list of songs for Lena's I took to the stage and rambled through whatever material I was familiar with. I also included the chorus to "Alice's Restaurant," but with little else it was just a little ditty that didn't make much sense, unless you knew the story. I began to tell the story of the garbage, "Officer Obie," the photographs, the blind judge. . . . It began.

On February 1st, I sent Chuck home and played Poor Richard's on my own. I remember being on stage doing "Alice's Restaurant" when a patron shouted, "Shut up and sing!" It wasn't but a few years afterward, when I quit doing "Alice's Restaurant," I was singing some song and someone yelled "Shut up and talk!" You couldn't please everyone. I drove home alone to Howard Beach after the five-night stint at Poor Richard's.

I had a ten-night gig at The Ashgrove, in Los Angeles, booked, so I flew out on February 24th to begin the run at Ed Pearl's Ashgrove. I was the opening act for Sonny Terry and Brownie McGhee. Ramblin' Jack was there, just being a friend. One of the first nights I was there someone (unknown) had laced my coffee with LSD. As I prepared to open the evening, I had a familiar metallic taste in my mouth and knew immediately what had happened. I went out onstage, and went through my set as best I could. The strings of my guitar were like rubber bands in slow motion. As I walked off the stage I thought I had completely blown the set, but Ramblin' Jack said, "It just looked like you had a little too much to drink." I was somewhat relieved, although not 100 percent convinced.

During March, April, and May, I had to deal with the local New York draft board. Since leaving college I no longer had an authentic deferment. As my status became known, I had to respond to questions regarding my eligibility for being drafted into the military. I sent and received letters to and from the local draft board, pleading my case. But nothing worked and I was finally ordered to appear at Whitehall Street for induction.

I went as instructed. After many hours I finally got to the end of the induction routine when I was asked if I'd ever been arrested. I couldn't lie, so I answered that I had been arrested for littering. They asked if I'd actually gone to court, and again I answered that I had. In the end, my draft card was unchanged from 1A, but I was found to be unfit for military service because of my arrest for littering. It was ridiculous, but I wasn't going to argue the finer points. I drove back to Howard Beach, when Lou Cooper met me outside the front door, with a glass of scotch. We toasted to my good fortune.

I began incorporating the true account of my experiences with the draft board, as it related to my littering arrest in the song "Alice's Restaurant." Although the events were totally separate, they seemed tied together in some surreal way. Toward the end of April and the first part of May I had a couple of gigs where I began to refine the tale now called "The Alice's Restaurant Massacree." I didn't really have to invent much, as the tale told itself: it was a time when many friends had gone through similar experiences.

On April 21 and 22, I did a couple of nights in Cambridge at the Club 47. On May 4 thru 7, I played in Bryn Mawr, Pennsylvania, at a place called the Main Point. On June 14 through 21, I played in Philadelphia at the 2nd Fret. On July 5 through 17, I played Gerdes Folk City in New York City. On July 19 through August 1, I played at Poor Richard's in Chicago. During all these nights onstage, I kept refining the Massacree. Through trial and error, each line was modified for nuance, timing, and effect. By the time summer had begun to end, it had become a piece that was more or less finished. It was included in all my performances and I began to love the effect it had on the unsuspecting audience.

In the early winter tour of 2006, Guthrie would crisscross the US and revisit the "Massacree" in full glory, adding sidebars and historical footnotes along the way. The song's reappearance certainly pleased audiences crowding into solidly sold-out venues. In the past, fans arrived at shows with no guarantee they would hear Guthrie perform his most famous song. Now it seemed a safe bet. Guthrie acknowledged the song had taken on a life of its own. "I'm still amused and amazed it has transformed from a '60s song to a Thanksgiving song. I don't know how that happened. But it's right up there with Bing Crosby's 'White Christmas.'"[74]

AG: In April we began modifying the old barn on The Farm, where we kept vehicles and animals, to a new office space. We had outgrown the office space in Sebastian, Florida, and the idea was to build a more suitable space, one which would also include our own family recording studio. Tim Sears, Abe's buddy and lead guitarist from Xavier, organized the effort and was the construction chief. We took the old aged exterior cedarwood and used it inside, while we faced the outside with manufactured stone.

On June 6, "The Guthrie Family Legacy Tour"—which was basically me with Abe and Gordon, along with Sarah Lee and Johnny—began in Alaska. That leg of the tour ended the last days of July. On that same day we closed our RSR offices in Sebastian, Florida, and moved our production offices back up to The Farm into the new space we had created.

On the final day of Guthrie's four-day stint at Disney's "Flower Power" concert series in Orlando, Rising Son issued a press release announcing the family's Legacy Tour. The Epcot residency allowed Guthrie to work out some of the material the family would perform over the course of the next year. At various times, Cathy, Annie, and Guthrie's grandchildren would join the revue, extending the legacy forward.

Cathy had recently become a recording artist in her own right. In 1996 she befriended Amy Nelson, the daughter of country music legend Willie Nelson. The two discovered they shared similar songwriting instincts—perhaps *tendencies* would be a better description—writing satirical verses dripping with stinging cynicism. Their songs offered sardonic commentaries on life's foibles and the shortfalls of old boyfriends. Calling themselves "Folk Uke," the pair released their first album in May of 2005. With such songs as "Shit Makes the Flowers Grow" and "Motherfucker Got Fucked Up," it was the first album recorded by a family member to carry a Parental Advisory label.

Though Woody Guthrie had written his share of ribald songs, they weren't generally well-known outside of a small circle. Though Woody's songs featured prominently on the Legacy Tour, the shows mixed old and new. The press release trumpeted, "The spirit of the Guthrie Family has been handed down from generation to generation," with the upcoming tour to explore "new ground as it weaves its way through generations of Guthries." Arlo Guthrie offered that the family tradition was rooted "in the songs, the humor, and the commitment to keep making the world a little better for everyone."[75]

The tour kicked off in Anchorage, Alaska, on 8 June and ended with a show at Long Island's Planting Fields Arboretum in Oyster Bay, New York, on 29 July. Guthrie had little time to rest as he and a more compact band were to directly set off on a two-month tour of England, Ireland, Scotland, Denmark, and Germany:

AG: On July 30, 2006, Abe, Krishna, Gordon, and I left home in some kind of big black van, loaded with all our gear and luggage. We were heading to Europe, flying out of JFK airport in New York. Just before the airport, and with a few hours to kill, we visited the home where I'd gown up in Howard Beach, Queens, New York. I pulled the van up to the house and we all got out. A car pulled up behind me. There was a woman with young children in the car. I overheard her telling the kids, "Don't get out of the car!" She was obviously quite nervous as I approached her. I told her that I had once lived in the house she now called home. She took a deep breath and relaxed telling me that, "In this neighborhood when you see a bunch of guys getting out of a big black van, it's not good."

She was referring to the fact that the neighborhood had changed from when I'd grown up, and was now considered to be mob territory. In fact, John Gotti had lived just down the same street. I didn't want to trouble her any further and declined to go inside. I visited some

neighbors who were still around, introduced my son and grandson, and
we left the area looking for a bite to eat. We visited what I consider to be
the best pizza parlor in the world on the occasion of their 50th anniversary: New Park Pizza on Cross Bay Boulevard in Howard Beach, only a
short distance from my old home. It wasn't quite as good as I'd remembered, but it was still better than anywhere else. After eating, we took off
and went to Europe.

Nigel Martin, our manager for the UK portion of the tour, met us at
the airport in London and whisked us away toward the north. I loved
working with Nigel. He was very organized, and a decent driver, so we all
felt comfortable sitting in the car driving on the left side of the road,
backwards to us, but normal for them. Nigel had been managing performers for quite some time, and knew all the little nook-and-cranny
places to stop along the route for food and drink and accommodations.
He was a little more budget conscious than I preferred, but we worked
well together. Nigel had done all the bookings for the tour and he handled all the business arrangements. All we had to do was play the gigs. I
loved it.

Though his appearances in England didn't attract much press,
Guthrie was a very popular figure in Ireland. On the eve of his gig at
Dublin's Vicar Street, a newspaper affirmed Guthrie as the "Son of US
folk icon Woody—and a damned good chip off the block he is, too."[76]
The Vicar Street gig was recorded by Ireland's RTÉ Radio 1 for several
rebroadcasts.

AG: On August 12, 2006, we visited Guthrie Castle in Forfar, Scotland.
The place is the ancestral home of the Guthrie family and had been in
the family for eight hundred years. I had first visited the castle around
1983 when it was still in the family, attempting to purchase the estate
with the help of family around the world. It didn't work out, and Jackie
couldn't even imagine moving to Scotland, where the weather was
cold, dark, and cloudy much of the year. I abandoned the project. But
we had a nice time visiting the grounds even though the new owners
were not overly enthusiastic at our being there. After the short visit we
continued north to Inverness.

In three and a half weeks we had done ten shows and, leaving Nigel's
care, we headed to Denmark for the Tønder Music Festival. I had been

to Tønder many times over the years, either doing the festival in August or just playing in the area at other times. I had become great friends with Carsten Panduro, who had founded the festival in the 1970s. And also with Rod Sinclair, who came aboard shortly after the festival began. In 1990 I went with Pete Seeger and performed at the Tønder Music Festival together as we'd done back home. Working with Carsten either as part of the festival or as part of some other tour was always a pleasure. I don't believe we ever had a contract in all the times we worked together. I especially loved going a few days early before the festival began. Then I could spend some free time with Carsten, Rod, or other friends. Abe, Krishna, Gordon, and I arrived a couple of days before the festival got underway and we enjoyed ourselves with a few days off.

Krishna left at the end of the festival, having to return to high school back home while Abe, Gordon, and I headed to Germany. My sister Nora had given some of my father's lyrics to a German cabaret singer who created some incredibly wonderful music and turned the lyrics into songs. Hans Eckardt Wenzel (or just Wenzel) and I had agreed to do a tour mostly in Germany of those songs, with his band merging with mine onstage. Although I am usually not fond of rehearsals, I realized that, in this case, it was necessary.

The genesis of Guthrie's collaboration with Wenzel was the result of a chance meeting. In February of 2000, Nora and Billy Bragg were attending the annual *Festival Musik und Politik* in Berlin. That festival was the successor to the original *Festival des politischen Liedes* (Festival of Political Songs). The topical-song festival was an international music gathering inaugurated by East Germany's Ockotoberklub in 1960. Its purpose was to bring together singer-songwriters who shared progressive politics. Over the course of the next twenty years, left-leaning artists traveled to East Berlin for several days of musical solidarity.

Since its inception, the festival would include artists from both East and West Germany, the Soviet Union, Eastern Europe, the Middle East, Africa, North Korea, Cuba, Greece, Argentina, Chile, Great Britain, Canada, and the US. Pete Seeger and Billy Bragg were guests of the *Festival des politischen Liedes* at the 1986 gathering in East Berlin. Both artists would subsequently appear on a rare LP issued by East Germany's Amiga Label, *16. Festival des politischen Liedes*.

In October 1990, the dissolution of East Germany brought an end to the original incarnation of the festival, and there was waning interest in radical song fests, state-sanctioned or otherwise. Folk festivals were still popular attractions in Western Europe, with big festivals in Tønder and Rudolstadt—neither oppressively political in design—stealing away many roots-music enthusiasts. But there was still some interest in topical and progressive songwriting. The *Festival Musik und Politik* was established in 2019, a third attempt at reviving the GDR-styled gathering of musicians with leftist pedigrees.

On 26 February 2000, Bragg was scheduled to perform at Berlin's WABE, where he shared the stage with Wenzel, a well-known cabaret performer from the former East Germany. On the afternoon of Bragg's formal concert a workshop was held, with Nora and the singer discussing Woody Guthrie and *Mermaid Avenue*. Nora was impressed with Wenzel's ability to connect with an audience in an approachable, easygoing manner, much as her father had.[77]

Described in the West as an East German dissident, Wenzel wasn't antagonistic to socialism, only opposed to East Berlin's totalitarian ways. He was a popular performer in German cabaret circles, often appearing in clown-face and playing an accordion. Due to his wearing a theatrical mask, Wenzel was able to communicate dissatisfaction with stifling East German governance, making satire of such *verboten* topics as the Berlin Wall, Stasi meddling, and puffed-up bureaucrats. Charmed by Wenzel's performance, Nora asked if he might consider putting his own spin on Woody's unpublished works.

Wenzel was taken back by the request. He didn't really know all that much about Woody Guthrie's music: he was familiar only with the legend. But these were the sorts of musicians Nora was interested in bringing into the fold, those who might approach her father's lyrics without the weight of preconception. "I've always wondered why people never mess around with folk music or Woody Guthrie lyrics," Nora sighed. "They're always kind of set in stone." Woody's best songs were, in Nora's description, "flexible and rubbery," and there was no reason they should exist only as sepia-toned curios.[78]

Musically, Woody Guthrie and Wenzel didn't have much in common. Wenzel's roots were in the cabaret tradition of Kurt Weill and Bertolt Brecht. His music wasn't even guitar-centered, instead employing accordion, tuba, bottles, piano, and brass. If Bragg and Wilco's *Mermaid Avenue* added a bit of "supersonic boogie," Wenzel would tie Woody's songs to cabaret and East European traditions.

Wenzel accepted the challenge, visiting the Guthrie Archives in New York City for two weeks in 2001, and poring over hundreds of unpublished works. He chose songs that best spoke to him—some appealing to the clown, some to his political inclinations. The end result was *Ticky Tock*, a collection of fourteen songs of little-known works. Two versions of the *Ticky Tock* album were issued, one in English and one in his native tongue.

Arlo Guthrie would meet Wenzel for the first time in February of 2003 at the Ryman's "Woody Guthrie 90th Year Celebration," the event neatly coinciding with the release of *Ticky Tock* in the US. Guthrie reminisced, "I usually rely on my sister's judgment, but I immediately could tell what a good musician he [was]. I thought it might be interesting to work with someone whose music is pretty different than my own, and which has a completely different background."[79]

Though it would take a few years, Guthrie and Wenzel would share the stage for eight shows in the first weeks of September 2006, near the tail end of his summer tour of Western Europe:

AG: Wenzel picked us up at the airport in Berlin and drove us to his farm in Bugawitz (far to the north), where we settled in to rehearse the merging of bands. We recorded the last show we did together in Eisenach, Germany, at the Wartburg Konzertsaal. The recording was not released in the US until 2010 (although it may have been released sooner in Germany). It was called "Every Hundred Years—Arlo Guthrie & Wenzel—Live Auf Der Wartburg."

The resulting live album remains one of Guthrie's more overlooked recordings. In musical terms it's also one of his most interesting. Wenzel and his wife, Karla, share vocals throughout, performing on piano and accordion, with Hannes Scheffler's guitar and Cornelius Ochs's bass accompanying. Guthrie plays guitar, harmonica, and piano, with Gordon Titcomb trading between mandolin and pedal steel and Abe on keyboards. Guthrie's version of his father's "My Peace" makes its first recorded appearance on this set—as does his short harmonica riff on the old fiddle tune "The Red Haired Boy." Otherwise, Guthrie's contributions are of songs routinely featured in his 2005–6 sets: "Green Green Rocky Road," "In Times Like These," "Ridin' Down the Canyon," St. Louis Tickle," "St. James Infirmary," and "Goodnight, Irene." Wenzel and Guthrie also duet on "Darkest Hour" (*"In meiner schwarzen Stunde"*), trading verses in their native languages.

> **AG:** I returned home and continued The Guthrie Family Legacy Tour, which ended at Carnegie Hall on November 25 with me, Abe, Sarah Lee, and Johnny. In December Jackie and I went back to Mokuleia, Hawaii. This time we stayed for about six weeks in our little cottage right on the coast of the North Shore. And although it was by far the most extended vacation I'd ever had, I could have stayed longer. We spent the holidays together in Mokuleia and most all of January away from the rest of the world.
>
> I resumed the Guthrie Family Legacy Tour in February, took off most of March at the CrabHouse, and picked up the tour again in April right through May 13 in Black Mountain, North Carolina. We arrived back at The Farm, where the boys were putting together the last pieces of the puzzle reconstructing the barn into our new office/studio space.

In June of 2007, Rising Son Records announced the folk singer was to embark on an ambitious eighty-four-date tour. The musical road trip would last through mid-May of 2008. Guthrie was calling this newest sortie the "Solo Reunion—Together at Last" tour, a jokey reference to the fact that he hadn't toured as a solo artist for a number of years. This tour would feature a "back to the starting point" vibe, Guthrie alone on stage with only a couple of guitars and piano. He was set to headline the Okemah celebration on 14 July—the anniversary of his father's ninety-fifth birthday.

He wasn't the only Guthrie performing at the festival that year. Both Folk Uke and Annie were scheduled to sing as well. Guthrie was not only pleased that the festival had blossomed since its inauguration in 1998, but happy to see his dad firmly embraced by the community as one of their own. When Guthrie first visited in 1971 he was bluntly told that Okemah's residents didn't want a flood of "hippie-types" to invade their town. Guthrie's response was succinct. "I think when America is 'invaded' by Americans it is a sad day. We've got to get it together so we don't have to have invasions between the young guys and the old guys."[80]

A week prior to the Okemah event, Guthrie—now age sixty and officially an "old guy"—took a call from the *Daily Oklahoman*. "I think my Dad has had enough time gone so that people around the world can decide whether they think he's any good or not, and I think the verdict is in," Guthrie opined. A year prior Woody Guthrie was an inductee to Oklahoma's

Hall of Fame, an honor unimaginable a few decades earlier. "Everybody finds it difficult to be a prophet in their own hometown," Guthrie mused, "and he was no exception. However, I think enough time has passed so that he may not be seen as a prophet, but he definitely is seen as being profitable."[81]

Guthrie confessed that while he was looking forward to going out on the road for his solo sojourn, he hadn't yet put together a working set list. "Part of me is reaching back and thinking, 'Well, what did you do back then?' Well, that's so long ago, I can't remember. So, I have no idea what I'm going to do. . . . I'm rehearsing for my geezer years."[82] There were actually a lot of surprises in store for fans. Guthrie not only brought back a few originals not performed on stage for years, but he also reached back to songs gleaned from his earliest mentors: Lead Belly, Cisco Houston, Mississippi John Hurt, Ramblin' Jack Elliott, and songster-guitarist Elizabeth Cotten.

Just before setting off on the "Solo Reunion" tour, Rising Son celebrated Guthrie's sixtieth birthday with the release of *In Times Like These*. In many respects the album was his most ambitious to date: the album was recorded with the University of Kentucky Symphony Orchestra in March 2006 at Lexington's Singletary Center for the Arts. The orchestra was conducted by John Nardolillo, the progenitor of the "Guthrie vs. the Symphony" collaborations. With James Burton's charts smoothed to perfection, the concert was recorded by legendary engineers George Massenburg and Al Tucker.

Rising Son issued a limited-edition vinyl version of *In Times Like These* in the US, and copies sold out quickly. Serious audiophiles refused to completely capitulate to digital formats, many preferring the warmth of vinyl. The album featured the first official appearance of the title track, a song composed following the devastation of Hurricane Katrina. Other songs making their first "official" appearance on a Guthrie live-in-concert album were "If You Would Just Drop By," "Epilogue," "Patriot's Dream," "You Are the Song," and "Goodnight, Irene." The string-supported arrangements were stunning.

Ironically, the 2007 album release of *In Times Like These* set Arlo Guthrie against a surprising marketplace competitor: Woody Guthrie. Six years earlier, the staff at the Woody Guthrie Archives received an unsolicited seventy-five-minute wire recording of the folk singer's 1949 appearance at Newark, New Jersey's Fuld Hall. No one had any idea what a wire recording was—Nora first thought the package might contain a bomb.[83] But the recording was a bootleg, and quite a rare one at that. Once the recording was painstakingly transferred to a safety copy, everyone marveled at what had been preserved. It was the most complete recording of a Woody Guthrie gig ever captured. Marjorie was also present on the recording, serving as moderator. She was tasked to coax her husband from an assortment of spoken-word tangents to actually sing a song or two.

Listening to the Fuld Hall recording was an experience for Arlo Guthrie, who noted, "This was the first time I had ever had the chance to hear a live performance of my dad." He admitted he really wasn't all that aware of his father's stage work because "When I talk to friends that were with him, guys like Pete Seeger or Cisco Houston or Ramblin' Jack, they generally would talk about their adventures. We never got into what a performance was like."[84] What it *was* similar to was an Arlo Guthrie concert. Songs were interlaced with winding homespun homilies spiked with wry humor, history, politics, and current-day matters. After listening to the initial playback, Guthrie mused, "You do begin to wonder how much of this is genetic."[85]

In mid-October of 2007, the latest issue of the glossy magazine *Vanity Fair* hit newsstands with an unusual multipage pictorial essay, *The Folk-Music Explosion! Its Biggest Legends and Newest Stars.*[86] The photographs were by Annie Leibowitz, whose work had famously been featured on hundreds of magazine covers over the years. Guthrie had a lifelong interest in photography, and the *Vanity Fair* shoot reignited that interest:

AG: On November 13 I did a gig in Ithaca, New York, at the State Theater, where I was introduced to Amelia Burns. She became our merch girl, and it was great having her out with us. She had an interest in photography, as I did.

I had an interest in photography since I was a little kid. For my tenth birthday I wanted a camera. Nothing fancy, just a Kodak Instamatic or whatever it was called back then. My mother only agreed if I would take photography classes from a neighborhood guy that had set up a darkroom in his garage where he had about six young kids coming every week. I was one of them. I learned how to develop film, and acquired a good sense of how cameras work. Manny Lebensfeld was the guy who taught me the first things I ever learned about photography. That knowledge has come in handy over the years and decades.

Even to this day I still tinker with cameras and take pictures. Sixty years after hanging out in his garage, I ran into Manny at a local restaurant in Pittsfield, Massachusetts. He was no longer the young man I had taken lessons from, but he told me he'd been looking online at some of the photographs I'd taken and was happy he had some part to play in my education. He passed away soon afterward, but I'm so thrilled we had a chance to meet again.

Though most of his 2007 tour were solo gigs, Guthrie continued to perform with both the Kentucky and Springfield Symphony Orchestras. The final show of the year was with the former at Carnegie Hall. Following the passing of Harold Leventhal, Annie Guthrie took over as producer of the annual staging. She also composed the program notes for the evening's *Stagebill,* recalling the time she and her sisters first joined their father on stage at Carnegie. As they were about to walk out on the proscenium, their father turned to say, "It's all downhill from here."[87] She also noted her father was recently blessed with three more grandchildren. Such arrivals would freshen the Guthrie Family Legacy in years yet to come.

AG: In December of 2007 we began the demolition of the CrabHouse. Forced by circumstances like hurricanes and local authorities, Jackie and I decided that if we were going to complete the project, we'd have to start from scratch and completely remove the years and decades of work we had invested in the building. With new architectural plans and a new construction loan in hand we began again. We designed the new plans to keep the historic facade of the building so that it looked almost the same as it had looked before the demolition.

We began 2008 at the Roseland House. The CrabHouse was pretty much gone, but Jackie and I would take the three-mile trip to the CrabHouse every morning, stopping at McDonalds for coffee (the only place in town). I'd take some photos while she read the newspaper sitting in the only remaining part of the house left standing. The walls were all that were left. In the evenings we'd go out for dinner at one of the local places. Our favorite was Basil's, a little Italian place with zero atmosphere but great food. We'd discuss plans, going over and over the changes I kept making, driving the architect a little crazy.

In February I picked up the guitars and headed back on the road. Amelia came out with us handling the merch with Killer driving. The tour was the next incarnation of "The Arlo Guthrie—Solo Reunion Tour—Together At Last," by far the best name for a tour we'd ever come up with. It went through the spring and into the summer. In June, the "Solo Reunion Tour" continued overseas in Australia, with Jodi Martin opening the shows. Naturally, I went by way of Mokuleia and took a week there before diving into the Australian tour. Richard James once again had put together a small series of shows, and I had a really great time.

By August, Abe and Krishna had joined me for what we were calling "Boys Night Out." We also had a new merch girl, Sam Barnes. We loved Sam, although her habit of not wearing footwear even on cold snowy days was a little odd. But each to their own, and she was Killer's niece. Sam was great to have on the road. Self-contained and ready to roll. I was happy to have her with us. With Abe, Krishna, BC, Sam, and Killer we crisscrossed the country until we were back on the East Coast for the holidays.

In September of 2008, a long-delayed recording project finally came to light. *Thirty-Two Cents: Postage Due,* the bluegrass album of Woody Guthrie songs recorded with the Dillards a decade earlier, was finally issued on Rising Son. Though an item in Guthrie's newsletter of 2002 suggested the recording's technical issues were mostly fixed, other glitches came to light and the album was shelved a second time.[88] On the eve of the album's release in September 2008, Guthrie posted a message on arlo.net alerting fans the CD was, at long last, pressed and ready for shipping:

AG: About ten years ago I sat down with my old friends, the Dillards, in Branson, Missouri, and spent a few days recording some of my father's songs together. We tried to do too much in too short a time and my voice turned to gravel after the third day. But we were having so much fun we just kept playing. Eventually we took the tapes home and tried to mix it all into a recording.

In those days we were recording on A-DAT format and had a number of A-DAT machines running in sync to record everything. When we got home we discovered that the machines were not quite as in sync as we'd thought, and my son Abe (our engineer) spent the better part of a year trying to remove the cracks and pops (digital artifacts) that were everywhere throughout the songs. By the time we got done, the songs had lost much of their original feeling. There didn't seem to be any way of fixing the problems, so we put it in the "we'll get to it" list of things to do.

As newer technology developed during the following years we thought we'd give it another shot. We were able to clean it up considerably, but then we started listening and there were more problems. So we shelved it again and a few more years went by.

Then one day I was walking around the house and my wife, Jackie, was playing the songs from the project. I hadn't heard it for years and I thought it sounded better than I had remembered. So I called Abe and asked him to start working on it again. I had plans to do a year-long solo tour and figured he could work on it while he was home and I was out on the road.

By this time everyone who knew of the project had given up hope of ever hearing it. But Abe kept at it, cleaning the tracks, separating the songs, all the stuff you do in the studio. Eventually my daughter Sarah Lee got involved and started working with Abe. She liked hearing all the talk and goofing off we were doing in the studio when we recorded it. And she began picking the songs that worked together best—creating a less formal recording then I'd originally planned. When I got back from the Solo Reunion Tour, they presented me with the recording and I told them to "put it out."

The resulting CD is not like the usual stuff we do. There are inherent problems with the sonic clarity, voices fading in and out, instrumentals where nobody is playing anything special, but it's all real. It's just the Dillards and me goofing off a decade ago singing and picking some of my father's most loved songs. Maybe there's a place for this somewhere. We decided not to try to "fix" it but rather to let it ride. This isn't the Dillards at their best. Not me at my best either. It's just what it was for a few days a long time ago.

If you ever wondered what it's like to just sit around a few microphones with some good friends singing and picking for the hell of it, this is for you. Thanks to Rodney, Doug, Dean and Mitch—THE DILLARDS—and thanks to Abe and Sarah Lee for getting this out there. This record was originally planned for when the US Post Office released a Woody Guthrie stamp worth 32¢. It's long overdue.[89]

Though the album was released without fuss or publicity, its rootsy, informal feel resonated with fans and critics. Glowing reviews came in from such folk music–centric publications as *Sing Out!* and *Dirty Linen,* but also in the Grateful Dead/Psychedelia–centric music magazine *Relix.* It was helpful that brick-and-mortar record stores were no longer the only option in getting music out into the world. Guthrie believed it a good time for indie record companies. He suggested "the biggest improvement for everyday musicians was the invention of iTunes—not so much the social communication stuff. The ability to market music through a world-wide network has made all the difference. You don't have to sell your soul to a record company to get your recordings out there."[90]

Guthrie saw social media as an important component of getting his music widely distributed. He offered, "The thing that might prompt some interest is the My Space and Facebook, stuff like that. But the way you actually buy the stuff, I think, has been revolutionary. Interesting that a computer company should develop the best anti-piracy device and not a record company. The thing that I love about the iTunes store is that the icon of my records label is no smaller than the icons of the biggest record companies in the world, pushing the biggest artists in the world. It's a level playing field. I don't know how long that will last, I can't believe that someone won't find a way to screw it up. But for now it's just wonderful—that it works on the merit of the music and not the hype. The simple word of mouth. There's a lot of power in that right now."[91]

AG: We ended the year as usual at Carnegie Hall, but this time I invited Pete Seeger to return and do the show together as we'd done so often. He was eighty-nine at the time and had talked with me on the phone about a week before the show. He said, "Arlo, I can't play like I used to play. And I can't sing like I used to sing." I said, "Pete! Look at our audience! They can't hear like they used to hear. It might not be a problem." He laughed and said he'd be there. We had a great time on stage swapping songs as our audience of almost fifty years sang along. An amazing night.

January 2009 started in the Roseland House. I went from Florida to Ireland, Scotland, and England for some solo shows before returning to the US in mid-February.

In late February Jackie and I sat on the ground by a contractor's truck and watched as the last of the old CrabHouse was completely taken apart by big machines. There was virtually nothing remaining of all the time and money we'd spent. Just a slab of concrete and two walls from the lanai we'd previously built. Our old hopes and dreams turned to bits of broken clay tile, chunks of concrete, and a lot of dust. But we had plans to rebuild it even better. New hopes and dreams replaced the old ones.

In March we began one of my all-time favorite tours. "The Lost World Tour" was a 180-degree turn from the solo shows I'd been doing. This was a big show. With Abe (keyboards), Bobby Sweet (guitar), Jody Lampro (bass), and Terry Ala Berry (drums), as well as Jeanie, Annie, and Marie Burns (vocalists), plus the crew, BC, and Killer. Everyone could sing, and it was such a fun show for me. I was sixty-two and probably at the highest point in my vocal and instrumental ability. There wasn't one bad gig. Everything about it was thrilling. May 19 was the last official show of The Lost World Tour. And I went back to doing the solo shows I had begun earlier. It was quite a change—and I was trying to find a way to simply do it again.

By June the new walls of the CrabHouse were going up and the building began to take shape. Jackie oversaw the project while I was out on the road, but I would return when I had a few days here and there. It seemed as if it were coming back to life at an incredible speed. She was sending new photos and movies of the progress almost every other day. By the end of July the roof was closed in on the CrabHouse.

August had one particular gig that I really looked forward to. It was me with Keith Lockhart conducting the Boston Pops at Bethel Woods—the site built on the hill where the original Woodstock Festival had taken place in 1969. Jackie and I made the trip from The Farm in a couple of hours. The highlight for me was a specially orchestrated version of "Coming into Los Angeles," with the Burns Sisters, and some of my band. We had wanted to create a humorous version that would incorporate elements of movies and TV shows that some in the audience would recognize. Pat Hollenbeck arranged it far beyond anything I could've imagined. It was stunning, funny, and it rocked.

We stayed at The Wild Rose Inn in Woodstock, New York, where we'd stayed previously—a great Victorian house with guest rooms, and easy walking to the center of town. Marti, the owner/operator, was just terrific and made us feel right at home. We became good friends. A week after the Bethel Woods show I was off to the Tønder Festival in Denmark again. When I returned I went immediately to Florida to see what was happening with the CrabHouse and spent a good deal of September fine-tuning the overall plans.

In the late summer of 2009, Guthrie's fans were surprised by the appearance of a brand-new CD archiving a fifty-year-old live set. Details of the source and origin of the 1969 recording were, at best, sketchy, but the tape featured a number of rarities sprinkled in its sixty-two-minute running time. The tape captured several early songs of Guthrie's: "If I Should See the Mountain," "Road to Everywhere," and "Hurry to Me." These were songs Guthrie confessed to having hardly any "memory of writing or singing."

The new album offered a peek into a fascinating time capsule. In a *New York Times Sunday Magazine* profile published in April of 1969, an assistant in Harold Leventhal's office had sighed that staffers needed to "weather Arlo's enthusiasms. Today he's doing a hippy Eastern thing. It's a phase." The assistant suggested their young client was still searching. "Next week he may be writing Beatle songs. Then the week after he may go on a Donovan toot. Or he may start writing something distinctly his own. Don't forget, he's just a baby, musically, a developing twenty-one-year-old baby."[92] The mentions of the Beatles and Donovan were appropriate in this context. Both were experimenting with Eastern melodies, writing songs with occidental scales, exploring ragas, and playing guitars in lush open tunings.

Only a handful of Guthrie's songs written in such style had been previously issued, most notably in "Meditation (Wave Upon Wave)," with percussionist Ed Shaughnessy tapping away at his tabla behind the shifting rhythm of Guthrie's guitar. One contemporary review of the *Arlo* album made note of Guthrie's experimentations with "Oriental-styled melodies and shifting meters."[93] It was the first and only album in which Guthrie's experimentations with Eastern music is evident. That second LP, issued in October of 1968, would not perform as well as *Alice's Restaurant*, the singer himself expressing disillusionment with his sophomore effort:

AG: In May of 1968 I was working on my second record in New York City. Fred Hellerman was again the producer. I was enjoying myself in the studio, experimenting with songs and sounds, using my time multitracking (essentially playing multiple instruments over previously recorded material), and building the songs rather than simply recording them. Fred was not as enthusiastic as I was playing with the varying technologies available. He was more old school while I was creating.

At some point, I was told that a comet had overflown New York and had erased all of my work left on the tape machines during the previous sessions. I was devastated. Not only that, but the album was due to be delivered to Reprise shortly and the only remedy was to record my live performance at a night club called The Bitter End, where I'd been scheduled to perform.

Over two nights, we recorded *Arlo Live at The Bitter End*. They may have been the two worst nights of my life as far as performances go. But Fred mixed the tapes and they were sent to Reprise on time. I was extremely disappointed with the final recording and for years would not even allow it in my house.

Several songs captured on this "new" CD, issued in late summer of 2009 as *Tales of '69*, are demonstrative of Guthrie's interest in Eastern melodies. Guthrie recalled the concert, preserved on a reel of quarter-inch tape, wasn't a properly engineered recording made for Reprise. Nobody was really sure where or when the tape came into Guthrie's possession. He recalled that the record was discovered by accident in a box wrongly labeled "Chicago." The only other clue was that the reel had been labeled "1969." The "1969" assignation proved to be correct, but the location of the recording was not. It wasn't until after the reel was transferred to a digital safety copy that Guthrie became aware the recording wasn't sourced from a Windy City gig at all.

The only real clues anyone had to determine provenance was Guthrie's brief onstage mention that "There's a lot of bread out here on Long Island." It was also apparent that the concert was recorded at an early 1969 show because the tape captured a very early—perhaps *the* earliest—recording of his future Woodstock anthem "Coming into Los Angeles." Guthrie's solo guitar break on *Tales of '69* demonstrates a Richie Havens–like rhythmic flourish rather than the electric single-string rock leads that eventually followed. Guthrie is accompanied on the tape by the string bass of Bob Arkin, the son of the actor Alan Arkin, another client of Leventhal's.

If the version of "Coming into Los Angeles" captured on *Tales of '69* seemed rough around the edges, it's understandable. The song was less than a month old, the recording capturing, perhaps, only its third stage outing:

> **AG:** I made the flight that inspired "Coming into Los Angeles" on January 4, 1969, so I must've written the song just around that time. I had spent Christmas at Caroly's flat in England with her parents just before that time. I had to get to LA for a gig at UCLA's Royce Hall on January 10. So I had to fly from London to LA directly (the shortest distance being over the North Pole). In those days, in Europe, weed was almost unknown—but they had hashish usually laced with opium (not well-known over on this side of the pond), and I probably had some small amount with me—nowhere near a couple of kilos (artistic license). Same problems either way for any amount of illegal substance. It was enough to inspire a song.[94]

There is no review or extant tape of the Royce Hall show to confirm "Coming into Los Angeles" was performed that night. Geographically speaking, the song's debut in the City of Angels would have been completely appropriate. It is certain the song was played a week later at Boston's Symphony Hall, one critic noting the performance of a new Guthrie song titled "Mr. Customs Man."[95]

This "Long Island" tape would have likely remained unheard had it not been for Guthrie's effort to preserve "family archival material." Such material consisted of radio interviews his mother and others had given over the years as well as other "personal" noncommercial recordings. Of the mysterious *Tales of '69* reel, Guthrie admitted, "No one knew it existed. It was just among twenty other boxes of stuff that we had sent in to be transferred from magnetic tape to digital format because I realized at some point the magnetic tape was disintegrating."[96]

When the box of tapes arrived back at The Farm on safety masters, Guthrie's children listened to the recordings, discovering the '69 concert recording mixed in with the batch. In Guthrie's recollection, his kids were "rolling around on the floor" in near-tears, laughing through the playback. Being 1969, there was no shortage of hippie-speak or references to recreational pharmaceuticals. "We've got to put this out," they pleaded. Guthrie's response was simply, "You can't put it out. It's not ready for prime time. It never really was." But their response gave him pause. "No, we've got to put this out," they begged. "It's too late in your career; it's not going to hurt you."[97]

Shortly after the recording's rediscovery, Guthrie received an email from an old West Coast friend, one including old photographs recently digitized. Guthrie had no recollection of where one photo was taken. His hair was wild, he was wearing a paisley shirt under a denim jacket, and he held several flowers in his left hand. He did notice that one photograph had a bit of writing on it. He was able to identify the handwriting as that of his ex-girlfriend, Caroly. He called her, asking if she had any memory of the time or place the photograph was taken. Describing the photo to her, she interrupted, "You mean the one where you're holding a flower, overlooking the Pacific?" She remembered that the photo was taken "right after the Monterey Festival and we were standing outside taking some pictures in the field. You had some crazy hair."[98]

In a moment of inspiration, Guthrie asked Caroly if she recalled anything about the old concert tape recently digitized. He described a bit about the songs and stories on that recording. She interrupted again. "Oh, I remember that gig. That show was on Long Island and the Grateful Dead were in the dressing room." Though that was all she could remember about the show, it was helpful in tracking down a date and venue. "She couldn't remember what town it was but remembers the Dead were in the dressing room and we were having a pretty good time."[99]

Though the CD was issued without any specific documentation, evidence suggests the tape released as *Tales of '69* was recorded on February 8, 1969, on the campus of Stony Brook University on Long Island. Guthrie had appeared on a double bill that night as a co-feature with bluegrass legends Lester Flatt and Earl Scruggs. There were actually two shows that night—7:00 PM and 10:00 PM—so it's still uncertain whether *Tales of '69* was sourced from the first or second set, but considering Guthrie's slow drawl and the Grateful Dead visiting backstage—it's reasonable to guess the tape was recorded at the second show. The packed-house audience—the show was free to students—seemed pretty relaxed and giggly as well.[100]

Stony Brook's student newspaper *The Statesman* ran a short item following the concert, noting Guthrie had consented to appear in a student film while visiting campus. The filmmakers were working on *The Death of Tamerlane,* and the folk singer was asked to simply sit in front of a fireplace, strum on his guitar, and look thoughtfully into the distance. Crouching at his side was a girl directed to brush back his hair while gazing adoringly upon him. The newspaper reported Guthrie's brief cameo, shot in the lounge area of a campus dormitory, was completed in "three takes for a scene that will appear for a period of five to ten seconds in the film." The paper reported, "Arlo was cool, with everything from contract to performance. . . . With one final handshake, he was off to the gym to get his head together for the next concert."[101]

AG: In October 2008 we reorganized the Guthrie Family Legacy Tour, this time calling the tour "The Guthrie Family Rides Again." For this tour we took the entire clan—Everyone was onstage, everyone played or sang or both. It was total chaos in a wonderful way. Everybody was onboard: Abe and Lisa's children, Krishna and Serena; Cathy's daughter, Marjorie; Annie's son and daughter, Mo and Jacklyn; Sarah Lee and Johnny's kids, Olivia and Sophia; and Izzy. Plus Terry, BC, Sam, and two drivers for the tour buses—band and crew numbered about twenty altogether. Jackie videotaped almost every show and traveled with me in the quieter bus. The tour continued through the fall, leading to the culmination at Carnegie Hall and Newark's New Jersey Performing Arts Center.

The Guthrie Family Rides Again tour continued into the New Year, beginning in mid-February. By April, Jackie and I had moved into the nearly completed CrabHouse. There were some small details to finish up, but after over twenty years it was essentially finished and habitable. By May we were moving our stuff from the Roseland House into the CrabHouse. With great help from close friends and neighbors we were pretty much living at the CrabHouse and completely moved in sometime in June.

In August 2010 I had a scheduled trip overseas. There were a few dates in Germany, a larger tour of Ireland, and a couple in Scotland and England before heading back to Tønder for the festival. There was a problem getting anywhere overseas because a volcano had erupted in Iceland, sending clouds of volcanic ash over Europe, and all flights were grounded. The only way to get there was by sea, so I booked passage on the Queen Mary 2 and traveled from New York to the port city of Southampton, England.

The trip took about a week and was fortunately uneventful. The oddest thing abroad the ship was the dress code obligating me to have formal attire for the evening dinners. Luckily, I was prepared with a black hand-made suit created by the company that the famous designer, Nudie Cohn, established in Los Angeles. It wasn't the typical performance suit with colorful images, but plain black and formal, much like Johnny Cash would wear. It worked perfectly—although I felt like a penguin.

September I was back at The Farm and preparing for the continuation of The Lost World Tour, which had evolved into a new tour called "Journey On"—named after a song by my good friend Hans Theessink. The plan was for me to create the new tour while Jackie returned to further set up the CrabHouse. On September 21 I was driving to Bradley International Airport with Jackie, as she had a flight to Sebastian. I dropped her off as usual, left her at the curb, and began the hour-and-a-half trip back home.

About a half-hour later, I received a call from Jackie saying that I needed to return to the airport immediately as she'd been arrested. The story unfolded and I was given directions by the local authorities as to how to retrieve my wife. They told me that they'd seen a piece of luggage with my name tag on it, and they wondered, "What kind of idiot was pretending to be Arlo Guthrie?"

They opened the luggage and found a small tin can that a fan had given me. It had a picture of a marijuana leaf on the top with the word "Amsterdam" written beneath. When the authorities opened the can, they found a small amount of the substance inside, and immediately arrested the imposter, not realizing that she was my spouse. She eventually convinced them that she was indeed Jackie Guthrie. We shared luggage from time to time. I had never opened the gift from the person who gave it to me, and had simply tossed it inside the suitcase and completely forgot about it.

Jackie was a serial hugger, and by the time they brought her out to the curb for me to take her home, she had made friends with all the police officers, knew all their names, the names of their kids, etc. They told me, "If we would've known it was her, we wouldn't have bothered with this. We really do have better things to do. But, once someone is arrested, well. . . . We can't un-arrest them." We recreated the arrest so I could take pictures and share them with our kids. She gave them all individual hugs and we drove back to The Farm. Naturally, she missed the flight that day, but the next day Jackie left for Florida on schedule.

Jackie only stayed for a short while in Florida and returned to The Farm about September 6th. From The Farm we were invited to attend an annual Amazon Camp Meeting, which was an event created by Jeff Bezos to gather a number of influential people in Santa Fe, New Mexico, for three days. I loved the idea and had always believed that events like this would be beneficial to humanity, just to gather together with no real formal agenda. We attended the event and met some incredibly wonderful people. It was mid-October. I flew from Santa Fe to Ann Arbor the day following the event to get the Journey On tour underway.

In November the family and I participated in the annual Macy's Day parade in New York City. I had never been asked to do that kind of event on such a large scale, so we were all pretty excited. I had become almost normal and acceptable—so it was a little odd. But a good time was had by all. The family and I stayed in New York during Thanksgiving, and we did our annual Thanksgiving concert at Carnegie Hall—this time with the University of Kentucky Symphony Orchestra, John Nardolillo conducting. Sarah Lee and the Burns Sisters added vocals to my performance. It went over very well. We returned to The Farm after the Carnegie Hall show and celebrated a late Thanksgiving on November 29th. The trek to New York for the events there had postponed our family time together, so we made up for it afterward.

In a beautiful set of program notes for the Carnegie event, Annie Guthrie recalled the previous year's show, sharing this poignant remembrance:

> Throughout the year my sister Cathy and I are reminded of the Annual Thanksgiving Concert at Carnegie Hall. Our calendars have reminders and important deadlines we need to meet to make this night happen. We have been coming here as a family for our entire lives. Last year we were setting up for sound check and when my dad walked out, I watched him. He paused just after the stage door and took a deep breath as he looked around the beautiful hall. He began to walk toward center stage. He stopped again and turned to me and said, "I just realized its 40 years. I've been here every year for 40 years."[102]

★ ★ ★ ★ ★

Chapter Nine

JOURNEY ON, 2011–2022

AG: By January, Jackie and I were firmly established at the CrabHouse and settling in to a routine of participating in events at Kashi Ashram, neighborhood restaurants, and the like. The family came to stay during the month, and I prepared to continue the Journey On tour in March. Jackie and I left the CrabHouse March 1st and the tour began with everyone in Easton, Maryland, at the Avalon Theater (a small but lovely venue), on the 2nd.

One of the cities "Journey On" would visit was Dallas. Technically, the swing through Dallas was part of a brief "Boys' Night Out" interlude: this time grandson Krishna was on spring break and had come along to play. As the tour passed through Ohio, Guthrie agreed to a phone interview with the *Dallas Observer,* the usual chat to help drum up ticket sales. Once a Democratic stronghold, Texas had made a strong turn to the right in the mid-1990s, with voters casting out Governor Ann Richards in 1994. Following her departure, Texans would mostly vote in Republican slates for the next fifteen-odd years.

It came as a surprise to some readers of the *Observer* when the paper reported that Arlo Guthrie, hero of the 1960s counter-culture, was now a registered Republican—and had been for several years running. "I can see where there would be a lot of eyebrow-lifting when people hear that I am a Republican," Guthrie acknowledged. But his ambition was to press the GOP to practice what they preached—less federal government interference in the rights of citizens. "I have my own ideas of what the Republican Party should be doing," Guthrie explained. "These are not the ideas that they are actually embracing, so I haven't been invited to any Republican clambakes as a result. There needs to be a lot more common sense in Washington," he continued. "And I like being a Republican so I can tell them what I think. They don't have to listen to me, by the way, and I don't expect them to."[1]

Guthrie's admission would not dissuade fans from turning out. Following his Texas concerts, the tour snaked through New Mexico, California, Nevada, Colorado, and Oklahoma. Guthrie's visit to Colorado's Boulder Theater was recorded and broadcast on *E-Town* radio. Two shows at Oklahoma City's Blue Door cabaret sold out so quickly that a third night was added to accommodate demand.

> **AG:** That leg of the Journey On tour ended in New Orleans at the Jazz Festival on May 1st. The show was recorded, and the festival released the recording. We thought the performance was really good, but the mix was not up to our standards. Abe remixed it as best he could given the time and money we had. It was still not quite good enough for us.

The two-CD set was released as *Arlo Guthrie—Live at 2011 New Orleans Jazz & Heritage Festival* (Munck Music). Munck was a self-described "live music recording and marketing company,"[2] specializing in the evolving business of supplying concertgoers with "official," near-instant CD recordings of live gigs. Munck would "record, mix and master" and burn directly to CD following gigs so fans could—literally—take the show home with them. Guthrie's set in New Orleans, taken from the soundboard, served as a wonderful document of the Journey On tour of winter/spring 2011.

The recording is an essential addition to any Guthrie collection, as it featured a number of songs, captured live, that were unique to this set: Guthrie's own "Days Are Short" (from *Hobo's Lullaby*), "Prologue" (from *Outlasting the Blues*), and the only official recording of Hans Theessink's bluesy "Journey On." As he was performing in Louisiana, Guthrie also included a few Lead Belly songs ("Alabama Bound" and "Pigmeat") featuring ringing 12-string guitar accompaniments. Technically, "Pigmeat" had already been recorded by the folk singer: captured at an appearance at Hunter College–CUNY on 15 March 1975. But that earlier recording of "Pigmeat" featured only Guthrie's solo piano, while the *Jazz Fest* CD captured a thundering full-band version. The new CD also featured Brownie McGhee's "Cornbread, Peas, and Black Molasses" and a superb cover of Hoyt Axton's "Evangelina." The Burns Sisters shared heavenly harmonies throughout. The sister's vocal contribution to "Days Are Short" arguably bests Guthrie's seminal, if more low-key, studio version of 1972.

AG: My touring partner from Australia, Jodi Martin, came to stay with us for a while with the intention of writing some songs together. She flew into New Orleans and joined us from then on thru the festival. We left that night after the gig for the CrabHouse. Jodi, Jackie, and I spent May mostly at The Farm, with occasional outings scattered here and there. The one notable gig was with Levon Helm in Cooperstown, New York, where we played at the Ommegang Brewery. Jodi sat in with us doing a song she'd written based on conversations with Jackie. It was called "Criminal," a really good song about how Mother Nature got turned into something illegal. At some point in late May, Jodi left The Farm and went to visit a boyfriend in Canada.

My sister Nora and her husband, Michael, had invited Jackie and me to come visit them in mid-June, and we left for Bonn, Germany, the day after the Clearwater Festival. We had a great time in Bonn, and Nora had organized an excursion to Paris about a week after we arrived.

Jackie and I had only been to Paris once before: to help promote the "Alice's Restaurant" movie when it was released overseas in early 1970. So for us it was fabulous to have some time off—no work, just enjoyment in that great city. We did all the tourist things—visited the Eiffel Tower, took a boat along the Seine and, for the first time ever, Jackie seriously went shopping.

She didn't have the shopping gene, preferring to wear cutoff jeans and tie-dyed T-shirts most of the time. But Paris has its charms and Jackie (sixty-seven at the time), a former Miss Malibu, had lost little of her natural beauty. We had to purchase another large suitcase just for the clothing she acquired during the trip.

We returned to Bonn and drove to Rudolstadt for the annual folk festival. Unlike my previous visit, I was not a performer, but a guest of the festival. We simply enjoyed the festival like normal people. There was only one gig lined up for me and that was in Bad Staffelstein, Bavaria, Germany. I was scheduled to perform with Wenzel at a large festival there, but wind and rainstorms limited our performance.

Jackie and I returned to the states afterward and went straight from Germany to Madison, Wisconsin, where street demonstrations were taking place in support of the We Are Wisconsin Worker's Emergency Rights Fund. I did a show at the Barrymore Theater that was both in support of the demonstrators and a celebration of the upcoming

100th birthday of my father. I roamed the streets meeting casually with everyday people and sang songs to help validate the demonstrations. Jackie and I became immersed in the crowds. We were thrilled to be able to have participated.

In September we were still working on The Bucksteep Project and hired someone to check the structural integrity of the buildings. Jackie and I went there almost every day imagining the changes we'd make. The results were not good since asbestos, well water problems, and other issues made themselves apparent. Still, even with all the problems, we believed we could make it happen. In October we set up to record some new material in the carriage house at Bucksteep. For three days we recorded with members of the band.

Guthrie's libertarian tendencies would again publicly surface in October. He surprised many by coming to the defense of country music superstar Hank Williams Jr. Williams's politics were far to the right, the opinionated singer suffering no sense of apologia. Williams found himself the center of controversy following his guest appearance on the solidly conservative *Fox & Friends* TV program. If Williams hoped to court publicity with that appearance, he succeeded. Describing President Barack Obama and Vice President Joe Biden as the "enemy," Williams opined Obama's recent round of golf with Republican House Speaker John Boehner was akin to "Hitler playing golf with Netanyahu."[3] Williams's comments were met with a wave of condemnation. Fearing blowback from advertisers, Williams's *Monday Night Football* theme song, "Are You Ready for Some Football?," was dropped as the program's musical intro.

Though Guthrie wasn't defending Williams's politics, he was wary when anyone's right to free speech was stifled. Shortly following the controversy, Guthrie offered that the right to speak one's mind—no matter how unpopular one's view might be—was worth defending. Guthrie mused there was nothing new about a politician or celebrity "saying something stupid." In fact, the public braying of inanities was, more or less, "the American way."[4] The network's decision to drop Williams's football anthem caused Guthrie to send the embattled country singer a letter of support.

"I said, 'Hank, we probably don't agree on anything, but it's more dangerous now to keep your mouth shut for fear of losing your job than it is to say the wrong thing. When people fear that by saying something or speaking out that they're going to lose something of value that is an evil omen for any nation.' So I said, 'You keep talkin'." It was puzzling to some that Guthrie would fire off a letter to someone whose politics were mostly at odds with his own. But as the son of Woody Guthrie, a compadre of Pete Seeger, and the subject of his own thick FBI file, to Guthrie free speech was a matter of more than theoretical interest. "To be at a place where you're so scared you can't say anything wrong or do anything wrong or think anything wrong," Guthrie mused, might signal "we're going to end up in an authoritarian nightmare."[5]

AG: I had agreed to do a tribute to George Wein, the founder of both the Newport Jazz and Folk Festivals in Rhode Island, as well as the founder of the New Orleans Jazz Festival. The tribute took place October 21st at Symphony Space in New York City.

The tribute to George Wein featured an impressive cast: Pete Seeger, Suzanne Vega, Lucy Kaplansky, Tom Paxton, Guy Davis, David Amram, Loudon Wainwright III, Toshi Reagon, and Richard Barone. The evening was to benefit the Clearwater organization. Wein, the eighty-six-year-old festival impresario, was to be honored with a Power of Song Award. While the tribute was memorable, the event directly following the concert would steal the morning's headline:

AG: Immediately following the show at Symphony Space, Pete wanted to walk downtown to Columbus Circle. He wanted to participate in the Occupy Wall Street Movement and knew that many young people were heading there coming from the other direction that same night.

I was more in favor of going to a bar and having a few beers with the other performers who'd showed up in support of George Wein. After all, it seemed unusual to leave one event and go to another. But, Pete insisted, and Pete was Pete: it would have been equally as unusual to see him in a bar after a gig. So I, along with David Amram and others, marched to Columbus Circle.

We walked (Pete using two metal crutches) through the cold October night, arriving at Columbus Circle two miles and an hour later. Most of the young people, walking from the other direction, seemed to have no knowledge of who Pete Seeger was, although there were a few who were thankful and excited to see him there. We sang some

songs together in support of the crowd gathered around the stone
monument.

The photographs of the ninety-two-year-old Seeger walking the thirty-
seven city blocks to support the young activists would hit newspapers and
social media outlets by storm. It wasn't surprising that many gathered at
the protest were unaware Seeger had joined them—many of the Occupy
activists were too young to have an inkling of who Seeger was and what he
represented. It *was* ironic that many in the crowd were singing the songs
Seeger helped bring to public attention: "We Shall Not Be Moved, "Down
by the Riverside," "This Little Light of Mine," and "We Shall Overcome."[6]

Shortly following the protest, Guthrie was asked to share his thoughts
on the Occupy Wall Street protests, specifically on how this new street
activism compared to social movements of the past. Guthrie responded
the protests were essentially the same as those of "forty, fifty years ago."
There were "so many things going on. You had the civil rights movement, the antiwar movement, you had the save the trees, the whales, burn
the lingerie, whatever was going on. Most of all of these things were lead-
erless. They weren't necessarily looking to do—to fix one thing one way.
There were a lot of different points of view. There were people who took
advantage of that—who sort of became de facto leaders—but nobody
really listened to them. It was really a groundswell, something just coming
out of the earth that poured people out into the streets, and it really did
change things. That's very reminiscent of what's going on today."[7]

The reporter then rolled tape of disparaging comments of the Occupy
movement made by Ben Stein, the author, pundit, and former speechwriter
for Richard Nixon. "The idea that you can help in a complex securities
fraud issue or complex banking fraud issue by banging on a drum and
sleeping inside a tent, is—it's just incredible," Stein suggested. "It's unbelievable. It shows the complete collapse of education in this country if
people think banging on a drum is going to solve this problem."[8] When
asked to comment, Guthrie didn't necessarily disagree. He conceded the
Occupy movement wasn't likely to bring Wall Street to its knees. But he did
believe critics were missing the message.

"I think the point that [Stein's] missing, and maybe some others also,"
Guthrie countered, "is that this is the first time in decades that you have
seen so many people of divergent points of view, politically and otherwise,

out in the street. They may be talking about Wall Street today, but what they're really doing is forming a sort of feeling of what it is to be somebody out on the street, what it is to feel like you're with hundreds of thousands of other people, not just in this country, but all over the world who are hoping that the world is going to improve."[9]

By February 2012 the Occupy movement lost a little ground in its struggle. On 11 November 2011, New York City's Zuccotti Park was cleared of protestors, police routing activists and dismantling tents. Occupy would eventually fracture into splinter groups—another "left" tradition—but the movement's "better angel" effects rippled on. At age sixty-four Guthrie wasn't engaged as deeply in the movement as he might have been four or five decades earlier. He was impressed by Occupy's grassroots activism, but not always in accord with some of their tactics and divisive messaging. Guthrie donated a new version of his "All Over the World"—recorded with family—to benefit the organization. The track appeared on the four-disc compilation CD *Occupy This Album*. Guthrie's new version features the revised closing line, "And I won't be satisfied/Until the whole world's occupied."

Though the Occupy movement had its critics, Guthrie wasn't one of them, at least not publicly. "I'm about supporting everybody who feels that their voice counts for something," he shared. "If you boil down what my father stood for, it was exactly that. That everybody's voice counts—and especially in a time when there are people who believe that government is best when it serves those with the most. I disagree with that. That is not an American philosophy. That is the kind of philosophy we had a revolution about. I don't see why people don't understand that these young people who are out there are motivated by the very same things that motivated the founding fathers who created our country in the first place. The government ought to represent everybody. My father's whole philosophy and his whole career was spent on making people feel that they had some value. That they counted! You don't have to agree with 'em. There's plenty to disagree about. But not that."[10]

AG: I had scheduled some rehearsals with the family to prepare for the few shows we'd be doing together which would culminate with our annual Thanksgiving show at Carnegie Hall. I wanted to remain near home as we'd planned to conclude negotiations with Judge Sacco to take possession of Bucksteep Manor on November 11th. Somehow the deal we had in place was now a moot point, as Bucksteep had been sold out from under us to someone else. The idea we had worked on for years fell apart, much to our disbelief.

Nevertheless we continued with the family rehearsals and eventually concluded the year at Carnegie. We had one more event, however, which was to participate in the annual Christmas tree lighting at Dante Square—part of the Lincoln Center holiday celebrations. Jackie and I, along with all the kids and grandkids, enjoyed a day off in New York City before the lighting event.

It was really a lot of fun to have all of us in one hotel at the same time. Everyone took their families out to eat or go shopping. We ended up singing a few songs outside while people gathered on the West Side to sing Christmas carols and other holiday songs and light the Christmas tree.

That year also was a little different as I'd agreed to do about a half dozen shows with my old friend Judy Collins in December. So we split up after New York. Jackie went to the CrabHouse and I began the series of shows with Judy. I would rejoin Jackie in Florida for the holidays.

On the first day of the new year, I left sunny Florida for what I was calling the "Scandinavian Winter Adventure Tour." During the last few months of 2011, Carsten Panduro and I had talked about my desire to return to Scandinavia. I wanted to perform in small venues, solo, at a time of year when no one in their right mind would be out touring. He put it together and had arranged with other promoters for me to perform under just those conditions. For me it was a return to a life I could hardly remember.

Years before I discovered something I'd rarely thought about. I had been playing great theaters, which had proven to be successful. Then one day, on a whim, I thought it would be a nice gesture to help out some of the smaller venues that retained the idea of paying performers to play—and not putting the burden of selling seats on the performers themselves.

Small music venues had, at some point, changed how business was done. They, in essence, sold the seats to aspiring young artists who became financially responsible for bringing music lovers to the venues. If people came, no problem. If people didn't show up, the performers still had to pay the venues for the empty seats. Nevertheless, a few "old school" venues did things the right way, as far as I was concerned, and guaranteed the artists at least something.

I decided to show my support to those few venues, by performing in much smaller places than I was capable of playing. I did about a half dozen of those kinds of venues and it was so much fun. But the following year when I wanted to return to the theaters, they said, "Well, he played at so and so, and he's a club not a theater performer." The bottom line was that it took me another couple of years to return to the theaters, which had become my bread and butter. I could no longer afford to perform in small venues around the country—not in the US anyway.

Overseas was completely different. So I arranged with Carsten to perform in small venues and explicitly told him, "Nothing over about four hundred seats." Håkan Olsson was the main promoter for Norway and Sweden, with Björn Pettersson arranging transportation, hotels, and serving as tour manager for the gigs there. Carsten Panduro and Rod Sinclair, who I had known from the Tønder Festival, arranged for things in Denmark. It was set, and I had a fabulous (although a little chilly) time.

I returned home to the states in early February and had a couple of days off with Jackie at the CrabHouse, before I once again hit the road continuing the "Boys Night Out" shows. The Boys Night Out tour was essentially a celebration of my father's 100th birthday. In addition to my own songs, I began to include many of the songs my dad had written.

On April 14th, my beloved teacher, friend, mentor, and guru, Ma Jaya Sati Bhagavati, passed away. I was in the northwest on tour when the news reached me. It was not unexpected as she had been ill with cancer, and Jackie and I had visited with her many times during those days following her diagnosis. There was nothing to say, except "Thank you" for all the years and work that had been poured out by her onto our family and everyone we knew.

On June 16th we started the "Guthrie Family Reunion Tour." Once again I took the entire family—all my kids and all of their kids—on the road. We did our first show, fittingly, at The Great Hudson Revival, which was another name for the Clearwater Festival. As it was so close to home it was the start of the tour, but it really wasn't a part of a tour. But it was the start.

July 7th was when we really got on the road and underway. The Guthrie Family Reunion Tour had us playing many outdoor venues, and the lingering daytime heat was catastrophic on the instruments, let alone on me. We were performing in what could only be considered ridiculous summer heat. Jackie filmed almost every show on better cameras as the tour continued. But it was exhausting.

The one exception was the gig in Ocean City, New Jersey, on the pier. We'd played there many times and the best thing about it was always the air conditioning. That and the fact that the venue was on a boardwalk with pizza and rides available to the little kids. It was always a fun time, put on by our friend Bob Rose. After the gig in Ocean City, the buses took everyone back to The Farm, while I took a flight to Denver for a gig at Red Rocks, in Morrison, Colorado, with Steve Martin and Emmy Lou Harris.

I had about a week off and then the real touring part of the tour began. We had a show in Newport, Rhode Island, as part of the Newport Folk Festival, but the very next gig was some three thousand miles away in Murphys, California. There were only eight shows scheduled for the tour scattered throughout the US and parts of western Canada. They all went great especially as it began to cool off a little. As the tour continued Jackie began to get weak and tired more often, needing help getting her cameras set up.

The tour officially ended August 19th at Ravinia, in Highland Park, Illinois. We were staying nearby at a favorite hotel in Skokie. Jackie didn't feel up to going out to dinner with the clan, opting to stay in the room. I was going to bring her something from the restaurant. When I returned with the food, she felt too tired to eat it. I didn't think much of it at the time as we were all pretty exhausted from the tour, and there is a usual deflation in energy when a tour ends.

The following day I left Chicago for the Tønder Festival in Denmark. Sarah Lee and Johnny accompanied me, the buses taking the remaining family and crew back to the Berkshires. After Tønder I had a solo tour of Ireland scheduled with my old friend and tour manager Nigel Martin. We began the tour as usual, playing smaller venues and enjoying ourselves. I even had arranged to play a gig in Milltown Malbay, where I'd first been in 1972. The show ended up being staged in the local Chinese restaurant which, although exasperating, was so freaking funny. I had never played in a Chinese restaurant before. But the sold-out gig was fabulous and everyone seemed to be happy.

In the middle of the tour, on September 12th, I received word from my kids that I needed to return as quickly as possible. Jackie was in the hospital in Great Barrington, Massachusetts, and had been diagnosed with cancer. I cancelled the remainder of the tour and flew home immediately.

I moved myself into the church as it was very near the hospital. That way I could be nearby. The Farm was about forty-five minutes away by car, so the church would provide a better place for me to stay for as long as needed. Every day I'd go see Jackie, meet with the doctors and nurses, and spend time with the kids, who'd all flown in from everywhere. Jackie's condition was terminal as far as the medical community was concerned, although they did suggest surgery. This would have, at best, prolonged her life for another few months. But the problem with chemo, radiation, and surgery was that once that path was begun there'd be no way back to alternate treatment.

So the choices were pretty clear. If we did nothing, or if we tried the surgery, she would die. If we wanted to try something off the books, we'd have to get her to Florida where we had friends who could be helpful. We set up the tour bus like a hospital room and drove straight through to Florida, where she entered the hospital system there.

It was a balancing act. As we tried the alternate medical protocols the tumors began to go away, but she was so weak her body couldn't eliminate the toxic stuff as fast as the treatment could kill it. And Jackie had been a staunch activist when it came to natural foods or foods produced artificially. She refused the immune boosting liquids when they tried to give it to her, because it was mass-produced artificially. The result was that she became weaker as days passed. Finally—less than a week after our forty-third wedding anniversary and exactly six months to the day after Ma had passed away—she left this world with family and friends at her bedside. The two most important women in my life were now gone. I felt very much alone.

I thought the best way forward was to get back to work as soon as possible. And after a series of shows in Canada, I resumed the US tour mostly staying around the northeast.

Though there were a few trailing shows in December, the 2012 concert season ostensibly ended at Carnegie Hall. The program was billed as "The Guthrie Family Reunion." Pete Seeger returned as well, as would Abe, Cathy, Annie, and Sarah Lee. This year Guthrie's grandchildren— Krishna, Shivadas (Mo), Serena, Jacklyn, Olivia, Marjorie, and Sophia— joined in, singing and playing in an unbroken circle. Johnny Irion complemented on guitar and vocals, Terry Hall on drums. It was a tough time. Pete's wife, Toshi, was ailing and confined to a wheelchair. She would pass in July of the following year. It was also the first Carnegie performance in which Jackie was physically absent. Annie Guthrie contributed a set of poignant program notes:

> I sat for a moment before I began this note, wondering exactly what I can say about this past year. It's not a loss of words. There is just so much I can say thinking not too far into the future what we all might be feeling this night. . . . When Mom was diagnosed with liver cancer she fought so hard. Every single one of us was taking care of her. We laughed, we cried, we prayed, we did everything we could until it was time for her to go. I can't say for sure what will happen tonight. But I know Mom will be with us.[11]

AG: In January I had to return to Ireland to make up for the shows that had to be cancelled due to my sudden return to the states. I flew from Orlando to Dublin leaving on the 12th and arrived on the morning of the 13th. I did about ten days of shows and went back to Florida on the 24th. The tour was notable for being part of the Woody 100th Birthday tour I was getting ready for back home.

In February I resumed working on the road for a few weeks, in what we called "Here Comes the Kid." It was a continuation of the Woody Centennial, but more focused on my dad's material.

The first leg of the Here Comes the Kid tour was a solo affair, Guthrie alone on stage with guitars, harmonica, and piano. Although having officially reached retirement age, Guthrie admitted to still being seen as "the kid" in the eyes of many. "I have been Woody Guthrie's son for as long as I can remember," he wrote. The one small change was some younger folks thought of him as "Sarah Lee, Cathy, or Annie Guthrie's dad or someone's grandfather. I'm not generally afraid of things like that."[12] He promised

Woody's songs would figure prominently on his solo tour but hoped fans would not race to the Internet to check out his recent set lists: "I hope they won't look them up, I want my audience to come without knowing what it's going to be."[13]

AG: After a show in Newark, Ohio, at the Midland Theater, I flew to Hawaii, en route to Australia. My old and dear friend, Cissy Van Kralingen, had a friend with a house near Haleiwa Town. I stayed for a few nights before flying to Australia.

For the tour down under I was accompanied by Abe and Sarah Lee and Johnny, who opened the shows. We met up in Sydney and spent a few days getting over any lingering jet lag. They were wonderful days, and we'd spend hours wandering around Sydney's Darling Harbour. There were plenty of restaurants and things to do while we geared ourselves up for the tour. Australia was wonderful. I'd enjoyed working with Richard James as our promoter and tour manager.

On March 18th I returned to Haleiwa, to the same house I had to myself going the other direction. This time I got to stay a little longer. Cissy stocked the house with food and flip-flops—all the things I'd need without having to go anywhere. As I didn't have a car, I relied on her for trips to Haleiwa Town for anything not already in the house. It was a lovely time, and I very much enjoyed the break from the road.

I returned to the continent and continued the Here Comes the Kid tour, with a stop in Boulder. My friend Lisa, Marti's sister, lived in Boulder. She was a doctor. Marti took time off from her innkeeping schedule and flew out to meet me with her sister, where they arranged some medical examinations and procedures for me, essentially a routine colonoscopy, while we had a few days off in Boulder before the gig at the Boulder Theater. As I had never been checked before, Lisa thought it was important that someone my age have the procedure. All went well, but I had to return a few times as the doctor recommended.

Most of April I was touring the West and the West Coast. We ended the West Coast leg in Eugene, Oregon, at the McDonald Theater on the 26th. The next day Lynn (driving) took the tour bus and headed to Madison, Wisconsin, while Bruce "BC" Clapper and I flew from Portland to Anchorage.

In May, BC and I did a short tour of Alaska. BC came to do the front-of-house sound, the business, and to help me schlep the guitars and gear from place to place. We had a grand time flying from place to place. After the four shows in Alaska, I flew back to Boulder to continue the medical work I'd initiated earlier. Marti once again left The Wild Rose Inn and helped me through the procedures. We had fun visiting with her sister Lisa and their mother, Barbara, who was in town for a visit. On May 8th, I left on a flight from Denver to Madison to meet up with Lynn and the tour bus. And we continued working our way east until we arrived at The Farm on May 20th.

The final show of the acoustic leg of the Here Comes the Kid tour was an appearance at the Dogwood Fine Arts Festival in Dowagiac, Michigan, on May 18. The solo tour had been an intimate affair conducted without much media attention. So it was interesting that Guthrie was first asked to ruminate on his father's legacy just as the tour was to wrap. "Well, it wouldn't be as a singer or as a musician," Guthrie answered. "He became well-known in spite of these things, not because of them. So my guess would be that it's something in the spirit of the man that still awakens interest in people these days. There's an honesty in his songs that is raw and uncompromising—which is also why some folks never liked him. And on top of that he had a wonderful sense of humor. He was fairly fearless in his art and in his life. That alone is worth admiring."[14]

AG: On June 6th I visited Marti at The Wild Rose Inn, where I came to do a photoshoot. She was hosting a semiannual event called "The Hooligan Dreamers," arranged by her dear friend Elizabeth Kemp. Elizabeth organized a workshop at the Wild Rose as part of her "Hooligan Dreams," teaching and acting coaching through the Actors Studio in NYC. For days they took over the inn, and I went to shoot some pictures of the workshop. I took a number of photos but one has become perhaps the best photograph in my catalog—"Absolution."

I took June off, spending time at The Farm, and didn't get back to work until we left July 6th for a few shows in Colorado. After the shows, I returned to The Farm for the remainder of July and the first part of August. I only had one event scheduled for August. It was in Jacksonville, Florida. A group of Vietnam veterans had invited me to their gathering to accept an award for my commitment to end the war and bring them back home. It was very close to my heart, and being with those guys brought me to the edge of tears.

I flew to the CrabHouse intending to stay only long enough to drive up to Jacksonville before returning to New England. I had never really stayed at the CrabHouse during the heat of the summer and now, being alone for the first time since I'd been married in 1969, I thought I'd see what it was like.

The CrabHouse is uniquely settled on the Indian River, and although the heat of summer could be felt on the side of the house facing the street, the river breezes kept the temperatures reasonably tolerable. I was actually enjoying myself. Every day, especially in the early mornings, I would grab a camera and watch the sun rise over the river. It was magical. Unlike the ocean, not far away, the river was full of visible life. Waterbirds and dolphins filled the camera lens every day. Although I missed having Jackie as part of my everyday life, I was making the best of it, and found I could be happy on my own.

My new friend, Marti Ladd, would occasionally take time off from her work and spend a few days with me. She was especially helpful when I began to plant new trees and make the place even more beautiful inside and out. It began to feel like a real home again. I took September off, enjoying the river and visiting my friends at Kashi Ashram, eating at local joints, and generally pretending to be normal. I left the CrabHouse on the 25th in order to be close to home for a show at the Mahaiwe Theater on the 28th.

I began a series of shows in the upper Midwest during October. The tour was an extension of the solo Here Comes the Kid tour, but this time we'd added Abe, Terry, and Bobby Sweet. The new tour was called "Here Comes the Kid(s)." Both tours were in celebration of my father's 100th birthday, and I continued to do a lot of songs that reflected the nature of the celebration.

It was with this new band that Guthrie pulled into town for two shows at Chicago's famed Old Town School of Folk Music. Both shows were recorded, the best performances seamlessly blended into the two-CD set *Here Comes the Kids: The Tour Celebrating Woody Guthrie's Centennial.* As one might expect, there were a lot of Woody's songs featured ("Oklahoma Hills," "Pretty Boy Floyd," "Deportee (Plane Wreck at Los Gatos)," "1913 Massacre," "Do Re Mi," and "This Land Is Your Land"). The CD also featured two pairings of Woody's extant lyrics with new original music: "My Peace," the first collaborative songwriting effort of father and son, and the poignant "Mother's Voice (I Hear You Sing Again)," to which Janis Ian contributed a haunting melody.

AG: I asked Pete Seeger if he would consider joining us again at Carnegie Hall for our annual Thanksgiving show. He said he would, but he also let me know that I'd have to carry the show, as he couldn't seem to remember the words to most of the songs we'd done over the decades. Pete was ninety-four years old at the time. I began to conceive a plan that would end up being a tribute to both Pete and the work he'd done without it appearing so. I knew if we'd suggested anything that smacked of a Pete Seeger tribute he wouldn't have shown up.

I began rehearsals with the family, going over all the Pete Seeger songs we could fit in an evening. Some were songs he'd written ("Where Have All the Flowers Gone?"); others were songs he'd helped popularize ("Guantanamera").

The evening came and as the great doors to the stage at Carnegie Hall opened up we walked out on stage. The audience, sensing the moment correctly, stood up and cheered Pete. They kept clapping and cheering for at least ten minutes, which seemed like hours to everyone on stage. They just wouldn't sit down and we endured the admiration that would not be detoured by any uncomfortableness onstage.

Finally we got started. I believed Pete hadn't actually forgotten any songs. It was just that he couldn't remember he knew them. When the kids and I would launch into one of those songs Pete would jump up and say, "Oh! I know that one." And he'd be singing and playing along as usual. The concert ended much like it had begun, the audience knowing that after decades and decades they would not see this man on a stage again.

On January 25 I was at the CrabHouse and received a phone call from the Seeger family, telling me that Pete was in a hospital in New York City. His body had begun to shut down, and he was asking for a chocolate cake which the doctors had refused. Pete was dying and wanted a chocolate cake, and the doctors and family had decided it wasn't good for his health. I shook my head in disbelief. I immediately called my daughter Annie and the Guthrie family sent a big chocolate cake to Pete in the hospital.

The next night I had a dream where Pete and I were together talking. Just everyday talk, nothing very serious. At some point he said, "Well, Arlo. Guess I better be goin.' See ya 'round."

I told him "Yep . . . See ya."

About 3 in the morning, I was woken up by a flurry of phone calls and texts that Pete had left this world. I wasn't surprised. He'd just said goodbye to me moments before.

Two weeks prior to the folk singer's passing, Tulsa's Woody Guthrie Center announced Seeger as the recipient of its first annual Woody Guthrie Prize. The press release informed: *The Woody Guthrie Prize will be given annually to the artist who best exemplifies the spirit and life's work of Woody Guthrie by speaking for the less fortunate through music, film, literature, dance or other art forms and serving as a positive force for social change in America.*[15]

Seeger's passing necessitated a change of plans. Nora Guthrie announced the ceremony would now serve as a commemoration—and not a solemn one. "The only thing I know for certain is that Pete would want us to gather together and make some music," read Nora's statement. "The power of song, as he constantly reminded us, can take us through everything that life, and death, throws at us. On Feb. 22, we won't take a moment of silence to remember him. We will take all the moments to sing—as loudly and with as many harmonies as we can muster."[16]

AG: Toward the end of February, Marti and I returned to Boulder to finish up the medical work, with my doctor there. We returned to the Crab-House and took most of March off. I resumed touring beginning March 29th in Mountain View, Arkansas, and continued on the road through April and most of May.

The spring tour brought Guthrie and the band through the Midwest and the western states, with a brief foray into British Columbia. It was a continuation of the Here Comes the Kid(s) tour, and Woody's songs continued to take prominence. The set lists were tweaked when geography dictated. Though Woody's "Roll On, Columbia" wasn't part of the tour's usual set list, an exception was made at gigs in the Pacific Northwest. "I've tried to weave together a show that includes a whole lot more of my father's songs than I would normally do in concert," Guthrie advised. "What I've tried to do is put together songs from early in his life that are well known, as well as the latest ones he wrote at the end of his life. I'll be putting them in context so you know where they're coming from."[17]

One song Guthrie was singing nightly was "My Peace." The words of the song—or of a poem, nobody was really sure—had been written by his father. Guthrie was particularly proud of this collaboration, describing the song as a "beautiful little summary" of his father's life. Woody had written the song, by his best estimate, while "in the hospital in, maybe, the late '40s."[18] The song served as the perfect coda. Guthrie explained, "For some people, there's always a place for writing about the human condition, especially when times get tough and people are finding it difficult to get jobs or make a living or be paid fairly." The folk singer explained that his father's best songs remained relevant and true and honest since everything was cyclical. "These things are in the news, just as they were in the news back in the '30s and '40s. The concerns and the compassion he was expressing in his work, in his books and in his music is still potent and still powerful."[19]

The message of "My Peace" transcended politics during a time in US history when rigid ideological battle lines were being drawn. The writer and broadcaster Studs Terkel once kiddingly asked Pete Seeger if there were "any Republican folksingers." Seeger replied in the affirmative—but added it all depended on how one defined such terms as "Republican" and "folk singer." It was often difficult to get through any interview, post-2006, without Guthrie's dalliance with the Republican Party being raised. Guthrie sighed, "I see comments like 'I don't like Arlo anymore. He's become a right-winger,' which is totally absurd. I haven't changed at all. I write a lot and I put that stuff online, and if people are interested they can see that it doesn't matter what I call myself, this is what I stand for, what everybody in this family has always stood for."[20]

"I think the world is in danger of becoming so grouped in tight-knit circles that nobody talks to each other anymore," Guthrie added. "The world needs to be able to work together on really critical issues. I'm not afraid to talk to anybody left, right, or center. If you're actually making friends with people you don't agree with, which I advocate, that's when you begin to change hearts and minds."[21] Guthrie's worldview differed little from Pete Seeger's own. Seeger's revolutionary fervor was tempered in later years, favoring "gradualism" as the best route forward. Seeger reminded audiences "controversy is a good thing. I wish every country in the world could learn it. I've even come around to the opinion if you want to have a healthy establishment, you *need* controversy." Seeger often cited Benjamin Franklin's suggestion to "Love your enemies, they point out to you your faults."[22]

AG: On June 2nd, I went to visit Marti at The Wild Rose Inn. I did another photoshoot with Elizabeth Kemp and The Hooligan Dreams. On June 7th we had a gig booked for just outside of Miami at Miccosukee Resort and Gaming. The event was to be held outdoors in a huge parking lot, with over ten thousand people expected to show up. We loaded the buses and headed to the casino, where a big stage had been erected.

It began raining and pouring before anyone got there, and so we began playing to a mostly empty parking lot with about seven people in attendance. It was like something out of Spinal Tap. Pretty soon the rain was coming into and onto the stage, blowing sideways in a fierce blustery wind. I had my wooden instruments removed from the stage and continued playing with a couple of composite-material guitars that could get wet with little effect. At some point, I noticed Abe's keyboards were playing notes that he couldn't possibly have meant to play, and I looked over at him. The rain had penetrated the instrument, and Abe lifted it up and tilted it over, and buckets of water came pouring out.

At about the same time I heard the main speakers on stage fizzle out, and soon the monitors died as well. There was no way to continue. The seven people in the audience were oblivious to the conditions and remained enthusiastic—DUI (dancing under the influence). We packed up the stage and went home thoroughly soaked.

On June 16th I participated in Theo Bikel's ninetieth birthday at the Saban Theatre in Beverly Hills. It was a wonderful tribute. I loved being able to hang out with Theo, as I'd known him for most of my life, although I rarely got time to hang out with him. He was the consummate actor and performer, uniquely himself and a real activist in the best sense. I'd taken Jackie and the kids to see him on Broadway doing "Fiddler on the Roof" decades earlier. Truly an amazing performance.

The show in Los Angeles was the only one I had scheduled until the Woody Guthrie Festival in Okemah on July 12th. From Okemah I flew back to the CrabHouse. I had only two shows scheduled for the remainder of July. One was in Riverhead, Long Island, and the other was one place I really loved playing—Cain Park just outside of Cleveland. Marti came with me for both remaining gigs.

While I was performing at Cain Park, a sudden thunder and lightning storm swept in. The stage manager told Marti, who was off in the wings, that the show had to be called as it would have been dangerous to me onstage—and to the audience. Marti, not accustomed to being onstage, nonetheless walked out while I was at the piano, and told me "DO NOT TOUCH THE KEYBOARD." She was adamant. I realized she was seriously determined to keep me from being electrocuted. So I made the announcement that park officials had called the show, and that everyone should return to their vehicles as safely and as quickly as possible before the storm hit. We left the area and returned to the Holiday Inn nearby, one of my favorite stops mainly because of Alfredo's Restaurant on premises. It was an earlier than usual night off.

Marti and I spent August together at the CrabHouse. Hurricane Irma was threatening the Sebastian area, so we decided to leave. On September 5th, Marti and I got the last two seats on the last flight out of Melbourne, Florida. We went back to The Farm. On September 13th and 14th, I attended an event that brought together various Native American tribes and others (like myself) to the Black Hills of South Dakota. I flew out to Rapid City and drove from there to some place out in the hills.

In October 2014 Guthrie published two books geared for the children's market. The first was *Whose Moose Am I?*, a volume wonderfully illustrated by Cindy Bradley. At first glance the book seemed a sequel to *Mooses Come Walking*, but it was a stand-alone tale. The second book, *Me and My Goose*, beautifully illustrated by Kathy Garren, was a retelling of Guthrie's whimsically grim "animal ballad" written in the tradition of Red Foley's "Old Shep." Guthrie would collaborate with Garren again on two subsequent books: *Old Bill: The Famous Berkshire Moose* and *Monsters*.

That same autumn Guthrie's memories were included on the audiobook documentary *My Name Is New York: Ramblin' around Woody Guthrie's Town.* The two-CD set offered an overview of street addresses figuring in

Woody's life and work in and around New York City. The superb documentary included spoken-word reminiscences by those who knew Guthrie best: Seeger, Ramblin' Jack Elliott, Bob Dylan, Mary Guthrie Boyle, Bess Lomax Hawes, Marjorie Guthrie, Jimmy Longhi, Millard Lampell, Harold Leventhal, Lee Hays, and Lead Belly's niece Tiny Robinson.

AG: In November we took the entire family to Manhattan for our annual Carnegie Hall Thanksgiving show. We also participated in the Christmas Tree Lighting in Dante Square. It was fun to have the family all there, but I missed Jackie very much in times when we'd all be together. It was just odd not having her there. Nevertheless, we did the best we could, and it was fine.

In January we began the most elaborate tour we'd ever done—celebrating the fiftieth anniversary of the actual events that led to the song, album, and movie of "Alice's Restaurant."

The show itself was bathed in lights, with a video wall that would show moments from the movie as I went through the song onstage. A big band allowed us to recreate anything we'd ever recorded—even better than the originals in many cases. We had two lighting engineers just to handle the lighting cues from song to song. It didn't leave a lot of room for spontaneity, but it covered just about everything else.

For the tour we resurrected the animated cartoon of "The Motorcycle Song" and used it to open the show. In April of 1978, they had filmed scenes of me riding a motorcycle for Peter Starr's movie *Take It to the Limit*. It was filmed along the local back roads of my hometown of Washington, Massachusetts.

Peter created camera angles never seen before as cameras were attached for the first time to motorcycles and riders to capture the pure thrill of motocross racing. To open the film, Peter used a Claymation cartoon of my "Motorcycle Song." We sang and recorded an upbeat version for the project, including characterizations and sound effects.

Jon Wokuluk was the master creator for the project, and for the tour we resurrected the animated cartoon of "The Motorcycle Song" and used it to open the show. Jon's Claymation masterpiece had been lost and forgotten for thirty years until it was discovered in a cardboard box under a desk in our offices. We wanted to bring it back to the big screen, this time as the introduction to the anniversary show. After it was digitized, Abe was able to make some serious edits to fit the time frame we had. The plan was for us to all come out on stage during the video and start playing so that when the cartoon ended we were already seamlessly into performing the song live onstage. It was magical.

The tour was both magical and *very* popular with ticket-buyers, many venues reporting fast sell-outs. It was helpful that the tour was attracting generous publicity. Having the "Alice" brand name-checked on the marquee gave fence-sitters the confidence to attend. During the tour's first few weeks, Guthrie gave an email interview to explain his decision to revisit his most famous song.

"Somewhere back in the mid-1970s," he wrote, "the song had become less immediate and more nostalgic. I continued to perform it for a little while but, like so many other songs tied to an event, when the events changed, the song became less relevant. And it still took almost twenty minutes to perform it. So I decided to take it off the set list. There were people who came demanding their money back, expecting to hear my 'hit.' Frankly, I was happier performing for people who came with no expectations. But I realized that for many people, the song was not simply tied to a single event but had become part of the soundtrack to their lives and to an era. So I compromised and decided that I would sing it for a year and a half every decade."[23]

Not every interview went smoothly. One ill-informed journalist expressed cynicism that the famously anti-authoritarian Guthrie would perform "Alice's Restaurant," despite now being a "Tea Party supporter." This was nonsense, of course, and the folk singer was quick to correct the misrepresentation. "Don't believe everything you read," he tartly responded. "I am not a sheep. I like thinking for myself, and I encourage that in others as best I can. I support everyone who speaks out whether I agree with them or not. This is America and I think everyone's voice should be heard. When everybody counts, the country stands stronger. That's what I believe and what comes out in my songs."[24]

AG: The show was doing really well, with most completely sold out. The tour included a filming for PBS at our hometown theater in nearby Pittsfield, Massachusetts—the Colonial Theater.

On May 21st and 22nd we filmed the event. The first day we did close-ups and did shots that required cameras onstage. The second

day we shot with a live audience. The filming was organized and produced by our friend Jim Brown, with whom we had worked many times
before. PBS released it for television and used it for their annual fundraising drives.

Guthrie brought the "Alice's Restaurant 50th Anniversary" tour to
Carnegie Hall that November. In the program notes, Abe, Cathy, Annie,
and Sarah Lee congratulated their father with the tease, "We are celebrating the 50th anniversary of your getting arrested. What family does that?"[25]
In his own notes, Guthrie shifted the attention to others. He recalled the
first time he visited Carnegie, age eight, to see the Weavers perform. "I
grew up loving the humor and the spirit of the songs they sang. And I
loved them individually as well. Their impact on me has remained strong
throughout my life. The spirit that came through their songs and tales,
through their voices and musicianship, was transcendent. It's hard to
describe, but you know it when you feel it."[26]

It was impossible to perform at Carnegie Hall without thinking of Pete
Seeger. A week or so prior to the concert, Guthrie offered that his old
friend thought himself a mere "link in a long chain of people singing and
dreaming about a better world for everyone. I am no different."[27] Seeger
was a firm believer that social and political change was possible, regardless
of what cynics and critics suggested. He knew change was possible. During
his ninety-four trips around the sun, the aged folk singer was witness to
such changes.

"Pete Seeger told me once that any big organization can be subverted
by governments or multinational special interests," Guthrie recalled. "They
have the resources to cast doubt and fear over any group they feel threat-
ened by. But no government or large organization has the resources to stop
millions of little people doing their own thing in their own hometowns. So
evolution continues unabated like a river turning right, then left, back and
forth." It was a message he took to heart, acknowledging the "purpose of
the Guthrie Center is to remind people that although there are twists and
turns, the river always goes to the sea. Remember that, and life becomes
more hopeful."[28]

AG: I picked up the Alice's Restaurant 50th Anniversary Tour January 16th at the Center for the Arts in Coral Springs, FL, after having
taken December and some of January off at the CrabHouse. Marti came

for visits occasionally, but most of the time I was there by myself enjoying the moist humid air. Marti flew down on January 21st and stayed at
the CrabHouse while I traversed the country with the big show. The
"Alice" tour continued throughout February, and although I'd had a
headache for much of that time, I didn't dwell on it. I continued the tour
until March, when I'd scheduled some time off by the river.

Guthrie was only a few days into his 2016 tour when Will Kaufman, a
Professor of American Literature and Culture at England's University of
Central Lancashire, posted an online essay that went viral. Kaufman, the
author of several highly respected and deeply researched academic books
on Woody Guthrie's life and works, was sorting through the Archives when
he unearthed several previously unpublished snippets of lyrics and free
verse written by Woody in 1952. Such discoveries were not unusual. What
was unusual is that some of the verses had tangential political relevancy in
2016. These concerned Woody's musings on the New York City real estate
baron Fred C. Trump, father of the current Republican presidential primary hopeful, Donald J. Trump.[29]

There had been a great deal of reportage as early as the 1970s that the
real estate empire of Fred Trump had been built unscrupulously. The elder
Trump had not only been investigated in 1954 for "profiteering off of public contracts" in his construction of public housing, but for employing
racially discriminatory practices in the leasing of units. Civil rights cases
would bring Trump's company under investigation by the US Justice
Department due to such allegations of racial bias.[30] What wasn't as well-
known was that in the years 1950–52, Fred Trump was landlord of the
Guthrie family's small apartment in Beach Haven. The recently discovered
writings demonstrated Woody displayed little goodwill to his landlord, cas-
tigating Fred Trump in such works as "Beach Haven Ain't My Home,"
"Racial Hate at Beach Haven," "Trump Made a Tramp Out of Me," and
"Beach Haven Race Hate."

Kaufman's original essay—published online 21 January 2016—was
picked up by newspapers and social media outlets and Woody was—again,
a half-century after his passing—a central figure in yet another political
imbroglio. With the presidential primary races picking up steam and rhe-
toric ratcheting, Arlo Guthrie acknowledged being approached to record
his father's damning "Old Man Trump." He chose not to, suggesting it

might be best "somebody else do it." His reason for not recording the song was personal, not political. "I've been attacked in my life by people who say, 'You're just like your father, you're no good.' I know what that's like. If there are things I don't like about Trump, I'll tell you. But I don't want to do a guilt-by-association thing. I think that's generally wrong. And the difference between right and wrong is important to me."[31]

When Donald Trump was elected to the presidency in November of 2016, Guthrie said much the same. But he was now less reticent to speak his mind. "There's enough not to like about Trump without resorting to guilt by association," he said. "This is America and everyone deserves a chance to be judged on their own merit. I personally think the idea of democracy has a lot of merit. So anyone who promotes or encourages some other form of government, whether it be far right or far left, is probably not hanging out with me. Present administration included."[32]

Though some saw Guthrie's views as those of an iconoclast, others saw the folk singer's libertarian-style musings as one more example of his dimming radicalism. In an essay appearing on a Socialist Workers website, the editor of *Red Wedge* even castigated Guthrie for singing "This Land Is Your Land" at Macy's Thanksgiving Day Parade. "Arlo has made his peace with the system the way his father could never stomach," the pundit bellyached."[33] The rebuke was a bit of a stretch, the ideologue managing to gloss over Guthrie's unblemished half-century of political and humanitarian benefit work.

For a half-century Guthrie donated time and talent to assist a myriad of political and social causes: antiwar resistance, the Black Panther Party, for Cesar Chavez's United Farm Workers, for antinuclear and antifracking causes, for pro-environmental groups, for community outreach programs, for local foodbanks, for unions, for striking workers, for veterans, for those suffering poverty and illness. If the *Red Wedge* editor had a better sense of history, he might have noted even a lifelong radical like Pete Seeger reminded audiences "history is made of steps and stages."[34] Seeger often prefaced the old spiritual "Jacob's Ladder" with the observation, "I decided that one of my disagreements with both religious people and revolutionary people, is that they think that everything is gonna happen in one big bang."[35]

The charge Arlo Guthrie was in some way a traitor to his father's legacy was ridiculous. It was no secret to anyone who admired Guthrie's music that the folk singer was consistently wary of authoritarianism regardless of political stripe. As early as 2003, Guthrie told readers of the *Rolling Blunder Review,* "The Democratic Party has many able candidates. What we need are some more good Republicans. There doesn't seem to be enough of those."[36] He didn't go so far in 2003 to suggest he might *register* as a Republican. Guthrie's very occasional endorsement of GOP moderates was his attempt to wrestle the party away from noisy far-right adherents.

Guthrie's politics were made public in July of 2009 when, in an interview with the *New York Times,* he made a more conclusive statement. "I became a registered Republican about five or six years ago, because to have a successful democracy you have to have at least two parties, and one of them was failing miserably. We had enough good Democrats. We needed a few more good Republicans. We needed a loyal opposition."[37] Not surprisingly, a media storm broke. Every editorial writer in the country seemed compelled to pontificate on Guthrie's dalliance with Republican politics.

Conservative pundits, in particular, filled editorials with comments ranging from mild amusement to outright gloating. Two of the more prominent conservative voices heard were those of George Will and Ronald Radosh. Discussing Texas congressman Ron Paul's *End the Fed* tome, George Will noted the book had been endorsed by Arlo Guthrie, "the son of a famous father—Woody Guthrie, the Depression-era composer and singer of leftist songs." At least Will's essay ended with his asking "Has American politics ever been this entertaining?"[38] Radosh's reaction was more mocking in tone. He congratulated Guthrie for courage "in telling the world about your political affiliation." But he ridiculed, "Should you prepare for some contentious moments during your next concert with Pete Seeger?"[39]

In truth, news of Guthrie's brush with Republicanism shouldn't have been surprising. A year earlier Guthrie had backed the candidacy of Ron Paul (R-Texas) in the 2008 Republican presidential primary. Hoping to sway voters to an agenda of less intrusive government, Paul had run as the Libertarian Party candidate some twenty years earlier, garnering some 431,000 votes. In a press release supporting Paul's 2008 candidacy, Guthrie offered, "I love this guy. Dr. Paul is the only candidate I know of who would have signed the Constitution of the United States had he been there. I'm with him, because he seems to be the only candidate who actually believes it has as much relevance today as it did a couple of hundred years ago. I look forward to the day when we can work out the differences we have with the same revolutionary vision and enthusiasm that is our American legacy."[40]

One of Paul's targets was the Federal Reserve. He suggested the reserve was an illegal institution since it was "not authorized in the Constitution." Paul also considered the reserve "immoral, because we have delivered to a secretive body the privilege of creating money out of thin air; if you or I did it, we'd be called counterfeiters." In his book of 2010, *End the Fed,* Paul outlined how the Federal Reserve corrupted American democracy. It was a study that caught the attention of many, including Guthrie. The folk singer would endorse the book, his blurb reading, "Rarely has a single book not only challenged, but decisively changed my mind."[41]

Guthrie didn't address his support of Paul or any personal politics on the concert stage. Anyone attending his concerts wouldn't sit through any soapbox sermonizing. His programs were, as always, an evening of great folk-rock music, interspersed with shaggy-dog storytelling and Will Rogers–like humorous commentaries on matters concerning "anti-stupidity." But as the outcries over Guthrie's alleged political shift raged on social media platforms—even on the fan-based arlo.net forums—the folk singer chose to seriously ruminate on a number of sensitive topics. On 21 July 2009, Guthrie published his online essay, "2 Cups of Coffee or My Two Cents":

> I haven't been home very much—yet. But that will change now that we're getting into the heart of summertime. I've been getting quite a few responses to the posts here at arlo.net concerning various subjects. I've been thinking it would be a good idea to further the conversation. There's controversy surrounding just about everything going on these days. And although I think discussing difficult subjects is good for the soul, I constantly have to remind myself that it ain't all there is.
>
> For example, about five or six years ago I left the Democratic Party and joined the Republican Party. I did so because I believed that my voice (and others like mine) needed to be heard where it would be most useful. Frankly, I still don't believe there's a whole lot of difference between the two. But a healthy democracy needs a loyal and healthy opposition. Without it we run the risk of a march toward totalitarianism that would be difficult to halt.

At the time, the Republicans were in power everywhere and they were seemingly taken over by ideas that ran counter to traditional Republican positions. They used to be for less big government intrusion into our lives. To me that's usually always a good idea.

So what was up with interfering in matters of who can marry who? That's a big invasion into personal freedoms and liberties. Those who try to control our personal lives are not only not for traditional Republican values; they're not even really for American values. The way I view it, the state has no business in the house let alone the bedroom. The way I would resolve the current controversy would be to insure that secular marriage be open to anyone. And that religious marriage not be infringed upon by the state—to marry or not as their traditions permit. Both religious and secular marriages would be acknowledged as it is now. That, to me, should be the Republican position.

What's up with the bail-outs, etc.? I hate to say it but the arguments in Congress and on TV miss the more important points. Talking heads and political animals arguing about how much to spend and where are not talking about the basic truth—that when more dollars get printed, the less each dollar is worth. With trillions of dollars being manufactured to pay for bail-outs and other tasks, each dollar buys less stuff. Not only have we given gazillionaires our tax dollars; we've made each dollar we still possess just about worthless. Saving and creating jobs may be an appropriate government intrusion in extraordinary times, but to do so in a way that makes our money worthless benefits no one in the long and endangers the nation. A return to real money—where the value is not up for discussion is the only protection a wage earner really has. That, to me, should be the Republican position.

What's up with rebuilding infrastructure? The best way to insure we'll have a 20th-century transportation system in the 21st century is to rebuild the existing infrastructure. I thought by now we'd be flying around in personal (automobile-size) vehicles. There's no reason we can't be building vehicles that use magnetic fields for flight and navigation . . . okay maybe I'm getting ahead of things. The point is that it seems easier to get to the freaking moon than it does to get from coast to coast. Who's thinking about that stuff? Constantly widening roads and bridges that devour the land with all the intersecting attributes of the same chains of crappola shops and fast (nutritionally worthless genetically modified and just plain bad) food restaurants can't be the next best hope for our nation's infrastructure. That, to me, should be a Republican concern.

What's up with health care? In a world where even the good guys (National Public Radio, Farm Aid, etc.) are sponsored and funded by organizations more powerful than any nation, it's hard to imagine that the bottom line will not be what's profitable, instead of what is beneficial. Can the two coexist? Sure. Do they? No. The sad truth looks to be that it's more profitable to have a nation filled with people who are in bad health, than a nation of healthy people. The current administration and the Congress have been talking about how to make health care accessible to everyone, because they all know that these multinational organizations will be more than happy to provide long-term drugs and services to a nation that permits and even encourages bad health whether or not a new health care plan comes into being. It's a win-win for government, insurance companies, pharmaceutical companies, hospitals, doctors, lawyers, and agriculture. Only you lose.

The march has already begun around the world to outlaw the use of natural medicines—vitamins, minerals, herbs, and other plants so that you will become a criminal and a lawbreaker when you try to care for your own family in your own way. You are no longer responsible for yourself or your family, as the state has in no uncertain terms made it clear that you belong to the nation, and the nation has every right to protect you and your family from yourselves—the child in the Midwest with cancer forced to undergo chemo and radiation being only the latest example. Is this not a cause for some loyal opposition? Where the hell are these guys when you need them? It's not a matter of being right or wrong. I've been both many times. It's a matter of having a real contest of ideas between different opinions. Sadly the Republican voice has drifted off to Neverland, while the larger issues of what health care actually is gets run over by arguments of how and who will pay for it.

I want government and big business out of my garden. I want insurance companies out of my way when I go visit my doc. I want to pilot my cool 21st-century flying electromagnetic car. I want real money. And I want to get out of the business of being in politics in either party. But someone has to say something. And these are just a few of the things I think need to be said. There's more . . . wars, interventions, useless government agencies, education policies, privacy issues, an end to criminalization of personal-choice things . . . all kinds of stuff.

Granted I've had two cups of coffee this morning, so I've gone on longer than I should have. And like I noted above, I don't expect to be right on anything. I'm perfectly capable of listening to a good argument and changing my mind. I'm not a piece of stone. Please feel free to take issue with me on anything—I enjoy changing my mind. I just wouldn't expect anything beyond a good friendly listen. There's more to this world than getting involved, but there's times you just feel like you have to do something, say something or be somebody—however uncalled for. There is, in my view, a larger, bigger picture where we are all stuck on some little tiny world in a very big universe of unimaginable largeness. Like ants figuring out which way back to the ant hill, our journeys however big they may seem to us, are small in the big picture of things.

That's no excuse not to get back to the hill. . . . An ant's gotta do what an ant's gotta do. Keeping the big picture in mind, knowing there's more to life than arguing about everything, but maintaining the basic nature of a free and democratic nation, taking care of each other in ways that encourage security, prosperity, and tranquility—Freedom, Liberty, Justice—You know, all the good stuff, these are worth talking about. I'll go on talking and thinking about these things wherever I think they need to be heard, even though I know full well they won't be inviting me to any clambakes or anything. Good thing I got my own clams . . . adg

Politics was not the only "big picture" issue to contend with in the first months of 2009:

AG: Marti flew back to Woodstock mid-March to resume her work as owner-operator of The Wild Rose Inn. I flew out to Arizona from the CrabHouse on March 30th. On April 1, 2016, I had a gig in Mesa. In the parking lot the morning before that evening's show, I was talking to Lynn (our bus driver) and a couple of others when I suddenly got very dizzy and my vision had become odd. I was seeing three of everything, and it was like looking through a moving kaleidoscope. I laid on my bed in the tour bus for about five or ten minutes until the dizziness passed. I thought nothing of it except how unexpectedly odd it was. We did the gig that night and everything went great. The same was true for all the following shows. Except that I had a persistent headache. Nothing that would keep me from doing the gigs, but annoying.

We left Mesa the next day and headed to Carpinteria, California, where we had about five days off before a show in Santa Barbara coming up. Marti, back in Woodstock, had arranged for her sister, Lisa (who was now living in Los Angeles) to check me out medically as the headache had been persistent for a few months. It was unusual and I hadn't been prone to headaches in the past. So Lisa drove up from LA and met me in Carpinteria where we were staying.

Lisa contacted a local clinic and scheduled some tests to be done while I had the time between shows. After a battery of tests it was determined that I had suffered a minor (mini) stroke in Mesa the week before. It was evident in the scans. They also told me that the headache was related to that experience and would wear off on its own. There was nothing further to do about it.

I asked Marti if she could get away from work and join me on the road. I needed help and someone I could trust to be there if things got serious. She met us in Palo Alto after the gig there at the Bing Concert Hall—Stanford University. She remained with me until May 11th in South Orange, New Jersey, when the tour officially concluded. Performing arts venues generally schedule their events from June through the following May. That's why their schedules usually say 2016–2017 season. They don't go by calendar-year dates. So it made sense for us to end the tour in May. That way we could plan another tour any time after June.

That same summer, Guthrie learned the writer Thomas Steinbeck, son of famed novelist John Steinbeck, had passed away on 11 August, age seventy-two, at his home in Santa Barbara. The lives of the Steinbeck and Guthrie families were forever intertwined due to their fathers' mutual chronicling of the dust bowl and migrant experience of Depression-era America. The friendship was sparked when Woody was introduced to John Steinbeck by the actor Will Geer in Los Angeles.[42] When Steinbeck first heard Guthrie's recording of "Tom Joad," Geer recalled Steinbeck's mock-anger that in his seventeen verses Woody managed to condense *The Grapes of Wrath* "story in just a few stanzas."[43]

The connection between the Steinbeck and Guthrie families outlasted the passing of the fathers. "Thom was friend and family," Guthrie noted. The folk singer wasn't merely speaking in metaphysical terms. Steinbeck was now *actual* family since Sarah Lee's husband, Johnny Irion, happened to be a grand-nephew of John Steinbeck. Though Guthrie conceded that while he and Thomas had very "different life experiences, we shared many things." They were both sons of "famous fathers whose line of work we continued."[44]

Only a few years earlier Steinbeck and Guthrie had visited several of the migrant camps their fathers passed through decades earlier. It was such visits in the 1930s that had inspired their fathers to tell the stories of the farmworkers and dispossessed Dust Bowl refugees. In 2000, Thomas and Arlo appeared on a television program examining *The Grapes of Wrath*. The idea behind that visit was to take a few photographs for their respective family scrapbooks, while filming the TV segment. Guthrie couldn't recall exactly which camp they had visited. He believed it was Weedpatch Camp, just south of Bakersfield, as that camp was the WPA era setting of Steinbeck's novel.[45] But their unannounced arrival—with a camera crew in tow—set off an unintentional exodus. Guthrie later told the *Bakersfield Californian*:

> As we pull up, there's some folks standing out there. They see these big cars coming with all the cameras—and they're fleeing! And I got out and said, "No, no, we're not the government." And I'm trying to explain in my Spanish, which isn't too good. I showed them the pictures, and [told] 'em, "That's my papa, and he was here then." Well, word went around and all these people came back, and they've got us signing pictures and everything. After we were done they brought us—I had never seen anything like this—they brought us a totally different fruit. The best, biggest, juiciest grapes I had ever tasted. Here are these hard-working people

living under these conditions, fine people, treating us to this wonderful thing. And we ate those grapes for weeks. I've been in the
fanciest, most uppity places in New York and they don't have anything on those folks.[46]

One month following Steinbeck's passing, Fred Hellerman, the former
Weaver and producer of Guthrie's first two LPs for Reprise, passed on 1
September 2016, age eighty-nine. Though Guthrie loved Hellerman, he
remained ambivalent over the recording of his two earliest albums. Though
the first, *Alice's Restaurant*, brought him his greatest commercial success—
Guthrie conceding Hellerman "actually did a lot of work" on both records—
the resulting albums were stripped-down musical affairs. Guthrie believed
neither Fred nor Harold Leventhal had "the sensitivity to what the songs
could have been."[47] Both men were contemporaries of Woody and Pete—
and mostly disinterested in rock 'n' roll and contemporary pop music.

AG: September 20th Marti Ladd moved in with me at the CrabHouse,
after selling The Wild Rose Inn, in Woodstock, New York. Our next big
tour, however, didn't begin until October, when we began our "Running
Down the Road Tour." For this tour I thought it would be great if we
could recruit some of the Shenandoah veterans—Steve and Carol
Ide, as well as Terry Hall. It began October 21st in York, Pennsylvania, at
the Strand-Capitol Performing Arts Center, and continued through the
next five weeks ending at Carnegie Hall.

The Running Down the Road tour wasn't initially designed to celebrate
the singer's 1969 album of the same title. The name had been appropri-
ated from a scheduled but doomed fundraising cross-country motorcycle
tour. "Unfortunately the bike thing never happened," Guthrie offered,
"but we had already named the tour Running Down the Road and had
begun accepting the gigs. We were stuck with the tour name, so we shifted
to focusing on the album of the same name."[48]

Guthrie was also beginning to hint that his days as a *studio* recording
artist were likely over. Many of Guthrie's original songs, post-*Someday*, made
their first appearances on the series of live recordings comprising the bulk
of his post-1990s discography. Guthrie's mentor, Ramblin' Jack Elliott, once
expressed his disinterest in the studio albums he recorded, sighing "I've
often wished that I could just record more of my shows."[49] In Elliott's view,

the stage was where the magic happened. Guthrie's vision seemed to now align with Elliott's.

Even at the beginning of his career, Guthrie expressed dissatisfaction with his earliest recordings. Writing in *This Is the Arlo Guthrie Book*, his song folio of 1969, he mused, "Maybe I would spend some time re-writing most of the songs and most positively re-record all of them."[50] Now, a half-century later, Guthrie volunteered, "I don't know if I'll make a studio album again. I prefer recording things live and in person. I got over making studio recordings when they began bringing in pitch control and other technologies that essentially took the artistic expression of a real human and substituted technology for talent and experience."[51]

Though the possible absence of future studio albums was disappointing to some, there was an upside. Fans were now routinely treated to full-length recordings documenting such sorties as the Journey On tour of 2010–11, the Here Comes the Kid(s) tour of 2013, and the Alice's Restaurant 50th Anniversary tour of 2015–16. The latter tour, captured on film by documentarian Jim Brown, was broadcast by PBS as the 2015 Thanksgiving holiday approached. The ninety-eight-minute-long program was later issued on Blu-ray and, in an extended version, as a two-CD set by Rising Son in 2016. Annie Guthrie also helped out PBS's fundraising campaign by compiling a wonderful two-CD retrospective of her father's career, offered as a premium to pledge drive supporters. That set, *Arlo Guthrie: The First 50 Years (Exceptin' Alice)*, was handsomely designed and packaged in a hardcover foldout book. The collection not only featured notes on each song, but also rare family photographs, original lyric sheets, and a handful of previously unreleased tracks.

On 20 January 2017, Donald J. Trump was sworn in as the 45th president of the United States, and his agenda was not terribly progressive. Within the first two weeks of taking office, Trump approved construction of the environmentally devastating Keystone XL and Dakota Access pipelines, ordered the building of a border wall between Mexico and the US, signed an executive order to prohibit citizens of seven Muslim-majority countries to travel to the US, nominated a conservative judge to fill the Supreme Court seat of liberal Antonin Scalia, made steps to repeal Obamacare, and suggested any criticism of his actions was "fake news." It was clear the elasticity of American democracy was going to be tested. Nine days following the inauguration, Guthrie was due back on the road.

AG: The Running Down the Road Tour picked up the next leg January 29th in Ft. Pierce, Florida, at the Sunrise Theater. That leg ended in Atlanta at the Woodruff Center February 26th. I decided to take March off with the exception of doing a couple of shows with my old friend, Taj Mahal. They were fun, just the two of us. One night Taj opened, the next I opened. It was friendly and we both had a lot of fun.

On 30 March, Guthrie consented to a telephone interview with the San Diego *Times-Union*. Guthrie was soon to visit the city on his West Coast swing. The writer was interested in getting the folk singer's assessment of the current American political scene—and on the country's swing rightward. "I think Nixon did some really stupid things," Guthrie mused, "but he also did some really smart things. We'll wait and see if the current administration comes up with the equivalent of something smart. It seems to be taking a little longer than some would hope."[52]

Guthrie wasn't excusing Nixon's politics of paranoia. The folk singer often joked that he *missed* Nixon and Spiro Agnew—if nothing else, they were both great foils for satire. Guthrie described Nixon as someone "who tried to fool *all* of the people *some* of the time." In contrast, Guthrie saw Donald Trump as someone with the ability to fool "*some* of the people *all* of the time." "There's a slight difference, and maybe it's an important difference," Guthrie opined, "but it doesn't work out well under either circumstance."[53] The recent Trump-led crusade against immigrants—most drawn to the US to escape poverty and repression back home—prompted Guthrie to resurrect his father's "Deportee (Plane Wreck at Los Gatos)." Due to the recent changes in political winds, Guthrie felt it was "an important song to add to our set list." Suddenly, in this era of Trump, the loss of Pete Seeger was more deeply grieved.

AG: Marti and I picked up the "Running" tour by way of flying to Tulsa, where we met the bus that would haul us to Solana Beach, California, at the Belly Up Tavern. While in Tulsa we visited the Woody Guthrie Center as they were preparing a Pete Seeger exhibit. I got to tune Pete's banjo for them. Pete had a unique sound that was in large part due to the banjo he played.

It originally had a lignum vitae neck that Pete had carved himself. The banjo was notable because of the extra length of the neck itself; no amount of tension from the strings would cause it to warp. But it was very heavy as the wood is known to be one of the more dense woods in existence. He eventually had another lighter neck made, and the extra length became known around the world as the Pete Seeger Long Neck Banjo. It also required special long-length strings that Pete had made for him. But the uniqueness of the sound had as much to do with how he played it. To anyone knowledgeable on the subject, all you had to hear was one plunk of one note, and you'd know it was Pete. Like Olatunji, Pete was a master.

As I played his banjo in the Woody Guthrie Center, in a back room off the exhibit hall, I had tears in my eyes. I dearly missed my old friend.

Was music alone enough to combat reactionary politics? Guthrie once enthused, "Folk music has always been the original social media," but it was becoming evident that songs were now a less effective tool for communication.[54] It was Guthrie's belief that in earlier times, "music was the cultural medium. It carried the ideas of a generation and passed them along. There are so many other ways of communicating now, so many other ways to reach into the world. The Internet has replaced popular music as the great voice of enlightenment and encouragement. The problem is that there are so many messages out there and no way yet to organize honest, organic dissent, the way Pete could do during the union marches in the 1940s and '50s when he conveyed powerful ideas and the history behind them just by singing in the street, walking along and picking his banjo. You can't expect every generation to learn from the past. But you can give directions to the well—and when people get thirsty enough, they'll drink."[55]

The simple truth was folk music had been sidelined as a prominent force in popular music. Protest music was no longer the sole property of folk singers brandishing acoustic guitars and 5-string banjos. Though singer-songwriters and acoustic performers continued to slip in and out of pop music favor, relatively few breakthrough artists held deep roots in traditional music-making. Guthrie slyly rebuked such deeply personal and introspective songwriting as "Songs in the Key of Me." Guthrie sighed that Seeger-style song-leading was simply "too Kum-Ba-Yah" for songwriters of the new millennium. Many tried to burnish their credentials by name-checking Woody, Cisco, Pete, and Lead Belly as influences. It was fashionable—perhaps even expected—for them to do so. But very few could recite a single verse of "Ludlow Massacre" or "Bourgeois Blues" if challenged.

It was the way of the world—and there was nothing anyone could really do about it. Except for a period in the early to mid-1960s, when the "folk boom" was all the rage and advertisers paid for pricey full-page spreads to sell their goods to a mostly youthful market, *Sing Out!*—the bible of US folkniks since 1950—was in constant financial struggle. The journal survived McCarthyism, political infighting, and the passing of public interest in folk music, but it couldn't outrun the clock. The magazine published its final issue in the spring of 2014. Guthrie had seen the signposts. He recalled the exact moment when he realized the times, as the song promised, had changed: "When people meet me for the first time and ask who I am—and they often do—I say, 'Woody Guthrie's son.' The next question is inevitably, 'Who's Woody Guthrie?' and I say, 'The guy Bob Dylan loved so much.' Then they want to know who Bob Dylan is."[56]

AG: From Tulsa we drove west, stopping along the way at some of my favorite places. The most notable was a funny little place just inside the boundary of Gallup, New Mexico. The El Rancho Hotel has the best corn tortilla enchiladas as far as I'm concerned. So we'd stop and eat, and sometimes even stay, at what appears to be an outdated tourist trap with gaudy advertising and very old rooms. But I loved it. Almost none of my friends, bandmates, or acquaintances shared my assessment of the place, but sometimes it's good to be the boss.

On May 19th the Running Down the Road tour ended in Lincoln, Nebraska, at the Rococo Theater. The crew bus took the band and crew back to Massachusetts, but I had one more show to do in Nashville—a performance at the Schermerhorn Symphony Center with the Nashville Symphony Orchestra, John Nardolillo conducting. I spent a few days off in Nashville awaiting the day of show. John and I reprised our "American Scrapbook" show and it was well received.

There were only a few things scheduled in June. One was a fundraiser for a film that had been made about the wonderful Chilean folksinger, Victor Jara, whose life I had recorded in song decades earlier. Peter Yarrow and I had agreed to do a concert that would make funds available to the filmmakers. It was a worthy project.

After the concert, Marti and I drove to Old Forge, New York, which was nearby a summer camp I had attended when I was a kid. Raquette Lake Camps (one for boys and one for girls) was located not far from Old

Forge. I met my sister Nora and her husband Michael and together the four of us visited Raquette Lake. [It being] June, the camps were preparing for the campers to begin showing up in a few weeks. It was nice walking around without the campers there, seeing how much had and hadn't changed. Nora found photos of us kids on the walls in typical camp photos. It brought back a lot of happy memories.

On July 12th the plan was for Marti to drop me off at the airport in Albany. I'd head to Okemah for Woody Fest, while she would take the car and visit her son still living in Woodstock. We'd both meet up upon my return. As I was going through the security check I realized I still had my car keys in my pocket. I called Marti and told her, "Don't turn the car off!" I explained that once she turned it off she'd need a key to restart it—the one I had. So she had to drive all the way back to The Farm, where I had a spare key on my desk.

July 18th we began to demolish the oldest part of The Farm, our living room. The memories of years came flooding back as the big machines tore into the old structure and ripped away the years where we watched the kids grow up, where we had our celebrations and spent the holidays. But, it had to be done. It was falling down without any assistance and, but for our intervention, would have taken the rest of the house with it. So we separated the part that was going to stay from the section that had to be removed. We had a big blue tarp covering the side of the house to keep out the wind and rain, and protect the insulation on the inside. It looked awful, but it was only temporary.

On September 27th, we began the "Re: Generation Tour." Abe, Sarah Lee, Terry, and I had a number of gigs scheduled October through November, ending with a performance at Carnegie Hall November 25th.

In his Carnegie program notes Guthrie would write,

For me, folk music was the original social media, it's the way people used to communicate. Traveling musicians, going from town to town not only to entertain, but to educate. The music spoke truth to power, and it made us talk to each other. The guys that did the fashion, the ones in theater, the folks that did art, we all knew each other, we were all hanging out with each other. There was a spirit to the times. And there's a spirit thing going on now too. It's a heart thing. You feel like, "Oh man, I'm here and something's happening. That changes you. It changes the chemistry in your brain. It changes your heart. It changes everything."[57]

AG: From Carnegie Hall I left driving my Chevy Tahoe, pulling a trailer filled with band gear: everything we'd need when we picked up the tour again in late January when we would continue the tour in Key West, Florida. I was also lugging my motorcycle so I could ride around Florida in December and January—something that couldn't be done at home on The Farm during the winter.

Marti and I stayed at the CrabHouse through January, enjoying the weather, the time off, and the comforts of home. Toward the end of the month, we resumed time on the road and went to play in Key West. We picked up regular road trips on February 2nd as we had a gig in Orlando at the Plaza Live.

We were trying to schedule less and less shows consecutively: space them out a little more as my voice was tiring more easily. With Sarah Lee along, I had a way of not overdoing it, swapping songs as we were both onstage at the same time. I also needed more and more time off between legs of the tours. I was getting tired more often, and needed time to recuperate.

The Re: Generation Tour was well underway, and Marti had come along for most of it, just to help me out. All went well until I began to lose my voice after a particularly grueling week. Five shows in six days had taken its toll, and I had to cancel three sold-out nights in Berkeley at the Freight & Salvage. I hated having to cancel the gigs, as it went against every instinct I had as a professional. But I had no choice.

With the three days to recuperate, I was able to do the two more shows on the schedule before taking a scheduled break back in Moku-leia. Marti and I stayed for two weeks in my rental cottage just outside Haleiwa Town. I didn't want to go anywhere or do anything other than listen to the waves and look for whales that occasionally drifted by out near the horizon. I was back in paradise for a much-needed vacation, away from everyone and everything.

We resumed the "Re: Generation" tour on May 2nd in Grand Rapids, Minnesota, at the Reif Center. For a little over the first three weeks of May we continued touring, working our way back to The Farm. After our annual HD [Huntington's disease] walk, Marti and I flew down to the

CrabHouse on June 3rd. On the 20th I flew from the CrabHouse to Seattle to play a couple of nights in Bow, Washington, at the Skagit Resort Casino. And from there I flew up to Alaska for a couple of shows. After the gig in Anchorage, I flew to Honolulu and had about nine days to myself in Mokuleia, back in my favorite little place in the middle of the Pacific.

It kind of made sense, as we had about twelve days between the show in Anchorage and the next one in Jacksonville, Oregon, where the tour would begin again. I would have to fly six hours to get to Jacksonville from The Farm or from Mokuleia. No brainer.

Marti stayed at the CrabHouse during that time, believing all was well enough as I had friends and family along with me. She'd been working on her own house nearby the CrabHouse, redoing it inside and out. Making it much nicer than when she'd acquired it about a year before. Every day she'd be out landscaping and planting and, little by little, the barren knoll became a botanical garden filled with tropical trees, shrubs, and flowers. It was a magical transformation.

Not everything that June was as idyllic as the beautiful garden. In an article on the history of Woody's song "Deportee (Plane Wreck at Los Gatos)," an editorial writer for *Urban Milwaukee* suggested Arlo Guthrie "may no longer be in sync with the sympathies expressed" in the plaintive song due to his conversion to Republican politics. The problem was the writer simply didn't have his facts straight. Guthrie was no longer affiliated with the GOP, and he hadn't been for some time. His good-faith attempt to steer the Republican Party away from its far-right trajectory had clearly failed. In some ways the writer from *Urban Milwaukee* couldn't be blamed. Though the media made much of Guthrie's original political "conversion," his abandonment of the GOP didn't receive the same degree of reportage.

Writing to *Urban Milwaukee*, Guthrie tried to set the record straight:

> I left the party years ago and do not identify myself with either party these days. I strongly urge my fellow Americans to stop the current trend of guilt by association, and look beyond the party names and affiliations, and work for candidates whose policies are more closely aligned with their own, whatever they may be. . . .
>
> What irked me was someone saying that I was a Republican, as if that alone meant that someone like me was supportive of the current administration's policies on immigration. . . . That is

absurd. There are many individuals in both parties (and neither party) who strongly oppose this administration's policies, not just on immigration but a host of other issues.

I remain deeply rooted and connected to my father's work and have been throughout my life. I remain distrustful of authority as I have been for over sixty years. And I get ticked off when someone insinuates that belonging to either political party makes them complicit when loudmouth buffoons of either side of the aisle pretend to speak for anyone associated with them, while in fact they only speak for themselves. I've posted innumerable times on my websites and social media noting my concerns and sharing my thoughts. I don't pretend to be right all the time, and sometimes I've gone so far as to change my mind from time to time.[58]

AG: On October 2nd we played the first gig of our new tour, "Alice's Restaurant—Back By Popular Demand." It was a long name for a tour. But, essentially, the success of the first Alice 50 Tour had sold out many venues, leaving some people who wanted to go in the lurch. So we decided to bring it back—the lights, the video wall, the whole thing—but with a different set list so that those who'd already seen the earlier tour would find it different enough in most respects.

The band consisted of Abe, Terry, Steve, and Carol. Sarah Lee opened the shows for us, and joined us onstage near the end of the program. The show was actually popular, and not just in name. We had to continue the tour long past the usual wind-up in May and into the summer, keeping at it until November 19th. The tour took us across the country to everywhere that wanted it.

The tour officially ended at the Mahaiwe Theater, in Great Barrington, Massachusetts, on November 17th. It was a little unusual in the sense that we'd often played the Mahaiwe in preparation for our family shows at Carnegie Hall. However, the show in New York was going to be with The Weight Band and not with the entire clan as we'd been doing recently.

The Alice's Restaurant—Back By Popular Demand tour continued through the first three months of 2019, hitting nineteen cities in the US South in early winter before heading west in March for more dates in

California. The tour was so well received that Guthrie even brought a "scaled-back version" of the show to Australia in April. In May and June, the US leg continued, Guthrie and the band playing shows out west before returning to the northeast for the annual church benefits and a Pete Seeger tribute at the Egg in Albany, New York. A month following the Seeger concert, Guthrie was honored with a tribute of his own.

Though Woody Guthrie once composed a song titled "I'm Living in Coney Island Till I Die," things didn't turn out as planned. But Brooklyn would forever loom large in the hearts and minds of his children:

AG: In June my sister and I were invited to be the king and queen of the annual Coney Island Mermaid Parade. We jumped on it as we were actually from Coney Island. On June 20th, my sister had organized a small family reunion. My brother Joady flew in from California and all of our kids and grandkids were on hand. Nora led a guided tour of the parts of New York where my dad had spent time with friends like Pete Seeger, Lee Hays, and others. We spent a day roaming through my old haunts as well, even visiting the Bitter End where my old pictures and posters were still on the walls.

The parade itself was freaking great, and I don't use the term lightly. It was a gathering of two hundred and fifty thousand–plus freaky people, and Marti and I were thrilled to be among them. Marti had spent time as a set and costume designer in her youth, which became completely apparent as she had designed an outfit for herself that wowed the crowd. The "Mother of Pearl" outfit was deliciously teasing, but because she had also chosen to use two bubble guns (plastic guns that shoot out soap bubbles), the crowd almost unanimously named her "Bubbles" as she danced her way through the parade. She also designed and constructed an outfit for me that captured the spirit of the regal person I'd been asked to portray: King Neptune—King of the Mermaids.

Guthrie's summer schedule of 2019 was full and varied. There were several "Alice" gigs, a few solo shows, and, of course, the usual slate of outdoor festival appearances:

AG: On July 4th I performed a few songs with my friend Keith Lockhart and The Boston Pops at The Esplanade. On July 11th I flew from Albany to Tulsa to attend the Woody Guthrie Folk Festival in Okemah.

On the occasion of the fiftieth anniversary of the Woodstock Festival I decided the best thing to do was to return to the same place and do a free concert for anyone who decided to show up. I'd had great financial offers for other events celebrating the anniversary, but they weren't in the same place.

There was also an offer to perform at Bethel Woods, which was located [near] the original festival but built up on the hill, leaving the original site virtually untouched. I appreciated that, but I declined both offers in favor of doing a free event on the original site, if I could arrange to do so.

The various agents and promoters kicked my idea around, and eventually the folks at Bethel Woods agreed to build a stage on the original site and to provide sound and lights so that we could bring our idea to fruition.

Bethel Woods had already booked Santana and Ringo Starr and other performers at their amphitheater up on the hill. Our show was scheduled on the 15th—the actual anniversary of my first appearance—which in 2019 fell on a Thursday so it wouldn't have interfered with their big acts playing the weekend.

We arrived on the 15th to find that nothing had been built for us: there was no stage, no sound, or lights, just a vacant field. I was furious. I had promised folks reading social media and other outlets that I would be there and perform. But there was no way to do it. Not at the original site anyway.

Bethel Woods had constructed a stage that attached to their amphitheater and I was asked if I would perform there instead of what we'd agreed to. I had already declined a small fortune to play at their venue, so the only option they presented me with was playing at their venue for nothing.

They had also limited the crowd expected to five thousand. But to get those free tickets, you had to call and give them information so they could contact you and deliver the free tickets. It reeked of a scam. You could now expect email and phone call advertising for life if all you wanted to do was participate in the free fiftieth anniversary celebration. It was corporate BS as far as I was concerned.

I stood on the hill overlooking the original site and said a few words to the spirits of those who may have been there, if not visibly so. I grabbed a guitar and walked down the hill to where I'd been fifty years to the day and sang "The Times They Are a-Changin'." There were a few reporters there, some with cameras. But at least I got to keep my word. I sang on the original site fifty years later. Not one of the original performers was there with me. The times had changed indeed.

When we performed on the stage they'd designed up near the amphitheater, I noticed lots of seats were in front of the stage in a roped-off area. That area was set aside for the friends of Bethel Woods and Live Nation (who worked with Bethel Woods), so our crowd stood in back.

The sound system they provided didn't project the sound to those standing there. It was a system like you'd see in a small club, nothing built for an outdoor concert. We turned it up as far as it would go, and the sound barely reached beyond the empty seats in front of the stage. We did the show as best we could, and Live Nation/Bethel Woods were thankful—but I drove off leaving the area disgusted with them all.

After the Bethel Woods/Live Nation fiasco, I went to Tulsa, where the Woody Guthrie Center had created an Arlo Guthrie Exhibit. It took a lot of going through archival material, old clothing, photos, instruments, memorabilia, etc., but it was fun working with Deana McCloud and the folks at the center.

The center had created a series of Woody Guthrie awards that they were giving to artists who had proven their commitment to social justice through their performances and activism. They had wanted to honor me with the award, but I kept refusing, believing it would be a little too uncomfortable for me to receive an award from a center based on my father's name. But they are good folks and have continued to provide visitors with wonderful events and exhibitions. It's not easy to get to or from Tulsa. Not from The Farm anyway. I did a few shows in New England before returning to The Farm for some time off during September.

We had picked up the Back By Popular Demand tour in October and we ran with it until November 23rd for a show at the Mahaiwe Theater in Great Barrington. As had become customary, I invited the entire family to perform with me as preparation for the annual gig at Carnegie Hall.

The Mahaiwe show was completely sold out, as was the upcoming gig at Carnegie. We wanted to make it good. I had decided, about a year beforehand, that the tradition of shows at Carnegie would end in

2019, a little over fifty years since I first performed there in 1967. The show at the Mahaiwe was bittersweet for that reason, but it went over really well and everyone in the family and in the audience enjoyed it.

The drive home after the show was short, only forty-five minutes away. Marti had left the Farm November 5th and returned to the Crab-House. She planned to spend the Thanksgiving holiday with her family at her mother's home about three hours south of Sebastian.

Our tradition was that we would have a family-gathering Thanksgiving dinner on the day before the actual holiday. Then on Thanksgiving some of us could go over to the church and help out serving our free "Thanksgiving Dinner That Couldn't Be Beat" to anyone who showed up. There were usually a couple hundred folks that would gather at the church and I wanted to be there too.

Abe decorated my still-unfinished living room with Christmas lights, while Cathy, Annie, and Sarah Lee cooked. Lisa brought food from the Abe family house and we had a fabulous time initiating the new living room as we hadn't used it yet for anything. There was no heat, no finished walls, no lights—not much of anything but four walls and a roof. That was good enough. We celebrated Thanksgiving by candlelight.

The following day—Thanksgiving Day—I was driving to the church when I realized I'd needed to stop and put some fuel in the car. As I opened the car door at the fuel pump, the world began to spin and I had trouble getting the car fueled up. I barely got the nozzle back in place on the fuel pump, when I realized I couldn't go any farther. Despite the loss of equilibrium, I managed to get the car away from the pump and pulled over to the side of the gas station.

I called Abe and an ambulance came and took me to Berkshire Medical Center in Pittsfield. Abe came and got my car and Annie rushed to the hospital. By the time I got to the ER, the dizziness had passed and I was able to walk around normally. Nevertheless the hospital staff insisted on running a battery of tests and told me I wasn't going anywhere for a few days.

They didn't understand. It was Thanksgiving! And I had a sold-out gig—the last one—at Carnegie Hall, the most prestigious theater in the world. There was no way I was going to miss or have to cancel that show. So, the next morning, without waiting for any results from the doctors, I escaped. I got on a small bus we had rented and left for New

York on Friday with the entire family. We stayed at a hotel across the street from the venue, and the next day, Saturday, the 30th of November, we played our last show at Carnegie Hall.

It was a whirlwind emotional experience for everyone. The kids and their kids had virtually grown up with a tradition that began before they were born. They had all accompanied Jackie and me to all the shows I had done there. It was family, it was tradition, and it was ending.

In previous years with the family onstage I had assigned time for everyone to do something that would shine a light on them individually. But given the nature of this last event, I did most of the heavy lifting myself and just wanted everyone to be there to help out. The show was a complete success and we finished up a lifetime of work to a standing ovation. I left the stage satisfied.

On the following day, Sunday, I flew down to the CrabHouse, where Marti picked me up at the airport and drove me home. The routine of decades was finally behind me; it was done. I began to relax into days along the river.

On December 4th I woke up at the CrabHouse disoriented. I was struggling to walk in a straight line, instead lurching from side to side. I walked down the hall to Marti's room and woke her up, saying that something was wrong. Luckily, we had scheduled a doctor's appointment early that afternoon nearby. We went to keep the appointment. The doctor suggested, quite strongly, that I go and get checked out at the hospital in Vero Beach, about twenty minutes away.

That afternoon I checked myself into the Cleveland Clinic in Vero Beach and they ran me through a battery of tests. It turned out I had suffered a stroke sometime the night before while in my sleep. I felt a little disoriented, but otherwise fine—although I had obviously lost some balance and had to be helped into the room at the clinic. I stayed for three days and nights and was dying to get out of there. Finally they let me go, but only as far as the rehabilitation center across the street.

I entered the Encompass Rehabilitation Center on December 7th. Marti stayed by my side and kept everyone in the family updated, with texts, phone calls, and pictures. As I couldn't walk very well, I was given a wheelchair and had a nice room at Encompass.

Every day, I had a schedule of routines I was asked to perform— such as walking, at first with crutches but graduating to using a cane in the first day or so. I also had to practice getting in and out of cars, walking up and down stairs, counting marbles, all kinds of things you wouldn't normally think about. I really wanted to get out of there and begin testing my ability to play guitar. Finally on the 13th (six days later) they let me go home. Marti drove me back to the CrabHouse, and I was so thankful to have her there as I needed all the help I could get.

By the time the holidays rolled around, I was walking without a cane and playing the guitar, although some of the coordination and grip in my left hand was noticeably weaker. It was going to take some steady practice to regain some of the ability I had lost. Luckily, we had a full schedule of dates planned for 2020. I had about two months to prepare for the upcoming tour, so I began walking and playing guitar every day, trying to strengthen my grip and balance.

The scheduled new tour didn't have a name, it was just called "Arlo Guthrie with Folk Uke." My daughter Cathy and her singing partner, Amy Nelson, were going to open the shows for me. This would help make it easier on my voice so I would only have about an hour's worth of work every night. My voice wouldn't get too tired and raggedy.

Marti kept encouraging me to walk, play music, and have a good outlook. And it was working. Every day I would be a little stronger, a little more like my old self. It was going to take time, but I had the time, and for that I was thankful. I also continued to see doctors who were monitoring everything—excessively so.

We began showing the CrabHouse to prospective buyers during January. A few people came to look it over, mostly people who wanted me to be involved in their ideas of what it could be used for. I had some misgivings about selling it, but although there were some interesting offers, none were outright buyers. Marti dealt with them, keeping me out of the negotiations.

Finally the tour began on February 9th in Clearwater, Florida, at the Capitol Theater. We had the usual adjustments to make as with the beginning of any tour. But it all went smoothly. Having Cathy and Amy out with us was fun. And they adjusted their more explicit material for my audience.

While I was on the road, Marti negotiated a deal for the sale of the CrabHouse. It was straightforward, no strings attached. The prospective buyers had come and looked it over while Marti and I kept in touch by phone. They loved it and had no interest in me being connected. It was perfect.

In March 2020 we did ten shows together before the venues were all closed due to rising concerns of the Covid-19 pandemic. I returned to the CrabHouse for a planned break in the tour, not realizing that our last show in Pelham, Tennessee, at the Caverns would be my last live stage performance.

I signed the preliminary CrabHouse sale documents when I returned, and we moved forward with inspections and the like. Marti began organizing for the sale, arranging for movers, tag sales, and giving away all the stuff I'd collected over decades. There was a lot of packing to do and I was not much help but did what I could in letting go.

Our scheduled concert appearances at first were postponed, then rescheduled, then finally cancelled. It was a nightmare. And I realized the Church would also need financial assistance if it was going to survive the crisis. So I began recording a number of songs at the Crab-House for a Church fundraiser that would become available via the Internet. The Church's Troubadour series of concerts were the primary source of income. When it came to an abrupt end, I had to find other means to support the Church. With the help and contributions of friends online, the Church survived the pandemic.

April 2020: It was difficult. I had no instruments I was familiar with, no recording equipment, and I still wasn't strong enough to play guitar as I'd been accustomed. I had a Gibson J-200 which I kept at the CrabHouse. At first I tried using it for the little videos we'd be making. But without the right cables and microphones it didn't sound all that great through the recording process, even if it sounded fabulous in the room. I borrowed a Martin D-18 from my dear friend Swami Anjani Cirillo, and the recording went much more smoothly. The slight difference in the size of the fretboard was noticeably easier for me on the Martin.

Much of the house was filled with boxes in preparation for moving and was off-limits for filming. But with Marti's help we'd do a few songs every week even as she'd be emptying the CrabHouse of decades worth of stuff we'd collected. Toward the end of April, Abe drove a rental car down and picked up my truck with a trailer attached, taking a full load of stuff back up to The Farm.

On May 9th, I awoke with the old Stephen Foster song, "Hard Times Come Again No More," rolling around in my head. I had no idea where it came from, only that it was there. I sent an email to Jim Wilson, whose musical sensibilities I admired, and asked if he would be interested in doing an arrangement of the song for me to add vocals. He wrote back saying he would indeed be interested in doing something together.

I continued recording songs for the church benefit while Marti continued packing. And by mid-May we'd moved enough stuff to her house to move in. We set up everything at her home in Micco, just over the San Sebastian River from where the CrabHouse now stood empty. I signed the final papers May 18th and after thirty years the CrabHouse was no longer mine.

We stayed in Little Hollywood, a section of Micco where Marti had her home. Luckily it was available to move into. Marti had purchased the property after selling The Wild Rose Inn, in Woodstock. The idea was to have some kind of supplemental income, as she no longer operated a business.

The home was supposed to have had renters, but the pandemic had changed everything, and her rental agreements were voided. So it was available to us and we stayed for two weeks before my tour bus picked us both up and drove us to The Farm, just in time to meet the moving company that would unload the stuff from the CrabHouse. The contractors working on The Farm addition were putting the finishing touches on the house while we moved back.

On June 6th, Jim and I had finally had a working track to "Hard Times," and I added an audio/video track to Jim's wonderful arrangement. On June 9th, Marti arranged for landscapers to come and rebuild the landscape around the house that had been decimated by a few years of construction. She planted new trees and flowers and created a number of beautiful areas that had been neglected over the years.

On the 27th, I began a series of recordings with the band at the Church. Bruce Clapper, Abe, Terry, Steve and Carol, and I gathered to see if we could get some songs on video that we would use for an as-yet-unknown destination. In July, I continued recording on weekends at the Church with the band. On July 30th *Rolling Stone* magazine would spotlight the video of "Hard Times" on their official website. It was released to the general public the next day. That August, still isolated at

The Farm, I continued to record with the band at the Church on weekends. September 7th was the planned release of the Church benefit I'd
been working on for months. On October 4th we did a live Zoom concert, although it was mostly me commenting on older videos that we
shared with the public.

On October 19th I called my dear friend Judy Collins and members
of my band and crew, telling them that I was cancelling the shows that
had constantly been rescheduled. I let them know how much I'd loved
them and working with them over the years and decades, but it was
time to let it go. I was also not going to take any more offers for upcoming shows. The days of being a road warrior were over.

I informed the public through my social-media outlets the following
day on October 20th that I had, officially, retired.

Guthrie titled his retirement post "Gone Fishing." The essay recounted,
in very personal detail, the recent health and life issues that led him to
acknowledge touring was no longer a viable option. It was a difficult decision. For more than a half-century, Arlo Guthrie had spent ten months of
each calendar year on the road, behind a microphone, singing songs of
triumph and despair, of victory and loss, of anger and joy, of peace and
war, of good times and bad—all while keeping a sense of humor about the
surrounding madness. Most importantly, Guthrie would optimistically
remind people that better times were still ahead—no matter what the
doomsayers moaned. He offered, in closing:

> A folk singer's shelf life may be a lot longer than a dancer or an
> athlete, but at some point, unless you're incredibly fortunate or just
> plain whacko (either one or both) it's time to hang up the "Gone
> Fishing" sign. Going from town to town and doing stage shows,
> remaining on the road is no longer an option.
>
> I don't remember answering the question on the other side of
> that piece of paper when I was asked, "Kid! Have you rehabilitated
> yourself?" But the short answer is now clearly "No!" In fact, I hope
> to be a thorn in the side of a new administration pretty soon. Tom
> Paine once wrote "To argue with a man who has renounced the
> use . . . of reason, and whose philosophy consists in holding human-
> ity in contempt, is like administering medicine to the dead." In
> other words, you cannot and should not argue with people who

don't care, or hold the caring of others in contempt. A healthy suspicion of authority, left, right, or center has been the hallmark of my career since the beginning, and I will continue to poke fun at cultural, political, or personal absurdities as I see it. I'm actually looking forward to it.

I'm happy, healthy, and good to go, even if I'm not going anywhere. I've taken back 6–9 months that I used to spend on the road, and enjoying myself with Marti, my family, and friends. In short—Gone Fishing.

Coda

AG: At sixty-five years of age (in 2012) I began to notice slight changes in my voice which affected my performing. It took more concentrated energy to maintain my performances at the same levels as they'd been previously. Over the next decade I gradually did less shows, at first taking more time between tours. Then less shows on consecutive nights in an effort to recoup. Then less time onstage every night. I transposed songs, lowering the keys to suit my ability.

By 2018 I could no longer do four nights in a row, and had to reschedule already booked shows to accommodate that reality. To help I recruited my daughters Sarah Lee and Cathy for my performances to either open the shows or spend time with me onstage. It helped a great deal, but by March of 2020 I could only do about forty-five minutes before my voice gave out. Then the pandemic hit and I was off the road as venues shut down.

At the same time I had sold the CrabHouse in May of 2020 and Marti and I moved into her house nearby for a couple of weeks before heading back to The Farm for the summer. The result of the continuing pandemic was that we stayed at The Farm throughout the rest of the year. The Farm was isolated and a safe haven. Well, it was semi-isolated at first. The constant coming and going of family, staff, delivery trucks, and all the business associated with RSR was problematic.

Eventually I relocated my daughter Annie, who was the sole survivor at RSR, to the Church (about forty-five minutes away). And with that move, The Farm became more like it had been when I first moved there in 1969. The times had changed. The building which housed RSR at The

Farm was repurposed as a guesthouse, although my son, Abe, still keeps our recording studio going on the lower level.

In November of 2021, after retiring and enjoying myself in Marti's company, we decided to get married. We'd been together as a couple for nearly a decade, and our commitments to each other had provided us both with the experience to be sure of what we were getting into. We were formally married December 8, 2021, at a courthouse in Delray, Florida, about an hour and a half from our home in Sebastian.

After the courthouse ceremony we drove to a celebratory dinner we had scheduled. We were met there by Marti's mother, Barbara, her sister, Lisa, and brother, Michael, and her aunt. But on the way, my rent-a-car was T-boned by another car making an illegal turn. No one was injured but my rent-a-car was not drivable and had to be towed away.

We awaited the arrival of the authorities, while eating pizza on the street corner. Marti and I were rescued by her sister, and we drove the few blocks away to our matrimonial dinner. We had a wedding cake that was so large that Marti delivered slices of it to anyone at nearby tables who expressed an interest in sharing it with us. We drove home to Sebastian the following day without incident.

Each morning I awaken before dawn and watch the light of the sun expand across the sky. At my age that's about twenty-seven thousand times the sun has risen, and while I can't honestly say I've enjoyed them all, I've certainly enjoyed the vast majority. It has been a privilege and an honor to have shared that enjoyment with everyone.

NOTES

INTRODUCTION

1. Gussow, Mel. "Arlo: Kids Want to Be Free." *New York Times,* January 11, 1970, 81.
2. Gussow.
3. Dooly, Susy. "Arlo's No Imitation." *Akron Beacon Journal,* March 6, 1966, 128.
4. Kiersh, Edward. *Where Are You Now, Bo Diddley?* (Dolphin/Doubleday, Garden City, NY), 1986, 64.
5. Hillier, Tony. "Arlo and a Song Like Alice." *Rhythms,* May 2008, 45.
6. Guthrie, Arlo. Guthrie Theater, Minneapolis, MN, April 21, 1989 (audience recording).
7. Klein, Joe. *Woody Guthrie: A Life* (Alfred A. Knopf, New York), 1980, 442.
8. Miller, Edwin. "Spotlight: The Hollywood Scene." *Seventeen,* February 1969, 54.
9. Hillier, "Arlo and a Song Like Alice."
10. Miller, "Spotlight: The Hollywood Scene."
11. Kiersh, *Where Are You Now, Bo Diddley?,* 66.
12. Braudy, Susan. "As Arlo Guthrie Sees It . . . Kids Are Groovy. Adults Aren't." *New York Times Magazine,* April 27, 1969, SM56+.
13. Whitman, Arthur. "The Apotheosis of Woody's Kid." *Chicago Tribune Magazine,* November 10, 1968, 16.
14. Klein, Joe. "Notes on a Native Son." *Rolling Stone,* no. 234, March 10, 1977, 52.
15. Bent. "Hipsters Get a New Hero in Arlo Guthrie Who Pulls SRO $7,800 in N.Y. Debut." *Variety,* November 15, 1967, 61.
16. Guthrie, Nora. "No Brooklyn Accent for Arlo." In Michael W. Robbins, ed., *Brooklyn: A State of Mind* (Workman Publishing Co., New York), 2001, 12.
17. Miller, "Spotlight."
18. Parker, Jeff. "Woody's Arlo." *Newsday.* August 23, 1969, 1W.
19. Davidson, Sarah. "Arlo Guthrie." *Boston Globe Sunday Magazine,* June 9, 1968, 27.
20. Gorlick, Adam. "Guthrie Center: Alice's Old Church Now a Community Space, Music Hall." *Salt Lake Tribune,* May 26, 2002, H4.
21. DeYoung, Bill. "Son Sets Dad's Lyrics to Music." *Sun Sentinel* (Fort Lauderdale), December 29, 2004, 61.

22. Seawell, Mary Ann. "Gentle Arlo's World for People, Not Machines." *Washington Post*, August 9, 1968, C4.

23. "Guthrie Jun—Singing without Anger: The New Voice of Youth." *Daily Mail* (London, England), April 15, 1968, 8.

24. McBride, Charlie. "Here Comes the Kid: Arlo Remembers Woody." *Galway Advertiser*, August 23, 2012.

25. Guthrie, Arlo. Email correspondence with author, March 5, 2000.

26. Yorke, Ritchie. "Arlo Doesn't Measure Up To Publicity." *Times Colonist* (Victoria, BC), November 29, 1969, 8.

CHAPTER 1

1. "Sound Business: Studio Tracks." *Billboard* 93, no. 9, March 7, 1981, 57.

2. Henke, James. "Arlo Guthrie a Home State Hit." *Rolling Stone*, April 2, 1981, 56.

3. Arlo Guthrie. "Oughttabiography." Email attachment (revised final) to author, December 5, 2020.

4. White, Timothy. "Lenny & Mo: How 2 Execs Taught Bugs Bunny to Rock." *Billboard* 106, no. 46, November 12, 1994, 1, 107.

5. Guthrie, Arlo. "Oughttabiography." Email attachment (revised final) to author, December 5, 2020.

6. "Sound Business: Studio Tracks." *Billboard* 93, no. 10, March 14, 1981, 47–48.

7. Menta, Peter. "Spirit of the '60s—1980 Style." *Connecticut Music Magazine* 1, no.7, September 1981, 1, 19.

8. Henke. "Arlo Guthrie a Home State Hit."

9. Christgau, Robert. "Christgau's Consumer Guide." *Village Voice* 21, no. 44, November 1, 1976, 79.

10. Henke. "Arlo Guthrie a Home State Hit."

11. "Billboard Top LPs and Tape." *Billboard* 88, no. 44, October 30, 1976, 78, 80.

12. Schorman, Rob. "Guthrie Goes Top 40 on LP." *Oakland Tribune*, September 2, 1981, B5.

13. "Albums: Arlo Guthrie Power of Love." *Philadelphia Inquirer*, June 12, 1981, 32.

14. "Billboard's Top Single Picks." *Billboard* 93, no. 33, August 22, 1981, 63.

15. Schorman, Rob. "Versatile Guthrie Can Play It Slick, Too." *Courier-Post* (Cherry Hill, NJ), September 9, 1981, 21.

16. Berman, Leslie. "Riffs: Arlo Guthrie Off the Record." *Village Voice*, August 12, 1981, 58.

17. Coppage, Noel. "Arlo Guthrie" (review of *Power of Love*). *Stereo Review*, October 1981, 90.

18. Menta, Peter. "Spirit of the '60s—1980 Style." *Connecticut Music Magazine*, 19.

19. Humphries, Patrick. Albums: Arlo Guthrie, "Power of Love." *Melody Maker*, September 5, 1981, 19.

20. Bohen, Jim. "Shortcuts." *Daily Record* (Morristown, NJ), September 20, 1981, D4.

21. Lawson, Michael. "Harrison Album Far from Boring." *Leader-Post* (Regina, Saskatchewan), June 24, 1981, C12.

22. Lawson, Michael. "Harrison Album Far from Boring."

23. "Albums." *Philadelphia Inquirer,* June 12, 1981, 32.

24. Marsh, Dave. "Records." *Daily Times* (St. Cloud, MN), August 29, 1981, 14D.

25. Marsh, Dave. "Rolling Stone Random Notes: Arlo Falls on His Face—Rickie Lee Doesn't Help." *Tuscaloosa News,* September 4, 1981, 5.

26. "Records." *Morning Call* (Allentown, PA), September 5, 1981, 69.

27. Petty, Moira. "Music Stage: Top Names for Critic's Marathon." *Stage and Television Today,* April 9, 1981, 9.

28. Denselow, Robin. First Night: "Jajouta Benefit." *Guardian and Observer,* April 15, 1981, 11.

29. *Karussell,* Swiss television broadcast, June 24, 1981.

30. "Top LPs & Tape." *Billboard* 93, no. 27, July 11, 1981, 71.

31. Arlo Guthrie and Shenandoah, Ramapo College, Mahwah, NJ, April 25, 1981 (audience recording).

32. Pousner, Howard. "On the Road with Arlo Guthrie." *Atlanta Constitution,* November 7, 1981, D28.

33. Provick, Bill. "Guthrie's Folk Defies Pigeonholes." *Ottawa Citizen,* July 6, 1981, 46.

34. Provick.

35. Provick.

36. Sanderson, Vicky. "Huge Crowd Relaxes with Arlo and Pete." *Globe and Mail* (Toronto), July 8, 1981, 16.

37. Morse, Steve. "Like Old Times for Guthrie." *Boston Globe,* July 13, 1981, 31.

38. Associated Press. "Guthrie to Be Released from Canadian Hospital." *Eugene Register-Guard,* July 26, 1981, 20D.

39. Associated Press. "Guthrie to Be Released from Canadian Hospital."

40. Associated Press. "Arlo Guthrie Out of Hospital." *Ellwood City Ledger* (PA), July 27, 1981, 8.

41. United Press International. "Guthrie 'Massachusetts' Is Compromise Subject." *Berkshire Eagle* (Pittsfield, MA), April 2, 1981, 29.

42. Henke, James. "Arlo Guthrie a Home State Hit."

43. "Hit Song." *Democrat and Chronicle* (Rochester, NY), March 15, 1981, 3C.

44. Zisson, Stephen. "Massachusetts: A Song Made for a State?" *Boston Globe,* March 12, 1981, 23.

45. Cooper, Kenneth J. "State Song? Now Mass. Has 2." *Boston Globe,* August 8, 1981, 1.

46. Zebora, Jim. "Nice to Have You Back, Arlo." *Record-Journal* (Meridian, CT), August 15, 1981, A11.

47. Zebora.

48. Berman, Leslie. "Riffs: Arlo Guthrie Off the Record."

49. Berman.

50. Berman.

51. Leonard, John. "Private Lives." *New York Times,* December 6, 1978, C12.

52. Seeger, Pete. "Singalong Demonstration Concert: Sanders Theatre, Harvard Campus, Cambridge, Mass." Booklet for Folkways Record (FXM 36055), 1980.

53. Arlo Guthrie and Shenandoah, Westbury Music Fair, Westbury, Long Island, NY, August 5, 1981 (audience recording).

54. Arlo Guthrie and Shenandoah, Westbury Music Fair.

55. Arlo Guthrie and Shenandoah, Westbury Music Fair.

56. Krasilovsky, Peter. "Arlo Guthrie: Pier 84, New York." *Billboard,* September 5, 1981, 45.

57. Pousner, Howard. "On the Road with Arlo Guthrie."

58. Joyce, Mike. "Performing Arts: Arlo Guthrie." *Washington Post,* August 17, 1981, B13.

59. Pousner, Howard. "On the Road with Arlo Guthrie."

60. Pousner.

61. Pousner.

62. Pousner.

63. Cromelin, Richard. "Seeger, Guthrie Team for Success." *Los Angeles Times,* September 2, 1981, G2.

64. Perlo, Ellen and Victor. "He Sang of and for Us." *Daily World,* October 9, 1981, 13.

65. Perlo, Ellen and Victor.

66. "Arlo Guthrie Now a Disciple of St. Francis." *Tampa Bay Times,* October 9, 1981, 3A.

67. Ball, Judy. "On the Road with Arlo Guthrie." *St. Anthony Messenger,* February 1980, 18.

68. Associated Press. "Folksinger Gets Degree from Franciscan College." *Observer-Reporter* (Washington, PA), October 9, 1981, B7.

69. Associated Press. "Arlo Guthrie Sings His Appreciation." *Schenectady Gazette,* October 9, 1981, 11.

70. Associated Press. "Folksinger Gets Degree from Franciscan College."

71. Associated Press. "Folksinger Gets Degree from Franciscan College."

72. "People." *Home News,* January 8, 1982, 2.

73. Holden, Stephen. "Cabaret: Vintage Arlo Guthrie at Bottom Line." *New York Times,* January 29, 1982, C23.

74. Radcliffe Joe. "Talent in Action: Arlo Guthrie." *Billboard* 94, no. 7, February 20, 1982, 56.

75. Associated Press. "Democrats Celebrate FDR Anniversary." *Telegraph* (Nashua, NH), February 2, 1982, 15.

76. Rashbaum, Drew. "Arlo Guthrie's Concert Evoked Memories of '60s." *St. Petersburg Times,* February 12, 1982, 3D.

77. Cribb, Charla. "Arlo Served Up-to-Date 'Alice,' but Other Offerings Substandard." *Evening Independent* (St. Petersburg), February 11, 1982, 7B.

78. Rashbaum, Drew. "Arlo Guthrie's Concert Evoked Memories of '60s."

79. Kent, Bill. "Arlo Guthrie, Player of Time and Music and Older Memories." *Philadelphia Inquirer,* March 6, 1982, 4D.

80. Kent.

81. Guthrie, Arlo. *Pete Seeger & Arlo Guthrie: Precious Friend* (Warner Bros. 2BSK 3644), 1982.

82. "Billboard's Recommended LPs." *Billboard* 94, no. 8, February 27, 1982, 57.

83. Schorman, Rob. "A Real Folk Story with a Mixed Ending." *Courier-Post* (Cherry Hill, NJ), March 9, 1982, 6B.

84. Johnson, Ronna. "Records." *Boston Globe,* April 1, 1982, Cal. 6.

85. Lacey, Liam. "Inside the Sleeve: Pop." *Globe and Mail* (Toronto), March 6, 1982, A6.

86. Aregood, Rich. "Records." *Philadelphia Daily News,* March 5, 1982, 46.

87. Schorman, Rob. "A Real Folk Story with a Mixed Ending."

88. Johnson, Ronna. "Records."

89. Horing, Allan. "Records." *Rolling Stone,* May 27, 1982, 57.

90. Fisher, Marc. "America's Best-Loved Commie: Even a Radical Can Become a National Treasure—Just Ask Pete Seeger." *Washington Post,* December 4, 1994, G1.

91. Kass, Bryna. "The Hired Brains." *Daily World,* July 17, 1982, 7.

92. "Counterrevolution Day, Part II." *Workers Vanguard,* February 19, 1982, 5.

93. Breindel, Eric M. "The Stalinist Follies." *Commentary* 74, no. 4, October 1982, 46–49.

94. Cohen, Bob. "Pete Seeger's Sound of Social Action." *In These Times,* March 17, 1982, 13.

95. Cohen.

96. Hitchens, Christopher. "Poland and the US Left." *Spectator* (London), March 6, 1982, 13.

97. Mano, D. Keith. "The Gimlet Eye: Poland and the Left." *National Review,* April 2, 1982, 371–72.

98. Dunaway, David King. *How Can I Keep from Singing? Pete Seeger* (McGraw-Hill, New York), 1981, 297.

99. Seeger, Pete. *Where Have All the Flowers Gone? A Singer's Stories, Songs, Seeds, Robberies* (Sing Out! Corporation, Bethlehem, PA), 1993, 238.

100. Marine, Gene. "Guerilla Minstrel." *Rolling Stone,* April 13, 1972, 48.

101. McLaughlin, Jeff. "Why Guthrie Gets Involved." *Boston Globe,* October 9, 1982, 8.

102. LeSage, Paul. "Woody's Name Is Used; Guthrie Family Is Irked." *Berkshire Eagle,* July 8, 1992, 1, 9.

103. LeSage, Paul. "Woody's Name Is Used; Guthrie Family Is Irked."

104. Maniace, Len. "This Honor Is Guthrie's Honor." *Journal-News* (Rockland County, NY), September 18, 1997, B1, B3.

105. LeSage, Paul. "Woody's Name Is used; Guthrie Family Is Irked."

106. "Guthrie Now Talent Scout." *Times Recorder* (Zanesville, OH), July 13, 1982, 4B.

107. Attwood, Alan. "Last Night: Arlo Guthrie Still Seeking." *The Age* (Melbourne), November 23, 1982, 2.

108. Schechter, Davis. "Guthrie, Bromberg Hear Different Drummers." *Record-Journal* (Meridian, CT), July 16, 1982, 9, 11.
109. Deane, Barbara. "Health Films Get Dose of Creativity." *Los Angeles Times*, July 25, 1982, Cal. 26.
110. "Isaac Bashevis Singer to Chair National Yiddish Book Exchange." *New York Times*, December 24, 1981, 19.
111. Morse, Steve. "Is Arlo Guthrie Still the Same? *Boston Globe*, August 9, 1979, A10.
112. Lansky, Aaron. *Outwitting History: The Amazing Adventures of a Man Who Rescued a Million Yiddish Books.* (Algonquin Books, Chapel Hill, NC), 2004.
113. Tugend, Tom. "A Jewish Visit to Guthrie's Land." *Jewish Journal*, December 2, 2004.
114. "Raitt to Open Mt. Watatic Festival." *Boston Globe*, June 3, 1982, 57
115. Wilson, Susan. "Issues and Good Times at Mt. Watatic." *Boston Globe*, August 17, 1982, 36.
116. United Press International. "No Hometown Homage for Woody." *Democrat and Chronicle* (Rochester, NY), September 7, 1982, 2C.
117. United Press International. "No Hometown Homage for Woody."
118. Seeger, Pete, *Where Have All the Flowers Gone?* 144.
119. Stein, David Lewis. "Seeger and Guthrie Keepers of the Faith." *Toronto Star*, October 7, 1982, G3.
120. Lacey, Liam. "Folk Concert March past Tired Era." *Globe and Mail*, October 7, 1982, 27.
121. McLaughlin, Jeff. "Why Guthrie Gets Involved."
122. McLaughlin.
123. Dreifus, Claudia. "Arlo Guthrie." *The Progressive* 57, no. 2, February 1993.
124. Dreifus.
125. Healey, Dorothy, and Maurice Isserman. *Dorothy Healey Remembers: A Life in the American Communist Party.* (Oxford University Press, New York), 1990, 224.
126. Dreifus, Claudia. "Arlo Guthrie."
127. Dreifus.
128. Brown, Jim (director), *American Masters: Pete Seeger—The Power of Song.* (Live Nation DVD, PS-1053), 2007.
129. Seeger, Pete, Rob Rosenthal, and Sam Rosenthal, eds. *Pete Seeger: In His Own Words* (Paradigm Publishers, Boulder, CO), 2012, 187.
130. Landry, Peter. "Offstage Arlo Guthrie Is Different Man." *Burlington Free Press*, March 1, 1976, 6.
131. Hedgepeth, W. "The Successful Anarchist." *Look*, February 4, 1969, 64.
132. Landry, Peter. "Offstage Arlo Guthrie Is Different Man."
133. Braudy, Susan. "As Arlo Guthrie Sees It . . . Kids Are Groovy. Adults Aren't." *New York Times Magazine*, April 27, 1969, 57–59+.
134. Arlo Guthrie and Shenandoah, Orpheum Theatre, Boston, October 9, 1982 (audience recording).

135. Arlo Guthrie and Shenandoah, Orpheum Theatre, Boston, October 9, 1982.

136. Arlo Guthrie and Shenandoah, Orpheum Theatre, Boston, October 9, 1982.

137. "Boxscore." *Billboard* 94, no. 46, November 20, 1982, 52.

138. Pembroke, J. Garland. "Guthrie Updates His Style of Political Protest Songs." *Atlanta Constitution,* November 10, 1982, 8B.

139. "Waronker Named Prez of WB Label." *Variety,* November 10, 1982, 95, 96.

140. Tannenbaum, Rob. "Is There Life after Majors?" *Musician,* July 1, 1987, 27.

CHAPTER 2

1. Guthrie, Arlo. "Oughttabiography." Email attachment (revised final) to author, December 5, 2020.

2. "Marjorie Guthrie, Singer's Widow, 65." *New York Times,* March 14, 1983, D11.

3. Hilts, Philip J. "Scientists Find Genetic Pattern in Fatal Illness." *Hartford Courant,* November 9, 1983, A1B.

4. "Longplay Shorts." *Variety* 310, no. 13, April 27, 1983, 138.

5. Morris, Erin. "Studio Track." *Billboard* 95, no. 22, May 28, 1983, 40.

6. Quinlan, Joe. "Folksinger Is Gently Aging, but 'Alice's Restaurant' Is Back." *Telegraph,* October 17, 1983, 18.

7. Milward, John. "Folk Music Regroups for the '80s." *USA Today,* September 17, 1984.

8. Tannenbaum, Rob. "Is There Life after Majors?" *Musician,* July 1, 1987, 30.

9. Tannenbaum.

10. Guthrie, Arlo. "One Thing Concerning You." *Rolling Blunder Review,* no. 7, Spring 1988, 3.

11. Guthrie, Arlo. "One Thing Concerning You," 3.

12. Guthrie, Arlo. "One Thing Concerning You," 3.

13. Guthrie, Arlo. "One Thing Concerning You," 1.

14. Kirby, Martin. "Rock 'n Roll Group Rehearses Its Act—With Reservations." *Philadelphia Inquirer,* February 16, 1967, 69.

15. Watson, Doc. Notes to *Southbound* (Vanguard VRS-9213, 1966).

16. Guthrie, Arlo. "One Thing Concerning You."

17. Kirby, Martin. "Rock 'n Roll Group Rehearses Its Act—With Reservations."

18. Guthrie, Arlo. "One Thing Concerning You."

19. Guthrie, Arlo. "One Thing Concerning You."

20. Klein, Chuck, and Rachel Rubin. "We're Putting Up with Philadelphia." *Broadside* (Boston), March 1, 1967, 26.

21. Klein and Rubin.

22. "Fifth Annual Broadside Poll Results." *Broadside* (Boston), March 29, 1967, 4.

23. "Record Reviews." *Variety,* January 15, 1969, 70.

24. Kirby, Martin. "Rock 'n Roll Group Rehearses Its Act."

25. Kirby.

26. Kirby.

27. Guthrie, Arlo. "One Thing Concerning You."

28. "Random Notes." *Rolling Stone,* May 3, 1969, 4.
29. Guthrie, Arlo. "One Thing Concerning You."
30. Lass, Don. "Record Previews: Singing at the Top." *Asbury Park Press,* November 23, 1969, 10C.
31. Guthrie, Arlo. "One Thing Concerning You."
32. Guthrie, Arlo. "One Thing Concerning You."
33. Guthrie, Arlo. "One Thing Concerning You."
34. Jahn, Mike. "Love Tales Sung by Arlo Guthrie." *New York Times,* December 27, 1969, C14.
35. Guthrie, Arlo. "One Thing Concerning You."
36. Scoppa, Bud. "Records." *Rolling Stone,* July 18, 1974, 64.
37. Guthrie, Arlo. "One Thing Concerning You," 3.
38. Guthrie, Arlo. "One Thing Concerning You," 2.
39. Guthrie, Arlo. "One Thing Concerning You," 3.
40. Himes, Geoffrey. "Seeger and Guthrie: A Tradition Continues." *Baltimore Sun,* July 22, 1983, B1.
41. Himes.
42. Himes.
43. Himes.
44. Klein, Joe. *Woody Guthrie: A Life* (Alfred A. Knopf, New York), 1980, 160.
45. Vites, Pablo. "Ramblin' Jack Elliott." *On the Tracks,* Spring 1995, 27–29.
46. Lewis, Randy. "Woody—This Man Is Our Man." *Los Angeles Times,* March 3, 1984, Sec. V, p. 12.
47. Lewis, Randy. "Woody—This Man Is Our Man."
48. Arlo Guthrie interview with Bryant Gumbel. *Today Show,* NBC-TV, March 7, 1984.
49. *Woody Guthrie: Hard Travelin'* (MGM/UA Home Video MV/MB600884), 1986.
50. *Woody Guthrie: Hard Travelin'.*
51. Lewis, Randy. "Woody—This Man Is Our Man."
52. Lewis.
53. Lewis.
54. Lewis.
55. United Press International. "Oregon Dam Taping Site for Woody Guthrie Documentary." *Greenville News* (SC), October 11, 1983, 5B.
56. United Press International. "PBS Schedules Film on Guthrie." *Alabama Journal,* October 14, 1983, 22.
57. Murlin, Bill, ed. *Woody Guthrie: Roll On Columbia—The Columbia River Songs* (Sing Out! Publications, Bethlehem, PA), 1991, 92.
58. Vandy, Greg, and Daniel Person. *26 Songs in 30 Days: Woody Guthrie's Columbia River Songs and the Planned Promised Land in the Pacific Northwest* (Sasquatch Books, Seattle), 2016.
59. Murlin, Bill. *Woody Guthrie: Roll On Columbia—The Columbia River Songs.*

60. Murlin, Bill. "Woody Guthrie and the BPA." In Murlin, *Woody Guthrie: Roll On Columbia—The Columbia River Songs.*

61. Associated Press. "Lost Woody Guthrie Songs Found." *Home News* (New Brunswick, NJ), September 2, 1983, C7.

62. Associated Press. "Lost Woody Guthrie Songs Found."

63. Arlo Guthrie interview with Bryant Gumbel.

64. Kaufman, Naomi. "Search on for Original Woody Guthrie Songs." *Oakland Tribune,* August 17, 1983, C8.

65. Guthrie, Arlo. *Vancouver Columbian,* April 28, 1985, as quoted in *Woody Guthrie: Roll On Columbia—The Columbia River Songs,* 8.

66. "1 Million across Europe Protest U.S. Nuclear Arms." *St. Louis Post-Dispatch,* October 23, 1983, 1, 3.

67. Arlo Guthrie and Shenandoah, Rutgers University, New Brunswick, NJ, November 5, 1983 (audience recording).

68. Arlo Guthrie and Shenandoah, Rutgers University, New Brunswick, NJ, November 5, 1983.

69. "A Day of Demonstrations against Missiles." *Boston Sunday Globe,* October 23, 1983, 22.

70. Arlo Guthrie and Shenandoah, Rutgers University, New Brunswick, NJ, November 5, 1983.

71. Gerstenzang, James. "Reagan: Invasion Is to Restore Democracy." *Pittsburgh Post-Gazette,* October 26, 1983, 1, 4.

72. Arlo Guthrie and Shenandoah, Rutgers University, New Brunswick, NJ, November 5, 1983.

73. "TSP Completes Series of Projects." *Back Stage,* December 3, 1983, 61.

74. Neal, Steve, and Jon Margolis. "Campaign: Political Notes." *Chicago Tribune,* February 28, 1984, 8.

75. Fritz, Sara. "McGovern Emerging as Party's Elder Statesman." *Los Angeles Times,* March 5, 1984, A8.

76. Arlo Guthrie interview with Bryant Gumbel.

77. Arlo Guthrie interview with Bryant Gumbel.

78. Arlo Guthrie interview with Bryant Gumbel.

79. Arlo Guthrie interview with Bryant Gumbel.

80. Guthrie, Arlo. *Pledge Drive Break* (WNET-13, New York), March 7, 1984.

81. Arlo Guthrie interview with Bryant Gumbel.

82. "Bay State Results Keep McGovern in Race." *Hartford Courant,* March 14, 1984, A8.

83. United Press International. "Mass. Voters to Give McGovern Verdict." *North Adams Transcript* (MA), March 13, 1984, 14.

84. Bruning, Fred. "His Time to Say Goodbye." *Newsday,* March 17, 1984, A1.

85. Hepp, Christopher. "McGovern Calls It Quits." *Philadelphia Daily News,* March 14, 1984, 22.

86. Brown, Jenny. "Woody's Ramblin' Boy Still on the Road." *The Age*, June 15, 1984, Weekend 3.

87. Brown.

88. Franckling, Ken. "Folk Singing Philosopher for the Common Man." *Schenectady Gazette*, January 31, 1986, 32.

89. Brown, Jenny. "Woody's Ramblin' Boy Still on the Road."

90. Brown.

91. Levinson, Arlene. "Arlo Guthrie: You Can Get Anything You Want. . . ." *Sydney Morning Herald*, June 15, 1984, 16.

92. Tulich, Katherine. "Folk: Arlo Guthrie, State Theatre, Tuesday, June 26." *Sydney Morning Herald*, June 29, 1984, 10.

93. Gibson, Mari. "Arlo Guthrie, Warm, Funny and Delighting His Fans." *Canberra Times*, July 2, 1984, 11.

94. Downie, Graham. "Hello Canberra, How Are Ya: An Accidental Entertainer Arrives." *Canberra Times*, June 29, 1984, 1.

95. Downie.

96. Takiff, Jonathan. "The Soul of Philadelphia's Folk." *Philadelphia Daily News*, August 24, 1984, 45.

97. Preston, David Lee. "Echoes of Past Will Fill the Air at Folk Festival." *Philadelphia Inquirer*, August 24, 1984, 18.

98. Preston.

99. Dunning, Jennifer. "Two Singers Whose Music Bridges a Generation Gap." *New York Times*, October 2, 1983, H29.

100. Wilson, Susan. "Ronnie Gilbert: Still Weaving Music and Politics." *Boston Globe*, April 7, 1983, A9.

101. Milward, John. "Folk Music Regroups for the '80s."

102. Milward.

103. Selvin, Joel. "Concert Review: HARP." *San Francisco Chronicle*, September 18, 1984.

104. Everett, Todd. "Seeger, Gilbert, Guthrie and Near." *Los Angeles Herald*, September 19, 1984.

105. Lacey, Liam. "Folk Singer Espouses 'Progressive Thought.'" *Globe and Mail* (Toronto), September 26, 1985, E4.

106. Guthrie, Arlo. Email correspondence with author, October 11, 2020.

107. Everett, Todd. "Seeger, Gilbert, Guthrie and Near."

108. Arnold, Thomas K. "Folkies Reunite for 'Celebration of Life.'" *Los Angeles Times*, October 19, 1984, SD C1.

109. Graybill, Elaine. "Arlo Guthrie's Comin' to Sing." *Pantagraph*, October 6, 1984, 6.

110. Guthrie, Arlo. "House of the Rising Son." *Esquire*, September 1984, 80–82.

111. Arnold, Thomas K. "Folkies Reunite for 'Celebration of Life.'"

112. Graybill, Elaine. "Arlo Guthrie's Comin' to Sing."

113. Arnold, Thomas K. "Folkies Reunite for 'Celebration of Life.'"

114. Pond, Steve. "Folk Tour Brings Back Bromberg." *Los Angeles Times*, October 19, 1984, J2.

115. Pond, Steve. "Folk Tour Brings Back Bromberg."

116. Pond.

117. Sonner, Gigi. "Seeger, Guthrie Sing with Students." *Daily Tar Heel*, November 21, 1983, 4.

118. Sonner.

CHAPTER 3

1. Dale, Steve. "Memories of Steve: Friends Unite for Goodman." *Chicago Tribune*, January 25, 1985, F2.

2. Dale.

3. Weine, Andy. "Folk Festival Is Fatiguing but Fabulous." *Michigan Daily*, January 29, 1985, Arts 6.

4. Harvey, Dennis. "Raitt's Blues Warms with Its Intimacy." *Michigan Daily*, April 10, 1985, Arts 5.

5. Wire Reports. "Arlo Guthrie Hospitalized, in Good Condition." *Evening Independent* (St. Petersburg), March 11, 1985, 2A.

6. United Press International. "Guthrie's Pain Puzzles Doctors." *Bulletin* (Bend, OR), March 12, 1985, C7.

7. United Press International. "Guthrie Resting at Farm after Aneurysm." *North Adams Transcript* (MA), March 22, 1985, 16.

8. Reid, T. R. "Louie Louie Sets Off Official-Song Battle." *Washington Post*, May 10, 1985, C1.

9. United Press International. "'Roll On Columbia' Praised." *World* (Coos Bay, OR), April 24, 1985, 17.

10. Lerten, Barney. "Arlo Guthrie Sings BPA Songs." *Bulletin* (Bend, OR), April 24, 1985, a9.

11. Associated Press. "Guthrie Gives Impromptu Concert at Plant." *News-Press* (St. Joseph, MO), April 24, 1985, 12B.

12. Lerten, Barney. "Arlo Guthrie Sings BPA Songs."

13. Associated Press. "BPA Gives Arlo Guthrie Tape of Woody's Songs." *Rochester Sentinel*, April 24, 1985, 6.

14. United Press International. "Guthrie Folk Tune Plugged by His Son." *News-Sentinel* (Lodi, CA), April 25, 1985, 9.

15. Associated Press. "Arlo Guthrie Loses Articles to a Thief." *Tuscaloosa News*, June 5, 1985, 32.

16. Morse, Steve. "Short Cuts: Dancing Lightly on the Waters." *Boston Globe*, June 20, 1985, A6.

17. King, Peter B. "Seeger & Guthrie: A Folk Duo That Binds 2 Generations Together." *Pittsburgh Press*, June 27, 1985, 47.

18. Paris, Barry. "Even His Mother-in-Law Thinks Arlo Is a Gem." *Pittsburgh Post-Gazette,* June 28, 1985, W4.

19. "Biggest Turnout." *Pittsburgh Post-Gazette,* July 2, 1985, 11.

20. Cromelin, Richard. "Pop Beat: For Joady Guthrie, an Unhappy, Fearful Legacy." *Los Angeles Times,* January 25, 1985, E1.

21. Iwata, Edward. "Joady Guthrie: Arlo's Brother Tries to Make It on His Own." *San Francisco Chronicle,* January 5, 1986, 37.

22. Paris, Barry. "Even His Mother-in-Law Thinks Arlo Is a Gem."

23. Lau, Steven. "Living Quietly in El Cerrito, Son of Woody Guthrie Looks Back on Life, Dad." *Pinole Patch,* July 12, 2012. https://patch.com/california/napavalley/woody-guthries-son-joady-lives-quietly-in-bay-area.

24. Hoffman, Louise. "Joady Guthrie." *Broadside,* no. 174, June–July 1986, 10.

25. McLaughlin, Jeff. "Folk Festival Will Return to Newport." *Boston Globe,* May 2, 1985, 77.

26. Santosuosso, Ernie. "Newport Folk and Jazz Line Ups Announced." *Boston Globe,* June 19, 1985, 65.

27. Santosuosso.

28. Wyman, Carolyn. "Newport Revival Strikes a Less Political Note." *Christian Science Monitor,* August 9, 1985, 23.

29. Ritter, Jeff. "Newport." *Broadside,* no. 166, September 1985, 10–11.

30. "Weavers Show Up at O. State Fair but Are Nixed." *Variety,* August 29, 1951, 49.

31. "Singers Banned at Fair in '50s Ready to Return." *Newark Advocate* (OH), August 14, 1985, 16.

32. "From Alice's Restaurant to the Carnegie Deli: Lean Years Are Over for Arlo Guthrie." *Daily News,* November 27, 1985, 67.

33. Woliver, Robbie. *Bringing It All Back Home: Twenty-Five Years of American Music at Folk City* (Pantheon Books, New York), 1984, 52.

34. Woliver, Robbie. Author's Note, in *Bringing It All Back Home,* x.

35. Holden, Stephen. "Folk City at 25: The Times They Are A-Changin.'" *New York Times,* September 13, 1985, C5.

36. Holden.

37. "Folk City Reflections." In Woliver, Robbie, and Marilyn Lash and Joe Hillesum. *Folk City 25th Anniversary Program Book.* 1985, unpaginated.

38. *Folk City 25th Anniversary Program Book.*

39. Kelp, Larry. "Guthrie Listens, Learns and Sings." *Oakland Tribune,* September 13, 1985, D1, 10.

40. Associated Press. "Farm Aid Concert: Stars Harvest 'Green' for Struggling Growers." *Courier-Post* (Cherry Hill, NJ), September 23, 1985, 3A.

41. Interview with Arlo Guthrie. TNN (The Nashville Network) simulcast, Farm Aid, Champaign, IL. September 22, 1985.

42. Interview with Arlo Guthrie. TNN simulcast.

43. Greenhouse, Steven. "Musicians Give Concert to Aid Nation's Farmers." *New York Times,* September 23, 1985, A16.

44. Seeger, Pete. "Notes on the Program: A Story You Should Know." Carnegie Hall *Stagebill,* November 1985, 10–11.

45. Bishop, Pete. "After 25 years, Arlo Guthrie is Still Living a Good Dream." *Pittsburgh Press,* May 11, 1986, F1, F4.

46. Oermann, Robert K. "Guthrie Relaxes with Own Label." *Press & Sun Bulletin* (Binghamton, NY), October 25, 1986, 3D.

47. "Now Read This." Rising Son Records Spring 1986 mailer (aka *Rolling Blunder Review,* Vol. 1).

48. "Crop Report Spring 1986." Rising Son Records Spring 1986 mailer (aka *Rolling Blunder Review,* Vol. 1).

49. "Music Industry Scorecard, 1985–87." *Billboard* 100, no. 18, April 30, 1988, 76.

50. Horowitz, Is. "CDs Keep Business on Even $ Keel." *Billboard* 98, no. 44, November 1, 1986, 1, 77.

51. "Get Stuff" mailer. *Rolling Blunder Review,* no. 5, Fall–Winter 1987.

52. "The Last Recordings Come Home." *Rolling Blunder Review,* no. 8, Summer 1988, 3.

53. "The Last Recordings Come Home."

54. "Outlasting the Blues." *Rolling Blunder Review,* no. 3, Winter 1987, 2.

55. Guthrie. "Oughttabiography." Email attachment (revised final) to author, December 5, 2020.

56. "Get Stuff in Trouble." *Rolling Blunder Review,* no. 5, Fall–Winter 1987, 1.

57. "Notes from Broadcast Markets in the U.S. and Abroad." *Variety,* February 5, 1986, 95.

58. Thomas, Jack. "Ingenious, These Yankees." *Boston Globe,* April 18, 1986, 36.

59. Bishop, Pete. "After 25 Years, Arlo Guthrie Is Still Living a Good Dream."

60. Bishop.

61. King, Peter B. "Guthrie, Prine Excel at Quiet, Moving Music." *Pittsburgh Press,* May 14, 1986, 48.

62. Mervis, Scott. "John Prine and Arlo Guthrie Express Folk Wit." *Pittsburgh Post-Gazette,* May 14, 1986, 25.

63. "Hummingbird and Guthrie Sing Praises of Dodge." *Back Stage,* June 6, 1986, 51.

64. Guthrie, Arlo. Text correspondence with author, November 13, 2020.

65. Neal, Anthony. "Hormel Talks Become Earnest." *Minneapolis Star and Tribune,* June 12, 1986, 01M.

66. Bark, Ed. "'Our World' Turns History into Pop Culture." *Asbury Park Press,* September 25, 1986, 56.

67. Bark.

68. Shales, Tom. "TV Preview: 'Our World'—ABC's Backward Glance." *Washington Post,* September 25, 1986, B1.

69. Promotional flyer for *Woody Guthrie: Hard Travelin'* (MGM/UA Home Video), 1986.

70. Cooke, Robert. "Test for Huntington's Disease Starts." *Newsday*, September 30, 1986, 4.

71. Guthrie, Arlo. "Despite the Shadow of His Father's (and Possibly His Own) Deadly Disease, a Folk Hero Celebrates Life." *People Weekly* 28, no. 10, September 7, 1987.

72. Guthrie, Arlo. "Despite the Shadow of His Father's (and Possibly His Own) Deadly Disease, a Folk Hero Celebrates Life."

73. Cromelin, Richard. "Pop Beat: For Joady Guthrie, an Unhappy, Fearful Legacy."

74. Goldsmith, Peter D. *Making People's Music: Moe Asch and Folkways Records.* (Smithsonian Institution Press: Washington, DC) 1998, 416.

75. Tuck, Lon. "Smithsonian Purchases Folkways Label: Company Noted for Diverse Recordings." *Washington Post*, April 1, 1987, D1.

76. Scharnhorst, A. "Arlo Guthrie Still Sending a Message." *Kansas City Star*, October 6, 1988, 4D.

77. Guthrie, Arlo. "One Thing Concerning You," *Rolling Blunder Review*, no. 7, Spring 1988, 4.

78. Guthrie, Arlo. "One Thing Concerning You," 4.

79. Guthrie, Arlo. "One Thing Concerning You," 5.

80. Associated Press. "Guthrie Show to Help Feed Unemployed." *Central Jersey Home News*, November 8, 1986, 2.

81. "Pizza Gonna Do It." *Rolling Blunder Review*, no. 2, Fall 1986, 1.

82. Williams, Stephen. "For Arlo Guthrie, the Travelin' Is Easy." *Newsday*, January 30, 1987, 13.

83. "Japan Trade War: Cancels Guthriesan." *Rolling Blunder Review*, no. 4, Summer 1987, 3.

84. Williams, Stephen. "For Arlo Guthrie, the Travelin' Is Easy."

85. Morse, Steve. "Pop Goes the Compact Disc." *Boston Globe*, December 7, 1986, B33.

86. Morse.

87. "The 9th Annual Readers' Poll Winners." *Boston Globe*, January 29, 1987, A1.

88. Morse, Steve. "Newport Folkfest to Mix Old and New This Year." *Boston Globe*, August 1, 1986, 32.

89. Wilson, Susan. "Masterful, Mixed Lineup Opens Newport Fest." *Boston Globe*, August 10, 1986, 44.

90. "Folkies Finished?" *Philadelphia Inquirer*, August 12, 1986, 2E.

91. Alarik, Scott. "On with the Folk Music!" *Boston Globe*, August 10, 1987, 22.

92. Franckling, Ken. "Guthrie Returns to Newport and Sings His Famous 'Alice.'" *Philadelphia Inquirer*, August 11, 1987, 4D.

93. Persky-Hooper, Marci. "At 40, Singer Arlo Guthrie Focuses on 'Having a Ball.'" *Sun-Sentinel* (Fort Lauderdale), July 23, 1987, 7E.

94. Persky-Hooper, Marci. "Arlo Got Everything He Wants from 'Alice's Restaurant.'" *Tampa Tribune*, July 25, 1987, F1.

95. Palmer, Robert. "A Tribute to a Pioneer of Folk." *New York Times*, October 9, 1987, C28.

96. "Guthrie Quits." *Rolling Blunder Review*, no. 6, February 1988, 2.

97. Braudy, Susan. "As Arlo Guthrie Sees It . . . Kids Are Groovy. Adults Aren't." *New York Times Magazine*, April 27, 1969, 57–59+.

98. Leonard, John. "Private Lives." *New York Times*, December 6, 1978, C12.

99. "Carnegie Hall: The Tradition Continues." *Baltimore Sun*, December 15, 1986, 1B.

100. Leventhal, Harold. "Meet the Artist." Carnegie Hall *Stagebill*, October 1987, 46.

101. Bazinet, Kenneth R. "Arlo's Last Serving of 'Alice.'" *Washington Post*, November 26, 1987, C12.

102. Reuters. "Arlo Guthrie Performing Last 'Alice's Restaurant.'" *Democrat and Chronicle* (Rochester, NY), November 28, 1987, 4C.

103. "The Massacree Celebrates Its 50th." *Rolling Blunder Review*, no. 4. Summer 1987, 3.

104. "From Alice's Restaurant to the Carnegie Deli: Lean Years Are Over for Arlo Guthrie."

105. Arlo Guthrie and Shenandoah, Coachhouse, San Juan Capistrano, CA, August 21, 1987 (audience recording).

CHAPTER 4

1. Hilburn, Robert. "McCartney's Absence Sparks Rancor at Rock Hall." *Los Angeles Times*, January 22, 1988, VI, 20, 22.

2. "Guthrie Folks the Big Time." *Rolling Blunder Review*, no. 6, February 1988, 1.

3. "Guthrie Folks the Big Time."

4. "Guthrie Folks the Big Time."

5. Faris, Mark. "A Legion of Legends: Parade of Stars, a Shining Night for Hall of Fame." *Akron Beacon Journal*, January 24, 1988, F1, 2.

6. Moore, Colleen. "'60s Legend Arlo Guthrie Sings, Plays for Manatees." *Florida Today* (Cocoa), February 5, 1988, 41–42.

7. Long, Phil. "Folk Singer Attuned to Plight of Manatees and Sea Turtles." *Miami Herald*, January 15, 1988, 83.

8. "Guthrie Rips Across Map: Europe in Tears." *Rolling Blunder Review*, no. 7, Spring 1988, 5.

9. Mac Connell, Sean. "Guthrie Makes 'Eat the Peach' Dream Come True." *Irish Times*, February 22, 1988, 12.

10. Guthrie, Arlo. Email correspondence to author, May 14, 2021.

11. Guthrie, Arlo. Email correspondence to author, May 14, 2021.

12. Mac Connell, Sean. "Guthrie Makes 'Eat the Peach' Dream Come True."

13. Oermann, Robert K. "Shenandoah's Fresh Start." *Nashville Tennessean*, August 15, 1992, D1.

14. Oermann.

15. Guthrie, Arlo. "One Thing Concerning You," *Rolling Blunder Review,* no. 7, Spring 1988, 3.

16. "Concert Planned May 15 in Memory of John Pilla." *Berkshire Eagle,* April 15, 1988, B7.

17. Hinckley, David. "Woody's Legacy." *Daily News,* January 3, 1988, 22.

18. Hinckley.

19. Hinckley.

20. Arlo Guthrie, Carnegie Hall, New York City, NY, November 24, 1989 (audience recording).

21. Arlo Guthrie, Carnegie Hall, November 24, 1989.

22. Arlo Guthrie and Pete Seeger, Carnegie Hall, New York City, NY, November 27, 1998 (sound recording).

23. McCoy, Brian. "Arlo Guthrie Is Back in Spotlight after Tribute Album, Tour." *Courier* (Waterloo, IA), October 26, 1988, 21.

24. McCoy.

25. Gerds, Warren. "Playing It Straight . . . with Himself." *Green Bay Press-Gazette,* September 29, 1988, 20.

26. Gerds.

27. Gerds.

28. Gallanter, Marty. "Pete Seeger." *Frets,* September 1979, 28.

29. Catlin, Roger. "Arlo Guthrie: On the Road for Earth." *Hartford Courant,* April 19, 1990, 87.

30. Linn, Amy. "Woodstock, 1989." *Philadelphia Inquirer,* March 27, 1989, D1.

31. Catlin, Roger. "Arlo Guthrie: On the Road for Earth."

32. Pine, Jon. "Reticent Rebel: '60s Music Still Relevant to Folk Singer." *Arizona Daily Star,* February 25, 1989, B12.

33. Pine.

34. Lannert, John. "Guthrie, Seeger Top Festival Bill." *Palm Beach Post,* February 10, 1989, 30.

35. "Pete Seeger Captured by Arlo's Annual Florida Concert." *Rolling Blunder Review,* no. 9, Fall–Winter 1988, 1.

36. Duffy, Thom. "Guthrie, Seeger Perform for the Love of Nature." *Orlando Sentinel,* February 12, 1989, 10.

37. Rovner, Sandy. "Genes, AIDS, and Ethics: TV Tunes In to Medical Issues." *Washington Post,* March 28, 1989, F20.

38. Rovner.

39. Morse, Steve. "Sebastian Wary of Woodstock Reunion." *Boston Globe,* March 30, 1989, 74.

40. Catlin, Roger. "Arlo Guthrie: On the Road for Earth."

41. Morse, Steve. "Just like Old Times." *Boston Globe,* May 5, 1989, 49.

42. Guthrie, Arlo. "Clams Surround Studio." *Rolling Blunder Review,* no. 11, Summer 1989, 1.

43. Guthrie, Arlo. "Clams Surround Studio."
44. Leiferman, Henry. "Sebastian: Escape from Burnout." *Sun Sentinel* (Fort Lauderdale), November 26, 1989, 18.
45. Guthrie, Arlo. "Clams Surround Studio."
46. Dunaway, David King. *How Can I Keep from Singing: Pete Seeger* (McGraw-Hill Book Co., New York), 1981, 273.
47. "Testimony of Arlo Guthrie" (in the Chicago Seven Trial), School of Law, University of Missouri–Kansas City, accessed January 20, 2023, http://law2.umkc.edu/faculty/projects/ftrials/Chicago7/Guthrie.html.
48. Arlo Guthrie, Club Casino, Hampton Beach, NH, July 3, 1989 (audience recording).
49. Linder, Lee. "Autopsy Confirms Suicide in Abbie Hoffman's Death." *Press & Sun Bulletin* (Binghamton, NY), April 19, 1989, 1.
50. Rice, Don. "Group Plans Honor for Woody Guthrie." *Daily Oklahoman,* September 29, 1965, 23.
51. Associated Press. "Guthrie Recognized by His Hometown." *Los Angeles Times,* July 15, 1971, 25.
52. Aarons, Leroy F. "Trouble Mars Woody's Big Day." *Austin Statesman,* July 14, 1971, C20.
53. Associated Press. "Town to Honor Guthrie." *Daily Oklahoman,* July 14, 1971, 45.
54. Associated Press. "Birthplace Will Honor Folk Singer." *Asbury Park Evening Press* (NJ), October 5, 1972, 13.
55. DeFrange, Ann. "Okemah's Children Honor Woody Guthrie with Song." *Daily Oklahoman,* December 2, 1988, 1–2.
56. Broyles, Gil. "Children Bring Guthrie Ballads to Life." *Okmulgee Daily Times,* December 2, 1988, 9.
57. Long, Larry. "Bringing Woody Home (Homemade Jam)." *Sing Out!* 45, no. 3, Fall 2001.
58. Associated Press. "Arlo Guthrie Slates Concert at Okemah." *Okmulgee Daily Times,* March 30, 1989, 2.
59. Hilburn, Robert. "This Town Is Guthrie's Town, at Last." *Los Angeles Times,* May 1, 1989, VI, 1, 4.
60. Phillips, Richard. "No RIP for Woody Guthrie." *Chicago Tribune,* April 27, 1989, 18.
61. Associated Press. "Woody Gets His 'Homecoming.'" *Manhattan Mercury* (KS), May 1, 1989, B8.
62. Broyles, Gil. "Arlo Guthrie Appearance Splits Woody's Hometown." *Fort Worth Star Telegram,* April 28, 1989, Sec. 5, 1.
63. Hilburn, Robert. "This Town Is Guthrie's Town, at Last."
64. Blackledge, Brett J. "Woody Guthrie's Hometown Honors." *Asbury Park Press* (NJ), May 2, 1989, C11.
65. Blackledge, Brett J. "Woody Guthrie's Hometown Honors."

66. Blackledge, Brett J. "Woody Guthrie Receives Homecoming after All These Years." *Okmulgee Daily Times,* May 2, 1989, 10.

67. Guthrie, Arlo. "Okemah Celebrates Pioneer Daze." *Rolling Blunder Review,* no. 11, Summer 1989, 4.

68. Guthrie, Arlo. "Okemah Celebrates Pioneer Daze."

69. Guthrie, Arlo. "Okemah Celebrates Pioneer Daze."

70. Guthrie, Arlo. "Okemah Celebrates Pioneer Daze."

71. Guthrie, Arlo. "Okemah Celebrates Pioneer Daze."

72. Guthrie, Arlo. "Okemah Celebrates Pioneer Daze."

73. Guthrie, Arlo. "Guthrie Gets the Third Degree." *Rolling Blunder Review,* no. 11, Summer 1989, 2.

74. "Singer Goes from Dropout to Doctorate." *Modesto Bee* (CA), April 26, 1989, A2.

75. "Singer Goes from Dropout to Doctorate."

76. "Ex-Rocky Chaplain Dies in Great Falls." *Billings Gazette,* September 27, 2005, 3B.

77. Guthrie, Arlo. "Guthrie Gets the Third Degree," 2.

78. Guthrie, Arlo. "Guthrie Gets the Third Degree," 2.

79. Guthrie, Arlo. "Guthrie Gets the Third Degree," 3.

80. Cacioppo, Nancy. "Arlo Guthrie: After Alice's Restaurant." *Journal News* (Rockland Co., NY), June 15, 1989, C3, C9.

81. John Motavalli. "Twenty Years Later." *Adweek's Marketing Week,* 27 March 1989 30, no. 1.

82. Seeger, Pete, and Arlo Guthrie, Tanglewood, Lenox, Massachusetts, July 4, 1989 (audience recording).

83. Guthrie, Arlo. "Journey to Blunderland: Fabulous Voyage Awaits." *Rolling Blunder Review,* no. 10, Winter 1989, 4.

84. "Blunderman's Fabulous Adventure," 3.

85. Curley, Suzanne. "Books for Children: The Gift of Imagination." *Newsday* (Suffolk, NY), November 24, 1985, 14, 16.

86. Guthrie, Arlo. "What's Gonna Happen Next." *Rolling Blunder Review,* no. 9, Fall–Winter 1988, 5.

87. "Visual Effects: Michael Sporn Completes Work on Several Animated Shorts." *Back Stage,* July 21, 1989, 39.

88. "Rashad, Kline Shine in Kids' Story Series." *Kitchener-Waterloo Record* (Ontario), December 26, 1991, D8; "Tape Series Brings Books to Life." *Press & Sun Bulletin* (Binghamton, NY), December 15, 1989, 49.

89. "Folk Singer Arlo Guthrie Puts Story-Telling Talent to Good Use." *Red Deer Advocate* (Alberta), November 14, 1991, C4.

90. "Guthrie Aims Stories at Kids." *Windsor Star* (Ontario), November 16, 1991, C7.

91. Ryan, Richard T. "Video Reviews." *Billboard* 102, no.4, January 27, 1990, 57–58.

92. Levine, Eric. "Babies Will Be Bored by 'Baby's Storytime.'" *Courier-Post* (Cherry Hill, NJ), September 9, 1991, 2D.

93. Levine.

94. Hinckley, David. "What? Woodstock for Dinner Again?" *Daily News,* September 8, 1989, 105.

95. Auerbach, Matthew. "Arlo: The Song (and Charm) Remains the Same." *Daily News,* November 27, 1989, 39.

96. Auerbach.

97. Holden, Stephen. "Arlo Guthrie: A Holiday Gathering" *New York Times,* November 27, 1989, C15.

98. Auerbach, Matthew. "Arlo: The Song (and Charm) Remains the Same."

99. Klein, Joe. "Notes on a Native Son." *Rolling Stone,* no. 234, March 10, 1997, 55.

100. Skelly, Richard. "Arlo Still Plays It Free and Easy." *Home News* (New Brunswick, NJ), December 4, 1989, C7.

101. Guthrie, Arlo. "Meet the Artist: My Oughta Biography." Carnegie Hall *Stagebill,* November 1989, 26.

102. Connell, Christopher. "Bush Hails the 'Dynamic Development.'" *Post-Star* (Glens Falls, NY), November 11, 1989, A2.

103. Arlo Guthrie at Carnegie Hall, New York City, November 25, 1989 (audience recording).

104. Skelly, Richard. "Arlo Still Plays It Free and Easy."

105. Guthrie, Arlo. "When A Soldier Makes It Home." *Rolling Blunder Review,* no. 12, Fall 1989, 5–6.

106. Jorgensen, Chris. "An Interview with Ramblin' Jack Elliott." *DISCoveries,* October 1990, 98–99.

107. Jorgensen.

108. Guthrie, Arlo. Email correspondence with author, November 21, 2020.

109. Guthrie, Arlo. "RSR Gets LA Artist; Guthrie Goes On." *Rolling Blunder Review,* no. 10, Winter 1989, 1.

110. Caporale, Patricia. "Brevard Comes Alive with Music." *Orlando Sentinel* (FL), February 9, 1990, F3.

111. Guthrie, Arlo. "Guthrie Goes On through Life Alone." *Rolling Blunder Review,* no. 10, Winter 1989, 1.

112. Guthrie, Arlo. "Earth Day." *Rolling Blunder Review,* no. 14, Spring 1990, 7.

113. Morse, Steve. "Singing for the Cause." *Boston Globe,* April 19, 1990, A12.

114. Catlin, Roger. "Arlo Guthrie: On the Road for Earth."

115. Arlo Guthrie, Hatch Shell, Boston Commons, Boston, April 20, 1990 (audience recording).

116. Morse, Steve. "Rock Notes: Guthrie to Play Concert for Human Rights." *Boston Globe,* May 11, 1990, 41.

117. Arlo Guthrie, Hatch Shell, Boston Commons.

118. Guthrie, Arlo. "China/Tibet Benefit." *Rolling Blunder Review,* no. 15, Summer 1990, 7.

119. Guthrie, Arlo. "China/Tibet Benefit."

120. Morse, Steve. "Singing for the Cause."

121. Ingrassia, Lawrence. "At Walden Pond, Two Liberal Causes Seem One Too Many." *Wall Street Journal,* April 24, 1990, A1.
122. Morse, Steve. "A Night of Rock Nirvana at the Centrum." *Boston Globe,* April 26, 1990, 86.
123. Scent, Dianne. "Pete Seeger Keeps Folk-Song Tradition Alive." *Courier News* (Bridgewater, NJ), January 5, 1989, B1, B5.
124. Robicheau, Paul. "Guthrie Picks up the Slack for Seeger." *Boston Globe,* July 3, 1989, 9.
125. Himes, Geoffrey. "Pete Seeger, Singing to the Choir." *Washington Post,* August 4, 1990, G9.
126. Guthrie, Arlo. "Oh, It's Prine Time Again." *Rolling Blunder Review,* no. 15, Summer 1990, 7.
127. Guthrie, Arlo (aka Irv, Investigative Reporter 5). "Interview with a Folksinger." *Rolling Blunder Review,* no. 30, Fall 1995, 2–3.
128. "FCC Warns Broadcasters to Watch Out for Lyrics That Glorify Drugs." *Variety,* March 10, 1971, 30.
129. "People: 'Fear of Music.'" *Fort Worth Star-Telegram,* August 13, 1990, 3.
130. "On Walden Pond: Rockers, Politicians, CEOs." *USA Today,* August 14, 1990, 3A.
131. "Who Will Control the Legacy of the Woodstock Nation?" *New York Times,* August 18, 1990, 1, 27.
132. Guthrie, Arlo. "'Whole Year Happens in One Day' . . . Says Folksinger." *Rolling Blunder Review,* no. 16, Fall 1990, 2.
133. "Popularity of U.S. Rights Hymn Irks German Reds." *New York Times,* March 5, 1967, 20.
134. Grossman, Victor. *Crossing the River: A Memoir of the American Left, the Cold War, and Life in East Germany* (University of Massachusetts Press: Amherst), 2003, 181.
135. Guthrie, Arlo. "Guthrie Says 'OK' to Movie: He's an Old Biker Who Says Something." *Rolling Blunder Review,* no. 17, Winter 1990, 7.
136. Holden, Stephen. "A Motorcycle Epic with Echoes of the '60s." *New York Times,* March 27, 1992, C10.
137. Morris, Chris. "On Screen: Roadside Prophets." *Billboard* 103, no. 50, December 14, 1991, 67.
138. Kehr, Dave. "'Roadside Prophets' Shoots for the Hip but Misses."
139. Rainer, Peter. "Shades of the '60s in Roadside Prophets." *Los Angeles Times,* April 3, 1992, F10.

CHAPTER 5

1. Guthrie, Arlo. "Blunderman's Fabulous Adventure II." *Rolling Blunder Review,* no. 15, Summer 1990, overleaf.
2. Guthrie, Arlo. "Israel in 1991." *Get Stuff Catalogue,* no. 17, October 1990, 4.
3. Vogt, Jenny. "Classic Arlo." *Palm Beach Post,* February 6, 1991, 1D.

4. Guthrie, Arlo. "The Folksinger's Notes." *Rolling Blunder Review,* no. 18, Spring 1991, 1.

5. Diamond, John. "The Congressman and the 'Kid.'" *Berkshire Eagle,* March 26, 1991, B1, B4.

6. Diamond, John. "The Congressman and the 'Kid.'"

7. Diamond.

8. Diamond.

9. Vogt, Jenny. "Classic Arlo," 10D.

10. Guthrie, Arlo. "4th Annual Indian River Festival." *Rolling Blunder Review,* no. 17, Winter 1990, 5.

11. Kennedy, Paul. "Arlo Guthrie: Always a Cause to Fight For." *Florida Today* (Cocoa), February 3, 1991, 47–48.

12. Vogt, Jenny. "Classic Arlo," 10D.

13. Guthrie, Arlo. "Notes: Indian River Festival." *Rolling Blunder Review,* no. 19, Summer 1991, 6.

14. Guthrie, Arlo. "Notes: Indian River Festival," 6.

15. Guthrie, Arlo. "The Troubadour." *Rolling Blunder Review,* no. 19, Summer 1991, 6.

16. Guthrie, Arlo. "Curse of the Northwest." *Rolling Blunder Review,* no. 19, Summer 1991, 2.

17. Guthrie, Arlo. "Ram Dass Revisited." *Rolling Blunder Review,* no. 19, Summer 1991, 7.

18. Guthrie, Arlo. "Rocky Mt." *Rolling Blunder Review,* no. 19, Summer 1991, 6–7.

19. Guthrie, Arlo. "Medical Mystery Tour: Interview by Irv." *Rolling Blunder Review,* no. 19, Summer 1991, 4–5.

20. Guthrie, Arlo. "Medical Mystery Tour," 4–5.

21. Guthrie, Arlo. "Curse of the Northwest," 2.

22. Radel, Cliff. "Guthrie in No Rush for New Music." *Cincinnati Enquirer,* May 17, 1991, C1.

23. Guthrie, Arlo. "What's Happening." *Rolling Blunder Review,* no. 18, Spring 1991, 5.

24. Guthrie, Arlo. "Miscellaneous." *Rolling Blunder Review,* no. 19, Summer 1991, 7.

25. Guthrie, Arlo. Notes to *All Over the World* (Rising Son Records RSR 0002), 1991.

26. Guthrie, Arlo. "In Record Time: Meanwhile. . . ." *Rolling Blunder Review,* no. 20, Fall 1991, 5.

27. Guthrie, Arlo. "In Record Time: Meanwhile. . . ."

28. Guthrie, Arlo. "What's Happening." *Rolling Blunder Review,* no. 18, Spring 1991, 5.

29. Guthrie, Woody, and Marjorie Mazia Guthrie. *Woody's 20 Grow Big Songs* (Harper Collins, New York), 1992.

30. Guthrie, Woody, and Marjorie Mazia Guthrie.

31. Campbell, Mary. "Guthrie's 'Grow Big' Songs on Disc." *Hanford Sentinel* (CA), September 27, 1992, 1.
32. Campbell.
33. Campbell.
34. Campbell.
35. Campbell.
36. Campbell.
37. Campbell.
38. Campbell.
39. Campbell.
40. McCormick, Moira. "Serendipitous Songbook." *Chicago Tribune*, September 2, 1992, 65.
41. Campbell, Mary. "Guthrie's 'Grow Big' Songs on Disc.".
42. Campbell.
43. Campbell.
44. Campbell.
45. McCormick, Moira. "Serendipitous Songbook."
46. Campbell, Mary. "Guthrie's 'Grow Big' Songs on Disc."
47. McCormick, Moira. "Serendipitous Songbook."
48. McCormick.
49. Campbell, Mary. "Guthrie's 'Grow Big' Songs on Disc."
50. Schnol, Janet. "A Collection of Folk Songs for a New Generation." *Publisher's Weekly*, October 5, 1992, 33.
51. Guthrie, Nora. "Notes from Woody Guthrie's Daughter." In *Woody's 20 Grow Big Songs: Woody & Arlo Guthrie and the Guthrie Family* (Warner Bros. 9 45020-2), 1992.
52. Schnol, Janet. "A Collection of Folk Songs for a New Generation."
53. Schnol.
54. Schnol.
55. Schnol.
56. Guthrie, Nora. "Notes from Woody Guthrie's Daughter."
57. Schnol, Janet. "A Collection of Folk Songs for a New Generation."
58. Schnol.
59. Guthrie, Arlo. Notes to *Son of the Wind* (Rising Son Records RSR 0003), 1991.
60. Guthrie, Arlo. Notes to *Son of the Wind.*
61. Guthrie, Arlo. Notes to *Son of the Wind.*
62. Arlo Guthrie and Pete Seeger, Carnegie Hall, New York City, NY, November 27, 1998 (sound recording).
63. Guthrie, Arlo. "Church for Sale." *Rolling Blunder Review*, no. 17, Winter 1990, 3–4.
64. Guthrie, Arlo. "There and Back Again." *Rolling Blunder Review*, no. 20, Fall 1991, 2.

65. Buckley, Daniel. "Guthrie Legacy Lives On As Arlo, Son Team Up." *Tucson Citizen*, March 7, 1991, 43–44.

66. Pratt, Abby. "But No Motorcycles, Please." *Berkshire Eagle* (Pittsfield, MA), November 20, 1991, B1, B4; Pratt, Abby. "Arlo Guthrie Allowed to Use 'Church.'" *Berkshire Eagle,* November 27, 1991, B1, B4.

67. Guthrie, Arlo. "There and Back Again." *Rolling Blunder Review,* no. 20, Fall 1991, 2.

68. Guthrie, Arlo. "There and Back Again."

69. Pratt, Abby. "But No Motorcycles, Please."

70. Pratt, Abby. "But No Motorcycles, Please."

71. Guthrie, Arlo. "Notes on the Program." Carnegie Hall *Stagebill,* November 1991, 18.

72. Holden, Stephen. "Arlo Guthrie: Carnegie Hall." *New York Times,* December 5, 1991, C20.

73. Guthrie, Arlo. "Notes on the Program."

74. Bellow, Daniel O. "Moving Day for Arlo." *Berkshire Eagle* (Pittsfield, MA), December 14, 1991, A1, A8.

75. "Great Barrington Journal: Folk Singer Hopes Fans Can Save 'Alice's Church.'" *New York Times,* December 6, 1991, A14.

76. "Seeking Sanctuary: Forget Alice's Restaurant; It's Alice's Old Church That Arlo Guthrie Wants to Buy." *People,* February 10, 1992, 89.

77. "Great Barrington Journal: Folk Singer Hopes Fans Can Save 'Alice's Church.'"

78. Guthrie, Arlo. "Alice's Church." *Rolling Blunder Review,* no. 22, Summer 1992, 2.

79. Pratt, Abby. "Arlo, Obie, Alice." *Berkshire Eagle* (Pittsfield, MA), January 31, 1992, A1, B6.

80. Pratt, Abby. "Arlo, Obie, Alice."

81. Pratt.

82. "Newsmakers: Arlo Guthrie." *Evening Sun* (Hanover, PA), February 9, 1992, 15.

83. Vogt, Jenny. "Brooklyn-Born Ma 'Teaches All Ways.'" *Palm Beach Post*, March 29, 1992, 12A.

84. Pratt, Abby. "Neighbors Call for Revocation of Guthrie's Permit." *Berkshire Eagle* (Pittsfield, MA), February 5, 1992, B1, B4.

85. Pratt, Abby. "Neighbors Call for Revocation of Guthrie's Permit."

86. Pratt.

87. Pratt.

88. Associated Press. "Musician's Plans Anger Neighbors." *New York Times,* February 18, 1992, A20.

89. Pratt, Abby. "Guthrie Says He Will Comply with Bylaws, Permits." *Berkshire Eagle* (Pittsfield, MA), February 6, 1992, B1, B8.

90. "New Menu for Alice's Restaurant." *Rockland Journal-News* (NY), February 6, 1992, 3.

91. Pratt, Abby. "'Arlo Had No Hidden Agenda': Friend Says Folk Singer 'Just Improvises.'" *Berkshire Eagle* (Pittsfield, MA), February 29, 1992, 7.

92. Guthrie, Arlo. "In Record Time: Son of the Wind." *Rolling Blunder Review,* no. 20, Fall 1991, 5.

93. Ferguson, Jon. "Arlo Guthrie Performs Live at The Village." *Intelligencer Journal* (Lancaster, PA), December 4, 1992, 50.

94. Guthrie, Arlo. "More Other News. . . ." *Rolling Blunder Review,* no. 22, Summer 1992, 3.

95. "Writers Hope Song Will Benefit Museum." *Hartford Courant,* August 5, 1992, D4.

96. Richmond, Dick. "An Earful of Kennedy Gossip." *St. Louis Post-Dispatch,* April 15, 1993, 64.

97. Bauers, Sandy. "Arlo Sounds like Woody in Guthrie Memoir." *Democrat and Chronicle* (Rochester, NY), May 23, 1993, 9D.

98. Guthrie, Arlo. "Blunderman's Fabulous Adventure: The Delta Queen." *Rolling Blunder Review,* no. 22, Summer 1992, 10, 16.

99. Guthrie, Arlo. "Blunderman's Fabulous Adventure," 10.

100. Rogovoy, Seth. "Arlo Guthrie Offers a Menu of Music and Politics." *Berkshires Week* (Pittsfield, MA), July 3, 1992, 9, 24.

101. Rogovoy, Seth. "Guthrie, Collins Shine for Holiday." *Berkshire Eagle* (Pittsfield, MA), July 6, 1992, 22.

102. Tommasini, Anthony. "Collins and Guthrie: The Years Have Dulled Their '60s Edge." *Boston Globe,* July 6, 1992, 37.

103. "Chronicle: Celebrating the Spirit of Woody Guthrie with a Birthday Party in Central Park." *New York Times,* July 9, 1992, B4.

104. Oermann, Robert. "Griffith Makes 'Rooms' for Heroes of Folk Music." *Tennessean* (Nashville), March 14, 1993, Showcase 6.

105. Hinckley, David. "It's Been Good to Know Him." *Daily News,* July 10, 1992, 61.

106. "'This Land Is Our Land, Y'all.'" *Austin-American Statesman,* July 12, 1982, 10.

107. Pratt, Abby. "Guthrie's Anti-stress Retreat Creates Tension in Barrington." *Berkshire Eagle* (Pittsfield, MA), August 5, 1992, B4.

108. Pratt, Abby. "Guthrie's Anti-stress Retreat Creates Tension in Barrington."

109. Guthrie, Arlo. "Guthrie Retreats! He Won't Back Down." *Rolling Blunder Review,* no. 23, Fall–Winter 1992, 14.

110. Margolis, Lynne. "Arlo Guthrie: 25 Years after 'Alice.'" *Observer-Reporter* (Washington, PA), September 2, 1992, B9.

111. Guthrie, Arlo. "IRV Creates National Blunder Team Cub Reporting Mission." *Rolling Blunder Review,* no. 23, Fall–Winter 1992, 8–9.

112. Guthrie, Arlo. "IRV Creates National Blunder Team Cub Reporting Mission."

113. "White House Honors Singer with 'Point of Light' Award." *Berkshire Eagle* (Pittsfield, MA), November 3, 1992, B5.

114. Associated Press. "Folksinger a 'Point of Light.'" *North Adams Transcript* (MA), November 3, 1992, 14.
115. Pratt, Abby. "Guthrie Cancels $1,000-a-Plate Dinner at Alice's Church for Lack of Guests." *Berkshire Eagle* (Pittsfield, MA), November 20, 1992, B3.
116. Guthrie, Arlo. "Notes on the Program." Carnegie Hall *Stagebill*, November 1992, 18–19.
117. "Small-Is-Beautiful Tour Brings Arlo to Ira Allen." *Burlington Free Press* (VT), December 9, 1992, D1.
118. "Guthrie Songs for Children Put Up for Grammy Award." *Berkshire Eagle* (Pittsfield, MA), January 10, 1993, B6.
119. McKeon, Diane. "No Spotlight Tonight for Seeger—And That's OK with Him." *Poughkeepsie Journal*, February 24, 1993, 1.
120. Guthrie, Arlo. "On the Road: Feb. 8, 1993—Arcata, CA." *Rolling Blunder Review*, no. 24, Spring 1993, 2.
121. Guthrie, Arlo. "On the Road: Feb. 23, 1993—Ketchum, ID." *Rolling Blunder Review*, no. 24, Spring 1993, 2–3.
122. Guthrie, Arlo. "On the Road: Feb. 8, 1993—Arcata, CA."
123. Associated Press. "A. Guthrie Sees Legacy of Mother in Discovery." *Boston Globe,* March 24, 1993, 20.
124. Arlo Guthrie interview, *Miller & Company.* Nashville Network broadcast, March 26, 1993.
125. Newman, Melinda, ed. "Continental Drift: Melbourne, Fla." *Billboard* 13, no. 105, April 10, 1993, 14.
126. Hickman, Breuse. "Arlo's Day of Music Moves North." *Florida Today*, May 14, 1993, TGIF 3.
127. Hickman.
128. Spitz, Katherine. "Man of All Religions." *Akron Beacon Journal*, August 21, 1993, A5.
129. Klein, Joe. "Notes on a Native Son." *Rolling Stone*, March 10, 1977, 57.
130. Spitz, Katherine. "Man of All Religions."
131. Donato, Maria. "A 'Peace Guy' Returns: '60s Troubadour Guthrie Comes Back to Chicago as Part of a Longtime Spiritual Quest." *Chicago Tribune*, September 14, 1993, Sec. 5, pp. 1, 4.
132. Associated Press. "Parliament of Religions Signs Global Ethics Pact." *Dispatch* (Moline, IL), September 5, 1993, A3.
133. Briggs, David. "Religious Leaders Commit to Quest for World Peace, Equality, and Respect." *Northwest Herald* (Woodstock, IL), September 5, 1993, 3.
134. Guthrie, Arlo. "Road Notes." *Rolling Blunder Review*, no. 26, Fall–Winter 1993, 2.
135. Polkow, Dennis. "Untimely Finale: Concert for Parliament Off-Key." *Chicago Tribune*, September 6, 1993, 12.
136. Polkow.
137. DiPietro, Ben. "Arlo's a Free Bird in 'Paradise.'" *New York Post*, March 8, 1993, 75.

CHAPTER 6

1. Bickelhaupt, Susan. "Bochco Mellows Out with Arlo's Aid." *Boston Globe,* January 14, 1994, 36.
2. Bickelhaupt.
3. Ryan, Tim. "The Genuine Arlo." *Honolulu Star-Bulletin,* February 8, 1994, B1.
4. Ryan.
5. DiPietro, Ben. "Arlo Guthrie Makes a Stab at Television." *Hanford Sentinel* (CA), March 3, 1994, 3B.
6. Schwartz, Jerry. "'Byrds of Paradise' Take Flight." *Advocate-Messenger* (Danville, KY), March 3, 1994, 21.
7. "Folk Singer Arlo Guthrie Tries His Hand at TV." *Ithaca Journal* (NY), February 26, 1994, 29.
8. Kravitz, Lee. "Fresh from Hawaii, Arlo Guthrie Can Sing, Too." *Fort Worth Star-Telegram,* May 27, 1994, 91.
9. "Hawaii-Based TV Series Cancelled." *Hawaii Tribune-Herald,* May 10, 1994, 4.
10. "Hawaii-Based TV Series Cancelled."
11. Guthrie, Arlo. "Byrds of Paradise." *Rolling Blunder Review,* no. 28, Summer 1994, 2.
12. Guthrie, Arlo. "Byrds of Paradise."
13. Guthrie, Arlo. "Byrds of Paradise."
14. Bell, Rick. "Arlo Guthrie Reaches New Generation." *North County Times* (Escondido, CA), March 25, 1994, 15–16.
15. Bell.
16. Kravitz, Lee. "Fresh from Hawaii, Arlo Guthrie Can Sing, Too."
17. Guthrie, Arlo. Notes to *Arlo Guthrie & Pete Seeger: More Together Again in Concert Volume Two* (Rising Son Records 0008), 1994.
18. Guthrie, Arlo. "Dear Paul 'Agent PS' Smith." *Rolling Blunder Review,* no. 27, Winter–Spring 1994, 6.
19. Guthrie, Arlo. "Dear Paul 'Agent PS' Smith."
20. Arlo Guthrie, "Return to Woodstock." Seaside Park, Coney Island, Brooklyn, NY, August 11, 1994 (audience recording).
21. Arlo Guthrie, "Return to Woodstock."
22. Scott, Janny. "Poor Tickets Sales Force Cancellation of a 'Woodstock.'" *New York Times,* August 2, 1994, A1.
23. Honey, Charles. "Others Going Back to the Real Garden." *Honolulu Star-Bulletin,* August 12, 1994, B1.
24. Hobson, Grace. "Arlo Guthrie Lights Up Free-Form Bethel Fest." *Poughkeepsie Journal,* August 14, 1994, 12A.
25. Hobson, Grace. "Arlo Guthrie Lights Up Free-Form Bethel Fest."
26. "25,000 Attend Free Concert at Original Site." *Baltimore Sun,* August 14, 1994, 20A.

27. Hobson, Grace. "Arlo Guthrie Lights Up Free-Form Bethel Fest."
28. Associated Press. "'THIS Is Woodstock.'" *Star-Gazette* (Elmira, NY), August 14, 1994, 3A.
29. Associated Press. "Alternative, Free Fest Now Happening in Bethel." *Bennington Banner* (VT), August 13, 1994, 3.
30. Guthrie, Arlo. "Shows Coming Up." *Rolling Blunder Review,* no. 28, Summer 1994, 8.
31. Stoute, Lenny. "Guthrie on Tour and Giving Back." *Toronto Star,* December 5, 1996, A28.
32. Jette, Rosemary. "Berkshire's Living Legend to Perform at Night Shift." *North Adams Transcript* (MA), May 24, 1996, 23.
33. McGarrigle, Dale. "Guthrie Coming to Maine." *Bangor Daily News,* May 22, 1996, 6.
34. Guthrie, Arlo. Notes to *Mystic Journey* (Rising Son Records RSR 0009), 1996.
35. Hickman, Breuse. "Arlo Serves It Up." *Florida Today* (Cocoa), November 13, 1996, 35.
36. Hickman.
37. Hickman.
38. Della Flora, Anthony. "Hospice Work Fuels Arlo's Intimacy on Stage." *Albuquerque Journal,* February 23, 1996, 66.
39. Della Flora.
40. Della Flora.
41. Butler, Janet. "Arlo Guthrie: Mystic Journey." *American Songwriter,* November 1995. https://americansongwriter.com/arlo-guthrie-mystic-journey/.
42. Harper, Colin. "Folk: Arlo Guthrie—Galway Arts Festival." *Independent* (London, England), July 25, 1996, 11.
43. Willens, Doris. *Lonesome Traveler: The Life of Lee Hays* (W. W. Norton, New York), 1988, 200.
44. Hinckley, David. "Arlo's Deep-Dish Restaurant." *Daily News,* May 15, 1996, 38.
45. Hinckley.
46. Dedolph, Meg. "Folk Songs a Family Affair for Guthries." *Wausau Daily Herald,* April 4, 1996, Weekend, 8.
47. Hickman, Breuse. "Arlo Serves It Up."
48. Reineke, Hank. "Ramblin' Jack Elliott: See How All Those Stories Get Twisted?" *Aquarian Arts Weekly,* April 17, 1985, 10–11.
49. Reineke.
50. Arlo Guthrie, Carnegie Hall, New York City, November 30, 1991 (audience recording).
51. Guthrie, Arlo. "Arlo and Cyril." *Rolling Blunder Review,* no. 29, Winter–Spring 1995, 6.
52. Guthrie, Arlo. "Notes on the Program." Carnegie Hall *Stagebill,* November 1993, 18–19.

53. Guthrie, Arlo. "Notes on the Program." Carnegie Hall *Stagebill*, November 25, 1994, 18.

54. Pareles, Jon. "For Once, Art Bests Politics as the Kennedy Center Honors 5." *New York Times,* December 5, 1994, C11.

55. Trescott, Jacqueline, and Roxanne Roberts. "A Weekend All about R-e-s-p-e-c-t." *Washington Post,* December 5, 1994, A1, B4.

56. Pareles, Jon. "For Once, Art Bests Politics as the Kennedy Center Honors 5."

57. National Medal of the Arts and Humanities Ceremony, White House South Lawn, Washington, DC, October 14, 1994, *Our Presidents* (National Archives), accessed January 17, 2022, https://ourpresidents.tumblr.com/post/10000768 4424/legendary-american-folk-singer-pete-seeger-passed.

58. Fisher, Marc. "America's Best-Loved Commie." *Washington Post,* December 4, 1994, G1, G7.

59. Pareles, Jon. "For Once, Art Bests Politics as the Kennedy Center Honors 5."

60. Breindel, Eric. "Celebrating Pete Seeger—A Man Who Stood by Stalin." *New York Post,* December 15, 1994, 39.

61. Podhoretz, John. "Dishonorable Mention for Kennedy Center Special." *New York Post,* December 28, 1994.

62. Pareles, Jon. "'Inconvenient Artist' Honored at Tribute." *Berkshire Eagle* (Pittsfield, MA), December 6, 1994, 7.

63. Trescott, Jacqueline, and Roxanne Roberts. "A Weekend All About R-e-s-p-e-c-t."

64. *The Kennedy Center Honors: A Celebration of the Performing Arts.* CBS-TV broadcast, December 28, 1994.

65. Williams, Jeannie. "Caroline Shares Spotlight at Kennedy Honors." *USA Today,* December 6, 1994, 2D.

66. Williams.

67. Guthrie, Arlo. "Taos, NM." *Rolling Blunder Review,* no. 29, Winter–Spring 1995, 4.

68. Guthrie, Arlo. "Taos, NM."

69. Guthrie, Arlo. "Crested Butte, Colorado." *Rolling Blunder Review,* no. 29, Winter–Spring 1995, 5.

70. Guthrie, Arlo. "Lots of Snow." *Rolling Blunder Review,* no. 29, Winter–Spring 1995, 6.

71. Guthrie, Arlo. "Crested Butte, Colorado."

72. Hinckley, David. "WNYC Celebrates 50th Ann'y of a Brand-Old, Folk-Music Show." *Daily News,* June 22, 1995, 94.

73. Reineke, Hank. *Arlo Guthrie: The Warner Reprise Years* (Scarecrow Press, Lanham, MD), 2012, 47.

74. "Circles and Arrows." *Boston Globe,* November 18, 1988, 2.

75. Associated Press. "Arlo and 'Alice' Anew." *Pantagraph* (Bloomington, IL), December 3, 1988, 3.

76. Trost, Isaiah. "Coney Island Okie." *Guitar World Acoustic* no. 24, 1997, 225–26, 91.

77. Tunis, Walter. "Guthrie Makes His Return to 'Alice's.'" *Lexington Herald-Leader* (KY), September 3, 1995, F1, F3.

78. Hickman, Breuse. "Arlo Guthrie on Activism, Career, and 'Massacrees.'" *Florida Today* (Cocoa), November 10, 1995, 67.

79. Gentile, Derek. "'Massacree' Turns 30: Arlo Guthrie Does New Recording of Classic." *Berkshire Eagle* (Pittsfield, MA), July 9, 1995, B1, B4.

80. Gentile.

81. Gentile.

82. Gentile.

83. "'Officer Obie' of 'Alice's Restaurant' Fame Dies at 69." *North Adams Transcript* (MA), September 13, 1994, 4.

84. "'Officer Obie' of 'Alice's Restaurant' Fame Dies at 69."

85. Guthrie, Arlo. *Mooses Come Walking* (Chronicle Books, San Francisco), 1995.

86. Rogovoy, Seth. "Alice and Arlo Again: Song-Famous Pair Do Book." *Berkshire Eagle* (Pittsfield, MA), December 3, 1995, B1, B4.

87. Rogovoy.

88. Rogovoy.

89. Rogovoy.

90. Rogovoy.

91. Bregman, Alice Miller. "Arlo with Antlers." *New York Times,* November 12, 1995, Book Review 3 Sec., p. 8.

92. "Notes, Footnotes & Queries." *Berkshire Eagle* (Pittsfield, MA), December 19, 1995, B1.

93. "Arlo Guthrie Writes of Mooses for Kids." *Brattleboro Reformer* (VT), December 5, 1995, 6.

94. Scribner, David. "Guthrie Takes Bull Tale by the Horns." *Berkshire Eagle* (Pittsfield, MA), December 17, 1995, B1.

95. Scribner, David. "Guthrie Takes Bull Tale by the Horns."

96. Guthrie, Arlo. "On to Woodstock, IL." *Rolling Blunder Review,* no. 30, Fall 1995, 7.

97. Guthrie, Arlo. "Notes on the Program." Carnegie Hall *Stagebill,* November 1995, 18.

98. Rising Son Records advertisement, *Radio & Records,* November 3, 1995, 63.

99. Belafonte, Harry. Introductory speech for Pete Seeger's induction into the Rock and Roll Hall of Fame, Waldorf Astoria, New York City, New York, January 17, 1996. YouTube, accessed November 29, 2022, https://www.youtube.com/watch?v=L8umOBPWrhc.

100. Guthrie, Arlo. Introductory speech for Pete Seeger's induction into the Rock and Roll Hall of Fame.

101. Hinckley, David. "Smooth Rock 'n' Roll Bash." *Daily News,* January 18, 1996, 3.

102. Bauder, David. "Seeger Appreciates Life's Little Ironies." *Post-Star* (Glens Falls, NY), May 29, 1996, B10.

103. Brown, Mark. "All Tuned Up, Arlo Guthrie Returns to His Musical Roots." *Daily Record* (Morristown, NJ), February 12, 1996, 7.

104. "Arlo's 'Mystic' Comeback." *Daily News* (Morristown, NJ), January 25, 1996, NOW 49.

105. Matsumoto, Jon. "Guthrie Gets His Show Back on the Road." *Los Angeles Times,* January 30, 1996, F3, F8.

106. "Names in the News." *Latrobe Bulletin* (PA), February 10, 1996, 7.

107. Della Flora, Anthony. "Hospice Work Fuels Arlo's Intimacy on Stage." *Albuquerque Journal,* February 23, 1996, 66.

108. Lamey, Mary. "Arlo Guthrie's Still Serving Up Activist Humor." *Gazette* (Montreal), December 5, 1996, 14.

109. Stoute, Lenny. "Guthrie on Tour and Giving Back."

110. Regenstreif, Mike. "Off the Beaten Track." *Sing Out! The Folk Song Magazine* 41, no. 2, August 1996, 146.

111. Gehman, Geoff. "Disc Reviews." *Morning Call* (Allentown, PA), March 2, 1996, A46.

112. Ide, Stephen. "Recordings." *Dirty Linen,* June 1996, 51.

113. Guthrie, Arlo. "Mystic Journey in a Store!" *Rolling Blunder Review,* no. 31, Spring 1996, 2.

114. Guthrie, Arlo. "Man Jumps Bus for Parts Unknown." *Rolling Blunder Review,* no. 31, Spring 1996, 2.

115. "Guthrie Sends Mahalo." *Honolulu Star Bulletin,* May 13, 1996, B4.

116. Harada, Wayne. "Arlo Guthrie Cooks Good Entertainment." *Honolulu Advertiser,* July 20, 1970, B8.

117. "Guthrie Sends Mahalo."

118. Hinckley, David. "Arlo's Deep-Dish Restaurant."

119. Brown, Mark. "With a New Album, Arlo Guthrie Returns to Singing." *Rockland Journal-News* (NY), February 17, 1996, C9.

120. Brown, Mark. "With a New Album, Arlo Guthrie Returns to Singing."

121. Guthrie, Arlo (aka Irv). "Interview with a Folksinger." *Rolling Blunder Review,* no. 30, Fall 1995, 3.

122. Guthrie, Arlo. Untitled article. *Rolling Blunder Review,* no. 25, Summer 1993, 1.

123. Shustack, Mary. "Share Some Music, and Laughs, with Arlo Guthrie." *Journal News* (White Plains, NY), September 30, 1999, 3G.

124. Buttars, Lori. "S.L.C. Woman Stands by Her Son-in-Law, Arlo." *Salt Lake Tribune,* March 6, 1992, D4.

125. Buttars.

126. "Headliners." *Salt Lake Tribune,* March 13, 1996, A2.

127. Guthrie, Arlo. Untitled article. *Rolling Blunder Review,* no. 33, Fall–Winter 1996, 1.

128. Guthrie, Arlo. Untitled article (Fall–Winter 1996).

129. "Arlo and Alice." *Boston Globe,* November 22, 1996, E14.

130. Guthrie, Arlo. "Going Back to Coney Island." In Robert Santelli and Emily Haas Davidson. *Hard Travelin': The Life and Legacy of Woody Guthrie* (University Press of New England, Hanover, NH), 1999, 34–41.

131. Nager, Larry. "Rock Hall Unplugs for Guthrie Benefit." *Cincinnati Enquirer,* October 1, 1996, C7.

132. Dart, Bob. "AIDS Memorial Quilt Reveals Patchwork of Lives Lost to Disease." *Chicago Tribune,* October 11, 1996, 2.

133. Dart.

134. Guthrie, Arlo. Untitled article (Fall–Winter 1996), 3.

135. Harris, Paul. "Arlo's Hawaiian Eye." *St. Louis Post-Dispatch,* September 26, 1996, 66.

136. Harris.

137. Hickman, Breuse. "Guthrie Will Perform in Melbourne." *Florida Today* (Cocoa), November 13, 1996, 1D, 2D.

138. Gentile, Derek. "Thanksgiving: And Arlo's on the Air." *Berkshire Eagle* (Pittsfield, MA), November 28, 1996, B1, B4.

139. *Alice's Restaurant Thanksgiving Massacree Concert,* broadcast November 28, 1996 (sound recording).

140. Guthrie, Arlo. Untitled article (Fall–Winter 1996), 2.

CHAPTER 7

1. Morris, Chris. "Koch International: The U.S.' 'Major Alternative' Marks a Decade of Big Changes and Steady Growth." *Billboard,* March 15, 1997, K3, K9.

2. Morris.

3. Morris, Chris. "Declarations of Independents." *Billboard,* February 15, 1997, 61.

4. Tamarkin, Jeff. "Arlo Guthrie at 50: In the House of the Rising Son." *Discoveries,* no. 111, August 1997, 40–49.

5. Tamarkin.

6. "Music News & Notes: Guthrie's Year." *Record* (Hackensack, NJ), June 4, 1997, YT 4.

7. Guthrie, Arlo. "Big Vacation." *Rolling Blunder Review,* no. 34, Spring 1997, 3.

8. Guthrie, Arlo. "Big Vacation."

9. Mattoon, Donna B. "Guthrie Concert Plans Face Obstacles." *Berkshire Eagle* (Pittsfield, MA), May 2, 1997, B1.

10. Dunne, Susan. "Kid Vid: This Land Is Your Land." *Hartford Courant,* May 8, 1997, 24.

11. Maes, Nancy. "Happy Gathering: Woody and Arlo Guthrie Recording Is Americana at Is Jubilant Best." *Chicago Tribune,* June 5, 1997, Sec. 5, p. 10B.

12. Reineke, Hank. *Ramblin' Jack Elliott.*

13. Rogovoy, Seth. "The Beat: Overdue Debut." *Berkshire Eagle* (Pittsfield, MA), November 21, 1997, D1, D5.

14. Associated Press. "Garcia Remembered for Youthful Spirit." *Leader-Telegram* (Eau Claire, WI), August 10, 1995, 3C.

15. Morse, Steve. "Further Festival: Life after Dead." *Dayton Daily News,* June 29, 1997, 10C.
16. Trost, Isaiah. "Coney Island Okie." *Guitar World Acoustic,* no. 24, 1997, 25–26, 91–92.
17. Catlin, Roger. "Not Fade Away: Memory of the Dead Ignites Fourth of July." *Hartford Courant,* June 29, 1997, G1, G8.
18. "Backstage Bits." *Berkshire Eagle* (Pittsfield, MA), June 12, 1997, 15.
19. Newman, Melinda. "Arlo Guthrie Tapped to Head Further." *Billboard,* May 31, 1997, 13.
20. Newman.
21. Passy, Charles. "Festival Fever: Why Everyone Is Imitating Lollapalooza." *Palm Beach Post,* June 19, 1997, 4D.
22. Livadas, Greg. "4 Picketers Arrested at Darien Lake." *Democrat and Chronicle* (Rochester, NY), July 9, 1997, B1.
23. Associated Press. "Guthrie Says He Got Protest Plans Too Late." *Democrat and Chronicle* (Rochester, NY), July 15, 1997, 5B.
24. Knapp, Tom. "Further Festival Charms Hershey." *Intelligencer Journal* (Lancaster, PA), July 12, 1997, B1, B3.
25. "Editorial: Work Out Plans for Guthrie Concerts." *Berkshire Eagle* (Pittsfield, MA), May 4, 1997, A8.
26. Rogovoy, Seth. "Guthrie's 'Alice's Restaurant Turns 30." *Berkshire Eagle* (Pittsfield, MA), October 7, 1997, B1, B4.
27. Rogovoy, Seth. "Guthrie's 'Alice's Restaurant Turns 30."
28. Scribner, David. "Notes, Footnotes & Queries." *Berkshire Eagle* (Pittsfield, MA), October 9, 1997, B1.
29. Arlo Guthrie interview with Bill Rosendahl. *Arlo Guthrie's Alice's Restaurant Reunion Concert.* November 27, 1997 (cable television broadcast).
30. Arlo Guthrie interview with Bill Rosendahl.
31. Fitzpatrick, Eileen. "Huntington's Group to Fete Guthrie Family." *Billboard,* October 11, 1997, 7, 108.
32. Fitzpatrick.
33. Fitzpatrick.
34. Fitzpatrick.
35. Fitzpatrick.
36. Forsberg, Helen. "This Dance Is Their Dance: The Piece of Americana That Introduced Woody Guthrie to His Bride." *Salt Lake Tribune,* November 23, 1997, D1, D4.
37. Forsberg.
38. "Reviews: Arlo Guthrie." *Folk Roots,* no. 174, December 1997, 68.
39. Morse, Steve. "Rock Notes: Arlo to Hang Out." *Boston Globe,* December 5, 1997, E16.
40. Morse.

41. Sukiennik, Greg. "Arlo Guthrie Eyes North St. Building." *Berkshire Eagle* (Pittsfield, MA), January 29, 1998, A1, A4.

42. Guthrie, Arlo. "The Return of Irv." *Rolling Blunder Review*, no. 36. El Niño 1997, 5.

43. Sukiennik, Greg. "Arlo Guthrie Eyes North St. Building. *Berkshire Eagle* (Pittsfield, MA), January 29, 1998, A4.

44. Sukiennik, Greg. "Arlo Guthrie Enthusiastic over Plans for Kresge Club." *Berkshire Eagle* (Pittsfield, MA), May 10, 1988, B1, B10.

45. Sukiennik, Greg. "Kresge Building Prospects Withdraw Offers." *Berkshire Eagle* (Pittsfield, MA), February 21, 1998, B1, B3.

46. Guthrie, Arlo. "Winter Tour Ends." *Rolling Blunder Review*, no. 36, El Niño 1997, 2.

47. Guthrie, Arlo. "Winter Tour Ends."

48. Guthrie, Arlo. "Winter Tour Ends."

49. Shuster, Fred. "Appealing to the Child—Another Side of Folk Singer Woody Guthrie." *Daily Advertiser* (Lafayette, LA), February 13, 1998, 4.

50. Rogovoy, Seth. "Berkshirites Got a Preview of Cream of Grammy Crop." *Berkshire Eagle* (Pittsfield, MA), February 26, 1998, A4.

51. Hill, Kendall. "Arlo the Old Hippie Gets Anything He Wants." *Sydney Morning Herald*, April 11, 1998, 9.

52. Hill.

53. Elder, Bruce. "Talkin' about Our Generation." *Sydney Morning Herald*, April 17, 1998, Arts 13.

54. Elder.

55. Elder.

56. Attwood, Alan. "Dead Singer's Fight Goes On." *Age* (Melbourne), November 2, 1979, 5.

57. Guthrie, Arlo. "Overseas." *Rolling Blunder Review*, no. 36, El Niño 1997, 3.

58. Guthrie, Arlo. "Overseas."

59. Sukiennik, Greg. "Guthrie, on TV from Park Square, Says He's Bought North Street Building." *Berkshire Eagle* (Pittsfield, MA), May 2, 1998, B1, B5.

60. Sukiennik, Greg. "Arlo Guthrie Enthusiastic over Plans for Kresge Club."

61. Sukiennik, Greg. "Arlo Guthrie Enthusiastic over Plans for Kresge Club."

62. Anstead, Alicia. "Minds Meet for Guthrie Symphony." *Bangor Daily News*, May 7, 1998, C1, C4.

63. Anstead.

64. Anstead.

65. Anstead.

66. Anstead, Alicia. "Guthrie's Move to Symphony a Heartwarming Surprise." *Bangor Daily News*, May 11, 1998, C1, C9.

67. Anstead, Alicia. "Guthrie's Move to Symphony a Heartwarming Surprise."

68. Fine, Eric. "Guthries Could Be the First Family of Folk Music." *Courier-Post* (Camden, NJ), July 30, 1999, 19T.

69. Buckstaff, Kathryn. "Song Compilation Could Help Branson: Entertainers Hope Arlo Guthrie's Recording of His Father's Songs Boosts Area's Status." *News-Leader* (Springfield, MO), June 17, 1998, 7B.

70. Buckstaff.

71. Guthrie, Arlo. Untitled article. *Rolling Blunder Review*, no. 37, Fall–Winter 1998, 1.

72. Shuster, Fred. "Bragg Album Revisits Woody Guthrie." *Rutland Daily Herald* (VT), December 18, 1998, C5.

73. Makin, Robert. "Gotham Nights: Hey Woody Guthrie." *Courier News*, December 10, 1998, 49.

74. Williamson, Nigel. "Tunes of Glory." *Uncut*, July 1, 1998, 40–43.

75. Williamson.

76. Williamson.

77. Levitan, Corey. "Bragging Rights." *Daily Breeze* (Torrance, CA), November 27, 1998, 65, 69.

78. Ganahl, Jane. "Bragging Rights to Woody Guthrie." *San Francisco Examiner*, March 23, 1998, 21, 24.

79. Levitan, Corey. "Bragging Rights."

80. Considine, J. D. "He's Writing Woody Guthrie Songs." *Record* (Hackensack, NJ), July 13, 1997, 142.

81. Klein, Joe. "Notes on a Native Son." *Rolling Stone*, no. 234, March 10, 1977, 56.

82. McDonald, Sam. "Soother of the Lost Souls." *Daily Press* (Newport News, VA), February 15, 2009, G2.

83. McDonald.

84. Palmer, Griff. "Fest Points Out Punk Appeal of Okemah's Native Son." *Daily Oklahoman*, July 16, 1998, 13.

85. Palmer.

86. Guthrie, Arlo. Untitled article (Fall–Winter 1998), 1.

87. Miller, Michael. "Daughter Continues in Musical Footsteps." *Leader-Telegram* (Eau Claire, WI), February 19, 2002, 7A.

88. Guthrie, Arlo. "Sarah Joins Show." *Rolling Blunder Review*, no. 37, Fall–Winter 1998, 4.

89. Guthrie, Arlo. "Sarah Joins Show."

90. Guthrie, Woody. "New People's Songster on Way." *People's World*, June 3, 1947, 5.

91. *Politically Incorrect*, with host Bill Maher (ABC-TV, broadcast October 26, 1998).

92. Applebome, Peter. "He Caught Folk on the Rise and Held On." *New York Times*, November 26, 1998, E1.

93. Somerville, Colin. "Country Life." *Scotland on Sunday* (Edinburgh), January 24, 1999, 9.

94. Adams, Rob. "Celtic Connections: Arlo Guthrie/James Grant, Glasgow Royal Concert Hall." *Herald* (Glasgow, Scotland), January 28, 1998, 17.

95. Shepherd, Fiona. "Celtic Connections: Arlo Guthrie/James Grant, Glasgow Royal Concert Hall." *Scotsman* (Edinburgh), January 29, 1999, 19.

96. Guthrie, Arlo. "Big Sky Country: Old Friends Show Up in Montana." *Rolling Blunder Review*, no. 38, Summer 1999, 2.

97. Guthrie, Arlo. "Locked and Dammed." *Rolling Blunder Review*, no. 38, Summer 1999, 3.

98. DuBois, Stephanie. "Soundtrack of Our Lives." *San Francisco Examiner*, September 24, 2001, C2.

99. DuBois.

100. Guthrie, Arlo. Untitled article. *Rolling Blunder Review*, no. 38, Summer 1999, 1.

101. Davis, Sandy. "Woody Guthrie's Influence Still Felt, Music Fest Proves." *Daily Oklahoman*, July 17, 1999, 1, 4.

102. Associated Press. "Day in the Garden a Nostalgic Trip for Original Woodstock Musicians." *Press and Sun-Bulletin* (Binghamton, NY), August 16, 1999, 3B.

103. Hill, Michael. "Woodstock Reunion." *Post-Star* (Glen Falls, NY), August 13, 1999, 15.

104. Mervis, Scott. "Papa Crosby: David Crosby Talks about His New Family, the Two Woodstocks, and His Reunion with SN&Y." *Pittsburgh Post-Gazette*, August 20, 1999, 28.

105. Associated Press. "'Day in the Garden' Revisits Concert." *Latrobe Bulletin* (PA), August 16, 1999, 2.

106. Barnes, Liz. "Letters: Missed Event." *Santa Fe New Mexican*, October 4, 1999, A11.

107. "Anti-nuke Activists Honor Their Own." *Albuquerque Journal*, September 25, 1999, 3.

108. "Arlo's Annual Thanksgiving Revival." *Rolling Blunder Review*, no. 38, Summer 1999, 4.

109. Guthrie, Arlo. "Sorry Guys! Sarah Lee Gets Married." *Rolling Blunder Review*, no. 39, Fall–Winter 1999, 4.

110. Szczechowski, Joe. "Introducing the Orchestrated Arlo Guthrie." *News Journal* (Wilmington, DE), October 22, 1999, D1–D2.

111. Guthrie, Arlo. Untitled. *Rolling Blunder Review*, no. 39, Fall–Winter 1999, 2.

112. Leonard, John. "Private Lives." *New York Times*, December 6, 1978, C12.

113. Guthrie, Arlo. "Notes on the Program." Carnegie Hall *Stagebill*, November 1999.

CHAPTER 8

1. Mandell, Jonathan. "Guthrie's First Bid for Glory: With a Paintbrush." *New York Times*, January 30, 2000, AR 44.

2. Brower, Steven, and Nora Guthrie. *Woody Guthrie: Art Works* (Rizzoli, New York), 2005, 243.

3. Mandell, Jonathan. "Guthrie's First Bid for Glory."

4. Guthrie, Arlo. Untitled article. *Rolling Blunder Review,* no. 41, Winter 2000, 1.
5. Guthrie, Arlo. Untitled article (Winter 2000), 1.
6. Renaud, Trisha. "Arlo Guthrie, Pete Seeger, Mime Troupe, and *Garzón* Highlight NY reunion." *Volunteer* 22, no. 3, Summer 2000, 1, 7.
7. Lomax, Alan, Woody Guthrie, and Pete Seeger. *Hard Hitting Songs for Hard-Hit People* (Oak Publications, New York), 1967, 62.
8. Hinckley, David. "Recalling Glory of Guthrie." *Daily News,* February 3, 2000, 48.
9. Hoffman, Jan. "A Daughter Who Shares Her Folks' Ways." *New York Times,* February 2, 2000, B2.
10. Guthrie, Arlo. "Program: Arlo's Note." Carnegie Hall *Stagebill,* November 2000, 30.
11. "Community Happenings." *Miami Herald,* February 15, 2001, 23.
12. Lindquist, David. "Arlo Guthrie Continues Support of Farm Aid Because He Admires Its Mission and Founder." *Indianapolis Star,* September 28, 2001, 5.
13. Goldscheider, Eric. "At Home with Arlo Guthrie." *Boston Globe,* November 22, 2001, H2.
14. Goldscheider.
15. Bahlman, D. R. "Grover, Guthrie Lead Musical Memorial at Park Square to Help Ease Kids' Fears." *Berkshire Eagle* (Pittsfield, MA), September 17, 2001, B1.
16. Gentile, Derek. "Islam Follower Details Misconceptions of Faith." *Berkshire Eagle* (Pittsfield, MA), September 27, 2001, A1, A4.
17. "Farm Aid 2001: Concert for America." *Times-Mail* (Bedford, IN), September 28, 2001, C5.
18. Lindquist, David. "Arlo Guthrie Continues Support of Farm Aid."
19. Lindquist.
20. Condran, Ed. "We Shall Overcome." *Central Jersey Home News* (New Brunswick), October 19, 2000, On the Go, 5.
21. Condran.
22. Blecher, Ian. "Bottom Line Massacre.' *New York Observer,* December 10, 2001, 3.
23. Rogovoy, Seth. "Guthrie Kin to Launch 1st Solo CD." *Berkshire Eagle* (Pittsfield, MA), January 11, 2002, D1.
24. Guthrie, Arlo. "End of the News." *Rolling Blunder Review,* no. 42, Winter 2002, 3.
25. Theessink, Hans. "The Making of the CD." In Guthrie, Arlo. Notes to *Banjoman: A Tribute to Derroll Adams* (Rising Son Records, RSR-2102-2), 2002.
26. Reineke, Hank. *Ramblin' Jack Elliott.*
27. Reineke, Hank. *Ramblin' Jack Elliott.*
28. Reineke.
29. Guthrie, Arlo. Notes to *Banjoman.*
30. *Arlo Guthrie: Live in Sydney* (Rising Son Records, RSR 1125-2), 2005 (sound recording).
31. Guthrie, Arlo. "A Year or So Later." *Rolling Blunder Review,* no. 42, Winter 2002, 3.
32. Guthrie, Arlo. "A Year or So Later."

33. "Rounder Records Releases 'Top of the World.'" *Polish-American Journal*, September 30, 2002, 13.

34. Guthrie, Arlo. "Some Interesting News!" *Rolling Blunder Review*, no. 42, Winter 2002, 3.

35. Guthrie, Arlo. "Some Interesting News!"

36. Barsness, Ann. "Authentic Arlo." *Leader-Telegram* (Eau Claire, WI), February 19, 2002, 7.

37. Havighurst, Craig "Talent Starts Strong, Never Fails the Songs in Tribute to Guthrie." *Tennessean* (Nashville), February 7, 2003, 2B.

38. Gerome, John. "Nashville Salutes Spirit of Guthrie." *Cincinnati Enquirer*, February 6, 2003, E7.

39. Havighurst, Craig "Talent Starts Strong, Never Fails the Songs."

40. Salome, Louis J. "This Land(mark) Was Made for You and Me." *Palm Beach Post*, March 12, 2003, 1D, 4D.

41. Salome.

42. Klein, Joe. *Woody Guthrie: A Life* (Alfred A. Knopf, New York), 1980, 366.

43. Dollar, Steve. "Guthrie's Jewish Music, from Archives to Stage." *Newsday*, December 14, 2003, D41.

44. Moskowitz, Jon. "Holy Folk! There Was More Inside Woody Guthrie's Mind—and Songbook—than the Plight of Farmers." *Forward*, December 12, 2003, 14.

45. Greenberg, Eric J. "Woody Guthrie's Songs for 'Bubbe.'" *New York Jewish Week*, December 19, 2003, 44.

46. Dollar, Steve. "Guthrie's Jewish Music, from Archives to Stage."

47. Guthrie, Arlo. Email correspondence with author, April 4, 2021.

48. Hochman, Steve. "Guthrie's Klezmer Clan: Who Knew Woody Guthrie Wrote a Trove of Jewish-Themed Songs? His Son Arlo, for One." *Los Angeles Times*, December 4, 2005, E1, E6.

49. Pareles, Jon. "Funny, Woody, You Don't Look Klezmer." *New York Times*, December 23, 2003, E3.

50. Guthrie, Arlo. Untitled article. *Rolling Blunder Review*, no. 44. Winter 2003, 3.

51. Guthrie, Arlo. Untitled article (Winter 2003), 2.

52. Guthrie, Arlo. Untitled article (Winter 2003), 3.

53. "Hey! This Doesn't Look like the RBR!" *Guthrie Center Newsletter*, Issue 1, no. 1. Spring 2001, 1.

54. Hillier, Tony. "Arlo and a Song like Alice." *Rhythms*, May 2008, 44.

55. Lauer, George. "Arlo Guthrie Delights Crowd with Sebastopol Benefit." *Press-Democrat* (Santa Rosa, CA), January 28, 2002, B1.

56. Guthrie, Woody. "Harry Bridges." In Lomax, Alan, Woody Guthrie, and Pete Seeger. *Hard Hitting Songs for Hard Hit People*, 327.

57. "Portrait of Historical Folksinger Woody Guthrie Dedicated at the State Capitol." Oklahoma Senate Press Release, July 15, 2004. https://oksenate.gov /press-releases/portrait-historical-folksinger-woody-guthrie-dedicated-state -capitol.

58. "Portrait of Historical Folksinger Woody Guthrie Dedicated at the State Capitol."

59. Lang, George. "In His Father's Footsteps: Arlo Guthrie Touched by Response of Fans and Artists to Woody Guthrie's Music." *Daily Oklahoman,* July 16, 2004, 1D, 10D.

60. Lang.

61. Freedman, Geraldine. "Telling a Lost Story: Guthrie, Klezmatics Kick Off Exhibit with Rousing Show." *Post-Star* (Glens Falls, NY), November 25, 2004, D3.

62. Guthrie, Arlo. "A Message from Arlo." Carnegie Hall *Stagebill,* November 2004, 34.

63. Guthrie, Arlo. "A Message from Arlo."

64. Hochman, Steve. "Dust Bowl Meets Matzo Ball." *Los Angeles Times,* December 26, 2005, 22.

65. "Arlo Guthrie's New Double CD, 'Live in Sydney,' Is Now Out on Rising Son Records." *PRWeb* (Austin, TX), August 25, 2005.

66. Levant, Ronald F. Notes to *Arlo Guthrie—Live at APA: My Peace* (APA Music), 2005.

67. *Arlo Guthrie: Live at APA—My Peace* (APA Music), 2005 (sound recording).

68. Fox, Margalit. "Harold Leventhal, Promoter of Folk Music, Dies at 86." *New York Times,* October 6, 2005, B10.

69. Guthrie, Arlo. "A Message from Arlo Guthrie." Carnegie Hall *Stagebill,* November 2003, 30.

70. Pensiero, Nick. "Arlo Guthrie's Riding the Rails." *Chicago Tribune,* December 2, 2005, 10.

71. "Interview with Arlo Guthrie." *American Morning,* CNN broadcast, December 16, 2005 (transcript).

72. "Interview with Arlo Guthrie." *American Morning.*

73. Interview with Arlo Guthrie." *American Morning.*

74. De La Paz, Diane. "Guthrie Out for a Good Time." *News and Observer* (Raleigh, NC), May 21, 2004, 16.

75. "The Guthrie Family Legacy Tour: A Multi-media Concert Tour with 'Woody' and Arlo Guthrie. Features Special Guests Abe Guthrie, Sarah Lee Guthrie and Johnny Irion." *PRWeb,* June 5, 2006.

76. "Roots." *Irish Times,* August 18, 2006, B2.

77. Kleff, Michael. Notes to *Arlo Guthrie & Wenzel: Every 100 Years—Live Auf Der Wartburg* (matrosenblau/12) (sound recording).

78. Taylor, Denise. "Guthrie's Unrecorded Lyrics Set to Music." *Boston Globe,* March 18, 2004, 7.

79. Kleff, Michael. Notes to *Arlo Guthrie & Wenzel.*

80. "Guthrie Family Anxious to Celebrate Woody's Birthday." *Daily Oklahoman,* July 14, 1971, 28.

81. McDonnell, Brandy. "Like Father, Like Son." *Daily Oklahoman,* July 6, 2007, 1D, 6D.

82. McDonnell, Brandy.

83. Rogers, John. "Lost Woody Guthrie Album Resurfaces." *Post-Star* (Glens Falls, NY), December 11, 2007, 23.

84. Rogers.

85. Rogers.

86. Robinson, Lisa, with Annie Leibowitz, photographer. "The Folk-Music Explosion! Its Biggest Legends and Newest Stars." *Vanity Fair*, no. 567, November 2007.

87. Guthrie, Annie. "Notes on the Program." Carnegie Hall *Stagebill*, November 2007, 32.

88. Guthrie, Arlo. "Some Interesting News!"

89. Guthrie, Arlo. "Post Subject: 32 Cents Postage Due." *Arlonet Forums: News and Announcements.* Posted September 15, 2008.

90. McDonald, Sam. "Soother of the Lost Souls." *Daily Press* (Newport News, VA), February 15, 2009, G2.

91. McDonald, Sam. "Soother of the Lost Souls."

92. Braudy, Susan. "As Arlo Guthrie Sees It . . . Kids Are Groovy; Adults Aren't." *New York Times Magazine*, April 27, 1969, 56+.

93. Sterritt, David. "New Guthrie—'Less Contented.'" *Christian Science Monitor*, November 2, 1968, 21.

94. Guthrie, Arlo. Email correspondence with author, April 17, 2021.

95. Santosuosso, Ernie. "Arlo Juggles Alice's Menu, Serves Up Witty Songfest." *Boston Globe*, January 20, 1969, 18.

96. Hallenbeck, Brent. "Guthrie Family Rides Again." *Burlington Free Press*, November 19, 2009, 1D, 2D.

97. Keyser, Tom. "Guthrie Clan Goes on the Road." *Record* (Hackensack, NJ), November 29, 2009, F11.

98. Ayers, Mike. "Arlo Guthrie Calls Up Ex-girlfriend for Lost Performance Details." *Spinner*, August 4, 2009. www.spinner.com/2009/08/04/arlo-guthrie-calls-up-ex-girlfriend-for-lost-performance-details/ (accessed March 3, 2011).

99. Ayers.

100. "SAB Presents Arlo Guthrie, Flatt & Scruggs, Saturday, February 8." *Statesman* 12, no. 26, February 4, 1969, 6 (advertisement).

101. London, Robin. "Arlo Stars in Student Flick." *Statesman* 12, no. 28, February 11, 1969, 5.

102. Guthrie, Annie. "A Note from Rising Son Records." Carnegie Hall *Stagebill*, November 27, 2010.

CHAPTER 9

1. Smyers, Darryl. "There's More to Arlo Guthrie than Protest Songs." *Dallas Observer*, March 24, 2011.

2. "About Us." Munck Music, accessed January 17, 2021, https://www.munck-music.com/pages/about-us.

3. "Flagged for Comment." *Daily Oklahoman,* October 8, 2011, 1a.

4. Chancellor, Jennifer. "Growing Up with a Legend: Arlo Guthrie Speaks about His Dad and the Concert to Commemorate Him." *Tulsa World,* February 26, 2012, WG2.

5. Chancellor.

6. Salazar, Christian. "Seeger, Friends Attend NYC protest." *Poughkeepsie Journal,* October 23, 2011, 4A.

7. Arlo Guthrie Skype interview with Randi Kaye, CNN television broadcast, November 3, 2011.

8. "What Would Ben Stein Do?" Video clip insert, CNN television broadcast, November 3, 2011.

9. Arlo Guthrie Skype interview with Randi Kaye.

10. Chancellor, Jennifer. "Growing Up with a Legend."

11. Guthrie, Annie, and the Guthrie Kids. "Welcome." Carnegie Hall *Stagebill,* November 24, 2012.

12. Miller, Michael. "Arlo Honors Father Woody as 'The Kid.'" *South Bend Tribune,* May 12, 2013, F5.

13. Miller.

14. Bonfiglio, Jeremy D. "'The Kid' Honors Father Woody Guthrie's Legacy." *Herald-Palladium* (Saint Joseph, MI), May 16, 2013, D1, D5.

15. "Woody Guthrie Prize to Honor American Folk Singer Pete Seeger: Annual Award Recognizes Artists Who Embody the Spirit of Woody Guthrie." *PR Newswire* (New York), January 9, 2014.

16. "Woody Guthrie Center and the Grammy Museum Move Forward with Plans to Honor the Late Pete Seeger with the First-Ever Woody Guthrie Prize." *PR Newswire* (New York), January 29, 2014.

17. Liberatore, Paul. "A Tribute to His Father." *Sacramento Bee,* April 11, 2014, B1, B3.

18. Liberatore.

19. Liberatore.

20. Liberatore.

21. Liberatore.

22. *Pete Seeger: Singalong—Demonstration Concert; Sanders Theatre, Harvard Campus, Cambridge, MA* (Folkways Records FXM 36055), 1980 (sound recording).

23. Catlin, Roger. "Fans Still Crave Arlo's 'Restaurant.'" *Washington Post,* February 1, 2015, E2.

24. Orel, Gwen. "'He'd Be Sittin' on the Group W Bench': Arlo Guthrie Spills the Beans." *Montclair Times* (NJ), November 26, 2015, D8.

25. Guthrie, Abe, with Cathy, Annie, and Sarah Lee. "The Artists." Carnegie Hall *Stagebill,* November 28, 2015.

26. Guthrie, Arlo, with Cathy, Annie, and Sarah Lee. "The Artists."

27. Paolino, Tammy. "'Alice's Restaurant' Turns the Big 5–0." *News Journal* (Wilmington, DE), November 13, 2015, 12 HR.

28. Paolino, Tammy. "'Alice's Restaurant' Turns the Big 5-0."
29. Kaufman, Will. "Woody Guthrie, 'Old Man Trump,' and a Real Estate Empire's Racist Foundations." *The Conversation*, posted January 21, 2016. https://thecon versation.com/woody-guthrie-old-man-trump-and-a-real-estate-empires -racist-foundations-53026.
30. Kaufman.
31. Varga, George. "Woodstock Veteran Arlo Guthrie Talks Music, Photography, Nixon, and Trump." *San Diego Union Tribune* (via Tribune Content Agency), March 30, 2017.
32. Biese, Alex. "Guthrie Uses Power of Music and Song." *Courier News* (Bridgewater, NJ), September 30, 2018, 2C.
33. Billet, Alexander. "This Song Is Our Song." *Socialist Worker*, December 16, 2012. https://socialistworker.org/2010/12/16/this-song-is-our-song.
34. Pete Seeger, Benefit for *Sing Out!* Bottom Line, New York City, May 13, 1974 (sound recording).
35. Seeger.
36. Guthrie, Arlo. Untitled article. *Rolling Blunder Review*, no. 44, Winter 2003, 3.
37. Solomon, Deborah. "Just Folk." *New York Times*, July 26, 2009, SM13.
38. Will, George F. "That's Entertainment." *Washington Post*, May 20, 2010, A21.
39. Radosh, Ron. "Hey Arlo! The Times They Are A-Changin'." PJ Media, July 26, 2009. https://pjmedia.com/ronradosh/2009/07/26/hey-arlo-the-times-they -are-a-changin-n182927.
40. "Legendary Singer-Songwriter Arlo Guthrie Endorses Ron Paul for President." *Business Wire*, January 29, 2008.
41. Guthrie, Arlo. Blurb on dust jacket of Paul, Ron. *End the Fed* (Hachette Books, New York), 2010.
42. Robbin, Ed. *Woody Guthrie and Me: An Intimate Reminiscence* (Lancaster-Miller, Berkeley, CA), 1979, 109.
43. Robbin, 108.
44. "John Steinbeck's Son, Fellow Author Thomas Steinbeck, Dies." *Journal Gazette* (Mattoon, IL), August 13, 2016, A2.
45. Price, Robert. "Guthrie on Guthrie at Fox." *Bakersfield Californian*, April 2, 2014. https://www.bakersfield.com/archives/guthrie-on-guthrie-at-fox/article _5c14275b-ce6e-5642-a526-b956e33cee4e.html.
46. Price.
47. Tamarkin, Jeff. "Arlo Guthrie at 50: In the House of the Rising Son." *Discoveries*, no. 111, August 1997, 45.
48. Biese, Alex. "On the Road Again." *Courier Post* (Camden, NJ), November 6, 2016, 2E.
49. Jarvey, Paul. "Ramblin' Jack Elliott Wanted to be a Cowboy." *Telegram & Gazette* (Worcester, MA), October 10, 1993, Sec. Datebook, 9.
50. Guthrie, Arlo. *This Is the Arlo Guthrie Book*. (Amsco Music, New York), 1969, 4.
51. Biese, Alex. "On the Road Again."

52. Varga, George. "Woodstock Veteran Arlo Guthrie Talks Music, Photography."

53. Varga.

54. Wolgamott, L. Kent. "Arlo Guthrie Keeps It Loose." *Morning Call* (Allentown, PA), July 23, 2017, Go 1, 6.

55. Quill, Greg. "Protest Is Guthrie's Birthright." *Toronto Star,* May 6, 2006, H14.

56. Quill.

57. Guthrie, Arlo. Quote from "The Program." Carnegie Hall *Stagebill,* November 25, 2017.

58. Murphy, Bruce. "'I'm Not a Republican,' Arlo Guthrie Says." *Urban Milwaukee,* July 2, 2018. https://urbanmilwaukee.com/2018/07/02/im-not-republican -arlo-guthrie-says/.

INDEX

References in italic type indicate images or image captions.